Case Studies in International Entrepreneurship

Managing and Financing Ventures in the Global Economy

The McGraw-Hill/Irwin Series in Finance, Insurance and Real Estate

Stephen A. Ross
Franco Modigliani Professor of Finance and Economics
Sloan School of Management
Massachusetts Institute of Technology
Consulting Editor

FINANCIAL MANAGEMENT

Adair
Excel Applications for Corporate Finance
First Edition

Benninga and Sarig
Corporate Finance: A Valuation Approach

Block and Hirt
Foundations of Financial Management
Eleventh Edition

Brealey and Myers
Principles of Corporate Finance
Seventh Edition

Brealey, Myers and Marcus
Fundamentals of Corporate Finance
Fourth Edition

Brooks
FinGame Online 4.0

Bruner
Case Studies in Finance: Managing for Corporate Value Creation
Fourth Edition

Chew
The New Corporate Finance: Where Theory Meets Practice
Third Edition

Chew and Gillan
Corporate Governance at the Crossroads: A Book of Readings
First Edition

DeMello
Cases in Finance

Grinblatt and Titman
Financial Markets and Corporate Strategy
Second Edition

Helfert
Techniques of Financial Analysis: A Guide to Value Creation
Eleventh Edition

Higgins
Analysis for Financial Management
Seventh Edition

Kester, Ruback and Tufano
Case Problems in Finance
Twelfth Edition

Ross, Westerfield and Jaffe
Corporate Finance
Seventh Edition

Ross, Westerfield and Jordan
Essentials of Corporate Finance
Fourth Edition

Ross, Westerfield and Jordan
Fundamentals of Corporate Finance
Sixth Edition

White
Financial Analysis with an Electronic Calculator
Fifth Edition

INVESTMENTS

Bodie, Kane and Marcus
Essentials of Investments
Fifth Edition

Bodie, Kane and Marcus
Investments
Sixth Edition

Corrado and Jordan
Fundamentals of Investments: Valuation and Management
Third Edition

Hirt and Block
Fundamentals of Investment Management
Seventh Edition

FINANCIAL INSTITUTIONS AND MARKETS

Rose and Hudgins
Bank Management and Financial Services
Sixth Edition

Rose
Money and Capital Markets: Financial Institutions and Instruments in a Global Marketplace
Eighth Edition

Santomero and Babbel
Financial Markets, Instruments, and Institutions
Second Edition

Saunders and Cornett
Financial Institutions Management: A Risk Management Approach
Fourth Edition

Saunders and Cornett
Financial Markets and Institutions: A Modern Perspective
Second Edition

INTERNATIONAL FINANCE

Beim and Calomiris
Emerging Financial Markets

Eun and Resnick
International Financial Management
Third Edition

Levich
International Financial Markets: Prices and Policies
Second Edition

REAL ESTATE

Brueggeman and Fisher
Real Estate Finance and Investments
Twelfth Edition

Ling and Archer
Real Estate Principles: A Value Approach
First Edition

FINANCIAL PLANNING AND INSURANCE

Allen, Melone, Rosenbloom and Mahoney
Pension Planning: Pension, Profit-Sharing, and Other Deferred Compensation Plans
Ninth Edition

Harrington and Niehaus
Risk Management and Insurance
Second Edition

Kapoor, Dlabay and Hughes
Personal Finance
Seventh Edition

Case Studies in International Entrepreneurship

Managing and Financing Ventures in the Global Economy

Walter Kuemmerle
Harvard Business School

Boston   Burr Ridge, IL   Dubuque, IA   Madison, WI   New York   San Francisco   St. Louis
Bangkok   Bogotá   Caracas   Kuala Lumpur   Lisbon   London   Madrid   Mexico City
Milan   Montreal   New Delhi   Santiago   Seoul   Singapore   Sydney   Taipei   Toronto

CASE STUDIES IN INTERNATIONAL ENTREPRENEURSHIP:

MANAGING AND FINANCING VENTURES IN THE GLOBAL ECONOMY

Published by McGraw-Hill/Irwin, a business unit of The McGraw-Hill Companies, Inc., 1221 Avenue of the Americas, New York, NY, 10020.
Copyright © 2005 by The McGraw-Hill Companies, Inc. All rights reserved. No part of this publication may be reproduced or distributed in any form or by any means, or stored in a database or retrieval system, without the prior written consent of The McGraw-Hill Companies, Inc., including, but not limited to, in any network or other electronic storage or transmission, or broadcast for distance learning.

Some ancillaries, including electronic and print components, may not be available to customers outside the United States.

This book is printed on acid-free paper.

1 2 3 4 5 6 7 8 9 0 CCW/CCW 0 9 8 7 6 5 4

ISBN 0-07-297784-1

Publisher: *Stephen M. Patterson*
Sponsoring editor: *Michele Janicek*
Editorial coordinator: *Barbara Hari*
Executive marketing manager: *Rhonda Seelinger*
Lead producer, Media technology: *Kai Chiang*
Senior project manager: *Lori Koetters*
Production supervisor: *Debra R. Sylvester*
Lead designer: *Matthew Baldwin*
Supplement producer: *Lynn M. Bluhm*
Senior digital content specialist: *Brian Nacik*
Cover design: *BrainWorx Studio*
Cover image: © *Alexander Svirsky*
Typeface: *10.3/12 Times Roman*
Compositor: *ITC*
Printer: *Courier Westford*

Library of Congress Cataloging-in-Publication Data

Kuemmerle, Walter.
    Case studies in international entrepreneurship: managing and financing ventures in the global economy / Walter Kuemmerle.
        p. cm. – (The McGraw-Hill/Irwin series in finance, insurance, and real estate)
    Includes bibliographical references.
    ISBN 0-07-297784-1 (alk. paper)
    1. New business enterprises–Management–Case studies. 2. New business enterprises–Finance–Case studies. 3. International business enterprises–Management–Case studies. 4. International business enterprises–Finance–Case studies. 5. Venture capital–Case studies. 6. Entrepreneurship–Case studies. I. Title: International entrepreneurship. II. Title. III. Series.
HD62.5.K845 2005
658'.049–dc22
                                                                                                    2004044874

www.mhhe.com

To Klara Abigail

About the Author

Walter Kuemmerle is Associate Professor of Business Administration at Harvard Business School. He teaches the popular MBA course "International Entrepreneurial Finance," which he conceived, and for which he developed all relevant course materials, including teaching cases and notes. He also teaches in various Harvard Business School executive education programs courses on entrepreneurship, entrepreneurial finance, general management and international business. Kuemmerle's research explores entrepreneurial activity and the interaction between financing and product-market decisions across a wide range of countries and in cross-border contexts. He is also studying multinational corporations' foreign direct investment in R&D. Kuemmerle's work has been published in the *Journal of Business Venturing, Harvard Business Review, Journal of International Business Studies, Research Policy* and *Strategic Management Journal*, among other venues. He has been retained for counsel and training by established industrial corporations, start-up firms, financial institutions, and government agencies around the world. Kuemmerle earned a Master's degree in Industrial Economics from the Otto Beisheim Graduate School of Management in Koblenz/Germany, a degree in Commerce from Ecole Superieure de Commerce in Lyon, France and has studied at both Kobe University and Keio University in Japan. He earned his doctorate from Harvard Business School. His work experience prior to joining Harvard Business School was in private equity, banking, and consulting and in the chemical and pharmaceutical industries. Kuemmerle serves on the boards of several private companies.

Preface

Dear Reader,

   This book presents a collection of case studies about entrepreneurs and those who finance them. The cases treat a variety of management and finance problems encountered at different stages in the development of entrepreneurial ventures across a wide range of countries and industries. I hope that the study of these cases will advance your career as an entrepreneurial manager or financier as it has those of many hundreds of Harvard Business School students. The book works well in a classroom setting where cases can be discussed with fellow students under the guidance of an instructor. It can also be a valuable component of a self-study program pursued by an aspiring entrepreneur.

   In the following introduction I will elaborate on the book's purpose and intended audience and provide additional information helpful to the study of the cases.

Walter Kuemmerle
Boston, MA
January 2004

Purpose of This Book

The creation of new ventures is a central part of economic growth in industrialized and developing countries alike. Risk capital and other critical resources for entrepreneurial ventures are now available in many countries. It is often assumed that globalization affects and is primarily driven by established multinational firms. This is not the case. The forces that have made globalization such a powerful phenomenon, including technology, geopolitical changes, and innovation in capital markets, are also very much at work in the world of new ventures. Entrepreneurship has thus an increasingly global character and understanding the differences and opportunities that exist across countries is a crucial part of the modern entrepreneurial framework. Also, because of the forces of globalization, international expansion, whether to access resources or markets, is a critical issue for entrepreneurial firms at a much earlier stage than has traditionally been the case.

   The case studies examined in this book relate how entrepreneurs, companies, and capital providers manage the entrepreneurial process and its financial aspects across a wide range of countries. They focus on ventures in industrialized countries, such as the U.S., Western Europe and Japan, and on ventures in the developing world. The case studies analyze a wide range of business models and suggest a wide range of solutions to overcome financing and valuation challenges. Thus, while many of the cases address the problems of valuation and finance that arise throughout the life of the entrepreneurial venture, the overall approach is much broader. It includes a focus on the analysis of the people and business models of entrepreneurial ventures as well as on the country context in which these ventures operate.

Intended Audience

The cases specifically target students of business and economics and practicing managers who plan to start a new or acquire an established business or to finance or work for a fast-growing enterprise. The book also has value for those who plan to join venture capital and private equity firms, investment banks, or multinational companies. It is intended to be useful no matter where one works; there is much to be learned from carefully comparing and contrasting opportunities, financing contexts, valuation approaches, and entrepreneurs in different countries. Finally, although the cases speak to the specific problems of international entrepreneurship and finance, they also address important issues in strategy, marketing, negotiation, organizational behavior, and operations and general management.

Philosophy of this Book and Learning Objectives

The case studies in this book all in one way or another address the following core question: "How do entrepreneurial managers and those who finance them design and execute ventures that effectively match opportunities and resources in an international context?" To answer this question one needs to apply the analytical lenses of entrepreneurship, international business, and finance. First, one needs to determine the optimal venture structure while considering constraints of the national context. This requires a detailed understanding of the opportunity at hand *and* the resources potentially available to the venture. Next, one needs to define an action plan to bring the venture to life. Third, one needs to think about contingency plans if the initial scenario for the venture does not work out. Answering the following questions (among others) will help to ensure an optimal structure for a venture. Where is capital for the present opportunity best sought? What should be the design of the pay-offs? Are mechanisms in place to mitigate cash flow shortages in the event of adverse contextual change? How are asymmetric information problems to be addressed? It is frequently concluded by those who study the cases in this book that a venture's *structure* determined its performance because it matched opportunities and resources available effectively.

A key insight of this book is that variance analysis is critical to learning about entrepreneurship in an international context. Variance can occur on many dimensions, including the nature of the entrepreneurial opportunity, the accessibility of resources and the quality of the local context. None of the cases in this book is purely an entrepreneurship, a finance, or an international business case; rather, all are located where these three areas intersect. Each case requires readers to think about complex trade-offs that involve not just business forecasts, but also the people who generated and are supposed to execute them. It is by design that the cases span a variety of industries, countries, and stages of entrepreneurial ventures; readers are expected to learn from variance and develop their own views of the spectrum of country contexts and entrepreneurial challenges. Variance analysis is thus a central organizing principle that helps students develop the skill of country assessment. It has been my experience that the *spectrum view* that results from analysis of variance across the cases in this book informs managers' assessments of other country contexts that they encounter in their careers.

All of the cases also offer readers opportunities to develop and discuss an action plan. Assignment questions for each case (see the Appendix) are helpful in this regard.

There are three overarching educational objectives of the cases analyzed in this book.

1. *To help students develop an understanding of what constitutes an optimal local context for entrepreneurial activity.* The cases introduce students to a variety of decisions that entrepreneurs and their financiers must make in an international context. The purpose is to help students understand the nature of those decisions and how the country context affects them. To give this analysis a frame it is useful to have an *archetype* of the entrepreneurial society in mind. The archetype of an entrepreneurial society can be defined as the context that gives any venture the very

best chance of success. This archetype context is characterized by strong property rights, broad and speedy access to financial and human capital, institutions that create new technologies, and a climate that both tolerates well-intentioned entrepreneurial failure and rewards entrepreneurial success. Students learn that no real-world context perfectly matches the archetype but that entrepreneurs are more likely to succeed in some contexts than others. The archetype optimal local context can be kept in mind as an anchor for subsequent country analysis and is a very useful tool to students as they become managers and launch their own entrepreneurial careers.

2. *To help students develop a comparative understanding of local contexts and improve financing, valuation, and deal structuring practices in entrepreneurial ventures across these contexts.* Many successful entrepreneurs have a keen eye for the few contextual factors that matter most to the businesses they started. This book provides opportunities to (1) compare and contrast across major industrialized countries and emerging markets the nature of opportunities and (2) apply to these opportunities rigorous valuation and management techniques. Often, the trickiest question that faces one who starts an entrepreneurial venture is, "What is it that I do not know that I do not need to know?" The cases in this book emphasize such relevant issues as determining the scope of an opportunity and valuation of a company. Considerations such as these feed into analysis of a venture's optimal deal structure. The cases reveal that a venture's success often depends on a deal structure that optimally matches opportunities and resources. From the case on Georgia Glass and Mineral Water one learns, for example, that an entrepreneur faced with weak property rights can nevertheless be successful by choosing a business in which assets are relatively easy to specify and protect. A *deep comparative understanding of country contexts* will inform choices around different business ideas that might be pursued in a given country and specific countries in which to pursue a particular business idea.

3. *To help students develop an understanding of the nature and benefits of an international expansion strategy.* International expansion strategies for entrepreneurial ventures involve consideration of costs, span of activities, and timing as well as of attendant benefits.

The cases in this book help students understand the costs of cross-border expansion. Entrepreneurs, I have found, frequently underestimate these costs, often with disastrous consequences for their ventures.

Entrepreneurial opportunities, moreover, can be construed to range from purely local to global. Whereas the Cityspace case, for example, revolves around a primarily local opportunity situated in London, United Kingdom, the opportunity to be pursued in the Internet Securities case requires that the company expand quickly into a range of countries. One can also think of the resources available to a venture as local or global. A typical venture initially pursues local opportunities with local resources and, as it becomes successful, gradually begins to seek opportunities in other countries supported by resources in those countries. Some of the cases in this book describe ventures that followed this classic path, that used local resources to pursue local opportunities and resources from multiple countries to pursue cross-border opportunities. Other cases describe ventures that deviated from this path, that pursued cross-border opportunities using only local resources or pursued local opportunities with resources from abroad. These alternative strategies, although they can be successful, generate tensions within a venture. Students who study the cases in this book become aware of such tensions and what can be done to ameliorate them.

Finally and most importantly, the cases go beyond the question of where and how it makes sense to expand. The cases show that no matter what the venture, entrepreneurs will make better decisions and create more effective ventures if they develop an *international expansion strategy*. In other words, entrepreneurs should develop an international expansion strategy during the very early stages of their venture. This insight builds on the earlier observation that the critical determinant of new venture performance is to connect opportunities and resources effectively.

Content and Organization

In selecting the cases for this book I looked for variance in entrepreneurial firms and contexts as well as in performance.[1] Case materials in this book cover more than 20 countries ranging from highly industrialized nations such as the United States and Japan to emerging markets such as Pakistan and Nigeria. Cases also cover a wide range of industries and management problems. A quest for general insights about international entrepreneurship guided the selection and development of all cases. Roughly three-quarters of the cases take the perspective of the entrepreneur, one-quarter the perspective of the financier. Cases that focus on ventures of a purely local nature complement cases on ventures that span borders.

The book is organized in five modules that reflect the cash flow curve typically followed by entrepreneurial ventures. **Exhibit 1** gives an idea of the book's organization. The development of entrepreneurial ventures can be divided into opportunity identification, mobilization of resources, management of contingencies as ventures grow, and further growth and harvesting or exit in later-stage entrepreneurial ventures. Valuation, a central activity for every entrepreneur and investor that is relevant at all stages of ventures, is treated in a separate module that follows the opening module on opportunity identification. Risk assessment, like valuation, also pertains to ventures at all stages. **Exhibit 2** summarizes the content of each case in terms of countries involved, business description, and topics covered. It also indicates whether a case is situated primarily within one country or involves a cross-border element. An extensive technical note on valuing cash flows

---

[1] I selected these cases from approximately 150 potential case sites to which I had access through a broad network of entrepreneurs and financiers. I selected only cases for which the protagonist was willing to release full and accurate information, even if it shed negative light on the venture, on the people involved, or on the local context. Note that in a few instances information might be disguised to protect confidential information.

EXHIBIT 1
Organization of the Book

Main Organizing Principle: The Cash Flow Curve of the Entrepreneurial Venture
Source: Author.

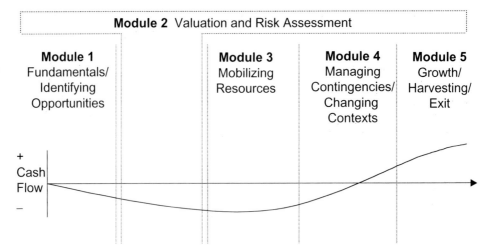

Module 2 Valuation and Risk Assessment

Module 1
Fundamentals/
Identifying
Opportunities

Module 3
Mobilizing
Resources

Module 4
Managing
Contingencies/
Changing
Contexts

Module 5
Growth/
Harvesting/
Exit

+
Cash
Flow
−

EXHIBIT 2   Overview of Cases in this Book

Case Number	Case Name (Abbreviated)	Countries Involved	Cross-border Orientation	Business Description	Topics
1. Fundamentals and Identifying Opportunities					
1	Singulus	Germany, U.S.		CD metallization machine mfg.	Opportunity. assessment, deal structuring, incentives
2	Officenet (A)	Argentina	x	Mail-order office supply distributor	Entrepreneurship, expansion finance, country context
3	Officenet (B)	Argentina, Brazil	x	Mail-order office supply distributor	Start-up merger issues
4	Term Sheet Negotiations	U.S.		Start-up firm / venture capital firms	Analysis of term sheets and financing alternatives
5	Cityspace	U.K.		Tourist information kiosks	P&L creation, strategy, sources of funding
6	Internet Securities	U.S., emerg. mkts.	x	Internet-based news provider	Business model, forecasting, expansion financing
7	@Hoc	Israel, U.S.	x	Internet software (incl. business plan)	Oppty./capital need assessment
2. Valuation and Risk Assessment					
8	Butler Capital & Autodistribution	France	x	Car parts distributor	LBO valuation and structuring, incentives
9	Absolute Sensors	U.K., U.S.	x	Commercialization of sensor technology	Technology spin-out valuation, options in start-up firms
10	Signature Security	Australia, NZ	x	Electronic security systems	Roll-ups, timing of exit, management issues
11	Ducati	U.S., Italy	x	Motorcycle manufacturer	Deal negotiations, LBO valuation, brand expansion
12	Infox	Germany, Switz.		Print materials distributor	Deal structuring, ownership transition, valuation
3. Mobilizing Resources					
13	Georgian Glass and Mineral Water	Georgia, CIS	x	Mineral water bottling	Property rights, Capex, alternative sources of capital
14	QI-TECH	China, NL, U.S.	x	Precision measurement machines	Joint venture valuation, negotiation strategy
15	Spotfire	Sweden, U.S.	x	Data analysis software	Cross-border coordination, VC funding, valuation
16	Mobile Communications Tokyo	Japan, U.S.	x	Telecom hardware design & mfg.	Organic financing, IPO in Japan versus U.S.
17	Capital Alliance	Nigeria		Telecom service provider	PE fund strategy, Capex assessment, valuation
18	TixToGo	U.S., Australia		Event platform	Fundraising, managing cash, new CEO
4. Managing Contingencies and Changing Contexts					
19	JAFCO	U.S., Japan	x	Venture capital fund	Managing VC fund, turnaround
20	Jinwoong	Korea, H.K., U.S.	x	Camping tents	Financial crisis, restructuring
21	Telewizja Wisla	Poland		TV stations	Expansion financing in emerging markets
22	Promise	Japan, U.S.	x	Consumer finance services	Growth in a restricted environment, regulat. change
23	Gray Security	South Africa		Building security services	Context change, IPO, international expansion
5. Growth, Harvesting and Exit					
24	TCS	Pakistan, UAE	x	Airfreight and delivery	Contextual obstacles, leasing, future expansion
25	TelePizza	Spain, Lat. Amer.	x	Pizza delivery	Entrepreneurship, franchising, directions of expansion
26	Sirona	Germany, U.S.		Dental chairs & equipment mfg.	Restructuring, PE auction bidding, valuation
27	Vacationspot.com	U.S., Belgium	x	Internet-based vacation rentals	Internat. expansion, x-border valuation differences
28	Infosys	India, U.S.	x	Customized software	Entrepreneurship, financing policies, U.S. listing
39	Mandic	Brazil		Internet access provider	Harvesting considerations, negotiations

xi

in an international context was developed specifically with the cases in this book in mind.[2] A brief conceptual overview of the financing of entrepreneurial ventures in an international context and a bibliography are also available.[3]

Module content is explained at the beginning of each module in an introductory chapter that includes synopses. Study questions for each case are provided in the Appendix. Even outside of a classroom setting it is advisable to review the study questions before reading the cases. These questions guide analysis and provide food for thought.

Case Exhibits Available as Excel Downloads

Analysis of the cases in this book is facilitated by having many of the case exhibits available as Excel spreadsheets. These spreadsheets can be downloaded from the website for the book: www.mhhe.com/kuemmerle. Cases for which Excel downloads are available are identified in the Appendix.

Supplemental Reading Materials and Videos

A manual of detailed Teaching Notes (ISBN 007297785x) for each case is available to qualified instructors through their McGraw-Hill/Irwin representative. These detailed notes each contain sections with overview/suggested assignments, analysis of case issues, teaching plan, update and key learning points.

Other materials that can inform the study of the cases in this book can be obtained from Harvard Business School Publishing. Copies of the following can be ordered by calling 1-800-545-7685 or visiting http://www.hbsp.harvard.edu. All the materials listed below are available to the general public.

Kuemmerle, Walter. 1999.
International Entrepreneurial Finance Overview (899-148). Boston: Harvard Business School Publishing. This document briefly introduces the kinds of entrepreneurship challenges that are considered in this book.

Kuemmerle, Walter. 2002.
International Entrepreneurial Finance Bibliography (802-186). Boston: Harvard Business School Publishing. This document identifies some useful sources of data and additional readings on the topic of international entrepreneurship and the financing of ventures.

Kuemmerle, Walter. 2002.
A Note on Depository Receipts (803-026). Boston: Harvard Business School Publishing. This document, which explains how a company can list its shares on a stock exchange in another country, is particularly relevant to the cases on Promise, Gray, and Infosys.

Kuemmerle, Walter. 2002.
Venture Capital Method: Valuation Problem Set Solutions (802-162). Boston: Harvard Business School Publishing. (Solutions for: Sahlman, William A., and Andrew S. Janower. 1995. The Venture Capital Method - Valuation Problem Set (396-090).

---

[2] Kuemmerle, Walter, and Matias Braun. 2002. *Valuing Cash Flows in an International Context (803-028).* Boston: Harvard Business School Publishing.

[3] Kuemmerle, Walter. 1999. *International Entrepreneurial Finance Overview (899-148).* Boston: Harvard Business School Publishing. Kuemmerle, Walter. 2002. *International Entrepreneurial Finance Bibliography (802-186).* Boston: Harvard Business School Publishing.

Boston: Harvard Business School Publishing.) These two documents, which describe the approach venture capitalists typically take to valuing companies, work particularly well with the Termsheet Negotiations for Trendsetter, @Hoc, Absolute Sensors, Spotfire, and VacationSpot cases.

Kuemmerle, Walter, and Matias Braun. 2002.
Valuing Cash Flows in an International Context (803-028). Boston: Harvard Business School Publishing. This document discusses extensively how cash flows, particularly with respect to entrepreneurial ventures, can be valued in an international context.

Kuemmerle, Walter. 2002.
The Entrepreneur: A Test for the Fainthearted. Harvard Business Review (May): 122-127. This article distills from the cases in this book some general lessons about entrepreneurship.

In the following videos (ISBN 0072977868) case protagonists reflect on the challenges they faced at the time of the case. Videos for other cases in the book are in preparation. Check the McGraw-Hill website for release dates and availability (www.mhhe.com/kuemmerle).

Kuemmerle, Walter. 2002.
Cityspace: Product Demonstration and Reflections by Marc Meyohas, Founder (HBS Case Video 802-806). Boston: Harvard Business School Publishing.

Kuemmerle, Walter. 2002.
JAFCO America Ventures: Reflections by Barry Schiffman, President (HBS Case Video 802-805). Boston: Harvard Business School Publishing.

Kuemmerle, Walter. 2002.
Spotfire Update: Reflections by Chris Ahlberg, CEO and Rock Gnatovich, President (HBS Case Video 802-804). Boston: Harvard Business School Publishing.

Kuemmerle, Walter. 2001.
Narayana N. Murthy and Infosys: Reflections by the CEO of a Leading Indian Software Firm (HBS Case Video 801-801). Boston: Harvard Business School Publishing.

Kuemmerle, Walter. 2001.
Singulus: Reflections by Roland Lacher (HBS Case Video 801-803). Boston: Harvard Business School Publishing.

Acknowledgements

This book would not have been possible without the support and encouragement of many people. I am grateful to all of them.

My Harvard colleague William A. Sahlman provided constant encouragement and guidance as I developed the cases. He read all of them and made numerous suggestions. Other colleagues in the Entrepreneurial Management Unit at Harvard Business School who devoted many hours to the review of the cases and underlying conceptual work include Howard H. Stevenson, Josh Lerner, Paul Gompers, Joe Lassiter, Teresa Amabile, Jay Light, Thomas McCraw, Tom Eisenmann, and Lynda Applegate.

Among many other HBS colleagues who provided comments, suggestions, and case leads were (in alphabetical order) Christopher A. Bartlett, Carliss Baldwin, Joseph L. Bower, George Chacko, Clayton Christensen, Dwight Crane, Rohit Deshpande, Ben Esty, Ken Froot, Bill Fruhan, Pankaj Ghemawat, Stuart Gilson, Felda Hardymon, Paul Healy, Carl Kester, Tarun Khanna, Lynn Paine, Krishna Palepu, Michael E. Porter, John Quelch, Richard Ruback, Peter Tufano, Louis T. Wells, and David Yoffie. Colleagues at other universities who provided valuable comments on cases or on the conceptual design of some of the materials include Steve Kaplan (University of Chicago), Glenn Hubbard and Murray Low (Columbia University), Rafael LaPorta (Dartmouth College), Juan Roure (IESE Business School), Simon Johnson, Don Lessard, Ken Morse, and Eleanor Westney (MIT), and Tomoaki Sakano (Waseda University in Japan). Finally, I am indebted to Richard Floor (senior partner at Goodwin Procter LLC) for advice on securities law issues and other legal questions pertaining to transactions described in the cases.

I am also indebted to the two principal case writers with whom I worked, Chad Ellis and William J. Coughlin. Both were willing to crisscross the globe with me for field visits, were resilient in dealing with contingencies, and performed exceptionally in the field and in the writing process. Ellis deserves additional credit for writing a record number of high-quality cases under extreme time pressure when I taught the International Entrepreneurial Finance course for the first time in spring 1999. Coughlin was also extremely productive during his tenure working on teaching notes as well. Other case writers to whom I am indebted for individual cases include Zahid Ahmed, Meredith Collura, Andrew Janower, Bokeun Jin, James Lee, and M. Frederick Paul. Finally, I am indebted to Kiichiro Kobayashi of Keio Business School in Japan who worked with me on the Jafco and Mobile Communications Tokyo cases while visiting Harvard Business School. My gratitude also goes to Alexander Berson and David Lane who provided skillful and timely assistance with the preparation of teaching notes.

Over the last five years I taught these cases to over one thousand MBA students and executive education participants at Harvard Business School. I am grateful to them. Their reactions in the classroom and their feedback were invaluable for sharpening and debugging the cases in this book.

Practitioners who provided access to companies as well as information and suggestions on case drafts and whose observations as class guests helped improve my teaching of the cases are acknowledged in the order in which the associated cases appear in the book (case titles are abbreviated). *Singulus:* Roland Lacher, Pete Denton, Friedrich von der Groeben. *Officenet:* Andy Freire, Santiago Bilinkis, Carlos Sicupira, Carlos Adamo, Linda Rottenberg. *Term Sheet Negotiations for Trendsetter:* Steve Hill, Richard Floor. *Cityspace:* Marc Meyohas, Nick Bohane. *Internet Securities:* Gary Mueller. *@Hoc:* Guy Miasnik, Ly Tran. *Butler Capital Partners and Autodistribution:* Walter Butler, Pierre Costes, Phil Cooper, Michael Miele. *Absolute Sensors:* Malcolm Burwell, Ian Collins,

John Harrington. *Signature Security:* Jim Covert, Howard Watson, Jeffrey Parr, Graham Rosenberg. *Ducati and Texas Pacific Group:* Abel Halpern, Frederico Minoli, Dante Razzano. *Infox:* Martin Halusa, Michael Phillips, Thomas Beer, Max Burger-Calderon. *Georgian Glass and Mineral Water:* Mamouka Khazaradze, Jacques Fleury, Ruud J. van Heel. *QI-Tech:* Bert Twaalfhoven, Roger Kollbrunner. *Spotfire:* Chris Ahlberg, Rock Gnatovich, Christopher Spray. *Mobile Communications Tokyo:* Hatsuhiro Inoue, Hitoshi Suga. *Capital Alliance:* Okey Enelamah, Thomas C. Barry, Dick Kramer, Steve Chapman. *TixToGo:* Steve Hill, Lee Taylor, Ralph Marx, Lu Cordova. *Jafco America Ventures:* Andy Goldfarb, Barry Schiffman, Hitoshi Imuta. *Jinwoong:* T. P. Lee, Scott Reeves, Chang Sun. *Telewizja Wisla:* Claire Hurley, Wojtek Szczerba, Simon Kenney. *Promise:* Hiroki Jinnai, David Richards. *Gray Security:* Dick Aubin, Eduardo Garcia, David Plane. *TCS:* Khalid Awan, *TelePizza:* Leopoldo Fernandez, Pedro Espanol. *Sirona:* Thomas Jetter, Franz Scherer. *VacationSpot.com & Rent-A-Holiday:* Steve Murch, Laurent Coppieters. *Infosys:* N. R. Narayana Murthy, Nandan Nilekani, K. Dinesh, S. D. Shibulal, Hema Ravichandar, Mohandas Pai. *Mandic:* Aleksandar Mandic, Carlos Sicupira, Alexandre Behring.

I am also grateful to my assistants, Jessica Dukas, Jessica Gagne, and Cheryl Druckenmiller, who over the years worked tirelessly to format and debug the cases. Among many other people at Harvard Business School to whom I am grateful for providing data for case exhibits, word processing support, and case services are Jeff Cronin and Erika McCaffrey, and Linda Olsen and her respective team. I also owe thanks to several individuals at Harvard Business School's California Research Center and Latin America Research Center, especially Chris Darwall and Gustavo Herrero for case writing support.

Finally I am indebted to Harvard Business School's Dean, Kim Clark, who provided generous intellectual guidance and financial backing. Developing this set of case studies and the underlying ideas that tie the cases together was an ambitious and costly endeavor that I do not think I could have accomplished at a similar quality level anywhere in the world but at Harvard Business School.

At McGraw-Hill/Irwin, among others I am grateful to Michele Janicek who served as a Sponsoring Editor, Barbara Hari who served as a Development Editor, Rhonda Seelinger who served as Executive Marketing Manager and to Steve Patterson, the Publisher. I am also indebted to the many academic reviewers selected by McGraw-Hill/Irwin for their helpful comments in the creation of this book.

All these acknowledgements notwithstanding, I am responsible for the materials in this book. I welcome suggestions or comments. You can let me know about your experience through McGraw-Hill/Irwin or by contacting me directly.

Walter Kuemmerle
Associate Professor
Harvard Business School
Soldiers Field
Boston, Massachusetts 02163
Email: wkuemmerle@hbs.edu
Website: http://www.people.hbs.edu/wkuemmerle/

(Please note that I am unable to offer any comments to students that would aid them in preparing these cases for class.)

Table of Contents/List of Cases

Fundamentals and Identifying Opportunities

This module introduces the fundamental aspects of cross-border opportunity assessment and local context analysis. The process of understanding opportunities works best from the bottom up, starting with assessment of the need addressed by the product or service and an estimate of market size. Often, superficial opportunity analysis leads to unreasonably optimistic forecasts and rosy assumptions about the ability of a start-up to capture part of an opportunity. One objective of the module is to introduce rigorous quantitative and qualitative analysis of opportunities.

Entrepreneurs might think quantitative analysis makes sense primarily for opportunities in industrialized countries in which context is predictable and reliable data are readily available. This module embraces the credo that quantitative analysis is absolutely essential for entrepreneurs and financiers *everywhere* in the world. The cases demonstrate that sources of data must be questioned in every instance, not just in emerging markets, and that there are sometimes creative ways to infer missing data needed for business decisions.

This book examines how entrepreneurs and those who finance them make sensible resource allocation decisions in an international context. This necessitates an introduction to the fundamental contracting problems of entrepreneurial ventures and the structures used to manage them. One can think of entrepreneurial ventures as webs of deals struck between entrepreneurs, financiers, employees, customers, suppliers and the communities in which the ventures operate. Within this web two deals are of particular importance: the deal between an entrepreneur and a private equity provider, and the deal between a private equity firm and its investors (see **Exhibit 1**). Two documents, a business plan and term sheet (the document in which a private equity investor proposes financing to an entrepreneur) pertain to the initiation and negotiation of the deal between a private equity firm and an entrepreneur; another document, a private placement memorandum, pertains to the deal between a private equity firm and its investors. This module discusses examples of these two important deals and how they vary across borders.

The module also considers the link between opportunities and resources. The availability of resources is generally determined by the characteristics and quality of an entrepreneurial venture. Financing and investment decisions are closely linked. For a start-up idea, for example, entrepreneurs might question whether they should first try to raise money from business angels or immediately approach venture capitalists. This module provides the basics needed to discuss the assessment of opportunities; the topic of mobilizing resources is covered in greater detail in the third module of this book.

EXHIBIT 1 Two Important Deals in International Entrepreneurial Finance

Source: Author.

This module suggests that national borders are quite permeable to entrepreneurial ideas, that opportunities exist in unexpected places, and that entrepreneurial ventures that seek to change the status quo or the rules of the game are worth careful study. Overall, the cases in this module raise a parsimonious set of insightful questions that aspiring entrepreneurs can ask in a broad range of settings. These include: Which aspects of the local context affect the venture most significantly? How do problems of uncertainty and agency manifest themselves and how can they be mitigated? Are there any cross-border aspects to the venture and what opportunities and risks do they imply? What data are missing and can they be inferred from existing data? Finally, this first module raises a number of questions that permeate the entire book and are treated in more detail in later modules. These include: What drives people who start entrepreneurial firms? Do entrepreneurial firms exhibit international differences? How can entrepreneurs assess the benefits and costs of international expansion?

Cases in This Module

The module consists of six cases. The module begins with Singulus, a case about a potential buy-out of a German manufacturer of CD metallization machines. The size of the opportunity is not clear; indeed, it seems highly uncertain, partly because there is a question of whether the forecast numbers can be trusted. A key executive is contemplating whether to join the company as entrepreneurial CEO. The case demonstrates that entrepreneurship is about not just starting new companies, but also restructuring existing ones.[1]

The next case, Officenet, examines a two-year-old start-up company in Argentina that distributes office supplies on the basis of catalog-generated telephone orders. Unlike most start-ups, it met or exceeded the numbers in its initial forecasts and has just become profitable. The case analyzes why the company has done so well. Specifically discussed is the need Officenet fulfills and how the entrepreneurs identified a profitable business model. The case also introduces the concept of sovereign risk, which is explored in greater depth in Module 2. At the time of the case Argentina's currency was pegged to the US$ 1:1, yet Argentina's government debt had a considerably higher yield. The case permits a discussion of the cost of capital and how it would be different if Officenet were in the United States. Finally, future opportunities for the company are considered. Various possibilities include expansion into other countries, into delivery to consumers, and into the online space. The (B) case describes how Officenet merged with Submarino, Latin America's

---

[1] The Singulus case has interesting parallels with the Cityspace case in the same module in which the size of the opportunity also is not clear. The Singulus case also has a connection to the Butler Capital/Autodistribution and Absolute Sensors (both Module 2) and Sirona (Module 5) cases, in all of which managers in established companies are considering switching to entrepreneurial careers.

would-be equivalent of Amazon.com, and how the entrepreneurs were considering undoing the merger after Submarino fell on hard times. The case thus points to an important aspect of successful entrepreneurship: the occasional need to shift strategies quickly.[2]

Term sheets are discussed in the third case, which describes how a team of two young entrepreneurs must decide between term sheets offered by two venture capitalists. The case contains two term sheets that incorporate all the terms and conditions frequently observed in practice. This is the only "synthetic" case in the book. The term sheets were constructed from 12 real term sheets obtained from venture capitalists. The choice between the two term sheets is not obvious and depends on the entrepreneurs' assumptions about how well their business will do as well as on a number of other factors. To better understand the term sheets one needs to develop payoff tables under different scenarios. Relevant terms such as "convertible preferred stock," "participating convertible preferred stock," and "ratchet" are introduced in this case.[3]

Cityspace, a recently founded company that plans to roll out a network of tourist information kiosks across London, is discussed in the fourth case, which emphasizes opportunity identification and assessment. The plan is to make money through advertising and online booking of restaurants and theaters. The opportunity looks attractive, if somewhat exotic, and the entrepreneurs already have 17 kiosks installed with plans for hundreds more. Case analysis requires preparation of a P&L pro-forma, which was intentionally left out of the case to permit its creation from the bottom up, a useful exercise for future entrepreneurs who plan to write business plans.[4–5]

Internet Securities, a venture capital backed start-up company that provides information on emerging markets to financial institutions, is considered in the fifth case. By the time of the case the company has consumed $15 million in cash, is not profitable, and is looking to raise an additional $12.5 million. The company already operates research offices in 18 emerging markets and is planning to establish offices in 13 more countries. A unique feature of the case is that it includes three sets of forecasts done at different times and real performance numbers for two years. Internet Securities is an important case about the cross-border expansion of young firms.[6] It generates discussion about four topics: the cash flow curve as a tool for analyzing entrepreneurial opportunities (data in the case enables creation of a cash flow curve); the cost of international expansion for

---

[2] The Officenet case provides an interesting juxtaposition with the AtHoc case in the same module, which also involves young entrepreneurs starting a company and wrestling with geographic expansion issues. Officenet also has interesting parallels with other cases that focus on context issues in emerging markets such as Georgia Glass & Mineral Water, QI-Tech, and Capital Alliance (all in Module 3).

[3] The Trendsetter case provides a basis for discussing the Spotfire and QI-Tech cases in Module 3, both of which contain financing proposals with elements similar to those in the Trendsetter case. The Trendsetter case also ties in well with the Jafco case (Module 4), which discusses a venture capital firm and its investment strategy. Finally, contrasting Trendsetter with cases on ventures that did not use venture capital such as TelePizza (Module 5) and Mobilecom Tokyo (Module 3) provides for an interesting discussion of the trade-offs that attend venture capital financing.

[4] A published video introduces the Cityspace product. Kuemmerle, Walter. 2002. *Cityspace: Product Demonstration and Reflections by Marc Meyohas, Founder. (HBS Case Video 802-806).* Boston: Harvard Business School Publishing.

[5] Cityspace has an interesting parallel with Singulus, the first case in this book, in that in both cases the forecasts can be doubted.

[6] Regarding cross-border expansion the case complements Officenet and @Hoc (Module 1), Absolute Sensors (Module 2), Spotfire (Module 3), and Vacationspot (Module 5).

start-up firms; the overconfidence bias among entrepreneurs and why it seems particularly pronounced in international ventures; and implications of missed forecasts for future pursuit of opportunities.

The sixth and concluding case of the first module, AtHoc, considers (1) the nature and content of business plans, (2) international expansion of start-ups, and (3) angel versus venture capital funding. The company's actual business plan is included in the case. AtHoc is a software/Internet company (started by two MBAs) that already has a headquarters in the United States and a team of R&D engineers working in Israel. Case analysis prompts a discussion of which elements of the plan are meaningful to potential investors and why. The case also supports discussion of two local contexts (the United States and Israel) and of the sustainability of two locations for a start-up company with a tight budget.[7]

---

[7] This topic is picked up again in the Spotfire case (Module 3).

Case 1

Singulus

I don't believe you understand what you are buying.

—*Roland Lacher to Friedrich von der Groeben, April 19, 1995*

Friedrich von der Groeben, HBS MBA '72 and Managing Partner of Schroder Venture's (SV) Frankfurt office, leaned back in his chair and gazed thoughtfully at the investment recommendation in front of him. Prepared by Rick Hoskins, HBS MBA '89 and SV partner, it described in fifty-two pages the observations of and conclusions reached by Hoskins and von der Groeben who had been researching the opportunity to purchase the Singulus CD metallizer business (Singulus) of Leybold AG. (See **Exhibit 1** for a glossary of terms relating to the metallizer business and **Exhibit 2** for a picture of a Singulus metallizer.) Looking through the familiar sections covering IRR calculations, strategic and market analysis, and financial projections, von der Groeben knew that in the end the deal would depend on judgement calls on a few basic issues. It was April 24, 1995, only two months after he first heard of the Singulus opportunity. Soon it would be time for a final investment recommendation to be made.

When the Singulus opportunity first arose, von der Groeben's instinct was to reject it sight-unseen. "We were being offered DM30 million (US$1 = DM1.66) in revenues and DM8 million in EBIT for a purchase price of DM30 million. It looked too good to be true, so I knew there had to be something wrong." (See **Exhibit 3.**) Indeed, the deal had not turned out to be a simple one. While the Singulus business had looked very attractive, it was not a company or a manufacturing plant that was for sale, merely the intellectual property associated with it. Serious personnel issues had to be solved, as SV had so far been unable to convince employees who had been involved with the Singulus line to stay with the business as an independent venture. Most unusual, perhaps, was the fact that the selling parent would be their main competitor, and clearly intended to win back any value in the business it was selling!

As he learned more, however, von der Groeben's interest in Singulus had grown. Clearly, if the challenges could be satisfactorily addressed, the deal offered excellent returns to SV's investors. It would also serve as a positive signal of SV's position in the

Professor Walter Kuemmerle and Charles M. Williams Fellow Chad Ellis prepared this case. HBS cases are developed solely as the basis for class discussion. Cases are not intended to serve as endorsements, sources of primary data, or illustrations of effective or ineffective management.

EXHIBIT 1
Glossary of Technical Terms

Source: Singulus.

Bonding	Permanent adhesion of two disc halves to each other, one of the DVD production steps.
CD	Compact Disc: optical medium for storage of prerecorded digital information, the information is permanently embedded into microscopic pits on the surface of the CD; this information can be read but not altered (audio, video, computer data); 650 megabyte storage capacity; 780 nanometer laser wavelengths; one polycarbonate substrate (120mm diameter, 1.2mm thick).
CD-R	Compact Disk-Recordable: optical data storage medium for workstation archiving of digital information (not rewritable); the CD-R can be recorded only once and can then be played repeatedly on a CD-ROM drive.
CD-ROM	Compact Disc-Read Only Memory: optical data storage medium for prerecorded computer data (Software).
Metallization	Application of a thin layer of metal (aluminum, gold, silver, or silicon) onto a CD or DVD disc; this reflective layer serves to reflect the laser beam; the cathode technology employed in the sputtering process has replaced the formerly used evaporation process.

EXHIBIT 2
Singulus Machine

Source: Singulus.

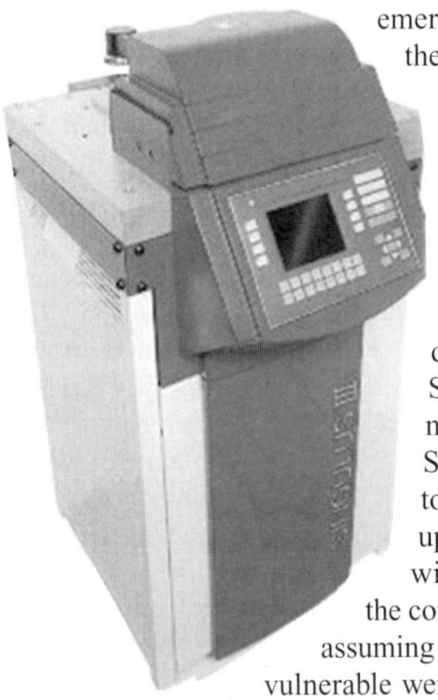

emerging market for corporate buyouts in Germany. By the same reasoning, however, Singulus offered the risk of a spectacular failure. If they bought a bundle of property rights and failed to turn it into a viable business, or if the sellers were able to capture their share of the market, SV would pay a considerable price in cash and reputation.

Von der Groeben knew he had to address several questions before he could make a final recommendation to SV's board on whether SV should invest in Singulus. Who were the people necessary to run the new venture as a successful business, and how could SV convince them to join? How difficult would it be to restructure Singulus as an independent entity, when up to then it had shared sales, marketing and service with other businesses of Leybold? How serious was the competitive threat—i.e., even with the right people and assuming the venture could get started on a healthy path, how vulnerable were the profit projections? And finally, if it was decided to go ahead, how should the deal be structured?

Private Equity in Germany

A large percentage of German equity was held in securities that were not traded publicly. Nevertheless, the market for private equity was less well developed than in the U.S. and Britain. Venture capital firms were fewer in number, and there was a clear shortage of qualified investment professionals. Furthermore, the exit opportunities in Germany were fewer, as the market for initial public offerings (IPOs) was less developed than in the U.S.

Private equity firms also found difficulty in recruiting strong managers for their portfolio companies. Germany's corporate culture favored larger companies, which

EXHIBIT 3
Singulus Historic
Profit and Loss
Statement, 000s
of DM

Source: Singulus.

	Year-End September 30		
	1991/1992	1992/1993	1993/1994
Sales	47,116	39,666	25,363
Material	12,290	12,907	7,612
Direct labor	2,672	1,797	1,388
Depreciation	105	63	44
Manufacturing OVH	728	425	370
Engineering costs	663	674	350
Travelling costs	30	95	123
Material handling	1,033	1,465	945
Gross profit	29,595	22,240	14,531
R&D expense	521	701	501
Sales and marketing	5,427	4,537	3,001
Warranty expenses	1,246	1,389	1,363
Other expenses	1,255	84	(70)
Operating profit before admin. and overhead	21,176	15,529	9,736

brought prestige to its employees. Conversely, there was a clearly perceived stigma to entrepreneurial failure significantly greater than in the U.S. A U.S. entrepreneur whose firm failed or who was forced to declare bankruptcy might well find financing for a second venture without undue difficulty; in Germany, such a recovery typically proved very difficult. This resulted in a more difficult cultural environment for the German private equity market (see **Exhibit 4**).

There were, however, positive signs that the potential of Germany's private equity markets was improving. Germany's large industrial conglomerates were beginning to respond to global competitive pressures by divesting non-core businesses, which was seen as likely to create opportunities for leveraged buyouts (LBOs) and management buyouts (MBOs). Furthermore, while finding deals was still harder than in the other markets, valuations were generally considered more attractive (see **Exhibit 5**).

Schroder Ventures started as the first LBO group (i.e., taking majority stakes in companies) in Germany in 1986, initially in Hamburg and in Frankfurt/Main since 1992. The first SV German fund had DM130 million in capital and generated an IRR to investors of 40%. The second fund had capital of DM230 million. Von der Groeben joined SV from the UK venture capital group 3i, whose German operation he had begun in 1986.

With the exception of one member of the SV Hamburg team, von der Groeben had to build a completely new team in Frankfurt, which by 1995 consisted of five professionals. Investments out of the 1992 fund had a slow start, with no investments in 1992 or 1993 and just five investments amounting to DM48 million in 1994. This had generated some internal pressure within the SV organization, reflecting both investor anxiety over the fund's progress and concerns in other offices that an underperforming fund could hinder their own fund-raising efforts. Von der Groeben wanted to increase his team's investment rate, although without sacrificing returns.

CD Metallization

Compact discs (CDs) had emerged in the 1980s as a powerful tool for storing and retrieving sound and data. Offering more precise sound and superior resistance to scratches and wear, CDs quickly rose to prominence in the music industry, ultimately replacing records.

EXHIBIT 4
International Comparison of Cultural Environment for Entrepreneurship

Source: Kuemmerle, Walter, Frederick M. Paul, and Henrik Freye. 1998. *Survey of Private Equity in Germany—Summary of Results and Analysis (Working Paper 98–112).* Boston: Harvard Business School, p. 8.

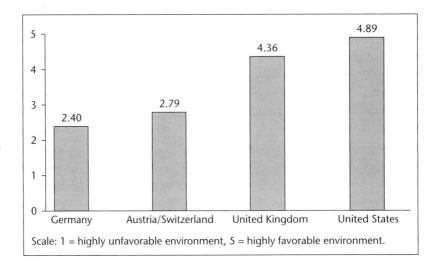

Scale: 1 = highly unfavorable environment, 5 = highly favorable environment.

EXHIBIT 5
International Comparison of Deal Flow and Valuation

Source: Kuemmerle, Walter, Frederick M. Paul, and Henrik Freye. 1998. *Survey of Private Equity in Germany—Summary of Results and Analysis (Working Paper 98–112).* Boston: Harvard Business School, p. 9.

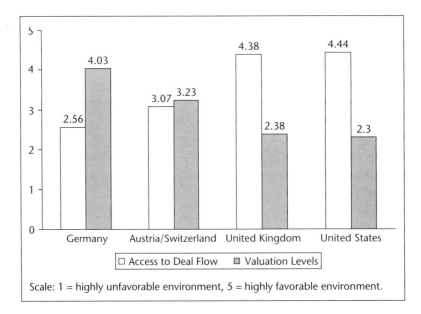

Scale: 1 = highly unfavorable environment, 5 = highly favorable environment.

Music continued to represent the largest portion of the CD market (representing approximately 86% of CD production in 1995), but other applications, notably CD-ROM (Read Only Memory) for computer software became popular as well.

CDs were produced through distinct steps in highly automated production lines (see **Exhibit 6** for an overview of the CD manufacturing process). After forming a disc through injection molding of polycarbonate, a thin layer of aluminum would be applied—this process was known as metallization. Afterwards, a clear coating would be applied to the disc, at which point it would be ready to store information (for example, audio or CD-ROM data). Along with the injection molding equipment, the metallizing equipment was the most expensive involved in the overall process, representing approximately 30% of the total cost of a line.

The market for CDs was highly seasonal, with heavy demand before Christmas and occasional spikes for a particular product when an artist ran on tour. Demand for a particular CD was also difficult to predict in advance. Furthermore, the variable cost of producing a CD was small—roughly 5% of the retail price. High demand fluctuation and low variable cost relative to the final price of the product had caused the large end-users

EXHIBIT 6
Overview of the CD Manufacturing Process

Source: Singulus.

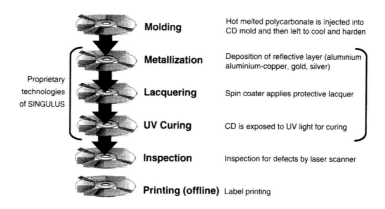

Molding	Hot melted polycarbonate is injected into CD mold and then left to cool and harden
Metallization	Deposition of reflective layer (aluminium aluminium-copper, gold, silver)
Lacquering	Spin coater applies protective lacquer
UV Curing	CD is exposed to UV light for curing
Inspection	Inspection for defects by laser scanner
Printing (offline)	Label printing

Proprietary technologies of SINGULUS

EXHIBIT 7
Metallizer Manufacturers' Installed Base (December 1994)

Source: Schroder Ventures.

Manufacturer	Installed Base	In Percent
Leybold	540	48.4%
Balzers	450	40.4
Tokuda/Shibaura	60	5.4
FTL	25	2.2
Nobler	20	1.8
Ulvac	20	1.8

(primarily music companies) to bring CD manufacturing in-house. Producers also maintained capacity that was considerably in excess of actual production and produced more CDs than were demanded by the market. In 1994, worldwide demand for CDs was 2.1 billion; output was 3.2 billion and capacity was 4.8 billion.

The market for metallizers was dominated by two companies, Balzers (a subsidiary of Swiss industrial conglomerate Oehrlikon-Bührle Holding AG [OBH]) and Leybold, with a combined market share estimated at nearly 90% in 1994. (See **Exhibit 7** for a breakdown of metallizer installed base.) Tokuda Shibaura, a Japanese competitor, held just over 5% of the market, due largely to business from Sony.

Customers for metallizers included both original equipment manufacturers (OEMs) and the end users themselves. OEMs, typically manufacturing automation companies such as ODME, 4M, Robi and Marubeni, bought components and assembled integrated lines for end users. End users, such as the 'Big 5' producers (Polygram, EMI, Sonopress, Sony and Warner) sometimes bought complete lines from OEMs and sometimes bought metallizer units directly from the manufacturers.

Because users tended to have dedicated service personnel (who were familiar with their particular equipment) and a fairly high level of spare parts, there tended to be little switching from one supplier to another among customers. Due diligence interviews conducted by Hoskins suggested that Balzers might have gained some market share recently due to customer uncertainty about Singulus's status regarding its disposal by Leybold. It was unknown how difficult it would be to regain any of this lost business.

An Unwilling Sale

In November 1994, OBH acquired Leybold from Degussa AG, a German industrial conglomerate that had experienced severe losses after its takeover of Leybold from Metallgesellschaft AG and had been forced to dispose of assets. The sale price was not disclosed but was thought to be low, due to Degussa's situation and losses incurred at Leybold.

Bringing Leybold under the same ownership as Balzers meant that roughly 90% of CD metallization equipment production would be under single ownership. While this did not violate German law, due to the relatively small size of the business,[1] the U.S. Federal Trade Commission (FTC) ruled that the acquisition of Leybold by OBH would require the disposal of one of the two metallization businesses.

This resulted in an unusual bidding situation. If the business retained by OBH were able to steal market share and ultimately dominate the metallization market, it would be unlikely to raise further anti-trust issues. The FTC would, however, have to give its approval to the acquirer of the other business. OBH therefore had an interest in selling Singulus to the weakest bidder acceptable to the FTC, rather than necessarily to the highest bidder. OBH also wished not to sell to companies it competed with in other areas of the coatings business, in which Singulus's technology or earnings potential might represent a competitive advantage.

The deal was further complicated in that OBH intended to sell only the intellectual property of the Singulus business. Component manufacturing was already largely outsourced, and Singulus shared facilities, sales and service organization, accounting and administration and even some of its key R&D people with other Leybold businesses. The FTC consent order stipulated that OBH had to allow employees to join the new venture—indeed, it had to give those that did a bonus equal to 25% of their annual salary—but OBH hoped to retain many people a new owner might wish to hire.

Further complicating the deal was the business interdependence between Singulus and Leybold after the deal was complete. Leybold supplied vacuum pumps to Singulus, representing roughly 20% of a metallizer's material cost, and had a virtual monopoly. Leybold's line business was also an important customer to Singulus. Any deal would have to ensure that Singulus was not excessively vulnerable to Leybold upon gaining its independence.

A Buyer is Found

Denton Vacuum Inc. (DVI) was a New Jersey-based manufacturer of vacuum deposition equipment for precision optics. It was owned and operated by Peter Denton, HBS '69, and had sales in 1994 of approximately $15 million. DVI had attempted unsuccessfully to enter the CD metallization equipment business in the 1980s and Denton had remained interested in the market. Denton was one of the people contacted by the FTC in the summer of 1994, during its review of the anti-trust implications of the acquisition of OBH by Leybold, and he had watched the outcome with keen interest. Denton recalled:[2]

> I was good friends with Leybold's U.S. sales manager, John Marcantonio. He told me, "Pete, you really want to take a look at this." At first it looked like the FTC would only require the disposal of Leybold's U.S. business. That would have been a very risky acquisition, and they practically would have had to give it to us. But the FTC finally decided that if they wanted any competition they would have to require a 100% disposal.

Denton continued to think about the possibility of acquiring Singulus, but took no action at first. Then, at his 25th HBS reunion, he mentioned the deal to a sectionmate, Don Nelson. Nelson, an investment banker, encouraged him at least to take some preliminary steps.

"He said, 'If it's a good deal, I'll get the money,' " Denton recalled. "Later, when I almost gave up, Don told me to send them (Leybold) an offer letter, since we had nothing

---

[1] German anti-trust law did not apply when an entity's total domestic revenues were under DM10 million, as was the case with the combined sales of Singulus and Balzers.

[2] Casewriter interview.

to lose." Denton drafted the letter, offering $18 million for the business, one third in cash, one third in delayed payments, and one third financed by advanced payments for Singulus metallizers that Leybold would still need during the first few years for its line business.

Leybold replied to the letter, saying that the offer was too low, and that they would only entertain cash offers for the business. Denton knew that without some sort of earn-out or seller financing, he would have to look for external sources of capital.

Schroder Ventures Moves In

Denton had hoped to retain substantially all of the equity in Singulus, and spoke with a number of banks in order to raise the necessary money. His efforts did not meet with success:

> This would have been a very safe loan—a stable business with good cash flow and leading market share. All the banks could see, though, was that there were no tangible assets to the business. I kept asking them, 'Do you want me to pay you back with assets, or with cash?' If this had been a business that had lousy margins but came with a big plant, they would have been more likely to go for it.

Denton also had trouble raising money from U.S. Venture Capital (VC) firms. "When you try to raise money from venture guys," Denton explained, "they look for reasons to say no." To U.S. VC firms, the risks of investing in Singulus seemed magnified by its location in Europe.

Denton realized if he was going to make the deal happen, he would have to raise money closer to the target. He and Nelson spoke again, and Nelson suggested contacting another HBS classmate, Eddie Miller, who was working in London and was familiar with the German market. Miller put Denton in touch with several European firms, including ING, Flemings, and SV. Miller and von der Groeben had known each other from their days at McKinsey. Despite his concerns about a deal that looked too good to be true, von der Groeben and Hoskins decided to examine the deal further.

Although ING and Flemings also expressed interest in the deal, Denton settled on SV, in part due to Miller's opinion that they would make the best long-term partner of the three. Denton went to Germany frequently over the winter months, working on details. While the HBS connection had facilitated bringing the team together, Denton recalled that it was not always a full solution:

> One Friday afternoon we were working on a revised offer letter that had to be faxed to Leybold by 5pm. We were crowded in Friedrich's office working on this thing, but none of us could get the computer to work! Five HBS MBAs and I would have traded four of us for a good secretary. At five o'clock we had to call Leybold to tell them the fax would be late, and the guy's secretary told us he'd gone home an hour ago and we could send it to them on Monday.

Despite such technical setbacks, the team was able to make considerable progress. They learned that while there were five other bidders, two were not serious and two would raise new anti-trust issues or were unattractive to Leybold for competitive reasons. DVI was seen by Leybold as an ideal acquirer for Singulus, and Denton ultimately persuaded Leybold to give him exclusivity to go ahead. By February, the basic structure of the deal had been worked out, and a letter of intent had been signed. Denton knew, however, that there were no guarantees the deal would go ahead unless his investors were convinced that it stood a good chance of success.

Can this Work? The Search for Credibility

On some levels, von der Groeben and Hoskins found the deal easier to evaluate than most. "The due diligence wasn't complicated," recalled von der Groeben. "There were only a few important customers, and no one thought there was a serious technological threat." What quickly became clear, however, was that several "soft" issues remained which would present serious problems if they were not solved.

In mid-March, von der Groeben and Hoskins met with the Leybold employees involved with the Singulus business. Von der Groeben told them that SV was negotiating to buy Singulus from Leybold/OMH and gave a presentation on his plans for the new company. With the exception of a few whose jobs were dedicated to Singulus, none of the key staff indicated any interest in leaving Leybold. Only a handful of people asked any questions, and von der Groeben heard from HR staff later that no one was interested in leaving. Von der Groeben was not surprised by this, explaining, "As a financial buyer you never have any credibility with employees." Nevertheless, he left the meeting wondering if it would be possible to establish Singulus as an independent company. Looking back, he reflected on the challenge:

> We weren't being offered a company, just a product line—some intellectual property, inventory, a list of customers and suppliers, but no equipment, no people. We couldn't just bring in a competent outside manager to run it. The key to making the deal viable would be finding a manager with enough credibility within Leybold to convince key people to leave their positions and take jobs with a new venture.

The challenge of attracting Leybold employees was complicated further by the nature of the two companies the employees would choose between. Leybold was an old and established German firm with a strong reputation. Under OBH, it would be part of a powerful manufacturing conglomerate. Working there offered a great deal of security and prestige. Singulus, by contrast, offered the uncertainty of a start-up venture. Von der Groeben knew that entrepreneurship was not held in as high esteem in Germany as it was in the United Kingdom or the U.S.

One key person who would almost certainly join the new venture was Reiner Seiler, then head of sales for the Singulus business. Seiler would be important for maintaining and developing customer relationships and would make a credible lieutenant to the CEO, but what Von der Groeben needed was to find and attract that CEO. The ideal candidate was as obvious as he was unlikely to join: Roland Lacher.

At age 53, Roland Lacher was an elder statesman at Leybold. A director of the company, he was the General Manager of the Coatings Division, a group of ten businesses (including Singulus) which shared a number of common resources (including sales, R&D and factory space) and which had combined revenues of roughly DM440 million and personnel of roughly 800 in 1995. His annual compensation was DM350,000. Lacher had been heavily involved in the disposal of Singulus. He wrote the bulk of the offering memorandum, had contacted a number of potential buyers, and it was his role to address any operating issues relating to the sale.

Von der Groeben knew that Lacher was an unlikely candidate to leave Leybold. He had three children in University and just twelve years before retirement; if the venture failed, it would likely be impossible for him to find a comparable position to the one he was leaving. Furthermore, his career had been established within Germany's large industrial companies—there was no entrepreneurship in his background. How could von der Groeben persuade him to give up management of a DM440 million business in favor of a much riskier DM30 million venture?

In November 1994, when Denton still hoped to acquire all of Singulus himself, he had met Lacher at a trade show in Kansas City. In a pre-arranged luncheon meeting, Denton asked Lacher who in his organization could run Singulus for him if he acquired it. When no likely candidates turned up, Denton had asked, "Why don't you run it for me?" Lacher's reply was characteristically blunt: "Why would I do that?"

Lacher's superiors at Leybold clearly thought von der Groeben's hopes of attracting Lacher were unrealistic. "When I approached them and said we were interested in hiring him, they said, 'Go ahead and talk to him, if you want to look foolish.' " Unless he could identify another candidate, however, von der Groeben felt he had to try.

There were some signs that Lacher wasn't entirely happy at Leybold. When the FTC had ordered that either the Leybold or the Balzers CDM business be sold, Lacher had argued that it made more sense to sell the Balzers operation as it was a stand-alone metallizer business. Singulus, by contrast, was part of a cluster of three CD-related businesses, including CD lines and mastering, each of which would be weakened if they were separated. Von der Groeben suspected that Lacher had not been happy with the final decision. "It looked like he had been dictated to, and was forced to sell off one of his businesses without his approval," von der Groeben recalled. "That may have made him angry."

Business Outlook

Schroder Ventures' due diligence process addressed several core issues, ultimately enabling them to estimate Singulus's future performance (see **Exhibit 8**). The key areas of concern were: technology, market outlook, competition, future strategy and dependence on Leybold.

Perhaps the easiest issue to address was the potential threat of new technology. Sputtering, the technology used by both Singulus and Balzers, had proved far superior to rival technologies. Von der Groeben explained:

> We surveyed the major customers and several OEM line replicators to ask them if they knew of any companies that were working on different approaches to metallizing CDs. In all our discussions, only one company mentioned an alternative, naming a development effort by Ulvac and Robi (two OEM suppliers of CD lines) to get evaporation metallization at under two seconds per CD. All other major customers could see no reason to test a new technology, since sputtering had proven to be quite effective. In the minds of customers, the question of technology revolved less around the metallization process and much more around the mechanical handling of the CDs during the metallization process.

EXHIBIT 8 Singulus Financial Projections: Current Year (8 months) through 1998

Source: Schroder Ventures.

DM 000s	May 1995–December 1995	1996	1997	1998
Sales	27,575	43,542	48,620	57,937
Cost of goods sold	9,512	18,166	21,530	29,141
Gross margin	18,063	25,376	27,090	28,796
R&D	928	1,392	1,462	1,535
Sales & marketing	2,093	3,114	3,245	3,382
U.S. operation	1,334	2,001	2,101	2,206
G&A/other	2,650	4,530	5,406	6,130
EBIT	11,058	14,339	14,876	15,543

EXHIBIT 9
Predictions for CD Demand (in million CDs)

Source: Schroder Ventures.

	1995	1996	1997	1998
CD audio	2,300	2,500	2,750	2,900
CD ROM	450	650	900	1,000
CD video	10	100	250	500
Total demand	2,750	3,250	3,900	4,400
Total capacity required	5,320	6,305	7,605	8,575

There were a number of other companies who employed sputtering technology for other products. DVI manufactured sputtering and evaporation equipment to coat precision optics, and Intevac made sputtering equipment for magnetic disk drives used in computers. DVI had tried to develop a machine for CDs but had been unable to achieve the necessary high-speed reliability and quality needed. SV's team believed that the large installed base of the two market leaders, and their resulting advantage in the learning curve, made it unlikely that a new competitor could enter the market with a superior product.

The market outlook for metallizers also looked promising. Orders and discussions with customers suggested that 1995 would be a record year for metallizer sales. The medium term demand outlook also appeared favorable. In 1994, only 60% of U.S. households and 45% of European households owned a CD player, compared with 80% for Japanese households.[3] With CDs continuing to gain popularity for audio recording and CD ROMs capturing more of the home computer software market, demand for CDs, and for CD metallizers, was expected to remain strong. 1996 sales would probably be lower than 1995, but SV believed the medium term outlook was for a doubling of CD production capacity over the next four to five years, which would require sales of between 800 and 1,000 metallizers. (See **Exhibit 9** for SV's market projections.)

With 90% of the market between them, competition essentially meant Singulus versus Balzers. Interviews with customers suggested that there was little difference between the two on the key performance measures of uptime, cycle time, quality and target usage. The only notable difference was in handling technology. Balzers had been successful in marketing its robot arm handling system. By comparison, Singulus's technology, based on a mechanical rotating turntable, had some difficulties in positioning CDs under the metallizer. Although it was cheaper and easier to repair than Balzers' system, SV felt that some improvements in the handling system were needed.

Strategic Issues—the Integrated Replication Line Strategy

One of the key issues that would face Singulus after an acquisition was whether to develop an integrated replication line to offer end-users. Leybold had entered this market in 1990 and the Singulus team strongly believed it would be right for them to pursue this approach. There were two business reasons for doing so. First, Singulus's management argued that they could build a lower-cost line than the OEMs. The metallizer was a key cost component that OEMs would have to buy from Singulus or Balzers, whereas a Singulus lines business would pay only the manufacturing cost. Moreover, Singulus could strip down their metallizers in such a way as to require only one central control unit for all components in the line, making it considerably (15%) less expensive to build than a line comprised of several stand-alone systems and multiple control units. This would enable Singulus to command higher margins than OEMs.

[3] Source: Schroder Ventures.

Second, OEMs were putting pressure on suppliers for lower prices, and might begin to push for stripped down metallizers themselves, in order further to reduce costs. Leybold had lost the ODME account (representing roughly 20 metallizers per year) to Balzers when Leybold refused to provide ODME with a stripped down metallizer. Singulus's management believed that a stripped-down metallizer would cost DM30,000 less to produce but commanded a price up to DM100,000 lower than a standard metallizer. Building integrated lines could reduce Singulus's dependence on OEMs and help maintain margins.

The Leybold lines business had achieved sales of DM41.3 million with EBIT margins of 14%. (See **Exhibit 10** for an abbreviated profit and loss statement for Leybold's lines business.) Discussions with managers at Singulus suggested that it would be possible to develop a new integrated line and re-enter the business with sales of perhaps DM10 million in 1996, rising to DM25 million by 1998.

In addition to the financial and competitive arguments, von der Groeben knew that the key people Singulus would need to hire were strong supporters of the integrated line strategy. If Schroder Ventures balked at the strategy, it might prove impossible to build the necessary team.

There were, however, concerns associated with entering the lines business. Most serious was the reaction of the OEMs. When Leybold entered the lines business, four of the seven significant OEMs shifted business away from Leybold to Balzers at least partly in response (see **Exhibit 11** for a breakdown of metallizers used by OEM line producers). Thus, much of the sales gained through selling integrated lines were lost as Balzers gained share among OEMs (see **Exhibit 12** for a breakdown of Singulus metallizer sales by customer type). While it was difficult to know how much of its metallizer sales were being cannibalized through the offering of integrated lines, it was clearly a significant concern.

The acquisition of Leybold by OBH had faced the OEMs with a difficult question. Previously, they had shifted business towards Balzers since it did not compete with them in integrated lines. Had Balzers now become their competitor through its joining with Leybold, who would continue to offer lines? During due diligence interviews with OEMs, SV learned that several who had shifted business towards Balzers were very interested in negotiating with the new owners of Singulus. There appeared to be an opportunity to recapture some lost market share, but only if Singulus credibly signaled that it was not going to re-enter the lines business. Entering the lines business could jeopardize this opportunity.

Moreover, there was some evidence that margins in the OEM business would not fall dramatically. Some of the key OEMs in particular had a strategy of open architecture. Stripped-down metallizers required tight integration of the control unit into the line; an open architecture approach would be inconsistent with this integration. Interviews with OEMs confirmed that most did not envision a dramatic shift towards stripped-down metallizers.

EXHIBIT 10
P&L for Leybold Lines Business

Source: Leybold AG.

DM 000s	1993/1994	% of Sales
Sales	41,345	100.0%
Cost of goods sold	26,289	63.6
Gross margin	15,056	36.4
R&D	1,735	4.2%
Sales	2,975	7.2
Warranties & accrual	4,162	10.1
Other	400	1.0
Operating profit	5,784	14.0%

EXHIBIT 11
Metallizers Used by
OEM Line
Producers (%)

Source: Leybold AG.

	Leybold Metallizer	Balzers Metallizer
ODME		
May 1989	100%	—
Present	—	100%
Toolex Alpha		
Mid-1994	90	10
Present	50	50
Robi		
1992	100	—
Present	10	90
DiskData		
1993	50	50
Present	30	70
Marubeni/USA	100	—
4M-Multimedia	—	100

EXHIBIT 12
Unit Sales of
Singulus by OEM
and Direct and for
Leybold Lines

Source: Leybold AG.

Year Ended September	Direct	OEM	Leybold	Total
1991	25	12	0	37
1992	48	46	0	94
1993	39	43	7	89
1994	43	12	21	76
1995E	63	39	30	132

Financing the Deal

Von der Groeben knew from experience that getting the structure of the deal right would have a large impact on SV's potential returns. After long negotiation, price was one of the remaining issues. It appeared that DM30 to 40 million would be required to purchase Singulus, including transaction costs of DM1.75 million, some of which had already been incurred. DM4 million of the purchase price would take the form of a contingency payment. SV would put up just over DM11 million, of which DM2.4 million would represent equity investment with DM8.65 million as a loan. Other shareholders would put up nearly DM1 million of equity and the remainder would be financed through loans. (See **Exhibit 13** for a breakdown of investors and their prospective debt and equity positions should the deal go ahead.) This represented a fairly typical debt/equity split for an LBO.

The deal would, if completed, be signed in June 1995 but, due to the need to await final FTC approval, would not be finalized until around December. Von der Groeben and Hoskins were uncomfortable about having the company run by Leybold for so many months after the acquisition, and Hoskins suggested a novel way to address the problem. It was agreed that May 1 would be the economic transfer date, after which Leybold would run Singulus on behalf of its new owners. Leybold would retain all profits earned by Singulus during that period, but those profits would be offset against the ultimate purchase price (paid after FTC approval), thereby reducing the payment of the equity investors.

EXHIBIT 13   Prospective Division of Acquisition Financing

Source: Schroder Ventures Investment Recommendation document.

000s of DM	Share Capital	%	Loan	%	Total	%
Schroder Ventures	2,400	75.0	8,650	98.1	11,050	92.1
Denton Vac (DVI)	400	12.5	150	1.9	550	4.6
Management	400	12.5	0	0.0	400	3.3
Total	3,200	100.0	8,800	100.0	12,000	100.0

Exit Strategy

A final consideration von der Groeben had to consider was how his fund would eventually harvest its investment. SV's time horizon for a typical investment was from three to five years. Von der Groeben hoped that that would be long enough to establish Singulus as a viable, independent entity, but even assuming that was successful it would be important for SV to find a suitable exit strategy. The German equity market was principally for large companies, and while there was some dicussion of the formation of a new 'small capitalization' market akin to NASDAQ in the U.S., it was uncertain whether a domestic IPO would be feasible. Would a foreign IPO or a trade sale be likely to realize a higher valuation, what might that valuation be, and what steps could be taken to maximize it?

Whether to Go Ahead?

As he re-read the investment report in front of him, von der Groeben knew his initial skepticism on the deal had been replaced by a fundamental belief it could be made to work. He also knew that pulling out of the deal at this late stage would not be without cost, perhaps financially and certainly in reputation.

Von der Groeben felt that SV's strength lay in making difficult deals happen, and there was no denying the potential to make an excellent return on Singulus. But what did he have to have in order to make the deal come together? How serious was the risk that the new venture would prove unviable in the face of competition from Balzers? Could he convince Lacher to join, and if not, what were his alternatives?

Case 2

Officenet (A): Making Entrepreneurship Work in Argentina

It was a warm afternoon in early October 1999, but Andy Freire was trembling. Not out of fear but because the entire edifice around him was shaking. He and his business partner, Santiago Bilinkis, were at La Bombonera, the soccer stadium of the Boca Juniors in the La Boca district of Buenos Aires. As the match between the Boca Juniors and Racing Club went on, Bilinkis was bouncing up and down with the rest of the hometown fans. Even though they were partners in their office supply start-up, Officenet, they were archrivals in *fútbol:* Freire supported the visiting Racing Club while Bilinkis was a fan of Boca Juniors. They had decided to attend the match as a way to gain some temporary relief from the pressures of their start-up.

For approximately three years, the two long time friends had been working together on Officenet and now the company was at a crossroads (see **Exhibit 1** for an Officenet organizational chart). Over that period of time, Officenet had grown from an idea in their heads to the leader in the fragmented office supply market in Argentina. Just that day, the company had met with Duff and Phelps to discuss the rating for their proposed commercial paper program and received very positive feedback from the rating agency (see **Exhibit 2** for the Duff and Phelps term sheet). After the meeting, it seemed that it was Officenet's decision whether to pursue the debt facility or not. Although the debt facility would provide a needed source of capital for growing their existing business, Freire and Bilinkis needed to consider this next stage of capital in relation to their long-term growth plans. They had several options on which they could develop their business: expand geographically, expand into the consumer segment, and expand more aggressively into Internet-driven commerce. All of these options had their unique risk/benefit tradeoffs.

Dean's Fellow William J. Coughlin (MBA '99) prepared this case under the supervision of Professor Walter Kuemmerle. HBS cases are developed solely as the basis for class discussion. Cases are not intended to serve as endorsements, sources of primary data, or illustrations of effective or ineffective management.

EXHIBIT 1
Officenet
Organizational Chart

Source: Officenet.

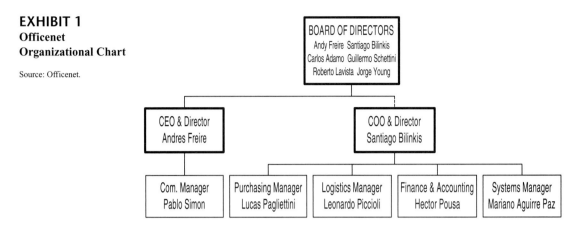

Note: Officenet total head count in October 1999 was 203 employees and 16 hired truck drivers versus 16 employees and 1 driver in May 1997.

EXHIBIT 2
Duff and Phelps
Commercial Paper
Term Sheet

Source: Officenet.

Commercial Paper Size:	US$ 3MM
Interest Rate:	14%
Liquidity:	(Current Assets − Current Liabilities)/Current Debt >= 1
Debt:	Total Debt/Book Equity <= 1.4
Debt:	Financial Debt/(Financial Debt + Book Equity) < 0.5

Also, the different entry strategies would determine the amount of capital the company would ultimately need—and from where it should be raised. As Freire and Bilinkis watched the match, they knew that their escape from reality would be short lived; soon they would have to go back and make a decision on how to proceed with the commercial paper program and, more importantly, on the direction of their growing company.

Background on Argentina

An Initially Promising, but Ultimately Rocky, Economic History

Argentina, a former Spanish colony, became independent from Spain in 1816. It occupied most of the southern half of South America and was often cited for its great natural beauty and varied landscapes. (See **Exhibit 3** for a map.) Starting in 1852, a stable Argentinean government succeeded in promoting liberal economic policies.[1] These policies, combined with abundant fertile land and an active immigration policy, led to strong economic growth, foreign direct investment, and industrialization. Around the turn of the twentieth century Argentina had become one of world's ten wealthiest countries in terms of income per capita.[2] This made Argentina an attractive destination for emigrants, particularly from Italy and Spain. At the time, many emigrants faced a choice of whether to sail to the U.S. or to Argentina, and to many, Argentina seemed like a more promising destination. Nothing displayed Argentina's wealth more ostensibly than the city of Buenos Aires, with its magnificent urban buildings and boulevards.

The Great Depression affected Argentina severely. Despite its rapid growth during prior decades, Argentina was not a fully developed industrial society. Its interior parts were largely focused on agriculture and its inhabitants were poor. The military seized power in 1930 and for much of the period until 1987, military governments alternated with civilian

[1] Rock, David. 1987. *Argentina 1516–1987: From Spanish Colonization to Alfonsin.* Berkeley: University of California Press, 1987, p. 131.

[2] *EIU Country Profile Argentina 1998–99.* London: Economist Intelligence Unit, 1998, p. 4.

EXHIBIT 3   Map of Argentina

Source: *EIU Country Profile Argentina 1998–99.* London: Economist Intelligence Unit, 1998, preface.

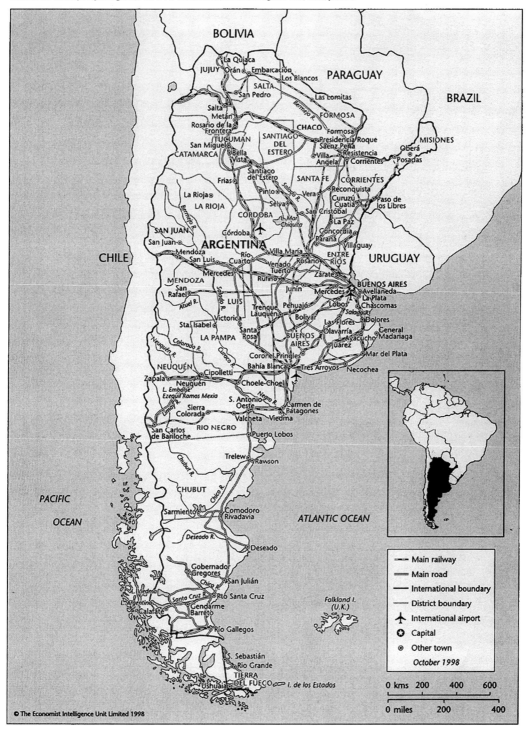

governments. Argentina's most famous politician of the twentieth century was Juan Domingo Peron, a career military officer. Peron was elected president in 1946 partially due to the growing popularity and political savvy of his second wife Eva, a previously unknown actress. During Peron's reign she stood for the "descamisados" (literally: the ones without shirts—i.e. the working poor).[3] Peron enacted legislation that promoted job security and pension reform. Eva passed away in 1952 and Peron was overthrown in 1955, at which point he fled to Paraguay. Nine different governments followed until 1973 when Peron was reelected, but he passed away the following year. The military seized power again in 1976 and became increasingly autocratic. During the period from 1976–1981, known as the "Dirty War," thousands of Argentines simply disappeared. Despite economic stagnation and general dissatisfaction among the population, the military was able to hold on to power until the ill-fated 1982 attempt to regain control over the Falkland Islands, which had been occupied by Great Britain since the early eighteenth century.

In 1983 a civilian, Raul Alfonsin, was elected president. He was a member of the moderate UCR party and sought to restart Argentina's economy by promoting austerity (measures included wage freezes and high taxes on gasoline). But after decades of military rule, Argentina's economic foundations had been shaken and Alfonsin's policies did not take effect in time. In 1989, Argentina experienced hyperinflation. Dissatisfied, Argentines turned their hopes back to Peronism. In May 1989, Carlos Menem, the leader of Partido Justicialista (the Peronist party), was elected president. Menem cultivated a playboy image and provided a stark contrast to Alfonsin. To the surprise of many he was respectful of the interests of private industry, forged moderate wage-increase pacts and promoted privatization. The Convertibility Plan, started in April 1991, pegged the peso to the U.S. dollar at a rate of one-to-one and made the U.S. dollar legal tender. In May 1995, Menem was reelected. During his second term, however, Argentina suffered increasing unemployment and there were signs that Menem was returning to populist policies. (See **Exhibit 4** for recent events and economic data.)

A Lack of Entrepreneurial Ventures

In 1999, there was very little entrepreneurial activity in Argentina. Freire offered his views on the subject:

> There is no real entrepreneurship in Argentina yet. We have only had maybe ten years of stability, which has prevented the entrepreneurial culture and spirit from developing in this country. With inflation running at 200% per *month* during some points in our history, it was impossible to build an agreement between investors and management about anything. As a result, the seeds of entrepreneurship are not sown in university as the curriculum focuses on how big businesses are run. With most of the companies in Argentina at least 100 years old, it is not a surprise to find this.

Carlos Adamo, a prominent member of Officenet's investor group, elaborated on the problems facing entrepreneurial activity in Argentina:

> The main difficulty in starting a business in Argentina is the difficulty to implement ideas. Implementation capacity is the most important element for any start-up and there are just not enough people who can deliver in Argentina. There are several reasons behind this. There is a cultural hurdle, not in terms of a fear of failure, but in a lack of discipline and a poor method of working in this country. In addition, the infrastructure in this country may be much better than ten years ago, but it is still very limited when compared to countries like the United States. Also, the cost of financing is just much higher than in many other countries simply because of the country risk factor; if the cost of capital in the United States is 15%, it is 25–30% in Argentina. Finally, the educational system trains students to be abstract generalists and individualists. We have a lot of creative people in this country, but it is one thing to talk and another thing to act. People not only

[3] Rock, David. 1987. *Argentina 1516–1987: From Spanish Colonization to Alfonsin.* Berkeley: University of California Press, 1987, p. 306.

EXHIBIT 4   Argentinean Information

Source: Data compiled from Economist Intelligence Unit. Section titled "Important Recent Events" verbatim from *EIU Country Profile Argentina 1998–99*. London: Economist Intelligence Unit, 1998, p. 6.

	Argentinean Economic Data				
	1994	**1995**	**1996**	**1997**	**1998**
GDP at market prices (Ps bn)	257.4	258.0	272.2	292.9	298.1[a]
GDP ($ bn)	257.7	258.1	272.2	293.0	298.3[a]
Real GDP growth (%)	5.8	−2.8	5.5	8.1	3.9
Consumer price inflation (avg; %)	4.2	3.4	0.2	0.5	0.9
Population (m)	34.3	34.8	35.2	35.7	36.1[a]
Exports fob ($ m)	16,023	21,162	24,043	26,431	26,221
Imports fob ($ m)	20,162	18,804	22,283	28,554	29,444
Current-account balance[b] ($ m)	−10,949	−4,938	−6,468	−12,035	−14,730
Reserves excl. gold ($ m)	14,327	14,288	18,104	22,320	24,752
Total external debt ($ bn)	80.3	93.9	105.2	123.2	135.0[a]
Debt-service ratio, paid (%)	31.1	34.3	44.2	57.2	54.7[a]
Exchange rate (avg.; Ps:$)	1.0	1.0	1.0	1.0	1.0

Important Recent Events
"November 1993:   Carlos Menem and Raul Alfonsin announce an agreement to reform the 1853-60 constitution (the Pacto de Olivos). A new constitution is adopted in July 1994 and Mr. Menem is able to run for re-election.
May 1995:   Mr. Menem is re-elected for a second term with 50% of the vote. The Partido Justicialista wins a majority in both houses of Congress. His second term is inaugurated in July 1995.
July 1996:   Mr. Menem fires the economy minister, Domingo Cavallo, the architect of the Convertibility Plan, but his departure goes unnoticed by the markets. His replacement by the president of the Banco Central de la Republica Argentina (the Central Bank), Roque Fernandez, ensures economic policy stability.
October 1997:   The Peronists are beaten by the newly created Alianza in the congressional election.
July 1998:   Mr. Menem formally declines to fight for a third chance to be re-elected in 1999."

[a] EIU estimate.
[b] Current-account estimates until 1997 are derived from the IMF, and are not compatible with revised Central Bank figures quoted in foreign trade and payments.

lack the ability to concentrate on the details, but are not trained to work in teams like they are in the United States. We just have the wrong type of ego in this country to make teams work.

That being said, Andy and Santi are different from the rest. They have the personal character to build a team and to work with a board that is at least two times their age. There seems to be an aversion of the old and young to work together in this country. The ability to build a team with a variety of ages and backgrounds and to get them to work together in times of adversity is not at all easy to find here. That quality is what makes Andy and Santi quite unique.

Life Before Officenet

Freire and Bilinkis met each other when they were sitting for the admissions test at San Andreas University in Buenos Aires. Over the course of their studies, the two forged a strong relationship as both held a burning desire to engage in an entrepreneurial venture after graduation. Six months before graduation, the two made a pact. "We promised each other that we would start something together after we graduated from school," explained Bilinkis. "Our dream was to have someone pay us to think together." Before graduation, however, both entered a contest organized by Procter & Gamble (P&G) that involved attending a seminar in Mexico. "It was really a recruiting event disguised as a training program," Freire said. "It was very elite as they had interviewed the 20 top students from every one of the best schools in each country in Latin America and were to invite one person per country to attend the event. Santi and I were the top two from our university and after much deliberation, they decided to bend the rules by sending two people from Argentina and thus extended an offer to both of us."

After the event, P&G began recruiting both Freire and Bilinkis heavily. After going to lunch with the Financial Director of Latin American operations, they both decided to join P&G. "We were really fooled," Freire reflected. "P&G really rolled out the red carpet for us. I mean, the Financial Director *knows* us; he called us 'unique.' Yet once we were hired, the guy didn't care—he couldn't even remember our faces, let alone our name, when we saw him a couple of months after joining. And all that hoopla made us forget the promise we made to each other."

Having started in March 1994, Freire left P&G in November of the same year to pursue an opportunity with Carlos Adamo, an investor Freire had known previously through a friend and, subsequently, through a summer job at university. The opportunity consisted of working with Adamo as the head of a $5 million private equity vehicle backed by Adamo and some of his close colleagues. When Freire left the firm, P&G gave Bilinkis a series of raises in order to encourage him to stay on. But in late 1995, Freire and Bilinkis decided it was time to chase their dream and they began working actively on developing their own business plan. Bilinkis, however, was still at P&G. Freire had already made three investments for Adamo, but the fund was not performing well. So they decided to work off-business hours to define a project and write a business plan.

The two began looking at a number of industries that would provide a good opportunity for a new venture. Adamo set a number of parameters for the two budding entrepreneurs. The business would need to eventually post sales of at least $500 million per year, would need to operate in an initially fragmented market, and would need to be able to develop entry barriers once the business began consolidating the market. Freire and Bilinkis had their own criterion as well. They decided from the start that they would run a business that was run ethically. "We both did not want to run a business like most other businesses in Argentina: one that succeeded based on accepting and giving bribes," Bilinkis stated emphatically. "We would either run our business cleanly or else we would shut it down." After looking at six business ideas, they short listed two and finally picked the office products segment. Freire described the discovery of Officenet:

> Two of Officenet's investors (Jorge Young and Guillermo Schettini) had earlier made an investment in a mineral water company that distributed coolers and water bottle refills to offices, like Sparklets in the United States. The portfolio company was interested in expanding into the coffee market and Jorge (the company's CEO) attended a seminar in the United States on how copy and office products companies were buying coffee companies. When returning from the meeting, the CEO dropped off a U.S. Office Products catalogue on my desk because he thought the catalogue was interesting; at that time there weren't any catalogues in Argentina. After investigating the industry further, Santi and I decided that this was the opportunity we were looking for.

Business-to-Business Office Supply Market

The Argentinean office supply market in 1997 was similar to the U.S. market in the early to mid 1980s.[4] In 1986, the North American market was dominated by 14,000 independent stationers and by a similar number of suppliers of ancillary business services.

[4] The three following paragraphs were adapted from an update to Officenet's original business plan by Matthew Hobart. Hobart, then an MBA student at Stanford University, spent the summer of 1998 working for Officenet with support from Endeavor. Endeavor (www.endeavor.org) is an international non-profit organization that supports entrepreneurial activity in emerging-markets countries. Endeavor identifies high-potential entrepreneurs with the help of expert panels consisting of international venture capitalists and successful local business leaders. Officenet's founders were selected as Endeavor entrepreneurs in January 1998.

Stationers were supplied in part by the manufacturers directly, but primarily by wholesalers (such as SP Richards and United Stationers). These wholesalers achieved purchase economies, offered one stop shopping, and maintained most items in inventory for rapid aggregation and shipment of orders. Also during this period, direct marketing suppliers (such as Quill and Viking) increased their presence in the market. These suppliers offered products through catalogue sales to small and middle market customers. Finally, in about 1986, the three leading big box retailers (BBRs), OfficeMax, Staples, and Office Depot, launched a new concept focused at providing supplies to small offices and home offices through very large "super stores" with up to 25,000 products and aggressive pricing under a matrix strategy.[5] In 1999, these companies dominated the home and ten employee and under office market.

Around 1990, national large contractors (NLCs) began developing a significant market presence. The NLCs offered similar products and pricing available from BBRs to larger companies with a focus on service quality generally through account representatives. These NLCs grew through acquisition and the pursuit of large corporate accounts, and had more recently expanded into various ancillary services. Medium and small dealers (stationers) attempted to serve medium and small sized local clients, and were beginning to feel the pressure of these larger players. In a response to this pressure, these stationers had banded into buying groups (such as Office Plus) in order to gain similar purchasing and marketing economies. As a result, there had been a dramatic consolidation and concentration of the U.S. office supply market, and most BBRs and NLCs have sought to expand their business models internationally. Staples and Office Depot had recently moved into the business-to-business segment by creating NLC divisions and had also acquired the main mail order companies Quill and Viking, respectively. The European market had attracted significant efforts from most of the major U.S. players. The Australia/New Zealand/Asian region (especially Japan) has also attracted significant interest, but the Latin American market had remained largely unexplored. The only activity seen had been minor, initial forays into Mexico and Colombia (see **Exhibits 5** and **6** for a description on the global players and for an illustration of the office supply market consolidation in the United States).

Though the office supply market in Argentina was still fragmented in 1997, there had been examples of new business models in other Argentine markets. In the food and general retail sector, significant displacement of old retail "mom and pop" stores had resulted. This displacement came from shifting distribution channels, capital constraints and the consolidation efforts of large hyper-market retailers such as Chile's Jumbo and Norte, France's Carrefour, and the U.S.'s Wal-Mart, which established entrenched positions in these emerging, competitive markets. A 1997 report by CCR International Research indicated that in the period since 1995, the mortality rate of retail shops in Argentina had reached a rate of 7,000 per month in the face of increasing hyper-market locations.

There were many major issues that surrounded the Argentine office supply market. The two largest issues were inherent infrastructure problems and corruption. Freire explained the impact of these problems on the office supply industry:

> There were no serious logistics companies in Argentina when we looked into the office supply market. There were some companies, such as Excel, that did exist, but they were utterly unreliable; if you tried to send a package to Cordoba it would end up in Santa Cruz. (Cordoba was the second largest city in the country and Santa Cruz was the region in the southern part of Argentina, almost unpopulated.) The only certainty you had in sending a letter via the post office was a certainty that it would never get there. No one, including the post office, invested in logistics. Furthermore, corruption was a rampant problem throughout the mail delivery industry.

[5] Prices were only low on some items, which acted as loss leaders to bring consumers into the store in order to sell them other higher margin products.

EXHIBIT 5   Global Players and Potential Partners

Source: Adapted from an earlier draft by Matthew Hobart; Officenet.

Company	Sales & Employment	Current International Presence	Preferred Entry Strategy	Interest in Retail	Interest in Multi-Country	Entry Timing into Argentina
Office Depot (ODP) and Viking (VKG) – (recently acquired by Office Depot)	$9.8 bn 44,000 people	**ODP** is in Mexico (17 stores), Israel (11), Poland (6), Columbia (5), France (5), Thailand (2), Japan (4), and Hungary (1). **Viking** Sales of **$814 mm** (63% of sales) through operations in UK, France, Australia, Netherlands, Belgium, Luxembourg, Ireland, Germany, Austria, and Italy	ODP has used licensing agreements in Israel and Columbia; JVs in Mexico, Poland, France, Thailand, Japan, and Hungary, but supposedly is trying to dissolve some of the JVs. Viking has entered new countries with greenfield operations, but post merger will consider entering new markets with partners.	High	High	**1–2 Years;** Viking is focused on entering the Japanese market right now and depending on their experience will move further into Asia. They are looking at Brazil and are interested n South America generally.
Boise Cascade Office Products (BCOP)	$8.4 bn 12,000 people	$520 mm (20%) United Kingdom, Canada, Germany, France, and Spain	Acquisition of 100% of stock	Low; Canada only	High	**Winter 1998/Spring 1999;** BCOP has completed a first round of meetings and is bringing its CEO to the Mercosur in the fall of 1998.
Staples (SPLS)/Quill	$4.7 bn 21,580 people	SPLS is in Canada, UK, and Germany Quill is 100% United States	SPLS has used JVs in Canada, UK, and Germany	High	NA	**5 Years;** SPLS is focused on United States and Europe and has no current plans for South America.
Office Max (OMX)	$3.3 bn 19,050 people	Mexico and Japan	JV in Mexico and Japan	High	NA	**1–2 Years;** OMX is on the verge of announcing its entry into Brazil and wants to enter Chile or Argentina next.
Corporate Express (CEXP)	$3.8 bn 25,700 people	Canada, UK, Germany, France, Austria, and New Zealand	Acquisition in Europe, JV in Japan and China	None	High	**Summer/Fall 2000;** CEXP is focused on executing agreements in China and Japan over the next 6–12 months and will then head to South America.
U.S. Office Products (USOP)	$2.6 bn 14,700 people	$829.9 mm (29.3%) New Zealand, Australia, and Canada	Acquisition of 100% of Stock	Low	NA	**5 Years;** USOP is 100% focused on rationalizing its U.S. business. USOP recently pulled out of Mexico entirely.
BT Office Products (BTF)	Sales N.A. 4,500 people	Germany, France, The Netherlands, Sweden and UK, Austria, Italy, Switzerland, and the Baltic States	Acquisition in Western Europe; licensing agreements in Austria, Italy, Switzerland, and the Baltic States	None	NA	NA

EXHIBIT 6   **Consolidation of the U.S. Office Supply Market**

Source: National Office Products Association, "Winning Strategies for the 1990s," 1988; Staples; Bloomberg.

1988

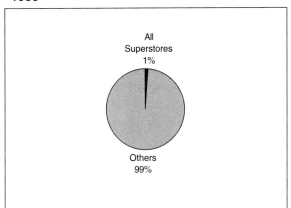

1998

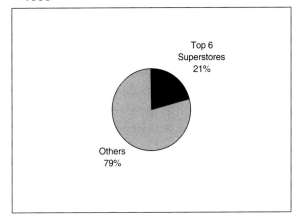

Note:
— In May 1986, Staples opened the first office products superstore
— In October 1986, Office Depot opened the second office products superstore
Over the years, industry players have come and gone:

# of Stores	1986	1988	1997
Staples	2	22	742
Office Depot	3	26	613
Office Max		14	713
Office America		5	
WORKplace		7	
HQ Office Supplies Warehouse			
Office Club		15	
HQ International			
BizMart		10	
Office Square		2	
Office World		4	
OW Office Warehouse		2	
National Office Warehouse		2	
Office Place		6	
Office Station		2	
Office Shop Warehouse		6	
Office Stop			
OP Club		6	
TOTAL	5	129	2068

Staples Financial Data	
1998 sales ($bn)	8.38
1998 EBITDA ($bn)	0.4478
1998 EBITDA margin	5.3%
EPS growth (last 5 years)	42.6%
EPS growth (next 5 years)	28.4%

Corruption as a whole in the Argentine office supply market was significant as well. When investigating the market, I was amazed at how these companies manage their businesses without any information system to speak of; it is like driving with your eyes closed. The lack of ethics has much to do with these companies' approach to doing business. It is normal practice for some companies to take bribes in selecting their office supplies provider. Also, many companies in Argentina would manage their business to maximize tax evasion, by cooking the books or by selling products for cash that had been written off as scrap. As a result, these competitors were excellent at cash management. For instance they only paid their bills with the endorsed check of a customer and would never account for that sale in the system. This way they knew the money coming in the door would go out the door to settle the bills.

It was clear to Freire and Bilinkis that they had to overcome the logistics challenge and that they had to be much more efficient than the incumbent players to compensate for the advantages these players gained through dubious behavior.

Officenet—Getting Started

Initial Diligence

In July of 1996, Freire and Bilinkis presented a preliminary business plan to Adamo and his group of investors. The investor group was impressed with the proposal and decided to give them $50,000 to develop a complete proposal. Over the following months, the two worked on putting together a detailed model on the business and in October 1996, they headed to the United States to round out their diligence on the industry and to validate the assumptions of their financial model. Bilinkis recounted the experience of the trip:

> We did a search on the Web for U.S. office supply companies of various sizes—$5 million, $20 million, and $40 million in sales. We wanted to get an idea of the issues we might face as we grew so we targeted firms at different sizes; we even had a chance to meet the head of a $2.5 billion firm—U.S. Office Products—after they purchased the largest company we targeted. What amazed me was how open and responsive these managers were. We took with us a list of 500 questions (see **Exhibit 7** for a sample of the list) ranging anywhere from how they segment the market to the size of their boxes. And they answered most of the questions in surprising detail. It was crazy; I only sent them an email and they set aside one, and even two, days for us. I don't know why they did it; maybe they were just curious about what Argentines were like!

Freire and Bilinkis both quit their respective jobs in September 1996, after they had completed a preliminary business plan, but before funds had been secured. All they had was $50,000 for research and took the risk of ending up jobless if they could not secure funding. In the preliminary plan, Freire and Bilinkis estimated they would need $2 million for start-up capital, but after their trip to the United States, they determined they would need closer to $4 million because of an accelerated growth rate in sales in the revised plan. In December 1996, Freire and Bilinkis presented their final business plan to the investor group. The group was surprised by the large increase in the capital requirements but decided to fund the investment. As part of the agreement, the investment would be staged, with $2,000,000 committed up front for 1997 and the balance of the funds subject to the achievement of certain milestones. With that, Officenet had begun.

Growing Pains: The Early Days of Officenet

"In January, we started off as two guys with two cell phones," Freire recalls, "and that was it. By May, we had built a company called Officenet. In hindsight, I am amazed that we pulled this off." After finding suitable office space, the two partners began hiring people and negotiating with suppliers. Freire continued:

> We wanted to make it look like we were a five star international company, so we got a room at a five star hotel in town and began the interview process . . . without disclosing the name of the company, of course. After receiving over 1,000 applications, we hired 23 people over

EXHIBIT 7
Sample from Officenet's Due Diligence List

Source: Officenet.

GENERAL/PRODUCTS
- Number of SKUs at the Beginning and Later
- ABC Classification: Rotation
- Sales by Company and by Employee
- Value Added by Logistics to the Consumer
- Measurements of Logistic Performance
- Cost of Logistics/Sales

LOGISTIC PROCESS
- Merchandise Receiving
- Fixed Time
- Unloading Area
- Admission/Quality and Quantity Control
- Bar Code

Storage/Warehousing
- Layout/Size/Location/Prices
- Preparation: Times, Stages
- Sectors: Expensive Goods/Fractioned/Small/Large
- Inventory Days/Size and Rotation
- Security/Fire/Insurance
- Employee Profiles
- Wages and Incentives

Order Taking
- Telemarketing
- Fax/Interface
- On line: EDI/Internet/Intranet; Check of Inventories
- Things they *don't* have

Picking
- Per Order or per Sector
- Printed Pick-list/Information
- Collector: Parallel/Core Process/Radiofrequency
- Interface with System if Batch
- Sequence/Internal Movements

Exit Control
- Everything or Sample
- Box ID

the first three months of operation–and it was probably the most thorough hiring process we have had yet. Everyone was scheduled to start on April 1, but on March 31, we still had not received our office furniture. Only twelve hours before our employees were set to arrive did we have chairs for them to sit in. We were worried that we were going to be this "multinational" corporation with people sitting on the floor!!

At the same time we were hiring our first employees, Santi and I began negotiating with potential suppliers. We gave a PowerPoint presentation to 80 vendors with the intention of picking 40 of them as our suppliers. To select the 80, we conducted research on all of the products sold by our competitors-to-be. Then we analyzed what brands were sold by which companies and we came to a list of 200 companies. Out of those, we selected the 80 that seemed most important. We decided to take a hard line with those 80 companies. We told them that they needed to give us their best pricing conditions or else we would not grow. Instead of starting off with bad prices and decreasing them in eight months we tried to convince them to just start off low. The few U.S. vendors we contacted could understand our situation but it was a little more difficult with the smaller, local vendors. They tended to be very traditional and stuck in their ways. Fortunately, most vendors eventually accepted our plan and we were able to get off the ground. We were even able to raise $180,000 in advertising from vendors to build the catalogue.

Building the catalogue was another challenge for the two partners. "Before designing the catalogue," Bilinkis explained, "we knew *nothing* about the products." Along with their first hire, a 19-year-old general assistant, Pablo Simon, they contacted the vendors and asked them to send Officenet a sample product with the net price attached to the product. By setting up 175 small signs identifying product groups and by dividing all of the samples into piles, the three learned to understand all the products and to conceptualize the catalogue. However, once they had the catalogue completed in July 1997, the education process was not over yet. Since this was the first catalogue in Argentina in any industry, it took some time before the customers were comfortable with the new format. (See **Exhibits 8** and **9** for sample pages from the catalogue.) Bilinkis described the process of designing and introducing the catalogue:

> We needed to keep the concept simple because people in Argentina were not used to the concept of a catalogue. We were fortunate in that most of the purchasing process with existing firms was impersonal in practice; customers would fax in their orders and would receive their products at a later, often undetermined, date. And they often did not know exactly what they were ordering. We felt that even though 80% of our focus group said they didn't want a catalogue, the increased service of Officenet would win them over. It was sort of like a computer; you don't have one and don't know why you should need one. But when you get one, you don't see how you could live without it. With the Officenet catalogue, not only were people able to see exactly what they wanted, but they were guaranteed free delivery within 24 hours on all products. This focus on service was what we believed would be our edge in consolidating the market.

Sales started taking off as customers became more comfortable with the new format of the catalogue (see **Exhibit 10** for historical monthly sales data). While the company was successful at generating sales, there were many challenges the company faced as it began to mature. Freire remembered the education they received in their early days:

> When the company launched, we decided to stock $250,000 in inventory. After the first couple of months, when sales were under $60,000 per month, this was more than sufficient. But then, in August, our inventory levels represented 2.5 months of sales and in September it was just one month of sales. Instead of increasing our inventories with the increases in sales, we kept inventory flat at $250,000. We first started running out of high rotation products, then low rotation products and then, before we knew what was happening, we found we didn't have one out of three products. The company grew so quickly and we were so focused on other things, we just missed it.
>
> So we went into crisis mode. We got each vendor to rush us products and in five days time, fifty vendors delivered goods all at once. We were so swamped we couldn't take proper inventory, so, as a result, we now had goods, but none were available for sale. So all four of us—Santi, Pablo, Lucas Pagliettini (the Purchasing Manager) moved into the warehouse and inputted the products into the system. But then payables were swamped! We thought we would never see the end of it.
>
> I think part of the problem is that when we traveled to the United States, we took them seriously on everything they did. Take for instance our receivables. The largest company we looked at had $40 million in sales and had only one guy in collections. After six months, we had sales of close to $350,000 but had collected nothing from our customers. I realized this problem in September 1997 when I met someone who didn't know I was affiliated with Officenet. This person told me, "Officenet? They are great! They have the best products, excellent service, and, best of all, you never have to pay them!" Things do not work the same in Argentina as they do in the United States. Today we have 10% of our payroll in collections. We need to pick up the payments in person or else we will never receive payment. We are doing better right now, but it is something we are constantly trying to improve upon.

EXHIBIT 8   **Officenet Catalog**

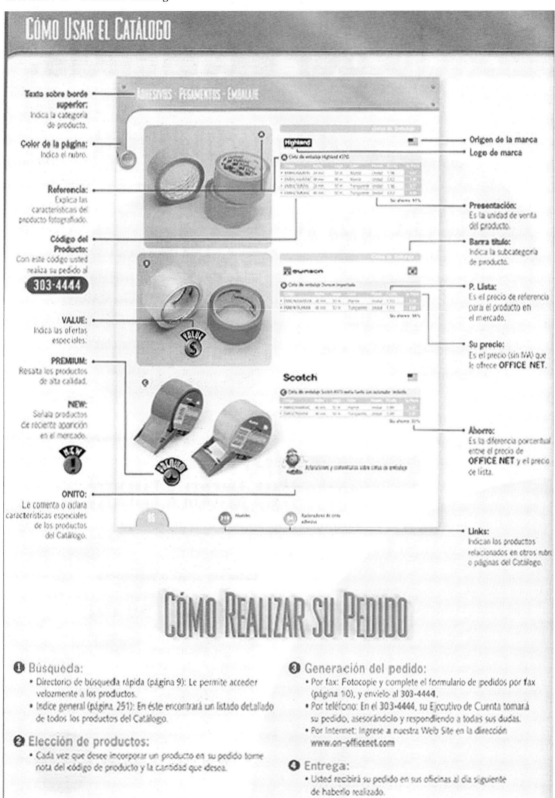

CÓMO REALIZAR SU PEDIDO

❶ Búsqueda:
- Directorio de búsqueda rápida (página 9): Le permite acceder velozmente a los productos.
- Índice general (página 251): En éste encontrará un listado detallado de todos los productos del Catálogo.

❷ Elección de productos:
- Cada vez que desee incorporar un producto en su pedido tome nota del código de producto y la cantidad que desea.

❸ Generación del pedido:
- Por fax: Fotocopie y complete el formulario de pedidos por fax (página 10), y envíelo al 303-4444.
- Por teléfono: En el 303-4444, su Ejecutivo de Cuenta tomará su pedido, asesorándolo y respondiendo a todas sus dudas.
- Por Internet: Ingrese a nuestra Web Site en la dirección www.on-officenet.com

❹ Entrega:
- Usted recibirá su pedido en sus oficinas al día siguiente de haberlo realizado.

EXHIBIT 9 **Officenet Catalog**

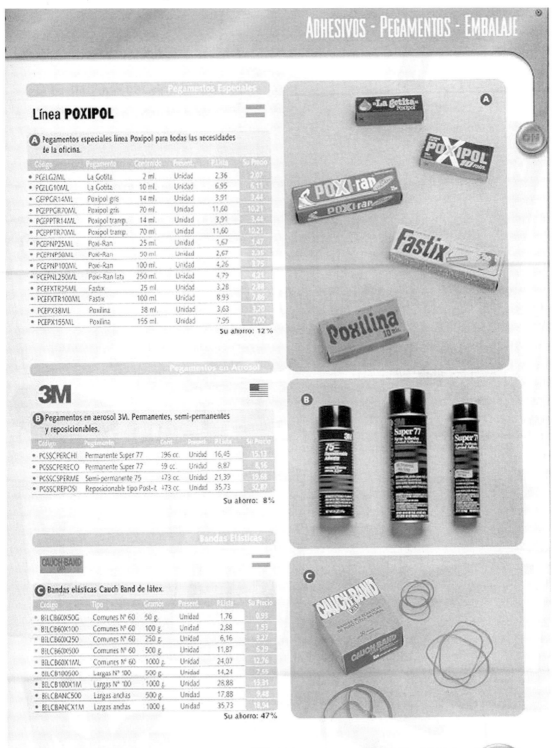

ADHESIVOS - PEGAMENTOS - EMBALAJE

Pegamentos Especiales

Línea **POXIPOL**

(A) Pegamentos especiales línea Poxipol para todas las necesidades de la oficina.

Código	Pegamento	Contenido	Present.	P.Lista	Su Precio
PGELG2ML	La Gotita	2 ml.	Unidad	2.36	2.07
PGELG10ML	La Gotita	10 ml.	Unidad	6.95	6.11
GEPPGR14ML	Poxipol gris	14 ml.	Unidad	3,91	3,44
PGEPPGR70ML	Poxipol gris	70 ml.	Unidad	11,60	10,21
PGEPPTR14ML	Poxipol transp.	14 ml.	Unidad	3,91	3,44
PGEPPTR70ML	Poxipol transp.	70 ml.	Unidad	11,60	10,21
PGEPNP25ML	Poxi-Ran	25 ml.	Unidad	1,67	1,47
PGEPNP50ML	Poxi-Ran	50 ml.	Unidad	2,67	2,35
PGEPNP100ML	Poxi-Ran	100 ml.	Unidad	4,26	3,75
PGEPNL250ML	Poxi-Ran lata	250 ml.	Unidad	4,79	4,21
PCEFXTR25ML	Fastix	25 ml	Unidad	3,28	2,88
PCEFXTR100ML	Fastix	100 ml.	Unidad	8.93	7,86
PCEPX38ML	Poxilina	38 ml.	Unidad	3,63	3,20
PCEPX155ML	Poxilina	155 ml.	Unidad	7,95	7,00

Su ahorro: 12 %

Pegamentos en Aerosol

3M

(B) Pegamentos en aerosol 3M. Permanentes, semi-permanentes y reposicionables.

Código	Pegamento	Cont.	Present.	P.Lista	Su Precio
PCSSCPERCHI	Permanente Super 77	196 cc.	Unidad	16,45	15.13
PCSSCPERECO	Permanente Super 77	59 cc.	Unidad	8,87	8,16
PCSSCSPERME	Semi-permanente 75	473 cc.	Unidad	21,39	19,68
PCSSCREPOSI	Reposicionable tipo Post-it	473 cc.	Unidad	35,73	32,87

Su ahorro: 8%

Bandas Elásticas

CAUCH BAND

(C) Bandas elásticas Cauch Band de látex.

Código	Tipo	Gramos	Present.	P.Lista	Su Precio
BELCB60X50G	Comunes Nº 60	50 g.	Unidad	1,76	0,93
BELCB60X100	Comunes Nº 60	100 g.	Unidad	2,88	1,53
BELCB60Q250	Comunes Nº 60	250 g.	Unidad	6,16	3,27
BELCB60Q500	Comunes Nº 60	500 g.	Unidad	11,87	6,29
BELCB60X1ML	Comunes Nº 60	1000 g.	Unidad	24,07	12,06
BELCB100500	Largas Nº 100	500 g.	Unidad	14,24	7,55
BELCB100X1M	Largas Nº 100	1000 g.	Unidad	28,88	15,31
BELCBANC500	Largas anchas	500 g.	Unidad	17,88	9,48
BELCBANCX1M	Largas anchas	1000 g.	Unidad	35,73	18,94

Su ahorro: 47%

 219 Muebles   **235** Productos de limpieza   **91**

EXHIBIT 10
Officenet's Monthly
Sales Data

Source: Officenet.

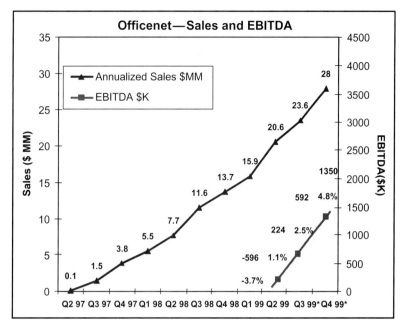

Officenet—Sales and EBITDA

Legend:
— Annualized Sales $MM
— EBITDA $K

Data points (Annualized Sales $MM): 0.1, 1.5, 3.8, 5.5, 7.7, 11.6, 13.7, 15.9, 20.6, 23.6, 28

EBITDA labels: -596 (-3.7%), 224 (1.1%), 592 (2.5%), 1350 (4.8%)

X-axis: Q2 97, Q3 97, Q4 97, Q1 98, Q2 98, Q3 98, Q4 98, Q1 99, Q2 99, Q3 99*, Q4 99*

* Estimated.

Despite some of these growing pains, the company was quite successful and came up with a number of innovations. In November 1997, the company decided to split its sales force into two groups: one called "hunters," which was responsible for generating new accounts, and one called "gatherers," which was responsible for servicing existing accounts. "This helped us increase the efficiency of our sales force immeasurably," explained Simon, who had become the Sales and Marketing Manager. They also had developed a new inventory control system for receiving, stocking and shipping under the guidance of Leo Piccioli, the Logistics Manager. "One thing we did was organize our inventory in a more efficient manner," explained Piccioli.

> After six months, we discovered that we could identify a small number of items that represented the lion's share of our sales. This inspired us to organize the warehouse around two areas, called Micro Centro and Macro Centro (respectively named after the downtown area and the district surrounding downtown area of Buenos Aires). Together, these areas represented about 70–80% of sales but only approximately 8% of the warehouse space. Combined with a new software system that tracked all aspects of inventory and warehouse control, we have been able to design routes that have increased the speed and accuracy of picking the products for delivery. Additionally, this software system has allowed us to track the efficiency of the individual picking worker and the firm as a whole in all areas of our warehouse and inventory management and we can work on improving the speed and accuracy of our business. We now have the ability to prepare our logistics for future large increases in sales that previously caught us off guard.

Because of the infrastructure problems in Argentina, Officenet had to develop their own delivery network to ensure the delivery of their product. There seemed to be an ample supply of delivery people with their own trucks as recent privatizations had put a significant number of people out of work due to cost cutting measures. While this measure allowed Officenet to overcome some infrastructure barriers in Argentina, it had two important side effects: a relatively high initial per order cost and a limit on the geographic area which they could serve. The management of this delivery system was an area where the company looked for improvement, both logistically and financially.

Initial Success: The Pressure Is On

These innovations helped the company reach operating levels that more than achieved the initial milestones required in the initial funding agreement (see **Exhibit 11** for the milestone requirements and the actual results). In March 1999, Officenet posted its first month of positive results (see **Exhibit 12** for historical financial information). By September 1999, the company had become the market leader in the business-to-business segment of the office supply market. Based on a September run rate of $30 million in annual sales, the company estimated that it had a market share of approximately 15% in the business-to-business segment of the office supply market. Officenet was almost four times as large as the number two player and was bigger than the second, third and fourth largest companies combined. In fact, September also saw the company launch their Web site, migrating 15% of sales to the Internet instantly. This positioned Officenet as one of the leading e-commerce companies in Argentina.

EXHIBIT 11
Milestone Requirements and Actual Results

Source: Officenet.

Description	Requirement	Actual Performance
1998 sales level	$268,000	$345,000
1998 cash flow level	$2,000,000	$2,000,000
1998 net income (loss)	($998,000)	($744,000)

EXHIBIT 12 Officenet Historical Financial Information—Fiscal Year Ended December 31, 1999.

Source: Officenet.

(In US$ thousands)	1997	1998	1999
Income Statement Information			
Revenues	1,526.4	10,019.7	21,718.0
Cost of Goods Sold	−1,066.4	−7,068.0	−15,989.0
Gross Profit	460.0	2,951.7	5,729.0
Selling and Administrative Expenses	−1,107.2	−3,472.8	−5,459.5
Other Expenses			
EBITDA	−647.2	−521.1	269.5
Depreciation	−45.1	−91.8	−243.0
Amortization	−51.6	−281.5	−281.5
Operating Income	−743.9	−894.4	−255.0
Net Interest Expense	0.0	0.0	−225.0
Profit Before Taxes	−743.9	−894.4	−480.0
Taxes	0.0	0.0	0.0
Net Income	−743.9	−894.4	−480.0
Balance Sheet Information			
Cash	276.4	164.6	0.0
Working Capital	922.8	2,191.8	2,734.5
Gross Fixed Assets	517.4	4,510.0	5,325.0
Less Accumulated Depreciation	−96.7	−470.0	−713.0
Net Fixed Assets	420.7	4,040.0	4,612.0
Other Assets	289.4	448.0	1,645.0
Total Debt	53.4	1,027.4	3,654.5
Total Equity	1,856.1	5,817.0	5,337.0
Other Information			
Capital Expenditures	517.4	3,992.6	815.0

Despite this initial success, however, there were many areas in which the company needed to improve. The collections process needed to be overhauled to operate in a more efficient manner. At this point in time, Officenet often made two trips to a customer in one day: once to deliver the products, and once to collect the payment. The company needed to redesign its routes, adjust its staffing levels, and retrain its personnel in order to improve this process. More importantly, the company wanted to consider automating more of its logistics. Greater warehouse automation and designing a delivery routing system similar to the system designed for preparing the items for delivery were only two proposals Piccioli was investigating for the company. In addition, as the company grew, Freire and Bilinkis needed to add more human and financial resources to the sales and marketing effort. All of this took money, which Officenet did not have enough of to complete most of these requirements. Freire wondered whether Officenet's capital expenditure forecasts were accurate and sufficient (see **Exhibit 13** for company forecasts).

The commercial paper program could help with many of these problems, but there were other, larger strategic issues the company was grappling with that could affect its financing decision. Officenet was slowly reaching a crossroads. "We need to figure out what we want to be when we grow up," Freire said. There were three ideas Freire and Bilinkis had for the business: geographic expansion, expansion into the business-to-consumer market segment, and a dramatic expansion into Internet-driven commerce. In order to achieve the long-term growth potential required to realize an exit for the business,

EXHIBIT 13 Officenet Forecasts—Fiscal Year Ended December 31

Source: Officenet.

(In US$ thousands)	2000	2001	2002	2003
Income Statement Information				
Revenues	35,803.7	44,754.6	53,705.6	61,761.4
Cost of Goods Sold	26,093.4	32,421.0	38,360.6	43,761.7
Gross Profit	9,710.3	12,333.6	15,345.0	17,999.7
Selling and Administrative Expenses	−7,957.7	−9,549.3	−11,077.2	−12,406.4
Other Expenses				
EBITDA	1,752.6	2,784.3	4,267.8	5,593.2
Depreciation	−264.0	−330.0	−396.0	−455.4
Amortization	−281.5	−281.5	−281.5	−281.5
Operating Income	1,207.1	2,172.8	3,590.3	4,856.3
Net Interest Expense	−510.6	−638.2	−510.6	−510.6
Profit Before Taxes	696.5	1,534.6	3,079.8	4,345.8
Taxes	0.0	0.0	−923.9	−1,303.7
Net Income	696.5	1,534.6	2,155.8	3,042.0
Balance Sheet Information				
Cash	0.0	0.0	0.0	0.0
Working Capital	2,226.2	2,615.8	3,139.0	3,850.1
Gross Fixed Assets	6,825.0	7,825.0	8,825.0	9,825.0
Less Accumulated Depreciation	−893.0	−1,013.0	−1,133.0	−1,253.0
Net Fixed Assets	5,932.0	6,812.0	7,692.0	8,572.0
Other Assets	1,645.0	1,645.0	1,645.0	1,645.0
Total Debt	3,769.7	3,504.1	2,752.0	1,301.1
Total Equity	6,033.5	7,568.1	9,724.0	12,766.0
Other Information				
Capital Expenditures	1,500.0	1,000.0	1,000.0	1,000.0

Officenet needed to begin preparing itself. Any shift in strategy would take time to complete and would affect its immediate funding decisions. Bilinkis outlined their thoughts on each of the three options:

Geographic Expansion

The first option was geographic expansion, which, for many reasons, would mean Brazil. The big benefit to the Brazilian market was the absolute size of the market (see **Exhibit 14** for a comparison of Argentina and Brazil). By expanding there, Officenet could benefit in two ways. First, they could potentially achieve enormous synergies in purchasing and, consequently, dramatically increase the purchasing power of the entire organization. "Scale is the name of the game in the United States," according to Bilinkis. "Companies like Staples can have their own private label products in things like paper." Although Officenet had started some private label products of its own, these efforts were quite limited due to the size of the company. The increased scale achieved through regional expansion could allow them to expand this dramatically. Second, a Brazil expansion could help on the exit by allowing Officenet to command a regional multiple, rather than a single-market multiple, upon a realization event. "Both the public markets and the strategic buyers see more value in a company operating in more than one country," Bilinkis explained. "The big opportunity is that no one is expanding in the region. We are the only ones in Latin America with a regional vision and our concept is well suited for expansion." Since the office supply market in Brazil was very fragmented and otherwise quite similar to Argentina, Officenet felt it could employ much the same entry strategy they did in Argentina—namely first via catalogue and then by expansion into the Internet. Bilinkis continued:

> That being said, there are tremendous risks involved in this option. There are huge cultural and language barriers in moving to Brazil. To begin with, they speak Portuguese and we speak Spanish. This risk can not be taken lightly as there have been many cases of Argentine companies entering the Brazilian market and destroying the entire business. We would be essentially risking the entire business; since the Brazilian market is three times the size of the Argentine market, the Brazilian operations would dwarf the operations here in Argentina. Moreover, there are personal risks involved and neither Andy nor I want to move to Brazil, but that would probably be necessary if we chose this route. Finally, there is a huge problem caused by another similarity with Argentina—corruption. As a result, we made Officenet a green field effort in Argentina because we thought existing entities were not suitable for us to use as a platform for growth. That is not really much of an option in Brazil, as we would probably need to partner with a local company because of the cultural differences. It may be difficult to find an attractive and ethical partner in there.

EXHIBIT 14 Comparative Economic Indicators, 1998

Source: Compiled from Economist Intelligence Unit data.

	Argentina	Brazil	Chile	Peru	Colombia	Mexico	United States
GDP ($ bn)	340.1	760.3	76.2	63.5	94.5	422.8	8,511.0
GDP per head ($)	9,414	4,745	5,139	2,566	2,310	4,382	31,488
Consumer price inflation (avg; %)	0.9	1.4	5.0	7.3	21.1	15.9	1.6
Current-account balance ($ bn)	−13.7	−34.8	−4.6	−4.0	−6.3	−15.8	−233.8
% of GDP	−4.0	−4.6	−6.1	−6.3	−6.7	−3.7	−2.7
Exports of goods ($ bn)	25.2	51.1	14.7	5.7	11.0	117.5	673.0
Imports of goods ($ bn)	−29.6	−57.4	−17.1	−8.2	−14.2	125.2	919.1
External debt ($ bn)	135.0	192.1	34.5	30.4	34.2	158.5	—
Debt-service ratio, paid (%)	54.7	39.5	20.0	28.7	32.2	28.1	—

Business-to-Consumer

The driver behind entry into the business-to-consumer segment was that it would provide a big increase in the size of the market Officenet served. The company estimated that in Argentina the business-to-consumer market was roughly the same size as the business-to-business market. By entering this segment, Officenet could effectively double the potential size of their business. From an operational standpoint, there were other benefits such as clear logistical and purchasing synergies that Officenet would benefit from by entering this segment. Moreover, they could potentially gain some of the scale necessary to expand their private label efforts. Finally, there were exit considerations. "This could also help our exit because this is a flashy segment in the eyes of the public and private markets," according to Bilinkis. Officenet felt they would probably be able to significantly increase the valuation multiple they would receive at exit by entering the segment. However, as Bilinkis explained, there was a downside to this strategy.

> The problem with expansion into this segment really boils down to a profitability issue. Right now our cost per order is about $40 and our average order size is around $190 dollars. In the business-to-consumer market the average order size would be significantly lower than in the business-to-business segment. There may be certain aspects of the business that we may be able to change to lower that cost, but we are not clear what those even are let alone the impact they would have on the business. We could also impose a minimum order size, but that could dramatically limit the effective market we would be targeting. Marketing is another issue. There might be better direct marketing information in this segment, but loyalty in this segment is a big question mark. This just expands us further into the unknown. That being said, there is a question if this even matters: if we sell to a strategic buyer based on a multiple of sales, then our profitability is a moot issue.

Internet Expansion

The goal on entering this segment would be to phase out the catalogue and conduct 100% of Officenet's business over the Internet. In the longer term, the founders envisioned they could even start line extensions into other businesses and become a "Wal-Mart of the Internet" in Argentina. Officenet would effectively become logistical experts in Argentina and would position the company in other markets where logistical expertise was important. "The big draw of this option is the *huge* multiples seen for Internet companies these days," Bilinkis said. "This would probably change our exit options—from a Staples or an Office Depot to an Amazon or a Star Media—but the line extension would bring about an even *greater* increase in the exit multiple."

However, the downside in this option was large as well. Even without the line extensions, the capital investment required would be enormous and the Internet penetration rate in Argentina was very low on an actual and a projected basis when compared to other countries. Bilinkis elaborated:

> We would risk becoming such a hybrid that no one would be interested in us. Also, with the line extension, the risks go through the roof; we could easily just vaporize the entire firm. Not only do we still have to develop much of the know-how to sell things like CDs, but we also would be grappling with even lower order sizes than in the business-to-consumer segment of the office supply market. Given the infrastructure problems we face in our existing business, this could be a formidable challenge.

As the game ended at La Bombonera, Freire and Bilinkis mulled over these problems. Not only did they soon have to make a decision on the commercial paper program, but they also had to make a decision on the long-term strategy of the company. In making the decision, they had to consider more than just the positive and negative aspects of each option but other interests as well. They needed to think about the interests of Carlos Adamo and the investor group and how each of the options fed into their original charge set out by Adamo back in 1996. Plus they had to think about the interests of their most likely exit opportunity, the BBRs, and what these firms considered important in a business partner or acquisition target. Finally, Freire and Bilinkis needed to think about their own interests and what they wanted to achieve personally and professionally. "Could we work for a firm that is like a P&G or rapidly becoming that way," Bilinkis asked. With the sun setting on a warm spring evening in Buenos Aires, Freire and Bilinkis left the stadium to head back to work. Soccer was great: 90 minutes of excitement and then you go home. Building a company was different: continued excitement, but no relief in sight.

Case 3

Officenet (B): After the Merger

Andy Freire and Santiago Bilinkis were sipping their morning coffee in Officenet's new warehouse in Sao Paulo, Brazil. As they looked out at the long rows of half-empty inventory racks, they could not help but wonder what would come next. A lot had happened over the last year to the company they had founded together in 1997 (see **Exhibit 1** for a timeline of events). Officenet had grown from a total of 203 employees and 16 truck drivers in October 1999 to 350 and 21 respectively in August 2000. Several months before, in February 2000, Officenet had been acquired for $31 million by Submarino.com, a business-to-consumer (B2C) Internet company that sold books, CDs, DVDs, cellular phones and other products in Brazil, Argentina, Mexico, Spain and Portugal. (Officenet and Submarino operated as independent businesses joined together by a holding company.) It was August 15th now, and Officenet had just successfully expanded its office supplies business into Brazil. Freire held the position of President and CEO of Officenet, while Bilinkis, who previously managed Officenet's operations in Argentina, became Chief Financial Officer for the company (see **Exhibit 2** for an organizational chart). The two founders hired a new country manager for Argentina, and Martin Escobari, one of Submarino's founders, was chosen to launch and run Officenet's Brazilian operations.

Freire and Bilinkis had spent the good part of the morning discussing the company's future, which was highly uncertain. By merging Submarino and Officenet, the companies had planned to leverage Submarino's e-commerce platform to sell office supplies online to small and medium-sized enterprises (SMEs). The merger had seemed like the ultimate thing to do in the "New Economy."[1] It seemed like a good match: Officenet's deep logistics expertise and business-to-business (B2B) acumen, combined with

---

[1] The "New Economy" referred to a rapid growth of Internet-based businesses during the late 1990s and the very early part of the 21st century.

E-Business Fellow Meredith Collura and Professor Walter Kuemmerle prepared this case with assistance from the HBS Latin America Research Center. HBS cases are developed solely as the basis for class discussion. Cases are not intended to serve as endorsements, sources of primary data, or illustrations of effective or ineffective management.

EXHIBIT 1
Timeline of Officenet Events

Source: Officenet.

January 1997	Officenet Argentina founded through US$4 million investment from PCP Investments (only US$2 million committed up-front for 1997)
September 1999	Officenet launched Version 1.0 of web site
December 1999	Officenet achieved annual net sales of US$21.4 million (EBITDA positive) and sold 13% of Officenet to Submarino for $4 million in cash (first of two-part sale)
January 2000	Officenet launched Version 2.0 of its web site
February 2000	Officenet sold remaining 87% of Officenet to Submarino for additional $9 million in cash and $18 million in Submarino stock (second part of two-part sale, totaling $31 million for 100% ownership)
April 2000	Officenet/Submarino filed for IPO on NASDAQ; weeks later cancelled plans for IPO (NASDAQ fell 35% between mid-March to mid-April)
July 2000	Officenet launched business service offerings in Argentina
August 2000	Officenet launched greenfield operations in Brazil and became leading retailer of office supplies to small and medium-sized enterprises (SMEs) in Latin America with US$36 million annualized net sales (40% online)

EXHIBIT 2   **Officenet Organizational Chart**

Source: Officenet.

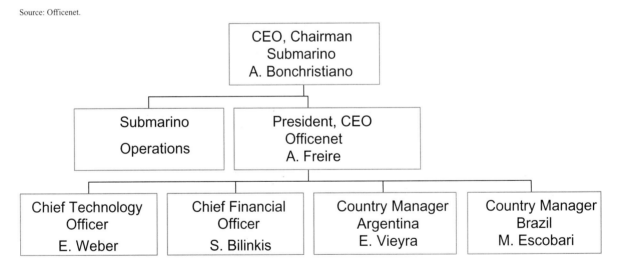

Submarino's e-retailing brand name, geographic presence in five countries and know-how. The company had filed for an Initial Public Offering (IPO) on the NASDAQ stock exchange in April 2000, just a couple of months after the sale had closed, to take the combined B2B and B2C company public. However, they were forced to abandon these plans soon after, when the NASDAQ slid during mid-March through April 2000 (see **Exhibit 3**). In fact, since then several "dot-coms"[2] had shut down their operations (see **Exhibit 4**).

[2] "Dot-coms" were companies with Internet-based business models.

EXHIBIT 3 NASDAQ Composite

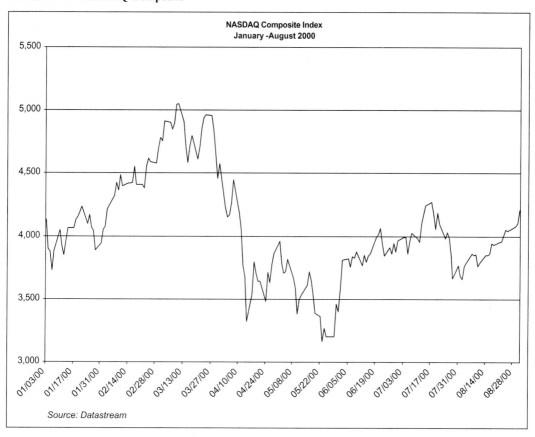

Source: Datastream

EXHIBIT 4 Dot-com Casualties During 2000

Source: Compiled from Webmergers.com data, *The Industry Standard* data.

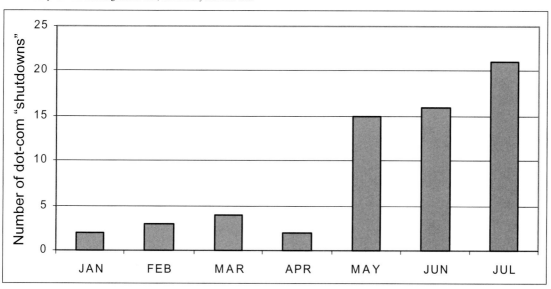

Notes:
• Total dot-com shutdowns through July 2000 totaled 62.
• Roughly 80% of the shutdowns were B2C, the rest B2B.
• Approximately 3,800 jobs were lost due to failures.

The Deal

Carlos Adamo, a partner at PCP Investments and a member of Officenet's Board of Directors,[3] explained Officenet's decision to sell the company:

> We sold Officenet because we needed to take the next step and expand regionally. To succeed as a business, Officenet needed to demonstrate that the concept that was successful in Argentina could be successful in other Latin American countries. To enter new markets we needed at least $30 million, but [my partners and I at PCP] were not ready to invest $30 million on top of the $7 million we had already put in. The size of the investment relative to the size of our fund would have been too large.[4]

Submarino acquired Officenet through a two-part deal in December 1999 and February 2000 for $31 million using cash and equity (see **Exhibit 5** for term sheet). Soon after the sale closed, Adamo joined Submarino's Board of Directors. Submarino's CEO Antonio Bonchristiano commented on the acquisition, which took place shortly before the NASDAQ's peak (refer back to **Exhibit 3**):

> We came across Officenet in September 1999. I met Andy Freire and Santiago Bilinkis and thought, "these guys are unique and I want to do something with them." We visited the company, and the more we learned, the more we were impressed. The company was in a very attractive sector. The office supplies market was huge, highly fragmented and ripe for consolidation.

[3] PCP provided Freire and Bilinkis with US$4 million in private equity funding in January 1997 (with only US$2 million committed up-front for 1997 and the remaining capital contingent upon certain milestones). By 12/99–2/00, at the time of Officenet's sale to Submarino, PCP had invested a total of US$7 million.

[4] Case author's interview with Adamo 5 December 2000.

EXHIBIT 5   **Termsheet for Sale of Officenet to Submarino**

Source: Officenet.

Basic Terms	
Valuation of Officenet	$31 million
Payment Structure	Submarino paid $13 million in cash, $18 million in equity (based on 2/00 valuation)
Timeframe/Ownership Structure	Submarino purchased 13% of Officenet in 12/99 (for $4 million in cash), and remaining 87% in 2/00 (for $9 million in cash and $18 million in equity)

"Dealbreaker" Terms (agreed upon at 12/99)

The sale of Officenet would *not* take place under any of the following circumstances:
1) Argentina devalued its currency.
2) Submarino was not able to close its second round of funding in the first quarter of 2000.
3) The pre-money valuation for Submarino was lower than $120 million or higher than $180 million.
4) Submarino raised less than $40 million.

Actual Conditions Relative to "Dealbreaker" Conditions

The following conditions existed at the time of the Officenet sale, and therefore the transaction closed as planned:
1) Argentina did *not* devalue its currency.
2) Submarino successfully closed its second round of funding in 2/00.
3) Submarino's pre-money valuation was $140 million.
4) Submarino raised $71.3 million during its second round of funding.

But at the time, we didn't have the money to do a deal. We started negotiating with Officenet anyway, and ended up doing a deal such that Submarino bought 13% of Officenet in December 1999 for $4 million in cash. (Incidentally, we borrowed $4 million from two of our investors, GP Investimentos and Warburg Pincus, as a bridge loan to be repaid after our second round of funding, which we knew would take another few months to complete.) Following this first part of the deal, we had the obligation to buy the remaining 87% of Officenet, once we closed our second round of financing. We agreed to pay Officenet an additional $9 million in cash (for a total of $13 million in cash), plus $18 million in Submarino stock. Officenet was willing to accept our stock at an undetermined future valuation because the market was so hot [in late 1999 and early 2000].[5]

For Officenet, operations continued as usual immediately after the acquisition. Adamo commented:

After the sale, it was business as usual for Officenet in Argentina for three or four months. The original plan was to have a Submarino/Officenet IPO in April or May. But the market blew up before then, and by June we learned that there was no chance for us in the @public equity: market. We had to find a different way to finance Submarino and Officenet. At that time, we chose to operate Submarino and Officenet as independent businesses and to provide each business with its own CEO and management team. However, we thought it made sense to keep them both under one umbrella.

Operating Initiatives

According to Pablo Simon, Officenet's Vice President of Business Development, Officenet had undergone three major operational changes since the sale: Officenet had 1) transferred 40% of its sales online, 2) launched operations in Brazil and 3) began offering business services in Argentina.

1. *Shifted sales online.* By August 2000, 40% of sales were done online. Simon commented that, "Submarino allowed Officenet to enter the New Economy. Officenet had only begun site testing (to Version 2.0 of its web site) in January 2000, so Officenet was very new to the New Economy." Because online sales were more profitable, Officenet began providing incentives for account managers and customers to buy online. For example, the company's site included features such as detailed product search, inventory availability and product recommendations. Despite its online presence, the company continued its use of printed catalogs and telemarketing as channels for closing sales; often account managers assisted customers with online buying on the phone. However, this was a very costly process.[6] Thus, the company planned to further expand sales via the Internet in the future.

2. *Launched operations in Brazil.* Officenet officially launched greenfield operations in Brazil on August 1, 2000. Officenet shared warehouse space in Submarino's new distribution facility located outside of Sao Paulo. Officenet offered 2,200 SKUs[7] and projected that it would achieve revenues of $50,000 during August, its first month of operation. According to Simon, as a result of the company's expansion into Brazil, the company became more international, as meetings were conducted in Spanish,

---

[5] Case author's interview with Bonchristiano 1 December 2000.

[6] For a reference based on another industry: studies at a major U.S. pharmaceutical company indicated that a customer order handled by an employee via telephone cost approximately $350 to process. On the other hand, a customer order processed online cost only $20, and was twice as likely than a telephone order to be resolved without additional follow-up. (Casewriter interview, March 14, 2001.)

[7] SKU referred to a Stock Keeping Unit, or a number associated with a product for inventory purposes.

Portuguese, and English, and as Simon described, "not everyone knew each other in meetings." In early August, the company had announced plans to enter Chile, Mexico, and Spain over the next couple of years.

3. *Expanded service offerings.* Since Officenet launched its web site in September 1999, it offered free content, such as news and downloadable tools, such as "how to conduct interviews of potential employees," "how to choose a supplier," and "how to organize one's daily agenda." But in July 2000, Officenet expanded its offerings to include business services, such as travel bookings, online English language courses, and shipment/delivery of documents and bulk packages. To provide these services Officenet partnered with local suppliers, who contributed a percentage of these transactions as commission to Officenet. Officenet also planned to launch a Request for Proposal (RFP) service for companies to submit and bid for contracts online.

Siamese Twins: Can We Afford a "Break-Up"?

While their original plan was to take the two businesses public under the holding company arrangement, it had become increasingly clear to Freire and Bilinkis over the last several months that Officenet and Submarino were in fact two very different businesses with distinct customer segments, economics and business models. Submarino was a pure-play Internet company launched in late 1999, whereas Officenet was established in 1997 and had both offline and online sales. In addition, there was still a good deal of optimism around B2B e-commerce in Latin America, which in 1999 was estimated to be a $350 million market, or twice the size of B2C in Latin America.[8] *Lehman Brothers* estimated that annual spending online was $1705 for the average business customer in Latin America, but only $306 for the average Latin American consumer. Hype and excitement around B2C, which Adamo referred to as the "bad boy of NYC," had waned in Latin America, due to low Internet penetration, high customer acquisitions costs, low credit card usage, and widespread customer concerns about security.

Adamo summarized some of Officenet's learnings:

We learned [from Submarino] that is very difficult to build a brand and build a customer base purely using the Internet as a channel. We learned first-hand at Officenet that moving existing customers online by leveraging an established operations and delivery platform was much easier. It was clear to us that the easiest way to grow a business was through a combination of offline and online channels.

The financial positions of Officenet and Submarino were also quite different (see **Exhibit 6** for Officenet's historical and forecasted financial statements). By August, Submarino's annualized 2000 revenues were only $15 to $20 million, relative to Officenet's projections of 2000 revenues that would likely exceed $40 million. Most significantly, Officenet had been profitable in 1999 based on annualized sales of $26 million, while Submarino had yet to make a profit. Freire and Bilinkis wondered whether potential investors would want to fund the different businesses as they existed now, as one company.

On that August morning, Freire and Bilinkis focused their conversation on how they were going to expand geographically, increase Internet sales, and enhance business service offerings. While on one hand they weren't sure whether Officenet would be able to grow its business if it stayed "married" to Submarino, on the other hand they owed a lot of their recent learnings to Submarino. And there would be a lot of potential synergies if Submarino's business continued to expand.

[8] Schleiein, M., "Latin America Online: Sizing the Internet in Latin America," *Lehman Brothers*, 06 July 2000, p. 5

EXHIBIT 6   Officenet Historical Financial Information

Source: Officenet.

(In US$ thousands)	1999 (12 mos)	2000 (6 mos)
Income Statement Information		
Gross Revenues	25,908	15,824
Net Sales	21,412	13,078
Cost of Goods Sold	(17,490)	(11,105)
Gross Profit	3,922	1,973
Selling and Administrative Expenses	(3,944)	(3,029)
Other Expenses	—	—
EBITDA	(22)	(1,056)
Depreciation	(177)	(122)
Amortization	—	(17)
Operating Income	(199)	(1,195)
Net Interest Expense	(195)	(194)
Profit Before Taxes	(394)	(1,389)
Taxes	(184)	(79)
Net Income	(578)	(1,468)
Balance Sheet Information		
Cash	289	124
Working Capital	8,127	8,200
Gross Fixed Assets	4,518	5,577
Less Accumulated Depreciation	(290)	(429)
Net Fixed Assets	4,228	5,148
Other Assets	22	508
Total Debt	8,176	10,958
Total Equity	4,490	3,022
Other Information		
Capital Expenditures	999	1,059

Note: Figures are for Officenet only.

EXHIBIT 6 (Continued) Officenet Forecasts—Fiscal Year Ending December 31

Source: Officenet.

(In US$ thousands)	2000	2001	2002	2003
Income Statement Information				
Gross Revenues	36,978	71,578	180,465	282,107
Net Sales	30,560	59,155	149,145	233,146
Cost of Goods Sold	(22,260)	(42,555)	(108,845)	(172,546)
Gross Profit	8,300	16,600	40,300	60,600
Selling and Administrative Expenses	(12,400)	(20,700)	(34,500)	(41,700)
Other Expenses	(1,100)	(800)	(1,700)	(2,300)
EBITDA	(5,200)	(4,900)	4,100	16,600
Depreciation	(380)	(720)	(915)	(1,005)
Amortization	(40)	(45)	(52)	(52)
Operating Income	(5,620)	(5,665)	3,133	15,543
Net Interest Expense	(350)	(180)	(80)	(10)
Profit Before Taxes	(5,970)	(5,845)	3,053	15,533
Taxes	—	(50)	(160)	(420)
Net Income	(5,970)	(5,895)	2,893	15,113
Balance Sheet Information				
Cash	26,500	12,500	3,500	500
Working Capital	11,500	18,500	25,000	45,000
Gross Fixed Assets	34,000	48,000	61,000	67,000
Less Accumulated Depreciation	(7,700)	(8,465)	(9,432)	(10,489)
Net Fixed Assets	26,300	39,535	51,568	56,511
Other Assets	500	500	500	500
Total Debt	9,800	21,930	28,570	35,400
Total Equity	55,000	49,105	51,998	67,111
Other Information				
Capital Expenditures	(4,000)	(14,000)	(13,000)	(6,000)

Note: Figures are for Officenet only.

Also, it was not clear whether Submarino would let Officenet go. Freire commented, "Officenet needs to raise money quickly to expand, as does Submarino. The questions are: who needs capital more urgently, Officenet or Submarino, and can we obtain capital at a lower cost if we stay together?"

Freire and Bilinkis agreed to move cautiously and not to force any major decisions. They discussed several questions. What financing alternatives would Officenet have if it were to split from Submarino? How long would it take potential U.S. strategic investors, such as Staples or OfficeMax, to perform due diligence? They estimated that a due diligence process by a strategic buyer would probably take a few months. Could anyone else provide equity capital faster? Would the terms be attractive, or would they have to substantially dilute their already small ownership stake in the company (4.5%)?

Case 4

Term Sheet Negotiations for Trendsetter, Inc.

Wendy Borg and Jason Kushdog had some big decisions to make on this muggy June 3rd, 2000. And probably for the first time since the founding of their company in March 2000 they were entirely uncertain what to do. They were the CEO and COO, respectively and co-founders of Trendsetter, Inc., a software start-up that would provide innovative warehouse and distribution solutions for clothing retailers. The software would contain a demand-forecasting module that was better than anything else in the industry. The entrepreneurs expected that their software would do for fashion retailing what the spreadsheet had done for accounting—not a small feat. The two had been meeting with several venture capital firms (VCs) and had just received offering documents known as term sheets from two of the VCs: Alpha Ventures and Mega Fund (see **Exhibits 1** and **2**). With neither having any experience in raising capital from venture investors, Borg and Kushdog were not sure where to begin evaluating each proposal—let alone deciding upon which one to take. "This is all very confusing," lamented Kushdog, "and scary as well. We are running out of the seed money that we have both contributed to the venture so we need to act fast." Kushdog estimated that Trendsetter, Inc. had about six more weeks of cash to burn. As the two sat across from each other for lunch at one of the tables of their "corporate dining room" (a local Weston restaurant called Ye Olde Cottage), they knew they should get a grasp of the relative merits of each proposal before they were finished with the day. The question was where to start?

Getting It Started: The Background of Trendsetter, Inc.

Wendy Borg had many years of experience as a supply chain management consultant and worked with many fashion retailers in the past. It was in this capacity that she and Jason Kushdog had met while she was working on an assignment. Kushdog had been the head

Dean's Fellow William J. Coughlin (MBA '99) prepared this case under the supervision of Professor Walter Kuemmerle. HBS cases are developed solely as the basis for class discussion. Cases are not intended to serve as endorsements, sources of primary data, or illustrations of effective or ineffective management. We wish to thank Stephen Hill and Andy Goldfarb (MBA '93), Managing Directors at JAFCO Ventures for their contributions to this case.

buyer for Livin' Large (LL), a bricks-and-mortar retailer of specialty fashion clothing for big and tall people. The two had worked with each other for a number of years and each individually had a desire to start his own business. One night while working late on a project for LL, Kushdog revealed to Borg his desire to start his own company. It just so happens that Borg had been working on an idea for a warehouse and distribution management software program for retailers and Borg suggested to Kushdog that the two start the company together. After thinking it over, Kushdog agreed to work with Borg and the two quit their jobs to start Trendsetter.

At first, the two operated with their own capital but knowing very well that they would need to raise outside money. Borg explained.

> This type of software solution will take a lot of money to develop. Also, we needed a partner firm for the development phase. Luckily, I was able to get a former client Waldo, a major fashion retailer, to commit to work with us while we were developing the product. Although we hadn't signed any contracts yet, I had a good relationship with the CEO and I was promised that we would get a signed agreement from them once we got funding. That's why we approached the VCs.

Borg and Kushdog were no fools and knew that most top-tier venture capitalists received more than 2,000 unsolicited business plans per year. In most of these venture capital firms all 2,000 plans made it straight into the garbage can—without receiving any consideration. Experience had shown VCs that it was not worth their time to look for needles in a haystack. Rather, VCs focused on plans that came with recommendations and endorsements (from other VCs, entrepreneurs whom the VC had previously backed, investors in the VCs' fund and from other "friends").

Fortunately, Borg and Kushdog knew two insiders who were well-connected in the venture capital community. "Our friends got us in the door at several firms," Kushdog recalled, "Once a first meeting had been arranged we knew that the ball had been teed up for us and we needed to hit it. We knew that we were on to something when our first meeting with a VC that was originally scheduled for 30 minutes ended up lasting 2 hours—and the VC did not complain."

Borg and Kushdog received a lot of interest from the VC community. They presented to seven VCs. And six of them really liked the plan and the team that was in place. The process of meetings and presentations took almost two months, however. This was longer than the entrepreneurs had expected. So it was a real relief for the two when they finally received term sheets from the VCs they wanted the most: Alpha Ventures and Mega Fund. Both funds were top tier VCs and had a lot of experience in retail and software. Plus the chemistry with both firms seemed good. Borg explained:

> With Mega everything went smoothly. Alpha I think really liked our idea but was pretty skeptical about our ability to get a five-star client like Waldo on board early. As a result they really liked us but wanted to invest at a lower valuation than other VCs because they did not think we could book $500,000 in revenues in the first year. After a lot of talking they came around and made a fair offer.

Since Borg and Kushdog thought that both VC firms, Alpha Ventures and Mega, were an equally good fit it would come down to who gave Trendsetter a better offer. Neither of the entrepreneurs had any experience in analyzing term sheets and although the topline valuations from both VC firms were not that different the entrepreneurs knew that they had to be very careful when comparing covenants in both term sheets. "I don't like lawyers but I think we need one, now," said Kushdog as they left the restaurant. "I agree," replied Borg, "but wouldn't it be reassuring if we could figure this out on our own first?"

EXHIBIT 1   **Alpha Ventures Term Sheet**

Trendsetter, Inc.
June 2000

Summary of Terms for Proposed Private Placement of Series A Convertible Preferred Stock

Issuer:	Trendsetter, Inc. a Delaware corporation (the "Company").
Amount and Securities:	4,761,905 shares of Series A Convertible Preferred Stock (hereafter simply called Series A Preferred) and Escrowed Shares (as described below).
Aggregate Proceeds:	$5,000,000
Pre-money Valuation:	$7,350,000, assuming an employee option reserved pool of 3,000,000 shares and no issuance of Escrowed Shares.
Escrowed Shares:	In addition to the 4,761,905 shares of Series A Convertible Preferred Stock, 501,253 shares of Series A Preferred are to be held in escrow and not issued unless the Company has not achieved fiscal year 2000 revenues of $500,000 ("Escrowed Shares")
Issue Price:	The weighted average issue price will be $1.05 if the Escrowed Shares remain in Escrow. If the Escrow Shares are released to the Investors, the Issue price will be $0.95.
Dividend:	The holders of Series A Preferred shall be entitled to receive noncumulative dividends in preference to any dividend on the Common Stock in the amount $0.08 on all Series A Preferred outstanding, when and as declared by the Board of Directors. For any other dividend or distributions, Series A Preferred participates with Common Stock on an as-converted basis.
Anticipated Closing Date (the "Closing"):	June 16, 2000
Founders:	Wendy Borg, Jason Kushdog
Investors:	Alpha Ventures ("Alpha") and Silicon Valley Partners ("SV") and other mutually agreeable investors ("Investors"). Alpha $2.25 million SV: $2.25 million Other Investors: $0.50 million
Liquidation:	Initial pay issuance Price plus declared but unpaid dividends on each share of Series A Preferred Stock. Thereafter each share of Series A Preferred Stock and Common Stock share on an as-converted basis until such time as each share of Series A Preferred Stock has received three times the initial pay issuance Price. A merger, reorganization or other transaction in which control of the Company is transferred will be treated as a liquidation.
Conversion:	The holders A Preferred shall have the right to convert the Series A Preferred, at any time, into shares of Common Stock. The initial conversion rate shall be 1:1, subject to adjustment as provided below.
Automatic Conversion:	The Series A Preferred shall be automatically converted into Common Stock, at the then applicable conversion price, (i) in the event that the holders of at least a majority of the outstanding Series A Preferred consent to such conversion or (ii) upon the closing of a firmly underwritten public offering of shares of Common Stock of the Company at a per share

(continued)

EXHIBIT 1 (Continued)

	price not less than $5.00 per share and for a total offering of not less than $15 million (before deduction of underwriters commissions an expenses) (a "Qualified IPO")
Antidilution Provisions:	The Series A Preferred shall have broad-based weighted average antidilution protection on issuances of shares. No adjustment will be made for the issuance of up to 3,000,000 shares of Common Stock (or any options for Common Stock) to employees, directors or consultants pursuant to board-approved equity incentive plans.
Voting Rights:	Series A Preferred votes on an as-converted basis, but also has class vote as provided by law. Also, approval of at least 60% of Series A Preferred is required for (i) the creation or issuance of any senior or *pari passu* security; (ii) an increase in the number of authorized shares of Preferred Stock; (iii) any adverse change to the rights, preferences and privileges of the Preferred Stock; (iv) an increase in the size of the Board of Directors; (v) repurchase of Common Stock except upon termination of employment; (vi) repurchase or redemption of any Preferred Stock (except pursuant to redemption provisions of Articles); (vii) any transaction in which control of the Company is transferred; (viii) any amendment to the Bylaws or Articles of Incorporation; (ix) any dividend or distribution on capital stock of the Company; and (x) any sale, pledge, license or transfer of all or substantially all of the Company's assets.
Representations and Warranties:	Standard representations and warranties from the Company.
Nondisclosure and Development Agreements:	Each officer, employee and consultant of the Company will have entered into a proprietary information and inventions agreement in a form acceptable to the Investors.
Right of First Refusal:	The Investors shall have a pro rata right, based on their percentage equity ownership of Preferred Stock, to participate in subsequent equity financings of the Company. If any shareholder of Common stock (or equivalents) wants to sell shares, he must offer them first to the holders of Series A Preferred.
Co-Sale Rights:	If a shareholder of Common or equivalent wants to transfer shares, holders of Series A Preferred have a right to participate on a pro rata basis (based on their percentage ownership of the Series A Preferred) in the sale. This does not apply to sales in a Qualified IPO or afterward.
Information Rights:	So long as any Investor of the Series A Preferred holds 250,000 or more shares, the Company will deliver to each Investor annual, quarterly and monthly financial statements; annual business plan and budget, within 45 days prior to the beginning of the fiscal year; and other information reasonably requested by an Investor. Each Investor shall also be entitled to standard inspection and visitation rights.
Board of Directors:	Five total. The Series A Preferred will be entitled to elect two representatives (Alpha will have the right to nominate one representative of Series A Preferred); the Common Stock will be entitled to elect one representative (Wendy Borg as Founders' representative and CEO); and the Common Stock

(continued)

EXHIBIT 1   (Continued)

	and Series A Preferred, voting together on an as-converted basis, will be entitled to elect two representatives—one outsider recommended by the Founders and acceptable to Investors; and one additional outside director acceptable to the board. In the case the escrowed shares are released, the Investors will have the option of replacing the fifth director (i.e. the outside director acceptable to the board) with a new director chosen jointly by the investors. Will set a reasonable board meeting schedule at the first board meeting.
Compensation Committee:	Three total. Two representatives of the Series A Preferred and one outside director. All senior management compensation will be approved by the Compensation Committee.
Indemnification:	Directors and officers will be entitled to indemnification to the fullest extent permitted by applicable law.
Counsel and Expenses:	Investor counsel to draft closing documents. The Company to pay all Investor legal and administrative costs of the financing, not to exceed $20,000 plus disbursements.
Registration rights:	(a) Beginning on earlier of three years from closing, or six months after Qualified IPO, two demand registrations upon initiation by holders of at least 30% of outstanding Series A Preferred for aggregate proceeds in excess of $7,500,000. Expenses paid by Company.
	(b) Unlimited piggyback registration rights subject to pro rata cutback permitted at the underwriter's discretion. Full cutback upon a Qualified IPO; 30% minimum inclusion thereafter. Expenses paid by Company.
	(c) Unlimited S-3 Registrations of at least $750,000 each, with no more than two per year. Expenses paid by Company.
	No future registration rights may be granted without consent of a majority of Investors unless subordinate to Investors' rights.
Key Person Insurance:	Company to obtain key person life insurance policy on Wendy Borg and Jason Kushdog, in the amount of $2 million each, with Company as beneficiary.
Founders Stock, Options and Vesting:	Except as approved by Board, employee option pool to have 48 month vesting with 12-month cliff and linear monthly vesting thereafter. Wendy Borg's and Jason Kushdog's shares vest 25% on purchase, with remainder vesting linearly over a 36 month period with the unvested portion subject to buyback provisions. The Company has the right to repurchase unvested shares at cost in the event of employment termination. The Founders will receive six months additional vesting in the event of a termination without cause, and will also receive accelerated vesting, following a change of control transaction. In addition, the Founders will receive six months salary as severance pay in the event of a termination without cause.
Restriction on Common Stock Transfers:	(a) No transfers allowed prior to vesting.
	(b) Right of first refusal on vested shares until initial public offering.

(continued)

EXHIBIT 1 (Continued)

	(c) No transfers or sales permitted during lock-up period of up to 180 days required by underwriters in connection with stock offerings by the Company.
Use of Proceeds:	The proceeds from the sale of the Series A Preferred will be used for working capital according to the Company's business plan.
Finders:	The Company and the Investors will each indemnify the other for any finder's fees for which either is responsible.
Other:	The Company agrees to file a qualified Small Business Corporation.
Conditions Precedent to Financing:	This summary of terms is not intended as a legally binding commitment by the Investors, and any obligation on the part of the Investors is subject to the following conditions precedent: Completion of legal and accounting documentation satisfactory to the prospective Investors. Satisfactory completion of due diligence by the prospective Investors. Execution by the Investors of definitive agreements approved by Investor's counsel and executed by the Investors and the Company.
Alpha Ventures, Inc.	Trendsetter, Inc.
_____	_____
Nancy Downard, Managing Principal	Wendy Borg, President & CEO

Post-Closing Capitalization Table

Common Stock outstanding:	[_____]
Employee Stock Options—Reserved Pool:	[_____]
Of which granted: 0	
Series A Preferred Outstanding	[_____]
Total fully-diluted shares	[_____]

EXHIBIT 2 Mega Fund Term Sheet

Trendsetter, Inc.
June 2000

Summary of Terms for Proposed Private Placement of Series A Convertible Preferred Stock

Issuer:	Trendsetter, Inc., a Delaware corporation ("Company").
Investors:	Mega Fund ("Mega" or "Investors").
Current Outstanding:	4,500,000 shares of Common Stock ("Common"). In addition, by closing the Company will have reserved for issuance under its stock option plan an aggregate of 2,500,000 shares of Common (the "Reserved Shares"), of which 929,889 shares are subject to previously granted options.
Amount of Investment:	$5,000,000
Type of Securities:	Series A Convertible Participating Preferred Stock ("Series A Preferred" or "Preferred").

(continued)

EXHIBIT 2 (Continued)

Number of Shares:	5,000,000 shares of Series A Preferred.
Price per Share:	$1.00 per share of Series A Preferred ("Series A Purchase Price").

Rights, Preferences, Privileges and Restrictions of Series A Preferred

(1) **Dividend Provisions:** A cumulative dividend on the Series A Preferred will accrue at the rate of ten percent (10%) per annum commencing on the one year anniversary of the issuance of the Series A Preferred (the "Accruing Dividends"). The Accruing Dividends shall cease to accrue when the per share amount of the Accruing Dividends total twenty-five percent (25%) of the Series A Purchase Price. Accruing Dividends shall be payable (a) if, as and when determined by the Board of Directors or (b) upon the liquidation or winding up of the Company. In addition, if a dividend is paid on Series A Preferred or Common, then Series A Preferred shall receive same dividend on an as-converted basis. No dividend will be declared or paid on Common without the consent of (i) the holders of at least 60% of the then outstanding shares of Series A Preferred.

(2) **Liquidation Preference:** In the event of the liquidation or winding up of the Company, the holders of Series A Preferred will be entitled to receive in preference to the holders of Common, an amount per share of Series A Preferred (the "Series A Liquidation Amount") equal to the sum of (a) one-and-one-quarter times the Series A Purchase Price and (b) all declared but unpaid dividends (including the Accruing Dividends) on such share of Series A Preferred. After payment in full of the Series A Liquidation Amount, the remaining amounts available for distribution shall be distributed ratably among all holders of Common and Series A Preferred on an as-if converted basis.

A consolidation or merger of the Company into or with any other entity or entities (other than a merger to reincorporate the Company in a different jurisdiction or a merger in which the shares of the Company outstanding immediately prior to the closing of such merger (a) represent or are converted into shares of the surviving entity that represent at least two-thirds of the total number of shares of the surviving entity that are outstanding or are reserved for issuance immediately after the closing of the merger and (b) have the power to elect at least two-thirds of the surviving corporation's directors) or the sale of 50% or more of the Company's assets or the acquisition in a single transaction or series of related transactions by any person or group of 50% or more of the Company's outstanding Common will be deemed to be a liquidation or winding up for purposes of the liquidation preference unless the holders of at least 70% of the then outstanding shares of Series A Preferred, voting together as a single class, elect not to treat any such event as a liquidation, dissolution or winding up.

(continued)

EXHIBIT 2 (Continued)

(3) **Redemption:** The Series A Preferred shall be redeemed at (I) a redemption price that shall equal the sum of (a) the Series A Purchase Price and (b) any declared but unpaid dividends on such shares of Series A Preferred (including the Accruing Dividends) and (II) there shall be no redemption of Series A Preferred upon an acquisition of the Company or upon a Qualified Public Offering (as hereinafter defined). If the Series A Preferred are not redeemed as required then the Investors shall have the right to designate a majority of the directors.

(4) **Antidilution Provisions:** The Series A Preferred shall have weighted average antidilution rights on issuances of shares at a price less than 100% and greater than 50% of the Series A Purchase Price (except for the issuance of the Reserved Shares); provided if new shares are issued at a price less than or equal to 50% of the Series A Purchase Price then the adjustment will be full ratchet; provided, however, that with respect to a Designated Financing, this ratchet adjustment shall be made only if the holder of Series A Preferred invests its Pro Rata Share. A Designated Financing shall be an equity financing of at least $100,000 made on a pro rata basis (based on ownership of Common) to all Investors that is designated by the Board as a Designated Financing. Each holder's Pro Rata Share equals a portion of the Designated Financing equal to the number of shares of Common owned by such holder divided by the number of shares of Common owned by all Investors.

(5) **Voting Rights:** The Series A Preferred will vote together with the holders of Common *on* an as-if converted basis on all matters presented to the stockholders. In addition to any other required vote, the Series A Preferred will be entitled to vote as a separate series as described under "Protective Provisions" below.

(6) **Protective Provisions:** Consent of the holders of a super-majority of the Series A Preferred will be required for certain corporate actions, which actions and consent thresholds shall be agreed upon by the parties and shall be more specifically set forth in the closing documents.

(7) **Conversion:** Each share of Series A Preferred may be converted by its holder at any time into a number of shares of Common equal to the Series A Purchase Price divided by the conversion price of the Series A Preferred. The conversion price will initially be equal to the Series A Purchase Price and will be subject to adjustment as specified in paragraph 4 above.

(8) **Automatic Conversion:** The Series A Preferred will be automatically converted into Common, at the then applicable conversion price, in the event of an underwritten public offering of shares of the Common at a public offering price per share that is no less than $20.00 (to be appropriately adjusted for any stock splits or stock

(continued)

EXHIBIT 2   (Continued)

	dividends) in an offering with aggregate proceeds to the Company of not less than $25,000,000 (a "Qualified Public Offering").
Information Rights:	So long as any of the Series A Preferred is outstanding, the Company will deliver to each Investor annual, quarterly and monthly financial statements, annual budgets and other information reasonably requested by an Investor.
Registration Rights:	(a) Beginning on earlier of three years from closing, or six months after Qualified IPO, two demand registrations upon initiation by holders of at least 30% of outstanding Series A Preferred for aggregate proceeds in excess of $7,500,000. Expenses paid by Company.
	(b) Unlimited piggyback registration rights subject to pro rata cutback permitted at the underwriter's discretion. Full cutback upon a Qualified IPO; 30% minimum inclusion thereafter. Expenses paid by Company.
	(c) Unlimited S-3 Registrations of at least $750,000 each, with no more than two per year. Expenses paid by Company.
	No future registration rights may be granted without consent of a majority of Investors unless subordinate to Investors' rights.
Use of Proceeds:	The proceeds from the sale of the Series A Preferred will be used for working capital.
Board Representation and Meetings	The charter will provide that the authorized number of directors is five. The Board arrangements will include one member elected by the Common Stock (Ms. Borg as founders' representative and CEO), two Series A investor elected representatives, one outsider company nominated and one outsider company-nominated and acceptable to all.
Preemptive Rights:	The Investors will be given preemptive rights to purchase securities issued by the Company (other than Reserved Shares) based on their percentage equity ownership of Preferred Stock. The integrated preemptive rights will be set forth in the Securities Purchase Agreement discussed below.
Reserved Shares:	The Reserved Shares will be issued from time to time to directors, officers, employees and consultants of the Company. Upon closing of the Offering, the Company will have reserved for issuance under its stock option plan an aggregate of 2,500,000 shares of Common (the "Reserved Shares"), of which 929,889 shares are subject to granted options. The Company shall not increase the number of Reserved Shares under the Incentive Plan or any similar stock option plan without the consent of the holders of a majority of the then outstanding Series A Preferred shares. Unless subsequently agreed to the contrary by the holders of 60% of the shares of outstanding Series A Preferred, any issuance of shares in excess of the Reserved Shares will be a dilutive event requiring the issuance of additional shares of Common as provided above in "Antidilution Provisions" and will be subject to the Investors' preemptive rights. The Reserved Shares will have 48-month vesting with a 12 month cliff and linear monthly vesting thereafter. Founder's shares vest 25%

(continued)

EXHIBIT 2   (Continued)

	on closing, with remainder vesting linearly over a 36 month period, and unvested portion subject to buyback provisions. The Company has the right to repurchase unvested shares at cost in the event of employment termination. By closing the founders will have executed an employment agreement mutually agreeable to the founders and the investors.
Nondisclosure and Developments Agreement:	Each officer and employee of the Company with access to proprietary information will have entered into a nondisclosure and developments agreement in a form reasonably acceptable to the Investors.
The Securities Purchase Agreement:	The purchase of the Series A Preferred will be made pursuant to a Securities Purchase Agreement drafted by counsel to Mega. Such agreement shall contain, among other things, appropriate representations and warranties of the Company, covenants of the Company reflecting the provisions set forth herein and other typical covenants, and appropriate conditions of closing, including, among other things, qualification of the shares under applicable Blue Sky laws, the filing of a certificate of amendment to the Company's charter to authorize the Series A Preferred, and an opinion of counsel. Until the Securities Purchase Agreement is signed by both the Company and the Investors, there will not exist any binding obligation on the part of either party to consummate the transaction. This Summary of Terms does not constitute a contractual commitment of the Company or the Investors or an obligation of either party to negotiate with the other.
Expenses:	The Company will pay up to $20,000 for expenses of Thatcher, Major & Blair, LLP, counsel to the Investors.
Finders:	The Company and the Investors will each indemnify the other for any finder's fees for which either is responsible.
Mega Fund, Inc.	Trendsetter, Inc.

—————————————————	—————————————————
Jessica Upbeat, Managing Principal	Wendy Borg, President & CEO

Post-Closing
Capitalization Table

Common Stock outstanding:	[ ]
Employee Stock Options—Reserved Pool:	[ ]
Of which granted:	
Series A Preferred Outstanding	[ ]
Total fully-diluted shares	[ ]

Case 5

Cityspace

It was Monday, July 6, 1998 and Marc Meyohas, managing director of Cityspace, was having lunch at Café Europa with Nick Bohane and Stuart Newman, the other two members of Cityspace's management team. Café Europa had opened in order to provide authentic food for the nearby Italian consulate to the United Kingdom, and had never advertised; it was, in Meyohas's view, one of London's undiscovered treasures. Now it provided a respite from the modest meeting room where the young entrepreneurs had been trying to gain support for their venture offering an interactive, multimedia information service for tourists.

Cityspace's management had spent the morning meeting with two different venture capital (VC) firms who might participate in the company's upcoming second round financing. The company hoped to raise at least £2.5 million ($4.2 million) to fund the expansion of its i$^+$ (information plus) network of information kiosks throughout London, as well as extending the service to additional platforms, such as hotel TV systems.

Since its incorporation in October 1995, Cityspace had accomplished a great deal. It had attracted industrial partners, developed a working kiosk prototype, secured agreements with prime London tourist areas such as the National History Museum and Madame Tussauds, and had launched its kiosk network which had grown to 17 kiosks throughout London. Sponsors had been secured for some of the content, and the company had also generated revenues through contracts with outside cities. The plan to extend the i$^+$ service to hotels had been well received by both hotel chains and the three leading providers of hotel TV services. Despite all this, however, securing VC commitments for the needed financing had proven difficult.

Time was beginning to run short. Although the company was temporarily generating positive cash flow from a contract with the city of Cardiff, they would not make it through the end of the year without additional financing. Meyohas hoped some of the VCs would commit soon, but if they didn't there were some difficult questions to be asked. Did the valuation they sought leave enough upside for a VC investor? If no VCs came forward, where else might Cityspace look for funding? Finally, was Cityspace really pursuing the right business model?

Professor Walter Kuemmerle and Charles M. Williams Fellow Chad Ellis, MBA '98 prepared this case. HBS cases are developed solely as the basis for class discussion. Cases are not intended to serve as endorsements, sources of primary data, or illustrations of effective or ineffective management.

Birth of a Venture

In 1992, a friend, Brendan MacNamara, who wanted to develop an interactive information service for the Sydney Tower in Australia, approached Meyohas. Meyohas adapted the concept and the two men formed a preliminary business plan for "Cityscape," which was to focus on the Parisian tourist market. They put together a business plan, but were unable to raise sufficient funds and ultimately abandoned the project.

Despite this setback, Meyohas remained convinced of the potential for developing a profitable information service for tourists. Returning to London, he had a brief stint at Lehman Brothers as a corporate finance analyst before leaving to set up a small team selling medical insurance. (See **Exhibit 1** for resumes of Cityspace management.) During this time Meyohas continued to think of ways to improve the original business model and soon determined to give his vision another chance. He persuaded Bohane and

EXHIBIT 1   **Resumes of Cityspace Management and Key Employees**

Source: Cityspace.

Marc Meyohas: Managing Director

Marc conceived and founded Cityspace three years ago since when he has been working solely on developing the concept and the Company. Marc has been involved in all aspects of the Company, including raising capital, finance and project management, investor relations, sales and marketing, business development and recruitment.

Prior to Cityspace, Marc worked briefly in corporate finance at Lehman Brothers as an analyst. Following this, he set up a sales and marketing team specializing in marketing medical services, which he ran successfully for two years. This involved marketing and selling the products of BUPA, PPP and other healthcare providers. The operation included direct marketing, telemarketing and direct sales activities. Marc then conceived and planned the Cityspace project and in November 1995 he secured start-up funding from London Merchant Securities.

Nick Bohane: Business Development Director

Nick has been working with Cityspace since its inception. He has been responsible for business development, including trade marketing, sites and trade relationships, public relations and brand development. Nick is also a founding investor in Cityspace.

Prior to Cityspace, Nick worked for ten years for Burson-Marsteller, part of Young & Rubicam Group, mainly in investor relations. His final two years at Burson-Marsteller were spent in various cities in Russia, Kazahkstan and Egypt, setting up representative offices for the company, recruiting local employees and working on privatizations.

Stuart Newman: Creative Director

Stuart has been working at Cityspace since March 1996 and prior to that he was involved with the Company as a consultant. Stuart is responsible for the Company's product offering which involves determining the creative direction of each product, the appropriate technical strategy and the resource requirements. Stuart's role is also to ensure consistency of development work across the product range.

Before joining Cityspace, Stuart was a founding director of an Internet marketing consultancy, with a client list that included Levi's, Diesel and the European Leisure Software Publishers Association. Prior to setting up this agency, Stuart held various positions in consumer marketing and public relations.

Lingan Vairavamoorthy: Programming Manager

Lingan is responsible for the technical development of the Company's products. This includes software development, networking and integrating with hardware platforms and managing the programming team.

Prior to joining Cityspace, Lingan headed up development teams for various multimedia companies. His work has included kiosks, award-winning CD ROMs and client server solutions for clients including Ford, Consumer Association, Madame Tussaud's and SWIFT.

Newman to join him[1] and, with seed money from his former boss at Lehman Brothers and from London Merchant Securities (LMS), formed Cityspace—the new venture's name indicating its origins.

Bohane had worked for Burson-Marsteller, a subsidiary of Young & Rubicam, for the previous ten years. He had met Meyohas through their mutual involvement with Place to Be, a children's charity. Despite what looked like a comfortable corporate career path, Bohane found the transition to a start-up venture fairly easy to make: "For the last two years my job had been setting up new offices in emerging markets. I managed a $6 million budget almost alone. I'd gotten used to working in a fairly entrepreneurial environment and I liked it. I liked the Cityspace concept, and found the idea of working for myself very attractive."

Meyohas also preferred entrepreneurship to corporate finance. "At Lehman, I worked stupid hours," he remembered. "Cityspace is still more stressful, but I leave work at the office when I leave and am able to enjoy myself. It has been a relatively good life in terms of hours."

Not all of Cityspace's founding members were as suited to the entrepreneurial lifestyle, however. In addition to providing financing, Meyohas's boss from Lehman left his position as a director of the firm in order to help start the new venture. Although his 14-year tenure in investment banking had prepared him for some of the rigors of starting a new venture, he was unable to cope with the uncertainties inherent in a start-up, and was prone to doing excessive analysis. Within months of joining Cityspace, he had returned to his old position.

At this time Cityspace noticed that the chairman of the British Tourist Authority, Ms Adele Biss, was leaving her post. Realising that they needed to build high-level links in the travel and hospitality world, Cityspace wrote to her asking if she might be interested in advising the company. Biss, who had previously created and sold her own marketing services company, took a liking to the operation and the entrepreneurial management ethos, and provided the team with valuable input and contacts.

The i[+] Service

Cityspace's core concept was simple. By presenting tourists with an interactive system that would provide information about popular attractions, events and places to shop or eat, they hoped to entice users to make bookings and advertisers to sponsor segments of the product. Bohane explained the need in the theater segment: "Over three million tickets are sold to London tourists each year in a highly fragmented retail market that leaves visitors poorly served. Over a third of overseas visitors still book in person at the venue, rather than through an intermediary. Even if our only added value was to eliminate the need to queue [wait in line] to buy tickets, the service would be useful."

Although at the time the i[+] was only available on a kiosk platform, management emphasized that the service was largely independent of the platform. Newman explained: "We're not a technology company; we use technology to deliver a product. Part of the strength of i[+] from a commercial perspective is that it can easily grow to fit new platforms with minimal adjustments."

The Kiosk

Although Cityspace believed that its service was substantially platform-independent, it was clear that for the venture to succeed, the first platform—the stand-alone kiosk—would have to succeed first.

---

[1] Newman originally worked for Cityspace on a consulting basis before becoming Creative Director in March 1996.

Cityspace looked at existing kiosk products and decided that they did not meet their functional or aesthetic needs. The company designed their own kiosks with the help of a local design firm. (See **Exhibit 2** for a picture of an i[+] kiosk.) Each kiosk contained a customized Pentium II computer, a 14.1" touch-sensitive flat screen, a 300 dpi thermal printer, a credit card reader for on-line bookings and speakers. Each kiosk had an estimated life of three years and cost approximately £7,500 to construct.

The start screen of a Cityspace kiosk offered the user a choice of six languages: English, German, French, Italian, Spanish and Japanese. With a language chosen, i[+] would automatically advance to a second screen, offering four basic categories of information:

- Eating out & Drinking. Cityspace's database contained information on over 1,000 restaurants and bars in London. Users could search by location, price range, or the type of food or atmosphere they were looking for.
- What's On. This category featured the popular musicals, shows and concerts in and around London. Users could see video clips of some of the most popular shows.
- Sightseeing—showed all of London's top attractions, often with either still pictures or video clips. Users could ask for an alphabetical listing, or ask for a list of attractions in a particular area in order to focus their search on where they expected to be.
- Shopping—a database of roughly 200 popular London stores sorted by category, location and price range.

In each category, the user could print out a map of selected destinations, including the closest Underground[2] station. The service was based on an intuitive, easy-to-use touch-screen system. Cityspace also took great effort to ensure that its i[+] offered significant content beyond a simple listing of options. Attractions were independently filmed by Cityspace, so that users saw a video clip, often with music and voice-over, to give them a better idea of what they were choosing from. Restaurant listings included ratings assigned by Harden's Guide, a popular London restaurant review which included ratings for quality of food, atmosphere and service.

Attracting Sites

No matter how good the i[+] service was, it was clear that it could only succeed if it was able to win good sites for its kiosks. "Our business has a lot of similarities to retail," explained Bohane. "Our service has to be in good locations or potential customers will never know it exists."

"There's also the competitive angle," added Meyohas. "Once a site has a kiosk they're not likely to want to add another. We think this gives us a good barrier to later entrants, but also means we have to move quickly to secure the best spots." From the outset, therefore, Cityspace strove to locate and contract prime kiosk sites. The company believed the best sites would be those frequented by tourists, such as popular attractions, transport hubs and hotels.

To convince site owners to allocate space for a Cityspace terminal, the company offered both financial and service arguments. From a service perspective, Cityspace pointed out that adding a free, useful service would add value to the location. From a financial side, site-owners were offered a share of revenues generated by the kiosk. Typically, a site owner had a choice of two options. They could pay Cityspace an installation and service fee, which essentially covered the costs of the kiosk. In that case, they would retain 25% of the booking commissions the kiosk generated. Or, they could simply provide a location and require Cityspace to bear all costs, in which case they typically received 10–15% of commissions. (Cityspace did not share advertising revenue with site-owners.)

[2] The name of London's public rail transit.

EXHIBIT 2 The i⁺ Kiosk

Source: Cityspace.

The i⁺ kiosk

- Kiosk designed with Seymour Powell
  - flat screen technology
  - illuminated glass panel with simple instructions

High quality print-outs
take-away information
1,000 print-outs stored

Credit card reader
on-line bookings

Kiosks are networked (ISDN2 links)
information up-dated automatically
kiosk constantly health checked

Although in name Cityspace was almost identical to its predecessor, there were significant differences between the i$^+$ product and that envisioned for Cityscape in Paris. Perhaps most significant was the different plan for revenue generation—whereas the Paris kiosk network had planned to charge users on a pay-per-view basis, Cityspace intended to keep its service *free* and to generate revenues from advertising and bookings. Meyohas explained: "There are really only three business models you can use for a broadcast medium: pay per view, commission from bookings and advertising revenues. While we feel that i$^+$ creates value for the tourist that could theoretically be paid for, the system will grow much more quickly as a free medium. It will be easier for us to capture the value we create through advertising and bookings."

Arguably, the largest obstacle to a pay-per-view model was the user. Since i$^+$ was aimed at tourists, Cityspace had to assume that many users would be unfamiliar with the system and might be unwilling to spend money on an unknown and unfamiliar service. The company had gone to great lengths to make their kiosks attractive and easy to use; it was important to make sure visitors to London had no disincentive to try them out. By contrast, the i$^+$ service lent itself very easily to a model based on advertising and booking.

Advertising

Cityspace felt that its i$^+$ service offered a powerful advertising vehicle. Since only tourists would be likely to use the service, almost every contact would be an ideal target—an individual with money to spend, looking for specific information. With advertisers able to customize their content, and with information printouts increasing the likelihood that a user would follow through and purchase, Cityspace believed it could charge a premium fee for access to its users.

Although Cityspace intended to list all of the most popular shows, attractions, restaurants, etc., on its service, not all listings were equal. Sponsors could pay to ensure that their listings were more likely to be seen and, hopefully, to be selected by the tourist.

The i$^+$ service was separated into four categories of advertisement. First, a single Premium Sponsor would appear on the main display page, along with a dedicated page displaying its services. Thomas Cook, London's largest foreign exchange provider, had already signed a sponsorship contract for £1,000 per kiosk per year. (See **Exhibits 3** and **4** for a summary of advertising opportunities.)

At the next level, each of the four categories (e.g., Eating and Drinking) would have a single sponsor. Cityspace estimated that it could charge such sponsors an annual fee equivalent to 4 pence per opportunity to see their page.

One level in from the category screen, but before the full listing, was another page with up to fourteen individual sponsors per category. Half of these were intended for advertisers who would pay for a listing on all of Cityspace's London kiosks, while the other half would be "enhanced" advertisers, who would select kiosks close to their own location. Thus, a major attraction or chain of restaurants could advertise London-wide, while a single restaurant or smaller attraction could concentrate its advertising spend on a smaller number of kiosks in easy walking distance.

Cityspace based its rates for these advertising spaces on a cost-per-lead basis, where a lead was assumed to be whenever a customer chose to advance from the category page to that of the sponsor. Cityspace estimated that they could charge 9 pence for each lead for advertisers using the entire network, and possibly 18 pence per lead for "enhanced" advertisers.

To date, Cityspace had generally been able to sell advertising space at higher rates than budgeted. It remained to be seen whether this could be maintained as the company worked to fill all of its advertising space, but the centralized i$^+$ gave the company some potent tools with which to convince potential advertisers. Cityspace was able to keep

EXHIBIT 3 Advertising Opportunities

Source: Cityspace.

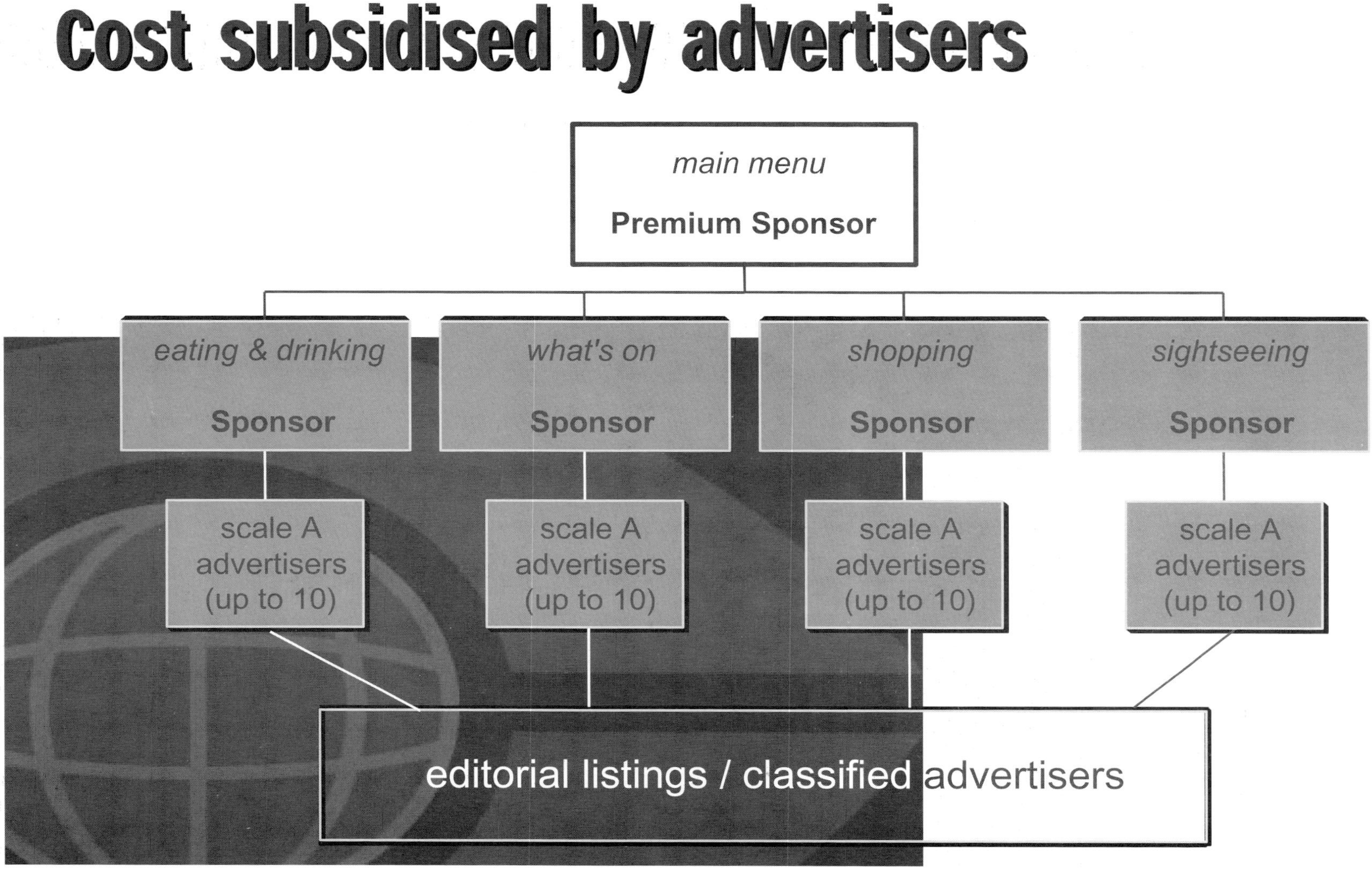

Cost subsidised by advertisers

main menu

Premium Sponsor

eating & drinking
Sponsor

what's on
Sponsor

shopping
Sponsor

sightseeing
Sponsor

scale A advertisers (up to 10)

scale A advertisers (up to 10)

scale A advertisers (up to 10)

scale A advertisers (up to 10)

editorial listings / classified advertisers

EXHIBIT 4   Sample Sponsor Page—Planet Hollywood

Source: Cityspace.

EXHIBIT 4 (Continued)

CATEGORY SPONSOR

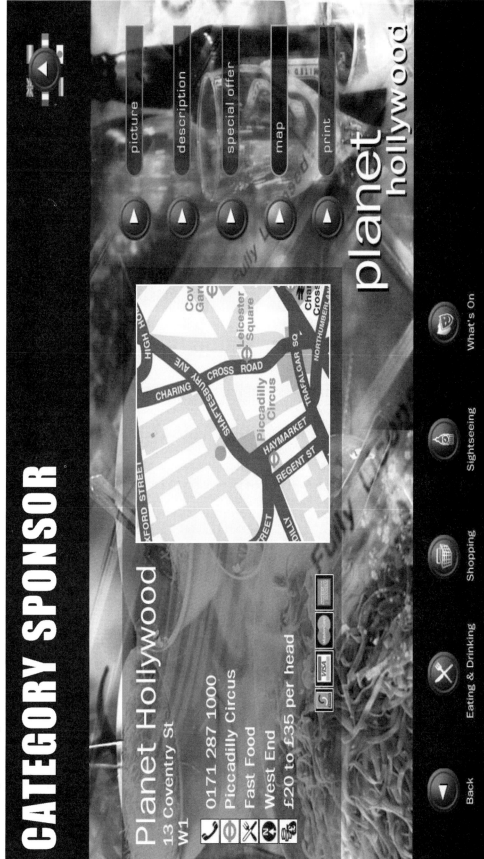

track of hits on each of its screens, enabling the company to offer an accurate estimate of future hits an advertiser could expect. Since these were focused users (i.e., someone selecting the page of a current musical would be more likely to buy a ticket than the average reader of a newspaper or *Time Out*[3]), Cityspace could reasonably expect to charge a premium over competing advertisements.

Bookings

Although Cityspace had already generated some advertising revenues, in the long run the company believed it could generate substantially more revenues from booking fees. Although the technology had not yet been developed, the company was confident that within a few months of completing its next round of funding its terminals would be able to accept credit cards and could therefore conduct transactions for users, for which Cityspace would gain a commission. Cityspace believed it could generate bookings from restaurant reservations, theater tickets and tours.

One of the problems plaguing restaurants was the customer who made reservations but then changed plans, making it difficult for the restaurant to manage its capacity. Cityspace offered a solution. Users of i[+] could make bookings for listed restaurants directly at the kiosk, at a charge of £2 per person. The kiosk would then print out a confirmation of the booking, which would entitle the diner to a discount of £2 per person from the final bill. Thus, the diner effectively put down a deposit on the table (rather than actually paying for the reservation), and the restaurant paid Cityspace £2 per person for customers who booked using the i[+] service. The booking itself would be handled electronically, ensuring that the restaurant had the necessary space and realized that it had been made. Cityspace estimated that the average booking would be for three people.

Another natural area for bookings was theaters. While Cityspace's kiosks couldn't print actual theater tickets, they could produce a receipt to be exchanged at the box office. Cityspace had signed a contract enabling i[+] users to book tickets through FirstCall's system,[4] with Cityspace capturing a commission. Cityspace estimated an average purchase price of £40 per booking, with a commission of 15%.

As the system developed, Cityspace anticipated being able to offer a value-added distribution service as well. Meyohas explained a dilemma Cityspace could help solve:

> If you're managing a theatre, your biggest problem is empty seats. All your costs are up front, so you'd gladly sell an empty seat on the day of the performance for almost nothing. But how do you distribute them? By the time you know the tickets are unsold it's too late for most channels, and you have to be careful that you don't upset the punters who have paid full price by shouting out that you're selling the rest at a discount.

Cityspace believed that the i[+] network was the ideal channel to distribute surplus tickets. Because it was connected live to the inventory of the ticket agency, it could offer a much more responsive service than any print media. Cityspace could also advertise special ticket prices as an i[+] offering, which would enhance the perceived value of the service while enabling the theater to avoid the potential stigma of announcing unsold tickets at discounted prices.

Cityspace was also negotiating booking arrangements with operators of sightseeing tours in and around London. An agreement had been reached with Golden Tours, a leading London tour company, whereby Cityspace would receive a 25% commission on tours booked through i[+].

---

[3] *Time Out* was one of London's leading magazines describing and listing current entertainment and attractions.

[4] FirstCall was a leading London ticketing agency, similar to Ticketmaster in the United States.

Since Cityspace had not yet developed the capability to handle booking transactions, it was impossible to know how much business the i$^+$ system would do. Management had projected an average of eight bookings per kiosk per day, once the system was well established, although originally the numbers were likely to be much smaller. Meyohas felt these projections were probably conservative: "Ultimately this should become like an ATM or a stamp machine. How often do you go to an ATM and not get money? How often do you go to a stamp machine and not buy stamps?"

Contract Projects

Cityspace also hoped to generate revenues from developing kiosk networks for cities on a contract basis. The company had won a contract with the city of Cardiff to build such a network ahead of the European Summit in June 1998, which would bring 3,000 delegates to the Welsh capital. The Cardiff contract generated revenues of £150,000, as well as some needed cash flow.

Current Usage—the Good News

Since each of the kiosks was centrally linked to Cityspace's central network, tracking usage details was relatively simple. An average kiosk was used 65 times per day, generating a total of roughly 50,000 uses per month. There was, however, considerable variation depending on location, with some kiosks generating over one hundred uses per day, while others had considerably fewer. Average time per use was 3.5 minutes, and the average user looked at two of the four main categories and five total listings. Cityspace could also demonstrate that buying advertising significantly improved the chances of a site being looked at in detail. Seventy-five percent of the final listings selected by users belonged to one of the (front screen) advertisers, with only 25% being sites that were included solely as part of the service's content.

Adding New Platforms

Cityspace believed that one of the core strengths of the i$^+$ service was that it could be easily adapted to new platforms. Two that the company was particularly excited about were Hotel TV and the Internet. (See **Exhibit 5** for projections on users by platform.)

EXHIBIT 5   **i$^+$ Platform Volume Projections**

Source: Cityspace.

At Period End	3 Months Ending June 1998	Year Ending June 1999	Year Ending June 2000	Year Ending June 2001	Year Ending June 2002	Year Ending June 2003
Number of Kiosks	30	69	108	147	186	225
Number of Hotels	0	9	27	45	63	81
Number of Bedrooms	0	2,160	6,480	10,800	15,120	19,440
000s of Hotel Users	0	128	984	1,859	2,734	3,609
Other Platforms:						
000s of Users	0	240	1,000	1,400	2,500	4,400

Hotel TV

Most London hotels offered an in-hotel TV service that included some free features (such as automatic checkout) and pay movies. The TVs were owned, and the service offered, by an independent company—in the United Kingdom the market leaders were Granada and Thorn, two U.K. media conglomerates, with On-Command Technology the only other significant player.[5] These companies offered hotels use of the televisions plus a share of revenues in exchange for access to the hotel's customers.

Not all in-hotel TV systems could support the i^+ system, but most of the major hotel groups were upgrading their systems to allow video on demand and games. Cityspace had spoken with system suppliers and was confident that these more advanced systems were capable of supporting i^+. Ten thousand hotel rooms already had these advanced systems installed, and Cityspace estimated, based on research by LTB Accommodation Services, that roughly 35,000 London hotel rooms would have them within the next five years.

Cityspace had already signed non-disclosure agreements with Granada and Thorn, and had met with the U.K. distributor of On-Command. Each company was preparing a pilot project to test the value of the i^+ system. Negotiations were complicated somewhat by the insistence by each of the three suppliers that any contract with Cityspace would be exclusive.

Hotel operators were enthusiastic about the service, which essentially represented free incremental revenues. Current usage of hotel TV was low—it had been estimated that even when a movie was paid for the average viewing time was only eleven minutes. Thus, there was little danger that adding Cityspace's service would cannibalize existing pay-TV business. Hotels would also receive a share of any revenues generated and would incur no additional cost, leaving them with little downside.

Cityspace expected to generate advertising revenues from hotel users comparable with those of kiosk users. For bookings, the company had projected an average of 14 bookings per 240-room hotel[6] per day by the year 2000, rising to 20 bookings per hotel per day by the year 2003.

Internet

Cityspace was in the process of developing a fully interactive web site that would support transactions and bring the entire i^+ service to the Internet. The company hoped to establish their site as a leading source of information for incoming tourists as well as to encourage visitors to London to book tickets and tours in advance. The company recognized, however, that while the potential of the Internet was vast, competition was already high and the barriers to entry that might exist for the kiosk and Hotel TV platforms were not present.

Costs

Cityspace had developed extensive cost projections as part of its business plan, based on variable costs associated with the revenues it hoped to generate as well as fixed costs needed to develop and operate the service.

Cityspace's anticipated direct costs included the share of revenues given to the hosts of its sites, as well as commissions paid to agencies who secured advertising revenue for the service, as well as various other costs associated with running the system, such as bank charges for handling bookings. Cityspace estimated that these costs would be fairly stable as a percentage of revenue by the year 2001, representing roughly 50% of total revenues.

---

[5] On-Command Technology dominated the U.S. market for in-hotel services; Thorn and Granada were market leaders throughout Europe.

[6] Chosen as an average size for major London hotels.

Cityspace's central costs (see **Exhibits 6** and **7** for projected central and operating costs) were largely fixed. They consisted of compensation of management and key employees, rent and utilities, and legal and professional fees (such as the annual audit) associated with running the company. Cityspace had also estimated the operating costs associated with each of its platforms as they came on-line.

Cityspace expensed development costs as they were incurred. Most of the development costs of the kiosk product had already been incurred, but the company anticipated further development costs relating primarily to the extension of i$^+$ to hotel TV and other platforms. Development costs of roughly £600,000 were budgeted for the year ending June 1999, by which time Cityspace expected to have i$^+$ developed for hotel TV and for the Internet.

EXHIBIT 6   **Cityspace Central Cost Projections**

Source: Cityspace.

£000s	3 Months Ending June 1998	Year Ending June 1999	Year Ending June 2000	Year Ending June 2001	Year Ending June 2002	Year Ending June 2003
Management	51	209	304	350	402	462
Key Employees	23	90	104	119	137	157
Employers NI	7	30	42	48	55	63
Office Costs	37	147	169	194	224	257
Professional Fees	13	51	59	67	78	90
Total Central Costs	**131**	**527**	**678**	**778**	**896**	**1,029**

EXHIBIT 7   **Cityspace Operating Cost Projections**

Source: Cityspace.

£000s	3 Months Ending June 1998	Year Ending June 1999	Year Ending June 2000	Year Ending June 2001	Year Ending June 2002	Year Ending June 2003
Total (Kiosk)	27	166	353	506	671	883
Administration	8	42	78	85	116	123
Marketing	10	69	161	240	326	442
Employers NI	5	22	35	46	54	65
Miscellaneous	4	33	79	135	175	253
Total (Hotel)	0	41	176	363	500	779
Administration	0	11	30	54	66	87
Marketing	0	16	77	167	231	374
Employers NI	0	8	21	34	44	53
Miscellaneous	0	6	48	108	159	265
Total (Other Platforms)	0	8	104	193	359	659
Administration	0	2	23	32	56	99
Marketing	0	3	44	87	163	303
Employers NI	0	1	14	23	43	75
Miscellaneous	0	2	23	51	97	182
Total Operating Costs	**27**	**215**	**633**	**1,062**	**1,530**	**2,321**

Financing

Cityspace raised approximately £250,000 of seed finance in 1995 to fund development of a prototype interactive information service and to assess the market potential. London Merchant Securities (LMS)[7] and Meyohas's former boss at Lehman Brothers each invested £100,000, with the rest coming from Meyohas and Bohane.

Once the service prototype had been developed, and reaction from the tourist industry seemed positive, Cityspace needed to raise close to £1 million in additional funds to develop the service and to create the kiosk network. In 1997, Cityspace approached U.K. venture capital funds, but was unable to secure the investment they sought at what they considered a fair valuation. Meyohas attributed part of the problem to the less-developed state of the U.K. venture capital industry: "To get VC funding in the United Kingdom you've either got to be lucky or have a relationship with one of the VCs. Otherwise you've got to do something crazy, like getting a $40 billion company to invest £400,000."

Cityspace's $40 billion company was NEC, one of the world's largest electronics and communications companies. NEC learned of Cityspace from EPIC Group, a U.K. interactive software house which had worked with NEC.[8] NEC's senior U.K. representative liked the i[1] concept and saw a potential fit with NEC's own multimedia businesses. After extended negotiations, the company agreed to invest £400,000.

The NEC deal wasn't an easy one to complete, and had its tense moments. Cityspace management never met the decision-makers in Tokyo, which made it hard to judge how likely they were to reach agreement. The U.K. representative had intended for NEC to invest £1,000,000 for a 30% position. A Tokyo representative, however, had already indicated that the investment size would be only £400,000, and to go against that would have caused him to lose face. Finally, when the deal was close to completion, a representative called to say that NEC wanted a larger share in Cityspace than had previously been agreed. Meyohas described his team's reaction: "We sat around our meeting table wondering what to do. We had about two weeks of cash, so if NEC didn't invest we would have to close up shop and go home. It was a pretty tense time."

Despite the stakes, Meyohas, Bohane and Newman decided to hold firm to the original terms. They called back the NEC representative and said they were prepared to go ahead, but would not increase the stake given NEC in the deal. NEC agreed to go ahead.

Another element to the deal was NEC's wish to invest the money in stages, with each subsequent investment triggered by performance hurdles, such as raising funds from additional investors, signing up a certain number of kiosk sites and securing booking partners. Cityspace was happy with this in principle, but Meyohas didn't like the hurdles NEC suggested. "They were all either much too easy or impossible," he explained. "Basically, they didn't really understand our business, so they didn't know what were reasonable hurdles for us to achieve." Meyohas went back to NEC with an alternative list, which they eventually accepted.

"We never actually met the person who authorized the NEC investment," Meyohas recalled. "He's very senior in the Tokyo headquarters, but I don't even know his name." Despite its advantages, and the timeliness of the cash injection, it was clear that the partnership with NEC would be an unusual one.

Shortly after securing NEC's investment, Cityspace was able to convince More Group to invest £285,000. With revenues of over £100 million, More Group was one of the

[7] London Merchant Securities was a listed U.K. firm specializing in property development and investments, particularly in health, leisure and communications companies. Revenues for the year ended March 1998 were £43 million.

[8] EPIC Group had been given a 5% share in Cityspace, in exchange for software and support in developing the i[+] service.

world's largest outdoor advertising companies, through street furniture panels, billboards, and advertisements in public transit booths. Like NEC, More saw opportunities in Cityspace's product.

In 1998, Cityspace prepared for a second round of funding. They hired Deloitte & Touche to prepare a detailed business plan and investment document. The plan, which was published in February, described a funding need of approximately £4 million over the next several years. Cityspace was hoping to raise £2.5 million in this round, for which management was prepared to give up 25%–30% of the company.

Industrial Partnerships—the Safety Net?

Quite separate from financial support, Cityspace had benefited considerably from its two partnerships in developing its product and in finding additional opportunities.

First, NEC had become involved with Cityspace on many levels. It had highlighted Cityspace's i[+] service in a commercial describing its own worldwide multi-media projects, and had reached a preliminary agreement to introduce i[+] to its BigLobe on-line service[9] in Japan, potentially giving Cityspace access to over two million Internet subscribers. Although NEC did not have any rights to introduce Cityspace's technology or service in other markets, it would make a logical partner for geographic expansion.

NEC had also supported Cityspace in developing its kiosks, providing them with needed equipment on favorable terms. The personal computer inside each kiosk had been custom-designed by NEC to fit within the kiosk shell and with a top-loading CD-ROM drive. NEC also supplied the touch-sensitive screens. Cityspace believed that working with NEC saved them roughly £1,500 per kiosk.

Second, More Group and Cityspace had found a link between i[+] and Adshel, More Group's street furniture business. Together, the two companies had been developing an outdoor version of the Cityspace kiosk to go into bus shelters. It was these kiosks which were being installed in Cardiff, and that contract had arisen in part out of ongoing work Adshel was doing for the city.

More Group had just recently been acquired by Clear Channel Communications of the United States, whose own outdoor advertising company, Eller, was to be merged with More to form the world's largest outdoor advertisement company with sales of over $750 million and operations in 24 countries. It was too early to know what impact this change in ownership might have on Cityspace's relationship with More.

Looking Forward

As the check arrived, Meyohas sipped his drink with uncharacteristic quiet. Raising venture capital had eluded him before, and while he was optimistic that Cityspace had demonstrated sufficient potential to bring in financial investors, he knew it might prove difficult to secure the money they needed. Although some VC firms had expressed interest in the company, Meyohas knew that the U.K. VC industry was geared more towards later-stage investments and buy-outs. More than one firm had said they would like to invest later in the company's development, but that Cityspace wasn't yet appropriate for their portfolio. With cash running out, Meyohas knew he had to raise capital somewhere. But where, and from who?

---

[9] BigLobe was roughly comparable to America Online, in terms of users and type of service.

Case

6

Internet Securities, Inc: Financing Growth

Gary Mueller, HBS MBA '94 and founder and CEO of Internet Securities (ISI), put down the private placement memorandum that had arrived that morning by messenger. The memorandum, prepared by investment bank Donaldson, Lufkin & Jenrette (DLJ), would be the foundation behind ISI's efforts to raise roughly $12.5 million dollars in new equity capital to fund its continued growth. Sixty-six pages and professionally formatted, it was a far more polished presentation of the company's prospects than the original business plan submitted to potential investors in May 1995. It was now October 12, 1998, and Mueller hoped that ISI's current round of financing would be sufficient to fund the company to the point where it began to generate positive cash flows.

Mueller thought about what he and his team at ISI had accomplished during the three and a half years between the two documents. ISI had successfully launched its Internet-based emerging markets information service, *ISI Emerging Markets,* and had expanded coverage to 27 different countries. (See **Exhibit 1** for a map of countries covered by ISI, and **Exhibit 2** for a timeline of company coverage.) It had attracted a large number of blue-chip financial and corporate customers, with whom it had an annual retention rate of roughly 88% and who were increasing the volume of business they did with ISI every year. Mueller believed the company had established credible barriers to entry in their niche of the information services industry, making it attractive both as a financial investment and as an acquisition target for a larger firm.

ISI had also handled the transition from a loosely run start-up to a professionally managed firm. While Mueller sometimes missed the chaotic days when he and his brother George ran the firm on a day-to-day basis, he was pleased with his current management team, which blended strength in information technology, sales and marketing, operations

Charles M. Williams Fellow Chad Ellis, MBA '98, prepared this case under the supervision of Professor Walter Kuemmerle. HBS cases are developed solely as the basis for class discussion. Cases are not intended to serve as endorsements, sources of primary data, or illustrations of effective or ineffective management.

EXHIBIT 1   **Current ISI Market Coverage**

Source: ISI.

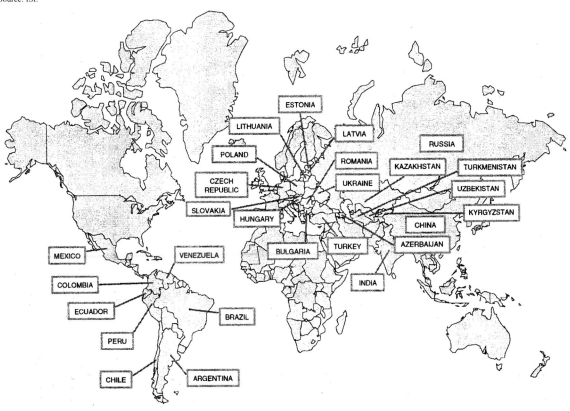

EXHIBIT 2
Coverage Timeline

Source: ISI.

1995: Poland, Russia, Czech Republic, Hungary, and the Baltic States
1996: Turkey, Ukraine, India, and China
1997: Colombia, Chile, Peru, Venezuela, Ecuador, Bulgaria, and Romania
1998: Brazil, Mexico, Argentina, and Central Asia

Plan for next eighteen months (lead country for each region in bold):
Greater China: **Korea**, Taiwan, and Hong Kong
Southeast Asia: **Thailand**, Malaysia, Indonesia, Singapore, and Philippines
Middle East/Africa: **Egypt**, Morocco, Lebanon
Former Yugoslavia: **Slovenia**, Croatia

Future prospects: Greece, Israel

and finance. (See **Exhibit 3** for ISI's organizational chart and **Exhibit 4** for management resumes.) Mueller knew that many entrepreneurial firms had stumbled after a period of rapid growth and felt that ISI's development had been relatively successful.

Mueller knew, however, that not all of ISI's prospective investors would see things as favorably as he did. ISI's 1995 plan forecasted positive net income in 1997; the current plan envisaged continuing losses until 2001. Mueller believed he had identified the causes of the shortfall and could explain to investors why the current projections should be looked at with more confidence. He knew, however, that some potential investors would wonder whether ISI was the type of investment where profitability is always two to three years away.

EXHIBIT 3 Internet Securities Organizational Chart

Source: ISI.

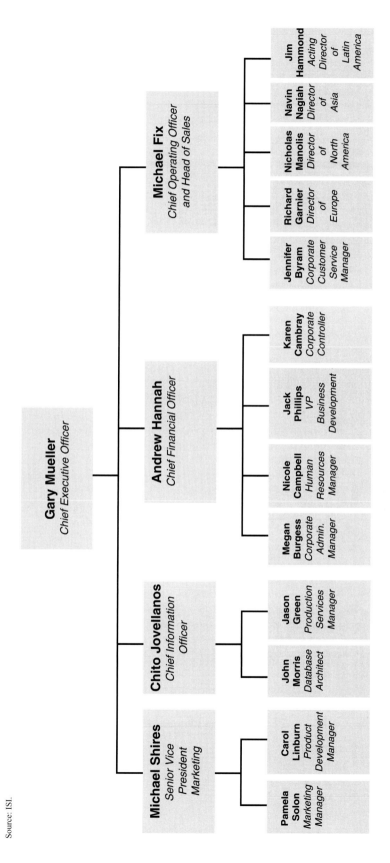

EXHIBIT 4 **Management Resumes**

Source: ISI.

Gary Mueller (Founder, Chairman of the Board, President and Chief Executive Officer). Mr. Mueller founded Internet Securities in 1994 and has led the Company every since. Mr. Mueller has worked extensively in the fields of emerging market finance and financial information. Prior to Internet Securities, Mr. Mueller spent three years working in emerging markets, primarily on privatization, and was part of the economic reform team that assisted Russia in its transition to a market economy. He spent two of those years working on privatization and fund formation in Poland and Russia with Graham Allison, Jeffrey Sachs and Stanley Fischer. He then worked for KPMG's privatization group in Poland. Mr. Mueller serves on the Board of Directors of Endeavor, a nonprofit organization supporting entrepreneurship in emerging markets, and The Fund for Civil Society in Russia. Mr. Mueller and Internet Securities are featured in both a Harvard Business School case study as well as a Babson Business School case study. Mr. Mueller is a graduate of Harvard Business School and Harvard College.

Michael W. G. Fix (Chief Operating Officer and Head of Sales). Prior to Internet Securities, Mr. Fix had 11 years of general management, sales management and sales experience in the online information industry. Most recently, Mr. Fix was Managing Director of Thomson's Electronic Settlements European operations. Prior to that, he was Director of Sales for Knight-Ridder Financial's Asian Operations and General Manager of Knight-Ridder Financial's Hong Kong operations. Mr. Fix holds a business degree from Copenhagen Business School.

Chito Jovellanos (Chief Information Officer). Prior to Internet Securities, Mr. Jovellanos served as Director of Research and Product Development of Thomson's Electronic Settlements Group (ESG) with a mandate to develop a worldwide product and technology infrastructure. Prior to that, he was Vice President of Business Planning at investment bank ScotiaMcLeod Inc. in Toronto, Canada. From 1985 to 1991, Mr. Jovellanos served in various capacities at Reuters PLC, most recently as Director of Product Development in the Transaction Products Group. Mr. Jovellanos received his M.Sc. from the University of Guelph (Canada) and a B.Sc. from Ateneo University (Philippines). Mr. Jovellanos has 10 years of experience in the financial information industry.

Andrew Hannah (Chief Financial Officer). Mr. Hannah is a Certified Public Accountant and prior to Internet Securities spent eight years in public accounting and consulting at Deloitte & Touche, most recently as a Senior Manager. He has served as the Chief Financial Officer of Internet Securities for the past three years. He graduated Salutatorian at the Katz School of Business at the University of Pittsburgh (1992) with an MBA (emphasis in Finance and Marketing) and has a B.S. in Accounting from Penn State University.

Michael Shires (Senior Vice President—Marketing). Mr. Shires is a veteran of the financial markets industry with his most recent position prior to Internet Securities being Senior Marketing Manager for Reuters, spending much of his time in Eastern Europe. He also brings a wealth of experience from his background as a fund manager with Barings and Morgan Grenfell and as a stockbroker with Robertson Stephens and NatWest Securities. Mr. Shires completed a D.Phil. Program at Oxford and has 22 years of experience in the financial information industry.

Jack Phillips (Vice President—Business Development). Mr. Phillips is a graduate of Williams College and Harvard Business School. He began his career in media and information as an investment banker at Morgan Stanley & Co. in New York, and at the Long-Term Credit Bank of Japan in Tokyo. After spending a year with McGraw-Hill in the MBA Associate Development Program, Mr. Phillips moved to Internet Securities in October 1995.

Mueller also knew that he had to balance the interests of several parties as he weighed his financing options. Many of his current investors, both individual "angel" investors and venture capital (VC) firms, hoped to realize their investment. (See **Exhibit 5** for a summary of current ISI ownership.) Their primary concerns were getting liquidity and doing so at the most favorable valuation possible.

Many key ISI employees also had an ownership stake in the company, either through equity or options, which they could exercise profitably if allowed to sell. While they would not expect to exit their stake completely, many would hope to gain some liquidity for their investment. Mueller himself wanted to realize some of the value of his 18.1% stake—he and his wife wanted to buy a house in the suburbs, and his salary was quite modest compared with the value of his equity in the company.

EXHIBIT 5   **Ownership as of August 31, 1998**

Source: Donaldson, Lufkin & Jenrette Offering Memorandum.

Common Stock	Shares	Percentage of Shares Outstanding	Options[a]	Total Shares and Options
Gary Mueller (CEO)	808,000	18.15	3,333	811,333
George Mueller	350,000	7.8	—	350,000
Michael Fix (COO)	—	—	85,000	85,000
Chito Jovellanos (CIO)	—	—	83,833	83,833
Andy Hannah (CFO)	—	—	83,333	83,333
Other Shareholders	447,113	10.0	364,398	811,511
Total Common Stock[b]	1,605,113	35.9%	619,897	2,225,010
Preferred Stock[c]				
Information Associates, L.P. (Trident)	853,067	19.1%	—	853,067
Advent International	521,740	11.7	—	521,740
Applied Technology	368,556	8.2	—	368,556
38 Newbury Managers B/Jeff Parker	247,155	5.5	—	247,155
Draper International India, LP	203,944	4.6	—	203,944
Other Investors	667,944	15.0	—	667,944
Total Preferred Stock	2,862,406	64.1%	—	2,862,406
Total	4,467,519	100.0%	619,897	5,087,416

[a] Excludes 120,000 options issued evenly to the COO, CFO, and CIO, with strike prices of $20.00 for the first 60,000 options and $30.00 for the remaining 60,000 options. The weighted average strike price for all other outstanding options is 40.90, excluding 60,000 options granted to senior executives with a strike price of $10.00.
[b] Excludes the conversion of subordinated debt to Common Stock.
[c] Converts into Common Stock on a share-for-share basis.

Mueller knew, however, that most of his net worth would remain tied up in ISI for the foreseeable future. Many of the options held by senior managers were "out of the money" and would only become profitable if the firm succeeded in the long term. For ISI's management, therefore, securing the future of the firm was more important than the precise valuation the deal took place at. As his CFO, Andrew Hannah had commented earlier that day, "I don't view this as the ultimate exit. The financing strategy is more important than simply getting liquidity."

From Eastern European Consulting to Internet Entrepreneur

After graduating from Harvard College as a Biology major in 1988 and studying in Germany under a Fulbright scholarship, Mueller worked as a consultant in Eastern Europe, advising the governments of Poland and Russia in the early stages of privatization. It was at that point that Mueller realized that there was a severe shortage of quality information on emerging markets, and that such information would be valuable to investors and businesses involved in those countries.

In 1992 Mueller returned to the United States. He enrolled in Harvard Business School, earning his MBA in 1994. During his MBA studies, Mueller did a field study in which he developed a business plan for an Internet-based service providing business information on emerging markets. Upon graduation, he and his brother George, an expert in computer engineering and systems integration, who had graduated from Carnegie-Mellon University with a BS in Computer and Electrical Engineering, decided to turn the plan into a new venture. They based their new company, Internet Securities, in Pittsburgh, PA, and began offering their service with coverage of Poland and, to a lesser extent, Russia.

The Muellers' belief in a market need was rapidly confirmed. Revenues grew by 600% from 1995 to 1996, by 330% from 1996 to 1997 and were expected to have grown by an estimated 114% from 1997 to 1998. Blue chip financial and industrial companies, such as Citibank, Deutsche Bank, Motorola and Siemens subscribed to ISI's service and ISI found that it was often able to sell new country services to many of its existing client base. (See **Exhibit 6** for a representative client list.)

Growing Pains—Reaching Critical Mass

In its early years, ISI was a typical start-up, both in terms of infrastructure and culture. Hannah recalled:

> At first, when the founders ran the company, everything was participatory. If they had to decide what color to make some part of the product they sent an email out to the twenty or so people working there and asked what they thought. Everyone would vote and they would go with the majority. As ISI grew, however, it had to develop professional management and people had to recognize that some decisions were theirs to make and some weren't.

Hannah had been hired in 1995 as part of the shift towards professional management. He first heard about the company through an email circulated through Deloitte & Touche (D&T), where he had worked for eight years. He explained:

> I worked in the D&T audit department for four years, but I got bored. I got my MBA at the University of Pittsburgh in an intensive 13-month program and went back to D&T in a group that was developing new products and services for clients, such as re-engineering and outsourcing of internal audits. It was an interesting idea, but at the time they weren't really putting in the resources necessary and it got a bit frustrating.
>
> Then, in early 1995 I got an email about a start-up company that was looking for a financial controller. I'd always been intrigued by entrepreneurship and had started a non-profit myself, so I knew what it felt like to grow an organization. I met with George and talked with him about what they were trying to do and what their vision for the company was. I told him they needed more of a financial engineer than just a controller, someone who could help build the financial infrastructure of the company.

EXHIBIT 6 **Representative Client List (June 1998)**

Source: ISI.

Int'l Investment Management Companies	Commercial and Investment Banks	Local ("In Country") Banks and Corporations	Multinational Corporations
AIG	Banque Indosuez	Bank Gdanski	Boeing
Brunswick Capital Management	Bear, Sterns & Co.	Bank Handlowy	Eli Lily
Creditanstalt	Citibank	Banque Paribas	Federal Express
Credit Suisse Asset Management	European Bank for Reconstruction Development	Brunswick	Lockheed Martin
Fidelity Management and Research	OFC	Lukoil	Lucent Technologies
Foreign and Colonial	ING Barings	Matav	Mitsubishi
GE Capital	JP Morgan	Menatep	Motorola
Putnam Investment Management	Merrill Lynch	Moscow Narodny Bank	Novell
The Pioneer Group	Morgan Stanley & Co.	Polski Bank	Polaroid
Wellington Management	World Bank	Raiffeisen	Price Waterhouse
Societe Generale	•	Wood and Company	Siemens
			Sun Microsystems
			United Technologies

The two brothers agreed with Hannah and hired him as ISI's Vice President of Finance, later appointing him CFO. At the time, ISI had little in the way of financial controls. "There were no systems to reconcile accounts, segregate duties or ensure accurate financial statements," Hannah explained. "There were accounting and billing systems that enabled Gary and George to keep close tabs on cash flows, but once we received our second round of financing in early 1996 the company needed to get serious about accounting."

Implementing financial controls and a budgeting process was fairly straightforward, given Hannah's experience at D&T. Designing an incentive and compensation system that would grow with the company was more complicated. Hannah explained:

> When you're small you can't afford to pay market [salaries] so you say to people, "Look, we can't pay you what you're making now but we'll give you these options." As you grow, and have more capital, you start paying higher salaries, which can create a gap between people who joined early and those who joined later. Looking back, I think we would have been better off if we just stepped up and hired people at market from the beginning.
>
> Designing an option-based compensation system needs strategy. It's easy just to say, "We'll give this person so many options," but that just causes problems. You need to think about what is a realistic expectation for the firm's exit valuation and how much you want each person to walk away with. Finally, you have to be careful not to let expectations get ahead of reality. It's easy for early employees in particular to believe the company is going to be the next Yahoo. Then, when you do an IPO or a strategic sale and they get liquidity at a more modest valuation, they can get disappointed, whereas someone who joined later might just say, "Great, I make $9 a share on my options!"

Mueller's original plan called for ISI to reach profitability in 1997. By the end of 1998, however, the company did not expect to break even before 2001. (See **Exhibit 7** for

EXHIBIT 7a **Projections at Different Stages of ISI's Development, March 1995**

Source: ISI Business Plan (March 1995).

	Actual Q1 1995	Projections			
		1995	1996	1997	1998
Sales	$3,550	$227,000	$1,330,000	$2,853,000	$5,388,000
Net profit	(48,005)	(406,000)	(121,000)	620,000	1,044,000

EXHIBIT 7b **Summary Financial Information, February 1996 (amounts in thousands)**

Source: ISI Business Plan (February 1996).

	1996	1997	1998	1999	2000
Revenue					
Developed countries	$ 2,043	$6,334	$10,759	$16,467	$24,102
Emerging countries	239	1,769	4,527	7,499	10,380
Total revenue	2,282	8,103	15,286	23,966	34,482
Costs					
Developed countries	2,985	4,825	7,778	11,853	15,762
Emerging markets	1,440	3,099	5,008	6,983	8,425
EBIT	$(2,143)	$ 179	$ 2,500	$ 5,130	$10,295

EXHIBIT 7c Projected Statements of Operations and Cash Flow, October 1998 ($ in millions)

Source: Donaldson, Lufkin & Jenrette Offering Memorandum.

	Fiscal Year Ending December 31, 1998					Projected Fiscal Year Ending December 31, 1999					Projected		
	Q1A	Q2A	Q3A	Q4E	Total	Q1	Q2	Q3	Q4	Total	FY2000	FY2001	FY2002
Revenues	$1.7	$1.9	$2.1	$2.3	$8.0	$2.6	$3.0	$3.5	$4.0	$13.1	$22.2	$32.9	$43.4
Cost of revenues	0.4	0.5	0.5	0.6	2.0	0.6	0.7	0.8	1.0	3.1	5.3	7.9	10.4
Gross profit	1.3	1.4	1.6	1.7	6.0	2.0	2.3	2.7	3.0	10.0	16.9	25.0	33.0
Operating expenses	2.8	2.8	3.0	2.9	11.5	3.9	4.3	4.4	4.5	17.1	19.3	21.3	22.8
(Loss) income from operations[a]	(1.5)	(1.4)	(1.4)	(1.2)	(5.5)	(1.9)	(2.0)	(1.7)	(1.5)	(7.1)	(2.4)	3.7	10.2
Cash flow adjustments[a]	0.4	(0.3)	(0.1)	0.2	0.2	0.2	0.1	0.2	0.5	1.0	2.0	2.5	2.7
Cash flow	(1.1)	(1.7)	(1.5)	(1.0)	(5.3)	(1.7)	(1.9)	(1.5)	(1.0)	(6.1)	(0.4)	6.2	12.9

	Fiscal Year Ending December 31, 1998					Projected Fiscal Year Ending December 31, 1999					Projected		
All figures are percentages	Q1A	Q2A	Q3A	Q4E	Total	Q1	Q2	Q3	Q4	Total	FY2000	FY2001	FY2002
Revenue growth													
Quarter over previous quarter	20.0%	11.8%	10.5%	9.5%		13.0%	15.4%	16.7%	14.3%				
Over same period previous year	200.2	169.5	98.3	64.1	114.0	52.9	57.9	66.7	73.9	63.8	69.5	48.2	31.9
Operating data as a percentage of revenues:													
Cost of revenues	23.5	26.3	23.8	26.1	25.0	23.1	23.3	22.9	25.0	23.7	23.9	24.0	24.0
Gross profit	76.5	73.7	76.2	73.9	75.0	76.9	76.7	77.1	75.0	76.3	76.1	76.0	76.0
Operating expenses	164.7	147.4	142.9	126.1	143.8	150.0	143.3	125.7	112.5	130.5	86.9	64.7	52.5
(Loss) income from operations[a]	(88.2)	(73.7)	(66.7)	(52.2)	(68.8)	(73.1)	(66.7)	(48.6)	(37.5)	(54.2)	(10.8)	11.2	23.5
Cash flow adjustments[a]	23.5	(15.8)	(4.8)	8.7	2.5	7.7	3.3	5.7	12.5	7.6	9.0	7.6	6.2
Cash flow	(64.7%)	(89.5%)	(71.4%)	(43.5%)	(66.3%)	(65.4%)	(63.3%)	(42.9%)	(25.0%)	(46.6%)	(1.8%)	18.8%	29.7%

[a] Includes amounts related to the purchase of capital equipment (net of depreciation and net borrowings for capital equipment), growth in deferred revenues as a result of pre-billings and growth of general liabilities.

financial projections at different stages in ISI's development and **Exhibit 8** for historic P&L data.) Mueller knew that, like many high-growth Internet companies, ISI's revenues and costs were difficult to forecast. Hannah explained some of the challenges:

> We were close to the revenue targets of our original '95 plan. The problem was that our costs were much higher than we expected. We didn't realize what it costs to run a global company so we underestimated the costs above and beyond those of the individual offices. Our advisors tell us, "You have all the issues of a Rockwell International but not all of the zeroes in your revenue line."
>
> Later plans were the opposite. We've gotten very good at rolling out country products and we understand the cost structure now, so our cost projections are pretty reliable. On the revenue side, unfortunately, we were really hit by the emerging markets crisis. Suddenly spending

EXHIBIT 8   Summary of Historical Financial Information

Source: Donaldson, Lufkin & Jenrette Offering Memorandum.

Condensed Consolidated Balance Sheets ($ in thousands)			
	As of December 31,		As of
	1996	1997	August 31, 1998
ASSETS			
Current assets			
Cash and cash equivalents	$1,890	$4,145	$1,997
Accounts receivable, net of allowance for doubtful accounts	610	1,224	1,415
Prepaid expenses	50	146	215
Total current assets	2,550	5,515	3,627
Net property and equipment	665	1,017	1,407
Deposits and other assets	296	277	210
Total assets	$3,511	$6,809	$5,244
LIABILITIES AND STOCKHOLDERS' EQUITY (DEFICIT)			
Current liabilities			
Current portion of long-term obligations	$96	$182	$363
Accounts payable	124	212	343
Accrued expenses	560	904	1,128
Deferred revenues	527	1,535	1,539
Total current liabilities	1,307	2,833	3,373
Long-term obligations—less current portion	327	782	1,032
Subordinated debt	—	—	1,500
Other liabilities	—	137	130
Stockholders' equity			
Redeemable convertible preferred stock	6,143	12,999	12,999
Common stock	2	2	2
Additional paid-in capital	361	366	391
Accumulated deficit	(4,615)	(10,293)	(14,104)
Cumulative translation adjustment	(11)	(14)	(76)
	1,880	3,060	(788)
Less—treasury stock, at cost	(3)	(3)	(3)
Total stockholders' equity (deficit)	1,877	3,057	(791)
Total liabilities and stockholders' equity (deficit)	$3,511	$6,809	$5,244

(continued)

EXHIBIT 8 (Continued)

Condensed Consolidated Statement of Operations ($ in thousands)

	Fiscal Year Ended December 31,		Eight Months Ended August 31,	
	1996	1997	1997	1998
Revenues	$875	$3,757	$1,947	$4,978
Costs and expenses:				
Cost of revenues	260	912	484	1,224
Technical and development	884	2,350	1,370	2,291
Selling, general and administrative	3,625	6,349	4,134	5,256
Total costs and expenses	4,769	9,611	5,988	8,771
Loss from operations	(3,894)	(5,854)	(4,041)	(3,793)
Net interest income (expense)	68	176	86	(17)
Net loss	($3,826)	($5,678)	($3,955)	($3,810)

Condensed Consolidated Statement of Cash Flows ($ in thousands)

	Fiscal Year Ended December 31,		Eight Months Ended August 31,	
	1996	1997	1997	1998
Cash flows from operating activities:				
Net loss	($3,826)	($5,678)	($3,955)	($3,810)
Adjustments to reconcile net loss to net cash used in operating activities:				
Depreciation and amortization	178	381	275	411
Increase (decrease) in cash from:				
Accounts receivable	(535)	(628)	(135)	(217)
Change in other assets and liabilities	323	529	252	395
Deferred revenues	511	1,030	493	92
Net cash provided by operating activities	(3,349)	(4,366)	(3,070)	(3,129)
Cash flows from investing activities:				
Purchases of property and equipment	(637)	(613)	(377)	(831)
Cash flows from financing activities:				
Repayment of capital lease obligations	(915)	(31)	(33)	(49)
Proceeds from bank borrowings	338	439	189	541
Proceeds from the issuance of convertible debt	250	—	—	1,500
Net proceeds from the issuance of preferred stock	4,664	6,856	6,875	—
Other	(14)	5	—	(166)
Net cash provided by financing activities	5,223	7,269	7,031	1,826
Effect of exchange rate changes on cash and cash equivalents	—	(35)	80	(14)
Net increase (decrease) in cash and cash equivalents	1,237	2,255	3,664	(2,148)
Cash and cash equivalents, beginning of period	653	1,890	1,890	4,145
Cash and cash equivalents, end of period	$1,890	$4,145	$5,554	$1,997

on emerging markets was cut across the board by many of our customers—it's pretty hard to get someone to pay for an emerging markets service when their CEO is talking about pulling out the investments they have in place.

As ISI grew it also had to rethink its sales strategy. Tom Grant of Applied Technology, one of ISI's earliest VC investors, explained how the early strategy hurt the company's efforts to hit its targets:

> We probably underspent in the New York region, on penetrating all the financial institutions there. We also underspent on multi-national accounts and on thinking through how to structure our pricing in order to get corporate accounts instead of just getting our nose in the door with one office. One of the things we wrestled with in early 1998 was hiring the right people and getting the right strategy in place to push sales forward more effectively, but I think we're doing much better now.

As ISI grew it became necessary to hire a larger number of software developers. Gary and George agreed that the firm should relocate in order to have access to a broader employee pool and in October 1996 ISI relocated to downtown Boston. It was at this time that George decided to leave the company. Gary explained:

> George had left one of his own ventures on hold to help start ISI, but he was more comfortable managing a smaller team than the one we were going to need. So he returned to his original venture, which has been doing very well.

ISI expected to continue with its rapid growth, but Mueller felt that critical mass had already been attained in many important aspects. With over 200 employees, 18 worldwide research offices and coverage of 27 different markets, ISI was well on its way to fulfilling its mission of becoming "the recognized leading provider of business and professional information on emerging markets."

The Product

ISI's core product was ISI Emerging Markets, an Internet-based service which aimed to provide information its clients could use to make significant decisions on investment and operations in emerging markets. ISI aggregated information about companies, industries, economic indicators, capital and financial markets as well as local laws and regulations and calendars of significant financial dates into a searchable and customizable web interface. (See **Exhibit 9** for sample screen displays.) ISI used over 650 content sources, including local newspapers, financial news agencies, stock exchanges, banks, brokerage houses and government bureaus. (See **Exhibit 10** for a description of the information ISI provided.)

About 50% of the information ISI provided on its twenty-seven markets was publicly available, but Mueller strongly believed that the service was much more than an amalgamation of information that could be easily found elsewhere. Many of the sources were public, but not published, such as the filings of financial statements by private companies. ISI's local offices would gather and aggregate data that was not widely available, providing information on individual companies as well as industry-wide statistics. Mueller felt that about 50% of the information ISI provided was "proprietary" as it was not available elsewhere in aggregated form. Mueller felt that the strength of his local research teams and the cost it would take to duplicate them formed one of ISI's strongest barriers to entry by competitors.

ISI's first-mover advantage also included relationships and licensing agreements with content providers, many giving ISI exclusive rights to distribute their content over the Internet. Although these agreements were not indefinite, ISI's management believed it would be very difficult for a rival to convince content providers to switch to another service.

EXHIBIT 9 Sample Screen Displays

Source: Donaldson, Lufkin & Jenrette Offering Memorandum.

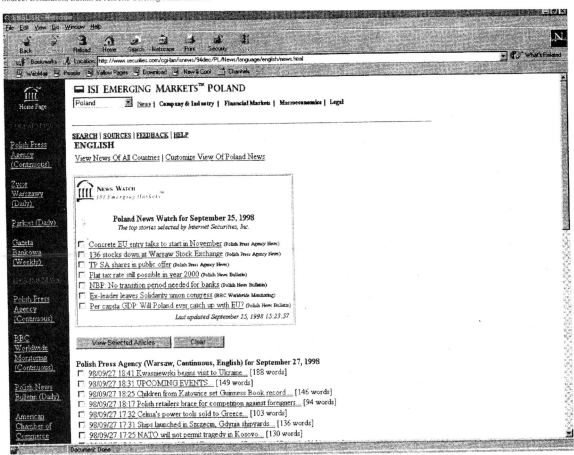

ISI believed it added additional value to the information it provided through its functionality, broken down as follows:

- Accessibility. Because ISI was provided over the Internet, customers could access the service from anywhere in the world. Many of its competitors required devoted terminals to access the service, making it less accessible for traveling professionals.

- Ease of retrieval. ISI had spent considerable resources organizing its data and designing its interface to enable users quickly and efficiently to retrieve information.

- Customizable presentation. Clients who wished to access particular data on a regular basis could create custom displays best suited to their needs. A fund manager, for example, could design a presentation that would display the same key data on different companies, enabling her to see quickly whether a company met her fund's investment criteria.

- Multilingual support. *ISI Emerging Markets* was presented in thirteen local languages in addition to English, and the service supported foreign language fonts.

- Analytical support. Because ISI used open systems architecture, users could easily transport reports, charts and other data into spreadsheets or other electronic documents, such as investment recommendation reports by securities analysts, which typically included a chart displaying recent share price performance.

EXHIBIT 9   (Continued)

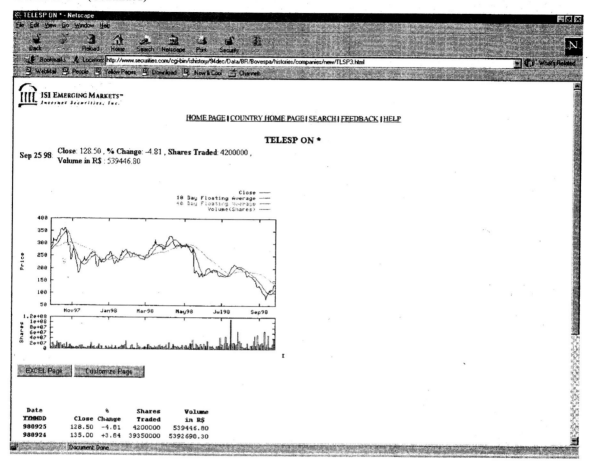

ISI strove to involve its customers as closely as possible in developing its product, both actively through focus groups, surveys and interviews, and passively by monitoring usage patterns. Determining what aspects of the service were of the greatest value to customers was complex, explained Hannah:

> Everybody reads the news each day. If you work on Wall Street you're going to read the [Wall Street] Journal every morning. If you work in an emerging market you're going to read ISI's news coverage. But that doesn't mean that's where we add the most value, since there are other ways of getting that information which are maybe not as convenient but not impossible either. Based on our own research, we believe our company and industry data is the most valuable to clients, even if it is accessed less frequently than are some of the bread and butter parts of the service.

ISI's customers included financial services firms, such as investment banks, investment managers and buyout funds and corporate clients, which included both large multinationals and local companies in the markets it served. Nearly 50% of ISI's revenues were generated in the very markets they were covering. Hannah estimated that financial firms accounted for two-thirds of total sales, but believed that the requirements of financial and corporate clients were not overly dissimilar:

> Much of the information our clients need in order to make decisions is fairly similar. Investment banks are looking for possible M&A targets; so are multi-nationals. Analysts use our industry data to help them assess the prospects of [publicly traded] companies they are

EXHIBIT 10
Internet Securities
Information
Providers

Source: ISI.

Internet Securities' information providers include news organizations, banks and financial institutions, government bodies, private companies, and research organizations which supply different types of data. Internet Securities signs contracts with these information providers from both the geographic focus areas ("in-country") and in the developed financial markets. In-country information providers are a particularly important part of ISI Emerging Markets service in that they are difficult to access from Western financial centers. In addition, Internet Securities includes developed market information providers to add summary analysis and "brand name" credibility to the ISI Emerging Markets service.

Sample of Branded Information Providers (June 1998)

Alliance Friday News Dispatch; ASIDA; Business Central Europe; Business World Update; CASE Research; CASH; CBnet; Citibank; Chip News; Duff & Phelps; Economic Daily; Economist Intelligence Unit; Financial & Economic Research International; First Investment Trust Research; Futures Market provided by UFIE Co. Ltd.; Horizon; Informed Business Services; Infotrade; PlanEcon; WEFA Group.

Sample of In-Country Information Providers (June 1998)

Brazil Agencia Estado; Agroanalysis; Advanstar Editora; Banco Hole Magazine; BM&F; BNDES; Bovespa; Carta Capital; Central Bank of Brazil; CVM; Economist Intelligence Unit; EFC Consultores; Enfoque Sistemas; Folha de Sao Paulo; Gazeta Mercantil; Jornal do Brasil; LCA Consultores; Macrometrica; Ministry of Finance; O Estado de Sao Paulo; O GLOBO; Previsa; Trend Consultores.

Poland Gazeta Bankowa; Gdansk Institute for Market Economics; GUS (State Statistical Office); KSH; Ministry of Finance; National Bank of Poland; NFI; Notoria; PAIZ; Parkiet; Pekao S.A.; Penetrator Brokerage House S.A.; Pentor; Pioneer Polish Securities Co.; Polish News Bulletin; Polish Press Agency; Pretor; Raiffeisen; Warsaw Voice.

China Bank of China; Business Beijing; CCPIT; China Chemical Week; China Contact Information (DCCB); China Daily; China Electric Power Information Center (CEPIC); China Law Information Service; China Petroleum Newsletter; China Watch; IDG China; Investment Institute of State Planning Commission; POT Market; Shanghai Stock Exchange; Shenzhen Stock Exchange; SinoScan; US Embassy, Beijing Daily Commercial Briefs; Xinhua News Agency (China Economic Information Service).

recommending or investing in; those same companies use the data to make better investment decisions. There are differences, of course. Goldman Sachs is going to look up stock prices more often than General Electric, but both firms want to know about local companies, industry statistics, economic indicators and political developments.

Operations

ISI had eighteen offices in seventeen countries. Global headquarters were in Boston, with European headquarters in London and sixteen other offices spread throughout the world. Other than Brussels and New York, which were exclusively sales offices, each of ISI's offices both sold and built information products. (See **Exhibit 11** for a list of regions along with average years in operation, number of personnel and rough profitability.)

ISI had developed considerable experience in rolling out new offices and believed that its current time from start-up to product launch and local revenue generation was less than seven months. Each office was designed to be self-sufficient and was considered a distinct profit center, with the number of personnel determined primarily on the local market for *ISI Emerging Markets*.

ISI's goal with respect to technology was to use its global infrastructure and the open architecture of the Internet to create a platform that was scalable, robust and extensible.

EXHIBIT 11
Regional
Profitability Analysis

Source: Donaldson, Lufkin &
Jenrette Offering
Memorandum.

Country/Region	Average Years in Operations[a]	Operations Personnel
Profitable:	3.0	
North America		10
Western Europe[b]		9
Czech Republic		11
Poland		10
Ukraine		4
Nearly Profitable[d]	2.5	
Russia[d]		14
Hungary		10
Romania		2
Bulgaria		6
Turkey		8
China		7
Chile		9
Preparation Stage:	1.5	
Brazil		10
Argentina		5
Mexico[f]		6
Other	2.5	
India		14
Total		135

[a] The average years in operation reflects the time since the office commenced significant business activities.
[b] The Western European operations include the U.K. and Belgian sales operations and exclude corporate marketing and regional headquarters personnel and costs.
[c] Nearly profitable is defined as operations within $8,000 per month of profitability.
[d] As a result of financial difficulties experienced by the Russian market, the performance of the company's Russian operations (9% of total company revenues) may vary significantly in the future.
[e] Excludes regional technology personnel and costs.
[f] Sales operations began in June 1998.

Each local office had a Web server from which it served the local market, and each local product would be mirrored across the company's other offices. ISI planned to develop its own private network in 1999 to ensure timeliness of data delivery.

Sales and Marketing

ISI's sales policy was to "penetrate and proliferate." Sales efforts aimed at bringing in new customers but at least as important was generating new revenues from existing customers. (See **Exhibit 12** for an organization chart of global sales operations.) Hannah explained:

> A lot of our customers have very localized decision making. An investment bank might buy our service in New York but not in London or Tokyo. At least half of our new revenues is coming from increasing our sales within firms that are already customers, and that will increase going forward as there are fewer and fewer potential customers who aren't already buying at least some of our service.

Pricing was on a subscription basis that ranged from $250 to $1,900 per user per month, depending both on the breadth of products purchased and the location of the customer. "Interest in FDI in Russia might be very small in the US," Hannah explained, "but larger in the UK. Our head of marketing sets the prices by country and product, with a set formula for discounts based on the number of products and number of users." A large user might get a discount of up to 50% on new products.

EXHIBIT 12
Global Sales Operations Organization Chart

Source: Donaldson, Lufkin & Jenrette Offering Memorandum.

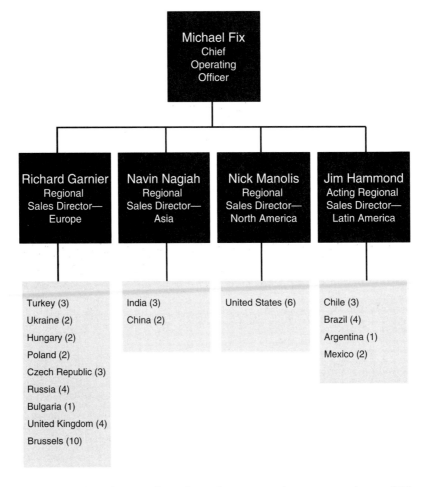

Determining the actual number of users wasn't an exact science. "When we sign a new account we offer training sessions for the people who will be using the service," explained Mueller. "Then our sales rep can go in to see the decision-maker with the number of people who attended and negotiate the contract."

Although the system wasn't perfect, ISI believed it was easier to manage and more efficient than charging on a variable rate based on total usage. "We did try charging by usage for a while," said Hannah, "but there are a lot of problems associated with that. It's very hard to set customer expectations when neither you nor they really know how much or how quickly their people will use the service, and it creates a very unpredictable revenue stream."

Instead, ISI used its usage data as a general negotiating tool, especially when it became apparent that a customer might have more users than it was paying for. "We can go to a customer and say, 'Here is how much you are paying us on a usage basis compared to the average,'" stated Hannah. "That makes it easier for us to argue that they are underpaying. If we have to—if they won't renegotiate—we will cut a client off. We shut off the World Bank and are probably going to renegotiate at about twenty times the level they were paying us before."

Competition

ISI competed with a number of large, established information service firms such as Bloomberg, Reuters, Thompson Financial Services and Pearson. These firms had global reach, excellent content and considerable expertise in product development and customer service. However, these firms concentrated on the more developed world markets, and provided only modest information on emerging markets, if any. Mueller believed that ISI's customers saw *ISI Emerging Markets* as a complementary product to the other information services they subscribed to, filling a niche that the larger players did not fill.

ISI also competed with smaller firms with an emerging market's focus, such as Porvenir, BradyNet and Emerging Markets Companion, as well as local providers within each of the countries in which it operated. ISI believed that the breadth of its product range, its international scope and the functionality of its service gave it a substantial competitive advantage against its smaller competitors. (See **Exhibit 13** for a summary of ISI's main competition.)

EXHIBIT 13   Main Competitors

Source: Donaldson, Lufkin & Jenrette Offering Memorandum.

Bridge Information Systems

Bridge is a leading financial information services provider with estimated 1997 revenues of $400 million. Bridge is part of the Global Financial Information Corporation (GFI) family of companies, which was created in 1995 through a series of investments and acquisitions by Welsh, Carson, Anderson and Stowe. Since 1995, Welsh, Carson has spent approximately $1 billion to build GFI into a leading financial information company. In 1996, GFI/Bridge acquired Knight-Ridder Financial for $275 million, and in 1998, the company acquired Dow Jones Markets (Telerate), rival Dow Jones' real-time financial news and online quotes service for $510 million. Bridge maintains coverage of more than 60 countries worldwide including first- and second-tier emerging markets.

Bloomberg L.P.

A leading financial news and data company, Bloomberg maintains approximately 100,000 proprietary terminals for which subscribers pay approximately $1,100 per month. The Bloomberg terminal provides institutional investors and other users with real-time news, market data, analyses, sports and advertising around the clock. The company is estimated to have generated $1.3 billion in revenues in 1997. Bloomberg's primary customers are institutional investors, financial intermediaries, issuers, and corporations. In addition, Bloomberg provides electronic trading access for several financial markets, including NASDAQ. Its founder, Michael Bloomberg, owns 80% of the firm.

The Dialog Corporation

Dialog was newly formed in November 1997 as a result of the merger between Knight-Ridder Information and M.A.I.D plc. The company serves over 20,000 corporate clients in 120 countries and maintains over 900 databases. Dialog's two main products are DIALOG and Profound, both of which are delivered via dial-up or over the Internet. DIALOG is the world's oldest and largest commercial online information service, with a powerful and precise search capability. The service contains nearly 500 databases from a broad range of disciplines, including business, U.S. and international news, patents and trademarks, science and technology, as well as consumer news. Profound provides market research reports, breaking and archived business news, company statistics, brokerage research, economic analysis, and up-to-date stock market and commodity prices.

Dow Jones & Company, Inc.

Dow Jones is a global provider of business news and information. The company's operations include business publishing (*Wall Street Journal*), financial information services and general interest community newspapers. In addition to its print publications, the company also sells Dow Jones Interactive, an Internet-based service that provides access to 5,500 publications. This year, Dow Jones exited the electronic financial information business by selling Dow Jones Markets (Telerate) to Bridge. The company has adopted the Internet as a future delivery platform by forming the Interactive Publishing Group, which manages the Wall Street Journal Interactive Edition.

Thomson Financial Services ("TFS")

TFS, with $1.1 billion in annual revenue, is a major subsidiary of The Thomson Corporation, a leading Canadian publisher with interests in specialized information and publishing worldwide as well as newspaper publishing in North America. The company serves the financial, legal, educational, and health care industries, among others. TFS businesses specifically serve retail and investment banks, institutionalized investment firms, securities brokers and dealers, corporations, underwriters of municipal bonds and syndicated loans, and consumers.

(continued)

EXHIBIT 13   (Continued)

In 1997, approximately 85% of TFS sales were to the U.S. market, with the balance coming primarily from Europe, Australia and other countries in the Asia-Pacific region, particularly Japan. TFS serves customers in more than 70 countries. Major companies within TFS include First Call, Investext, ILX, Securities Data Company, The Electronic Settlements Group, and Technical Data Corp.

Reuters Group PLC

Reuters provides real-time financial data, transaction systems, numerical and textual historical databases, news, graphics, still photos, and news video to the global business community and news media. The company recently released the Reuters Markets 3000 series of products, which are designed to deliver real-time data, news and television, as well as extensive historical and reference information covering the money, equity, and fixed income markets. Reuters' Instinet service, with its broker-dealer affiliates, provides agency brokerage services to security industry professionals in 30 countries and enables quick and cost-effective trading of global equities. Reuters' 1997 sales were approximately $4.7 billion, with only 15% of revenues coming from the Americas. Europe, Middle East, Africa and Asia/Pacific accounted for 70% of revenues. Reuters has also recently migrated their traditional Reuters Business Briefing product to an Internet delivery platform.

Pearson plc

Pearson is most noted for its flagship print publication, the *Financial Times* ("FT"). The company is a leading global media company with stakes in print publishing, television, and educational book publishing. Pearson's FT group owns 50% of the Economist Intelligence Unit, which publishes the *Economist* magazine and produces a wide range of electronic information products for the financial and business community. In 1997, Pearson plc's revenues were $2.9 billion.

Porvenir

Covering only Latin American markets, Porvenir's Internet-based subscription service catalogs and organizes information and data about Latin American business. The company was started within the last two years and is based in San Francisco, California. To date, Porvenir has not created original editorial content or sourced proprietary financial information. The information catalogued is otherwise available for free on the Internet.

BradyNet

BradyNet has emerged as a leading source of emerging market fixed income securities information, with a strong focus on Brady Bonds. BradyNet also has online chat areas for fixed income investors. Much of the data sourced and cataloged on BradyNet is free on the Internet. BradyNet's business model primarily relies on advertising as its main source of revenue.

Emerging Markets Companion ("EMC")

EMC primarily relies on advertising revenues to fund operations. EMC also recently introduced a premium service, which offers additional information for interested subscribers. EMC aggregates financial data on emerging markets from a number of freely available sources, and aggregates that information in an online product delivered free over the Internet.

Local Providers

While the company competes with certain local providers in its markets, these companies are typically characterized by good local expertise but limited product offerings and limited international distribution.

Financing

ISI received seed financing from the Mueller brothers and several wealthy individuals during 1994 and 1995. Many of these individuals were experts on information services or entrepreneurship and joined either ISI's Board of Directors or its Advisory Board. (See **Exhibit 14** for a summary of ISI's financings to date and **Exhibit 15** for a description of the company's board members and advisors.) Tom Grant, of Applied Technology, invested in the company's "Angel round" in the fall of 1995:

EXHIBIT 14   **Summary of Historic Financings ($ in thousands, except post-money valuation and per share data)**

Source: Donaldson, Lufkin & Jenrette Offering Memorandum.

Investment Type	Amount	Date	Post-Money Valuation	Price per Share
"Seed Capital"	$ 350	1994/1995	Various	Various
"Angel"	1,200	Fall 1995	$ 5.4 million	$ 2.36
Round 1	250	Spring 1996	7.8 million	3.31
Round 2	4,700	Spring 1996	15.2 million	4.42
Round 3	6,900	Spring 1997	27.9 million	5.75
Total Equity	$13,400			
7% Sub-debt	$ 1,500	Spring 1998	$50.0 million	$10.00

EXHIBIT 15   **Board Members and Advisors**

Source: Donaldson, Lufkin & Jenrette Offering Memorandum.

Gary Mueller (Founder, Chairman of the Board, President and Chief Executive Officer)

Robert McCormack (Director, Investor). Mr. McCormack is a founding partner of Trident Capital, Inc., a private equity investment firm that invests in information and business services companies. Prior to that he was the Assistant Secretary and Comptroller of the Navy. Mr. McCormack has also held positions as Vice President, Principal and Managing Director of Morgan Stanley's Chicago office and as a Senior Vice President of Dillon Read. Mr. McCormack serves on the Board of Directors of several companies.

J. Carter Beese, Jr. (Director). Mr. Beese is the President of Riggs Capital Partners, and formerly was Chairman of BT Alex. Brown International. Prior to rejoining Alex. Brown, he served as a Commissioner of the SEC from March 1992 until November 1994. While at the SEC, Mr. Beese was particularly active in the areas of cross border capital flows, the derivatives market, and corporate governance.

Nicholas Callinan (Director, Investor). Mr. Callinan is a Senior Vice President and Managing Director of Emerging Markets at Advent International, where he is responsible for developing and overseeing private equity investment in emerging markets. He joined Advent in 1994 to establish the firm's Central and Eastern European investment activity. Prior to joining Advent, Mr. Callinan founded his own venture capital group in Australia (which subsequently became affiliated with Advent). He spent most of his early career with various engineering and industrial groups and was eventually appointed Managing Director of Cummins Engine Co.'s Australian operation.

Thomas Grant (Director, Investor). Mr. Grant is a managing partner at Applied Technology, a venture capital fund focusing on innovative information technologies and media. Previously, Mr. Grant served as a group president at Data resources Incorporated and a senior management member of Softbridge Microsystems, a PC-software development company.

Jeffrey Parker (Business Advisor, Investor). Mr. Parker is the CEO of CCBN (a recent venture created by Mr. Parker) and President of 38 Newbury Managers (a venture investment firm). He was the founder and CEO of other successful financial service companies, such as Technical Data Corporation and the First Call Corporation. He sold both companies to Thomson Corporation, and under his leadership, Thomson Financial Services became a major provider of proprietary financial information to the investment community. His entrepreneurial activities are the subject of several case studies at the Harvard Business School.

Esther Dyson (Business Advisor, Investor). Ms. Dyson is President and owner of *EDventure Holdings*, a company focused on emerging information technology worldwide, and on the emerging computer markets of Central and Eastern Europe. She is also Chairman of the Electronic Frontier Foundation. EDventure Holdings publishes Release 1.0 and manages EDventure Holdings, a venture capital fund dedicated to active investing in software and information companies in Eastern Europe.

(continued)

EXHIBIT 15 (Continued)

Bill Draper (Business Advisor, Investor). Mr. Draper is the President of Draper International India, LP. Among his many achievements, he co-founded Sutter Hill Venture Capital and was the former head of the ExIm Bank and the UN Development Program. Mr. Draper has invested in more than 140 companies in his career. His current company, Draper International India, LP, invests in companies with business activities in India.

Bill Sahlman (Business Advisor, Investor). Dr. Sahlman is the *Dimitri V. D'Arbeloff—Class of 1955* Professor of Business Administration at Harvard Business School and is internationally recognized for his work in entrepreneurial finance and venture capital. Mr. Sahlman is a member of the editorial advisory boards for the *Journal of Business Venturing* and the *Journal of Small Business Finance*.

Robert Reid, Sr. (Business Advisor). Mr. Reid was an Executive Vice President at Reuters (now retired), in charge of Instinet, an online, NYSE equities trading system. During his eight years at Reuters he helped grow Instinet to its present size of 1,100 large institution investor clients. Before his tenure at Reuters, Mr. Reid served as a Senior Vice President at the NYSE. He also spent five years as a Vice President at Bridge Information Systems, where he helped to expand Bridge's online information service.

Joan McArdle (Business Advisor, Investor). Ms. McArdle has been a Vice President at Massachusetts Capital Resource Company ("MCRC"), a private investment company in Boston, since 1985. Prior to joining MCRC, Ms. McArdle was a Vice President of multinational/large corporate banking at the First National Bank of Boston.

Jeffrey Timmons (Business Advisor). Dr. Timmons is internationally recognized for his work in entrepreneurship, new ventures and venture capital. He is currently the Chairman of the Board of the Ewing Kaufman Foundation, which supports entrepreneurship and venture capital development. He formerly held the *MBA Class of 1954 Professor of New Ventures* and the *Frederick C. Hamilton Professor of Free Enterprise Development* chairs at the Harvard Business School.

Peter Grossman (Business Advisor, Investor). Mr. Grossman was Managing Director–Western Hemisphere for American Express Bank where he successfully developed international private banking and correspondent banking businesses. Prior to that, he was Senior Vice President for Latin America and Head of International Private Banking at Bankers Trust Company.

I was friends with Jeff Parker and had invested with him before. I'd spent eleven years in the information services business, so I had a good comfort level with the favorable economics of the subscription model and felt I could help them to grow the company. The key due diligence issues were the people—we spent a lot of time with Gary and George—understanding the economics of the business at the time, which was basically just Poland, and how the country roll-out model would work.

From fall 1994 to spring 1998 ISI raised a total of $14.9 million in equity, including $1.5 million of convertible debt, in six separate stages, each with a higher per-share valuation. Mueller believed that raising $12.5 million in new equity would be sufficient to fund the company to positive cash flow and self-sufficiency. Raising new equity would require a valuation of ISI. Mueller wondered how helpful the valuation comparisons provided by DLJ (see **Exhibit 16**) would be for this process and what types of companies were most comparable to ISI.

Weighing the Options: IPO or Strategic Investor?

One of the central questions Mueller had to address was whether ISI should attempt an initial public offering (IPO) on the public markets or try to find a strategic buyer for the company. Both options looked attractive. Gary explained:

It's hard not to look at some of the Internet IPOs that have been done. We have a unique product, fast growth and a good story to tell—it's quite possible that we could be a "hot" IPO. There are a lot of advantages to finding a strategic buyer, too. The stock market doesn't bring you a database of a million customers and high-level contacts that can help you win firm-wide deals.

EXHIBIT 16 Valuation Comparisons

Source: Donaldson, Lufkin & Jenrette Offering Memorandum.

Comparable Companies	Price 12/21/98	% of 52-Week High	Fully Diluted Market Value	Enterprise Value (1)	Enterprise Value/Revenue (1)		Price/EPS		Revenue Growth 98/99
					CY 98	CY 99	CY 98	CY 99	
Functional Driven Content:									
Excite	$50.38	85.9%	$3,038.6	$3,028.3	20.4x	12.9x	NM	109.5x	57.9%
Infoseek	47.94	96.8	1,687.8	1,633.3	20.7	10.5	NM	NM	96.3
Lycos	58.56	85.2	2,737.0	2,571.3	29.8	16.3	NM	1,952.1	82.7
Yahoo!	247.50	98.7	29,921.4	29,490.3	132.1	80.6	773.4x	392.9	63.9
Average		91.7%			50.7x	30.1x	773.4x	818.2x	75.2%
Edit Driven Content:									
broadcast.com	$91.00	94.5%	$1,740.6	$1,682.4	86.5x	41.1x	NM	NM	110.6%
CNET	58.75	78.9	1,090.4	1,046.6	17.5	12.1	NM	94.8x	44.4
DoubleClick, Inc.	48.50	62.9	1,021.6	971.9	12.1	7.6	NM	NM	58.5
Geocities	39.94	77.7	1,437.6	1,337.7	77.0	28.6	NM	NM	169.1
Sportsline USA	15.88	40.1	337.5	232.8	8.0	4.4	NM	NM	79.1
Average		70.8%			40.2x	18.8x	NM	94.8x	92.3%
Online Services:									
America Online	$117.00	98.0%	$66,218.2	$64,948.3	17.6x	12.7x	248.9x	169.6x	39.0%
@Home	67.00	89.0	9,162.6	8,989.0	192.3	57.6	NM	NM	234.0
Average		93.5%			105.0x	35.1x	248.9x	169.6x	136.5%
Average of all Internet Companies		82.5			55.8	25.9	511.2	543.8	94.1
Financial Information Companies:									
BARRA Inc.	$26.75	92.2%	$400.7	$368.3	2.3x	2.0x	15.6x	13.0x	15.6%
Dialog Corporation PLC (formerly MAID)	3.63	22.3	141.1	383.6	1.2	1.2	11.3	6.7	7.2
FactSet Research Systems Inc.	58.31	99.3	645.5	614.5	7.9	6.5	43.8	36.7	22.1
NewsEdge	7.50	38.0	130.4	87.5	1.0	0.7	NM	NM	34.5
Primark Corp.	23.75	53.4	564.9	552.3	1.3	1.2	27.6	19.8	9.2
Reuters Group PLC	63.75	82.3	16,240.7	14,781.7	3.0	2.9	22.0	20.2	5.2
The Thomson Corp.	24.29	74.9	14,751.2	19,125.2	3.0	2.8	7.2	6.7	6.8
Value Line Inc.	39.75	79.7	396.6	353.7	NA	NA	NA	NA	NA
Average		67.8%			2.8x	2.5x	21.3x	17.2x	14.4%

(1) Enterprise value is defined as market value, plus debt, plus minority interests, plus preferred stock, less cash and cash equivalents.

93

EXHIBIT 16 (Continued)

Comparable Transaction Analysis

($ in millions, except per share data)

Acquiror / Target	Lycos Inc. / Wired Digital Inc.	Lycos Inc. / Tripod Inc.	Sportsline USA, Inc. / GolfWeb.Com, Inc.	Wolters Kluwer / Ovid Technologies	Bridge Info. Systems / Dow Jones Markets	MAID PLC / Knight-Ridder Info.	Pearson plc / Interactive Data	Primark Corp. / Disclosure, Inc.	Reed Elsevier / Mead Data Central	Dow Jones / Telerate Inc.	Knight-Ridder / Dialog Info Srvcs.
Announcement Date	6-Oct-98	3-Feb-98	15-Jan-98	29-Sep-98	18-Mar-98	2-Oct-97	20-Jul-95	26-May-95	4-Oct-94	21-Sep-89	11-Jul-88
Closing Date	—	3-Feb-98	30-Jan-98	—	29-May-98	14-Nov-97	31-Aug-95	30-Jun-95	2-Dec-94	3-Jan-90	30-Aug-88
Status of Transaction	Pending	Closed	Closed	Pending	Closed	Closed	Closed	Closed	Closed	Closed	Closed
LTM Period Ended	31-Dec-97	31-Oct-97	30-Sep-97	31-Dec-97	31-Dec-97	28-Sep-97	31-Dec-94	31-Dec-94	2-Oct-94	30-Sep-89	31-Dec-87
Market Value of Common	$83.0	$58.0	$15.3	$154.4	$510.0	$420.0	$201.0	$200.0	$1,500.0	$1,996.5	$353.0
Net Market Value of Options/Warrants (1)	NA	NA	NA	40.0	NA	NA	NA	NA	NA	9.8	NA
Equity Market Value (EMV)	$83.0	$58.0	$15.3	$194.4	$510.0	$420.0	$201.0	$200.0	$1,500.0	$2,006.2	$353.0
Plus: Book Value of Preferred Stock	NA	11.5	11.1	0.0	NA	0.0	NA	0.0	0.0	0.0	0.0
Plus: Total Debt	NA	0.0	1.7	1.3	NA	0.0	NA	12.1	22.0	68.5	5.5
Plus: Minority Interests	NA	0.0	0.0	0.0	NA	0.0	NA	0.0	0.0	0.0	0.0
Less: Cash & Equivalents	NA	(5.9)	(1.4)	(2.6)	NA	0.0	NA	(1.6)	0.0	(15.2)	0.0
Less: Unconsolidated Investments	NA	NA	0.0	0.0	NA	0.0	NA	(3.1)	0.0	(17.0)	0.0
Total Enterprise Value (TEV)	$83.0	$63.6	$26.7	$193.1	$510.0	$420.0	$201.0	$207.4	$1,522.0	$2,042.6	$358.5
Valuation Multiples											
TEV/LTM Revenue	4.74 x	93.86 x	19.24 x	4.68 x	0.69 x	1.68 x	3.01 x	2.10 x	2.39 x	4.16 x	3.65
TEV/LTM EBITDA	NA	NM	NM	81.3	7.1	NA	NA	8.7	12.2	9.3	16.0
TEV/LTM EBIT	NA	NM	NM	NM	NM	NA	14.8	15.9	26.1	12.7	21.0
TEV/Total Assets	NA	9.2	7.7	4.8	NA	1.0	NA	2.0	NA	3.4	11.5
EMV/LTM Net Income	NA	NM	NM	NM	NA	22.3 x	NA	29.8 x	33.5 x	24.0 x	38.4
EMV/LTM Net Cash Flow	NA	NA	NA	79.4 x	NA	NA	NA	10.4	13.4	14.1	24.3
EMV/Book Value of Common Equity	NA	NM	NM	20.6	NA	1.3	NA	4.2	NA	5.0	37.6

I also think there are some risks to taking the IPO route. If you look at the really success-ful Internet IPOs they are all very consumer-based . . . not a lot of business to business. We can also get a lot out of a partner with good expertise, beyond just reducing redundant infra-structure costs. I'm not a big brand guy. I'm a sales guy. Our company name is probably wrong. There are a lot of companies in our industry who can probably help us do some things a lot better. They all have a lot of cash and are generating a lot of cash. And what do they do? They buy companies like us.

Grant was undecided about the relative attractiveness of a trade sale vs. an IPO. He explained:

The basic model that Gary and George outlined worked, although as the company grew it be-came clear that the trade-off between reaching break-even and continuing to grow was less favorable than we had hoped. A strategic buyer is going to worry less about some of the P&L issues. They will see this as an opportunity to acquire expertise on using the Internet and on understanding news coverage in emerging markets. They will also see it as an opportunity to get some top managers as well as the financial side.

For us, however, the bottom line is valuation. Based on recent deals it might be possible to get as much or more in an IPO than we would get from a strategic investor. That also would give us the option of retaining some of our investment and capturing future upside if the ulti-mate valuation doesn't meet our aspirations. A strategic buyer is unlikely to want to keep the VCs at the table.

Mueller knew he wouldn't have to look far to find potential buyers—he had been in regular contact with them almost since ISI's founding:

I've been getting calls from the big IS companies at least once a month for the past few years. I used to tell them that talking with us was like trying to date someone with over-protective parents in junior high school. We could have lunch, but we're too young to have dinner and certainly couldn't get married. Now we're talking more seriously.

Decision Time

Standing up from behind his desk, Mueller stretched. It wasn't easy separating all the is-sues relating to what could amount to the sale of his business. Whether ISI ultimately chose to do an IPO or to sell to a strategic buyer, Mueller knew that the company would change from what it was in the earlier years. The decision he and his team were about to recommend to the company's Board of Directors would have significant implications for its existing investors, its employees and for Mueller himself. But what was the best path to follow? As he looked at the skyline of Boston's financial district from his corner office near South Station Mueller wondered whether it was possible somehow to combine the virtues of an IPO and a trade sale.

Case 7

@Hoc: Leveraging Israeli Technology in the United States

On a late afternoon in July 1999, Guy Miasnik (MBA '99) and Ly Tran (MBA '99) were sitting in Kresge, the Harvard Business School cafeteria, eating pizza. Though both had just graduated from HBS that June, they still had ties to the campus through their start-up, AtHoc, Inc. ("@Hoc"). Miasnik and Tran were about to head into a meeting with one of their faculty advisors to discuss their fundraising campaign that had just started (see **Exhibits 1 and 2** for Miasnik's and Tran's resumes). They had just completed their business plan (**see Exhibit 3** for @Hoc's business plan), a document that found its genesis from some of the field studies the two had taken during their second MBA year at HBS. The two had several questions in store for their meeting, the most important of which was from whom to raise money: angels or venture capital firms. While in business school, the two had already raised $400,000 in a seed-round of capital. This seed-round was in fact a convertible bridge loan whose strike price was dependent on the valuation of the first round of financing. Along with the HBS field studies and Miasnik's connections in Israel, the seed money of $400,000 had allowed them to move slightly beyond a prototype for their product, which was developed during their field studies. It was clear that @Hoc needed much more capital to formally launch the company. Miasnik and Tran were also wondering how much capital they should raise. They estimated they would need approximately $1–$1.5 million to complete the product and ramp-up operations, but should they raise more capital than that?

Also concerning were some of the strategic issues facing the company. R&D for the company was located in Israel but the company's headquarters were in Boston. R&D had been conducted out of Israel because Miasnik's partners lived and worked there. But should R&D remain there and for how long? The entrepreneurs also had some other marketing and distribution concerns that they had been careful *not* to highlight in the business plan. These concerns could affect the amount of money required and the source from which it should be raised. As Miasnik and Tran finished their pizza (cold by now)

Dean's Fellow William J. Coughlin (MBA '99) prepared this case under the supervision of Professor Walter Kuemmerle. HBS cases are developed solely as the basis for class discussion. Cases are not intended to serve as endorsements, sources of primary data, or illustrations of effective or ineffective management.

EXHIBIT 1 Miasnik's Resume

Source: @Hoc.

GUY MIASNIK

Experience

1996–1998 **KINETICA INTERNETTING SOLUTIONS**   HERTZELIA, ISRAEL
Co-Founder and CEO. From zero capital, built Kinetica into the leading high-end Internet solutions firm in Israel. Specialized in delivering sophisticated e-commerce and intranet customized solutions for clients.

- Achieved $1M revenue run rate within eight months. Reached and sustained profitability within one year and maintained 30% quarterly growth rate.
- Partnered with Microsoft, Sun and Oracle to market and design solutions for clients. In joint development with Microsoft, introduced the first commercial solution for developing Hebrew Web content; immediately became the market leader.
- Attracted over 30 clients, including large corporations, government ministries and startups. 25% sales to US-based clients. Major projects include the first Online Brokerage in Israel (Analyst.co.il), an Online Investment Game for the US teenage market (MainXchange.com), a Virtual Community for school teachers and an Intranet for Discount Bank (third largest in Israel).
- Researched, analyzed and developed company's strategy and business plan. Built financial models and forecasts. Managed cash flow. Deployed managerial control system.
- Successfully completed the sale of Kinetica in a cash and equity deal to NetVision, Israel's largest ISP (a subsidiary of Elron Electronic Industries; NASDAQ: ELRNF).

1991–1996 **ISRAEL DEFENSE FORCE, TECHNOLOGY UNIT**
1994–1996 **Project Manager and Team Leader–Captain.** Managed development teams of multi-million dollar technological projects, specializing in state-of-the-art communication systems.

- Evaluated operational requirements, performed top-level system design, developed hardware and software based system, and coordinated industrial subcontractors.
- Managed engineers, programmers and technicians in multiple projects.
- Established internal GPS technology knowledge base. Worked with industry experts.
- Technologies used included: TCP/IP, Windows NT, SQL, C++, OOD, Client-Server Architecture.
- Promoted from R&D Engineer (Lieutenant: 1991–1993). Received top performance ranking.

1990–1991 **INTERBALCO A.G.**   SHANNON, IRELAND
R&D Engineer. Designed and developed a new computerized product for the automobile market.

Education

1998–1999 **HARVARD BUSINESS SCHOOL**   BOSTON, MA
Candidate for Master in Business Administration degree, June 1999. Co-Chair, HBS Business Plan Contest. Co-Editor, HBS-Israel Alumni Journal. Field study projects: Internet Promotion Plan for TMSI's MoversNet.com; Hong Kong Online Financial Services–Analysis of market potential.

1992–1998 **TEL AVIV UNIVERSITY** (evening program)   TEL AVIV, ISRAEL
Candidate for LL.B. degree in business law, 1998.

1987–1991 **TECHNION–ISRAEL INSTITUTE OF TECHNOLOGY**   HAIFA, ISRAEL
Bachelor of Science degree in Electrical Engineering, summa cum laude.

Community

1994–1996 **YOUNG ENTREPRENEURSHIP FORUM**   TEL AVIV, ISRAEL
Co-founded national forum supporting new business initiatives.

1988–1990 **PROGRAM FOR THE ADVANCEMENT OF TECHNOLOGICAL MANPOWER**   ISRAEL
Director of Computer Education. Program aimed at under-privileged high school students.

Personal   Fluent in Hebrew and English. Enjoy photography, squash, hiking, skiing and traveling.

EXHIBIT 2 Trans's Resume

Source: @Hoc.

LY K. TRAN

Education

1998–1999   **HARVARD UNIVERSITY**   **BOSTON, MA**
                         GRADUATE SCHOOL OF BUSINESS ADMINISTRATION
                         Candidate for Master in Business Administration, June 1999. Venture Capital & Principal Investment Club. High Tech & New Media Club. 1999 Business Plan Competition Co-Chair. HBS WesTrek 1999 co-organizer.

1988–1992   **PRINCETON UNIVERSITY**   **PRINCETON, NJ**
                         Bachelor of Arts in History. Wrote thesis on U.S. policy of resettling war refugees from the Vietnam conflict. Argued that Government absolved itself from guilt of withdrawal by selecting a limited number of collaborators to resettle in America. Won 1st place in Eastern Sprints–freshman lightweight crew.

Experience

1998—present   **Ancestry.com.** Recruited by CEO and founding shareholders to bring in strategic partners and raise capital (the company provides online genealogical content over the Internet).
- Solicited and successfully raised $2.0MM venture financing from Intel Corp. (Nasdaq: INTC).
- Participated in negotiating $10.0MM investment from CMG*i* (Nasdaq: CMGI).
- Created partnerships for commerce, content and community services.

1995–1997   **Citicorp Emerging Markets SA.** Retained as financial consultant to create, launch, and manage Citicorp's principal investment business in the Socialist Republic of Vietnam.
- Developed investment strategy and wrote business plan with team of bankers from Hong Kong, Singapore, Vietnam and London. Presented strategy to Vice-Chairman of Citicorp. Recommended investment focus on consumer goods opportunities as a play on Vietnam's 77 million (and growing) population.
- Negotiated terms and drafted MOU for investment in mineral water company. Managed complex international deal team involving French entrepreneur, Swiss food conglomerate, Citibankers, and lawyers from Vietnam, Singapore and Hong Kong.

1995–1996   **Vietnam Fund Management Co.** Retained as financial entrepreneur to turn-around portfolio companies and assess venture capital opportunities for $55MM private equity fund.
- Worked with team of French architect, Thai hotel operator, financial investor, and local partner in development of Ana Mandara, Vietnam's first international beach resort (located near Cam Ranh Bay). Created financial control system and trained chief accountant. Resort received great review in *Condé Nast's Travel & Leisure.*

1996–present   **Moca Café Roasting Co.** Founder and co-owner. Vietnam's first specialty coffee roasting company. Voted best café & coffee in 1997 & 1998 by the *Vietnam Investment Review.*
- Identified unique opportunity to transform Vietnam's specialty coffee industry. Investigated technology behind specialty coffee roasting. Created and built "Moca" brand. Recruited and trained team of young managers to operate coffee roasting business.

1994–1995   **SMITH BARNEY INC.**   **NEW YORK, NY & HONG KONG, PRC**
                         Principal Investments, Mergers & Acquisitions
                         Developed valuation analyses, performed due diligence, prepared offering memoranda, and analyzed strategic issues for companies in various industries.
- Represented Boston-based LBO group in $1.0BN bid for Prudential Home Mortgage. Worked on Ssangyong Motors sale to Mercedes Benz AB. Worked on principal investments deals in Hong Kong, China, Indonesia and Thailand.

1992–1994   **THE CHASE MANHATTAN BANK, NA**   **NEW YORK, NY**
                         Global Mergers & Acquisitions Group
- Represented Nextel in strategic sale to Nippon Telegraph and Telephone. Advised Tokuyama Soda in joint venture with Mineral Export Co. of Vietnam. Represented Tetley Tea in joint venture with Te Laggs Mexico.

Community   Volunteer in **Operation Smile**, an organization that brings American surgeons to developing countries to perform cleft-lip surgeries on children. Built OpSmile's accounting system in Hanoi and acted as general advisor.

Personal   Master coffee roaster (prefer Colombian and Javanese beans). Created world's best spring roll recipe. Terrible but avid squash player. Speak some French. Speak fluent Vietnamese.

they looked at each other. They needed to make up their mind soon on these questions. The clock was ticking and every moment they lost in fundraising was another moment they gave to the competition.

Who Are These People? Background on the Two Entrepreneurs

Guy Miasnik

Guy Miasnik was a native of Israel who had started his career as an officer in the Israeli army. In the army he worked for five years in a technology R&D unit that developed communications technology, eventually rising to the rank of Captain. "So much of the commercial technology in Israel comes from the armed forces," explained Miasnik, "that it was actually the perfect place to begin my career right out of school. The army gave me the opportunity to manage technological development at an early stage of my career." In 1996, after leaving the army, Miasnik co-founded and ran an Internet consulting and solutions company in Israel called Kinetica. After building the company into the leading high-end solutions company for the Internet in Israel, he sold the company to NetVision, the largest Internet Service Provider in Israel. With the deal in the works, Miasnik decided to head to HBS. Miasnik explained his decision:

> I decided to attend business school because I really wanted to make a transition to the United States. The United States is where the Big Game is located and if you are going to work in the technology industry, that is where the Big Leagues are—the cutting edge of everything is there. As an entrepreneur, I felt that being close to the U.S. market was key for any future venture I would be involved in. At the same time, Israel's distance creates a major hurdle that few startups can manage to overcome. That is why once we made the decision to sell Kinetica, I left Israel to attend HBS. The timing couldn't have been better.

Ly Tran

Ly Tran was born in Vietnam and left the country for the United States in 1975 with his family. After graduating from Princeton, he worked at Chase for a year in mergers and acquisitions in New York City. While working on a transaction in Asia, he went back to Vietnam for the first time since his emigration and fell in love with the country. Tran recounted his journey:

> When I went back to Vietnam, I absolutely fell in love with the place. Culturally, it was energizing because everyone was speaking "my language" and I felt like I was able to get in touch with my roots. Professionally, the place was terribly underdeveloped, but had this incredible energy. I just saw it as this huge opportunity. So when my then-girlfriend—now-wife—moved to Vietnam after college, I lined up a consulting job with Citicorp based in Hong Kong where I acted as the "local advisor" and helped them source deals. In doing so, I came across the Moca Café coffee roasting idea for Vietnam. Moca Café was developed entirely from scratch and funded by my partners and me. With the exception of the equipment, we were able to source everything locally, and so we did not need a lot of capital. That is where I got my first real whiff of entrepreneurship, and I was hooked!
>
> When my girlfriend applied to Harvard Law School, I decided it was time to head to business school so I applied to HBS. I wanted to transition into the technology area and HBS looked like the perfect opportunity to do so. While at HBS, I was itching to do a deal when I received a business plan from Ancestry.com, a CD-ROM genealogy database company that was transitioning into the Internet. I decided to help them with the company's fundraising during my second semester at HBS, not only because I liked their plan a lot, but because it would help me transition into the Internet space.

During their first semester at Harvard Business School in Section I, Tran and Miasnik sat near each other and began to forge a relationship. While discussing their mutual goals and aspirations, the two felt they might be a good fit and started working on several business ideas together during their second year through field studies offered at HBS. Although they had a specific opportunity to work together at Ancestry.com, they decided to start @Hoc instead. Tran explained:

> We both thought the @Hoc idea was by far the best idea we had come up with. During the field studies we found out that we could work together. And @Hoc simply offered the opportunity to build something from scratch. So we took a leap of faith of sorts and decided to head out on our own with @Hoc.

So Many Choices—Strategic Issues

Although they felt relieved that they had completed their business plan, Miasnik and Tran knew that they still had a number of important issues outstanding. The first was the location of their R&D unit. Should it be kept in Israel or moved to the United States? There were two reasons why R&D should remain in Israel. First, Miasnik not only had access to engineering talent in Israel, but he basically had an entire team lined up there and ready to move on the project. In an industry where being first to market can make or break a company, this was a major value. Second, it was difficult to find engineering talent in the United States, at the right price. A Boston-based C++ or HTML programmer with four to five years experience demanded about $60,000–80,000, compared to Tel Aviv where the cost was about 25% less. Miasnik knew that @Hoc would need more engineering talent as the company grew. And he knew the labor pool and sources for engineers in Israel well. The Kinetica sale was completed by June 1998 and some of Miasnik's former co-workers were ready to move on with him. "We had to fill in the team a bit," recalled Miasnik, "but we had the core there."

While these were two reasons for keeping R&D in Israel, there was one major concern: the distance. It would be difficult for the management team in the United States to communicate with the R&D engineers in Israel, not just because of communication and travel costs but because the engineers were so far from the market that they may not understand the real product needs. "The Internet changed product development and launch cycle times from years to a few months. To get it right, you must have a direct and close loop between your market and R&D," explained Miasnik.

Miasnik and Tran had mentioned in their business plan that the R&D group would eventually move to the United States, but in reality this was not a finalized decision. The good news was that most of the Israeli engineers seemed to be willing, even eager, to move to the United States. It would be "just" a question of getting the immigration papers. Whether, and when, they were going to move the team was a major issue for the two entrepreneurs.

A second concern was how to approach the market. There were several questions. Should they self-promote the product, or focus on an infrastructure play, where @Hoc provided a type of private-label infrastructure for customers to brand (i.e. Inktomi, BeFree). A related concern was how to distribute the product. Should @Hoc distribute the product on their own site or via the customers' site? Finally, there was the question about whether to develop a mass-market product or focus on vertical segments, and in that case which vertical segment was best suited for initial entry. In the business plan, the team pointed out all the benefits of going into the finance segment. It seemed like a good choice but the entrepreneurs knew that they did not understand other vertical spaces equally well. "All of these choices are very important," warned Tran, "as they have dramatic consequences for our budget and capital requirements. If we distribute off of our own site, that would have dramatic implications for our advertising and marketing budget."

Another concern was the execution side of product development. They had already developed a working prototype, but during their studies at HBS they had learned about many prototypes that fizzled. "It really comes down to our ability to move from a high-level concept prototype to marketable product," explained Miasnik. "Also, this is not just a question of writing good code but also of user acceptability. At this point we know very little about how well users will understand and accept our product." Finally there were some of the more typical start-up issues: human resources and team building, as well as competition. Miasnik and Tran had never built a team in the United States before. Regarding competition, they knew that other companies in a similar space were currently being funded but in the emerging Internet economy it was very hard to identify a competitor until they hit you—hard. All of these concerns had important implications for how the company should be developed and funded.

Funding Issues

The team wanted to raise between $1 to $1.5 million in capital during the first round. Miasnik explained the rationale:

> We want to raise enough money to get to the next milestone in our company's development. We now have a prototype, a plan and the core of a team, but we need some cash to get us to the next level. We define the next milestone as getting the product fully developed and ready for launch, getting five clients signed up and paying us, and getting valuable user feedback to determine the next steps we should take in growing the company.

Tran, on the other hand, argued for a larger round of financing:

> There are certainly arguments for having a smaller first round of financing. This will keep us focused on doing things step by step. But we also have some other issues. If we decide to bring the guys over from Israel, we would probably want more money. Not only would we need the money for moving expenses, but we would also want to make sure we are well capitalized before we have the R&D team move over. We and the R&D team would not feel comfortable with the move otherwise.

The other question was from whom they should raise money: VC firms, angel investors, or both. In the team's eyes there were several positives and negatives with going down each route. Venture capitalists offered the branding, the access to customers, partners and financing, and the help in recruiting @Hoc really felt it needed. On the downside, VC firms tended to be much slower in the funding process, were often quite conflicted because they saw a lot of deals and could potentially incubate @Hoc's idea on their own. VC firms were also expensive with regards to the amount of equity they required. Angel investors offered much quicker decisions on fundraising, could be well connected and were a little "cheaper." On the downside, raising money from angels could turn the management of the investor group into an assignment from hell for the entrepreneurs. Because angels generally invested as individuals, a company often had to raise money from several angels to complete a round of financing. This could be difficult to manage both during the fundraising process and later during board meetings, especially when things went "South." "Plus, we just are not sure *how* valuable angels really are," explained Tran. "We know they are connected but how much of the VC services in branding and recruiting can they really deliver?"

Regarding both types of investors, Miasnik and Tran had put together some parameters for valuation purposes. Based on discussions with numerous friends and advisors, Miasnik summarized their thoughts on the valuation parameters a VC and an angel investor uses in evaluating a potential investment:

> In the first round of financing, we think that a VC will require a 30% equity stake at an absolute minimum. Quite often they will take from 40% to even 50% of a company in the seed round or sometimes even in the first round. That is why we call them "expensive." With angels, we think that, on average, they put a $3 to $4 million valuation on a seed round. All of these parameters apply for a team with an idea and a business plan. We think we offer much more than that. We have a prototype, some clients, lots of experience in starting ventures, and a team that has proven it can execute. That should go a long way. But how far it goes remains to be seen in the negotiations.

With these questions spinning in their heads, Miasnik and Tran walked across the HBS campus towards Morgan Hall. They knew that their faculty advisor would not have an answer for all of these questions but they were fairly certain that the meeting would clarify some of their thinking.

EXHIBIT 3
@Hoc's Business Plan

Source: @Hoc.

AtHoc Inc.
1105 Massachusetts Ave., Suite 7C
Cambridge, MA 02138
Tel: (617) 576-0081
Fax: (617) 868-8781
www.athoc.com

@Hoc Business Plan

Guy Miasnik guy@athoc.com
Ly Tran ly@athoc.com

This document is not an offer to sell securities but is provided for information purposes only. Estimates or projections contained herein involve significant elements of subjective judgment and analysis. This plan does not purport to contain all of the information that may be required to evaluate the Company and any recipient hereof should conduct its own independent analysis.

Table of Contents

I. Executive Summary

Management Team

@Hoc's management is composed of a seasoned and diverse team of Internet entrepreneurs. The members of this team have worked with each other in the past and have collectively achieved:

- founding, developing and successfully selling Kinetica, Israel's leading Internet solutions company, to NetVision, the largest Israeli Internet service provider;
- developing the business strategy and bringing Intel Corp. as an investor in the $12 million Series A financing for Ancestry.com;
- cumulating 50 years of experience in technological research, development and management;
- sharing over 15 years of experience in marketing, business development and product management.

We have assembled a Board of Advisors comprising entrepreneurs and leading business scholars. The biographies of the management team as well as the advisors are included in the section that follows.

Business Concept

AtHoc Inc. ("@Hoc" or "Company") focuses on a user's *ad hoc* behavior, which is poorly addressed in the online space. The Company is creating a new channel for commerce and content that caters to the *ad hoc* behavior of online users. Specifically @Hoc enables instant, context-sensitive information retrieval and shopping from anywhere in the Web or desktop. The technology and service are patent pending.

@Hoc allows the user to activate any word in any Web page or desktop application and make that word behave like a hypertext link even though no hypertext link previously existed in relation to that word. The users can then direct the activated word to their choice of services, be they stock quotes, search engines, news sites, shopping destinations or other options. In doing so, @Hoc enhances the user's experience by integrating personalized services into the online and desktop environment. Most observers refer to @Hoc as a personalized impulse portal which promotes stickiness and provides a service that taps an unexploited usage behavior, thereby creating opportunities for customer acquisition, impulse buying and context-sensitive advertising.

Value Propositions

We have three constituents in the @Hoc service network: end-users, content partners, and commerce affiliates. The Company creates value for each of its constituent in the following ways.

For the end-users, we create value by enhancing their online experience. @Hoc gives users the freedom to access content and engage in commerce from any application and context. @Hoc learns more about the users with the frequency of usage and leverages its growing database of user behavior to further enrich the user's experience by offering goods and services that are personalized and context-sensitive.

For the content partners, @Hoc is a sticky application and provides a direct pipeline between their Web sites and their users. This pipeline increases user traffic and retention, extends the content reach, and reduces customer acquisition cost. We are able to capture a share of this value creation by splitting ad revenues with the content partners. We will also be able to charge content suppliers slotting fees for placement of their services on the @Hoc client.

For the commerce partners, @Hoc creates value by driving traffic for unintended purchases to their shopping sites. According to Jupiter Communications, 23% of online purchases are unintended.[i] The Company will be able to capture a share of this value creation from the commissions earned as commerce affiliates.

Business Model

As the Company fulfills the *ad hoc* needs of online users, the Company will generate revenues from several sources:

- **Slotting fees**—we will sell listing space within the @*Hoc* pop-up menu. Slotting fees are typical sources of revenues for portals that can drive traffic to content and commerce sites.

- **Transaction fees**—because the activation of an @*Hoc* panel enables a topically-relevant impulse sales platform, we will be able to facilitate online purchases on a regular basis and earn commissions on sales.

- **Advertising fees**—each time a user activates @*Hoc* to request a service (i.e. retrieve stock quotes), a pop-up window showcasing the requested content will open. This window is a new premium real estate created and owned by @*Hoc* for banner ads, sponsorships and icon placements. Revenues from these ads will be split with the content partner who supplied the requested service.

- **Bundled subscription fees**—using the cable-TV subscription model, we will bundle premium content services that cater to online *ad hoc* needs and offer those services as paid subscription. We will split the subscription revenue with the content providers.

- **Other sources**—these revenues could include money from data mining, private labeling @*Hoc,* hosting other people's content and even licensing the @*Hoc* technology.

Sustainability of Business

Long-term sustainability does not depend on the long-term success of the @*Hoc* client. Arguably, software application companies as well as portals could readily introduce comparable clients to activate *ad hoc* services. Accordingly, we will develop our core strength in the back-end, providing *ad hoc* services for all clients be they the @*Hoc* client, private-labeled clients operated by the Company, @*Hoc* embedded clients or third-party clients. In doing so we will focus on developing the following competitive advantages:

- **Accumulating and leveraging knowledge of the user**—because we will maintain and constantly expand our database of users' preferences and online *ad hoc* habits, we will develop a valuable and personalized service for every user, thereby creating a barrier to switching.

- **Creating a catalog of services with a broad network of partners**—our network of partners, who will work with us to provide content and commerce services as well as to proliferate @*Hoc,* represents the key to our success. We will work on enlarging the network and add services to further build on our relationships with content and commerce providers.

- **Aligning with strategic partners**—we will develop industry alliances, whether with leading new media partners, broadband players or hardware/software manufacturers. These relationships, combined with our swiftness to the market as the first mover, will result in creating a barrier of entry. We will leverage these alliances to acquire new users and to position the Company as the *de facto* provider of *ad hoc* services.

- **Developing a state-of-the-art back-end technology**—we will be investing significant efforts in building the back-end technology, utilizing our knowledge of the user and the *ad hoc* online space to provide the most advanced services. We will incorporate through partnerships, acquisitions and in-house development, a wide range of back-end services such as digital wallets, billing and content retrieval.

- **Creating a world-class business development team**—we recognize the importance of building strong relationships with content and commerce partners. The artistry of well crafted deals and relationship management depend on intellect as well as experience. As such, we will focus on recruiting the best individuals to create a world-class business development team.

As a result of these efforts coupled with being the first mover, we will create barriers of entry for our competitors. These barriers include switching cost for the users, an intensive "catalog" of services, knowledge of the space and technology, and strategic industry alliances.

Market Segmentation

The Company will develop the user base by first segmenting the Web universe into vertical markets and then offering *@Hoc* services tailored to the needs of users within those markets. Examples of vertical markets include personal finance, sports and education. Our goal is to develop an active user base so that we maximize the life time value of every customer.

We have identified the personal finance market as the first point of entry to distribute the *@Hoc* client and acquire users. The reason for personal finance reflects the size and profile of the user base. According to Jupiter Communications, the number of households with online trading accounts is expected to grow from 6.8 MM in 1998 to 15.2 MM in 2002.[ii] Twenty-percent of the web population already use the Internet for personal finance purposes. Also, the profile of these users make them attractive customers; as a group, they are wealthier, better educated and more active Internet users than the average Web population.

The customer groups that we will next target are users who depend on the Web for reference information (white collar professionals) and users who depend on the Web for sports information. With respect to users of reference information, the number of individuals in higher education alone exceeds 15.1 million, according to the National Center for Education Statistics.[iii] With respect to sports users, Jupiter Communications "discovered that for over a third of the Internet news audience, sports scores and information were the number one reason to go online."[iv] Education and sports vertical markets represent logical extensions of the *@Hoc* customer target.

Marketing and Distribution

The Company's content partners will distribute the *@Hoc* freeware. The economics of affiliate distribution is as follows: in return for promoting and distributing the *@Hoc* client via a link from their web sites, the content affiliates earn default slotting for their services on the *@Hoc* pop-up menu. Thus, a user who downloads the *@Hoc* client from an affiliate's site will automatically receive that affiliate's services as default in addition to other non-competing services offered by *@Hoc*. By yielding premium default slotting in exchange for distribution, we create a win-win-win situation. We expose *@Hoc* to millions of visitors across our content partners' network and acquire new users, the content partners receive default slotting for their *ad hoc* services, and the user is able to access his or her favorite services from anywhere on the desktop and web.

We also plan to partner with companies who already have a client presence on the user's desktop, such as Eudora, RealNetworks and AOL. We will bundle *@Hoc* by providing a client kit to these companies.

Finally, we will use viral marketing techniques to propagate *@Hoc* as well as traditional marketing methods such as press releases, trade shows, banner ads, and bounty purchases. We believe that in the immediate future, however, the main distribution channel for *@Hoc* will be through the network of content affiliates.

Current Status

The following is an update of our progress.

- **Business Development:** We have signed Letters of Intent ("LOI") to develop *@Hoc* with CBS MarketWatch.com, TheStreet.com, Quote.com, RagingBull.com and Ancestry.com. Preliminary discussions are also underway with Ask Jeeves and Google.com. In addition, the Company is an affiliate of Amazon.com and intends to become affiliates of BarnesandNoble.com, 800Flowers.com, eToys.com and other commerce providers. We will soon engage in preferred affiliate relationships where the commerce partners pay to have the default slots for certain goods and services on *@Hoc*. We are opening an office in San Francisco in July, and we are also actively recruiting to fill key roles in marketing, sales and business development.

- **Technology Development:** In April 1999, we developed a working prototype of *@Hoc*'s technology and filed a provisional patent for the technology and business process. In June 1999, we established a research and development center in the Herzelia Industrial Center in Israel to scale-up the technology. Beta testing is expecting to commence by the end of the summer.

- **Financing Development:** We have raised over $400K in seed financing from individual investors. The proceeds will be used to develop Version 1.0 of the technology, create an affiliate network of roughly 20 content and commerce partners, ramp-up operations and launch *@Hoc*. We will then aim to raise a venture round to further build the business and engage in a major marketing effort.

Summary of Projected Income Statement

@Hoc Financial Projections	1999	2000	2001	2002	2003
Revenues					
Advertising	$35,912	$670,627	$3,987,322	$14,723,757	$31,836,147
Transactions	30,864	467,244	4,961,188	27,572,436	60,486,865
Slotting	—	478,420	3,287,006	12,234,840	36,280,509
Bundled Subscription	—	43,058	613,574	3,513,147	9,070,127
Total revenues	66,776	1,659,349	12,849,091	58,044,180	137,673,648
Cost of goods	183,532	649,136	1,703,875	5,382,523	11,521,446
Depreciation	500,000	500,000	1,000,000	2,000,000	5,000,000
	683,532	1,149,136	2,703,875	7,382,523	16,521,446
Gross profit	−616,757	510,213	10,145,216	50,661,658	121,152,202
Salary	1,320,000	6,975,000	12,030,000	23,200,000	46,100,000
Selling and marketing	1,986,400	5,775,000	12,612,500	19,650,000	27,750,000
General admin	74,750	563,750	1,200,000	1,970,000	4,018,000
	3,381,150	13,313,750	25,842,500	44,820,000	77,868,000
Operating profit	−$3,997,907	−12,803,537	−$15,697,284	$5,841,658	$43,284,202
Head count	32	65	120	220	420
Revenue per employee	$2,087	$25,528	$107,076	$263,837	$327,794
Expense per employee	$127,021	$222,506	$237,886	$237,284	$224,737
Revenue mix					
Advertising	54%	40%	31%	25%	23%
Transactions	46%	28%	39%	48%	44%
Slotting	0%	29%	26%	21%	26%
Bundled Subscription	0%	3%	5%	6%	7%

II. Team

Guy Miasnik, CEO

Guy was the co-founder and CEO of Kinetica (www.kinetica.com), Israel's leading high-end Internet solutions company. Guy orchestrated Kinetica's growth from a zero-capital start-up to profitability in less than two years, attracting blue-chip clients such as Discount Bank, Ministry of Foreign Affairs and Israel's top stock brokerage house (www.analyst.co.il). His tenure at Kinetica culminated in the recent sale of the company to NetVision. (NetVision is Israel's largest Internet Service Provider and a subsidary of Elron Electronic Industries–NASDAQ: ELRNF.) Prior to Kinetica, Guy was a Captain in the Technology Unit of the Israel Defense Force where he managed the development teams of multi-million dollar technological projects specializing in state-of-the-art communication systems.

Guy graduated *summa cum laude* with a BS in Electrical Engineering from the Technion–Israel Institute of Technology. He has recently completed his MBA from Harvard Business School (June 1999). An avid squash player, Guy gives his best whenever in the glass court. Aside from squash, Guy happily posts digital photos of Ron, his first child, on the Web.

Ly Tran, VP Business Development

Ly has been the Strategic Advisor to Ancestry.com (www.ancestry.com) where he has helped develop the business strategy and raise $12.0 million of venture financing. Ly continues to serve as an advisor to the CEO and the Executive Committee of Ancestry.com in the area of electronic commerce strategy and strategic alliances. His flexibility as an entrepreneur has enabled him to apply his business development skills across multiple industries including finance, hospitality, and coffee roasting. Ly built Citicorp's private equity business in Vietnam, co-developed the Ana Mandara Resort (a 68-room bungalow beach-front resort near China Beach), and founded Moca Cafe, Vietnam's only specialty coffee roasting company.

Ly holds an AB in History from Princeton University and has earned his MBA from Harvard Business School (June 1999). An avid runner, Ly is trying to lose weight from the damage caused during his recent honeymoon in Italy.

Aviv Siegel, CTO

Aviv was a co-founder of Kinetica and also served as its Chief Technology Officer. He is recognized by industry participants as one of the leading experts in Internet technology in Israel. Aviv was the lead developer of Kinetica's WISE methodology for Internet project development, which is being taught and implemented in major Internet projects. Aviv has consulted to the most prestigious private and government institutions in Israel such as RAFAEL, Ministry of Foreign Affairs, Discount Bank, brokerage houses, insurance companies, and universities on issues about Internet security, electronic commerce and networking. Aviv has designed and managed the development of an online insurance sales system for Direct Insurance Ltd., the first commercial electronic commerce system in Israel. He has also led the development of Analyst—the first online brokerage system in Israel. Prior to Kinetica, Aviv served five years in the army and obtained the rank of Captain. Aviv was in charge of several multi-million dollars high-bandwidth communications and imaging systems.

Aviv holds a B.S. *cum laude* in Electrical Engineering from the Technion–Israel Institute of Technology. Outside of work, Aviv is adjusting to his new role of manhood as he has recently become the proud father of two twin boys. Other members of Aviv's family includes Tuvya and Arik (his cat and dog, respectively).

Roy Sharon, VP Product Management

Roy was also a co-founder of Kinetica and served as its head of marketing and product management. Under his leadership, Kinetica has introduced several Internet and Intranet products that have earned the company its lead position in Israel's Internet market.

Roy has deepened Kinetica's influence on Israel's burgeoning Internet industry by launching an advisory service where Kinetica assesses the impact of the Internet on business organizations. Roy has played a key role in positioning and branding Kinetica's WISE methodology for Internet project development, transforming it into one of Kinetica's competitive advantages. In the sale of Kinetica, Roy played a critical role both in the negotiations and due diligence process.

Outside of computing, Roy spends time with his two children. During the rare spare moments that he can find between work and family, Roy enjoys a good game of bridge.

Roey Ben-amotz, Server-side R&D Team Leader

Roey joined *@Hoc* from Israel Online ("IOL"), Israel's largest Internet portal, where he served as its Chief Technology Officer since its inception in 1996. In addition to managing a team of 18 developers, his responsibilities at IOL covered all technology oriented services such as development, production, administration and support. Prior to IOL, Roey was in the Israeli Defense Force and obtained the rank of Lieutenant. While in the military, his technological expertise enabled him to also provide consulting services for the World Bank.

Roey holds a B.A. in Computer Information Systems and Economics from Israel Open University. He is fluent in Visual Basic, SQL, asp, MTS, MSMQ, Java, JavaScript, Pascal, C++, DHTML, and XML.

Shay Kochan, Product Development

Prior to *@Hoc,* Shay was a senior technologist at Partner Communications Ltd., a leading wireless communications services company in Israel. As a large-scale DBA specialist, he created, tested and adminstered the database systems required to operate Partner Communications. Shay graduated with a BA in Information Systems from the College of Management in Tel Aviv and spent several years in the Israel Defense Force where he developed training programs and electronic warfare models.

Shay Sharon, Product Development

Prior to *@Hoc,* Shay was a co-founder and the Director of Applications Development at Internative Solutions Ltd. in Tel Aviv. Shay graduated from the IDF computer science academy and has eight years of experience in software development, specializing in database application. Shay also has four years of experience in the development of content management web-based tools. In this area, he was the lead developer in an enterprise application platform team for implementing business-critical document management solutions over distributed Intranet/Internet networks.

III. Definition of Opportunity

Usage Behavior

Ad hoc behavior can be characterized as the sudden need to seek information or make purchases while in the middle of an activity. It is generally triggered by context association. In the real world, there are practical solutions that fulfill the needs of *ad hoc* behaviors. Examples include pulling down a dictionary from the home bookshelf to track the meaning of a word, referring to a trusted source such as *Standard & Poor's* for a quick company profile, or purchasing a merchandise displayed in the window of a store. These solutions are intuitive and convenient; they satisfy the *ad hoc* needs by giving instant gratification and permitting individuals to return to their activity with little disruption.

By comparison in the online world, someone who needs information *ad hoc* or wishes to make purchases on impulse faces few intuitive and practical solutions. That person usually disengages from the current online activity and goes through several steps before retrieving the content or completing the purchase initially sought. The prevailing processes are inconvenient and fall short of meeting a user's *ad hoc* needs.

Market Need

In order to better understand *ad hoc* behavior and its uniqueness to the online world, we compare the following usage types in Table B:

TABLE B:
Research vs. *Ad Hoc* Usage

Research Behavior		*Ad Hoc* Behavior
■ Search triggered (on keywords)	vs.	■ Context triggered
■ Linear surfing through sites	vs.	■ "In and out"
■ Access specific destination site	vs.	■ Access multiple sites from each context
■ Research material/news	vs.	■ Reference material
■ Intended purchase	vs.	■ Impulse purchase

Most current online usage falls under the model of research behavior. For example, we use portals to search for information about specific items and then link from the search result to a destination site (or another section of the portal). This process might be repeated several times during a research session. Alternatively, more advanced users might know their target destination sites and go there directly via URLs or bookmarks. In all cases the process is linear in nature—one site after the other—and requires us to disengage from a current activity.

Online *ad hoc* behavior is different than research behavior and is usually triggered by context association. For example while online, reading an article could trigger a sudden need to check the stock quote of a company or to purchase a related product. In the absence of hypertext links, retrieving the information or conducting the *ad hoc* transaction would require leaving the article, visiting one's favorite online financial service or commerce site, and entering the company's name or product. In addition to being cumbersome, this process usually disrupts the user's current activity or causes the user not to seek the content or perform the transaction at all. Well planned hypertext links may partially solve the *ad hoc* problem, yet many key words are often unlinked or direct the user to unrelated information. Although there are many sites that can satisfy this need for information or commerce, gaining access to them in an intuitive and convenient manner requires services and tools that are not currently available in the market.

The *@Hoc* Requirements

Based on an analysis of the user's needs, we conclude that five functions must be featured in any offering of online *ad hoc* services:

- **Accessible:** The *@Hoc* service must be accessible from anywhere on the Web and desktop since *ad hoc* behaviors can occur anywhere. Without ease-of-access, efforts to satisfy the *ad hoc* need becomes moot.

- **Context Triggered:** The *@Hoc* service must be able to "zoom in" on contextually relevant information. Whether a specific word, phrase, graphical image or ad, the service must be able to interpret a user's needs against a backdrop of historical usage behavior and contextual meaning. Improving the relevance and utility of information is critical to enhancing the user's online experience.

- **Comprehensiveness:** The *@Hoc* service needs to offer multiple choices regarding the activated word. For example, assuming that we would like *ad hoc* information about "Intel," we may want Intel's stock quote, Intel's company profile, or alternatively buy a book about Intel. Limiting the *ad hoc* options to only one service makes the solution incomplete.

- **Personalized:** While *@Hoc* must provide comprehensiveness, most users have a preferred and limited number of sites from which they like to get their information. The *@Hoc* service does not need to provide all the options available on the Internet, but rather personalize the choices according to the user's preferences and appropriate context.

- **Non-Disruptive:** The *@Hoc* service must provide its content in a way that will not disrupt the user's current activity. Thus if a user is currently reading a *Wall Street Journal* ("WSJ") article, accessing a stock quote through *@Hoc* must also allow the user to stay in WSJ's site.

The *@Hoc* Solution

Our solution is to create a new channel for content and commerce that caters to the *ad hoc* behavior of online users. Specifically *@Hoc* enables instant, context-sensitive information retrieval and shopping from anywhere in the Web or desktop. In doing so, we enhance the users' Internet experience by integrating personalized services into the online and desktop environment.

@Hoc aims to establish itself as a new online infomediary, differentiated by its unique approach to connecting users with content and commerce providers. With our patent-pending technology, the Company will provide a solution for the *ad hoc* needs in the following manner:

- *@Hoc* users will be able to activate any word or phrase on the Web or desktop application for *ad hoc* purposes simply by highlighting and clicking on the *@Hoc* button. This one-click will then trigger a list of context related services from which the users can select. For example: highlighting a name of a company in a Microsoft Word document and clicking the *@Hoc* button will result in a list of services which may include: company's quote, company's profile and latest company news.

- *@Hoc* will provide access to a broad network of customized *ad hoc* services from the leading content and commerce providers. We will work with our content and commerce partners to define the services that are most suited for the *ad hoc* behavior.

- Upon selection of the desired service by the user, *@Hoc* will provide the relevant result in a pop-up window. The result appears in a pop-up window on the same page that the user activated *@Hoc*. The pop-up window that does not disrupt the user's current activity, once the user becomes satisfied with the *ad hoc* content, the pop-up window gets closed. Alternatively, the user will be able to chose additional relevant *@Hoc* services or link to the content provider's Web site for more detailed research.

- From our Web site, *@Hoc* users enter their profile and may customize their preferred content and commerce providers, thereby creating a library of personalized, user-oriented content and commerce services. *@Hoc* recognizes the environment under which the user works and leverages this context sensitive capability to offer complementing services and goods for every *ad hoc* content retrieved or purchases initiated by the user. For users who do not customize their selection of preferred services, *@Hoc* will provide a set of default services that matches the user's profile.

- *@Hoc* will capture user information and leverage it for the user's benefit on future transactions. For example, shipping information entered while performing one transaction would be saved and then offered as a default for the next transaction.

Thus, *@Hoc* will become a central repository of user information and creates value through personalization and facilitating one-click access to *ad hoc* services. The value that *@Hoc* provides the user increases with any additional usage.

Powerful Integration of Content and Commerce

Trends in the Internet space show a growing interdependence between content and commerce activities. Sites offering content services are striving to give users a more complete experience by integrating commerce services. Content sites can achieve this by becoming affiliates of commerce services, or, provide commerce services directly such as iVillage.com offering iBaby.com and MyBasics.com. Likewise, leading commerce sites are beginning to provide content-related services. An example of this development is Amazon.com offering e-cards and acquiring Alexa to enhance its member's shopping experience.

This industry trend suggests that current implementation of digital wallets lacks an integration of content and commerce. The usage frequency of digital wallets is limited only to commerce occasions, which occurs a few times a year. In addition to other reasons, the infrequency of usage explains why digital wallets have not yet been accepted by users. *@Hoc* evades the inevitable haplessness of the digital wallet functionality by incorporating compelling content services with a commerce solution, giving the users a robust tool for a more complete and satisfactory online experience.

Sustainability of Business

Long-term sustainability does not depend on the long-term success of the *@Hoc* client. Arguably, software application companies as well as portals could readily introduce comparable clients to activate *ad hoc* services. Accordingly, we will develop our core strength in the back-end, providing *ad hoc* services for all clients be they the *@Hoc* client, private-labeled clients operated by the Company, *@Hoc* embedded clients or third-party clients. In doing so we will focus on developing the following competitive advantages:

- **Accumulating and leveraging knowledge of the user**—because we will maintain and constantly expand our database of users' preferences and online *ad hoc* habits, we will develop a valuable and personalized service for every user, thereby creating a barrier to switching.

- **Creating a catalog of services with a broad network of partners**—our network of partners, who will work with us to provide content and commerce services as well as to proliferate *@Hoc,* represents the key to our success. We will work on enlarging the network and add services to further build on our relationships with content and commerce providers.

- **Aligning with strategic partners**—we will develop industry alliances, whether with leading new media partners, broadband players or hardware/software manufacturers. We will leverage these relationships to acquire new users and to position the Company as the *de facto* provider of *ad hoc* services.

- **Developing a state-of-the-art back-end technology**—we will be investing significant efforts in building the back-end technology, utilizing our knowledge of the user and the *ad hoc* online space to provide the most advance *ad hoc* services. We will incorporate through partnerships, acquisitions and in-house development a wide range of back-end services such as digital wallets, billing and content retrieval.

As a result of these efforts coupled with being the first mover into this space, we will create a high barrier of entry for our competitors. These barriers include a high switching cost for the users, an intensive "catalog" of services, knowledge of the space and technology, and strategic industry alliances.

IV. Value Proposition and Business Model

Value Propositions

We have three constituents in the @*Hoc* service network: content partners, commerce affiliates, and @*Hoc* users. The Company creates value for each of the constituents in the following ways.

For the content partners, @*Hoc* provides a direct pipeline between their Web sites and their users. This direct pipeline increases traffic and user retention, extends the content reach, and enables customer acquisition through cross-promotion. We are able to capture a share of this value creation by splitting ad revenues with the content partners, charging bounty fees and slotting fees.

For the commerce partners, @*Hoc* creates value by driving traffic for unintended purchases to their shopping sites. According to Jupiter Communications, 23% of online purchases are unintended.[v] We are able to capture a share of this value creation from the commissions earned as commerce affiliates.

For the users, we create value by enhancing their online experience. @*Hoc* solves the problem of *ad hoc* behavior by giving users the freedom to access content and engage in commerce from any application and context. @*Hoc* also learns more about the users with the frequency of usage. Leveraging its growing database of user behavior, @*Hoc* further enriches the user's online experience by offering goods and services that are personalized and context-sensitive.

Revenue Sources

@*Hoc* intends to capture a share of the value that our service creates from the following four revenue sources:

- *Advertising Fees:* Each time a user activates @*Hoc* to request a service (i.e. retrieve stock quotes), a pop-up window showcasing the requested content will open. This window is a new premium real estate created and owned by @Hoc, for banner ads, sponsorships and icon placement. Revenues from these revenues will be split with the content partner who supplied that requested service.

  Unlike traditional online advertising models where ads are served based on content-specific themes or low-quality user data, @*Hoc*'s service will offer marketers the potential to deliver promotional messages to users based on a deep understanding of each user's online usage behavior, demographics and interest profile. @*Hoc*'s advertising service will integrate these sources of information to provide advertisers with qualified communication opportunities and above average transaction conversion rates. @*Hoc* will also offer suggestive selling opportunities triggered by a user's impulse activation of the @*Hoc* service, thus further increasing the attractiveness of this real-estate to advertisers.

  As a result, @*Hoc* believes it will be able to command CPM rates above the current industry norm of $25 CPM.[vi] @*Hoc*'s ability to received premium prices for its advertising space will be further enhanced by the services' capabilities in the facilitation of convenient, one-click purchasing. Because @*Hoc*'s digital wallet service will remove barriers to the completion of a transaction, the service will also drive higher response rates and lower costs per transaction for @*Hoc* advertisers.

- *Transaction Fees:* According to Jupiter Communications, 23% of all online purchases are unintended.[vii] Because the activation of an @*Hoc* panel provides a context sensitive impulse sales platform, we believe that @*Hoc* will be able to facilitate online impulse transactions. Accordingly, @*Hoc* plans to negotiate revenue-sharing and commission-based agreements with product vendors and service providers in appropriate transaction categories. In addition to independently negotiated revenue-sharing agreements, the Company will also participate in traditional affiliate and associate sales programs and will position itself as a source of qualified lead generation and customer cross-sell data.

@*Hoc* believes that transaction-generated revenue will become an increasingly large portion of the Company's top-line earnings growth in the future. @*Hoc*'s evolving knowledge of user's personal cross-site data will enable it to facilitate transactions and simplify the purchasing process. Thus, it can be argued that @*Hoc* will be able to extend its commerce reach from the non-intended purchasing space (23%) into the intended purchasing space (77%) as the usage of @*Hoc* increases.

- ***Slotting Fees:*** Default positions in the @*Hoc* panel will be provided to content partners in exchange for facilitating downloads of the @*Hoc* client from their site. Additional non-competing services will be offered as default by @*Hoc*. These default positions will be sold to preferred content and commerce partners for slotting fees. With slotting fees at major portals and destination sites fetching upwards of $20 million dollars per year, @*Hoc* believes that it is well positioned to capture significant value from slotting sales even if its user base remains a fraction of a traditional portal's size. Based on the importance of slotting fees in generating traffic and awareness on the internet, Jupiter Communications estimates that by 2002 54% of all online transactions will stem from slotting and tenancy deals.[viii]

- ***Bundled Subscription Fees:*** To build traffic while stratifying users' willingness to pay for content, many Internet sites offer visitors tiered levels of content access. Most initial levels of access are free for all users but many sites also offer premium content levels for customers willing to pay for access to proprietary content. To enhance our user-utility and help generate additional subscription revenue for content producers, @*Hoc* will introduce a subscription bundling service.

  The @*Hoc* service will splice "best of breed" content from a number of sources into bundled targeted packages. These packages will be offered to @*Hoc* users for a subscription fee. An Internet user who would not normally subscribe to discrete sites for content due to increased costs and logistical challenges may subscribe to @*Hoc*'s bundled service because it delivers access to multiple content sources in a convenient and low-cost manner. For example, a WSJ site subscriber may be reluctant to also subscribe to TheStreet.com site due to the potential for overlapping content and interface hassles. @*Hoc* service would provide the best content from both sources for the cost of one subscription and then split the revenue with the content partners accordingly.

  A recent report by Jupiter Communications estimated that in 1997 only 1.4 million individuals paid for access to online content but Jupiter estimates that this number will increase to over 8.8 million in 2002.[ix] As content providers on the Internet face increasing challenges in their ability to monetize their product, they may seek solutions such as @*Hoc*'s bundled subscription service in order to extend the reach of their content before its value evaporates. @*Hoc* believes that its subscription bundling service is a strategically important part of the Company's business model as it provides value to @*Hoc* users while also strengthening @*Hoc*'s relationships with content providers.

- ***Other sources:*** these revenues could include money from data mining, private labeling @*Hoc,* hosting other people's content and even licensing the @*Hoc* technology.

V. Strategy

Market Segmentation

@*Hoc*'s technology and service can create significant value to the entire online community, making @*Hoc* potentially a mass market product. Yet, in order to build a customer base, create sufficient barriers to entry for competitors and establish @*Hoc* as a leader in this space, *@Hoc* must provide a comprehensive experience to the users. Comprehensive implies a sufficiently large number of services that would answer most of the user's *ad hoc* needs. Yet providing such a comprehensive service to all online users at the launch does not seem realistic.

Accordingly, we will develop our customer base by first segmenting the Web universe into vertical markets and then offering *@Hoc* services tailored to the specific users within each specific vertical market. We will prioritize these vertical segments by maximizing the added value *@Hoc* creates for the users in these markets. Examples of vertical markets include personal finance, sports and education. Our goal is to foster and nourish active users so that we maximize the life time value of every *@Hoc* customer.

We have identified the personal finance market as a logical point of entry. The reason for personal finance reflects the size of the user base, their profile, as well as their usage patterns which fit the *ad hoc* usage. According to Jupiter Communications, the number of households with online trading accounts is expected to grow from 6.8 MM in 1998 to 15.2 MM in 2002.[x] Moreover, twenty percent of the Web population use the Web for personal finance purposes.

The customer groups that we will next target are users who depend on the Web for reference information (white collar professionals, students in higher education) and users who depend on the Web for sports information. With respect to users of reference information, the number of individuals in higher education alone exceeds 15.1 million according to the National Center for Education Statistics.[xi] With respect to sports users, Jupiter Communications "discovered that for over a third of the Internet news audience, sports scores and information were the number one reason to go online."[xii] Education and sports vertical markets represent logical extensions of the *@Hoc* customer target.

The vertical segmentation approach affects many other aspects of our strategy— selection of content and commerce partners, communication strategy and distribution strategy.

Distribution Strategy

The Company will market and distribute *@Hoc* initially using four different marketing channels. The first and primary channel will be through *@Hoc*'s content affiliate network. Complementing channels will include viral marketing, software download sites, and *@Hoc*'s home page.

- ***Content Affiliate Network:*** On the site of every *@Hoc* content affiliate, there will be an *@Hoc* icon linking the user to *@Hoc*'s download page. In return for promoting *@Hoc* via this link, the content affiliate receives default slotting for its services on *@Hoc* for every download which originates from that affiliate's site. Thus whenever a user accesses *@Hoc,* the affiliate content partner's services appear under the appropriate category (i.e. Finance). For example, a CBS MarketWatch user encounters *@Hoc*'s icon on MarketWatch site. Clicking on it will link the user to *@Hoc*'s registration page offering MarketWatch as default financial services (i.e. stock quotes, news and analyst columns).

  By giving premium default slotting in exchange for distribution, the Company is creating a win-win-win situation. We expose *@Hoc* to millions of visitors across our content partners' network and acquire new users; the content partners receive default slotting for their *ad hoc* services; and the user is able to access his or her favorite services from anywhere on the desktop and Web. This default slot creates value for the content providers by increasing content usage, traffic, brand awareness, and user retention. In the event that someone already has the *@Hoc* client when he or she visits a content partner's Web site and clicks on the *@Hoc* icon, the *ad hoc* services related to that site will be added to the user's menu of services, but lower in hierarchy. Indeed, the user will have the option to change the settings, including the default.

The default slotting model allows for "preferred" relationships with content partners who agree to promote @*Hoc* in additional ways (co-promotion in physical media etc.) or pays for default slotting. For example, a user who downloads @*Hoc* from CBS MarketWatch would also have Alta Vista as the default search engine service because Alta Vista would have bought a "preferred" partner relationship with @*Hoc*. In this case, Alta Vista would be promoting @*Hoc* across its Web sites.

- **Viral Marketing:** @*Hoc* will support viral marketing by integrating communication services into the client. One example of a viral marketing technique is to provide a "Send to a Friend" service which will allow the user to send the result of an *ad hoc* query to a friend's e-mail. That e-mail will also contain a link to @*Hoc* so that the recipient will be able to download the @*Hoc* client. Another technique of viral marketing which will be used is "Refer a Friend" whereby the user will be asked to input e-mails of friends who would also be interested in *ad hoc* services. We will then send an email to those addresses inviting them to download and use @*Hoc*. In the latter case the user might receive access to promotional services or other loyalty-oriented programs.

- **@*Hoc* Web site:** We will also use traditional marketing techniques such as press releases, trade shows, banner ads, and bounty purchases to drive traffic to our site. The purpose of this marketing strategy is to locate users who would not find his or her way to @*Hoc* because they normally do not visit @*Hoc*'s content affiliates. The cost of this marketing approach is likely CPM driven.

- **Download sites:** These sites include C | net, ZDNet, TUCOWS and others who focus on promoting new software for downloads. According to Media Metrix, the number of unique visitors visiting C | net's software download site during March 1999 exceeded 4.3 MM. Although the composition of the visitors may not perfectly match those focused on personal finance, buying exposure on these well visited sites will contribute to generating the "buzz" around @*Hoc*.

The approaches described above represent the principal marketing and distribution methods at the launch. In the future, we will use additional distribution methods such as:

- **ISP:** Cooperate with ISPs to include the @*Hoc* client as part of the communication utilities offered by ISPs to their customers.
- **Hardware OEM:** Cooperate with computer manufacturers to have @*Hoc* pre-installed on shipment of computers.
- **Software OEM:** Embed @*Hoc* client in 3rd party software applications by providing the developers with a software development kit ("SDK").
- **Affinity Packages:** Tailor packages of *ad hoc* services for specific affinity groups. These groups will include universities, corporations, virtual communities and targeted user groups.

Acquisition Strategy of Content Partners

Our goal with content partners is twofold: leverage their user base to distribute @*Hoc* and provide access to their content and service via the @*Hoc* channel in return for splitting the financial reward from ad sales. Unlike acquiring commerce partners where affiliate programs are established, acquiring content partners will require more time and effort because of independent negotiations and various lead time.

The value we create to our content partner is fivefold:

- Extending their reach by allowing their user access to their content and services not just on their site, but from any place on the Web and desktop.
- Simplifying access to their content and services for their users.

- Increasing traffic and therefore potential revenues.
- Increasing user retention through closer relationship with the user.
- Increasing brand awareness.
- Acquiring new users through slotting presence.

These values will provide the motivation for our content partners to work with us.

The position we will take *vis à vis* content partners is that in return for distributing *@Hoc* through their Web sites, we will give them the default slots for their services, be they stock quotes, company news, or message boards. Excluding AOL and Yahoo!Finance, Table D below shows the leading 20 investing and finance Web sites and the ones with whom we have entered into a Letter of Intent. We are actively in the process of lining up the other content partners.

TABLE D
Personal Finance
Web Sites

		Unique Visitors (000)		
		Home/Work	Home	Work
1	QUICKEN.COM	2,603	1,630	1,076
2	INTUIT.COM	2,373	1,711	809
3	MONEY CENTRAL	2,327	1,422	1,157
4	ETRADE.COM	1,644	1,021	744
5	CNNFN.COM	1,567	793	885
6	**MARKETWATCH.COM (*@Hoc* Letter of Intent)**	1,536	824	822
7	FOOL.COM	1,140	668	558
8	BLOOMBERG.COM	1,115	621	559
9	SCHWAB.COM	975	636	499
10	BIGCHARTS.COM	964	589	494
11	**THESTREET.COM (*@Hoc* Letter of Intent)**	942	456	515
12	WSJ.COM	928	459	547
13	**RAGINGBULL.COM (*@Hoc* Letter of Interest)***	894	NA	NA
14	**QUOTE.COM (*@Hoc* Letter of Intent)**	735	475	274
15	NASDAQ.COM	703	347	356
16	HOOVERS.COM	560	362	248
17	TRADERONLINE.COM	542	351	248
18	NASDAQ-AMEX.COM	507	249	293
19	STOCKMASTER.COM	461	245	250
20	WATERHOUSE.COM	433	334	156

MediaMetrix, March 1999.
*Company provided source.

The high number of unique visitors to many of these sites create opportunities to expose and distribute *@Hoc*. For example according to Media Metrix, the average number of unique visitors who visit the sites belonging to content suppliers who have already signed LOIs with *@Hoc* exceeds one million visitors per month.[xiii] The aggregated user-base exposure *@Hoc* has with sites who already signed LOIs exceeds 2.5 million users.[xiv]

Acquisition Strategy of Commerce Partners

In most cases, acquiring commerce partners for *@Hoc* is relatively simple. Most commerce providers have programs whereby affiliates earn between 3% and 25% commissions on sales driven from the affiliate's site. In the case of Amazon, over 1.6MM people visit Amazon.com through its affiliate network during the last quarter of 1998 making this method of customer acquisition a significant part of Amazon's marketing effort.

Among the many options for commerce affiliates, our review of online purchasing patterns leads us to focus on book and gift sellers. Table E shows that among several online shopping habits, buying books is the most popular, with 20% of the personal finance Web users making an online book purchase during the last six months compared to 5% for clothes and apparel.

TABLE E   **Online Shopping Behavior**

			@Hoc Content Partners		
Profile Point	**% Comp. Web Population**	**Investing & Finance Websites % Comp.**	**CBS Marketwatch % Comp.**	**Quote.com % Comp.**	**The Street.com % Comp.**
Books (p/online/6 mo.)	15.0	19.9	21.1	26.6	33.5
Any Internet Travel Purchase (Last 6 months)	12.4	18.2	19.6	23.4	22.0
Any Internet Investment Transaction (Last 6 months)	5.9	14.5	34.4	25.9	37.3
Any Computer Software (p/online/6 mo.)	9.8	13.9	12.0	20.9	17.5
Airline Ticket/Reservation (p/online/6 mo.)	9.1	13.7	14.4	18.3	14.6
Stocks (t/online/6 mo.)	4.8	12.1	30.9	24.5	34.6
Computer Hardware (p/online/6 mo.)	8.2	11.9	11.5	22.3	15.8
Musical CD's/Tapes (p/online/6 mo.)	7.2	9.0	8.4	9.6	10.2
General Software (p/online/6 mo.)	5.9	8.6	8.9	12.3	10.3
Hotel/Motel Reservations (p/online/6 mo.)	4.6	7.2	9.0	10.1	11.4
Home Banking (t/online/6 mo.)	3.6	6.0	5.6	8.8	6.3
Flowers (p/online/6 mo.)	3.7	5.4	4.0	7.5	6.1
Clothes/Apparel (p/online/6 mo.)	4.2	5.0	5.7	5.5	7.6

Data is based on US Adult active Web population (18+).
Copyright @plan., Inc., Spring 1999 Release.

Although the table also shows that buying airline tickets as a popular shopping behavior, we argue that the decision process required to purchase an airline ticket requires more research and is less *ad hoc* than buying books or gifts. Therefore, an airline ticket shopping service would not be highly prioritiz*e*d for *@Hoc*. Listed below are samples of potential commerce partners who have affiliate programs:

Company	Products	Commission to *@Hoc*
Amazon.com	books, music, vides & gifts	3–15%
eToys	toys & video	25%
800Flowers	flowers & gifts	6–8%
JCrew.com	clothes	5%

Joining affiliate programs would be a preliminary approach. As our service matures and user base expands, we will aim to create a closer relationship with the commerce partners. This relationship will include distribution deals, slotting deals and perhaps preferred commissions.

Pricing Strategy for Content Partners

Unlike the commerce affiliate networks whereby the terms are well defined, content partnerships vary deal-by-deal. In our case, there is another twist. Because *@Hoc* will initially depend on its content partners to distribute the client, *@Hoc* will waive the typical slotting fee and give the content partners a default placement in the *@Hoc* client for content retrievals. With respect to sharing ad revenues, the industry practices suggest the following ad split or bounty structure:

Ad revenues:	Split 50/50 between content provider and *@Hoc* if ads appear on the *@Hoc* channel *in addition* to cut of the residual value of the user once he leaves the *@Hoc* channel for the content provider's site.[xv]
	To the extent possible, *@Hoc* will aim to control the banner ad space and sell that inventory through its own network, relying on achieving a higher CPM due to *@Hoc*'s user knowledge. In cases where this will not be appropriate, the partner's ad inventory will be used and *@Hoc* will get its split from the partner.
Bounty:	The logo of the content partner will appear in the popup window holding the service result. Clicking on this logo would link to the partner's site. This creates the possibility of charging click-through rate for each *@Hoc* user who links to the partner's site.
Duration:	Six months in order to provide the flexibility for upward or downward adjustments.
Slotting fees:	As discussed above, *@Hoc* will unlikely charge slotting fees at a time when the content partners are also distributing the *@Hoc* client. Yet *@Hoc* will charge content partners for slotting in clients downloaded from other sites.

Ad Management Strategy

Central to *@Hoc*'s ability to monetize its business model is the ability to utilize user's knowledge to gain a significant premium on the CPM rate *@Hoc* will charge advertisers. In addition, *@Hoc* needs the flexibility to share ad revenues with partners. Therefore the requirements for ad management are sophisticated.

@Hoc plans to outsource the Company's advertising management requirements to one or more service bureaus during the initial stages of the Company's build-out. We have developed a relationship with DoubleClick and examined the DART technology. DART offers solutions for our advanced requirements:

- DART Syndicated Network Service—manages and tracks ad revenues split between *@Hoc* and its network partners.
- DART user information—allows using knowledge about user to improve targeting of ads.

Other vendors active in the advertising management arena include AdBureau by Engage/Accipter, AdCenter by NetGravity, ClickWise by AdKnowledge and Adforce by Imgis. In general, the market's service bureau offerings are priced based on various tiers of application sophistication and are more expensive than in-house solution but will offer

@Hoc greater strategic flexibility during the Company's initial launch and scale-up. Similarly, outsourced vendors active in the online media measurement arena include PC Meter, RelevantKnowledge, @Plan and NetRatings.

As time advances, we will consider developing in-house advertising and transactive content management functionality. Doing so will allow the Company to have higher control and better optimization of our user knowledge for creating revenues from ads and ad-driven transactions. While it is difficult to project the cost implications of shifting from a service bureau model to in-house capability at some point in the future, Forrester Research estimates the current three year cost of buying and maintaining a large scale ad server to be around $700,000.[xvi]

Technological Development Strategy

Currently, our technological development efforts are centered around developing a working prototype of the *@Hoc* service. The prototype works online and includes 18 different services from 10 different content and commerce providers.

In order to facilitate a quick ramp-up of the technological development upon financing, we are creating a plan of the development process. This detailed plan includes design of the technology, resource allocation, time table and other details. The plan is documented in the "*@Hoc*—Technology Ramp-Up Plan" working paper.

In addition, we plan to contract a team of experienced developers from Kinetica (Internet solutions company previously founded and sold by the current founders of *@Hoc*'s) with whom we have worked. A draft of the Terms Sheet with Kinetica has already been drafted.

Partner's Interface Strategy

We have developed the *@Hoc* solution around XML technology (extendible mark-up language). Although there are several XML-based companies who serve the business-to-business market ("B2B"), few pay attention to the business-to-consumer market ("B2C"). *@Hoc* is one of the first companies in the B2C XML space. Our belief is that the major providers of online content and commerce will embrace XML technology and will offer an XML interface to their services. This vision is rapidly being implemented in the B2B space by WebMethods, but owing to a lack of clear end-user benefits, the business-to-consumer market has not yet embraced XML technology. With its *ad hoc* content retrieval solution, *@Hoc* provides a clear and compelling consumer benefit. When the number of individuals who use *@Hoc* reaches a critical mass, their *ad hoc* needs will drive the other consumer oriented Web services to embrace XML. Accordingly, *@Hoc* will be well positioned to capitalized on the technology shift.

Wherever possible, *@Hoc* will partner with WebMethods or an equivalent XML technology company to help the content providers make their Web sites interface with XML protocols. Enabling XML interfaces will make content retrieval faster, easier and better for *ad hoc* services. Partners who will not have XML interface available will be able to provide us with access to their information using their Web site or alternatively through traditional feed lines. We will then be able to convert this Web interface (HTML) or feed into XML and interface it to *@Hoc* back-end.

VI. Market Analysis & Industry Landscape

Market Analysis

Though estimates of the Internet's future growth vary, most analysts agree that the next five years of online development will be characterized by robust expansion in the number of users and quality of access. Jupiter Communications, for example, projects that by 2002, 123 million US users or 55% of the US population will be online.[xvii]

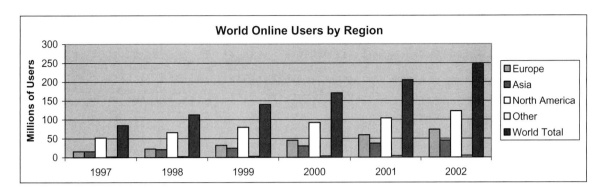

While the internet's rapid growth is integral to the long-term health of *@Hoc*'s market, the Company plans to target two very specific sub-segments of the Internet community during the first months of service roll-out. Specifically, *@Hoc*'s market entry strategy with focus on penetrating the online financial services and education markets.

The profile of people using personal finance Web services also make them attractive customers. As a group, they tend to be wealthier, better educated, and more engaged in the Internet than the average Web population. Table C below compares the profile of the Web population to that who visit personal finance Web sites. The data shows that finance-oriented Web users are 33% more likely to be on the Web everyday then the average user, 27% more likely to make a purchase online, 47% of them download software each month, and 41% of them are more than 3 years online.

TABLE C   **Profile Comparison of Web Users**

Profile Point	% Comp. Web Population	Investing & Finance Websites % Comp.	@Hoc Content Partners		
			CBS Marketwatch % Comp.	Quote.com % Comp.	The Street.com % Comp.
Access from home	82.4	86.9	88.7	90.8	90.0
Access from work	51.7	60.6	64.4	66.7	63.6
3+ years online	33.5	41.6	44.9	53.1	52.2
Download Software (Last 30 days)	39.0	47.1	50.9	57.6	50.2
News/Info (Last 30 days)	76.6	87.6	93.2	89.2	93.1
Research for Personal (Last 30 days)	64.0	71.5	72.6	73.4	72.5
On Web every day	30.4	40.6	52.8	54.9	61.0
Any Internet Purchase (Last 6 months)	43.5	55.3	63.8	69.6	74.3

Data is based on US Adult active Web population (18+).
Copyright @plan., Inc., Spring 1999 Release.

The second target market segment *@Hoc* plans to pursue during its service launch is the online teen and college student market. Projected by eMarketer to be about 8.9 million online users or 16.1% of the US's total online population, the student market represents a vibrant community of users whose online usage profiles and behavior patterns closely mirror that of an ideal *@Hoc* user.[xviii] Additionally, the online student market represents online purchasing power of nearly $900 million or over $100 per student per year.[xix]

The rationale behind *@Hoc*'s decision to target the online student community is based on the market's size, behavior and adaptability. Top content sites visited by students include sport, entertainment and news related destinations—all of which are information intensive and navigationally complex.[xx] *@Hoc* also believes that the student markets' proclivity to conduct research and reference-based activities is significantly above average and that the *@Hoc* service would benefit from the rapid adoption curves traditionally observed in student and youth markets. Confirming *@Hoc*'s fit with the student market is a recent report by Jupiter Communications which indicates that 8 out of 10 of the top online activities are primarily utilitarian in nature (researching products, accessing news, etc.) and tended not to be entertainment-focused as is commonly assumed within the online student market.[xxi]

In sum, the two markets that *@Hoc* plans to target in its initial launch collectively represent several million Internet users. Because both the financial service and student markets are easily identifiable, *@Hoc* believes it will be able to create compelling value for both these target segments by working with the leading content partners to provide enhanced online functionality to these user groups. Following the service's initial launch, *@Hoc* anticipates expanding into other high-value target segments where the users experience in data-rich transactive content environment can be enhanced using *@Hoc*.

Industry Landscape

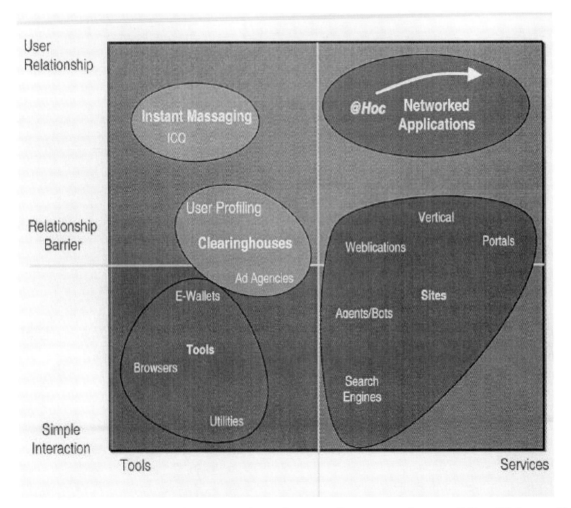

The industry map above shows no direct competitors to *@Hoc*. While e-wallets and other tools provide some *ad hoc* services, none offers services as comprehensive as *@Hoc*. It is conceivable that Microsoft, Yahoo! and other portals may enter the *ad hoc*

space, but they are also likely to be buyers of an *ad hoc* service company once the business is proven.

VII. Discussion of Financial Projections

Overview

The projected income and cash flow statements have been prepared on a cash basis. Although we could have used accrual accounting methods, we are interested in reflecting the cash needs of the Company. The projections show a net zero working capital balance even though it is likely that @*Hoc* would benefit from up-front cash payments for slotting and advertising from its content and commerce partners. In addition, no cash benefit has been factored to show the potential for equipment leases. Finally, the financial statements do not reflect tax benefits stemming from operating losses associated with the early years of operations.

@*Hoc* Financial Projections

	1999	2000	2001	2002	2003
Number of active @*Hoc* users	56,840	382,736	1,460,892	3,495,669	6,046,752
Revenues					
Advertising	$35,912	$670,627	$3,987,322	$14,723,757	$31,836,147
Transactions	30,864	467,244	4,961,188	27,572,436	60,486,865
Slotting	—	478,420	3,287,006	12,234,840	36,280,509
Bundled Subscription	—	43,058	613,574	3,513,147	9,070,127
Total revenues	66,776	1,659,349	12,849,091	58,044,180	137,673,648
Cost of goods	183,532	649,136	1,703,875	5,382,523	11,521,446
Depreciation	500,000	500,000	1,000,000	2,000,000	5,000,000
	683,532	1,149,136	2,703,875	7,382,523	16,521,446
Gross profit	−616,757	510,213	10,145,216	50,661,658	121,152,202
Salary	1,320,000	6,975,000	12,030,000	23,200,000	46,100,000
Selling and marketing	1,986,400	5,775,000	12,612,500	19,650,000	27,750,000
General admin	74,750	563,750	1,200,000	1,970,000	4,018,000
	3,381,150	13,313,750	25,842,500	44,820,000	77,868,000
Operating profit	−$3,997,907	−$12,803,537	−$15,697,284	$5,841,658	$43,284,202
Head count	32	65	120	220	420
Revenue per employee	$2,087	$25,528	$107,076	$263,837	$327,794
Expense per employee	$127,021	$222,506	$237,886	$237,284	$224,737
Revenue mix					
Advertising	54%	40%	31%	25%	23%
Transactions	46%	28%	39%	48%	44%
Slotting	0%	29%	26%	21%	26%
Bundled Subscription	0%	3%	5%	6%	7%

User Base

Revenue is driven by the projected growth in active users. The growth of active users is driven by user acquisition as influenced by the user's exposure to @*Hoc* and the rates of download, activation and retention. The assumptions are as follows:

- **Exposure**—Immediately following the launch, @*Hoc* will be exposed to millions of potential users because there will be an @*Hoc* icon on the Web site of the content partners. With twenty content partners in 1999, @*Hoc* will be exposed to an estimated 11.2 million people, net of traffic duplication. The breadth of user exposure increases as the Company grows the number of content partners.

- **Downloads**—The rate of user download begins at 0.5% in 1999 and grows to 2.0% by 2003 for all who are offered the opportunity to download @*Hoc*. This is a minimal expectation based on the rate of banner ad click-through. It is reasonable to expect that @*Hoc* downloads will be greater than the projected rates because over 50% of the targeted users (visitors to finance and investing Web sites) downloads a software at least once a month. There will also be an @*Hoc* icon button on the content partners' sites; an icon button as opposed to a banner ad conveys permanency and tacitly endorses @*Hoc* to the Web site visitor.

- **Activation**—One out of three users would find the @*Hoc* service compelling and robust enough to use it with frequency. As the @*Hoc* service improves, we assume that 50% of the users who download it would frequently use it.

- **Retention**—We factor in a user retention rate starting with 40% in 1999 and increasing it to 75% by 2001. The assumption is that the more robust the service, the more satisfied the user, which consequently increases the retention rate.

The results of these assumptions yield the following user base:

User Base Projections	4Q 1999	2000	2001	2002	2003
Total Number of Distributed Clients	162,400	900,000	2,462,500	4,800,000	6,850,000
Number of New Active Users	56,840	360,000	1,231,250	2,400,000	3,425,000
Net Total Number of Active Users	56,840	382,736	1,460,892	3,495,669	6,046,752

Revenue

There are four sources of revenues, three of which are driven by the number of users and frequency of usage while the fourth one is driven by the number of salable slots on the @*Hoc* client. The revenue components depending on the users and frequency of usage are advertising, transactions and bundled subscription while the non-user dependent one is slotting fees.

- **Frequency of usage**—On average, @*Hoc* will be activated once every two hours and increase to at least once every hour by the user. This estimate is then multiplied by the average hours online according to Jupiter Communications and a related rate of ad revenues. The figures used are conservative considering that financial users are advanced and active users of the Internet. Usage estimates are also predicted to grow with time.

- **Advertising**—The Company aims to sell one ad fifty percent of the time for every pop-up window triggered by @*Hoc*. Ad rates begin at $25 per CPM and increase to $30 per CPM owing to customer targeting; it can be argued that ad rates on the @*Hoc* frame will be greater than $30 per CPM because the context sensitive capability makes targeting even more customer-specific. Ad revenues will be split on a fifty-fifty basis with content partners.

- **Transactions**—According to Jupiter Communications, 23% of online shopping reflects unintended purchases. Since @*Hoc* provides convenient one-click buying functionality, @Hoc will capture a share of this buying behavior and earn the commissions for provoking and executing the impulse purchases. Commission rates will increase from 3% in 1999 to 6% by 2003 because of preferred relationship with commerce partners.

- **Slotting Fees**—Slots on the *@Hoc* client provide content and commerce suppliers with a customer acquisition tool as well as a channel to extend their content and goods. The services on the *@Hoc* client will also be user-specific, and therefore each slot represents premium real estate for tenancy. Pricing for slots will be CPM based, starting at $25 per CPM and increasing to $40 per CPM owing to user-targeting.

The result of these assumptions is shown in following revenue composition:

Revenue Projections	4Q 1999	2000	2001	2002	2003
Annual Ad Revenue	$35,912	$670,627	$3,987,322	$14,723,757	$31,836,147
Annual Transaction Revenue	$30,864	$467,244	$4,961,188	$27,572,436	$60,486,865
Annual Slotting Revenue	$0	$478,420	$3,287,006	$12,234,840	$36,280,509
Annual Bundled Subscription Revenue	$0	$43,058	$613,574	$3,513,147	$9,070,127
Gross Revenue	**$66,776**	**$1,659,349**	**$12,849,091**	**$58,044,180**	**$137,673,648**
Advertising Revenue Percentage	53.8%	40.4%	31.0%	25.4%	23.1%
Transactive Revenue Percentage	46.2%	28.2%	38.6%	47.5%	43.9%
Slotting Revenue Percentage	0.0%	28.8%	25.6%	21.1%	26.4%
Bundled Subscription Revenue Percentage	0.0%	2.6%	4.8%	6.1%	6.6%

Expenses

Due to the inefficiencies involved in jump-starting a new venture infrastructure, a significant gap is projected to exist between per employee revenue and per employee expenses during the first few years of operation. The main drivers of costs are as follows:

- **Cost of sales**—Drivers in this category include information technology expenses, full depreciation of capital expenditures (cash accounting), and costs associated with servicing ads.
- **Salary**—This expense is driven by the headcount and the market rate for salaries associated with hiring the talent needed to build a successful start-up. Head count will be a modest 32 employees by year-end 1999 and ramp accordingly.

Assumptions	6-12/99	2000	2001	2002	2003
Number of Managerial & Sales Staff	10	25	50	100	200
Number of Technical & Product Staff	16	25	40	80	160
Number of Administrative & Customer Suppl.	6	15	30	40	60
Fully Loaded Management Salary	$100,000	$140,000	$120,000	$120,000	$120,000
Fully Loaded Technical Salary	$80,000	$100,000	$102,000	$105,000	$110,000
Fully Loaded Administrative Salary	$60,000	$65,000	$65,000	$70,000	$75,000
Avg. IT/Comm Spend Per Person	$6,000	$6,500	$4,000	$4,000	$4,000

- **Selling, general & admin**—The Company's operating expense is expected to reduce as content partner acquisition and support costs are shifted from a direct face-to-face sales model to a telephone-based online demonstration model. The Company also anticipates lower cost per download marketing expenditures as it gains greater sophistication in its ability to target download solicitations. The drivers of operating expenses are summarized as follows:

Assumptions	6-12/99	2000	2001	2002	2003
Avg. Square Feet Per Person	175	175	250	250	250
Average Cost Per Square Foot	$20	$25	$30	$30	$35
Avg. Admin. Cost Per Content Partner	$0	$3,500	$3,000	$2,000	$2,000
Avg. Admin Cost Per Employee	$2,000	$2,000	$1,500	$1,000	$800
Cost Per New Content Partner Acquisition	$10,000	$7,500	$5,000	$5,000	$5,000
Marketing & Distribution Cost Per Download	$11	$6	$5	$4	$4
Advertisment Serving Costs (per thousand)	$2	$1	$0.5	$0.25	$0.25

Cost Structure Variability

@Hoc's financial model has been structured to maximize the variable costs associated with the service's implementation while reducing the need for fixed-asset requirements. Specifically, the Company's two largest cost drivers—staffing and marketing—are both variable and will expand or shrink in tandem with the growth of *@Hoc*'s content partner universe. As the *@Hoc* user base expands, the Company anticipates that it will need to incur greater fixed costs in two areas: internal information technology infrastructure and advertising sales network development. Both of these fixed-cost expense items will require step-function investments but will only be incurred when justified by appropriate increases in top-line revenue volume.

Revenue Model Strengths

In addition to understanding the critical assumptions driving the Company's Revenue Model, it is also important to recognize several unique strengths inherent in *@Hoc*'s business model. Some characteristics of the Company's model that distinguish its ability to generate attractive returns include:

- **Distribution Leverage**—Unlike many software, service or Internet tool companies that struggle to find cost-effective distribution channels, the *@Hoc* model will capitalize on our content partner's pre-existing scale to speed the introduction of the *@Hoc* client. By harnessing the user-base aggregation strength of our content partners, *@Hoc* will be able to gain significant distribution leverage by offering tacitly-endorsed downloads from a wide variety of distributed gateways. The financial benefits of this leveraged distribution strategy are significant. Capital will need to be committed to general awareness marketing and online advertising efforts but the total cost per download that *@Hoc* bears will be relatively small in comparison to other Internet-related customer acquisition figures.

- **Content Leverage**—In many Internet-based businesses, content management (content generation, maintenance and monetization) is the single largest expense a company must bear other than variable marketing costs. Because *@Hoc*'s model legally re-purposes other sites' content under the *@Hoc* moniker, the Company is able to offer *@Hoc* users content utility without incurring any content management costs itself. As such, *@Hoc* can leverage best-of-breed content resources drawn from a variety of partners to create value for its user base while avoiding the expense of overseeing proprietary content development.

- **Scalability**—Because the cost structure associated with the *@Hoc* service model does not ramp linearly as the number of *@Hoc* users increases, the Company's business model scales very elegantly and provides increasing returns to its shareholders.

Similarly, *@Hoc*'s model of leveraging content and distribution partnerships to provide greater value and functionality to each individual *@Hoc* user means that the company will benefit from the network effects of a growing universe of content partners without incurring proportionally increasing operational costs. The net result is a robust financial model that faces very few internal constraints to growth.

End Notes

i   "Consumer Internet Economy: Portal Landscape, Revenue Strategies, Five Year Projections" June 1998." Jupiter Communications.

ii   "Online Investing Report—Navigating the Discount Brokerage Revolution." Page 14. Jupiter Communications 1998.

iii   National Center for Education Statistics. Enrollment in Higher Education: Fall 1995. Reported in May 1997, NCES 97-440; http://nces.ed.gov/pubs97/97440.html.

iv   "Net Sports," Andrew Zipern, *Silicon Alley Reporter,* Issue 23—1999, Vol. 3, #3, page 62.

v   "Consumer Internet Economy: Portal Landscape, Revenue Strategies, Five Year Projections" June 1998. Jupiter Communications.

vi   24/7 Media Rate Sheet estimate for typical banner advertising with area, SIC code, domain and country targeting capabilities.

vii   "Consumer Internet Economy: Portal Landscape, Revenue Strategies, Five Year Projections" June 1998. Jupiter Communications.

viii   Peter Storck, "Consumer Internet Economy" Jupiter Communications, June 1998.

ix   Peter Storck, "Consumer Internet Economy" Jupiter Communications, June 1998.

x   Online Investing Report—Navigating the Discount Brokerage Revolution, page 14. Jupiter Communications 1998.

xi   National Center for Education Statistics. Enrollment in Higher Education: Fall 1995. Reported in May 1997, NCES 97-440; http://nces.ed.gov/pubs97/97440.html.

xii   "Net Sports," Andrew Zipern, *Silicon Alley Reporter,* Issue 23—1999, Vol. 3, #3, page 62.

xiii   March 1999—Media Metrix.

xiv   Assuming two sites per unique user.

xv   "Consumer Internet Economy—Portal Landscape Revenue Strategies Five Year Projections" June 1998. Jupiter Communications.

xvi   Susan Gertzis, "Ad Serving and Measurement" Forrester Research Report, May 1997.

xvii   Peter Storck, "Consumer Internet Economy" Jupiter Communications, June 1998.

xviii   Gary Galati, "Almost 50% of US Teens on Web By Year End", Internet News, September, 1998.

xix   Dianna See, "Net Firms Hope to Cash in On the College Market" The Industry Standard, September 2, 1998.

xx   "Where Teens Are Clicking On the Web" Media Metrix, May 1998.

xxi   "Defining the Internet Shopper: Attitudes, Objectives and Behavior" Jupiter Communications, October 1998.

Module II

Valuation and Risk Assessment

An overarching insight of this book is that the notions of risk and reward are as important in privately held as in publicly held firms. In privately held firms, however, entrepreneurs and financiers are often forced to make assumptions based on woefully incomplete data. This book's contribution to valuation and risk assessment is its focus on privately held companies domiciled in countries around the world. This module provides some of the tools needed to value these companies. It is not intended to substitute for a traditional text or casebook on international financial management. Rather, it illuminates and extends topics in international finance that are particularly relevant to entrepreneurs. I suggest that readers who are not familiar with principles of international finance review an extensive technical note on the valuation of cash flows in an international context that I developed specifically to accompany the cases in this book.[1]

This module also considers how start-up firms in different countries might think about granting equity-based compensation. A final component of the module deals with the valuation of subscription-based businesses, the cash-flow characteristics of which are attractive to entrepreneurs (the cash flows being highly predictable and often prepaid reduce the need for working capital).

This module (and the entire book) builds on the theory and practice discussed in core finance books and courses. Specifically, it builds on the capital asset pricing model, option pricing techniques, and free cash flow valuation. Above all, the module applies discounting and option pricing techniques to the valuation of entrepreneurial firms. An extensive literature in finance explores a model world in which all firms' financing decisions are independent of their investment decisions and a real world in which firms' investment decisions are clearly influenced by their access to financing.[2] Fazzari and Hubbard, for example, found in a sample of 450 publicly listed firms in the United States that fast-growing firms relied more heavily on internal financing than on the issuance of new equity, which one would not expect in a perfect capital market. Possible explanations

[1] Kuemmerle, Walter, and Matias Braun. 2002. *Valuing Cash Flows in an International Context (803-028).* Boston: Harvard Business School Publishing.

[2] Fazzari, Steven M., Glenn R. Hubbard, and Bruce C. Petersen. 1988. Financing Constraints and Corporate Investement. *Brookings Papers on Economic Activity* (1): 141–195. Modigliani, Franco, and Merton H. Miller. 1958. The Cost of Capital, Corporation Finance and the Theory of Investment. *American Economic Review* 48 (3): 261–297.

for this observed behavior include transaction costs, tax advantages of internal financing (if capital gains on retained earnings are taxed at a lower rate than paid out earnings are taxed), cost of financial distress, agency costs, and the distribution of asymmetric information. This module demonstrates that financing and investment decisions are often highly interdependent for privately held ventures. The module also illustrates how a global perspective on access to resources permits entrepreneurs to choose optimal resources, or to not pursue a venture at all. This enhances the performance of ventures and increases the likelihood of venture survival.

The module proposes that, given the uncertainty associated with the evolution of entrepreneurial ventures, it is particularly useful in valuations to analyze ranges of possible scenarios rather than just point-estimates. It is also suggested that entrepreneurs and their financiers should anticipate, and develop different action plans for, both good and bad news for a venture. Finally, many analysts skilled in valuation seem to be better at criticizing than at giving advice on how to fix a given venture. A good valuation analysis will point to the drivers of value creation as well as to a venture's weaknesses. The challenge and opportunity is thus to draw constructive conclusions from a valuation.

The cases in this module emphasize five topics that are repeated and extended in cases later in the book. First, entrepreneurial firms must focus on managing cash. The negotiating position of an entrepreneurial venture that is not generating free cash flows deteriorates disproportionately as the venture's cash dwindles. The cases permit discussion of this. Simple scenario analysis techniques for assessing the likely future position of an entrepreneurial venture can be used in this context.[3] Attention is also paid to estimating operating cash needs in determining working capital requirements for a young company. Relevant cases in this regard are Infox and Spotfire (Module 3).

Second, entrepreneurs need to understand the so-called venture capital method, which values start-up firms based on an assumed multiple of net income after a number of years (typically three to five) using a very high discount rate, often between 25% and 50%. Several cases permit the reader to think about how to dissect the components of this rate. Analysis shows that this method can be useful for all equity-financed firms with no intermediate free cash flows, but should always be used with great caution. Serious misestimates can result from "fudging" a range of unknown factors into the discount rate. Relevant cases are Absolute Sensors (this module), Spotfire and TixToGo (Module 3) and Vacationspot (Module 5).

Third, the process by which entrepreneurs and those who finance them structure and value entrepreneurial buy-out deals is often iterative, with senior debt, high-yield debt, and equity as financing components. Several cases permit the application of cash flow valuation methods such as capital flows and adjusted present value that are convenient for firms with changing capital structures. Relevant cases include Butler Capital Partners and Ducati (this module) and Sirona (Module 5).

Fourth, cases in this module allow for the application of option valuation techniques. Even though it is challenging to apply these techniques in start-up firms, they work demonstrably better than rules of thumb. This is an important subject inasmuch as many start-up firms use options as part of their compensation. Early-stage employees in start-ups are often found to have little understanding of how to think about these options.

---

[3] Module IV (Managing Contingencies/Changing Contexts (especially the case on Telewizja Wisla)) revisits and delves deeper into this topic.

Entrepreneurs can influence prospective employees to join young firms by communicating the value of these contingent claims succinctly. Relevant cases are Absolute Sensors and Butler Capital Partners (this module).

Fifth, entrepreneurs need to understand cash flows in an international context. The cases enable an examination of the cost of capital in countries outside the United States using a stylized distinction between the integrated capital market (countries among which capital flows relatively freely) and segmented capital markets. Many cases in this module and throughout the book allow for a discussion to what degree spreads of US$-denominated bonds can be used to account for sovereign risk in segmented capital markets and how sovereign risk is related to firm risk. An extensive technical note, "Valuing Cash Flows in an International Context," covers this topic in detail.[4]

Finally, the module considers the valuation of subscription-based businesses, the cash-flow characteristics of which are attractive to entrepreneurs (the cash flows being highly predictable and often prepaid reduce the need for working capital). The per-subscriber valuations are shown to depend on assumptions about acquisition cost, profitability, and lifetime of subscribers. Relevant cases are Signature Security (this module) and Mandic (Module 5).

Cases in This Module

The module consists of five cases. The first case of the module deals with leveraged buy-outs in entrepreneurial settings. The case "Butler Capital Partners and Autodistribution: Putting Private Equity to Work in France" is about a young French buy-out firm's attempt to acquire the largest after-market car parts distributor in France. Autodistribution was created by a group of entrepreneurs who are approaching retirement. Because the company, although profitable, is not very transparent, the entrepreneurial buy-out manager must make certain assumptions about operating improvements and their financial impact. The case provides inputs for the buy-out valuation in a convenient way. Financing structure and purchase price are fixed and pro-forma financial statements are provided.[5] The case also considers what incentives to offer the senior manager at a French car manufacturer who is the candidate for CEO. (Cultural aspects clearly play an important role in mobilizing resources and motivating key employees.) In summary, the case provides an introduction to buy-outs of entrepreneurial firms in a country context in which such transactions are thought to be nearly impossible to execute because of archaic corporate governance structures.[6]

The second case focuses on a U.K.-based sensor company, Absolute Sensors, and explores the valuation of start-up firms. The case allows for a discussion of the company's business model and the valuation of the company using the venture capital method. Also, the reader can examine the diverging interests of the three founders and determine

---

[4] Kuemmerle, Walter, and Matias Braun. 2002. *Valuing Cash Flows in an International Context (803-028)*. Boston: Harvard Business School Publishing.

[5] Cases on entrepreneurial buy-outs later in the book (for example, Ducati (this module) and Sirona (Module 5)) are more complex because they do not provide these inputs.

[6] The Butler case also expands aspiring entrepreneurs' understanding of opportunities by distinguishing between external opportunities in the marketplace and opportunities internal to a firm (restructuring). The QI-Tech case (Module 3) provides an interesting parallel that supports a continuation of this discussion.

whether granting them a set of options might mitigate the impact of their differences on the business. The case offers an opportunity to think rigorously about the difficult problem of valuing these options.[7]

The third case, Signature Security, focuses on the valuation of subscription-based enterprises, a type of business that exists in many industries (e.g., entertainment, publishing, services) and has been the source of numerous entrepreneurial fortunes. Analysis of the positive impacts of subscriptions on cash flows (predictability and prepayment) points to three critical aspects of valuing subscribers: acquisition cost, lifetime, and steady-state profitability. The case demonstrates that the per-subscriber valuation metrics often used in industry are nothing more than a reduced form of a set of specific assumptions about the future of the industry and the firms within it.

Signature Security, an Australian home-alarm systems company, also illustrates the trend towards globalization in international entrepreneurship. A U.S. home-alarm industry entrepreneur had raised money in Canada in anticipation of rolling up an industry in Australia. Within two years the company had made more than 60 acquisitions, overpaying for some of them because the entrepreneur and his team had insufficient understanding of the Australian context. Less stringent contracts than in the United States led to poaching of customers and debt financing was not as readily available because Australian banks were less proficient in lending against cash flow.[8]

The buy-out of the famous Italian motorcycle brand Ducati by U.S.-based Texas Pacific Group is the subject of the module's fourth case. The buy-out fund and turn-around managers have entrepreneurial profiles; both are unfazed by what must have been one of the wilder negotiation roller-coaster rides in entrepreneurial finance. The sellers, a family in financial trouble, only wanted to sell as much as 49%. The buyers wanted at least 51%. The relevant case analysis involves detailed forecasting about stretching payables and collecting receivables more quickly. One also must think about a potential financing structure in the Italian context. The case provides insight into the challenges of valuing a mismanaged family-owned firm and illustrates how Italy's corporate governance needs to be considered to make the deal work. The Ducati case reinforces the insight that opportunities in existing companies can be viewed as both internal and external.[9]

Infox, the fifth case in this module, sets up the valuation and possible acquisition of a small but highly profitable Germany niche business in print materials mailing by a private equity firm. The case emphasizes not valuation per se, but how to determine operating capital requirements and capital expenditures. Because capital expenditures associated with management's plan to expand into several new businesses are unclear, a thorough analysis is warranted. The case is especially intriguing because the firm has

---

[7] The Absolute Sensors case has interesting parallels with the Vacationspot case (Module 5). Both consider differences in local context and the respective motivations of entrepreneurs in Europe and the United States and make the case that these differences need to be managed carefully to improve venture performance. Both cases also demonstrate how a global perspective on access to resources improves the quality of deal structures. Absolute Sensors also has much in common with the several cases about entrepreneurship involving managers from established firms (Singulus (Module 1), Butler Capital Partners and Ducati (this module), and QI-Tech (Module 3)).

[8] Signature Security is one of several cases (@Hoc (Module 1), Spotfire (Module 3), Jinwoong and Gray Security (Module 4), and TelePizza (Module 5) that discuss the opportunity and need for global expansion. Signature also has commonalities with other cases involving buy-out strategies (Ducati and Butler Capital (this module) and Sirona (Module 5)).

[9] Also see Butler Capital (this module) and QI-Tech (Module 3).

a quasi-monopoly in its market. Were it to be taken public, Infox might sacrifice a portion of its profits to the attendant publicity and subsequent pressure from customers. The
case exhibits a common pattern in entrepreneurial firms with two founders: one wants to
sell, the other is unsure. A savvy investor can exploit such a situation. The case offers interesting parallels with other cases in which entrepreneurs built successful and profitable
businesses without a great deal of external financing and faced questions about harvesting (e.g., Infosys, Mandic, and TelePizza (all Module 5)).

8

Butler Capital Partners and Autodistribution: Putting Private Equity to Work in France

Walter Butler was watching the traffic that rolled past his office along the River Seine in Paris. It was late in the afternoon on April 29, 1999, and he had just been in touch with the investment bank, Lehman Brothers, about a new investment proposal. His private equity firm, Butler Capital Partners, had just raised their $180-million second fund, France Private Equity II, and was considering submitting a proposal on Autodistribution S.A. (AD), the leading independent auto parts supplier in France. "By most accounts, it is a wonderful opportunity, " lamented Butler as he looked out of his office in Paris' 8th arrondissement. "Every time I look out the window, more than 10% of the cars I see have parts that come from Autodistribution. And I see a lot of cars." Yet, Butler had some significant concerns due to the context of the deal.

At the beginning of February 1999, the privately held Autodistribution had entered into an agreement with Strafor Facom (SF), a publicly owned industrial products company, to be sold for a combination of cash and SF stock; AD shareholders were to become the largest shareholders of the new entity. However, at the end of March, Fimalac, another publicly owned industrial products company, made a bid for the entire organization shortly before the sale had closed. Fearing that Fimalac would neglect the Autodistribution business, the AD shareholders were forcing the SF management to find an alternative solution for Autodistribution. The major requirement was that the new buyer complete a deal on the same terms (i.e. at the same price of FF 3,455 million[1] ($552 million) and under the same conditions, including the same warranties) on which SF had agreed to purchase AD. Butler highlighted his concerns:

> The AD business is a very attractive opportunity, but some of the constraints of the proposal put quite a strain on the investment decision. Due to the specifics of the deal, not only do we have no flexibility on price, but we also have very little time to evaluate the investment thoroughly. With a little over two weeks to complete the transaction, we not only need to complete our due diligence, but we also need to secure financing. That is no small order, as this could be the biggest buyout in Europe for 1999 if completed. To make things more interesting, it would require an equity commitment 1.5 times the size of our firm's largest investment to date. This is challenging even if it is perfectly in line with our fund's charter. The question becomes, should we even bid on this deal given these difficult circumstances? One thing is clear: if we do bid, life will become interesting.

The French Private Equity Market

1998 was a banner year for the venture capital/private equity market in Europe. According to the European Private Equity and Venture Capital Association (ECVA), not only did investment in this region rise by 50% that year to EURO 14.5 billion ($15 billion), but it also saw a record level of funds raised of EURO 20.3 billion ($21 billion). (See **Exhibit 1** for fundraising and investment data.) According to Paul Waller, outgoing chairman of the EVCA, there was still room for growth as the U.S. venture capital market was four times the size of the European market even though the gross domestic product was of similar size to the United States. (See **Exhibit 2** for economic data.)[2]

Outside of the UK, France was considered the largest and most mature private equity market in Europe. Like many other continental European markets, France was characterized by a large number of small- and medium-sized family-owned companies. As a result, much of the deal flow in France was generated from succession issues within these companies. In addition, there was an increasing emphasis amongst large companies in France to streamline operations and dispose of non-core assets.[3] These trends were reflected in the types of transactions seen in the market. While seed and start-up investments in Europe were accelerating, the most significant portion of the investments were in management buyouts and buy-ins, representing 46% of investment in France and over half of the amount invested in the UK.[4] European buyout funds also posted the best returns in the 1990s, demonstrating 30% returns over the period (see **Exhibit 3** for returns by fund type).[5] However, with these trends, the main concern for the future was that the big increases in funds raised would result in "too much money chasing too few deals"—a trend that was already visible in the increased competition seen in the large end of the market, according to Butler.

---

[1] The French Franc exchange rate is FF6 : US$1.

[2] McCurry, Patrick, and Andy Thomson. 1999. Investors Jump on Europe's Private Equity Bandwagon. *European Venture Capital Journal* (July/August), p. 18.

[3] Davisson, Anita. 1999. Adopting a Pan-European Focus: The European Marketplace Comes of Age. *UK Venture Capital Journal* (May/June), p. 39.

[4] McCurry, Patrick, and Andy Thomson. 1999. Investors Jump on Europe's Private Equity Bandwagon. *European Venture Capital Journal* (July/August), p. 19.

[5] Ibid.

EXHIBIT 1   **Fundraising and Investment Data**

Source: McCurry, Patrick, and Andy Thomson. 1999. Investors Jump on Europe's Private Equity Bandwagon. *European Venture Capital Journal* (July/August), p. 21.

New Funds Raised in Europe: 1997–1998

	1997 (Em)	1998 (Em)	Growth (%)
United Kingdom	12,245	8,959	26.8
France	**1,078**	**3,811**	**253.5**
Germany	2,573	1,875	−27.1
Netherlands	859	1,162	35.3
Sweden	984	999	1.6
Italy	1,072	936	−12.7
Spain	408	692	69.5
Norway	77	442	474.1
Belgium	190	415	118.2
Finland	230	365	58.6
Switzerland	76	222	192.2
Ireland	29	164	464.2
Austria	61	123	101.2
Greece	56	70	25.5

Investments in Europe: 1997–1998

	1997 (Em)	1998 (Em)	Growth (%)	1997 (#)	1998 (#)	Growth (%)
United Kingdom	4,428	7,105	60.5%	1,686	2,018	19.7%
Germany	1,326	1,948	46.9	1,087	1,513	39.2
France	**1,248**	**1,777**	**42.4**	**1,551**	**1,544**	**−0.5**
Netherlands	760	1,059	39.3	425	707	66.4
Italy	603	933	54.7	234	267	14.1
Spain	262	363	38.7	244	244	0
Belgium	179	259	44.6	169	233	37.9
Switzerland	55	215	291.8	47	86	82.7
Sweden	351	203	−42.3	120	115	−4.2
Finland	113	189	67.0	193	274	42.0
Norway	170	165	−2.8	170	161	−5.3
Ireland	36	64	77.1	66	106	60.6
Austria	19	50	164.0	40	93	132.5
Portugal	63	50	−21.4	79	68	−13.9
Denmark	22	40	84.1	55	50	−9.1
Iceland	5	22	332.5	54	120	122.2
Greece	16	20	22.1	32	29	−10.4
European total	9,656	14,462	49.8	6,252	7,628	22.0

Note: # = number of deals; Em = Euro millions.

Walter Butler and Butler Capital Partners

Walter Butler was born in Rio de Janeiro, Brazil in 1956 to an American father and a half-French, half-Brazilian mother. After spending his early childhood in Brazil, Butler moved back to France with his mother after his parents divorced. In 1983, Butler graduated in the top five in his class at the prestigious École Nationale d' Administration (ENA) and went to work with the French Treasury as Inspecteur des Finances (see **Exhibit 4** for the biographies

EXHIBIT 2 Comparative Economic Indicators, 1997

Source: Compiled from Economist Intelligence Unit and Eurostat data.

	France	Germany	Italy	U.K.	U.S.
GDP ($ bn)	1,392.5	2,092.4	1,145.4	1,312.3	8,110.9
GDP per head ($)	23,760	25,506	19,919	22,255	30,306
Consumer price inflation[a] (%)	0.7	0.7	2.0	1.5	1.6
Unemployment rate[a] (%)	11.8	9.7	12.4	5.5	4.6
Exports of goods fob ($ bn)	284.2	511.1	238.2	281.3	681.3
Imports of goods fob ($ bn)	256.1	439.3	191.5	300.8	877.3
Current-account balance ($ bn)	39.5	−2.8	33.4	10.0	−155.38

[a]EU harmonized figures, except for U.S., 1998.

EXHIBIT 3
European Private Equity Fund Returns in the 1990s

Source: Compiled from McCurry, Patrick, and Andy Thomson. 1999. Investors Jump on Europe's Private Equity Bandwagon. *European Venture Capital Journal* (July/August), p. 20.

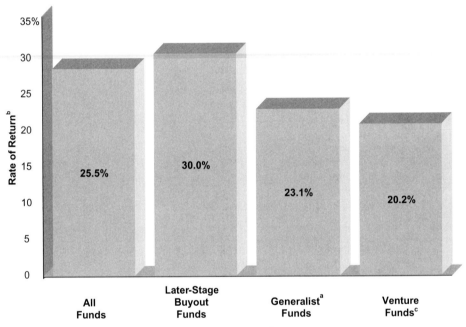

[a]Fixed-life and evergreen funds investing in both venture and buyout opportunities.
[b]For top quarter funds.
[c]Including early-stage.

of the Butler Capital Partners team). In 1986, he became head of privatizations in the media sector for the French Government. In 1988, he left the Government to become an executive director in the investment banking division at Goldman, Sachs. Butler explained his move.

It was a different world at Goldman, Sachs. Being French was not necessarily a plus and being a former civil servant was definitely not a plus. But this was where I learned everything, not only about finance, but also about business in general. Everything in life is possible, but you need to make the right moves to be successful.

One day, while working on an M&A assignment, I was putting together a book on strategic alternatives for a European company. As part of the presentation, we listed the various parties that could be interested in purchasing the client. In the end, we had a couple of strategic buyers and tons of U.S. financial buyers of all types, but no European financial buyers. At that very moment, it struck me that this was a tremendous opportunity that I needed

EXHIBIT 4   **Biographies of the Butler Capital Partners Team**

Source: Butler Capital Partners.

Walter Butler, 43—Prior to founding Butler Capital Partners in 1991, Walter Butler was executive director in the Investment Banking Division of Goldman Sachs. From 1986 to 1988, he was in charge of privatization in the media sector, within the French Government. He had previously held, from 1983 to 1986, the function of Inspecteur des Finances for the French Treasury, after graduating from ENA in 1983. Walter Butler has been the chairman of the French Venture Association (AFIC) since 1997.

Pierre Costes, 30—Pierre Costes, chartered accountant (CPA), joined Butler Capital Partners in 1998, having spent the previous seven years at Arthur Andersen where he was director in the Acquisition and Special Operations department. He graduated from Ecole Superieure des Sciences Economiques et Commerciales (ESSEC).

Karin Jacquemart-Pernod, 31—Karin Jacquemart-Pernod joined Butler Capital Partners in 1991, having spent the previous three years at Goldman Sachs, as an analyst in the Corporate Finance Department. She graduated from Ecole des Hautes Etudes Commerciale (HEC).

Laurent Parquet, 33—Laurent Parquet joined Butler Capital Partners in 1997, having spent the previous six years at Andersen Consulting where he was director in the Media and Communication Group. He graduated from Ecole Superieure des Sciences Economiques et Commerciales (ESSEC).

Michel Vedrines, 53—Michel Vedrines joined Butler Capital Partners in 1991, having spent the previous three years as the chief executive of a medium-sized manufacturing company. From 1983 to 1988, he worked at the Institut de Developpement Industriel, a French investment company. He spent the previous 17 years at a subsidiary of Elf Aquitaine. He graduated from "Ecole Superieure de Chimie de Marseille" (Chemical Engineering) and obtained an MBA from ISA in 1983.

Jean-Pierre Pipaud, 47—Chief Financial Officer—Jean-Pierre Pipaud joined Butler Capital Partners in 1999, having spent the previous two years as chief operating officer of NatWest Markets (Asset Management Department) in France. From 1990 to 1996 he was financial controller of SBC Warburg in France, where he managed the internal Financial Control Service. He spent the previous 13 years at Credit Agricole. Jean-Pierre Pipaud holds a master degree in business law.

to pursue. Though the risk was significant, I felt that in 1989 I was able to handle it; ten years later I probably would not. With that in mind, I moved back to France to begin raising the fund.

Initially the experience was a case of the extremes: it was much worse than my worst nightmares, but much more exciting than my wildest dreams. I had no team and no track record—I had a U.S. brand but initially there was just me and . . . me. Six months after starting I hired an assistant, and the next person to join was Michel (Vedrines, director) but that was after the fund was raised. I still do not know how I did it.

The first fund, European Strategic Fund, closed in 1991, 18 months after Butler began the fundraising process. Focusing on small family owned companies and on divisions of larger companies, the FF 300 million ($50 million) fund was very successful during a very difficult period in the French economy (1991–1996), attaining gross returns of 38–39% (see **Exhibit 5** for the investments in the first fund). On the back of this success, Butler Capital Partners closed its second fund, French Private Equity II, in September 1998 at FF 1.1 billion ($180 million), becoming one of the largest independent funds in France. The new fund would focus on investments in France and would continue to make traditional capital investments similar to those from the first fund, but on a larger scale. Given the development of Butler Capital Partners, the roll-up envisioned in the Autodistribution transaction could be the perfect opportunity for the fund—at least under normal circumstances. "In order to decide on the investment, we first need to get smart on the company and the industry . . . and in a hurry," Butler instructed his team.

EXHIBIT 5 Investments from Fund I

Source: Butler Capital Partners.

Company Name	Strategy	Type of Business	Initial Inv. Date	Realization Date	Cost	Proceeds	Total Value	IRR	Multiple of Cost
Realized Investments									
I	Build up	Market research	Sep-97	Jul-99	144.0	488.5	488.5	60.9%	2.3
			Dec-97		64.0				
B	Buy-out	Logistics/express delivery	Oct-92	Jan-99	25.0	117.2	117.2	28.2	4.7
N	Buy-out	Mailroom equipment producer	Mar-92	Sep-97	15.2	34.7	34.7	18.7	2.3
D	Turnaround	Global advertising	Oct-94	Apr-97	30.0	76.0	76.0	46.7	2.5
Total realized					*278.2*	*716.4*	*716.4*	*37.6%*	*2.6*
Unrealized Investments									
F	Buy-out	Labels for food packaging	Jan-92		32.6	0.0	5.0	−31.3%	0.2
C	Buy & build	Specialist directories	Aug-92		9.3	0.0	19.9	11.6	2.1
G	Buy-out	Office supplies products	Jul-93		17.0	0.0	37.5	13.9	2.2
O	Turnaround	IT services	Dec-97		60.0	0.0	300.0	162.8	5.0
Total unrealized					*118.9*	*0.0*	*362.4*	*27.0%*	*3.0*
Total Investments					**397.1**	**716.4**	**1,078.8**	**32.8%**	**2.7**

Note: Companies names were intentionally eliminated.

Autodistribution: A Dominant Force in the European Auto Part After-Market

The European Automotive Part After-Market

The four largest markets in Europe for automotive after-market supplies were Germany ($15.8 billion), France ($13.3 billion), the United Kingdom ($6.7 billion) and Italy ($6.7 billion).[6] Every market was very fragmented, with no company holding a share of any significance. In the UK and in France there were companies that began to exhibit some size ($500+ million in sales), but at the same time, had a relatively small share of the total market (around 10%). "It was amazing," mused Butler. "I had never seen an industry where a company (AD) was number one in Europe, but had no real presence outside the home market." Nevertheless, throughout the early to mid 1990s, the European auto supply market saw steady growth. Between 1992 and 1996, the European market was led by Italy (5% CAGR), the United Kingdom (3.5% CAGR) and France (3.3% CAGR). (See **Exhibit 6** for an overview of each of the major markets.) The French market had seen most of its growth in the period from 1992 to 1994 (3.5% CAGR) and the market continued to grow by 2% to 3% from 1994 onwards. As for future growth, at the start of 1999, the market was expected to grow by 2% to 3% for the foreseeable future. Factors for growth included a growing number of cars in circulation, an aging car fleet, an increased technical complexity of car parts, new legislation requiring more frequent compulsory vehicle inspections, and deregulation to meet European standards (see **Exhibit 7** for the impact of deregulation).

The French automotive parts market was organized around three main distribution channels—the car manufacturers channel, the independent wholesalers channel (AD's business), and the "new distribution" channel (see **Exhibit 8** for a diagram of the industry channels). Historically, legislation in France insulated car manufacturers from competition

[6] Based on 1996 data (source: Butler Capital Partners company documents).

EXHIBIT 6   **Overview of the Major European Markets**

Source: Butler Capital Partners.

- In **Germany, the car manufacturers' channel is very strong** with a reported market share of 60%. The "nothing but the best" German philosophy has led car users to often have their car serviced at the main dealer, expecting premium quality and premium products. As a result, there are fewer auto-centers or fast-fits than in other European countries. AD's German counterpart is the firm CARAT (FF 13 bn in sales) which has recently integrated with the ADI network for its auto parts distribution activity.
- **The British market's structure resembles that of France**: significant position held by car manufacturers (45%) and strong development of the "New" distribution channel (around 1/3 of the market for auto-centers and fast-fits). Great Britain used to have many small traditional wholesalers, which were about half the size of their French counterparts. But many of the smaller wholesalers have disappeared and have been replaced by so-called "super factors" such as Partco (FF 4.2 mn), Finelist (FF 3.7 bn) or the successful buying group FSG.
- **Spain seems to mirror French distribution trends, but is still 15 years behind.** Car manufacturers hold 38% of the market and the traditional wholesalers started forming buying groups. There are 2 main international organizations: Group Auto Union and ADI. The emerging "New" distribution channel has grown rapidly over the last few years as the needs in car servicing increased, with French-owned firms taking the lead (Norauto, Carrefour, Auchan).
- **The Italian automotive after-market** is fairly traditional but **car dealers are not very strong**: Italians prefer to have their car serviced in small outlets. New distribution emerges slowly but is confined to extreme North and cities.

EXHIBIT 7   **Impact on Deregulation**

Source: Butler Capital Partners.

A positive evolution of the European legislation towards a more deregulated market should lead to stiffer competition between independent distributors and car dealers. This legislation should:
- allow car dealers, previously exclusively supplied by their car manufacturer, to buy their auto parts to independent wholesalers,
- allow wholesalers to sell auto parts manufactured by car manufacturers,
- allow wholesalers to manufacture and sell body parts that are today proprietary components, only handled by car manufacturers.

EXHIBIT 8
**Automotive Parts
After-Market
Industry Channels**

Source: Butler Capital
Partners.

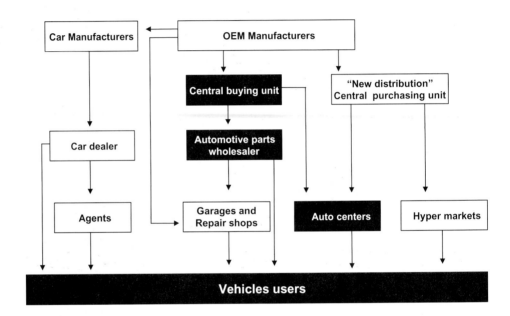

from independent wholesalers. Unlike the rest of Europe, the car manufacturers tied up car dealerships and agents with exclusivity deals that prohibited them from purchasing parts from independent wholesalers. Moreover, there were certain parts sold by car manufacturers that independent wholesalers were simply prohibited from selling. "AD can supply about 95% of the number of parts for a car," explained Vedrines. "In the past, they could not sell body parts, but deregulation should change much of this in 2002."

"The main trend during the 1990s had been a boom in the "new distribution" channel comprised of new auto centers and fast-fit body shops. These new distribution businesses saw a huge increase in market share during a seven year period through 1994 as they took business from gas stations, independent garages, and agents, while car manufacturers and independent wholesalers were able to retain market share. However, the boom seemed to end in the mid 1990s as market shares had remained steady throughout the industry since 1994. (See **Exhibit 9** for market share data.)

Autodistribution History

Robert Gerbois created Autodistribution in 1962 as an automotive parts-purchasing association controlled by independently owned affiliates. Originally a loosely organized, central-buying cooperative, AD acted as an intermediary between its affiliates (wholesalers in automotive replacement parts) and their suppliers. The intent was to pool together a group of independently owned wholesalers to gain purchasing power and price discounts

EXHIBIT 9   Automotive After-Market Structural Overview

Source: Butler Capital Partners.

Channel evolution has stabilized after radical pruning amongst independents and others.

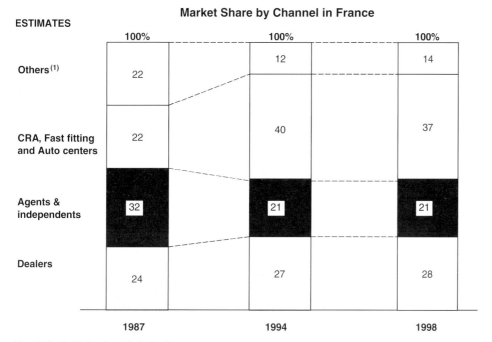

Market Share by Channel in France

ESTIMATES

Note (1): Service/Fuel stations, Wholesales, Scrappers.

through the volume generated by their aggregated purchase orders. When Gerbois died in 1976, the son of one of the major affiliates, Pierre Farsy, assumed control of the buying unit and proved to be a dynamic and influential figure in the organization. By the early 1980s, AD had begun using the profits generated by the central buying unit (CBU) to acquire wholesalers—not only affiliates, but unaffiliated companies as well. Many of these companies were financially or operationally troubled companies that AD was able to rehabilitate through its increasing financial power and industry expertise. Over time, the purchasing power of AD grew as it continued to increase the volume of the parts purchased through the CBU.

While integrating affiliates and consolidating the group in France, Farsy also turned towards Europe and began developing an international brand through a subsidiary, AD International (ADI). Started by Gerbois in 1976 in Belgium, Farsy expanded the network to seven buying units in seven different countries, with each country's network owning an equal share in ADI. The increased purchasing volume generated by the international buying unit enabled each international affiliate to obtain an additional 2% to 3% discount off the prices negotiated locally, with such additional discounts distributed to the local buying units based on purchasing volume. After registering the AD brand in 1984, Autodistribution began incorporating it throughout the network of wholesalers and garages in France and the rest of Europe.

By the end of 1998, Autodistribution had become the largest independent wholesaler in France, with a market share of 33% in the independent wholesaler segment and 10% overall (see **Exhibit 10** for market share information). With approximately FF 5.4 billion ($900 million) in sales and a network that represented over FF 7.0 billion ($1.2 billion) in combined revenues, AD was also the largest independent wholesaler in Europe

EXHIBIT 10 French Automotive Part After-Market Information

Source: Butler Capital Partners.

Aggregate Revenues of the Main Central Buying Units or Co-operative Affiliates

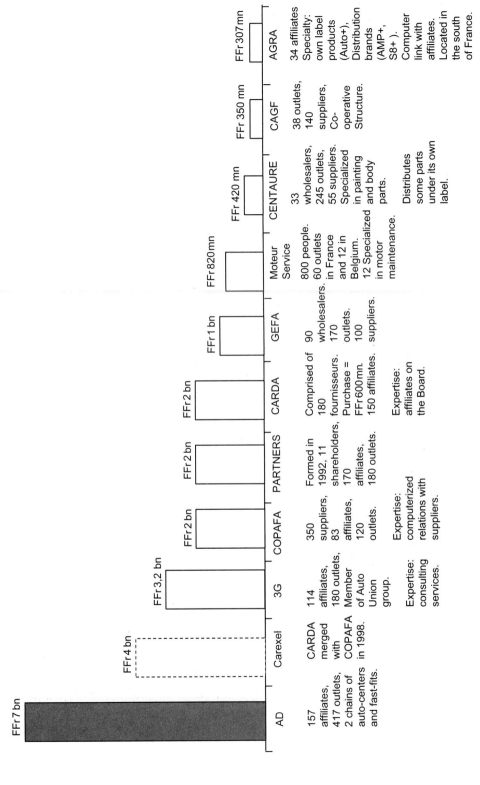

(see **Exhibit 11** for AD's historical financial information). Autodistribution was organized around three business functions: the CBU, company-owned wholesalers, and auto centers (see **Exhibit 12** for an organization chart). The CBU was at the center of the AD organization. It represented a group comprised of 58 subsidiary wholesalers and 99 affiliated wholesalers and negotiated with over 350 suppliers. The company-owned, subsidiary wholesalers accounted for approximately 50% of the purchases made by the CBU. The auto centers conducted AD's business-to-consumer activities through Maxauto, a 75-store garage chain, and Axto, a 24-store exhaust and brake replacement shop. Since the unit was still early in the expansion phase, its FF 350 million ($58 million) in

EXHIBIT 11   AD Historical Financial Information

Source: Butler Capital Partners.

Autodistribution—Historical consolidated P/L

Thousand of FFr	1994		1995		1996		1997		1998	
Turnover (n-1 perimeter)	n.d.		4,323,000	95.6%	4,498,000	97.2%	4,805,000	95.8%	5,263,000	97.5%
% / n-1 without acquired n-1 turnover	*n.s.*		*n.s.*		*(0.6%)*		*3.8%*		*4.9%*	
% / n-1 including acquired n-1 turnover	*n.s.*		*n.s.*		*4.0%*		*6.8%*		*9.5%*	
Turnover of purchased companies	n.d.		200,243	4.4%	129,372	2.8%	211,576	4.2%	137,532	2.5%
Total net turnover	**4,228,968**	*100.0%*	**4,523,243**	*100.0%*	**4,627,372**	*100.0%*	**5,016,576**	*100.0%*	**5,400,532**	*100.0%*
% / n-1	*n.s.*		*7.0%*		*2.3%*		*8.4%*		*7.7%*	
	-	-	(2,617)	(0.1%)	188	0.0%	424	0.0%	-	-
Raw material and goods purchases	(2,981,168)	(70.5%)	(3,166,984)	(70.0%)	(3,208,175)	(69.3%)	(3,463,077)	(69.0%)	(3,699,596)	(68.5%)
Gross margin	**1,247,800**	*29.5%*	**1,353,642**	*29.9%*	**1,419,385**	*30.7%*	**1,553,923**	*31.0%*	**1,700,936**	*31.5%*
% / n-1	*n.s.*		*8.5%*		*4.9%*		*9.5%*		*9.5%*	
Other variable costs	(346,775)	(8.2%)	(368,000)	(8.1%)	(381,872)	(8.3%)	(421,463)	(8.4%)	(441,165)	(8.2%)
Value added	**901,025**	*21.3%*	**985,642**	*21.8%*	**1,037,513**	*22.4%*	**1,132,460**	*22.6%*	**1,259,771**	*23.3%*
% / n-1	*n.s.*		*9.4%*		*5.3%*		*9.2%*		*11.2%*	
Personnel and social charges	(633,009)	(15.0%)	(662,100)	(14.6%)	(713,079)	(15.4%)	(787,251)	(15.7%)	(833,358)	(15.4%)
Employee profit sharing	(6,436)	(0.2%)	(8,739)	(0.2%)	(7,830)	(0.2%)	(8,638)	(0.2%)	(11,627)	(0.2%)
Taxes	(47,318)	(1.1%)	(55,709)	(1.2%)	(56,402)	(1.2%)	(64,326)	(1.3%)	(69,687)	(1.3%)
State fundings	-	-	941	0.0%	1,912	0.0%	1,675	0.0%	-	-
Other products and expenses	17,301	0.4%	20,772	0.5%	(11,262)	(0.2%)	17,730	0.4%	24,710	0.5%
EBITDA	**231,563**	*5.5%*	**280,807**	*6.2%*	**250,852**	*5.4%*	**291,651**	*5.8%*	**369,809**	*6.8%*
% / n-1	*n.s.*		*21.3%*		*(10.7%)*		*16.3%*		*26.8%*	
Depreciation allowance	(44,404)	(1.1%)	(46,130)	(1.0%)	(51,196)	(1.1%)	(58,784)	(1.2%)	(64,889)	(1.2%)
Risk allowance	(80,055)	(1.9%)	(85,625)	(1.9%)	(87,384)	(1.9%)	(101,153)	(2.0%)	(100,286)	(1.9%)
Reprises & transferts de ch.	86,277	2.0%	92,281	2.0%	120,170	2.6%	114,795	2.3%	105,939	2.0%
EBIT	**193,381**	*4.6%*	**241,332**	*5.3%*	**232,442**	*5.0%*	**246,509**	*4.9%*	**310,573**	*5.8%*
% / n-1	*n.s.*		*24.8%*		*(3.7%)*		*6.1%*		*26.0%*	
Operations in common	317	0.0%	342	0.0%	(19)	(0.0%)	(74)	(0.0%)	226	0.0%
Cash discount on purchases	n.d.		n.d.		22,000	0.5%	23,810	0.5%	22,500	0.4%
Other financial income	33,052	0.8%	38,405	0.8%	8,682	0.2%	6,502	0.1%	8,324	0.2%
Financial charges	(50,763)	(1.2%)	(46,814)	(1.0%)	(30,823)	(0.7%)	(20,167)	(0.4%)	(13,958)	(0.3%)
Financial depreciation	-	-	1,167	0.0%	5,623	0.1%	4,055	0.1%	579	0.0%
Financial result	**(17,394)**	*(0.4%)*	**(6,900)**	*(0.2%)*	**5,463**	*0.1%*	**14,126**	*0.3%*	**17,671**	*0.3%*
EBIT after interest	**175,987**	*4.2%*	**234,432**	*5.2%*	**237,905**	*5.1%*	**260,635**	*5.2%*	**328,244**	*6.1%*
% / n-1	*n.s.*		*33.2%*		*1.5%*		*9.6%*		*25.9%*	
Extraordinary profits	21,027	0.5%	27,575	0.6%	41,366	0.9%	15,725	0.3%	27,814	0.5%
Extraordinary expenses	(34,894)	(0.8%)	(27,442)	(0.6%)	(35,053)	(0.8%)	(21,949)	(0.4%)	(19,904)	(0.4%)
Extraordinary allowance	-	-	(24,495)	(0.5%)	(25,186)	(0.5%)	(620)	(0.0%)	520	0.0%
Extraordinary result	**(13,867)**	*(0.3%)*	**(24,362)**	*(0.5%)*	**(18,873)**	*(0.4%)*	**(6,844)**	*(0.1%)*	**8,430**	*0.2%*
Tax penalty					-		-		(25,000)	(0.5%)
Income tax	(54,829)	(1.3%)	(85,916)	(1.9%)	(92,735)	(2.0%)	(115,592)	(2.3%)	(145,033)	(2.7%)
Net result before goodwill amort.	**107,291**	*2.5%*	**124,154**	*2.7%*	**126,297**	*2.7%*	**138,199**	*2.8%*	**166,641**	*3.1%*
% / n-1	*n.s.*		*15.7%*		*1.7%*		*9.4%*		*20.6%*	
Goodwill amortization	(3,334)	(0.1%)	(4,761)	(0.1%)	(5,810)	(0.1%)	(15,121)	(0.3%)	(13,624)	(0.3%)
Consolidated net result	**103,957**	*2.5%*	**119,393**	*2.6%*	**120,487**	*2.6%*	**123,078**	*2.5%*	**153,017**	*2.8%*
% / n-1	*n.s.*		*14.8%*		*0.9%*		*2.2%*		*24.3%*	
Minority interests	1,122	0.0%	1,116	0.0%	(946)	(0.0%)	(528)	(0.0%)	4	0.0%
Group consolidated net result	**102,835**	*2.4%*	**118,277**	*2.6%*	**121,433**	*2.6%*	**123,606**	*2.5%*	**153,013**	*2.8%*
% / n-1	*n.s.*		*15.0%*		*2.7%*		*1.8%*		*23.8%*	

n.s. = not meaningful
n.d. = not available

(continued)

EXHIBIT 11 (Continued)

Autodistribution—Historical Balance Sheets				
Thousand of FFr	**1994**	**1995**	**1996**	**1997**	**1998**
Non called-up capital	-	120	60	-	1,159
Net intangible assets	26,084	31,498	33,533	44,213	45,521
Goodwill	118,417	103,880	84,577	80,959	79,530
Net tangible assets	271,411	286,241	293,411	349,538	359,510
Investments and financial assets	32,929	50,835	48,098	28,437	29,571
Long term assets	**448,841**	**472,454**	**459,619**	**503,147**	**514,132**
Net inventories	603,545	682,354	688,747	718,979	736,071
Accounts receivables	1,104,809	1,136,858	1,115,275	1,253,580	1,303,184
Other current assets	466	112,050	40,138	44,863	30,273
Current assets	**1,708,820**	**1,931,262**	**1,844,160**	**2,017,422**	**2,069,528**
Cash and time deposits	**229,769**	**141,951**	**220,537**	**206,595**	**219,903**
Prepaid expenses	37,951	34,536	33,417	36,081	37,680
Total Assets	**2,425,381**	**2,580,323**	**2,557,793**	**2,763,245**	**2,842,402**
Common stock	50,778	24,508	73,523	308,095	308,095
Consolidated retained earnings	503,086	632,869	695,683	516,998	596,319
Profit and loss account	101,964	118,277	121,433	123,606	153,011
Equity	**655,828**	**775,654**	**890,639**	**948,699**	**1,057,425**
Other equity	**18,743**	**11,435**	**18,380**	**15,339**	**14,082**
Provision for liabilities and charges	**36,237**	**53,943**	**51,024**	**46,629**	**45,227**
Other long term debt	490,525	360,665	217,200	271,686	59,417
Short term borrowings	n.d.	n.d.	159,359	107,420	165,255
Accounts payable	1,159,893	1,148,741	1,000,267	1,134,485	1,197,772
Other debts	61,427	226,801	217,898	235,018	300,171
Total debt	**1,711,845**	**1,736,207**	**1,594,724**	**1,748,609**	**1,722,615**
Prepaid charges	2,728	3,084	3,026	3,969	3,053
Total liabilities	**2,425,381**	**2,580,323**	**2,557,793**	**2,763,245**	**2,842,402**
Off balance sheet engagements					
Pensions	n.d.	24,406	25,930	33,221	33,566
Leasing for tangible assets	n.d.	46,907	39,653	34,218	32,858
Leasing—other tangible assets	n.d.	20,856	17,250	14,991	12,797
Total – Leasing	**n.d.**	**67,763**	**56,903**	**49,209**	**45,655**
Net debt					
Financial debts	490,525	360,665	376,559	379,106	224,672
Leasing *(1)*	n.d.	38,053	31,902	27,603	25,387
Cash and time deposit	(229,769)	(141,951)	(220,537)	(206,595)	(219,903)
Net debt	**260,756**	**256,767**	**187,924**	**200,114**	**30,156**
Increase in net debt		n.s.	(68,843)	12,190	(169,958)
% of increase in net debt		*n.s.*	*−26.8%*	*6.5%*	*−84.9%*
Increase in net debt (leasing excluded)		n.s.	(62,692)	16,489	(167,742)
Debt / equity / cap. propres	**40%**	**33%**	**21%**	**21%**	**3%**
Net result / equity/ cap. propres	**15.7%**	**15.2%**	**13.6%**	**13.0%**	**14.5%**

n.s. = not meaningful
n.d. = not available

(continued)

EXHIBIT 11   (Continued)

Thousand of FFr	1994	1995	1996	1997	1998
Autodistribution—Historical Balance Sheets					
Working capital requirements					
Inventories	701,509	773,003	771,284	801,347	817,616
Accounts receivable (net)	1,174,589	1,210,892	1,170,053	1,312,290	1,364,460
Other current assets	38,888	146,723	74,437	82,520	68,847
Accounts payable	(1,159,893)	(1,148,741)	(1,000,267)	(1,134,485)	(1,197,772)
Other liabilities	(64,155)	(229,885)	(220,924)	(238,987)	(303,224)
Working capital requirements	**690,938**	**751,992**	**794,583**	**822,685**	**749,927**
Change in WCR		61,054	42,591	28,102	(72,758)
Inventories	61 days	62 days	61 days	58 days	55 days
Accounts receivables	101 days	98 days	92 days	95 days	92 days
Othe assets	3 days	12 days	6 days	6 days	5 days
Accounts payables	(100 days)	(93 days)	(79 days)	(83 days)	(81 days)
Other liabilities	(6 days)	(19 days)	(17 days)	(17 days)	(20 days)
Working capital requirements	**60 days**	**61 days**	**63 days**	**60 days**	**51 days**

Autodistribution—Historical Cash Flow Statements

Thousand of FFr	1994	1995	1996	1997	1998
Consolidated net results	103,957	119,393	120,487	123,078	153,017
Depreciation allowance	44,404	46,130	51,196	58,784	64,889
Risk allowance	(6,223)	16,672	(13,223)	(17,077)	(6,752)
Goodwill depreciation	3,334	4,761	5,810	15,121	13,624
Funds provided by operations	**145,473**	**186,957**	**164,270**	**179,906**	**224,778**
Tangible acquisitions	n.d.	45,734	61,953	93,756	61,032
Intangible acquisitions	n.d.	10,027	10,178	13,871	6,486
Investments and financial assets	n.d.	36,622	38,505	27,337	36,419
Additions to long term assets *(1)*	**n.d.**	**92,383**	**110,636**	**134,964**	**103,937**
Long term asset disposals		(21,298)	(33,052)	(8,796)	(12,559)
Net capital expenditure *(1)*	**n.d.**	**71,085**	**77,584**	**126,168**	**91,378**
Change in WCR	**n.d.**	**61,054**	**42,591**	**28,102**	**(72,758)**
Attributed dividends	**n.d.**	**3,536**	**6,383**	**33,447**	**43,144**
Cash used—total	**n.d.**	**135,675**	**126,558**	**187,717**	**61,764**
Net cash	**n.d.**	**51,282**	**37,712**	**(7,811)**	**163,014**
Changes in perimeter & ajustments		(9,240)	24,980	(8,678)	4,728
Total	**n.d.**	**42,042**	**62,692**	**(16,489)**	**167,742**
Increase in net debt (2)	**n.d.**	**(42,042)**	**(62,692)**	**16,489**	**(167,742)**

Notes : - *(1) excluding additions financed through leasing*
- *(2) excluding leasing*

n.s. = not meaningful
n.d. = not available

EXHIBIT 12 **Organization Chart**

Source: Butler Capital Partners.

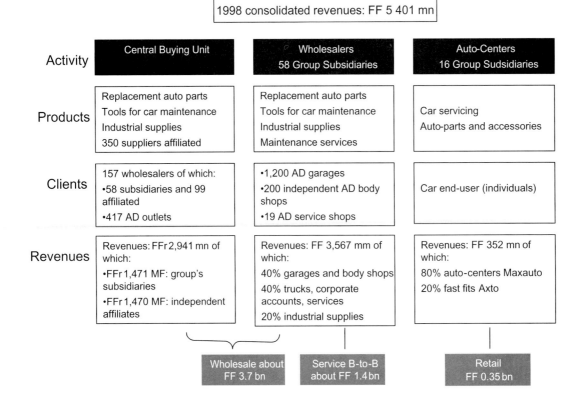

revenues placed each business well behind the industry leaders in each segment and the unit had yet to reach breakeven. Moreover, the auto center business remained a small part of the operations, having accounted for less than 7% of AD's sales.

Why AD is for Sale (Again): Deal History

Strafor Facom was a leading industrial product manufacturer of specialized tools in France. The company had very close ties with Autodistribution, having been a long-time supplier of products to AD. Almost immediately after becoming CEO of SF in June 1998, Paul-Marie Chavanne began negotiations with AD about a potential merger (see **Exhibit 13** for Chavanne's biography). Chavanne explained his career and interest in AD.

> I have always been interested in cars for as long as I can remember. I left Peugeot not because I wanted out of the automotive industry, but because I came to the realization that I was too much of an entrepreneur to stay at such a large corporation. I always had the feeling that I wanted to run an entrepreneurial organization but at the start of my career, I did not know for sure. Then, after a number of years at Peugeot, I found that I was acting more as an organizer than an entrepreneur. Moreover, Peugeot was really a player in the French market only, and I wanted to be a part of a business that had broader interests in an international context. I accepted the position at Strafor Facom because of the chance to lead an entrepreneurial organization that had a broader focus. I was interested in merging with AD, not only because of the

EXHIBIT 13
Chavanne's
Biography

Source: Butler Capital
Partners.

Paul-Marie Chavanne (48) was chairman and CEO of Strafor Facom (a publicly listed company manufacturing industrial tools, with a turnover of FF 8.8 bn in 1998). He joined Strafor Facom as COO in 1997 and became CEO in 1998. From 1992 to 1997, he was a manager and member of the Board of the French car manufacturer Peugeot-Citroën (PSA). He had previously held, from 1978 to 1989, various functions of Inspecteur des Finances for the French Treasury and the French Finance Ministry, after graduating from ENA in 1978 (where he graduated as one of the top five students) and from Ecole Centrale as an engineer in 1976.

EXHIBIT 14
Autodistribution
Transaction History

Source: Butler Capital
Partners.

Date	Event
February 3, 1999	Agreements signed between SF (Strafor Facom) and shareholders of AD (Autodistribution)
March 24, 1999	Fimalac announced their intention to launch a tender offer on SF
April 1, 1999	Terms of the Fimalac tender offer accepted by market authorities
April 1, 1999	Butler Capital Partners' 1st meeting with Lehman Brothers. Lehman Brothers looking for "white knight" for Fimalac's hostile takeover bid on Strafor Facom (SF)
April 8, 1999	SF Board rejected the Fimalac tender offer
April 23, 1999	Butler Capital Partners' 1st access to the data room
April 28, 1999	Butler Capital Partners had meeting with Lehman for presentation of AD management's business plan. 2nd access to the data room

automotive connection, but also because of the tremendous growth opportunities the company had throughout Europe. AD was not just a French company, but an entire international network that was built around the AD concept, the AD brand and the AD process. Given the fragmentation in both the French and the European market, I believed there was a tremendous opportunity for growth given adequate access to capital and the right operating environment.

The discussions with AD began in June of 1998 at the instigation of Rothschild, the French merchant bank and advisory firm (see **Exhibit 14** for a history of the transaction). After a couple of meetings with AD, in which Farsy and Chavanne shared their views on the auto parts market, the two companies began discussions about a merger. Chavanne explained the nature of the discussions.

We shared very similar views on the direction of the auto parts market and the strategic direction of AD. The initial phase of growth for AD would be to purchase these independent affiliates to consolidate our position in France before tackling European expansion. SF not only had the capital to commit to this strategy, but was also publicly traded. Since many of the owners of AD were also the owners of the independent affiliates and were approaching retirement age, this was an important point. A merged entity created a vehicle where they could sell their independent businesses—the importance of which was being dwarfed by their interest in AD anyway—while creating liquidity for their AD holding by trading it in for SF shares. Most importantly, as the largest shareholder group post-merger with a 20% stake, they would retain effective control over the entire combined entity.

At the end of February 1999, Strafor Facom entered into an agreement with Autodistribution's shareholders to purchase 100% of Autodistribution in 1999. However, soon afterward, publicly owned Fimalac, another diversified industrial products manufacturer, placed a hostile takeover bid on Strafor Facom's shares. This bid was rejected both by

Strafor Facom's management board and by Autodistribution's shareholders. Strafor Facom tried first to find an industrial company or a financial investor willing to place a counter takeover bid against Fimalac. Chavanne recounted the experience.

> Since we had already made a deal with AD and since AD shareholders would then be the largest shareholder of SF, we needed to get approval for any Fimalac proposal from AD shareholders, which effectively meant we needed approval from Pierre Farsy. Even though AD was a broadly held organization, Pierre had run the organization for a number of years, was the owner of an independent himself, and more or less had the complete trust of all of the shareholders. His influence was significant. In the Fimalac proposal, Pierre knew that Fimalac would not have the resources to develop both the combined Fimalac/SF business and the AD business at the same time. In fact, the offer to include AD was more of an afterthought for Fimalac when they placed the hostile bid for SF. As a result, we needed to either find a white knight for the entire SF organization including AD or we needed to find a separate buyer for AD that could guarantee its development and implement a build-up strategy. Our initial attempts focused on finding a white knight for the entire business, but this proved too difficult due, at least in part, to the time constraints imposed by the closing of the AD transaction. As a result, we turned our attention to finding a separate buyer for Autodistribution. That is when we became aware of Butler Capital Partners.

Rolling It Up: Autodistribution's Strategy

There were four key elements to AD's strategy going forward under Chavanne. The first element of the strategy was to pursue an aggressive acquisition program to build up the organization set in two stages. Stage one focused on opportunities within France, with the goal to acquire around FF 1 billion ($167 million) of turnover each year. Around half of these acquisitions would be AD affiliates, on many of which AD had a right of first refusal, and half independent wholesalers not affiliated with AD. After approximately three years, most of the acquisition opportunities in France would be exhausted, so the company would focus on acquisitions outside of France. The first targets here would be European wholesalers affiliated with the ADI network. The second element of the AD strategy was to increase efficiency within the organization's existing subsidiaries. "About one third of the subsidiaries were highly profitable," said Chavanne, "one third were of average or adequate profitability and one third were under-performing or loss making subsidiaries. We need to take measures to ensure the last two categories increase their efficiency. These include everything that goes from the implementation of best practices to the re-evaluation of management."

The third element of the AD strategy was to improve the central organization through the elimination of back-office expenses and through better coordination of logistics. "At the time of the AD purchase by SF," explained Chavanne, "there was very little centralization of the administrative aspects of the business. In addition, we needed an investment in logistics of approximately FF 50 million ($8.3 million) to centralize the control of the inventory flows throughout the organization." The final element of the strategy was to increase the purchasing power of the CBU. Part of this would be accomplished through the increased demand garnered through the acquisitions described above. Another method would be to increase the percentage of purchases affiliates and subsidiaries made through the CBU. "Since we assumed our market share in the existing business would remain stable and since we expected the market to grow at two to three percent over the near term," Chavanne explained, " we needed to find incremental growth in the existing business. Therefore we wanted to get the subsidiaries to increase their purchases from 65% to 70% over the subsequent three to four years." Another method by which the management expected to increase the CBU purchasing power was through increasing the supplier base. "Currently, most of our suppliers are in France," Chavanne said. "By expanding throughout Europe, we also expected an enlargement of our supplier base that would allow us to arbitrage automotive part prices in other markets." Through these four strategic elements, Chavanne and AD management expected to make Autodistribution a powerful presence not only in France, but in the broader European market as well.

. . . And Along Comes Butler Capital Partners

History of Involvement

In early April, Butler Capital Partners first approached Lehman Brothers about the Autodistribution opportunity. Karin Jacquemart-Pernod of Butler Capital Partners explained the initial development of the deal.

> Walter had contact with Lehman on April 1, 1999 when the Fimalac offer became public. Lehman was looking for a white knight to fend off the hostile takeover attempt of SF. Our discussion at first centered on a Butler Capital Partners buyout of the entire entity, but after two to three weeks, the discussion shifted to a buyout of Autodistribution alone. Aside from getting a brief overview of the market, the company and the opportunity, we really received little information from Lehman. Then, for three or four weeks, we heard nothing at all from them but continued working on the deal by studying AD and the related businesses from an outside perspective. Lehman's bankers were trying to get authorization to release more information, but I suppose they were really just focusing everyone's efforts on trying to sell the entire business. For a while there, we thought we were out of the running and then, all of a sudden, we were allowed access to a data room on April 23rd for our first look at AD's internal numbers. On April 29th, we had a second shot at the data room and a second meeting with Lehman, where they provided a much more thorough presentation of the management's plans for the business. From that meeting, we could see that we were in the running, but we only had a little over two weeks to finalize a bid if we decided to make one.

Based on the information gathered in the data room and from the meetings with Lehman Brothers, there were some concerns that developed due to the constraints of the deal that were put on potential investors. Aside from the constraint created by the short evaluation period, the absolute valuation seemed in line with the market for the industry. However, compared to the prices paid in Butler Capital Partners' other investments, the valuation looked rather "fully priced." As a result, the team needed to make sure they could justify the valuation as reasonable for this particular transaction. Also, there was limited information available in the data room. This was not only a concern for Butler Capital Partners' in-house investment decision, but also for the evaluation of financing by the banks. However, the information they did receive was quite useful, as the numbers had been audited only two months prior in connection with the original Autodistribution acquisition by SF. Finally, there were the potential liabilities associated with the company. While Butler Capital Partners would receive the same representations and warranties as SF and could review all SF due diligence reports available in the data room, the team had a limited ability to investigate the company's liabilities due to the lack of time and information.

In light of the numerous constraints put on Butler Capital Partners, the one area in which they felt had some flexibility was the capital structure. Since the price of the transaction was already determined, the one source of value for the fund was in structuring the deal. Butler commented on his fund's approach to structuring the transaction (see **Exhibit 15** for the proposed capital structure).

> When thinking about the deal structure, the first thing that we must be cognizant of is the nature of the business. Since AD is pursuing a build-up strategy, we want to build as much flexibility into the capital structure as possible in an effort to avoid limiting AD's ability to pursue their strategy. That being said, we want to ensure we are able to achieve an equity return that is

EXHIBIT 15
**Butler Capital
Partners' Proposed
Capital Structure (in
FF millions)**

Source: Butler Capital
Partners.

Senior debt		1,450
Subordinated debt		600
Equity		
Butler Investment Group	792	
Existing AD shareholders	559	
New shareholders (AD's affiliates)	39	
Management	15	1,405
		3,455

commensurate with the risk and our objectives in the fund. Since we cannot negotiate on price, the only way to enhance the return is through the different levels of financing—especially debt—in the capital structure. Our capital structure needed to reflect a balance between these two goals.

Another consideration was the amount of capital Butler Capital Partners could, or wanted, to put in the deal. Butler Capital Partners' covenants required that they put no more than 20% of the FF 1,100 million ($180 million) into any one deal. In order to complete the deal, the fund needed to find alternative sources of equity capital outside of the fund. One potential source was management; this provided the additional benefit of aligning incentives. For example, the equity stake the CEO had in the company could provide a significant incentive.[7] But management could only contribute so much cash toward the offering and Butler could not afford to give away free equity—for a variety of reasons. Another source was other private equity funds. But this source was also limited, as these funds faced even sterner timing issues for diligence than Butler since they would come into the deal even later than Butler Capital Partners. A final source of capital came from the existing AD shareholders who would exchange one third of their existing stock for stock in the new entity. When Butler developed the proposal for the capital structure, the composition of this group and their objectives needed to be taken into consideration. Pierre Farsy had significant influence over the group, but even he had limited persuasion power.

Even with this flexibility, the complex developments of the deal history unveiled some additional constraints. "Since we were brought into the deal at such a late point in the process," explained Pierre Costes of Butler Capital Partners, "the availability of financing had become quite tight. When the various interests put together their proposals for the transaction between SF and AD, they made sure they secured financing for the deal. In the process of doing so, they conflicted many potential sources of debt and mezzanine financing. Thus, four out of the six major French banks were effectively eliminated from providing us with financing."

One potential source of financing was from a French bank with which Butler Capital Partners had worked before—Banque Nationale de Paris (BNP). Although they had not yet guaranteed funding, BNP did give Butler Capital Partners a term sheet that outlined their indicative pricing levels and amounts (see **Exhibit 16** for the preliminary term sheet). Although the team was pleased to find a bank that was not conflicted, there were still some serious issues over the terms of the financing. Butler explained his concerns.

There were several elements to the original term sheet that concerned us. First of all, the pricing levels were quite high. The spread levels were at least 25 basis points (bps) too high across the board. Second, BNP required that most of the fees to them were due even if our bid was not selected. That is something that was simply unheard of. Third, BNP required that a formal working capital facility be put in place. AD already has a working capital facility in place, just not a formal one. By making the facility a formal arrangement, AD would incur

[7] Chavanne's last salary at SF was FF 3 million.

EXHIBIT 16
BNP Preliminary Term Sheet Proposal

Source: Butler Capital Partners; Bloomberg.

	Size (FF mn)	Coupon[a]	Term	Warrants[c]
Senior debt:				
Tranche A	1,100	E+ 2.0%	7 years	0.0%
Tranche B	350	E+ 2.5%	8 years	0.0%
Subordinated loan	600	E+ 5.5%[b]	10 years	9.5%

[a]Represents a margin over EURIBOR (E). EURIBOR was at approximately 2.6% at the time of the proposal. In addition, the rate of the 30-year French government bond was 4.88%.
[b]200 bps of the coupon represented capitalized interest. The balance was to be paid in cash.
[c]Warrants levels expressed as a percentage of fully-diluted equity.

a fee that was unnecessary. Finally, the term sheet required that all the equity would be paid up front, even though about 3% of the equity would not be purchased until 2001.[8] Not only would we rather delay that equity infusion, but we would also like to use the cash flow from operations to finance the transaction if AD is ahead of budget.

Although none of these elements pleased us, we were in somewhat of a bind. There was very little time available to us before we needed to submit our proposal, and we could not negotiate on all of these issues. Moreover, there did not seem to be many other alternatives outside of BNP available to us; because of the dynamics of the deal, only a couple of banks could possibly finance this. As a result, we had to prioritize our concerns carefully and decide which elements we could accept, which elements we could renegotiate at a later date, and which elements were deal breakers.

To Invest or Not to Invest?

Despite all of the constraints caused by the dynamics of the transaction and the deal history, Butler and his investment team believed there was an investment case for an AD buy-out and build-up. Vedrines believed that the market throughout Europe was ripe for consolidation. "I am quite sure the auto parts market will consolidate," he said.

> The driver of the industry is securing the best purchase price. Before, the buying associations similar to the original structure of AD were sufficient for that and were the only practical way of organizing the industry. Logistically, it was impossible to consolidate in an efficient manner, as the dynamics of the business did not allow for much in the way of eliminating costs. For example, take inventory control. The dynamics of the business required that a particular wholesaler needed to have a part in his hands within as little as 1/2 an hour for many parts in order to serve the needs of repair garages in his environment. Often the mechanic wants to keep the car on the lift while getting a part he had not anticipated needing; by definition, there would be a significant amount of inventory overlap as the market drove this requirement. But with the recent changes that have come forth in information technology and logistics, there are ways to fix this problem. For instance, we can now identify high-turnover parts and low-turnover parts very quickly. The former will be stored close to final customers. The latter will be stored in central storage. And we can reassign parts to different storage locations very speedily. It is these changes in information technology that will bring about the opportunity to see margin improvements through consolidation and will bring about the opportunity for a pan-European market to develop.

Butler Capital Partners also believed AD had several other attractive attributes that warranted consideration (see **Exhibit 17** for a detailed account of Butler's investment case). As his team put together a financial model for the transaction, Walter Butler was able to better quantify the investment opportunity. "We thought we had one edge over the competitors," Butler recollected. "That was a vision of the opportunities e-business could bring to the industry. These e-commerce opportunities could greatly increase the value at exit." Also, the internal growth opportunities presented by the acquisition of the independent affiliates could also help grow sales. Not only would AD get the affiliate's

[8] For tax reasons, certain shareholders could not close the transaction before 2001.

EXHIBIT 17 **Butler Capital Partners Investment Case**

Source: Butler Capital Partners.

Development opportunities

- Increase in the penetration rate of AD's central buying unit among the affiliates by setting up an efficient IT system for purchasing.
- External growth opportunities in France: integration of affiliates or acquisition of independent wholesalers.
- Many expansion opportunities in Europe provided by the fragmentation of the industry.
- Low competition on acquisitions because of the lack of players able to afford a dynamic build-up strategy
- Strong growth potential of the industrial supplies segment.
- Potential of development of fleet maintenance and agreements with insurance companies.

Profitability improvements

- Natural increase in gross margin as a result of the integration of affiliated wholesalers: for an acquisition representing 10% of revenues, the group's gross margin increases by 1 point and the operating margin by 0.2 points.
- The acquisition of independent wholesalers brings an additional gross margin of 8.8%, increases the CBU's purchasing power and therefore puts more pressure on parts manufacturers' prices.
- Potential of reduction of operating costs trough a centralization of IT systems for purchasing and sales tariffs databases, a progressive centralization of administrative tasks and a rationalization of the legal structure.

e-business

- Many e-business opportunities (mainly B2B)

Strategy

The investment purpose is to strengthen AD's platform so that it can support a build-up strategy whose first step will consist in an expansion nationwide, followed by an IPO around 2001–2002 and eventually targeted acquisitions in Europe or the purchase of a major European player.

- AD's **organic growth** will be limited to 1 to 3% per year but the group's strong market position, that should not be weakened by the evolution of the market, protects it from the risk of losing market shares.
- **Targeted acquisitions in France** should bring from FF 800 mn to FF 1 000 mn of revenues each year to the group. According to the management forecasts, AD should double its revenues within 5 years. This objective is ambitious but can be achieved with the contribution of:
  - a dynamic new CEO,
  - the appropriate financial partners (banks and shareholders) ready to support the expansion. A FF 400 mn capital expenditure line has been recently negotiated.
- **Profitability** is expected to increase thanks to the natural increase of margins subsequent to the integration of new wholesalers and to a rigorous centralized management control.

---

revenues but the CBU would stand to benefit as well; independent affiliates made 55% of parts purchases through the CBU compared to 65% for AD-owned subsidiaries. Externally, the purchase of other nonaffiliated wholesalers would continue, but the acquisition opportunities in France, both internally and externally, would really run out after two to three years. Therefore the acquisition opportunities in the fragmented European markets were very attractive. Finally, potential margin improvements were significant. For an acquisition of an affiliate representing 10% of revenues, the group's gross margin increased by 1 percentage point and the operating margin by 0.2 percent. The acquisition of independent wholesalers could bring even greater margin improvement (see **Exhibits 18 and 19** for Butler Capital Partners' assumptions for the AD business and for comparable company information).

However, there were risks involved in the deal that were significant. First, there was the fact that no one at AD had had any real international experience except for Chavanne even though most AD managers were internationally aware thanks to the ADI network. After the transaction there would be a new AD with European ambitions, but with limited

EXHIBIT 18   Butler Capital Partners' Assumptions for AD

Source: Butler Capital Partners.

	1999	2000	2001	2002	2003	2004	2005	2006
Growth								
Organic sales growth	2.0%	3.9%	3.7%	3.5%	3.0%	2.5%	2.5%	2.5%
Sales from acquisitions	378,457	582,407	676,137	762,195	778,440	871,750	701,900	706,600
Margins								
Gross profit	32.2%	33.2%	34.2%	35.2%	36.0%	36.3%	36.5%	36.6%
EBITDA	7.500%	7.750%	7.975%	8.225%	8.625%	8.700%	8.825%	8.925%
Depreciation	1.20%	1.23%	1.23%	1.23%	1.23%	1.23%	1.23%	1.23%
Financial income	3,000	2,000	2,000	2,000	2,000	2,000	2,000	2,000
Interest expense[a]								
CapEx debt	1.875%	1.875%	1.875%	1.875%	1.875%	1.875%	1.875%	1.875%
Other debts	0.750%	0.750%	0.750%	0.750%	0.750%	0.750%	0.750%	0.750%
Goodwill	16,000	20,000	25,000	29,000	34,000	40,000	45,000	50,000
Extraordinary expenses	5,000	8,000	9,000	10,000	11,000	12,000	13,000	14,000
Other Information								
Tax rate	40.0%	36.7%	36.7%	36.7%	36.7%	36.7%	36.7%	36.7%
Net working capital	55 days	55 days	55 days	55 days	55 days	55 days	55 days	55 days
CapEx	60,000	68,000	77,000	88,000	99,000	110,000	121,000	132,000
Acquisitions multiple[b]	0.275x	0.275x	0.300x	0.300x	0.350x	0.350x	0.350x	0.350x
Debt levels								
CapEx debt	50,000	250,000	400,000	400,000	400,000	400,000	400,000	0
Other	215,000	255,000	355,000	445,000	625,000	820,000	890,000	910,000

[a]Margins over Euribor (2.6% in all periods).
[b]Purchase price as a multiple of target's current year sales.

EXHIBIT 19A   Comparable Company Information

1998 Multiples	U.S. Companies							Parts Source	UK Companies			
	Genuine	AutoZone	Pep Boys	O'Reilly	Discount	Keystone	Universal	Source	Partco	Fine List	Average	AD
Revenues	0.92	1.58	0.75	1.84	1.20	0.99	0.48	0.57	0.49	0.75	1.08	0.61
EBITDA	9.25	17.77	11.89	16.49	8.01	9.97	10.59	20.82	N/A	6.96	11.61	8.96
EBIT	10.3	13.4	33.2	20.0	10.3	11.7	17.2	56.3	9.1	7.9	12.69	10.67
Net income	15.1	20.09	184.45	31.40	14.00	19.14	N/A	−28.42	11.6	7.60	18.44	21.63

Other Information	U.S. Companies							Parts Source	UK Companies			
	Genuine	AutoZone	Pep Boys	O'Reilly	Discount	Keystone	Universal	Source	Partco	Fine List	Average	AD
Revenues (US$ mn)	6,614.00	3,242.90	2,389.70	616.30	447.50	263.80	63.90	46.10	696.96	620.96		884.40
Revenue CAGR	7.5%	20.3%	14.5%	54.2%	20.6%	51.3%	0.6%	31.2%	46.0%	19.5%	15.5%	8.0%
Gross margin	30.3%	41.7%	23.8%	41.8%	34.4%	43.2%	20.5%	36.5%		89.7%	15.5%	8.0%
EBITDA/margin	10.0%	8.9%	6.3%	11.2%	15.0%	10.0%	4.6%	2.8%		10.8%	9.3%	6.8%
EBIT/margin	8.9%	11.8%	2.3%	9.2%	11.6%	8.5%	2.8%	1.0%	5.3%	9.5%	8.5%	5.8%
Stocks	91.6 days	108.8 days						63.6 days	118.3 days		53.3 days	
Net debt	705	538	877	169	156−10	21	17	55	227		30	
Equity market value	5,385	4,578	917	967	381272	10	10	286	187		NA	
Working capital (% sales)	26.9%	7.7%						7.6%	19.5%		11.2%	
Equity betas	0.69	1.05	0.68	0.78	0.62	0.66	1.00	−0.50	0.50		0.73	

Source: Butler Capital Partners; Bloomberg.

EXHIBIT 19B   Comparable Transactions—The Fast-Fit Sector

Source: Butler Capital Partners.

Target	Target Activity	Date	Bidder (Country)	Bid Value for 100% (£m)	Net Debt/(cash) (£m)	Enterprise Value (EV) (£m)	Multiples (except cost/outlet)						
							EV/Sales	EV/EBITDA	EV/EBIT	EBT	PER	Cost/Outlet (£000)	Net Asset
Kwik-Fit Holdings	Operation of tyre, exhaust, and automotive repair centres	Apr-99	Ford	1008.0	91.6	1099.6	2.13x	15.5x	18.9x	18.2x	26.9x	687	5.1x
International Tyre Brands	Operation of tyre centres in the UK	Aug-98	Just Tyres Holding	11.0	3.5	14.5	0.45x	10.1x	13.5x	14.8x	18.6x	n/a	4.0x
Universal Tyres & Spares	Tyre wholesalers, retailers and distributors	Jan-98	Montinex	0.5	−0.6	−0.1	neg.	neg.	neg.	3.4x	4.4x	neg.	0.6x
A5 Tyre & Exhaust	Supply and fitting of tyres, exhaust systems and batteries, and the undertaking of MOT testing	Dec-97	Montinex	1.1	0.1	1.2	n/a	n/a	n/a	n/a	n/a	197	2.7x
Haslemere Tyre & Battery	Tyre and battery centre	Dec-97	Montinex	0.5	n/a	0.5	n/a	n/a	n/a	n/a	n/a	500	n/a
Humphries Tyre & Exhaust	Fitting of exhaust systems and tryes	Feb-97	Kwik Fit	5.2	0.6	5.8	1.61x	44.2x	50.6x	9.1x	30.9x	n/a	3.3x
Northway/Imaco	Retail supply of tyres and other spare parts	Jan-97	Montinex	3.9	−0.5	3.4	0.28x	3.6x	4.1x	4.9x	7.6x	572	1.9x
Super Fit Exhaust	Fitting of exhausts	Dec-96	Montinex	1.1	0.1	1.2	0.78x	1.3x	18.0x	22.0x	28.9x	248	18.4x
Albany Tyre & Exhaust	Tyre and exhaust centres	Oct-96	Montinex	1.0	n/a	1.0	n/a	n/a	n/a	n/a	n/a	200	n/a
Ebley/Autospec/Manor Tyre	Automotive fitters	Apr-96	Kwik Fit	12.3	n/a	12.3	0.62x	n/a	n/a	10.3x	15.8x	273	3.0x
Tyre Sales (Birmingham)	Wholesale and retail of tyres and exhausts	Dec-95	Kwik Fit	12.0	2.8	14.8	0.70x	55.4x	88.6x	60.0x	92.3x	344	neg.
Charlie Brown Autocentres	Autocentre stores	Apr-95	Montinex	19.0	3.4	22.4	0.47x	89.1x	neg.	neg.	neg.	298	neg.
Malvern Tyres	Sale of tyres and other related products	Mar-95	Montinex	1.5	−0.2	1.3	n/a	n/a	n/a	n/a	n/a	436	2.1x
Superdrive Motoring Centres	Operator of retail outlets for the supply and fitting of motor vehicle parts	Oct-94	Kwik Fit	21.5	13.0	34.5	0.83x	neg.	neg.	neg.	neg.	766	n/a
Exhaust Despatch	Distribution of motor parts	Oct-94	Montinex	0.5	−0.1	0.4	0.50x	3.8x	4.2x	5.7x	8.1x	138	n/a
Chessington Tyres	Operator of tyre centres	Jul-94	MBI (Montinex)	7.5	1.7	9.2	0.45x	10.3x	12.4x	11.3x	17.1x	249	1.9x
						Mean	0.80x	25.9x	26.3x	16.0x	25.1x	378	4.0x
						Median	0.62x	10.3x	15.8x	10.8x	17.9x	298	2.7x

EXHIBIT 19c Comparable Transactions—Autoparts Distribution/Retail Sector

Source: Butler Capital Partners.

| Target | Target Activity | Date | Bidder (Country) | Bid Value for 100% (£m) | Net Debt/(cash) (£m) | Enterprise Value (EV) (£m) | Multiples (except cost/outlet) | | | | | | |
							EV/Sales	EV/EBITDA	EV/EBIT	EBT	PER	Cost/Outlet (£000)	Net Asset
Partco Group	Distribution of components to the automotive after-market in the UK and western Europe	Apr-99	UGC Ltd	178.9	34.2	213.1	0.49x	7.3x	9.2x	9.9x	14.9x	426	n/a
Dixons Motors (parts distribution business)	Distribution of automotive parts	Nov-98	Speedpart	6.5	3.0	9.5	0.61x	n/a	n/a	n/a	8.1x	n/a	5.4x
Port Brake Services	Motor factors—commercial vehicle servicing, repairs, parts and accessories	Jul-98	Partco Group	2.4	0.4	2.7	0.58x	9.4x	15.8x	18.1x	23.9x	300	4.6x
Bancrofts	Distributor of automotive paints and associated products	May-98	Finelist Group	14.5	1.5	16.0	0.76x	13.8x	17.8x	16.1x	n/a	800	3.9x
SVG	Supplier of body panels, lamps and crash repair components to the automotive after-market	May-98	Partco Group	4.5	5.3	9.8	0.47x	neg.	neg.	neg.	neg.	3,267	1.3x
Emergency Spares	Retailer of motor vehicle parts	Jan-98	Finelist Group	3.1	0.5	3.6	n/a	5.5x	5.7x	4.9x	7.2x	241	2.9x
Wheels Motor Factors	Supplier of automotive parts	Nov-97	Finelist Group	6.8	n/a	6.8	0.97x	n/a	n/a	n/a	9.7x	567	n/a
Regor	Cash and carry distributor of automotive parts	May-97	Finelist Group	3.0	1.68	4.7	n/a	22.9x	52.2x	neg.	neg.	n/a	1.8x

Target	Target Activity	Date	Bidder (Country)	Bid Value for 100% (£m)	Net Debt/(cash) (£m)	Enterprise Value (EV) (£m)	EV/ Sales	EV/ EBITDA	EV/ EBIT	EBT	PER	Cost/ Outlet (£000)	Net Asset
Maccess Group	Distributor of motor vehicle components and spare parts	Apr-97	Finelist Group	23.0	9.60	32.6	0.55x	14.8x	16.3x	11.5x	n/a	n/a	10.8x
First Line	Wholesale packaging and distribution of automotive parts	Feb-97	Finelist Group	7.2	n/a	7.2	n/a	n/a	n/a	n/a	n/a	n/a	6.5x
Brown Brothers	UK warehouse distribution operations	Feb-97	Partco Group	103.0	n/a	103.0	0.46x	4.2x	4.6x	4.6x	6.3x	n/a	2.5x
Ferraris Piston Services	Distributor of automotive parts	Jan-97	Finelist Group	52.0	9.00	61.0	1.30x	14.1x	17.0x	14.5x	14.6x	n/a	7.4x
Motor World Group	Retail of auto parts, consumables and ancillary products to the DIY motor sector	Jul-96	Finelist Group	48.1	3.2	51.3	0.93x	8.2x	10.9x	12.4x	16.1x	155	2.8x
Gordon Plunkett	Distribution of vehicle parts and factoring	Jul-96	Dixon Motors	6.0	1.4	7.4	0.49x	n/a	n/a	8.2x	n/a	n/a	1.7x
						Mean	0.69x	11.1x	16.6x	11.1x	12.6x	822	4.3x
						Median	0.58x	9.4	15.8x	11.5x	12.1x	426	3.4x

159

experience in that market aside from this experience with ADI. This brought about the more important concern: execution risk. There was definitely an opportunity in AD, but that was because the firm lacked structure. It was a loosely organized, entrepreneurial business run by men and women who were entrepreneurs. This entrepreneurial spirit had been a key to the success of the enterprise, but there was a dire need to centralize control for the LBO to be viable and to produce the 30% IRR Butler's fund would require. The key to success was to change the culture of the company from one of an association to one of a corporation without destroying the organization in the process.

Chavanne shared Butler's concerns on the cultural challenges facing AD going forward.

> The biggest surprise I had when acquiring AD was how old the management was. Pierre was a dynamic personality in the organization, but he was in his 70s. It became clear that this was really the end of the founder generation. While the founders might be considered irreplaceable, there was a definite need to reinforce each level of the organization with new blood without losing the spirit of the company. The greatness of the organization was that it was an open-minded organization; an organization of free men who felt free to put forth new ideas and to level criticism. But it was tough to run. The key would be to convince people to decide to change and to implement those changes. It would be a delicate and slow process.

Walter Butler was also concerned about the due-diligence process. A problem was that his firm was somewhat late in the game. There had been several funds that had more time to perform due diligence on the company and, more importantly, to allow AD and the fund to get comfortable with each other on a personal level. In fact, Butler was aware of one group, led by BC Partners (of the ING Barings Group), which had been in the process from the very start and had produced a much more aggressive proposal. At the same time, BC Partners' build-up strategy was more limited than the one proposed by Butler's team. Butler knew that BC Partners was a serious contender.

As Walter Butler walked out of his beautiful "art nouveau" office building along the River Seine, he looked up at the Eiffel Tower in the distance rising above the cafes that lined the street in front of him. With cars full of AD parts whizzing past him, he knew Autodistribution could have the potential to become a power in the French and European markets. At the same time, he thought that an investment of this scale could represent a considerable amount of risk for his new fund, even though the business was counter-cyclical. Moreover, the history of the deal and the constraints of the proposal had only increased the potential risks involved in the transaction. Finally, while Chavanne had indicated a strong interest in the CEO position, he had not yet signed on; the question about his compensation was still an open one. With the sun setting in the distance, he knew that time was running out on his decision.

Case 9

Absolute Sensors

As he walked along the path running between the main building of The Generics Group (Generics) and the old mill building that housed its new spin-off, Absolute Sensors Limited (ASL), Ian Collins allowed himself a moment to enjoy the scenery. Generics had chosen a lush and remote section of Cambridge, England, for its head office; and as managing director of ASL, Collins was often too busy to appreciate it fully. It was September 10, 1998, and the weather was still mild; Collins felt that over the last few months he might have been well-advised to take more time to reflect rather than simply working on current projects.

Since joining Generics in 1990, Collins, 49, had come to believe that some of the technologies the company developed could best be exploited by spinning them off into new ventures, rather than using them primarily to generate consulting work. Originally, he had tried to encourage others to pursue such opportunities, but eventually he decided to take the initiative himself. "I often see something I think someone ought to do," he remarked. "Some of the big steps I've taken in my life have come from seeing something I wanted done and realizing no one else was going to do it."

Over the past year and a half, Collins had done just that. Convinced that a new sensor technology Generics had developed, dubbed Spiral, could form the basis for a new company, he and two colleagues had gradually convinced Generics' top management and won their parent company's support. Now he had the chance to prove his case.

Collins was pleased with the progress he and his team had made so far. Two substantial license deals had demonstrated some of Spiral's potential, ASL had been formally incorporated and provided with seed capital, and the three men had identified new markets they wished to attack. While progress had not always been rapid, it had been steady, and so far there had been no major stumbles along the way.

Collins knew, however, that many of the greatest challenges were yet to come. ASL's next round of financing would probably require outside investors. This meant the young firm had to demonstrate the kind of progress and potential such an investor might require.

Charles M. Williams Fellow Chad Ellis, MBA '98, prepared this case under the supervision of Professor Walter Kuemmerle. HBS cases are developed solely as the basis for class discussion. Cases are not intended to serve as endorsements, sources of primary data, or illustrations of effective or ineffective management.

Collins and his colleagues would also have to consider what benefits and limitations each type of investor might entail.

On an operational level, ASL had to transform itself from a technology-based service company into a provider of specific applications. None of ASL's six current employees had substantial experience in manufacturing, and the decision had not yet been taken as to whether ASL would attempt to develop such capabilities or concentrate on product development while outsourcing production. Whichever path he and his colleagues took, Collins knew the challenges and competition they faced would be different from those they encountered while working for Generics.

In many ways, being a consultant had been great. However, Collins knew that at this stage in his career ASL was a better fit. Consulting meant intellectually challenging work and a reasonably high and steady stream of income. Entrepreneurship at ASL meant freedom, the chance to create something truly lasting, along with both greater risk and potential return should he succeed.

Background—The Generics Group

Founded in 1986, Generics had a diverse range of interests, all related to the development and use of innovative technology. Most of the group's £19.4 million (£1=$1.65) in revenues came from its consulting business, known as Scientific Generics (SG). SG offered a range of services, from developing new technologies on a turnkey basis, to advising clients on developing their own research and development teams. SG had a staff of over 200, and provided services in the United Kingdom, on Continental Europe and in the United States. Roughly one-fourth of SG's staff filled some administrative role. Of the remainder, 60% were practicing scientists or engineers and roughly half had advanced degrees, most commonly a Ph.D. or MBA. (See **Exhibit 1** for the financial statements of the Generics Group.)

SG also generated revenue by licensing technologies that it had developed. When a client hired SG to develop a new technology for a specific application, the contract typically assigned SG all rights relating to the technology in other applications. SG was then free to think of other possible uses for the technology and seek licensing arrangements with companies that could exploit it.

More typically, however, SG used its proprietary technologies to help generate new consulting work. A senior consultant explained, "When you are a consultant you are constantly trying to convince potential clients that they want to talk to you. Having a new technology that you can apply to a client's business will almost always get you that first meeting with the CEO or Vice President. It gives you the leverage you need to sell yourself."

Generics Asset Management (GAM), a small fund management subsidiary, attempted to exploit the group's superior understanding of nascent technologies by investing in early-stage technology companies which Generics felt had strong prospects. GAM had also provided seed financing to start-up ventures on occasion.

Generics prided itself on nurturing an atmosphere of innovation and individual initiative. Employee's contributions to the Group were evaluated across a broad range of criteria and, provided general profitability targets were met, group leaders had great flexibility in how they built their business. Generics was publicly committed to enabling its employees to pursue a wide range of paths towards value creation.

EXHIBIT 1
Generics Group
Consolidated
Financial Statements

Source: The Generics Group
Annual Report.

Profit and Loss Account (For year ended December 31, 1997)		
	1997	1996
	£000	£000
Turnover	14,949	13,329
Operating expenses	(13,743)	(12,131)
Gross profit	1,186	1,198
Share of associates' operating loss	(440)	—
Operating profit	746	1,198
Profit on disposal of fixed asset investments	1,028	217
Investment income	130	104
Amounts written off investments	(125)	—
Interest payable and similar charges	(49)	(99)
Profit on ordinary activities before taxation	1,730	1,050
Tax on profit on ordinary activities	(554)	(370)
Profit on ordinary activities after taxation	1,176	1,050
Minority interest	29	37
Profit for the fiscal year	1,205	1,087
Dividends paid and proposed		
Additional final dividend for 195 following conversion of options	—	(6)
Interim paid October 31, 1997 of 16p (1996–14p) per share	(124)	(109)
Final proposed of 35p (1996–31p) per share	(272)	(241)
Retained profit for the year	809	731
Earnings per ordinary share (p/share)	154.9	142.4

Development of Spiral

In 1994, SG was hired by an elevator manufacturing company to design and develop a location sensor. Computers controlling modern elevators needed accurate location data in order to ensure that the elevators stopped in a position level with the floor. The conditions a location sensor for an elevator had to endure, however, were testing. The sensor had to be resistant to dirt, temperature changes and other environmental factors associated with being on the outside of a working elevator. It also had to be non-contacting, as a sensor that relied on contact with the elevator shaft was almost certain to develop serious problems due to wear. SG met this challenge by developing the Spiral sensor.

Spiral was a very innovative positioning technology. It used a fixed sensor track, attached to processing electronics, and a moving unit comprising a resonant coil and capacitor. The track extended over the range of possible locations, while the unit was attached to the object whose location needed to be determined. The system then operated using magnetic induction. The processing electronics generated a current which in turn generated an alternating magnetic field, causing the resonant coil in the unit to resonate. The resonant field, in turn, generated AC voltages which would be passed back to the processing electronics. A radiometric, phasor-based algorithm then determined the unit's position. (See **Exhibit 2** for a descriptive article on Spiral.)

EXHIBIT 1
(Continued)
**Generics Group
Consolidated
Financial Statements**

Balance Sheet (As at December 31, 1997)		
	1997 £000	1996 £000
Fixed assets		
Tangible assets	3,385	3,519
Investments	—	198
	3,385	3,717
Current assets		
Debtors due within one year	3,898	3,853
due after one year	68	—
Investments	1,055	—
Cash at bank and in hand	2,421	2,361
	7,442	6,214
Creditors: amount falling due within one year	(5,093)	(4,182)
Net current assets	2,349	2,032
Total assets less current liabilities	5,734	5,749
Creditors: amounts falling due after more than one year	—	(752)
Provisions for liabilities and charges	(568)	(648)
Net assets	5,166	4,349
Capital and reserves		
Called-up share capital	207	195
Share premium account	3,279	3,266
Profit and loss account	1,642	836
Shareholders' fund—all equity	5,128	4,297
Minority interests	38	52
Total capital employed	5,166	4,349

Spiral combined a number of attractive features. In addition to being non-contact and environmentally robust, as needed for the elevator application, it offered high precision, low cost and could be applied to both 2-dimensional and 3-dimensional measurement. With superior characteristics in some areas and a competitive manufacturing cost, it seemed clear that the technology could find uses in other applications. Collins explained:

> The things customers will value varies by application. In some applications, Spiral is up to 50% cheaper than rival technologies. For customers who need a sensor that can work under difficult conditions, Spiral is ideal; you can misalign components and put it in a greasy, noisy, vibrating environment and it will still work. Optical technologies [one of Spiral's main rivals] are fine as long as everything is clean and dry. Spiral also offers a comfort factor to companies that are reluctant to adopt new technologies. The manufacturing risk is low because Spiral is a new use of mature circuit-board technology.

The Vision: From Technology to Start-up

Collins, in whose group at SG Spiral had been developed, felt that Spiral offered sufficient promise to serve as an example of how SG could capture more of the value in its technologies through spin-offs than by consulting and licensing alone. He recalled:

> I wanted to show Generics that creating a new company is sometimes the right way for us to exploit new technology. We have tended to use new technologies to win consulting contracts or to get some license fees, but that doesn't capture as much of the value as if we develop

EXHIBIT 1
(Continued)
Generics Group
Consolidated
Financial Statements

Cash Flow Statement (For the year ended December 31, 1997)		
	1997	1996
	£000	£000
Cash flow from operating activities	1,662	913
Returns on investments and servicing of finance		
Interest received	126	103
Interest paid	(49)	(94)
Dividend received	2	—
	79	9
Taxation		
UK corporate tax (paid)/received	(308)	2
Capital expenditure and financial investment		
Purchase of tangible fixed assets	(532)	(611)
Purchase of investments	(1,255)	(4)
Sale of fixed asset investment	1,587	272
	(200)	(343)
Equity dividends paid	(372)	(218)
Net cash inflow before financing	861	363
Management of liquid resources	(1,249)	(282)
Financing		
Issue of share capital	25	169
Repayments of loans	(826)	(574)
Issue of shares of subsidiary undertakings to minority interests	—	272
	(801)	(133)
Decrease in cash in the period	(1,189)	(52)

applications and products ourselves. That was my main motivation for doing this [pushing for the creation of ASL]. I would certainly like to make some money from it, but I'm not concerned with becoming hugely rich.

Technically, SG had supported perhaps a dozen technology-based spin-offs, but what Collins was proposing was still quite new. Previous spin-offs had been run more like separate departments within SG, with managers still employed by SG and rewarded by conventional salary and incentive schemes. SG retained full ownership of both the technology and the new company, even if it was legally incorporated. Collins was pushing for a "true" spin-off, with managers employed by the venture itself and with a direct equity stake.

As an elder statesman at Generics, Collins was able to bring considerable internal credibility to bear on building his case for a new venture. He explained:

The people at Generics knew that I believed this was the right way for the firm to go, that I wasn't just trying to grab a bigger piece for myself. That's important, since Generics really believes in giving people the chance to try things they think will work, but is less interested in supporting people who just want to get rich for themselves. Since we're trying to change the part of the Generics culture that prefers exploiting technology through consulting, it's important that we are consistent with the rest of the culture—collaborative, cooperative and working towards what is best for the Group.

This could dramatically change the way Generics exploits new technologies, because while the risk is certainly higher we have the potential to capture far more of the value than if

EXHIBIT 2 **Article on Spiral**

Source: Paul Stevenson, *BTR Technology Review,* May 1998.

BTR's Sensor Technology Acquisition

In response to an ever growing sensor market, Paul Stevenson reveals why BTR has acquired a revolutionary, new, noncontact position sensing technology called SPIRAL.

FASCO Controls Corporation is a subsidiary of BTR Sensor Systems and Paul Stevenson is program manager for SPIRAL technology.

BTR Sensor Systems has obtained an exclusive global license in the automotive industry (patents pending worldwide) for SPIRAL, a noncontact, position sensing technology with significant advantages over other technologies. BTR Sensor Systems is developing applications for this market, with a team of engineers at FASCO Controls Corporation in Shelby leading the development effort.

An aerospace license has also been acquired and, in order to utilize this, FASCO has teamed up with Electro Corp., Sarasota, in a joint BTR Sensor Systems development.

Competitive Advantages

SPIRAL is a noncontact linear and rotary position sensor technology that offers definite competitive advantages to auto makers with benefits such as:

- Large operating air gap capabilities
- Absolute position measurement at "key on"
- Virtually nonexistent thermal draft
- Robust against alignment tolerances for packaging and mounting
- Environmentally robust
- A variety of output formats

Leapfrog Technology

Car manufacturers are constantly faced with challenges from government and consumers to produce vehicles at lower cost with reduced emissions, increased fuel economy, extended vehicle life and enhanced features. In order to meet these challenges, the manufacturers rely on the use of electronic systems to continuously adjust vehicle functions and optimize performance.

These electronic systems rely on real time, accurate feedback from the vehicle for performance and safety. This feedback information is provided by the use of sensors in the vehicle. Due to the increasing variety of electrical systems, the number of sensors per vehicle is expected to be 24 or more in 1999.

For years, linear and rotary position sensors have been dominated by technologies such as resistive potentiometers (contact), Hall effect devices (active noncontact) and VR (Variable Reluctance) devices (nonactive, noncontact) with smaller numbers of MR (Magnetoresistive), GMR (Giant Magnetoresistive Ratio) and optical sensors (noncontact devices).

Car makers have had to work within the limitations of the technologies available to them for position sensing. Until now, "leapfrog" technologies have failed to emerge and prove themselves capable in the market, leaving systems designers with no new capabilities to meet the ever increasing demands placed upon them. SPIRAL is that "leapfrog" technology.

How it Works

SPIRAL consists of a sensing track and a small, lightweight, passive target. The name SPIRAL comes from the appearance of the traces on the sensor board. They are overlapping sine waves that "spiral" across a printed circuit board. The target is a stand alone device that does not require leads or bearing surfaces. The sensor track determines the position of the target in a linear or rotary system using phase based processing methods with an accuracy and resolution that exceeds other technologies.

An electromagnetic field is generated on an excitation trace on the sensor track board. This electromagnetic field is coupled to the resonator which is mounted to a moving device. The resonator then creates its own electromagnetic field, reflecting the coupled energy onto the sensor traces on the sensor track board. This reflected energy creates varying voltage waveforms on the sensor traces that can be processed and interpreted into a precise position measurement.

(continued)

EXHIBIT 2   (Continued)

Operating Air Gap Capabilities For Rotary Sensors

This technology can be used with much larger air gaps than are possible with Hall or VR devices and this gives it a distinct competitive advantage. The sensor is robust to air gap variations during position measurement, which results in less position error. The large air gap capability allows the components to be individually encapsulated and mounted on a vehicle as two separate components without bearing surfaces, which results in a long life, highly reliable product.

Contacting devices such as potentiometers rely on surface contact between a set of contacts and a resistive film material for operation. This surface contact creates wear on the device, shortening its operating life. Along with the contacting surfaces, bearing surfaces are also required to maintain tight tolerances between the contacts and the resistive film for a constant contact pressure. These bearing surfaces are also a source of wear in the device which results in shorter life. Both of these wear sources are eliminated with SPIRAL technology.

The development team at Fasco is working to bring this technology into the automotive market. SPIRAL technology can be used in a range of applications in the existing automotive speed/position sensor market which exceeds $400 million. Fasco has chosen to target applications where characteristics such as high accuracy and resolution, absolute position, long life and environmental robustness add value to vehicle systems.

The primary targeted applications include:

• Camshaft/crankshaft position sensing
• Steering position sensing
• Throttle position sensing
• Suspension height sensing
• Pedal position sensing
• Temperature control vent cover position

Product Development

Rotary and linear prototype samples have been produced and limited testing has been performed, confirming initial development data. Improvements have been made through the use of computer modeling, both for the electromagnetic fields and the processing electronics. The electronics for the low speed application devices have been optimized and tested using individual components, and development for the ASIC (Application Specific Integrated Circuit) chip has begun. The ASIC chip offers a low cost packaging solution to a complex electronic circuit. High speed devices (cam/crank sensors) have been modeled and prototypes were due to be ready for testing at the end of April 1998.

With an understanding of lead time testing requirements in the automotive industry, active production programs have targeted vehicle model year 2002 for chosen applications, which means that they must be production-ready in the fourth quarter of 2000. Product demonstrations have been performed for customers, and enthusiastic feedback was unanimous. Familiar with the current technologies, customers are excited about the benefits that SPIRAL has to offer.

Patent applications have been submitted worldwide. The patents have been granted in Australia and should be granted in Europe by May. The remaining applications are expected to be granted during the first half of this year.

Adding Value

BTR Sensor Systems recognized the value of this technology immediately. Hall effect devices have historically been the most chosen method for active position sensing in the automotive market, and SPIRAL can compete against these devices, giving more value and functionality at the same cost.

Based on those aspects in the table below, it is believed SPIRAL can offer innovative solutions to sensing applications with improved component features, as well as adding overall system value to customers.

Hall Effect Devices	Spiral Devices
Require costly targets	Low-cost, lightweight printed circuit board arrangement
Required fixed magnets	No fixed magnets required
No absolute position data	Provide absolute position information
Square wave pulsed output	Variety of outputs (analog, PWM, digital)
Operating air gaps approx. 2mm	Operating air gaps tested beyond 7mm
Susceptible to thermal drift	Extremely low thermal drift

we limited ourselves to consulting or licensing. As for myself, if this works I might try to do it again with another Generics technology or I might decide that I'd had enough and go back to running my own division.

Assembling the Team

Although Collins had a picture of where he wanted to take Spiral and had a strong position within SG against which to lever his ambitions, he knew that he would need to form a strong core team in order to put the project on the best path. Fortunately, two complementary partners were already present in SG.

David Ely, 27, had joined SG in 1993, immediately after earning an undergraduate degree in engineering from Cambridge University. Ely and Andrew Dames (who had since left SG) were the main inventors of Spiral, and Ely was a specialist in resonance systems and position sensors. Ely brought to the table his expertise in the Spiral technology and his understanding of how it could be applied to new fields and markets, as well as a youthful hunger to turn his product into a big success.

Like Collins, Ely felt that SG should try to capture more of the value represented by its technologies. "Consulting is an incredibly inefficient way of exploiting technology," he argued. "You never get more than a fraction of what it's worth." Ely also had a strong entrepreneurial bent and wanted to capture some of the value of his work himself. "I enjoy developing new products," he explained, "but I don't want to do it without a stake in the outcome."

Malcom Burwell, 40, was an experienced technology consultant. Born in Philadelphia, he had spent half of his life in the United States and half in the United Kingdom. He was therefore comfortable with working in either country over the medium term, although for personal reasons he could not live outside the United States for long. "My in-laws are in their seventies," he explained. "If I tell them I'm going to take my wife to live overseas permanently, they'll have my guts for garters."

Burwell joined SG in 1996, but with the express intention of finding an opportunity like Spiral:

> I'd done hands-on technology consulting for over 15 years. Typically I was managing teams of 20–30 people, working on the hardest problems and the most ridiculous schedules. It's not a bad life, but eventually I wanted to get out of hourly work and do something where I had an equity stake in what I was doing.

Burwell had approached SG with a novel approach. He would sell SG's consulting services in the U.S., but with the understanding that he would be putting some of his energies into figuring out how SG could make money outside of consulting. Ultimately, he told SG, he hoped to use the consulting business as a stepping stone for creating his own company. SG agreed. When Collins sought to develop Spiral beyond consulting, Burwell joined on, ultimately becoming ASL's marketing director. (See **Exhibit 3** for resumes of ASL's founding management.)

Early Development—Winning the Right to Play

The team's first challenge was to create a belief within SG that Spiral could generate substantial earnings for SG through methods other than using it to win consulting contracts. Only then could they convince SG to create a new company dedicated to exploiting Spiral.

Collins, Ely and Burwell began working to find an application and a partner that would generate substantial licensing revenues. The next few months were spent building demonstration units, brainstorming possible applications and meeting with prospective licensees to show what Spiral was capable of. Even at this stage, however, there were some internal challenges to overcome. Collins explained:

EXHIBIT 3 **Absolute Sensors Limited Management Resumes**

Source: Absolute Sensors Limited.

Ian Collins, Managing Director

Ian Collins is a Chartered Engineer with 30 years experience in the design, development and evaluation of a wide range of products.

He graduated in Engineering with First Class Honors from the University of Cambridge in 1971 and was awarded an MBA from City University in 1976. His initial engineering training and development was when working for the UK Ministry of Defense in a variety of roles. He then spent five years as a senior consultant at PA Technology, managing the design and development of a diverse range of products, ranging from a modular medical endoscope to a sophisticated piece of food manufacturing equipment.

Ian then spent four years as Head of Laboratories for Consumers' Association. His team of 65 was responsible for the testing and evaluation of all types of consumer products, from cookers to computers to cars. During his time at CA, Ian managed the process of obtaining NAMAS quality approval (equivalent to ISO 9000), introduced fast-track testing processes and established the feasibility and desirability of relocating the laboratory.

In 1990 Ian joined Scientific Generics, initially as a senior consultant, where his first project was to lead the design and introduction to manufacture (in China) of the first Dymo electronic label makers. Ian has taken on a wide range of management responsibilities within SG: he managed the Engineering Division and increased its size by 50% whilst maintaining profitability; he planned and managed the move of SG to Harston Mill; and is currently operations director.

Ian has been involved with SPIRAL technology since the beginning. He was responsible for planning and implementing the exploitation route that led to the sale of the SPIRAL automotive license to BTR. This was the first time that SG had successfully exploited technology through a pure licensing route and has stimulated a radical change in SG's approach to technology exploitation.

Malcolm Burwell, Commercial Director

Malcolm Burwell graduated in 1979 from the University of Cambridge with a degree in Electromechanical Systems Engineering. After a six-year apprenticeship in the textile industry, Malcolm then joined a leading UK-based engineering consulting firm. Initially in the UK, Malcolm spent seven years on the design and implementation of novel manufacturing systems, for a diverse range of products such as chocolate bars, dry batteries and nuclear fuel.

On moving to the United States, Malcolm took responsibility for managing major multi-million dollar product development programs: examples include surgical staples, blood-diagnostic equipment and a low cost photocopier.

Malcolm joined Scientific Generics in 1995. As director of U.S. Ventures, Malcolm has played a major role in developing SG's business in the United States. In particular, Malcolm has been responsible for the marketing of SPIRAL to U.S. companies, and carried out the commercial negotiations that led to both the BTR and Interval license deals.

David Ely, Technical Director

After a year with Thorn EMI Defense Systems, where he developed designs for a number of elements of a specialized radio frequency system, David studied for a degree in Engineering at the University of Cambridge.

After graduation in 1993, David joined the Sensors group in Scientific Generics. One of his responsibilities was to lead a team of ten engineers and software designers in a project to design a safety critical position sensing module for a transport application, based on novel technology.

His particular skill is to take new ideas and develop them rapidly into working systems that are optimized for real applications. Examples of such developments include fluid flow sensors, precision position transducers, retail security systems and anti-counterfeiting devices.

David invented SPIRAL technology in 1994. Since then, he has been at the center of SPIRAL development and has taken his, and other inventions, from initial concept to technology prove out and product development.

Our goal was to get a large up front payment and substantial fees in exchange for an exclusive contract [for a particular application]. That meant finding the right partner. In order for us not to have legal or even perceived obligations [towards potential licensors] it was important that our demonstrations not cost anything to the prospective licensors. Even though the Generics Board understood this, it went against the consulting grain. From time to time, someone would ask something like, "Why not just charge them something small, like $5,000?"

Although SG's culture was heavily oriented towards consulting, it also had a strong commitment to individual initiative, which the company felt was essential to maintaining a successful track record of innovation. While questions were sometimes raised, the Spiral team generally found it easy to move forward within SG. Collins recalled:

I found the money [for the early development] within my own division, because we were profitable enough. We were more than able to hit our [profitability] targets and do this, so nobody bothered us. Actually, I was surprised at how few questions we had on areas such as manufacturing. This is probably the biggest step we're taking away from the normal Generics path and it's something I would have expected to have been more of an issue. It's sort of the dog that didn't bark, because we're all very aware of it but haven't heard much about it from the Group.

Burwell added, "We did a lot of this by cajoling, bootstrapping, talking to people on the side. Generics is unusual because it really values this kind of behavior . . . the environment is deliberately very unstructured."

The team's efforts paid off in June 1997, when they signed a contract with Fasco Controls, a North Carolina subsidiary of BTR, a leading UK automotive components company. BTR saw applications for Spiral in a number of automotive functions, such as throttle position sensing, engine timing and fuel performance and emissions control, and expected to be able to introduce Spiral in U.S. cars by 2002. In exchange for an exclusive license for the use of Spiral in the automotive segment, SG won an up-front payment and license fees[1] of more than $2 million combined.

In July 1998, the Spiral team signed another deal with a toy company (Toyco[2]) that wanted to use Spiral to provide location data for computer-based games. Spiral would be used to locate playing pieces on the board and inform the computer opponent. While other technologies had been used for similar games, Spiral was substantially (30%) cheaper and offered superior functionality. Toyco received an exclusive license for the use of Spiral in gaming applications, in exchange for license fees comparable to those in the BTR deal.

These licensing deals demonstrated the potential for SG to capture more of the value created by Spiral than it would through consulting alone. Burwell explained, "It cost us around $200,000 [in marketing, travel and demonstrations] to win our first contract, so let's say the profit [in NPV terms] is around $800,000. The consulting business has profit margins of roughly 10%. That means this deal is equivalent [in profit terms] to an $8 million consulting job." By contrast, Spiral had helped to generate roughly $1.6 million in consulting fees for SG in the four years since its development.

A New Venture Is Born

With the BTR deal complete and the Toyco deal nearly so, the Spiral team was able to convince the Generics Board of Directors that a new company should be formed to pursue non-consulting opportunities for Spiral. On July 1, 1998, Absolute Sensors Limited was formally incorporated. Collins, Burwell and Ely were respectively named managing,

[1] The terms of the deal included royalties, technology transfer payments and milestone fees in addition to the up-front payment.

[2] For confidentiality reasons, Toyco's name has been disguised.

commercial and technical directors of the new company, and the intellectual property (IP) rights associated with Spiral were transferred from Generics into ASL.

As of July 1, however, ASL had no funding and its shares were held entirely by Generics. Internal negotiations continued over exactly how the company would be financed and how its managers would be rewarded if they were successful. While ASL was not the first new company Generics had supported or invested in, there was a great deal of uncertainty as to how much equity should be given to the Spiral team. Collins explained:

> Generics already has a system in place for rewarding employees who develop new technologies that lead to significant revenues. So, from their perspective, Spiral is theirs and we're all their employees. They're great in terms of giving us flexibility and encouraging us to try new things, but they don't have the American mindset that says, "If we want to grow the pie as much as possible, we have to give away some of it."

Structuring management compensation for the venture was complicated further by British tax law on options. Burwell explained:

> Options motivation doesn't work very well in the English tax system. In England, when an executive exercises an option, he or she is immediately liable for income tax on the gain. In the States, you are only taxed when the shares themselves are sold, and on a [lower] capital gains basis. This means in England you get a lower payoff and often have to sell the shares right away in order to meet the tax bill.

Finally, SG's policy was to encourage its culture of sharing and cross-fertilization by ensuring that even employees who had not been directly involved in a major development might have a chance to participate in its benefit. SG's bonus scheme, for example was based on profits at the group level. To this end, Generics wanted to set aside some shares in ASL for a general offering within the company.

It was not until early September that the internal discussions were complete and ASL received its seed financing and became a truly independent entity, with defined shareholdings and balance sheet. In addition to the Spiral IP and some ongoing license revenues associated with it, ASL raised £570,000 through sale of shares at £1 each. 500,000 shares were bought by Generics itself, 50,000 shares were sold to SG employees in an oversubscribed firm-wide subscription offer, and the remaining 20,000 were bought by the employees of ASL, principally Collins, Burwell and Ely.

Consistent with SG's policy of rewarding innovators, Ely was awarded 11,250 shares (from the 500,000 subscribed by Generics) as the co-inventor of Spiral, replacing what would otherwise have been a cash payment. Geoff Foote, one of ASL's founding employees and two other SG employees were awarded 600 shares each for their contribution to Spiral's creation.

Each of the three ASL directors was also awarded options to buy shares in ASL: 9,000 options each at an exercise price of £1, 9,000 each at £4 and 8,250 each at £10. The options were exercisable over periods ranging between three and seven years.

Looking back, Collins reflected on his dual role in the negotiations as both agent for Generics and advocate for himself and his team. "All this discussion about shareholding, options and ownership is as much emotional as rational. I've often found myself arguing for what my team and I feel we deserve but at the same time still thinking like a Generics insider who cares about what's best for the Group." He was also struck with what he'd been able to do within the Generics umbrella. "I don't think I'd be in this position of becoming an entrepreneur if I'd been working for any other company. I'd just be a corporate man."

Ely considered the Generics contribution differently. "Generics's value-added [to me] is it gave me a chance to play, it taught me a bit and it gave me two good people to work with. They [Generics] were helpful, but this could probably have been done without them. While Generics was still using Spiral to win consulting contracts, we could already have been producing products and going after venture funding."

Moving Forward

As ASL's structure and shareholdings were being formalized, the Spiral team continued to map out its future. There were a number of issues to be addressed, but two basic questions were central. For the long term, what should ASL's strategy be to maximize the opportunities offered by the Spiral technology? And, more immediately, how should ASL approach its first-round financing? The team knew these questions were not entirely independent, as decisions taken on one issue could affect their options with respect to the others.

Raising Money

ASL had a burn rate of roughly £50,000 per month, representing salaries, travel, ongoing legal work associated with Spiral patents and some consulting work being done by SG. This was offset by license income of roughly £20,000 per month, but expenses would surely rise as the company moved forward.

Collins expected the first-round financing to take place around February 1999. At that point he expected ASL would want to raise £2 million. "By that time," he explained, "there will be more maturity in the business. We'll have a lot more people then, so our monthly burn rate could be £100,000 and we'll want funding that will last for more than a year." Collins expected to give away up to 30% of ASL in the first round. "If the number was more than 30%, we would rethink the plan."

Apart from how much money was to be raised, ASL's management had to consider who they might approach as potential investors. None of the three had ever raised money before, but they knew that each potential shareholder could have different consequences for the business.

First, and most obvious, Generics itself was likely to want to invest in the second round. The company had recently paid off the mortgage on its home office and had ended 1997 with virtually no debt. Participation by Generics would make the financing substantially easier to arrange, providing some of the money as well as signaling "insider" commitment to other prospective investors. The team was somewhat concerned, however, that if Generics remained the dominant shareholder they might miss the insights and opportunities a new investor might bring to the venture.

ASL could also approach one or more industrial investors. BTR, for example, had expressed interest in taking a stake in ASL, and an American sensor company had suggested it might buy ASL outright. In addition to financing, an industrial investor could provide additional technical expertise, key personnel, and access to new markets. The concern was that getting too close to such a partner might constrain ASL from entering markets outside the partner's expertise. "I don't see any partner who will have a fit in every area that we wish to exploit," observed Ely.

Finally, ASL could seek private equity from a financial investor. SG knew some technology-oriented venture capitalists through its investment arm, and Burwell knew several private equity firms in the United States. "A venture capitalist would impose the tightest restraints on us," opined Collins. "We would have to plan an exit strategy instead of just growing the business, and might not be able to pursue our long term strategies the way we would like."

Defining the Opportunity

Collins's original goal of showing Generics that consulting was not always the best method for capturing the value of new technologies had largely been achieved; with license profits already ahead of what could reasonably have been achieved by consulting, all that remained was for ASL to develop and market some of its own products. Burwell was concerned that this might be all they would do if they weren't careful:

> There's an emotional willingness [in the United Kingdom] to settle for a lower target, which lets them look for a lower risk profile. Cambridge in particular tends to produce "lifestyle companies." I don't want us to become just another sensor company with $20–30 million in revenues. This company has to have a $100 million vision, which means finding a "game-changing" application somewhere. It also means we probably have to make things [i.e. manufacture] because it's hard to reach that level otherwise. I worry that we will let near-term issues distract us from that longer-term goal.

Ely, by contrast, wasn't concerned about ASL ending up as a $30 million company, and was more concerned with the one to two year plan and getting applications developed:

> It's more important to me that we move forward and make our mistakes but make progress, too. In a year's time we'll have fifteen to twenty people, of which maybe half will be technical. We'll have gone through a lot of the pain of developing applications and will have some up and running. Then we can license the less-interesting stuff and concentrate on the most promising bits.

Despite the differing visions, the three men felt very comfortable with their shared future. Referring to Burwell's '$100 million vision,' Ely joked, "Malcom gets quite disturbed when I agree with him. But the point is that while we disagree on things, we all respect each other and each other's viewpoint. Each of us brings something very different to the table, and so we all know we have to recognize each other's expertise and experience."

Three Preliminary Markets

ASL's research to date had identified three target markets for which to develop applications. The first was the general market for industrial sensors. For example, Spiral-based sensors could be used to determine positioning of various parts on machine tools. "It's a good place for us to start," explained Burwell. "The customers are willing to tolerate unknowns (due to the small size of many of the players) and the contracts are small, giving us room to learn." Ely continued, "We've never made more than fifty sensors in a batch, so it's good for us to start in an area where we can move up the scale curve gradually."

ASL also believed that Spiral offered a qualitative improvement for the electronic pen interface between palm-top computers and their users. Ely explained:

> Current palm-top technology requires a sensitive coating on the outside of the screen which registers contact with the pen. Spiral is the only technology we know of that would allow the manufacturer to put the pen location sensor behind the screen. This means the resolution will be better and the position sensing should be more reliable, too. We even think using Spiral may improve handwriting recognition. This opportunity could be large.

ASL was in early negotiations with a manufacture of palm-top computers and was hopeful that Spiral could capture a significant share of that market.

ASL's "Holy Grail," as Ely liked to put it, was to enable server motors to duplicate the output of stepper motors. Ely explained:

> Stepper motors are used for precise and reproducible movement, like the carriage on a computer printer. They're very reliable, but not quick. Server motors are quicker, but haven't been able to replace stepper motors because the feedback mechanisms to determine the motor's current position have always been too slow or too expensive. Spiral could solve that.

Stepper motors were used in a wide range of applications. If Spiral could enable server motors to duplicate the functions of stepper motors at a reasonable cost, the speed of server motors would make them very attractive in a number of applications. "This could easily be Malcom's $100 million vision," stated Ely, who estimated that the development effort was approximately where the automotive initiative (now licensed to BTR/FASCO) was two years ago.

Risks

While ASL's management knew they could not anticipate all the problems they would face with their new venture, they had identified several risks they would have to address going forward. Ely was concerned that the company might pick the wrong application investing in a product where the added value of ASL's management team turned out not to be that high. There was also patent risk. Even with a technology patent for Spiral, gaining application patents was tricky. Much of the license income Spiral had generated was contingent on successful patent approvals, and the prices the company could command for products it would develop would be strongly affected by their success at establishing patent protection.

On the people side, Collins added a few concerns to Burwell's fear that ASL might become a small, Cambridge, lifestyle company. "We have to make sure we have the cohesion and leadership needed to push through decisions. Generics is a supportive parent, but perhaps a somewhat stodgy investor as well. They won't put much pressure on us, so we have to make sure we put it on ourselves."

Burwell added, "All of our technologists [from Generics] are development engineers and young—not blooded. We will probably have to bring on some more experienced manufacturing-oriented engineers if we're to develop products successfully. The challenge will be to find them."

Looking Ahead

Collins threw a leaf into the stream below and watched it float away with the current. He didn't want to wait too long; Burwell and Ely were already inside and the three of them had plenty to accomplish. Financing had to be secured, strategies had to be developed and prototypes manufactured. But what were the priorities? Should he be meeting with venture capitalists right away or did it make more sense to concentrate on lining up companies that could support ASL's manufacturing requirements? Although at times ASL's resources seemed large, Collins knew that they were not without limits and there seemed to be an unlimited number of "priorities" he and his team had to focus on. Shaking his head, Collins mused that being an entrepreneur wasn't always simpler than being a consultant.

Case 10

Signature Security: Providing Alarm Systems for the Countries Down Under

Life was going well for Jim Covert, CEO of Signature Security (Signature). It was August 15, 1999, and he had just walked out of a board meeting for his company. As he headed home from his office in downtown Sydney, Covert saw several smaller office buildings that had a discreet but visible sticker on the door that said "Protected by Signature Security." Covert smiled. Twenty-six months before, these stickers had not been there. Covert was a longtime executive in the electronic security industry but this was his first foray into a foreign market. Signature Security represented a roll-up of electronic security companies in Australia and New Zealand that had begun in June 1996 after Covert had made a few visits to Australia. Signature was now the leader in the residential and small to mid-sized commercial alarm market following 67 acquisitions by Covert and his team and after pioneering a contract leasing method of selling alarms to customers.

While there was much to be proud of, the company was at a crossroads now. Much of the goals in the acquisition program had been achieved and the best acquisition targets had already been purchased by Signature. Moreover, through its aggressive acquisitions, Signature had driven up the price for purchasing companies to a level at which the company needed to rethink its strategy. Rumors were circulating that Signature's two largest competitors, Chubb and Tyco, were about to launch leasing programs of their own and Signature's investors had raised questions at the board meeting about the company's proper strategic direction. Privately, these strategic questions laid ground for another question in Covert's mind: his continued involvement in the company. A 30-month non-compete agreement in the United States, which he had signed when he sold his last company in June

Dean's Fellow William J. Coughlin (MBA '99) prepared this case under the supervision of Professor Walter Kuemmerle. HBS cases are developed solely as the basis for class discussion. Cases are not intended to serve as endorsements, sources of primary data, or illustrations of effective or ineffective management.

1996, had just expired and Covert was free to pursue other opportunities back home. Could this be the right time for him to leave the business he had built or was this precisely the time when his company needed him most?

Australia and New Zealand: The Countries Down Under

Australia was the world's smallest continent but the sixth-largest country by size.[1] It had a land mass roughly the size of the continental United States but a population of just 19 million people. (See **Exhibit 1** for a map of Australia, New Zealand and the Pacific.) Australia's population lived primarily along the southeastern and eastern coast. The main cities were Sydney (4 million) and Melbourne (3.4 million). Captain James Cook claimed Australia in 1770 for the British. Australia was originally designated as a penal settlement, but word of the new territory with vast grazing land also attracted increasing numbers of regular settlers from the early nineteenth century onward. Even though only 7% of Australia's territory was arable, farming proved to be an important industry.[2] So did mining, with coal and iron ore being major natural resources. The growth of these industries helped develop infrastructure and railroads. The Commonwealth of Australia was established in 1901 and consisted of six states.

After World War II, Australia attracted immigrants from a wide variety of countries, especially Europe and Asia, and its population became increasingly diverse. By 1999 Australia still operated an active immigration program, admitting about 80,000–90,000 people per year.[3] As a result of immigration Australia's population was quite young, especially when compared with the population of other industrialized countries. Due to free trade policies and technological advances, Australia's economy gradually shifted away from its dependence on agriculture and mining. By 1999, service industries accounted for about 71% of GDP and manufacturing for about 26%. There were approximately 990,000 non-agricultural businesses.[4] Tourism had become a major source of revenue. Australia's major export partner was Japan (19% of exports); its major import partner was the U.S (18% of imports).[5] While Australia thrived as an open economy, there were resurging protectionist tendencies in the late 1990s. A rising inflow of political asylum seekers, primarily from Asian countries, also created racial tensions at a level not previously experienced in Australia. In 1999 Australia was ruled by a Liberal-National coalition under Prime Minister John Howard (who had been elected in 1996), which replaced a previous Labor government. Despite its declared intention to do so, the government was struggling to reduce government intervention and public ownership of commercial assets. (See **Exhibit 2** for economic data on Australia and New Zealand.)

Although it shared a common history with Australia, New Zealand had a much smaller population (roughly 4 million people) and had seen more political and economic uncertainty in recent years. The agricultural sector represented about 8% of GDP (versus 3% for Australia) and was vital for the country's exports.[6] Main exports were dairy products, meat, and wood. New Zealand's largest trading partner for both imports and exports was Australia. Nationalism had been rising in New Zealand through the mid-1990s as the New Zealand First Party (NZFP) gained power. After the 1996 elections, the

---

[1] *CIA World Factbook—Australia.* Accessed online at www.cia.gov/cia/publications/factbook on February 13, 2004.

[2] *CIA World Factbook—Australia.* Op.cit.

[3] *EIU Country Profile Australia 1999–00.* London: Economist Intelligence Unit, 1999, p. 11.

[4] Signature Security company materials.

[5] *CIA World Factbook—Australia.* Op.cit.

[6] *CIA World Factbook—Australia.* Op.cit. and CIA *World Factbook—New Zealand.* Accessed online at www.cia.gov/cia/publications/factbook on February 13, 2004.

EXHIBIT 1

Source: Map of Australia: *EIU Country Profile Australia 1999–00.* London: Economist Intelligence Unit, 1999, preface. Map of South Pacific: *EIU Country Profile Pacific Islands 1999–00.* London: Economist Intelligence Unit, 1999, preface.

Map of Australia

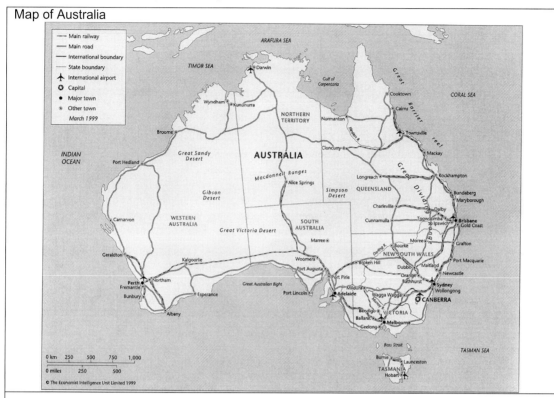

Map of South Pacific

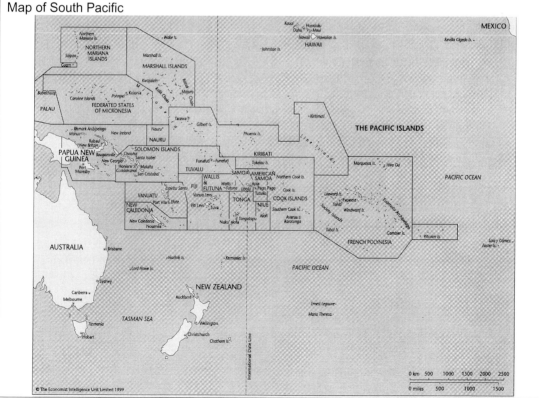

EXHIBIT 2 Comparative Economic Indicators, 1998

Source: Compiled from Economist Intelligence Unit data.

	Australia	New Zealand	Canada	U.K.	United States	Japan
GDP (US$ bn)	366.1	62.1	598.4	1,415.8	8,508.9	3,771.7
GDP per head (US$)	19,010	13,630	19,598	23,945	31,514	29,798
Population (mn)	18.7	3.8	30.5	59.1	270.0	126.6
Consumer price inflation (av; %)	0.8	1.3	0.9	2.7	1.6	0.7
Current account balance (US$ bn)	−18.2	−4.1	−13.1	−6.1	−224.3	119.6
Exports of goods (US$ bn)	55.8	13.3	213.8	266.1	674.3	386.4
Imports of goods (US$ bn)	60.9	12.4	200.8	302.0	921.7	275.9
Foreign trade[a] (% of GDP)	32.8	49.3	69.3	40.1	18.8	17.8

[a]Merchandise exports plus imports.

conservative and free-trade oriented National Party struck a coalition agreement with NZFP. The core of this agreement was to increase social expenditures and slow privatization. In 1997 Jenny Shipley, a member of the National Party, became New Zealand's first female prime minister. New Zealand suffered through a recession in the first half of 1998 as it was hurt both by side effects of the Asian crisis and by severe drought conditions for the vital agricultural sector.

Birth of Signature Security

Jim Covert: Building on a Secret Service Career

Jim Covert started out working for 10 years in the U.S. Secret Service at the White House during the Nixon, Ford, and Carter administrations. During this time, he supervised the introduction of electronic security by the U.S. Secret Service. Upon his retirement from the Secret Service he was solicited to head a number of in-house security operations for private companies, which was normal for a former member of the Secret Service. But Covert wanted to get in on the independent operations side of the business and took a position as vice president of operations at American Protection Industries (API). "I didn't want to be head of security at a place like Chase Manhattan," Covert explained. "I wanted to be on the business side, so I took a step backwards in salary to learn the alarm business."

Over time, American Protection grew to become the largest privately held alarm company in the United States. After becoming COO for a period, Covert left API to become Executive Vice President of Somitrol, another security company. But in 1986, Covert was approached by Stewart Resnek (the head of the Franklin Mint, a maker and marketer of collectable items) to purchase half of API's operations for US$16 million.[7] Covert explained:

> Not only didn't I have US$16 million, but I also had no idea how to raise that kind of money. So I called up a buddy from the Nixon Administration, Alan Greenspan, and asked him for help. I must have called the right guy. Within two weeks, I had everything together—met the executives, closed the deal and arranged financing. Alan introduced me to the private equity arm of Tucker Anthony in Boston (Now TA Associates and New Media Partners) and I came in with a prospectus asking for US$24 million, but they figured I ought to be thinking about more like US$32 million. We changed the name to SecurityLink and we were in business.

[7] All references to the Australian dollar are denoted by "$" and U.S. dollars by "US$." The exchange rate on September 30, 1999 was A$1.53:US$1.

Over the ensuing years ending in 1994, SecurityLink executed a roll-up strategy, made 64 acquisitions and had US$40 million in revenues. But right when things seemed to be at their best, problems started with the board. Covert had arranged to purchase a security company called National Guardian and had received board approval for the transaction. Then at the last second, Tucker Anthony killed the transaction. "They had just completed investing their current fund and were now starting to think about an exit," reasoned Covert. So Covert called the CEO of Ameritech, a major telecommunication services firm, to discuss a deal. Telecom companies were looking to bundle services and the security industry looked like a good fit for Ameritech. On Christmas Eve 1994, Covert sold his company to Ameritech but stayed on as CEO of the securities business and was able to complete the National Guardian deal, which turned the company into a business with US$310 million in revenues.

The security business proved to be one of the best performing units at Ameritech. But Covert felt that the large company culture was not for him. However, he was locked up by a non-competition agreement with Ameritech that prohibited him from operating in any U.S. state where Ameritech operated a security business for 30 months after he left the firm. On a telecommunications-related business trip to New Zealand for Ameritech, Covert casually looked at the security business and was surprised at what he saw. The market was even more fragmented than in the United States as there was no clear market leader in the industry. Moreover, alarm penetration rates were a fraction of those found in the United States—2% penetration in the residential business (vs. 15% in the United States) and 40% in the commercial business (vs. 70% in the United States). While taking three additional trips to Australia and New Zealand for Ameritech, he came across a company called Securitas. In June 1996 he resigned from Ameritech and entered into an agreement (letter of intent) to purchase Securitas. Covert explained his decision to leave Ameritech:

> I was having a bit of a tough time at Ameritech. I am really an entrepreneur at heart and working for a big organization like that can be stifling. For example, I wanted to buy 45 trucks to replace an aged fleet of service vehicles. This would have taken five minutes at SecurityLink but it took six months at Ameritech. Moreover, Ameritech was a telecommunications company and as I rose in the firm, I began doing things like giving presentations on the competition in the telecommunications market to shake up the brains of middle managers. That's not what I wanted to do.

After Covert had signed the letter of intent to buy Securitas and had developed a rough financing structure for the deal he went out to raise capital for the transaction. But this proved easier said than done. A number of private equity firms had solicited Covert in the past, including Chicago-based roll-up specialist Golder, Thoma, Cressey & Rauner, but when Covert approached them they were not interested due to the fact that the operations were in Australia. Then he ran into a friend named Lessing Gold, a longtime lawyer in the electronic security industry. Gold mentioned he should look at Clairvest, a publicly held Canadian private equity firm (see **Exhibit 3** for information regarding Clairvest). Clairvest sought to invest in companies with high internal growth, stable revenues and cash flows, and the ability to consolidate due to high fragmentation. The fund took a top-down approach to investing and had identified the industry as attractive but had not yet identified a company to invest in. After speaking with Clairvest, the two sides agreed to do a deal, but not necessarily in Australia and New Zealand. "Clairvest had never invested outside North America," Covert explained. "So they were wary of Australia." But after looking into a number of situations in the United States, Covert convinced Clairvest to go with him to Australia. "Purchase multiples were just too high in the United States," said Covert. "Competition was just too intense. And the only way to beat the competition is to go where they aren't, and that was Australia." So in December 1996, Covert completed the deal with Securitas and renamed the company Signature Security.

EXHIBIT 3
Information
Regarding Clairvest

Source: Clairvest.

Clairvest Group Inc. is a Toronto-based merchant bank that forms mutually beneficial investment partnerships with entrepreneurial corporations. It invests in both established and emerging companies, which have the potential to create above-average returns. Clairvest contributes financing and strategic expertise to support the growth and development of its entrepreneur partners in order to create long-term value for all shareholders. Clairvest realizes value through eventual disposition of its investments once its objectives have been achieved.

Statement of Income ($000 Except per share information)

	1999	1998
Net investment gains		
Gains on sale of investments (net)	$669	$4,727
Unrealized gains on investments (net)	1,558	31,166
Reversal of previously recognized gains	—	(790)
	2,227	35,103
Other investment income		
Interest and other income	2,500	2,848
Dividend income	1,507	7,569
Fees	782	794
	4,789	11,211
Administration and other expenses	3,824	4,648
Income before income taxes	3,192	41,666
Provision for (recovery of) income taxes	(661)	12,424
Net income	$3,883	$29,424
Net income per share	$0.21	$1.58
Fully diluted net income per share	$0.20	$1.46

Statement of Retained Earnings for Years Ended March 31 ($000)

	1999	1998
Retained earnings beginning of year	$47,541	$20,153
Net income	3,853	29,242
Unrealized gains on investments (net)	51,394	49,395
Dividends	(1,860)	(1,854)
Retained earnings (end of year)	$49,534	$47,541

Balance Sheet as of March 31

	1999	1998
Assets		
Cash and short-term investments	$4,679	$23,063
Accounts receivable	666	258
Corporate investments	157,809	133,069
Other assets	671	462
	$163,825	$156,852
Liabilities		
Accounts payable	$5,277	$819
Deferred income taxes	13,362	14,023
Total liabilities	18,639	14,842
Share capital	95,652	94,469
Retained earnings	49,834	47,541
Total equity	145,188	142,010
	$163,825	$156,852

Investment Case of Australia vs. the United States: Back to the Future

When Covert investigated the Australian/New Zealand market, he saw a situation that was much like the one found in the United States 15 years earlier. The market was very fragmented and there were no industry leaders to speak of. Moreover, the companies that were operating in the industry were relatively unsophisticated in terms of marketing and operations (i.e., the implementation of best practices). Aside from the competition, there were other elements that appealed to Covert. The rate of non-violent crime was very high in both Australia and New Zealand, much higher than those found in the United States (see **Exhibit 4** for crime statistics). Despite these high crime rates, the alarm penetration rates in both Australia and New Zealand were very low (see **Exhibit 5** for penetration rates). This penetration gap potentially allowed for strong internal growth of the business. As far as acquisitions were concerned there was something of a gap as well; whereas a typical M&A transaction in the United States would be valued at 60–70x RMR[8] (Recurring Monthly Revenue), multiples in Australia were much lower as evidenced by the 25x RMR Covert had paid for Securitas. "Most importantly, Covert and his team had done it before," said Michael Taranto from Sydney-based Macquarie Bank, a later-stage investor. "Even though the planned rapid growth was a concern of ours from an integration standpoint, we felt that Covert and his team were the best guys for the job."

[8] RMR multiples are the standard valuation measure in the electronic security industry. Signature's RMR in August 1999 was $3.14 million.

EXHIBIT 4
Crime Rates

Source: 1995 Australia Yearbook; Signature Security.

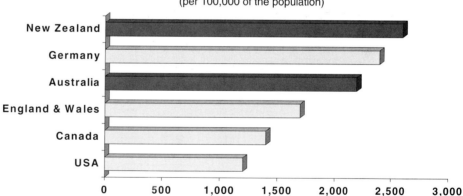

Burglary offences in selected countries, 1995
(per 100,000 of the population)

EXHIBIT 5
Penetration Rates
(August 1999)

Source: Derived using data from IBIS report, ASIAL estimates, Australian Bureau of Statistics; Signature Security.

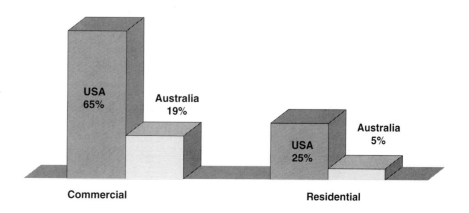

Going into the transaction, the key risk was in the selling process. The United States had long used a leasing model, similar to mobile telephones, where a customer would acquire the hardware in exchange for signing a long-term contract (5 years for Signature). The question became: would this work in the Australian market? All other companies were selling their alarm units outright to their customers and on-going service was not contractual. Many people believed that the Australian and New Zealand electronic security market would not accept this method of service by entering into a contract. But Covert was convinced it would work. "Whenever a U.S. style service was introduced into Australia, people migrated very quickly to that service," reasoned Covert. "Take cellular phones. Penetration rates for cellular service are much higher than in the United States. What those people are doing is signing a three year contract and lease program. And that is exactly our business."

In setting out for Australia, Covert had established a few goals for the company. Through an aggressive acquisition program, Signature would look to set a national footprint across Australia and New Zealand. "Pepsi used as many as 200 firms for its security business in the two countries, because no one could provide national coverage," Covert said. "Establishing a national footprint would make winning those accounts much easier." In relation to the footprint, Covert wanted to build a strong dealer network across both countries to enhance the sales and marketing effort. After the acquisition program was underway, Signature would begin applying the best practices that Covert and the team had learned from operating in the United States to bring about operational efficiency in the organizations they purchased. Finally, over the long-term, there was a thought of expanding to the United States after Australia had reached a critical mass. (See **Exhibit 6** for industry growth drivers and business model.) In the end, Clairvest decided to invest $9.6 million in the company at $53.00 per share. Covert and his team invested $1.0 million by way of interest-bearing, full-recourse loans from the company. Signature's banker together with another small investor invested $0.5 million. Also, management was given the option to increase its stake from 8.9% to 17.3% on a fully diluted basis.

EXHIBIT 6
Electronic Security Industry Growth Drivers and Business Model

Source: Signature Security.

Industry Growth Drivers

- Media coverage of increased crime heightens awareness and instills fear
  - Average cost of break-in: $30,000
  - Break-in 15x less likely if alarm system installed
- Insurance companies are beginning to provide discounts to property owners with security systems
- Insecurity of an aging population
- Increasing number of dual income families has increased the amount of property left unattended during the day
- Increasing number of people working at home increases need for equipment and document protection
- As penetration increases, customers without security systems feel more vulnerable to crime

Business Model

- Predictable cash flows due to contractual revenues
- High EBITDA margins with low volatility
- Pricing of services fixed with ability to increase
- Recession resistant
- Industry attrition rates historically stable
- Low penetration rate
- Rapid payback period and high ROI

Signature's History: Rolling It Up

As soon as Covert received funding for Signature from Clairvest, he began assembling a team of former colleagues. At first, the intention was to operate the company remotely from the United States, with the officers making periodic trips to Australia and New Zealand. But Clairvest was against the idea and headquarters was set up in the Darling Harbor area of Sydney. Andy Knott, Vice President of Marketing, explained some of the early days of Signature.

> Those early days were brutal. We had this studio in Darling Harbor where the whole management team worked for around 18 hours a day. We didn't even have real conference space, just a table where we could have two meetings going on at once. We worked so long and so hard together we would wind up either loving each other or absolutely hating each other! But there was a pretty good chance we would get along with each other. Most of the senior management team had been with Jim for over 15 years at API and SecurityLink; only Howard (Watson, CFO) and I were the real outsiders and my wife had run Jim's PR in the United States for years, so we knew each other on a personal level. The others knew each other well and had worked with each other for a number of years so that gave us a sense of stability. (See **Exhibits 7 and 8** for Signature's management team and biographies of management.) That demonstrates a lot about Jim. Not only is he a great company builder and a visionary, but a strong team builder and leader.

The Signature electronic security system consisted of a combination of a central unit with motion sensors and/or point-of-entry detectors. Using his relationships in the United States, Covert persuaded a leading U.S. security device manufacturer to purchase an Australian company in order to manufacture the security device in Australia using U.S. technology, important both for cost purposes and branding purposes.[9] Using outsourced installation services, the alarm would typically take six hours to install in a home. Once installed, the system would usually use the home's existing home telephone line to communicate with the central station in the area, which would then contact a person dictated by the customer in case of an emergency (i.e., another family member or a mobile telephone number). Once the contact person was reached, an outsourced emergency response unit would be sent to the premises if deemed necessary and the customer would be charged for the visit.[10] The police would also be contacted once there was sufficient evidence of a break-in. The largest central station, the Sydney Central Station, received 25,000 signals a day which, on average, were triggered by around 1,000

[9] The alarm had the Signature name and "made in Australia" printed on it, an important selling point in the Australian market.

[10] A customer could choose to pay a $5 per month premium to cover these costs.

EXHIBIT 7
Signature Management Team

Source: Signature Security.

Manager	Title	Fully-Diluted Shares Held	% FD Ownership
James Covert	President	34,035	4.47%
Joe Nuccio	Chief operating officer	3,405	0.45
Howard Watson	Chief financial officer	11,287	1.48
Bob Pierce	Vice president, Sales	3,405	0.45
Andy Knott	Vice president, Marketing	3,525	0.46
Steve Johnson	Vice president, Corporate Services	3,462	0.45
Steve Welsh	Vice president, Budget & Systems	3,525	0.46
		62,644	

Note: Steve Nicholson, former executive vice president—Acquisitions who left in early 1999, owns 10,574 fully-diluted shares representing 1.39% of the company.

EXHIBIT 8 Management Biographies

Source: Signature Security.

James Covert, President and Chief Executive Office

James Covert co-founded Signature Security Group (SSG) in November 1996 with Steven P. Nicholson. SSG's president and chief executive officer, Mr. Covert is regarded as one of the leading executives in the security industry worldwide. He has more than 26 years experience in the security industry, including 16 years in executive management positions with providers of electronic security services. Prior to this, Mr. Covert spent 10 years of United States Secret Service duty at the White House serving Presidents Nixon, Ford and Carter. During this time, he supervised the introduction of electronic security by the United States Secret Service. Mr. Covert has a bachelor's degree in criminology and graduated with salutatorian honors from the United States Secret Service Academy. He also holds the equivalent to a master's degree in administration of justice from American University.

Joe Nuccio, *Chief Operating Officer*

Joe Nuccio has over 15 years of industry experience. Mr. Nuccio joined SecurityLink in 1984 and remained there until 1997. Mr. Nuccio held a number of positions at SecurityLink, including as vice president and general manager in a number of regions, and as corporate director of Product Services. In these roles, Mr. Nuccio directed over 40 major acquisitions, including the integration of financial, sales, operational, and human resource systems and procedures. Mr. Nuccio also reduced attrition through aggressive customer service and reduced receivables through organized collection procedures. Mr. Nuccio holds a bachelor's degree in information science from Northeastern University.

Howard Watson, *Chief Financial Officer*

Howard Watson joined SSG as its chief financial officer in August 1997, following his immigration to Australia from South Africa in early 1997. He is a chartered accountant and was, until February 1997, the senior partner in Papilsky Hurwitz, an accounting firm in Johannesburg. Throughout his 17-year career at Papilsky Hurwitz, Mr. Watson served as a strategic financial advisor to several private South African companies where he implemented various management reporting systems, conducted turnarounds and directed successful listings on the Johannesburg Stock Exchange. Mr. Watson holds a bachelor's of accountancy (major in accounting auditing and tax) from the University of Witwatersrand and has been a chartered accountant (South Africa) since 1983.

Andy Knott, *Vice President, Marketing*

Andy Knott was recruited by Jim Covert to join SSG in December 1996 as vice president of Marketing. He oversees all legal and marketing aspects for SSG. Most recently, Mr. Knott served as an executive assistant prosecutor to the State's Attorney of Cook County (Chicago) where he served as press secretary and lobbyist for the second largest prosecutor's office in the United States, managing all marketing and public communications. He also served as crisis management consultant and political adviser and managed the media image for one of Chicago's most popular politicians. Mr. Knott has more than 18 years of marketing experience and was associate publisher of *Pro Football Weekly*, a Chicago-based national publication. During eight years as a reporter for the *Chicago Tribune* in the 1980s, he distinguished himself with three nominations for the Pulitzer Prize. Mr. Knott holds a bachelor's degree in communications from the University of Tennessee and a *juris doctor* degree from John Marshall Law School in Chicago.

Steve Johnson, *Vice President, Corporate Services*

Stephen Johnson was recruited by Jim Covert in November 1996 to join SSG as vice president of Corporate Services. A former owner of Hawkeye Security Systems from 1973 to 1988, Mr. Johnson has been involved in the design, sale, installation and service of industrial, commercial and residential alarm systems since leaving the United States Air Force, where he served in the communications electronics field. Mr. Johnson grew his company to become the third largest independent alarm company in Illinois before selling to SecurityLink in 1988. After the sale, he continued with SecurityLink in the capacity of director of technical services and director of engineering.

(continued)

EXHIBIT 8   (Continued)

Steve Welsh, *Vice President, Budget & Systems*

Steve Welsh was recruited by Jim Covert in July 1997 to join SSG as vice president of Budget and Systems. Mr. Welsh has been at the forefront of the industry consolidation of American alarm companies, having started with API Alarm Systems in 1984 as an accounting manager, supervising a 10-person department in a company with annual revenues of US$6 million. In 1988, Mr. Welsh joined SecurityLink as a regional controller, ultimately supervising the acquisition of 40 smaller alarm companies. After the acquisition of SecurityLink by Ameritech, Mr. Welsh instituted and managed the alarm industry's first and only centralized purchasing and distribution department, resulting in direct savings of US$6 million per annum. Mr. Welsh holds a bachelor's of science degree from Penn State University.

Bob Pierce, *Vice President, Sales*

Bob Pierce was hired by Jim Covert in April 1997 to serve as vice president of Sales. Mr. Pierce has more than 25 years of sales and management experience in the security and communications industries. After completing a master's of business administration degree (majoring in marketing and management) from the University of California at Los Angeles, Mr. Pierce began his career by leading a team of account executives at IBM to three consecutive top honor awards. Mr. Pierce later served as Executive Vice President of API Alarm Systems, where he orchestrated growth of a US$2 million company into a US$165 million company in 10 years. Mr. Pierce later served as Vice President of Sales at NEC America, where he headed a number of major telecommunications projects. Mr. Pierce's most recent role was Senior Vice President of Sales at SecurityLink in Chicago, where he was responsible for more than 1,000 employees, 75 branch offices and an operating budget of US$75 million per annum. Mr. Pierce's team generated more than US$133 million in new sales and increased recurring revenue by 36% each year.

"events" per day for both residential and commercial coverage. Five to ten of these 25,000 signals represented actual break-ins. "The key driver to success in the electronic security," explained Rod Acland, General Manager of the Sydney Central Station, "is to minimize the amount of human intervention without a loss in monitoring quality."[11]

Over time the company grew to become the largest electronic security company in the Australian and New Zealand markets focusing on the residential and the small to mid-sized commercial segments (see **Exhibit 9** for Signature's historical financials). After completing 67 acquisitions, Signature had developed the footprint and a 240-strong dealer network Covert envisioned when he set out for Australia. Moreover, in the second year, the company grew by 70% with EBITDA increasing more than 4 times. "From an operational standpoint, we are light years ahead of the two main competitors Chubb and Tyco," explained Acland. "Everything Jim said about Australia came true," said Graham Rosenberg of Clairvest. "I was shocked at our ability to go into the market and to succeed in attacking it from an internal sales point of view. Also, I was positively surprised by the potential for acquisitions."

There were many other positive surprises for Signature. The economics of internal growth were much better than anyone had anticipated as new recurring revenue creation stood at about $80,000–90,000 per month. "I never imagined we would get higher than $50,000," confessed Covert. Moreover, the lack of a competitive response from industry players surprised Covert and his team. Since both of the main competitors were affiliated with large global players with access to large amounts of capital, Covert thought they would begin to become more acquisitive and implement the leasing strategy much sooner than they eventually did. As a result, the acquisition multiples stayed lower for a much longer period of time than the team had first imagined.

[11] Due to longer vacations, more restrictive labor laws and other factors, central station operators in Australia who earned between $35,000 and $40,000 per annum were approximately 15% more expensive on an hourly basis than operators in the United States with the same qualification.

EXHIBIT 9
Signature's
Historical Financials
($000) (Excerpt)

Source: Signature Security.

Fiscal Year Ended March 31,	1998	1999
Income Statement Information		
Recurring revenues	16,001	34,409
Total revenues	26,497	45,875
EBITDA	2,345	10,018
Interest expense	2,188	6,672
Balance Sheet Information		
Working capital	(7,160)	(6,056)
Net fixed assets	5,079	6,887
Subscriber accounts	10,839	27,001
Goodwill, financing & acquisition costs	91,525	85,227
Total debt	52,000	90,000
Total equity contributed	45,000	50,000

But with the positives, there were negatives. By far the biggest surprise was the lack of a local financing source, a key concern for a roll-up that was in constant need of cash (see **Exhibit 10** for Signature's financing history). Although private equity was available, the local debt providers focused more on asset-backed financing than on cash-flow-backed deals. Initially, Signature had to rely on financing from a Sydney branch of Toronto Dominion, a Canadian-based bank with whom Clairvest had a strong relationship. Howard Watson, CFO, a native of South Africa, outlined some of his frustrations with the financing process:

> I was surprised at how conservative the Australians were in their capital markets sophistication. They seemed to have never seen a cash flow based business. All they would look at was earnings and they couldn't get their arms around the fact that the reason why we didn't have earnings was because we had a great deal of depreciation and goodwill amortization flowing through our books and because of the economics of our leasing program. On a cash flow basis we were doing fine. By comparison, the North American banking community is more switched on and more advanced due to the maturity of industries with similar cash flow characteristics such as cable, mobile phones, etc.
>
> Australian alarm companies sold the alarms outright to the customer for around $1,000, which represented the cost of the equipment itself. Our equipment costs are roughly the same, but this is not the all-in cost which includes marketing and sales costs and adds about another $200 to the full-in cost. Instead of selling the product to our customers, we lease it to them for $295 down, for a net creation cost of 30x RMR, plus a $1 per day monitoring fee. But that $1 per day is locked up in a five-year contract, net of attrition of course, but we estimate the life of a customer to average around 10 years. With the marginal cost of monitoring and servicing a unit at around 25%, depending on the capacity-utilization level of the central monitoring station, the incremental returns of a leased system are attractive for Signature.

Another concern surrounded the acquisitions themselves. From a strategic standpoint the acquisitions were critical. However, after integrating many of the companies into Signature, the economics of the acquisition, while solid, did not look quite as good. Since most of the target companies did not have their customers tied up in contracts, many of them would leave after the purchase of the company—often to a new company set up by the original owner. Moreover, the operating characteristics were sometimes not as good as advertised when Signature closed the deal. Signature fixed part of that problem by making payment of the purchase price contingent on actual receipt of revenues over the following year. But there were also problems with the implementation of uniform operating systems and the integration of acquired companies, which were run without systems by "mom and pops." Joe Nuccio, COO, provided an example of how an acquisition could go wrong:

EXHIBIT 10 **Signature's Financing History ($000 except price per share in $)**

Source: Signature Security.

Round	Original Deal (3/97)	Second Round (12/97)	Third Round (2/98)	Fourth Round[a] (9/98)	Fifth Round (6/99)	Total Financing on Aug 15, 1999	# of Shares owned on Aug 15, 1999	% of Shares owned on Aug 15, 1999
Debt Financing								
Credit Facility[a]	20,000	85,000	85,000	115,000	115,000	115,000		
Subordinated debt	—	—	—	—	35,000	35,000		
Total Debt Financing	20,000	85,000	85,000	115,000	150,000	150,000		
Equity Financing								
Clairvest	9,600	3,500	2,600	2,500	900	19,100	274,788	36.0%
Management[b]	1,000	900	800	100	100	2,900	62,644	8.2%
GE Equity	—	8,000	2,500	—	—	10,500	106,207	13.9%
GS Private Equity	—	—	—	—	10,200	10,200	81,600	10.7%
Macquarie	—	—	9,600	2,000	4,000	15,600	153,871	20.2%
Others[c]	600	2,100	3,800	400	—	6,900	84,184	11.0%
Total Incremental Equity Financing	11,200	14,500	19,300	5,000	15,200	65,200	763,294	100%
Price per common share	$53.0	$98.4	$98.4	$98.40	$125.0			

[a]Represents debt facility size.
[b]Management owes $2.0 million (on loans for underlying shares) and up to $2.7 million to exercise options.
[c]Represents investors owning less than 10% each, on a fully diluted basis.

An example of this problem can be seen in an acquisition we made in Gisborne, New Zealand. We negotiated a purchase based on a RMR of $75,000, but the thing ended up a disaster. They had a *much* higher attrition rate than we had been told in our diligence process and many of the customers were simply stolen by the previous owner. Stolen! There just aren't the same protections here as there are in the States. In the United States, a trade association certifies electronic security companies and if a company tried a trick like that, they would get their license pulled. Such trade associations exist neither in New Zealand nor in most states in Australia. Also, Gisborne was very far away from our main facility in Auckland and it was difficult to monitor attrition. As a result, we lost a lot on the deal. We paid a really low price but lost customers and valuable management time.

Finally, work mentality in the companies that Signature acquired was mixed. This was partially due to the fact that the acquired companies had grown more slowly in the past and had not always attracted the most entrepreneurial managers. Another country-specific reason was high tax rates. "With marginal income tax rates at 48%, there is not always a lot of desire to work hard," said Covert. "It was hard to find people willing to shift from a flat salary to an incentive-based compensation program, especially in sales. By contrast, in the United States everyone in sales *wants* to work on commission. Signature, however, succeeded by hiring younger people who were willing to take the chance since it offered them a chance to strike it rich quicker than normal. Or we brought in guys like Joe who knew how to get the job done. It took about a year to replace several of the former managers and create a top quality core team."

Although there had been a couple of surprises for the Signature Security team, most of the surprises were positive and the management team had accomplished many of the goals they had set out for themselves. But given these accomplishments, the question became what to do next.

Strategic Choices

Covert and his team had built the company they had imagined but a couple of things had become clear over the 26 months of operations. Australia and New Zealand were much greater opportunities than anyone had previously imagined. As a result, the team, and their investors, no longer believed that an entry into the United States was a viable and necessary alternative, unless it was done on such a scale that it would facilitate an exit for Signature's investors. Covert had three strategic options he was considering for the company: keep growing through acquisitions; stop the acquisition program and grow organically; or exit the business completely. Based on an equity and debt financing completed in June 1999 that totaled $50 million, Signature was well capitalized to finance its growth for the next two years. The company's relationship with bankers was good, the company's investors were "deep-pocketed," and pleased with Signature's performance to date.

Keep on "Rolling"

Although Signature had come a long way and had garnered a 19% market share by August 1999, the market still looked very similar to when Covert first arrived in Australia (see **Exhibit 11** for market share data). Covert explained:

> The penetration rates in Australia still trail the United States by a significant distance. We expect that gap to narrow over time as more players enter the market and as people become more aware of the crime situation. The multiples for purchasing these businesses are still low when compared to the United States, so there is still good value out there for us and we have a solid infrastructure in place for handling these deals.

EXHIBIT 11
Market Share Data

Source: Signature Security.

Company	Description	Market Share
Chubb	Large commercial accounts. Primarily manpower security services	24%
Signature	Residential and small- to mid-sized commercial accounts	19
Tyco	Primarily fire prevention industry	12
Others	More than 3,000 independent operators in Australia and 300 in New Zealand	45

Note: The combined market share of the top three to five firms in the United States and Canada was similar to the combined market share of Chubb, Signature and Tyco in Australia. The top firms in the U.S. were SecurityLink, Brinks, Chubb, Tyco and ProtectionOne. The top firms in Canada were Chubb, Tyco, Security Link, Voxcom and Microtec. The rest of the market in the U.S. and Canada was occupied by thousands of small firms.

However, there were some strong considerations for curtailing the acquisitions program. The company had accomplished its goal of building a national footprint and a national dealer network with the purchase of Consolidated Security in February 1998. This purchase also illustrated the dramatic rise in purchase prices that had occurred in the industry since Signature arrived in Australia. The initial purchase of Securitas was for 25x RMR but the valuation for Consolidated was in the 40–50x RMR range. Although some of this had to do with the particular investment (Consolidated was dominant in the Perth region, the only place where Signature had very little presence, and Consolidated had outstanding growth potential), it still demonstrated how the multiples had risen in the industry over two years. Moreover, through its aggressive acquisition program, Signature had taken most of the prime candidates for acquisition. "We didn't expect Signature to buy so many companies," confessed Rosenberg.

End the Acquisition Program

Another option for Covert and his team would be to focus on growing the existing business organically and end the aggressive acquisition program. Nuccio highlighted some of Signatures thoughts behind this option:

> Since we have our footprint and our dealer network, it is now time to focus on improving efficiencies and complete the consolidation and rationalization. We have made so many acquisitions that we have had to put aside some of integration elements and the best practices implementation that we wanted to execute at the company. When it was critical to gain scale in the market, we could leave these things aside. But now that we have accomplished many of our goals for the acquisition program, we need to hunker down and get the business running efficiently. As we do, the numbers will get much better (see **Exhibit 12** for company projections).
>
> Moreover, the economics of new account generation have been much better than we had imagined. We are growing at a faster rate and with better margins than we had figured we could when we came to this market. Combined with that are the rumors that the competition will start imitating our leasing program starting next month. Up to now, we had a monopoly on the best product and service but now there will be real competition. That calls for a greater focus on the sales effort.

The downside of this strategy was on the competitive level. If the company ended its acquisition program, then those companies were available for their competitors to acquire. Also, the competition had started poaching some key dealers from Signature. This trend could continue if competitors gained more scale in a growing market while Signature stopped growing.

EXHIBIT 12 **Signature Security Group 5 Year Forecast—Fiscal Years 2000–2004 (ending March 31)**

Source: Signature Security and casewriter estimates.

Statement of Net Income ($000) (Excerpt)

	Fiscal 2000	Fiscal 2001	Fiscal 2002	Fiscal 2003	Fiscal 2004
Net recurring revenue(a)	37,824	45,832	53,944	62,032	69,986
Total revenues	48,659	58,424	68,349	77,940	87,193
EBITDA	13,013	21,231	27,734	33,958	40,626
Interest	10,031	12,372	14,844	17,174	19,340

Balance Sheet ($000) (Excerpt)

	Fiscal 2000	Fiscal 2001	Fiscal 2002	Fiscal 2003	Fiscal 2004
Assets					
Current assets	8,049	8,941	9,933	10,917	11,862
Fixed assets	6,442	5,682	4,522	4,667	4,856
Installed subscriber systems	49,741	76,188	100,755	123,270	144,513
Goodwill, acquisition and financing costs	84,181	81,512	80,014	78,501	77,329
Liabilities					
Current liabilities	7,959	9,783	12,205	14,761	17,375
Total debt	107,114	134,205	159,419	183,241	204,991
Total equity contributed (b)	63,200	63,200	63,200	63,200	63,200

Statement of Changes in Financial Position ($000) (Excerpt)

	Fiscal 2000	Fiscal 2001	Fiscal 2002	Fiscal 2003	Fiscal 2004
Cash flow from operations	5,885	13,194	16,985	20,292	24,278
Investment activities					
Fixed assets	(1,975)	(2,000)	(2,000)	(2,000)	(2,000)
Subscriber systems	(30,957)	(34,522)	(36,248)	(37,974)	(39,700)
Acquisitions	(4,245)	(3,763)	(3,952)	(4,140)	(4,328)
Financing activities					
Financing fee	(1238)	0	0	0	0
Issuance of subordinated debt	35,000	0	0	0	0
Issuance of equity	15,000	0	0	0	0
Cash generated (used)	17,470	(27,091)	(25,214)	(23,821)	(21,750)

aThe majority of the decrease in net recurring revenue between FY 1999 and FY 2000 was due to the sale of Signature's guard and patrol business.
bIncludes loans to management to acquire shares.

Exit Options

The strategic choice between external and internal growth had some impact on exit timing and options. Essentially, Signature could carry out an IPO or sell to a strategic player. An IPO in United States would be most attractive from a valuation perspective (see **Exhibit 13** for comparable trading data). The only concern with this alternative was whether it was feasible for the company in its current state. It was not clear to Signature's management that U.S. investors would embrace an Australian company of Signature's size without a U.S. presence. The company could form an alliance or make an acquisition in the United States to gain that presence, but there were concerns about diverting management attention away from the Australian and New Zealand markets.

Also, Protection One, the only "pure" home alarm systems company of similar size that was publicly listed in the United States, had recently attracted negative publicity when

EXHIBIT 13 Data on Comparable Companies

Sources: Bloomberg, Firstcall, OneSource, GlobalVantage.

Security Alarm Companies (data in US$ millions)

Company	Ticker	Exchange	Stock Price 8/13/99	Market Value 8/13/99	Market Cap	LFY Revenues	LFY EBITDA	EPS Estimates 1999 FYE	EPS Estimates 2000 FYE	Multiples: Market Cap/ Revenues	Multiples: Market Cap/ EBITDA	Multiples: P/E 1999	Multiples: P/E 2000
Tyco International	TYC	NY	50.16	83,334.6	87,686.4	12,311.3	2,337.0	1.51	2.03	7.1x	37.5x	33.2x	24.7x
Williams PLC	WLMS	London	598.78	4,369.9	5,710.5	3,845.1	763.0	n/a	n/a	1.5x	7.5x	n/a	n/a
Voxcom Inc	VOX	Canadian Venture Exchange	4.70	10.6	14.5	9.9	3.0	n/a	n/a	1.5x	4.9x	n/a	n/a
Microtec Ent.	EMI	Toronto	1.86	10.1	36.3	13.7	7.3	n/a	n/a	2.7x	5.0x	n/a	n/a
Protection One	POI	NY	4.19	531.4	1,488.9	421.1	157.2	2.11	2.50	3.5x	9.5x	2.0x	1.7x
Guardian International	GIIS	OTC BB	0.75	6.4	13.1	15.2	n/a	n/a	n/a	0.9x	n/a	n/a	n/a
Pittston Brinks Guards	PZB	NY	24.13	985.8	1,058.9	1,451.3	224.4	2.16	2.49	0.7x	4.7x	11.2x	9.7x
Ameritec	AIT	NY	72.19	79,362.3	84,780.3	17,154.0	6,772.0	2.74	3.00	4.9x	12.5x	26.3x	24.1x

LFY: Latest Fiscal Year.
n/a: Not available.

EXHIBIT 13 (Continued)

Source: Salomon Smith Barney; Signature Securities.

Australian Companies

Valuation Mutiples Year Ending 30 June	Stock Price[a] A$	Mkt Cap (A$M)	EPS Growth 1999–2000	P/E 1999	P/E 2000	Debt/ Equity[c]	Firm Value/ EBITDA[b] 1999	Firm Value/ EBITDA[b] 2000	Firm Value/ EBIT[b] 1999	Firm Value/ EBIT[b] 2000	ROA LTM
Outsourcing											
Spotless Services Limited	$1.28	$415	5.6%	14.4x	13.6x	23.6%	7.5x	7.3x	10.0x	9.6x	12.6%
Ausdoc Group Limited	2.70	208	15.2	15.8	13.7	45.2	7.6	7.0	12.0	10.6	10.1
Skilled Engineering	3.01	222	25.4	17.0	13.6	66.0	9.1	7.8	10.8	8.8	14.1
Tempo Services Limited	2.18	93	16.4	13.7	11.8	36.3	6.5	5.9	9.2	8.1	18.8
Cande Australia Limited	2.60	71	26.0	17.3	13.8	42.1	10.0	7.9	10.7	8.4	19.2
Recruitment Solutions Ltd	1.77	42	11.0	15.0	13.5	27.3	NA	NA	NA	NA	51.1
Pracom Limited	1.31	100	73.0	35.4	20.5	9.4	24.5	9.0	31.3	10.8	NA
Other											
United Group Limited	3.04	194	6.2	8.5	8.0	30.6	5.1	5.1	6.3	6.1	NA
TDG Logistics	1.30	59	20.6	13.4	11.1	52.4	NA	NA	NA	NA	NA
Median	—	—	16.4	15.0	13.6	36.3	7.6	7.3	10.7	8.8	16.5
Mean	—	—	22.2	16.7	13.3	33.6	10.0	7.1	12.9	8.9	21.0

NA: Not available.

[a]Stock price in A$ as of 8 May 1999

[b]SSB estimates as of 8 May 1999.

[c]Short-term borrowings plus long-term borrowings divided by book value as of date of latest results.

it was investigated by the SEC for its accounting practices. This could make an IPO somewhat more difficult in the U.S. even for a strong company like Signature. An IPO in Australia could be a more feasible option, especially from a country risk perspective. Even though there were no security companies that were publicly listed in Australia, the Australian investor was becoming familiar with companies with similar cash flow characteristics as Signature (like cellular telephone and cable companies) and the stock market was hungry for an outstanding growth story.

Several companies had made overtures to Signature about purchasing the company in the past and perhaps this was the time to act. Both of the major players in the Australian market were backed by large multinational security companies that operated in different segments of the market than Signature, leading management to believe that Signature could be a good fit as there would be little direct overlap. Furthermore, several European and North American players had indicated an interest in the company in order to expand their geographic reach and build an international presence. Finally, Australian utilities looking to augment services to their local customers and to bind these customers in the face of deregulation in the natural gas, electricity and telephone business also provided an exit alternative.

Moreover, valuation levels for electronic security companies of Signature's size were still near their high in the market (see **Exhibit 14** for M&A comparable data). The question for management became: Was this the right time to exit? An IPO would not only provide an opportunity for a realization event for investors but would also provide the cash-hungry company with another source of capital. There were a number of areas where the company felt they could gain efficiencies in their business and not everyone was convinced Signature should sell out before those efficiencies were gained. "I guess it all depends on whether a prospective investor wants to pay us for those projected efficiencies or not," explained Watson.

Covert's Challenge: Should I Stay or Should I Go?

On a personal note, Covert also had an important decision to make: should he stay with the company or head back to the United States. Management and investors had always

EXHIBIT 14   Security Alarm Company Transactions (Greater than US$1 million of RMR—Last Three Years)

Source: Signature Security.

Year	Transaction	Purchase Price ($ millions)	RMR ($ thousands)	Price/RMR Multiple
1996	Sentry to Entergy	$48.0	$1,000	48x
	Westinghouse Security to Western Resources	426.0	8,000	53
1997	Masada to SecurityLink Ameritech	130.0	2,100	62
	ADT to Tyco	5,223.0	75,000	70
	Republic Security to SecurityLink Ameritech	655.0	9,500	69
	Rollins Protective to SecurityLink Ameritech	210.0	3,100	68
	Network Multi-Family to Westar Security	175.0	2,000	88
	Centennial Security to Westar Security	97.5	1,500	65
	Protection One to Westar Security	498.0	8,200	61
	Multimedia to Protection One	242.0	3,450	73
	Holmes Protection to ADT Security	147.5	3,190	46
1998	Comsec Narragansett to Protection One	68.0	1,300	52
	Westec to Southern California Edison	310.0	4,400	70
			Average	63x
			Median	65

realized that Covert would eventually go back home, but with these strategic choices lingering, Covert wondered if this was the best time for him to do so:

> When I first looked at Australia, I not only saw a great opportunity in the electronic security industry but I also said: "Hey! This is a nice place to visit. Wouldn't it be fun to serve out my 30 months down there?" Well, my 30 months are up and I would be free to pursue other opportunities in the United States if I chose. But is this *really* the best—or in fact the worst—time for me to depart? We are heading into an exciting and crucial time for the company. Competition is catching on to our strategy. This is good from the standpoint of growing the market opportunity but we must remain ahead of the competition. Also, there are a lot of things to improve at the company—things that we kept putting aside. But I feel that the rest of the management team is one of the strongest in the industry worldwide today. It may be a clean break for me personally but is this the time when the company needs me most?

Joe Nuccio, a longtime friend and co-worker of Covert, added:

> Jim is really a company builder and a visionary. He had the charisma to pull off 67 acquisitions in two years. That means something. He is able to convince owners who have built their businesses slowly over the years to sell out in a heartbeat. Jim and I and most of the senior managers at Signature have been working together for a long time. In our team we all have our jobs and deliverables. Jim's job was to identify the opportunity, secure initial financing and give a vision and mission to the company. Jim's job really is not in the details of acquisition due diligence or in the details of implementing a uniform operating system or marketing plan. Jim delivered on his part. Given the flux Signature's strategy is in right now, it is really a tough call for Jim whether he should stay. After all, he has quite a bit of equity tied up in this.

As Jim Covert continued walking towards his apartment close to Circular Quay in Sydney Harbor, he could see the Opera House and the Harbor Bridge. Sydney was not a bad place. It would be nice to be around for the Olympic Games in 2000. He stopped for a minute and pondered his choices. What was the right decision for his company? What was the right decision for him? He knew he had some tough decisions to make and he had better make them sooner rather than later.

Case 11

Ducati & Texas Pacific Group—A "Wild Ride" Leveraged Buyout

"Well, at least our lawyers are *here*!" exclaimed Dante Razzano, Managing Director of Deutsche Morgan Grenfell (DMG), as he addressed one of the advisors of Ducati, the Italian motorcycle company. With that statement, Razzano representing Texas Pacific Group (TPG) in their attempt to acquire Ducati, set off a scene of shouting and screaming by the advisors to Ducati. Abel Halpern, HBS '93, Partner at TPG, looked on as his 48-year-old banker defended the position the two TPG lawyers at the table had taken towards the deal. As the shouting ended, Razzano, suddenly with a placid calm, looked at Halpern and gave him a knowing, almost fatherly wink, as if to say, "don't worry Abel, now *we* have got the advantage." "The scene was unbelievable," Halpern recalled. "And then again, it wasn't. Inconceivable things had happened throughout this negotiation."

It was July 21, 1996, and Halpern and Razzano were in the final stages of negotiating the purchase of a majority stake in Ducati from Cagiva, a conglomerate owned by the Castiglioni family. TPG had already signed a detailed Letter of Intent with Cagiva and was now hammering out the details of the deal in the definitive purchase agreement. But as with everything in this deal, nothing was easy for Halpern and his team. Halpern believed that Cagiva had tried to shop the deal to other buyers, even though the Letter of Intent included an exclusivity clause for TPG. Moreover, the negotiations had been nothing short of acrimonious, with the Cagiva team reverting to tactics such as re-opening items that had been agreed upon and taking a highly confrontational stance in the discussions. "They even started calling me *macellaio* or 'butcher' because they began to hate me so much," Halpern said. Halpern recalled the scene surrounding the brawl:

> We had nearly finalized all of the points in the purchase agreement. The only major concern was that the Castiglioni brothers had failed to show up for any of the sessions. This would not have concerned me but for the fact that the brothers had done this repeatedly throughout

Professors Walter Kuemmerle and Dean's Fellow William J. Coughlin (MBA '99) prepared this case. HBS cases are developed solely as the basis for class discussion. Cases are not intended to serve as endorsements, sources of primary data, or illustrations of effective or ineffective management.

the transaction in order to try to back out of the deal. Now, I had my boss, David Bonderman [founder of TPG] and Senior Partner Jeff Shaw flying to Italy to sign the closing documents and we had this! No Castiglioni brothers—just a brawl between our investment banker and Ducati's advisors.

About 30 minutes later, during a negotiation break, Halpern and his business advisor Federico Minoli, a Partner at the consulting firm Bain & Co. conducting the due diligence with TPG, retreated to a dimly lit store room off the Ducati factory floor to reflect. "This is Italy," said Minoli to his visibly pensive client as they stood surrounded by carcasses of unfinished and defective motorcycles. "Abel, you must embrace this madness and make it work for you, otherwise it will all end in tears." Digesting Minoli's words Halpern thought: "Do I *really* want to do this deal?"

The Road to Italy Goes through Mexico: Texas Pacific Group, Abel Halpern and Their Interest in Italy

Abel Halpern was raised in Philadelphia and graduated from Yale University in 1988. After Yale, Halpern worked as a labor organizer, focusing on workforces in the casino industry in Las Vegas. Looking for a change, Halpern decided to apply to Harvard Business School, more or less on a whim. "They didn't require test scores, just essays," explained Halpern, "so I had nothing to lose." After getting accepted, Halpern decided to enroll at HBS after his interest was piqued during class day. At the end of working a summer at Bain & Co. in Boston, Halpern accepted a permanent job with Bain, working part time during his second year and starting work right after graduation in June of 1993. Halpern explained his experience with Bain:

> At Bain, I worked mostly on Latin American cases as I had an interest and an aptitude in the area. I spoke Spanish and also had some prior work experience in the Latino community. I lived in Mexico as an exchange student in a rural public school when I was 14 and I spent most of my time focusing on Latino workers when I was a union organizer. I suppose it was this expertise and interest that helped me land a job with TPG, which is known to be a bit eclectic in its approach to life.

A year after he joined Bain, his then-girlfriend (and later wife and fellow HBS alumnus) introduced him to some people at a relatively new private equity firm, Texas Pacific Group. David Bonderman formed TPG in 1993 out of a special fund called Air Partners, which purchased Continental Airlines and AmericanWest Airlines. Prior to forming Air Partners with TPG founder Jim Coulter and Bill Price in 1992, Bonderman worked for nearly a decade with Robert Bass, one of the four celebrated brothers from Fort Worth, TX who were some of the early industrialists/leveraged buyout investors. While working with Bass, Bonderman focused on troubled, out of favor companies and reportedly achieved annual investment returns in excess of 60%. TPG had already had international exposure via a joint venture with Newbridge Asia, but Halpern was the fund's first international employee when they hired him to open the Mexico City office in June 1994. Since that time, TPG had built upon the success Bonderman had achieved with Bass (see **Exhibit 1** for some information on TPG Partners).

Halpern's first potential deal target from Mexico City was ironically a Turin, Italy based fashion company Gruppo Finanziario Tessile ("GFT"), the licensee of Italian designers such as Giorgio Armani. Although TPG did not win the deal, Halpern worked with two key people that would become partners in his later transactions. One was Dante

EXHIBIT 1   **Summary Description of TPG Partners, L.P.**

Source: TPG.

The Partnership is being established primarily to acquire control of companies through acquisition and restructuring, and to a lesser extent to take minority positions in private and public debt or equity securities. The Partnership is being formed by David Bonderman, who for nine years was Chief Operating Officer of the Robert M. Bass Group, Inc. and its successor Keystone, Inc. (collectively "RMBG"); James G. Coulter, a former key investment officer for RMBG; and William S. Price, former head of Business Development at G.E. Capital, Inc. ("G.E. Capital"). Mr. Bonderman, Mr. Coulter and Mr. Price (jointly or in any combination, the "Principals") conduct their investment activities as the Texas Pacific Group, Inc.

Mr. Bonderman and Mr. Coulter have extensive experience making private and public investments. From RMBG's inception in 1983 through August 1992, Mr. Bonderman was responsible for structuring and coordinating all of RMBG's investments in private and public securities and real estate. Since 1986, Messrs. Bonderman or Coulter have had lead roles on behalf of RMBG and certain related entities (the "Keystone Investment Group") in 18 transactions similar to those contemplated for the Partnership involving over $1.1 billion in capital commitments. During their tenure, the Keystone Investment Group achieved a cumulative annual internal rate of return of 63.1% on the 14 of these investments that have been realized.

Mr. Price has extensive acquisition and business integration experience which he developed as head of Business Development for G.E. Capital and as a partner at Bain & Company ("Bain"). While at Bain, Mr. Price worked with Messrs. Bonderman and Coulter in the strategic evaluation of American Savings Bank, F.A. ("American Savings Bank"), one of the Keystone Investment Group's most significant investments.

Consistent with their historic practice, the Principals will generally seek investments for the Partnership of from $20 million to $100 million in companies with market values that typically range from $100 million to $2.0 billion. The Partnership will target a minimum portfolio internal rate of return of 35% on invested capital. In all acquisitions and recapitalizations and in many private and public strategic minority investments, the Partnership will be represented on the boards of portfolio companies and will take an active role in their strategic direction.

The Partnership will be distinguished from most investment partnerships by three characteristics. First, the Partnership will use a unique investment strategy which relies principally upon: (a) pursuing complex transactions; (b) focusing on industries undergoing change; and (c) applying cautious contrarianism. Second, the Partnership will be able to participate in a variety of investment types, including buyouts, restructurings, bankruptcies and, to a limited extent, strategic public security investments. This flexible investment mandate should enable the Partnership to take advantage of the most compelling private and public opportunities, allowing it to exert influence over a developing corporate situation or seek to gain control of a company through a variety of investment methods. Third, the Principals believe their relationships with three historically affiliated investor groups will bring specialized expertise to, and provide a substantial competitive advantage for, the Partnership over other similar pooled investment funds.

Razzano, one of the leading M&A bankers in Italy, and CEO of Deutsche Morgan Grenfell Italia. The second was Federico Minoli, an Italian Partner with Bain & Co. who focused on the consumer products and luxury goods sectors and who was based in Boston. Halpern highlighted his relationship with these two men and how they led to his interest in Italy:

> Although I was disappointed we didn't get the GFT deal, I was excited to have worked with Dante and Federico. We all just seemed to click. I really didn't know Federico well at Bain, but I knew his reputation and his experience as CEO of the U.S. subsidiary of Italian clothing and designer firm, Benetton. From a practical perspective I now had an Italian insider and an Italian CEO with whom I could partner on deals. However, Italy piqued my interest for other reasons as well. First of all, few international private equity firms saw Italy on their radar in 1994. As TPG always attempts to conceive tomorrow's idea, to go where no one else went was in itself interesting. Second, I saw two economies in Italy. One was one that I would call "statist"—big, inefficient companies that were either run by the state or were big,

mega-conglomerates that operated like state owned companies. The other economy consisted of smaller, middle market companies created by entrepreneurs. Many of these companies typically had between $100 and $300 million in sales, were mostly born or reborn after World War II, and were private. After a period of dramatic growth from the sixties through the eighties, many of these businesses struggled with the complexity of scale, a global market-place and frankly the challenge of generational succession. However, what I really liked about these companies was that in order to be successful in the high wage and high tax environment of Italy these companies focused on high value-added niches in high margin businesses, where the relative cost differentials are absorbed by the customer.

Most of the companies Halpern was interested in were companies that had grown rapidly but still had the corporate structures of very small companies, causing great stress to the management of the businesses. Moreover, these companies usually faced succession issues as the younger generation inherited the business from the founding generation. As many of these younger owners spent more time working out how to divide their assets than on working on how to improve their businesses, these companies were ripe for a LBO. However, one added complexity to doing these deals was their practice of what Halpern liked to call "fiscal efficiency." In order to minimize their tax liability, these companies could have Byzantine structures even if they were small. "It is not uncommon to see a company with $100 million in sales and 50 subsidiary entities," explained Halpern. As a result, some of these companies' subsidiaries would appear to be losing money when in fact they were quite profitable. Deciphering the numbers was often quite difficult, if not impossible. "Remember, that these companies were privately owned," warned Minoli, "and the owners could do as they pleased with their assets. If that meant siphoning off profits of one division to fund another division, so be it. The upside was that most of these companies had been plowing money back into the business to minimize their current tax liability so they often had very advanced manufacturing equipment."

"Many of these issues were reflected in Ducati," Halpern recalled. "That's what made the deal so interesting . . . and difficult."

Ducati—A Great Brand and a Wild Ride

Ducati—A History of Invention and Technical Leadership

Founded in 1926 by the Ducati family, Ducati was at one point the second largest manufacturing concern in Italy. The company had a long history of invention, becoming, as Minoli described, "consumer electronics before there was electronics." The company invented new types of razors, cameras and movie projectors for the Italian market. During World War II, the company produced materials for the Italian army and, as a result, was razed to rubble by the Allies in 1943. After the war, the founders were left penniless, so the Italian government took over the company through the state holding company, *Istituto per la Ricostruzione Industriale* (Institute for Industrial Reconstruction) or IRI.[1] Under IRI, the company was split into two concerns—Ducati Energia, a consumer electronics company, and Ducati Meccanica, the motorcycle company. In the late 1940s, the company designed and built the first motor bike in Italy, popularly called *cucciolo* or "the puppy," which became the most popular mode of mass transportation in Italy at the time.

What really got Ducati Meccanica started, however, was the engine designed by Fabio Taglioni, who Minoli described as "the genius of engine mechanics. He was responsible for the creation of the myth of Ducati." The avant-garde Taglioni design, also called the

[1] IRI had been set up in 1933 as a state holding company to take over the stakes in industrial companies held by three large Italian banks that were facing bankruptcy.

Desmodromic Distribution System, was partially designed out of necessity. As quality steel was unavailable at the time in Italy, Taglioni invented a new type of engine that could allow valves to open and close at high revolutions without the use of springs. When the motorcycles started racing, the Ducati quickly became one of the top racing brands in Italy. However, while the technical side was inventing state of the art products, the State was running the company into the ground. As a result of massive losses suffered by the State, in 1983, IRI decided to dispose of its motorcycle assets and an Italian conglomerate, Cagiva, purchased the company.

Cagiva stood for "Castiglioni Giovanni Varese" and was named after the founder and the town in which the company was based. Cagiva originally assembled Harley Davidson motorcycles, but began producing its own motorcycles in 1979. Cagiva's motorcycles were lower end models compared to Ducati, but Cagiva also added one important element to the Ducati motorcycle. "Cagiva had great frames but no engine," Minoli explained. "And Ducati had a great engine but no body. When the two were put together by Cagiva, that is when the real Ducati was born." However, Cagiva ended up having their share of problems as well. In addition to the motorcycles, Cagiva owned a wide range of other companies, everything from metal stamping businesses to hotels. By the mid-1990s, the company, now being run by the sons of the founder, had become excessively leveraged and was bleeding cash in many of its business lines. It was believed that the profits of Ducati were being used to support the other failing businesses. It was because of this financial difficulty that the Castiglioni brothers began a search for new financing for their troubled entity.

The World Motorcycle Industry in 1996

Motorcycles sold around the world basically fell into two categories: bikes that were used as an essential means of transportation and bikes that were used primarily for recreational purposes. Virtually all cruising bikes such as Harley-Davidson, dirt bikes (such as some of Yamaha's bikes), and street bikes (BMW, Honda, Ducati) with an engine volume >500cc were purchased for recreational purposes. Material affluence among empty nesters, the midlife crisis of baby boomers and other "life-style factors" contributed to a surge in bike demand for large cruising and sports bikes starting in the mid-1980s. Many baby boomers seemed to derive more utility from owning a bike than from riding it frequently. In fact, the bike brands that were more difficult to ride often commanded a price premium. Harley-Davidson was the most prominent recent example for the revival of a motorcycle brand. By 1996 the average waiting period for an entry-level Harley cruiser was six months. In the United States, street bikes >500cc represented only about 26% of the total bike market, while cruising bikes represented 36%. In Europe and Japan, cruisers represented only about 15% of the total bike market while street bikes >500cc represented 37%. (See **Exhibit 2** for European and U.S. market segment evolution.)

While in 1995 Harley-Davidson held a 65.0% share of the total U.S. cruiser market, corresponding to a 23% share of the total U.S. bike market >750cc (cruising and street combined), they only held a 21% share in the much smaller European cruiser market, corresponding to a 2.5% share of the total European bike market >750cc. European growth had been strong for Harley-Davidson in recent years, however, and an analyst[2] estimated that Harley-Davidson's worldwide sales growth could average 15% p.a. over the next seven years. Harley-Davidson, the only publicly listed motorcycle "pure play" in the world, was an intriguing role model for Halpern as he considered an investment in Ducati. Harley-Davidson had succeeded in creating a life-style brand with about 15% ($200m) of 1995 sales derived from highly profitable clothing and mechanical accessories rather than bikes and replacement parts. And, even better, there seemed to be

[2] Robert W. Baird & Company, Milwaukee, WI, 1996.

EXHIBIT 2A   **European Bike Market Segment Evolution (# of units)**

Source: Giral, Eurstat, Bain analysis.

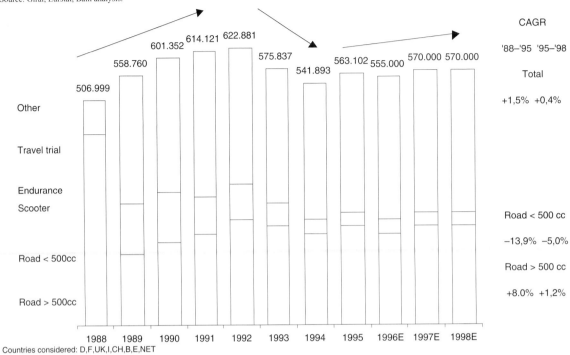

Countries considered: D,F,UK,I,CH,B,E,NET

EXHIBIT 2B   **U.S. Bike Market (# of units)**

Source: Ducati.

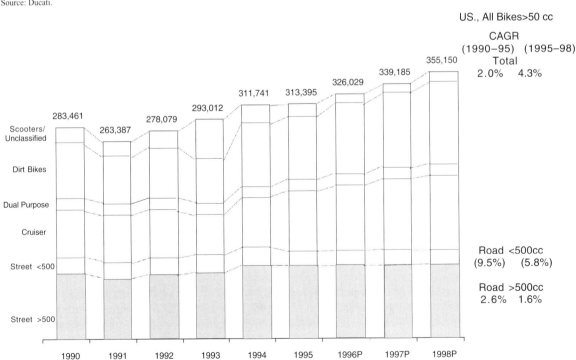

potential for further growth of clothing and other products. (See **Exhibit 3** for Harley-Davidson sales.) The price-earnings multiple of Harley-Davidson seemed to reflect only some of this growth potential, however. (See **Exhibit 4** for a table of comparable companies.) In July 1996, Harley Davidson had a market capitalization of $3.17 billion on 1995 sales of $1.35 billion and no long-term debt.

In many ways Ducati was in a great position to replicate with street-bikes what Harley-Davidson had done with cruisers. Ducati bikes had won the 1990, 1991, 1992, 1994, and 1995 World Superbike championships against strong competition.[3] Ducati's brand was well known even though marketing efforts in the past had been small. Also, Ducati had considerable growth potential in its core business. In 1995 the company sold 20,017 bikes while Harley-Davidson sold 105,104 and BMW sold 50,246. Only 2,402 of Ducati's bikes were exported to the United States in 1995. Ducati's world market share for street/road bikes >500cc was around 5%. (See **Exhibit 5** for Ducati's international sales distribution and **Exhibit 6** for Ducati's 1995 market share.)

Also, while several new competitors were rumored to re-enter the market for cruisers (e.g. Excelsior-Henderson, Indian Motorcycle Company) there were no significant new entrants foreseen for street bikes. Street bike customers liked technical excellence, as indicated by racing performance. And the high upfront costs of successfully designing and racing bikes seemed to deter entry.

Working Capital Problems and Product Line Issues

While Ducati looked like an attractive brand with development potential, TPG quickly discovered several "yellow flags" in the course of its due diligence. First, Ducati faced severe manufacturing and financing bottlenecks and had gotten itself into a vicious circle. Delays in payments to some key suppliers led to a large number of almost-finished bikes that remained "work in progress" because one or two key parts were missing. This in turn led to lower sales and extended customer wait lists. (See **Exhibit 7** for supplier dependence on Ducati and **Exhibit 8** for Ducati's pent-up demand.) The big question for any buyer would be what the working capital needs of Ducati were in the short and long term. By March 1996, accounts receivable were at 90 days sales. TPG believed that this number could eventually be reduced to 60 days but was not sure. Inventory had ballooned

[3] Honda had won in 1988 and 1989 and Kawasaki in 1993.

EXHIBIT 3
Harley Davidson Sales Mix (1995E, millions of dollars)

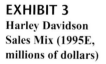

Source: Ducati.

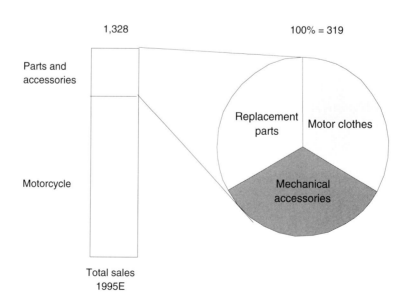

EXHIBIT 4 Comparable Companies (Amounts in US$000)

Source: Compiled from Bloomberg, Thomson Financial Datastream, Investext, Lexis Nexis, SEC filings data.

Motorcycle Companies

Company	HQ Country	Sales 1994	Sales 1995	Net Income 1994	Net Income 1995	Market Capitalization	Net Assets 1995	Sales Multiple	PE Multiple	Equity Beta June 1996	Units Sold 1995	Employees (12/31/95)
Harley Davidson	USA	1,158,887	1,350,466	104,272	112,480	3,166,944 (7/18/96)	955,679	2.16	22.6 (1996E)	1.09	105,104	4,800
Titan Motorcycle	USA	0	625	n.a.	n.a.	n.a.	n.a.	n.a.	n.a.	n.a.	n.a.	n.a.
BMW	Germany	425,174	511,189	n.a.	n.a.	6,696,788 (7/18/96)	3,527,729	2.04	18.6 (1996E)	1.10	50,246	1,900
Excelsior-Henderson	USA	0	0	n.a.	n.a.	n.a.	n.a.	n.a.	n.a.	n.a.	n.a.	n.a.
Indian Motorcycle	USA	0	0	n.a.	n.a.	n.a.	n.a.	n.a.	n.a.	n.a.	n.a.	n.a.
Honda	Japan	5,213,925	5,519,886	516,028	559,509	23,594,943 (7/18/96)	22,876,160	4.04	34.9 (1996A)	1.22	5,300,000	96,800
Ducati	Italy										20,017	

Notes:
Fiscal years for 0Honda are Japanese fiscal years (ending on March 31 of the following year).
Sales data for BMW and Honda are for motorcycles only. Net Income data for Honda are for motorcycles only. Net assets and market data for BMW and Honda are for entire company.
Motorcycles at BMW represent about 2% of sales.
All market data and multiples are for entire companies and for June/July 1996.
Titan Motorcycle was founded in 1994. Excelsior-Henderson is a traditional brand refounded in 1993 and rumored to enter the market with a cycle soon.
Indian Motorcycle was a traditional brand currently in re-founding.

Luxury Goods Companies

Company	HQ Country	Sales 1994	Sales 1995	Net Income 1994	Net Income 1995	Market Capitalization	Net Assets 1995	Sales Multiple	PE Multiple	Equity Beta June 1996	Units Sold 1995	Employees (12/31/95)
Bulgari[1]	Italy	177,333	242,948	15,402	24,926	5,328,000 (7/18/96)	319,500	21.34	207.98 (1995)	1.59	n.a.	573
LVMH[2]	France	5,231,388	6,076,531	685,933	825,918	20,707,443 (7/18/96)	11,205,200	3.46	25.43 (1995)	1.41	n.a.	18,617
Hermes[3]	France	641,171	780,816	54,433	82,449	9,181,580 (7/18/96)	753,400	11.99	113.58 (1995)	1.27	n.a.	3,366
Gucci[4]	Netherlands	263,576	500,064	17,921	82,878	3,666,145 (7/18/96)	329,458	7.18	43.34 (1995)	1.18	n.a.	1,176

[1]1995 Revenue by product category: jewels (44%), watches (42%), perfume (12%), royalties (2%). Bulgari went public in 1995.
[2]1995 Revenue by product category: champagne/wines (20%), cognac/spirits (18%), luggage/leather goods (25%), perfumes/beauty products (31%), other (7%).
[3]1995 Revenue by product category: scarves (20.2%), leather goods (20.3%), ready-to-wear (12.5%), ties (8.5%), watchmaking (8.8%), perfumes (6.7%), arts de la table (4.8%), other sectors/products (18.2%).
[4]1995 Revenue by product category: leather goods (51.6%), shoes (17.7%), ties & scarves (6.6%), ready-to-wear (12.1%), watches (3.1%), other (3.2%), royalties (5.7%).

EXHIBIT 5
Ducati Sales
International
Distribution (units)

Source: Ducati.

100% = 19,840

1995

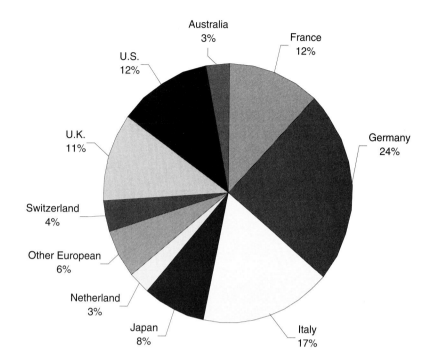

to almost 120 days sales. Here TPG was optimistic that this figure could be dropped to about 40 days. Accounts payable had "mushroomed" to about 100 days sales by March 1996. While this was good news in the very short term for Ducati's cash position, it did not exactly help that some of the unpaid suppliers were suffering severe financial problems. A realistic long-term goal for accounts payable was 60 days.

Second, since Ducati was heavily entangled with Cagiva, the details of its financial performance were not at all transparent. TPG was able to assemble profit and loss statements for 1993 to 1995 but a reliable balance sheet was only available for 1995 after some serious number crunching by a "Big 6" accounting firm. (See **Exhibit 9** for historic P&Ls, balance sheets and pro formas for Ducati.) As a result of bad management rather than lack of demand Ducati would most likely show a negative EBIT in 1996. In fact, bankruptcy was a real possibility.

On the positive side, while Ducati's product family seemed quite expansive given its low production volume (Ducati offered 15 models in four families based on seven different engines), the company had strong manufacturing fundamentals. Ducati had a low fixed cost base due to a high level of outsourcing. Approximately 85% of product cost were outsourced components. Also, Ducati had a high level of standardization of its engines. Crank cases and cylinder heads were by far the most expensive components of an engine. With only two crank cases and three cylinder heads Ducati produced seven engines. Among competitors only Harley-Davidson came close to this level of standardization. (See **Exhibit 10** for product line complexity and **Exhibit 11** for photos of Ducati motorcycles.)

The Beginnings of a Deal

When Cagiva's financial problems became apparent in the Spring of 1995, the Castiglioni brothers approached Razzano about a bridge loan from DMG to help the company through its troubles. After Razzano met with Cagiva, he was not interested in

EXHIBIT 6 **Ducati 1995 Market Share**

Source: Ducati.

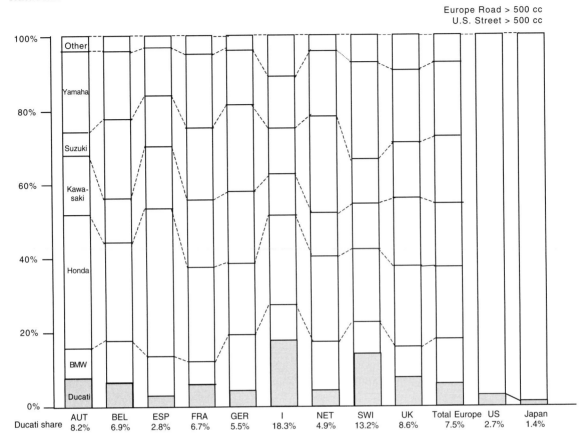

providing a loan to the company but thought that the company might have the elements he and Halpern were looking for in an investment. After several meetings between Cagiva and the TPG team in the Fall of 1995, Halpern told the brothers that TPG was not interested in an equity investment in Cagiva, but they were interested in purchasing Ducati. Halpern explained his interest in the motorcycle company:

> I loved the fact that this was a company that operated in a niche part of the motorcycle market for high performance vehicles. They were a high value added business and despite the high labor costs, were thought to be a low cost producer—remember, entrepreneurs and owners don't like fat. But we also didn't know exactly how profitable the company was as it was entangled in the Cagiva conglomerate's businesses. So we would need to do a lot of due diligence work. What we did know was that we had a great product and a great brand with what seemed to be a great deal of demand. Plus, this was *our* deal; not an auction.

Minoli agreed with Halpern and was very interested in the company:

> What I saw was a great product, a great group of product developers and a great consumer franchise, but no real company. In order to be successful in both our bid and a build out, we would need to try to figure out what the company *should* be making and we would need to build a real global company around these assets. But, in all my work in luxury goods, I have learned one thing: great global brands are few and far between. And global brands with a great technology are even more rare. Ducati was a bit like Ferrari. A lot of people who will never drive a Ferrari know what it is and what it stands for.

EXHIBIT 7
Supplier Dependence on Ducati

Source: Bain, Cuneo (compiled for Ducati).

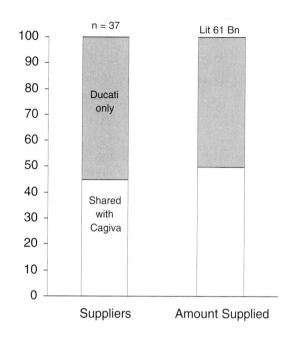

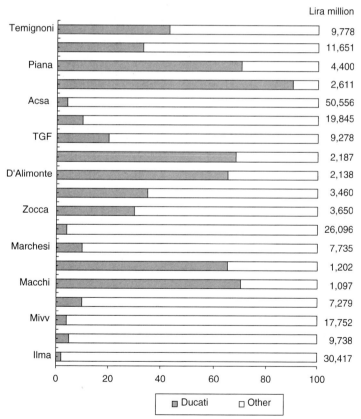

EXHIBIT 8
Ducati's Pent-up
Demand (# of units)

Source: Ducati.

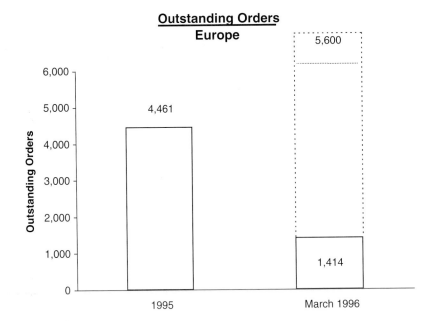

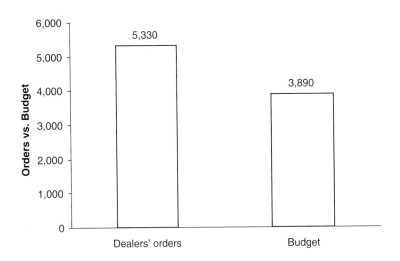

In order to build the business, Halpern and his team knew that they would need to find a world class management team to run the operation—one that could build the brand and that could build the company. "That was our ace in the hole," Halpern explained. "We had Federico."

Federico Minoli began working at Proctor & Gamble (P&G) in Italy in 1974 as a brand manager. As he advanced in his career he joined International Playtex Inc. where he spent his time in both Italy and the U.S. as an international marketing manager. After taking off a year to travel throughout Africa, Minoli began working at McKinsey & Co in Italy. "I hated almost every minute of it," Minoli reminisced. "But that is where I started getting

EXHIBIT 9A Ducati: Historic P&L Statements and Forecasts

Source: TPG.

	1993	1994	1995	1996
Total motorcycle volume (#)	16,507	18,163	20,017	13,480
Average unit price per cycle (million Lira)	8.3	10	12.8	14.8
Motorcycle revenue	137.0	181.6	256.2	199.5
Potential Cagiva North America mark-up	0	0	0	0
Adjusted motorcycle revenue	137.0	181.6	256.2	199.5
Apparel revenue	0	0	0	0
Other revenue / adjustments	26.6	23	35.8	0
Total revenues	163.6	204.3	292.0	199.5
Materials	93.2	119.3	156.9	109.1
Direct labor and other direct expenses	11.0	12.3	16.5	13.1
Variable sales expense	1.0	1.1	3.8	6.0
Apparel expenses	0.0	0.0	0.0	0.0
Total variable expense	105.2	132.7	177.2	128.2
Variable Contribution	58.4	71.6	114.8	71.3
Total SG&A	30.3	34.5	54.4	46.0
EBITDA	28.1	37.1	60.4	25.3
Depreciation	6.0	6.0	6.0	6.0
Amortization	0.0	0.0	0.0	20.7
EBIT	22.1	31.1	54.4	-1.4

	1993	1994	1995	1996	1997	1998	1999	2000	2001	2002	2003
Summary of Operating Ratios (1997 and onward are assumptions)											
Motorcycle volume growth		10.0%	10.2%	-32.7%	110.9%	23.9%	14.3%	10.0%	6.5%	5.5%	5.5%
Motorcycle average unit price growth		20.5%	28.0%	15.6%	-8.8%	0.0%	0.0%	0.8%	0.8%	0.9%	1.0%
Apparel revenue growth		0.0%	0.0%	0.0%	0.0%	0.0%	0.0%	0.0%	0.0%	0.0%	0.0%
Other revenue growth		-14.7%	57.7%	-100.0%	0.0%	8.8%	15.1%	17.1%	8.1%	0.0%	0.0%
Total revenue growth		24.9%	42.9%	-31.7%	92.3%	23.9%	14.3%	10.9%	7.4%	6.4%	6.6%
Percentage of total revenue											
Materials	57.0%	58.4%	53.7%	54.7%	53.5%	53.5%	52.0%	51.6%	51.1%	50.6%	50.4%
Direct labor & other direct expenses	6.7%	6.0%	5.7%	6.6%	5.6%	5.6%	4.8%	4.8%	4.8%	4.8%	4.8%
Variable sales expense	0.6%	0.5%	1.3%	3.0%	1.3%	1.3%	2.4%	2.4%	2.4%	2.4%	2.4%
SG&A	18.5%	16.9%	18.6%	23.1%	16.1%	15.8%	15.8%	15.8%	15.8%	15.8%	15.8%
Resulting EBITDA/sales	17.2%	18.2%	20.7%	12.7%	23.5%	23.8%	25.0%	25.4%	25.9%	26.4%	26.6%
Depreciation	3.7%	2.9%	2.1%	3.0%	1.9%	1.9%	2.0%	2.2%	2.4%	2.6%	2.8%
Amortization	0.0%	0.0%	0.0%	10.4%	6.4%	5.2%	5.2%	4.7%	4.4%	4.1%	3.9%
Resulting EBIT/sales	13.5%	15.2%	18.6%	-0.7%	15.2%	16.7%	17.7%	18.4%	19.1%	19.6%	19.9%

(continued)

EXHIBIT 9A (Continued)

	1996	1997	1998	1999	2000	2001	2002	2003
Proforma Resulting from Assumptions								
(see first part of Exhibit 9a)								
Total motorcycle volume (#)	13,480	28,429	35,224	40,261	44,287	47,166	49,760	52,497
Average unit price per cycle (million Lira)	14.8	13.5	13.5	13.5	13.6	13.7	13.8	14.0
Motorcycle Revenue	199.5	383.7	475.4	543.4	602.6	646.9	688.6	733.7
Apparel Revenue	0	0	0	0	0	0	0	0
Other Revenue	0	0.00	0.00	0.00	0.00	0.00	0.00	0.00
Total revenue	199.5	383.7	475.4	543.4	602.6	646.9	688.6	733.7
Materials	109.1	205.3	254.4	282.6	310.9	330.5	348.4	369.8
Direct labor & other direct expenses	13.1	21.5	26.6	26.1	28.9	31.0	33.1	35.2
Variable sales expense	6.0	5.0	6.2	13.0	14.5	15.5	16.5	17.6
SG&A	46.0	61.8	75.1	85.9	95.2	102.2	108.8	115.9
EBITDA	25.3	90.2	113.2	135.9	153.0	167.5	181.8	195.2
Depreciation	6.0	7.3	9.1	11.1	13.5	15.7	18.1	20.7
Amortization	24.7	24.7	24.7	28.5	28.5	28.5	28.5	28.5
EBIT	−5.4	58.2	79.4	96.3	111.0	123.3	135.2	146.0
Net Interest Expense	11.0	31.1	28.9	28.1	23.1	17.9	12.3	6.3
EBT	−16.4	27.1	50.5	68.2	87.9	105.4	122.9	139.7
Taxes (@53.5%)	0.0	14.5	27.0	36.5	47.1	56.4	65.7	74.7
Net Income	−16.4	12.6	23.5	31.7	40.9	49.0	57.1	64.9
Tax rate 53.5%								

All figures except percentages and where noted are in billion Lira.
On 07/01/96: 1US$ = 1534.6 Lira.
Some figures are approximate as Ducati's accounting was highly interviowen with Cagiva Group.
1996 figures are estimates based on preliminary figures for January through June.
THE FINANCIAL INFORMATION IN THIS EXHIBIT WAS PREPARED BY TPG FOR PURPOSES OF EVALUATING A POTENTIAL INVESTMENT IN THE DUCATI BUSINESS IN 1996. SUCH FINANCIAL INFORMA-
TION FOR YEARS THROUGH 1999 DOES NOT REFLECT THE ACTUAL FINANCIAL RESULTS OF DUCATI MOTOR HOLDING SPA, AND FINANCIAL INFORMATION FOR YEARS FOLLOWING 1999 IS NOT IN-
DICATIVE OF THE RESULTS THAT WILL BE OBTAINED BY DUCATI MOTOR HOLDING SPA. SUCH FINANCIAL INFORMATION IS NOT CURRENT, HAS NOT BEEN UPDATED AND MUST NOT BE RELIED UPON
FOR ANY PURPOSE.

Capital Expenditures

	Amount	Years	1993	1994	1995	1996	1997	1998	1999	2000	2001	2002	2003
Maintenance			2.1	4.2	4.3	6.0	6.0	6.0	7.0	7.0	8.0	8.0	8.0
Capacity expansion						4.6	1.5	4.0	4.0	4.0	5.0	5.0	5.0
Technical investment			3.5	1.9	3.5	2.3	3.0	3.0	5.0	5.0	5.0	5.0	5.0
Additional investment (TPG estimates)							5.0	7.0	8.0	6.0	6.0	6.0	8.0
Total			5.6	6.1	7.8	12.9	15.5	20.0	24.0	22.0	24.0	24.0	26.0
Depreciation			6.0	6.0	6.0	6.0	7.3	9.1	11.1	13.5	15.7	18.1	20.7
Amortization (Italian GAAP)													
Ducati brand name	207.2	10				20.7	20.7	20.7	20.7	20.7	20.7	20.7	20.7
Transaction costs	40	10				4.0	4.0	4.0	4.0	4.0	4.0	4.0	4.0
Performance goodwill hurdle (paid in 1998)	38	10							3.8	3.8	3.8	3.8	3.8
Total						24.7	24.7	24.7	28.5	28.5	28.5	28.5	28.5

THE FINANCIAL INFORMATION IN THIS EXHIBIT WAS PREPARED BY TPG FOR PURPOSES OF EVALUATING A POTENTIAL INVESTMENT IN THE DUCATI BUSINESS IN 1996. SUCH FINANCIAL INFORMATION FOR YEARS THROUGH 1999 DOES NOT REFLECT THE ACTUAL FINANCIAL RESULTS OF DUCATI MOTOR HOLDING SPA, AND FINANCIAL INFORMATION FOR YEARS FOLLOWING 1999 IS NOT INDICATIVE OF THE RESULTS THAT WILL BE OBTAINED BY DUCATI MOTOR HOLDING SPA. SUCH FINANCIAL INFORMATION IS NOT CURRENT, HAS NOT BEEN UPDATED AND MUST NOT BE RELIED UPON FOR ANY PURPOSE.

209

EXHIBIT 9C Ducati Balance Sheet (1997 onward are assumptions)

Source: TPG.

	1995 (pre-buyout)	1996	1997	1998	1999	2000	2001	2002	2003
Cash	9.4	11.3	22.6	8.0	9.8	37.2	59.9	87.2	132.2
Accounts Receivable	80.0	84.5	83.2	124.5	139.9	141.6	152.0	161.4	170.6
Inventory	55.0	37.2	49.2	65.4	61.7	68.1	72.6	76.3	80.2
Other current assets	3.3	2.2	2.7	3.2	15.0	16.8	18.0	19.1	20.2
Total current assets (non-cash)	138.3	123.9	135.1	193.1	216.6	226.5	242.6	256.8	271.0
PP&E	28.1	64.8	75.5	86.4	99.3	107.8	116.2	124.1	129.4
Ducati trademark	0.0	200.3	179.6	158.9	138.1	117.4	96.7	76.0	55.3
Goodwill	0.0	27.5	27.5	65.0	61.3	57.5	53.8	50.0	46.3
Capitalized transaction costs	0.0	38.7	34.7	30.7	26.7	22.7	18.7	14.7	10.7
Total long-term assets	28.1	331.3	317.3	341.0	325.4	305.4	285.4	264.8	241.7
Total assets	175.8	466.5	475.0	542.1	551.8	569.1	587.9	608.8	644.9
Accounts payable	40.0	30.3	50.4	78.7	94.4	104.1	110.9	116.6	122.6
Other current liabilities	11.3	9.4	10.5	13.2	7.8	8.7	9.4	9.9	10.5
Total current liabilities	51.3	39.7	60.9	91.9	102.2	112.8	120.3	126.5	133.1
Staff severance reserve	7.3	6.2	8.5	10.6	15.3	17.8	20.4	20.4	20.4
Total long-term liabilities	7.3	6.2	8.5	10.6	15.3	17.8	20.4	20.4	20.4
Existing mortgage	44.9	0.0	0.0	0.0	0.0	0.0	0.0	0.0	0.0
Existing bank debt	136.8	0.0	0.0	0.0	0.0	0.0	0.0	0.0	0.0
New senior debt	0.0	280.0	247.5	240.0	195.5	149.5	99.3	46.3	0.0
New subordinated debt	0.0	0.0	0.0	0.0	0.0	0.0	0.0	0.0	0.0
Total debt	181.7	280.0	247.5	240.0	195.5	149.5	99.3	46.3	0.0
Total liabilities	240.3	325.9	316.9	342.5	313.0	280.1	240.0	193.2	153.5
Capital contribution	0.0	140.0	140.0	152.5	152.5	152.5	152.5	152.5	152.5
Retained earnings	−64.5	0.5	18.1	47.1	86.3	136.4	195.4	263.0	338.7
Net shareholders equity	−64.5	140.5	158.1	199.6	238.8	288.9	347.9	415.5	491.2
Total liabilities and equity	175.8	466.4	475.0	542.1	551.8	569.0	587.9	608.7	644.7
Check	0.0	0.1	0.0	0.0	0.0	0.1	0.0	0.1	0.2

THE FINANCIAL INFORMATION IN THIS EXHIBIT WAS PREPARED BY TPG FOR PURPOSES OF EVALUATING A POTENTIAL INVESTMENT IN THE DUCATI BUSINESS IN 1996. SUCH FINANCIAL INFORMA-
TION FOR YEARS THROUGH 1999 DOES NOT REFLECT THE ACTUAL FINANCIAL RESULTS OF DUCATI MOTOR HOLDING SPA, AND FINANCIAL INFORMATION FOR YEARS FOLLOWING 1999 IS NOT IN-
DICATIVE OF THE RESULTS THAT WILL BE OBTAINED BY DUCATI MOTOR HOLDING SPA. SUCH FINANCIAL INFORMATION IS NOT CURRENT, HAS NOT BEEN UPDATED AND MUST NOT BE RELIED UPON
FOR ANY PURPOSE.

EXHIBIT 10   **Ducati Product Line Complexity (1995)**

Source: Ducati.

	Carters	Heads	Motors	Segments	Models
Ducati	2	3	7	4	15
Harley Davidson	2	2	3	1	21
BMW	5	5	6	3	15
Triumph	2	2	3	4	12
Honda	12	12	20	6	26
Yamaha	13	13	19	6	28
Suzuki	10	10	12	6	18
Kawasaki	8	8	13	6	19

involved with turnaround management." Minoli rotated into one of McKinsey's clients, Benetton, as CEO of the U.S. subsidiary to turn it around. After three years, his work was completed and since in the meantime, half of the Italian McKinsey team left to start Bain & Co., in Italy, he joined Bain. Minoli explained his time at Bain:

> I liked to do the stuff that no one else wanted to do. I got involved in the "messy" industries like fashion and entertainment working with companies that had great products but crazy people in the organization. After a while, I transferred back to the Boston office to appease my wife and to head the global brands practice and I work mostly on due diligence cases. My wife is American and she worked as a lawyer focusing on discrimination litigation. There just was not much of that type of work in Italy and she really wanted to raise her children in the United States. But then came GFT where I worked with Abel for the first time. I had a lot of fun working with him—we just seemed to share the same vision and had complementary personalities. After that, I became something of an in-house partner for TPG at Bain. And Ducati was the perfect entrepreneurial opportunity I had always looked for.

Halpern's idea was to build the Ducati organization with Minoli as its CEO along with a few other high level executives Halpern and Minoli had lined up through various contacts. As a result, TPG entered into a verbal agreement on exclusivity on the deal and were busy preparing a Letter of Intent. "That's when things got crazy," lamented Halpern.

The History of a Deal—No Safe Ground Anywhere

As Halpern's team got ready to begin serious due diligence in December 1995, suddenly there was utter silence from the Cagiva group. After some sniffing around, Razzano found out that Sam Zell, the U.S. investor famous for his media and real estate transactions, was in talks with Cagiva about buying Ducati. Halpern and his team were disappointed but Halpern believed the deal would come back to them. He explained:

> I did not know Zell personally. However, as his reputation was well known, I suspected he might have limited patience for the Ducati shareholders. Zell was a motorcycle fanatic, and when he heard that Ducati was for sale he was interested. Though of course I was not there, I heard stories to suggest that Zell grew tired of the owners' inconsistent and erratic approach to negotiating the deal. Typically you negotiate in a linear fashion—once you have addressed a topic it is closed. These characters adopted a more circular approach in their negotiations. They thought of a negotiation more like a buffet you could keep coming back to. What is more, is that the Castiglioni brothers not only had strong egos, but they also possessed unique personalities with extensive color and drama. At one point in the process the deal was

EXHIBIT 11   Photos of Ducati Motorcycles

Source: Ducati.

M900

900

916

750

even evaluated by an African shaman, an advisor to one of the brothers. These difficult personalities combined with exotic business practices and a constantly shifting deal terrain led me to believe that the deal with Zell would explode.

The Castiglioni brothers had retained a number of advisors on the transaction, many of whom had conflicting interests with the others. Halpern and his San Francisco partners Bonderman and Shaw kept in touch with all advisors throughout the period of uncertainty around the Zell deal. In March 1996, TPG got the deal back and signed a detailed Letter of Intent in April. In the Letter of Intent, the main aspects of the deal structure were outlined and TPG was given exclusivity over the deal—meaning Cagiva could no longer shop it around. (See **Exhibit 12** for a trade press article on the Zell deal.)

Deal Structure

In crafting the deal structure, the TPG deal team made sure that certain interests of both parties were met. As regards the Castiglioni brothers and Cagiva, the main concern was to allow the brothers to create the appearance that they were only selling a 49% stake. They expressed a strong desire not to sell control of their company to anyone, especially not to Americans. Yet it seemed very unlikely that anyone would acquire a non-control minority position in the company. As a result, the TPG team came up with a structure where TPG would attain control and Cagiva could perpetuate the notion that they in fact had retained control. TPG would directly purchase 49% of the equity. TPG would also buy another 2% of the equity and register it in the name of an independent fiduciary company. Cagiva would retain 49% of the company outright and would also have an option to repurchase the 2% held by the fiduciary company in the event of an IPO. "That way, they could say at the country club they screwed the Americans and only sold 49%," Minoli explained.

EXHIBIT 12
Trade Press Article about Zell/Ducati Deal

Source: Jon F. Thompson, *Cycle World,* vol. 35, issue 6 (June 1996), p. 23.

ZELL/DUCATI DEAL FIZZLES

While Cagiva is busy touting its forthcoming new superbike, rumored financial troubles inside the Castiglioni Brothers' empire may mean that a proposed deal to sell a majority interest in Ducati to an American investor is dead.

Under the terms of the proposed deal, Chicago financier Sam Zell was negotiating for purchase of up to three-quarters of Bologna-based Ducati. The result would be a new firm, to be called New Ducati, which would have replaced Ducati's existing worldwide structure (see *Roundup,* March, 1996, and April, 1996).

Now, however, those close to Zell and the Castiglionis suggest that the deal has come apart. The companies are, however, reluctant to speak on the record. Said one Zell confidant, "We're not making any comments about the rumors, but I wouldn't dispute them."

A source inside Ducati responded to a *Cycle World* query by suggesting that rumors about the collapse of the deal were untrue. A faxed response read, in part, "We kindly ask you to wait a moment before dealing with this matter in your magazine."

Sources inside the Italian motorcycle business community say the completed deal would have given Zell 70 to 80 percent of Ducati for an undisclosed purchase price. The problem, these sources suggest, is that Cagiva is deep in debt to the powerful and much-feared *Guardia Finanza,* the Italian equivalent to the Internal Revenue Service.

If Cagiva does indeed owe money to the government agency, sources suggest that one possible reason is that an untoward percentage of Cagiva's profits may have been applied not toward the company's tax responsibilities, but to the debt service on loans taken in the late 1980s and early '90s to finance expansion into Eastern Europe, and also the purchase of MV Agusta, Moto Morini and several hotels.

The Zell/Ducati deal is falling apart, sources suggest, because Zell's purchase monies would have gone to pay part of this tax bill instead of toward upgrades that would make Ducati better able to compete on the world motorcycle market. Said one observer, "Zell backed out because the value wasn't there."

In addition, TPG had a shareholders agreement that stipulated that TPG controlled the board—and effectively controlled the company—until TPG's interest dropped below 10%. Additionally, as any IPO would most likely include the issuance of new shares, the existing shareholders would be diluted, thus precluding the likelihood that anyone would have a majority of the public shares. Finally, TPG would allow the older brother, Claudio, to stay on as "chairman" even though he would have limited executive powers.

Another part of this creative exercise was to have a big headline number in the purchase price as part of the deal. "Again, so they could look good with their peers," Minoli explained. But again there were some strings. First, the purchase price of somewhere between Lit. 400 and 500 billion for 100% of the company (subject to final due diligence), was not all to be paid to Cagiva. As it was impossible to determine the results of Ducati as a stand alone entity, TPG would need to perform a significant amount of due diligence. A particular concern was with working capital levels. Since TPG did not believe that the working capital contributed to the new entity was sufficient, part of the purchase price would be paid directly to the company in the form of a working capital adjustment, the amount of which would be determined after TPG completed its due diligence. Moreover, TPG intended to structure the purchase to include a Lit. 100 billion earn-out subject to the company meeting certain EBITDA targets in 1996 and 1997.

TPG also had some concerns of their own. In addition to the appropriate working capital adjustment, TPG was concerned about Italian insolvency laws. If Cagiva were to go bankrupt after the deal, there was a risk that the bankruptcy courts would unwind the deal for up to four years in some circumstances. As a result, the deal would be structured as an asset sale. TPG would create a NewCo that would be funded by TPG and DMG. The NewCo would then purchase the brand and patent rights of Ducati from Cagiva. Then, the other assets of Ducati would be swapped for a 49% interest in the NewCo. Once the asset sale was approved by the courts, the bankruptcy risk period was cut down to one year. Additionally, TPG negotiated a covenant that would prohibit certain actions by the legal entity selling Ducati to technically preclude the possibility of insolvency.

Due Diligence—A Multimillion Dollar Effort

As Halpern began to mobilize his troops to conduct intense due diligence in May 1996, he heard that the company was trying to shop the deal—again. "The company was teetering on insolvency and the Castiglioni brothers were trying to rustle up another deal!" Halpern lamented. Fortunately, this stopped after a short period and the TPG team conducted its due diligence. Halpern explained the diligence process:

> The key for us was to figure out what the business should be making given the assets, what we knew of the sales levels and the macro environment. What we had to do was build a model from the ground up on a unit by unit basis to see if the company was indeed profitable. The problem was we had no real numbers to go by. The two companies were so intertwined that it was difficult to separate: Ducati made engines for Cagiva, Cagiva made frames for Ducati, they shared the same distribution system, etc. Moreover, Ducati had guaranteed Cagiva group debt and Ducati had stopped paying its suppliers. It was an amazing situation and required us to come up with a theory of what the numbers would have been if it were a standalone entity.

Upon the completion of due diligence, Halpern, Minoli and Razzano felt just a little more comfortable about the deal, if it could be done at the right valuation. They were still a little surprised at what they found. Minoli explained:

> It was amazing. We had a company making the best motorcycles in the world, which had a long waitlist for products and was winning all of the races. Yet, the company had no cash, couldn't produce its products, couldn't get financing and was heading towards bankruptcy. Since they hadn't paid suppliers they had a countless number of bikes sitting off to the side of the factory floor unsold because they were missing one part—either because they were cut

off by a supplier or the supplier went bankrupt. Yet the economics of the company *should* look good; that is important, as we want to make sure we achieve our payback goal of around 3x in three to five years. We really needed to make sure we could meet our production ramp up targets—especially since this was a levered transaction. Because of the backlog of accounts payable the buyer literally needed to write a thousand checks on the first day on the job to get the company going again.

Financing Structure

Halpern wanted to keep a conservative financing structure. LBOs in Italy, and Europe in general, were not the same as in the United States as the high-yield market was not equally developed, making it difficult to achieve the leverage levels in the United States. As a result, Halpern figured the debt to equity ratio would be 2:1 as opposed to the 3:1 found in the United States. TPG's advisor Dante Razzano from DMG had requested the opportunity to co-invest from the newly raised DMG private equity fund. As TPG had developed a good relationship with Razzano, they offered him to put up 20% of the TPG commitment. But there was still the issue of options to management. "Cagiva didn't want us to give any options," Halpern recalled. "We wanted to give senior management 10%, but the Castiglioni brothers were not going to have any part of it."

Securing debt financing was quite tricky because of the lack of transparency at Ducati. Originally one European bank was interested in leading the financing, but could not get comfortable with the deal. The working capital concerns, the complexity of the transaction and the Cagiva credit risk was too much. So in June, with Razzano calling every favor he could, DMG stepped up and got preliminary approval for syndicating the debt portion of the transaction. Also, originally, TPG had planned to use senior and subordinated debt. However, negotiations around the structure of the sub-debt proved quite complex. Also, time was an issue and placement of the subordinated debt might have delayed the deal. So TPG decided to go just with senior debt. After intense negotiations the banking consortium agreed to provide up to Lit. 280 billion in senior debt with a coupon of 11.25%. Disbursement and repayment was tied to a set of cash-flow covenants. Halpern recalled: "TPG had a reputation to lose. This was TPG's first deal in continental Europe and it would be the largest LBO ever in Italy. We did not want this deal to backfire because of a myopic financing structure."

Public Equity Markets and Corporate Governance in Italy

Another concern of TPG was the eventual exit from their potential investment in Ducati. The product was easy to understand for investors and the brand was well known. If it was managed well, Ducati should be a profitable company within a few years. All this suggested that an IPO might be feasible. Halpern also felt that an IPO of Ducati might fetch a higher price than a trade sale. On the other hand Halpern was somewhat concerned about the state of equity markets in Italy.

On the negative side, the public equity market (Borsa Italiana) was much less developed than in the United States. Up until 1991 trading took place by means of an "open outcry auction system" on 10 regional stock exchanges (Milan accounting in the 1980s for 99% of total trading volume). As of December 29, 1995, there were 221 companies listed with a total market capitalization of $192.6 billion. This compared to a total market capitalization of $7,277.9 billion for the United States (NYSE, NASDAQ, AMEX). In July 1995, the total capitalization of the Borsa Italiana amounted to less than 20% of GDP, compared with around 40% for France, 98% in the United States and more than 100% for the United Kingdom. Also, corporate governance structures in Italy were much less developed than in other industrialized countries and Halpern was wondering how soon this would change. (See **Exhibit 13** for Italy's ranking on various corporate governance related indicators on the World Competitiveness Scoreboard.)

EXHIBIT 13 1996 World Competitiveness Scoreboard (Selected Indicators)

Source: *The World Competitiveness Yearbook*, 1996, pp. 19, 463, 455, 512, 513.

	Overall Competitiveness	Banking Sector (The banking sector exercises a positive influence on industry)	Venture Capital (Venture capital is readily available for business development)	Corporate Credibility (Companies that enjoy the public trust)	Corporate Boards (Corporate boards are safeguards for proper practices in corporations)
1	USA	Luxembourg	USA	Singapore	Chile
2	Singapore	Hong Kong	Hong Kong	China	Singapore
3	Hong Kong	Chile	Singapore	Chile	Canada
4	Japan	Singapore	Israel	Malaysia	New Zealand
5	Denmark	Malaysia	Netherlands	Finland	Luxembourg
6	Norway	South Africa	United Kingdom	Hong Kong	Denmark
7	Netherlands	Switzerland	Chile	Colombia	Netherlands
8	Luxembourg	Norway	Malaysia	Switzerland	Australia
9	Switzerland	Netherlands	Taiwan	Denmark	Norway
10	Germany	Thailand	Canada	Norway	Sweden
11	New Zealand	USA	Finland	Philippines	China
12	Canada	Indonesia	Sweden	Netherlands	Finland
13	Chile	Belgium	Luxembourg	Ireland	Ireland
14	Sweden	New Zealand	Denmark	Sweden	Malaysia
15	Finland	Philippines	Norway	New Zealand	South Africa
16	Austria	Taiwan	New Zealand	Iceland	Belgium
17	Belgium	Denmark	Thailand	India	Austria
18	Taiwan	Sweden	Ireland	Canada	Germany
19	United Kingdom	Canada	France	Japan	Taiwan
20	France	Australia	Australia	Luxembourg	Switzerland
21	Australia	Austria	Belgium	Austria	Israel
22	Ireland	Germany	Indonesia	Taiwan	Philippines
23	Malaysia	Ireland	Spain	Israel	United Kingdom
24	Israel	Turkey	Philippines	Germany	Colombia
25	Iceland	Israel	South Africa	Thailand	USA
26	China	India	Colombia	Belgium	Hong Kong
27	Korea	Finland	Switzerland	Turkey	Japan
28	Italy	Colombia	Germany	Brazil	Turkey
29	Spain	Spain	Portugal	South Africa	India
30	Thailand	China	India	Australia	Portugal
31	Philippines	France	Austria	USA	Iceland
32	Argentina	United Kingdom	Korea	France	Spain
33	Colombia	Portugal	Italy	Portugal	Italy

(continued)

EXHIBIT 13 (Continued)

	Overall Competitiveness	Banking Sector	Venture Capital	Corporate Credibility	Corporate Boards
34	Czech Republic	Greece	Iceland	Italy	Brazil
35	Turkey	Brazil	Japan	Argentina	Hungary
36	Portugal	Japan	Brazil	Spain	France
37	Brazil	Czech Republic	Greece	Czech Republic	Greece
38	India	Poland	Turkey	Greece	Thailand
39	Hungary	Iceland	China	Mexico	Czech Republic
40	Greece	Korea	Argentina	United Kingdom	Argentina
41	Indonesia	Argentina	Mexico	Indonesia	Mexico
42	Mexico	Mexico	Poland	Poland	Korea
43	Poland	Italy	Czech Republic	Hungary	Indonesia
44	South Africa	Russia	Russia	Korea	Poland
45	Venezuela	Venezuela	Venezuela	Venezuela	Venezuela
46	Russia	Russia	Hungary	Russia	Russia

On the positive side, IPO activity had recently accelerated, especially among smaller companies with annual sales of $200 to $400 million. (See **Exhibit 14** for a list of recent IPOs and **Exhibit 15** for data on equity markets, interest rates and exchange rates.) Many of these companies had experienced rapid growth and needed additional capital for international expansion. At the same time, generational change drove IPOs as more founders of firms that were created in the post WWII era stepped down. There had also been some legislative initiatives to make public listings more attractive. The 1994 "Tremonti Law" allowed companies going public in 1995 to deduct 16% from their taxes for the next three years. Companies listing in 1996 would get two years' relief. But that was not enough incentive for many companies. An extensive article in the *Institutional Investor* noted:

> . . . a public listing in Italy implies a radical change in outlook that for many firms does not make sense. The days when Italian firms kept three sets of accounts—one for the shareholders, one for the taxman and the real one for the boss—may be largely over, but being small is still not necessarily a disadvantage. Notes Roni Hamaui, chief economist at Banca Commerciale Italiana in Milan: "In Italy it makes a lot of sense to be a small firm. You have fewer problems. You pay less tax.[4]

The Final Stages of the Negotiation—Back to Square One

The purchase agreement was scheduled for signing on July 21 with only a few details to be hammered out. With things looking like they were wrapping up Halpern went on his honeymoon (in Italy) in early July. Things were safe. Or so he thought. Halpern was called in from his honeymoon due to another crisis in the negotiations. Halpern explained this experience:

> It was crazy. We had a deal done and they reopened a couple of issues so I came back one day early from my honeymoon. When I got there on July 21, the Castiglioni brothers were nowhere to be found and my banker was instigating brawls with the other side. I was getting pretty nervous as David Bonderman had been calling me every couple of days since May to see when the deal was going to close. Now that we had spent $7 to $8 million on this deal and he was ready to board a plane, I did not know if we had a deal or not.

After the shouting fight broke up on that hot July day, both sides continued negotiating. At the end of the day it seemed like everything was set, except for the fact that nobody had heard from the Castiglioni brothers. Suddenly Halpern got a phone call. It was another private equity investor telling him that the Castiglioni brothers were shopping the deal again. Enraged, Halpern felt he had to stop this once and for all. He grabbed a piece of paper and wrote the following press release:

> Texas Pacific Group regrets that it must walk away from the Ducati transaction and can no longer take responsibility for the demise of this great company.

Handing it to one of the Cagiva advisors, Halpern threatened to release the document if he had not heard from the Castiglioni brothers within twelve hours. After twelve hours had passed, the TPG team had yet to hear from the Castiglioni brothers. Minoli looked to Halpern and said, "All right, what do we do now?" Halpern replied, "I don't know, Federico, but I think we should rethink this deal and the long term ramifications of completing it."

[4] John Glover, "Beyond family capitalism," *Institutional Investor (International Edition)*, July 1995, pp. 63–65.

EXHIBIT 14 Italian IPOs 1991 through 6/30/96

Source: Compiled from Securities Data Corporation data.

Issue Date	Issuer	Business Description	Industry	Proceeds (US$ mil)	No. of Italian IPOs	
11/01/91	Banco di Napoli SpA	Bank	Commercial Bank	185.7		
05/13/93	Industrie Natuzzi SpA	Mnfr. leather furniture	Manufacturing	126.0	1991	1
05/26/93	Fila Holding SpA	Manufacture footwear	Manufacturing	135.0	1992	0
12/09/93	Credito Italiano SpA(IRI)	Bank	Commercial Bank	208.5	1993	3
					1994	5
02/08/94	Istituto Mobiliare Italiano	Bank	Commercial Bank	1,446.4	1995	11
03/10/94	Banca Commerciale Italiana SpA	Bank holding company	Commercial Bank	983.8	1996	11
06/18/94	Finanza & Futuro(Cofide SpA)	Provide fund management svcs	Investment Fund	60.1		
06/25/94	INA(Italy)	Life, casualty insurance co	Insurance	2,886.5		
07/18/94	FINMECCANICA(SIFA/IRI/Italy)	Mnfr aviation control systems	Manufacturing	1,123.5	Mean: $472.5 million	
05/19/95	IMA(Finvacchi)	Mnfr packaging machinery	Manufacturing	26.2	Median: $62.3 million	
06/23/95	Brembo Kelsey-Hayes SpA	Manufacture automotive parts	Manufacturing	62.3		
06/26/95	Stayer SpA	Mnfr electrical welding equip	Manufacturing	18.2		
06/30/95	Bulgari SpA	Own,operate Jewelry stores	Manufacturing	42.6		
10/19/95	De Rigo SpA	Mnfr opthalmic goods	Manufacturing	123.8		
11/01/95	Carraro SpA	Mnfr m/v parts & equip	Manufacturing	16.9		
11/07/95	La Doria SpA	Produce canned fruits	Manufacturing	13.6		
11/20/95	Ente Nazionale Idrocarburi	Oil and gas exploration, prodn	Manufacturing	2,221.9		
11/27/95	ENI SpA	Oil and gas exploration, prodn	Manufacturing	1,726.8		
12/06/95	Pagnossin	Mnfr pottery products	Manufacturing	24.9		
12/09/95	Gildemeister Italiana SpA	Mnfr machine tools	Manufacturing	7.7		
02/02/96	Savino del Bene	Shipping company	Transportation	21.7		
05/17/96	Mediolanum SpA(Fininvest)	Insurance company	Insurance	88.4		
05/22/96	SAES Getters SpA	Mnfr electronic components	Manufacturing	52.7		
06/05/96	Roland Europe SpA	Mnfr musical instruments	Manufacturing	15.8		
06/08/96	Esaote SpA	Mnfr electrical indl apparatus	Manufacturing	55.8		
06/25/96	Reno Dei Medici SpA	Manufacture paper products	Manufacturing	18.1		
06/30/96	Mediaset SpA(Fininvest)	Own,op TV bdcstg station	Radio/TV/Telecom	1,063.5		

EXHIBIT 15 Data on Equity Markets, Interest Rates and Exchange Rates

Source: (1) Italian Exchange, *Facts & Figures on the Italian Exchange 1998*, Milan: Borsa Italiana, 1999, p. 61.
(2) *World Stock Exchange Factbook 2003*, Vol. 1, Plano, TX: Meridian Securities Markets, 2003, p. 202.

Italian Equity Market Data

	Total Market Capitalization (Euro ml) (1)	Performance of the Italian Equity Market Index (MIB) (2)
1990	86,838	8,007
1991	91,886	7,830
1992	89,468	6,916
1993	120,983	9,500
1994	151,614	9,813
1995	168,142	9,138
1996	199,433	9,291

Data for 1996 are up 6/30.
Base for MIB Index: 100 (01/02/75)

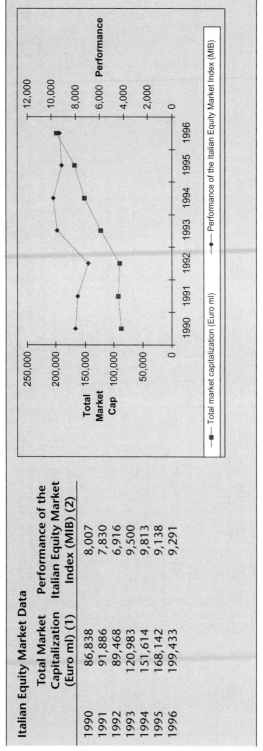

Interest Rates

7/1/96	US Treasury Bill (3 months)	5.10%
7/1/96	US Treasury Bond (10 years)	6.74%
7/1/96	Italian Treasury Bill (3 months)	8.25%
7/1/96	Italian Treasury Bond (10 years)	6.74%

EXHIBIT 15 (Continued)

Source: Compiled from EIU Country Data and Thomson Financial Datastream data. (above the Exhibit)

GDP Growth Rates

	Italy GDP	US GDP
1985	12.1%	7.1%
1986	10.3%	5.7%
1987	9.3%	6.5%
1988	11.0%	7.7%
1989	9.3%	7.5%
1990	9.8%	5.7%
1991	8.9%	3.2%
1992	5.2%	5.6%
1993	3.2%	5.1%
1994	5.7%	6.2%
1995	8.1%	4.9%

Exchange Rates (Italian Lira to US$)

12/31/93	1703.97
12/31/94	1629.74
12/29/95	1584.72
7/1/96	1534.57

Case 12

Infox System GmbH

Martin Halusa and Michael Phillips, both partners of the German office of Apax Partners & Co., looked out of the large window in the Apax conference room. It was March 18, 1995, and the clear morning sky had turned dark shortly after lunch. The two men were concerned that the coming blizzard, as unseasonable as it was unexpected, might delay their flight to Bonn, scheduled to leave in less than eight hours. The upcoming flight was not their only concern, however. They had spent the past couple of hours reflecting about Apax Partners' role within Germany's fast-growing private equity market and about the position of their firm. They knew that the imminent investment decision regarding Infox System GmbH would be an important one for the partnership, despite the investment's relatively small size. No one firm had yet established itself as the dominant private equity player in the German market. Even a small deal such as Infox could significantly impact the firm's reputation, with positive or negative repercussions for Apax's fund-raising power and its ability to attract scarce human capital.

Infox looked like an interesting deal. The company currently enjoyed a quasi monopoly in the distribution of advertising materials to travel agencies. In 1994 Infox had achieved net income of DM 4.4 m on sales of DM 28.5 m (US$1 = 1.6 DM). Sales had grown at an annualized rate of 25% over the past eight years. The management team seemed strong and business prospects were at least average. But there were several problems associated with the deal. The owners' asking price still seemed high, and one of the sellers in particular seemed unlikely to accept much of a reduction. The exit route for Apax was not entirely obvious, given a limited number of strategic buyers and the relatively weak state of the German IPO market. Finally, Halusa and Phillips were not sure about what the optimal deal structure would be, an issue that was complicated further by the reluctance of German banks to finance the acquisition of a business with little in the way of tangible assets.

Halusa and Phillips had been analyzing the transaction repeatedly during the past six weeks of intensive due diligence work. They were determined to complete their final analysis of the Infox opportunity before they would meet again with the two selling

M. Frederick Paul, MBA '98, prepared this case in collaboration with Charles M. Williams Fellow Chad Ellis, MBA '98, under the supervision of Professor Walter Kuemmerle. HBS cases are developed solely as the basis for class discussion. Cases are not intended to serve as endorsements, sources of primary data, or illustrations of effective or ineffective management.

shareholders in Bonn for a last round of interviews. Halusa popped open another can of soda as the two partners refocused their thoughts on the company's cash flow projections on the computer screen. Could it be that this investment opportunity was really as good as it seemed or had they overlooked a central flaw in the company's business model?

Apax Partners & Co.[1]

Apax Partners was among the world's leading private equity groups, advising more than $3 billion of international investment funds. Operating as an association of largely independent partnerships on both sides of the Atlantic, the group had offices in New York, Philadelphia, Palo Alto, London, Leeds, Paris, Munich, Madrid and Zurich. Rather than specializing in one narrow field of investment, Apax invested in all sectors of industry and in companies at all stages in their development. The group's private equity business was complemented by investment banking services, advising small and medium-sized corporations on all issues of corporate finance. In order to avoid potential conflicts arising from the two business areas, investment-banking activities were kept independent from private equity activities and staffed from a separate pool of professionals.

In addition to achieving exceptional returns through superior execution, the group sought to differentiate itself by means of its dedication to entrepreneurial business. In contrast to some of its competitors, Apax had a philosophy of "hands-on" investing which implied the close monitoring and active management support of the companies in its portfolio throughout the investment cycle. As the group defined itself:

> We are entrepreneurs: those we serve—both the corporate clients we advise and the companies in which we invest—are entrepreneurial businesses. We have grown because we understand the entrepreneurial spirit and culture. As a finance house for businesses which need that understanding, we are committed to working as close corporate partners in creating new and profitable enterprises and in realizing the full potential of well-established businesses.[2]

Alan Patricof founded the first office of Apax—Alan Patricof Associates—in New York in 1969. After graduating from Columbia Business School, Patricof had begun his career at investment advisers Schroders, Naess and Thomas, and later joined Lambert & Co, an international development capital fund, and Central National Corp., specializing in private equity.

The London and Paris operations were co-founded in 1972 by Ronald Cohen, HBS '69, and Maurice Tchenio, HBS '70, to provide international corporate finance advice and invest in high-growth companies. In 1977, the US and European operations joined forces and expanded further in 1989 with the addition of Corporate Finance Partners (CFP) of Zurich. Max Burger-Calderon, HBS '81, and Dr. Michael Hinderer had founded CFP in 1986. The two originally met at the University of St. Gallen in Switzerland. After Harvard Business School and the University of Innsbruck, respectively, they had gained experience in consulting, investment banking and industry and subsequently formed CFP to invest in private equity opportunities and provide corporate financial advice in the German-speaking region and Spain.

Four partners managed the Munich office of Apax Partners private equity operations, which had come into existence as a result of the merger with CFP. Burger-Calderon and Hinderer were joined by Dr. Martin Halusa, HBS '79, in 1991 and by Michael Phillips

---

[1] "Apax" in classical Greek means something that occurs once, and once only. The name was supposed to symbolize the group's unique role and the full integration of that role across activities and frontiers.

[2] Source: Company brochure.

in 1992. Holding degrees from Georgetown University, Harvard Business School and University of Innsbruck, Martin Halusa had begun his career at the Boston Consulting Group in Munich, where he left as the group's youngest German partner ever. Prior to joining Apax Partners, he had been the Head of Marketing and Sales at the Daniel Swarovski Corporation AG, Austria's largest private industrial company. Phillips, an MBA graduate of INSEAD, had spent 4 years at Ciba-Geigy and then subsequently several years at Germany's leading waste management company before joining Apax in 1992.

Apax Partners Germany was formally a Division of a Swiss Corporation, Apax Partners & Co. Beteiligungs AG. The first fund it advised, APA German European Ventures L.P. ("APA"), a Delaware Limited Partnership, was raised in 1990 and had total committed capital of DM 100 million. By the beginning of 1995, one third of APA was invested (at cost). Principal sources of funds were US pension funds, insurance companies and endowments. There were no German institutions among APA's limited partners, as private equity funds were a relatively unknown product to German institutional investors.

Deals were sourced through a variety of channels, the most important of which were the partners' proprietary network of contacts and unsolicited investment proposals sent in by independent entrepreneurs and shareholders. Only about 10% of the proposals were scrutinized further, and very few of those were finally pursued as realistic investment opportunities. Once the investigating partner concluded that an investment made sense, he prepared a recommendation that was then submitted to the main board for approval in principle. If the board approved, a second partner joined the deal team and a comprehensive due diligence process was initiated that would take from one to three months, with legal agreements a further one to two months. The total time from receiving the investment proposal to an investment being completed could be anywhere between two to six months, with an average of four months.

The German Private Equity Industry in 1995

The development and structure of the US and German private equity industries had been widely divergent. In sharp contrast to the US, the German market for private equity in 1995 was still in its early stages. Germany's principal private equity association, BVK, estimated that only about 760 private equity investments were made in Germany in 1995, with a total investment value of DM 1.25 billion (at cost).[3] Private equity funds raised in 1995 represented only 0.01% of GDP in Germany, a significantly smaller proportion than the 0.06% of GDP raised in the US. Similarly, cumulative funds raised were just 0.25% of GDP in Germany, compared to 0.53% in the US.[4] Only about 3% of funds invested in Germany could be attributed to "true" venture capital. The dominant investment category in Germany was expansion financing, with less than 10% of capital flowing into leveraged buyouts.[5]

There were at least five principal explanations for the absence of a strong private equity industry in Germany: lack of easily available funds, an underdeveloped entrepreneurial culture, regulatory obstacles, the lack of qualified human capital, and the absence of adequate exit opportunities, especially a liquid stock market for small cap companies (see **Exhibit 1**).

[3] Source: Infox company documents based on data compiled from BVK (German Venture Capital Association) 1995 annual report.

[4] Source: Casewriter calculation based on data provided by Infox and OECD data for 1995 GDP.

[5] Source: Infox company documents based on data compiled from BVK (German Venture Capital Association) 1995 annual report.

EXHIBIT 1 **Obstacles to Expansion of Private Equity Industry in Germany (1995)**

Source: Author. Based on Kuemmerle, Walter, Frederick M. Paul, and Henrik Freye. 1998. "Survey of Private Equity in Germany," Harvard Business School Working Paper, 98–112.

Obstacle	Issues
Limited access to funds	• There are a number of captive private equity firms (focus exclusively on investing funds from their parent companies (mainly banks)) but few non-captive private equity firms. Main reasons: absence of private pension funds, legal restrictions for insurance companies to invest in private equity. • Most funds raised by non-captive firms are raised from US investors.
Entrepreneurial culture underdeveloped	• Risk-taking not encouraged by bankruptcy laws. • Financial success alone does not entail high social status. No acceptance of "rags to riches" ideal. Lawyers enjoy higher social status than entrepreneurs.
Red Tape	• Multitude of local, state and federal tax laws. • Seemingly insignificant changes to operation of manufacturing facilities can require considerable paperwork. • Complex labor laws.
Few deal captains	• Only very few qualified "deal makers." • Recruiting of qualified employees extremely difficult for private equity organizations. • Specialized university system focuses on teaching knowledge rather than skills. • Very few MBA programs.
Limited exit opportunities	• Domestic market smaller than in the US which entails smaller number of strategic buyers. • Underdeveloped capital markets make public exit route difficult. • Most venture-backed German IPOs happen via NASDAQ.

The Company

Elmar Brandschwede and Jochen Krause, two German entrepreneurs who had spent the first years of their professional careers in the travel industry, founded Infox in 1975. Recognizing inefficiencies in the coordination of information flows between tour operators and travel agents, Brandschwede and Krause had collected data on booking vacancies from tour operators, transferring them onto microfilm and distributing them to travel agencies on a weekly basis. With the introduction of on-line computer booking systems in the late 1970s, however, the demand for Infox's microfilm service declined markedly and the business had to be stopped in 1983. In its place, Infox entered a new market segment that would become its core business for the next two decades. Acting as a remailer in the distribution of advertising information to travel agents, Infox took full advantage of the economies of scale of the German postal system and was thus able to provide substantial savings to tour operators through its services. As other travel product providers ("TPPs") realized the value created by Infox's service, the company's customer base expanded rapidly to include airlines, hotels, cruise lines, etc. and the cash flows generated enabled Brandschwede and Krause to enter new business areas.

Infox in 1995

In 1995, Infox employed 40 full-time and 600 part-time employees. By now, the company had expanded its operating activities into four different business areas: Advertising Distribution, Printing Services, Document Distribution and Catalogue Delivery.

(1) Advertising Distribution

This was the company's principal operating activity. Infox acted as a remailer of travel information on behalf of TPPs, collecting advertisements from their various TPP customers in bulk, repackaging them and then redistributing them to thousands of travel agencies in Germany.

TPPs mailed their advertisements to the company's central warehouse in Bonn from Friday through Wednesday. The warehouse had 17,500 "mailboxes," one for each travel agency served. Once the bulk mailings from the TPPs arrived at the warehouse, they were sorted and distributed to these mailboxes according to customer specifications. Distribution patterns could vary by TPP size and preference. Smaller TPPs usually preferred to have their information distribution limited to travel agencies in a particular region, defined by the first digit of the postal code (there were 10 major regions in Germany). Larger customers often had mailing lists of travel agents tailored to their particular target groups.

Sorting of incoming advertisements was done manually. The process was only automated to the extent that machines collated up to 50 individual pages into small "bundles" which could then more easily be distributed to the mailboxes. Each Thursday, the contents of the 17,500 mailboxes were placed in large Infox mailing bags labeled with the respective addresses of the travel agencies. Individual packages were then picked up by Trans-o-Flex, a private courier service, and delivered overnight to the various travel agencies throughout Germany.

The economics of the company's core business were driven by the economies of scale of the German postal delivery system. Germany had some of the highest mailing rates in the world, but rates did not increase proportionally with an increase in package weight. Thus, the per-unit mailing cost of a piece of advertisement decreased significantly when several of these units were bundled. This bundling advantage was even greater for customers of Trans-o-Flex. In contrast to the state owned German *Bundespost,* this private delivery service could guarantee Infox a fixed rate per package of DM 4.60 up to a weight of 7lbs. As a single letter-sized sheet of advertising weighed only about 5 grams, Infox could send up to 700 single sheets in one mailing for the same low cost of DM 4.60. Thus, a typical weekly mailing of materials from 50 TPPs to 17,500 travel agents would cost Infox only DM 80,500. In contrast, the total cost to the 50 operators for the same mailing without using Infox would amount to DM 875,000 in postage costs alone (not taking into account the substantial office costs incurred in the process), more than ten times the cost incurred by Infox. (See **Exhibit 2** for illustrations of Infox's cost advantage.) Given this cost differential, Infox was able to create a win-win situation with its customers and still generate substantial margins.

EXHIBIT 2   Economics of Infox Core Business (DM)

Source: Apax Partners & Co.

	Cost via Direct Mail		Cost via Infox		Infox Internal Cost	
	1 Letter Delivery	50 × 17,500 Deliveries	Cost per Delivery	50 × 17,500 Deliveries	1 Package Delivery	17,500 Deliveries
Postage	1.00	875,000	0.49	428,750	4.60	80,500
Office Costs	0.30	262,500	0.00	0.00	0.00	0.00
Mail Info to Infox[a]	0.00	0.00	0.01	5,000	0.00	0.00
Total	1.30	1,137,500	0.50	433,750	4.60	80,500

[a]Each tour operator must send ca. 90kg of paper to Infox in bulk. This translates into total costs of DM 100 per delivery to Infox x 50 tour operators = DM 5,000 total cost.

Customers were billed on the basis of the total weight of advertising materials shipped for them times the number of travel agents receiving the information (in the example above, the cost for a mailing via Infox would amount to only DM 433,750). Infox was the only remailer of travel-related information of its kind in Germany. The company's pre-tax profit margins were accordingly strong, averaging around 38% for the past eight years.

(2) Printing Services

The second most important activity for Infox was a service to design, layout, and print customized advertisements for its customers. This service appealed primarily to the smaller TPPs, as they could benefit most from Infox's economies of scale and design expertise. The advantages to the TPPs were fourfold. First, smaller TPPs often did not have sufficient experience to design and layout effective travel advertisements in-house. Infox, with its long-term experience in dealing with travel advertisements as well as agents could naturally add a high degree of value here. Second, Infox could usually secure significantly lower printing costs due to the high volume of its business. Third, outsourcing design and printing to Infox led to shorter lead times, as a TPP could send the information to Infox by Fax on Wednesday and have the materials printed by Thursday. Finally, TPPs could save on logistical costs, as they did not have to bulk-mail their advertisements to Infox.

While Infox conducted most of the design of the advertisements in-house, the bulk of production (approximately 85%) was outsourced to local printers who had to compete for the company's business on a regular basis. Margins in this bread-and-butter business were not as attractive as in the core remailing business, but at 10–15% were still high enough to provide a valuable source of stable cash flows to the company.

(3) Document Distribution

As a complement to their advertisement remailing services, Infox offered TPPs the opportunity to include other travel documents such as confirmations and general correspondence in their mailings. The documents were mailed in separately labeled envelopes inside the standard Infox package. To ensure consistent quality, a dedicated team performed document handling every Monday and Tuesday. Although the business was limited to a certain degree by timing constraints, most travel documents allowed for relatively long lead times as travel products were booked and paid for several weeks in advance.

(4) Catalogue Delivery

A further extension of the company's weekly mailings of (mostly short-term or last minute) travel advertisements was the distribution of catalogues for the larger tour operators. In Germany, the vast majority of holidays were booked through tour operators who offered a catalogued standard program of travel products in addition to their short-term travel arrangements. Out of the approximately 1,500 tour operators active in Germany, nearly 300 issued regular catalogues and mailed them directly to travel agencies all over the country. Each tour operator usually issued two main catalogues per year, one for each major holiday season. In addition, a variety of specialty catalogues was issued, covering nearly any travel need from budget holidays in Spain to round-the-world trips on Concorde.

Until 1994, tour operators had no choice but to label and mail the catalogues themselves, incurring substantial costs in the process. In November of that year, Infox acquired a second warehouse in Troisdorf near Bonn, negotiated more flexible terms with Trans-o-Flex (a typical catalogue mailing weighed approximately 100 lbs), and began catalogue remailing in addition to its other activities.

Apart from just remailing catalogues as short-term advertisements, Infox could offer an additional service element: the after-mailing of catalogues on request. To this end, catalogues were stocked at the warehouse and supplied to travel agencies that had run down their inventory. TPPs were not charged extra for this service, as warehousing costs were included in the distribution price. This was of significant value to a TPP, as otherwise catalogues were distributed in similar quantities to all travel agents, alternately resulting in shortages or oversupply at different locations. By delivering a lower volume initially and then after-mailing to those travel agents with a higher demand, both the travel agent and the TPP derived service and cost advantages.

In addition to these four business areas, Infox had entered into a joint venture with Dillon Communication Systems (DCS) of Hamburg in late 1994.[6] The resulting company, Infox Electronic GmbH, had just published the second version of a software package that enabled travel agents to book last minute travel products on-line. The software provided an efficient and user-friendly information interface between travel agents and TPPs, allowing travel agents to automatically search for vacancies in the booking systems of connected tour operators. Software was handed out free of charge, but Infox Electronic received a 3% booking commission on each travel product sale.

Potential Future Opportunities

To enhance the services currently provided, further cement customer relationships and diversify sources of cash flows, Infox management was contemplating entering several new business segments related to their core activities. No final decision had been made about entering any of these segments and no capital had yet been allocated to them.

Database Administration

In the course of building its four existing business areas, Infox had acquired the most comprehensive and up-to-date database for both TPPs and travel agents in Germany. As becoming a tour operator or travel agent in Germany did not require state certification or registration with any professional association, there was no other institution in Germany that had assembled a similar breadth and depth of information on either of these groups. To translate this wealth of information into cash flows, Infox management was planning to introduce a standardized numbering and database administration system. For a monthly charge of only DM 390, the company would maintain and update databases for customers who did not have the resources to build up their own nor the staff necessary to constantly update it. Management estimated that about 500 TPPs would take advantage of this service.

Fax-Broadcasting

As management expected fax broadcasting of "last-minute" advertisements to increase dramatically with the growth of this product sector, Infox was also planning to offer fax-broadcasting services to its customers. Fax broadcasts used modern computer technology to transfer printed information to a large number of recipients within a very short time frame. This way, urgent, perishable information could be communicated before it lost its value. While Infox did not have the necessary know-how and technology in-house, the company was contemplating the acquisition of TourFax, a small German fax broadcasting company specializing in the tour operating segment.

Travel Agent Tours

Given its comprehensive network of contacts in the travel industry, management was further planning to offer selected package tours to travel agency staff. Recognizing that the typical German travel agency had an average staff of five employees (who would most likely want to travel with a companion), and that Infox had a captive market of 17,500 travel agencies, there seemed to be a large amount of untapped revenues being left on the table. The average travel package would sell at DM 1,000 and Infox believed it could generate a 10% margin on the packages.

---

[6] The joint venture came officially into effect on January 1, 1995.

The Market: Germany's Travel Industry Value Chain

The dynamics of the market for Infox's services were influenced primarily by three groups of constituents—travel product providers, travel agents and end consumers.

Travel Product Providers

The company's direct customers were Germany's TPPs, including tour operators, airlines, hotels, cruise lines and vacation clubs. Among these customer groups, tour operators had traditionally accounted for the bulk of the company's business, due to their constant need for the distribution of short-term information. With the expansion of Infox into the catalogue distribution business, primary service providers such as airlines and hotels became progressively important, adding a growing degree of diversity to the customer pool.

Total revenues for tour operators in Germany—which constituted the company's major customer group—were DM 26.5 billion in 1993/1994. The market had been growing steadily at 10%–15% for the past few years and was expected to grow again at a rate of about 11% in 1994/1995. There were approximately 1,500 tour operators in Germany, which could be roughly divided into three groups of equal number: there were about 500 large regional and national tour operators, 500 medium-sized local tour operators and 500 smaller "mom and pop" tour operators. Infox's target customer group was limited to the first group of larger tour operators which were established organizations serving a sizable market of travel agents. The smaller tour operators would use their own distribution channels, selling through personal contacts. The larger tour operators had an average customer number of about 1,000 travel agents each. Within this top group of larger tour operators, revenues concentrated again in the top players. The top 60 tour operators generated overall revenues of DM 19.9 billion in 1993/1994, representing 75% of the market.[7]

As illustrated in **Table 1** below, Germany's top 60 tour operators generated roughly three-quarters of Infox's total sales, but the company was not dependent on its five largest customers.

The breakdown of tour operators' revenues also affected the business of Infox as more complicated travel products required heavier advertising and travel agent support. In 1993/1994, air tours accounted for 70% of total tour operator revenues, with 23% of revenues generated by car tours, 3% by train tours, 3% by cruise tours and 1% by bus tours. The trend was continuing towards air tours, which was good news for Infox as tours involving air travel tended to involve the most complicated booking scenarios including flight, accommodation, meals and other products.

Travel Agents

The second major group of constituents influencing the company's service-profit equation were the travel agents. Infox billed its customers according to the number of travel agents on their distribution list. More "points of sales" in the form of travel agents implied a higher flow of revenues to Infox from existing customers and thus improved profitability. It also put the company in a better position to win over new customers as

[7] Source for statistics on the German travel industry: FVW International.

TABLE 1
Infox Customer Pattern

Source: Infox.

Infox Customer	% of Market Sales	% of Infox Sales
Top 5	60%	18%
Top 60	75%	78%
Top 500	90%	99%

mailing costs to those TPPs who still distributed their information directly increased even further.

Over the past few years, the number of travel agents in Germany had been increasing constantly. At the same time, the percentage of chain-owned travel agencies increased even faster. Infox's revenues had historically been linked to the absolute number of travel agents but had not yet been affected by the degree of chain affiliation among them. (**Exhibit 3** gives a summary overview of the development of travel agent offices and chains from 1991 to 1993.)

Due to the competitive nature of the business, German travel agents operated on very slim margins. On an average tour price of DM 1,100 a travel agent gained a commission of about DM 110, which in turn yielded net profits of only DM 6–10. Given this operating model, a travel agent needed at least DM 2 million in annual sales as a rule of thumb to stay in business. Consequently, travel agents viewed materials received through Infox as a welcome way to strengthen their marketing efforts and increase their sales and profits.

German Consumers

The health of both the TPP and travel agency industries was ultimately driven by the consumption of travel products by the end consumer. Germany was notorious for its negative macroeconomic trade balance with respect to travel. As a result of high wages and generous vacation time allowances, Germans had become the world champions of international tourism, with a tourism trade deficit of DM 38 billion in 1994[8] (Japan was

[8] Source: Borrmann, C., and Marisa Weinhold. 1994. *Perspektiven der deutschen Tourismuswirtschaft im EWR.* Baden-Baden: Nomos, p.16.

EXHIBIT 3
Development of Number of Offices of Travel Agent Chains, 1991–1993

Source: Infox company documents based on data compiled from FVW International.

Travel Agent Chains	1991	1992	1993
ITS	193	325	307
First/BS&K/Hartmann	136	192	287
DER	153	166	194
Atlas	96	144	194
Hapag-Lloyd	123	143	182
Quelle	164	167	172
ABR (DER)	55	60	66
NUR	112	118	127
Karstadt	112	119	122
NVAG	91	91	93
Euro-Lloyd	58	72	78
Thomas Cook	38	53	72
Wagon Lits	30	34	39
AMEX	22	28	35
Kuoni	20	23	25
Alpha	16	16	17
Brewo	15	16	17
TRD	11	13	14
Ferien Welt	15	14	11
Schenker Rhenus	11	12	11
Other	103	146	178
Total travel agent chain offices	**1,574**	**1,952**	**2,241**
Total number of travel agent offices	**16,200**	**17,392**	**17,924**
Chains as percentage of total	**9.7%**	**11.2%**	**12.5%**
Total sales of all chains (DM m)	**n/a**	**10,970**	**12,134**
Average sales/chain office (DM m)	**n/a**	**5.62**	**5.41**

second with a deficit of minus DM 38 billion). Historically, demand for travel products had been relatively stable even in times of economic recession. Given the growing elderly part of the population with high disposable income and sufficient time at hand, no significant decrease in German travel activity was expected.

Competition

Unlike its customers, Infox enjoyed a quasi-monopoly for its services. The company was the only redistributor of physical travel information in Germany and had thus far successfully defended its monopoly position against the threat of new entrants. Several attempts had been made to enter the profitable remailing segment, but they were all squeezed out of the business quickly through Infox's commanding market presence. The most significant barriers to entry were Infox's accumulated experience, databases and contacts as well as significant economies of scale, which allowed Infox to win any price war.

A new threat might be posed by potential substitutes for the company's services. While there was currently no product available that could deliver the benefits of all Infox services, it was believed that CD-Roms and on-line services could potentially replace certain elements of the company's services and lure cost-conscious customers away from the company.

Although catalogues could be easily scanned onto CD-Roms, which would lead to a significant reduction in the weight of TPP mailings, this technology had thus far been largely neglected. Principal reasons for this were the insufficient hardware availability among German consumers,[9] the inadequacy of CDs for the distribution of short-term information, and the cost factors associated with the manufacturing of CDs.

More serious was the threat from on-line services. Essentially all the information distributed through Infox was also accessible through the START/AMADEUS booking system. START was a privately owned, centralized online booking system covering all major travel products available in the German market. Travel agents paid a monthly fee of DM 1,400 to access the service, and received a booking terminal free of charge. While START offered travel agents the same information as TPP advertising sheets, however, it could not be used as a marketing tool. For example, the travel agent could not show a flashy catalogue to the consumer. Nor could he or she enter a vacation destination and get all available offers on-screen automatically. Instead, the design of the service allowed the agent to search only one TPP's product portfolio at a time, making it inefficient for booking vacant capacity.

Due diligence suggested that START, in its current form, was not a serious threat. Less than 10% of tours were sufficiently standardized to work on the START platform and usage was very low. Moreover, START's data was not up to date and the system would sometimes offer spots on tours that were already sold out. Despite the shortcomings of START, however, Infox management feared that a more sophisticated on-line service could be developed that would combine ease of use with high quality graphics that could be printed out locally. Such a system could theoretically replace the traditional advertisement mailings.

The Deal: Whether and How to Go Ahead?

The Decision to Sell

Like many successful entrepreneurs who had proven their business concept, Brandschwede and Krause had moved on to new challenges and had reduced their involvement with their business. Halusa explained:

[9] In 1995 only 15% of German households owned a computer, and most of those did not have a CD-ROM drive. (Casewriter interview with Apax.)

The business had lost some of its challenge for them. In 1991 they had founded another company selling tour packages. It only advertised through Infox and in 18 months it had sales of DM 100 million. Infox's customers complained and they sold the company to another operator for a gain of DM 30 million, but they had proved that Infox worked. By 1995 they were spending less than 30% of their time with the company and probably hadn't seen a customer in years.

Brandschwede suggested that the two men sell the business and, with Krause's agreement, approached Berenberg Bank, a local investment bank. The entrepreneurs had felt that the company was worth at least DM 50 million, but the banker suggested that the company might sell for as much as DM 100 million and this number had captured the imagination of both men.

Apax Sees the Deal

Berenberg showed the deal to several potential buyers, including Apax, 3i, CVC and another local bank in November 1994. Apax began serious due diligence work in early February, during which time most of the bidders withdrew, leaving CVC and Apax as the main competitors. Apax had hoped to acquire the business at a valuation closer to Brandschwede's original DM 50 million. They knew, however, that CVC had a reputation for offering high bids with conditions and then cutting their price over details. This was likely to make the negotiations difficult.

Proposed Transaction Structure[10]

The objective of the proposed transaction was to acquire 100% of Infox Systems GmbH ("Infox" or "the company") and 50% of Infox Electronic GmbH, a new company with no revenues. The sellers would guarantee that the company would have available cash of at least DM 7 million at the time of the transaction. Consolidated net book value of the two companies at the time of the transaction would be DM 6.3 million. On top of the purchase price, potential transaction costs had to be considered. Total transaction costs were estimated at DM 1 million,[11] comprising banking fees of DM 520,000 (1.25% on debt), legal costs of DM 120,000, financial auditing costs of DM 80,000, APA administration costs of DM 150,000 and miscellaneous expenses of DM 130,000. All transaction costs would be charged to the Newco.

Originally the transaction was envisaged as a pure management buyout in which the two selling shareholders, Brandschwede and Krause (each owning 50% of the company), were to sell all of their shares and leave the company. In this scenario, the second-level directors, Thomas Beer and Jens Schnacke, would have become the active buyout managers. During the negotiations, however, the founders' interest changed. Halusa recalled:

> During the due diligence, they fell in love with the business again, particularly Brandschwede. It suddenly became very hard for them to let go, and at one point they came to us and said they had decided not to sell. However, it also became apparent to them that they had exhausted their friendship. There wasn't bad blood between them, but they weren't ready to continue together as business partners.

Ultimately, a new structure was agreed on. Krause would sell all of his shares and leave the company. Brandschwede would reinvest part of his sales proceeds and stay on as managing director for at least another two or three years and thereafter remain an active board member. Thomas Beer would also remain and become a shareholder in Newco. Finally, Jens Schnacke would be offered the option to invest or to receive a performance-related annual bonus (see **Exhibit 4** for summary biographies of envisaged post-buyout management).

---

[10] Some figures are disguised.

[11] Not including notary costs for the contract attestation, which would be paid by the purchaser.

EXHIBIT 4
Information on Infox Key Management

Source: Apax Partners & Co.

Elmar Brandschwede, 55

One of the two co-founders of Infox, Brandschwede spent his entire life in the German tourism industry and knew the business inside out. His wife operated a travel agency in Bonn. Brandschwede was the creative side, or Infox's brain. It was mostly his impetus that led to the leveraging of the existing remailing business into the other three related business segments. Apart from his creativity, Brandschwede was recognized in the travel industry for his intelligence and good sense of humor. In contrast to his management colleagues, Brandschwede preferred to focus on long-term strategic issues rather than the day-to-day operations of the company.

Jens Schnacke, 52

Schnacke was a 12-year veteran of Infox. He was responsible for the operating side of the business and for the daily contact to customers and travel agents. In contrast to Brandschwede, Schnacke did not attempt to contribute to the strategic development of Infox. His strengths were in his thorough understanding of the operating side of the business, his strong network of contacts among TPPs and travel agents and his ability to get along well with the 600 part-time work force. Schnacke was a loyal and hard-working manager who enjoyed solving day-to-day operating problems. He stood 100% behind the company.

Thomas Beer, 32

Beer represented the new generation of management at Infox. He was recruited in 1994 by Brandschwede and Krause (the co-founder of Infox who was planning to exit his investment through the buyout and leave the company) in order to ensure continuity of management. Beer had started his management career at Lufthansa AG, Germany's then state-owned carrier. After having gone through their obligatory trainee program and spending time as a manager in both Lufthansa's passenger airline and cargo business, he left Lufthansa in 1992 to join ITS, Germany's fifth largest tour operator which was owned by Kaufhof, one of the country's leading retailing groups. At ITS, Beer was appointed General Manager for a subsidiary which specialized in direct sales of packaged tours via catalogues, newspapers and direct advertising to corporations, and succeeded in building up sales to more than DM 100 million. Beer left ITS when it became apparent that the parent company was in financial difficulties, and joined Infox on the basis of his personal contacts to Krause. Beer was perceived to be an intelligent, hard-working and highly analytical manager who had the potential to serve as a counter-weight to Brandschwede's creativity and Schnacke's lack of leadership skills.

The new deal structure added a complication to the negotiations. Brandschwede became slightly less interested in price, as he was to remain a substantial shareholder and would realize most of the value of his investment later. Krause, by contrast, was far more interested in selling to the highest bidder.

Funding for the transaction would consist of the company's DM 7 million of available cash, at least DM 25 million in additional equity and shareholder loans and at least DM 25 million in senior bank debt. Equity and shareholder loans would come from Elmar Brandschwede (DM 8 million), Thomas Beer (DM 0.6 million) and funds advised by Apax UK (approximately DM 5 million) and IBG, a local private equity fund that was 100% owned by a German bank (DM 8.2 million). The remaining equity would come from APA German European Ventures L.P., through its subsidiary APA Beteiligungs GmbH. Senior debt financing would be provided by a consortium of German commercial banks that was to be selected based on the terms offered.

Ideally, Apax would have wanted to finance the transaction with a higher proportion of leverage, but this appeared difficult. Phillips explained:

Normally [when valuing an acquisition] you just apply a multiple of EBIT and assume you can leverage it at least 60%. In this case, however, we couldn't get support from the banks for more than DM 41 million of debt. I think this was simply because the business didn't have much in the way of tangible assets. EBIT had also been flat compared to the previous year, which may have made them nervous, even though Brandschwede was a good manager and the market was still growing.

Halusa and Phillips knew that the limited debt capacity for the deal could affect the price they were willing to pay. The greater the proportion of equity they were forced to invest, the harder it would be to generate the levels of return required in the private equity market.

Tax Considerations

In order to minimize tax liabilities in a country that was notorious for its rigid tax system, the transaction structure was to take full advantage of the new *Umwandlungs-steuergesetz* (conversion tax law*)*, a tax law that had only come into effect in Germany a few months earlier. The goal was to ensure that the goodwill created in the transaction could be depreciated in the P&L over 15 years, effectively creating a tax shield. Corporate income tax in Germany was 45%. Under the old tax laws, it would have been necessary to tax the goodwill arising from an acquisition at a rate of 15–20%. The tax was payable at the time of purchase, thereby reducing the value of the tax shield. The new *Umwandlungssteuergesetz* allowed for the conversion of the legal form of a company and the merger of two or more companies owned by the same shareholders, with no tax liabilities on unrealized gains and/or goodwill. In the Infox transaction, goodwill equal to the purchase price minus DM 6.3 million net book value minus DM 5.1 million tax credit would be created. To ensure the creation of a tax shield and the avoidance of paying taxes on the goodwill, the transaction would occur in several steps. First a Newco owned by management and the investors would acquire 100% of Infox Verlagsgesellschaft mbH, which in turn would hold 100% of Infox Systems GmbH and 50% of Infox Electronic GmbH. Following this acquisition, Infox Verlagsgesellschaft mbH and Infox Systems GmbH would be merged into one company. This new company would be co-owned by management and the financial investors. More specifically, five steps were planned for the transaction. (See **Exhibits 5A** and **5B** for an overview of the changes to the legal structure of the group.)

It was envisaged that the board of the Newco would consist of five members, two of whom would be management and two of whom would be investors, with one seat left for an external director. While management and investors would be reimbursed for travel costs only, the external director would also receive DM 10,000 in annual compensation.

Valuation Issues

The purchase price for Infox had not yet been decided. While the sellers recognized that they were not likely to get DM 100 million for the business they were still very resistant to Apax's counter-proposal of DM 50 million. Phillips and Halusa believed that CVC had offered something close to DM 90 million, although they suspected that CVC's offer involved difficult conditions and would ultimately be for less. They knew that if the investment did not meet APA's minimum return expectations of 25% at the agreed valuation level, the deal would fall through, and wondered what was the highest price they could offer and still earn a sufficient return.[12] (See **Exhibit 6** for summary financial statements and forecasts.)

[12] In March 1995, the average yield for a one year German Treasury bond was 5.2%, for a ten-year German Government bond it was 7.13%.

EXHIBIT 5A
Proposed Changes in the Legal Structure of the Group

Source: Apax Parterners & Co.

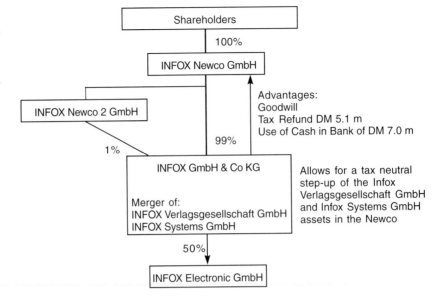

EXHIBIT 5B
Steps Required to Achieve Proposed Changes in the Legal Structure of the Group

Source: Apax Partners & Co.

Step 1 Establishment of a new company in the form of a "GmbH & Co. KG." This was a unique German legal company form, which combined the flexibility of Limited Partnership ("KG") with the limited liability of a Limited Company ("GmbH"). The GmbH & Co. KG would be owned 99% by the Newco (acting as the KG) and 1% by a 100% owned subsidiary of the Newco (Newco 2, acting as the GmbH).

Step 2 Merger of Infox Verlags GmbH and Infox System GmbH into the new GmbH & Co. KG. The two previous companies would cease to exist and their assets would be merged at book value into the new GmbH & Co.

Step 3 For the purposes of consolidated financial statement preparation and tax declaration the assets of the new GmbH could be treated as one with those of the Newco. This would enable the investors to fully integrate the goodwill and depreciate it over 15 years through the P&L.

Step 4 Through the merger the Newco would receive a tax refund of approximately DM 5.1 million from the German government. This was due to the fact that Infox Verlagsgesellschaft mbH and Infox System GmbH would have combined retained earnings of DM 6.2 million, which were taxed at 45%. This tax would be refunded within 12 months of the merger and would be available to the Newco for additional liquidity. It would not have to be declared as income on the P&L. Instead, it would simply mean that the DM 6.2 million of equity in the GmbH & Co. KG was fully taxable by the shareholder should any dividend payments be made.

Step 5 The goodwill in the Newco would be depreciated over 15 years as allowed by German tax law. Once the transaction had occurred, Apax would investigate the possibility of accelerating part of the goodwill depreciation by allocating it to existing fixed assets (German tax law allowed for this). If successful, Apax would increase the depreciation charge, thereby lowering tax payments.

Since Infox enjoyed a virtual monopoly position in its field in Germany and the German travel industry had a unique structure, there were no appropriate comparables for the transaction. There was neither a similar publicly traded company in Germany, nor had there been any similar transaction in the private market for corporate control. Valuation was thus solely based on the expected cash flows and expected exit multiples,

EXHIBIT 6   Infox Summary Financial Statements (DM millions)

Source: Apax.

	Historical		Forecast						
	1993	**1994**	**1995**	**1996**	**1997**	**1998**	**1999**	**2000**	**2001**
Sales									
Advertising distribution		21.9	22.5	23.2	23.9	24.6	26.4	26.1	26.9
Printing services		5.0	5.5	60.	6.5	6.8	7.2	7.5	7.9
Document distribution		1.4	1.8	2.3	2.5	2.6	2.8	2.9	3.0
Catalog delivery		0.0	1.5	3.0	4.0	4.2	4.4	4.6	4.9
Other		0.2	0.6	2.7	5.4	5.7	6.0	6.3	6.6
Total sales	**28.1**	**28.5**	**31.9**	**37.2**	**42.3**	**43.9**	**46.8**	**47.4**	**49.3**
Cost of goods sold	11.3	11.5	13.1	15.3	17.4	18.0	18.7	19.5	20.2
Gross profit	**16.8**	**17.0**	**18.8**	**21.9**	**24.9**	**25.9**	**28.1**	**27.9**	**29.1**
Operating Costs									
Personnel	3.9	4.4	4.5	5.2	5.9	6.2	6.4	6.6	6.9
Sales & marketing	0.0	0.1	0.4	0.4	0.5	0.5	0.5	0.6	0.6
Overhead & administration	1.2	0.8	1.1	1.3	1.5	1.6	1.6	1.7	1.8
Miscellaneous	0.0	0.5	0.6	0.7	0.8	0.9	0.9	0.9	1.0
EBITD	**11.7**	**11.2**	**12.2**	**14.3**	**16.2**	**16.7**	**18.7**	**18.1**	**18.8**
Depreciation (assets)	0.5	0.5	0.5	0.7	0.8	0.8	0.5	0.5	0.5
Depreciation (goodwill)[a]	0.0	0.0	3.9	3.9	3.9	3.9	3.9	3.9	3.9
EBIT	**11.2**	**10.7**	**7.8**	**9.7**	**11.5**	**12.0**	**14.3**	**13.7**	**14.4**
Less:									
Interest expense	0.0	0.0	3.3	3.3	2.4	1.8	1.1	0.4	0.1
Plus:									
Interest income	0.5	0.4	0.0	0.0	0.0	0.0	0.0	0.0	0.2
EBT	**11.7**	**11.1**	**4.5**	**6.4**	**9.1**	**10.2**	**13.2**	**13.3**	**14.5**
Exceptional items	0.0	0.0	1.0	0.0	0.0	0.0	0.0	0.0	0.0
Taxes	7.1	6.8	2.2	3.8	5.5	6.3	7.2	8.1	8.8
Net income	**4.6**	**4.3**	**1.3**	**2.6**	**3.6**	**3.9**	**6.0**	**5.2**	**5.7**
Margin Analysis									
Gross margin	59.8%	59.6%	58.9%	58.9%	58.9%	59.0%	60.0%	58.9%	59.0%
EBITD margin	41.6	39.3	38.2	38.4	38.3	38.0	40.0	38.2	38.1
EBIT margin	39.9	37.5	24.5	26.1	27.2	27.3	30.6	28.9	29.2
EBT margin	41.6	38.9	14.1	17.2	21.5	23.2	28.2	28.1	29.4
Net income margin	16.4	15.1	4.1	7.0	8.5	8.9	12.8	11.0	11.6

[a]Hypothetical case. The actual amount of depreciation of goodwill will depend on the purchase price.

with the latter being derived more by rule of thumb than scientific analysis. During the due diligence process, Martin Halusa and Michael Phillips found only one publicly listed company in a somewhat similar business. The company, Hays plc, operated only in the UK and was listed on the London Stock Exchange (ticker symbol: HAS). Their principal business was document distribution to law firms. In fiscal year 1994, Hays had sales of 632 million British Pounds and net income of 59 million British Pounds. On March 1, 1995, Hays traded at a price-earnings-multiple of 20.1.

EXHIBIT 6
(Continued)
Balance Sheets (DM millions)

Source: Apax.

	Historical 1994
Assets	
Cash & liquid securities	6.7
Accounts receivable	1.8
Other	1.1
Prepaid expenses	0.1
Inventories:	0.1
Raw materials	0.0
Work in progress	0.0
Finished goods	0.0
Current assets	9.8
Net Fixed assets	0.8
Total Assets	10.6
Liabilities & Equity	
Accounts payable	0.8
Other payables	1.4
Tax accruals	2.0
Other accruals	0.3
Prepayments	0.0
Current liabilities	4.4
Total debt	0.0
Paid-in capital & capital reserve	0.1
Profit for current year	4.4
Retained earnings	6.2
Shareholders equity	6.3
Total Liabilities and Equity	10.7

Note: Some figures may not match due to rounding.

The Final Investment Decision

Having conducted a thorough due diligence of the business, Phillips and Halusa felt well prepared for the meeting with Infox management. Their task now was to make a final decision on whether to recommend this investment to APA. The decision would have to weigh the strengths of the business against its perceived weaknesses, all in relation to the envisaged purchase price and the proposed transaction structure. Attempting to mentally set aside the obvious strengths of Infox, the two were now focusing on only the weak spots. To organize their thoughts for the upcoming meeting, they divided their concerns into five categories of risk: business, management, operating leverage, cost and exit.

Exit Risk

The most obvious risk for APA was that it might not find a buyer once it had been decided to exit the business in four to five years time. Given the weakness of the German public equity markets and the limited universe of strategic buyers, who would want to acquire the company at the end of the investment cycle? Furthermore, if the threat of substitutes was a real one now, would it not be reasonable to expect that this threat was to be even more acute in the future, given the rapid developments in the information technology sector?

Operating Leverage

Another perceived risk was resident in the company's high operating leverage. Even a small decrease in sales could presumably lead to a significant hit on profits. If the company lost part of their revenue for some reason, would it still be able to cover its debt obligations? Would a minor decrease in sales significantly impact the company's valuation in five years time?

Cost Risk

Mailing costs were the bulk of Infox's fixed costs base. Any increase here would adversely affect profits. Trans-o-Flex was losing money and could be out of business soon. While other private courier services offered similar pricing structures and each of them would have been likely to embrace Infox as one of their customers, it was always conceivable that there could be industry-wide upward pricing adjustments, significantly impacting the company's profitability.

Management Risk

Beer, despite his steep career in the travel industry and his obvious qualities, was not a proven manager at Infox. Would he be up to the job of playing the role of a counterweight to Brandschwede? Would he be able to live out his career ambitions in a small company like Infox?

Business Risk

Another key question was that of potential business risk. Infox was after all essentially a fixed cost business. Structural changes such as a reduction in the number of tour operators or travel agents, decreasing demand for travel products, lower levels of advertising etc. could presumably harm the business. Were these just risks for the remote future? Were the next five years really predictable or could change occur more quickly than anticipated?

As Halusa and Phillips pondered these questions while boarding the Lufthansa Airbus to Bonn, they were still unsure about what the decision should be. Their partners had backed the proposal to go ahead with the Infox investment at the "right" purchase price, and trusted Halusa and Phillips' judgment in making the final decision. The investment decision was an important one for the firm and they were determined not to let management go with their questions unanswered.

Module III

Mobilizing Resources

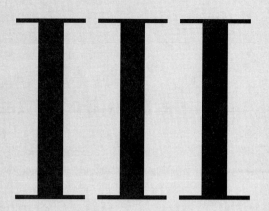

It is essential that entrepreneurs and those who finance them understand the process of how resources are mobilized. Entrepreneurship can be defined as the pursuit of opportunities without regard to tangible resources currently controlled.[1] Entrepreneurs typically first see an opportunity and then think about how to accumulate needed resources. When they do seek resources, entrepreneurs often face a catch-22 problem: they need resources to demonstrate that they can capture the opportunity they have identified, but without proof that they can capture the opportunity it is difficult to secure resources.

This dilemma is clearly reflected in the financial management of entrepreneurial ventures. Entrepreneurs typically can secure only staged commitments from capital providers. Given sufficient capital to demonstrate their ability and validate their ideas on a small scale, they are then in a position to raise additional capital needed to pursue the idea further. It is generally in the best interest of entrepreneurs to raise only enough capital to get to the next stage of a venture since its value increases with each milestone that is reached. Those who manage this process optimally will give away increasingly smaller shares of the equity pie at increasingly higher valuations without running out of cash.

The dilemma of how to mobilize resources for entrepreneurial ventures is exacerbated in countries that lack a developed market for risk capital (e.g., Japan, China, Nigeria, and Georgia). The cases in this book consider cross-country variance in the availability of capital to entrepreneurs and the possibility of cross-border access to resources.

This module also addresses the important questions of whether, where, and which activities entrepreneurial ventures should expand abroad. Entrepreneurs who try to mobilize resources stimulate financiers to make funding decisions. Because it is important to overcome stereotypes in order to be able to focus on common ground in a cross-border negotiation, it is useful to understand, in a comparative manner and across countries, what motivates people in general and entrepreneurs in particular. It is equally vital to understand the institutional underpinnings of cross-country differences.

[1] Stevenson, Howard H., and David E. Gumpert. 1985. The Heart of Entrepreneurship. *Harvard Business Review* (March–April): 85–94.

Two topics receive particular focus in this module. One is that the interaction of product-market and financing strategy is a key driver of the performance of entrepreneurial ventures. The second is a framework of motives for international expansion.

Interaction of Product-Market and Financing Strategy

An entrepreneur needs to determine whether a discovered opportunity is purely local or global in nature and then identify an optimal source of financing.[2] Analysis of the cases in this module suggests that prospective entrepreneurs should be aware of the entire set of funding choices potentially available to them before making a decision. This is particularly the case if venture capital is not well developed as a funding system in the local context or if a venture targets a global opportunity.

It makes sense for entrepreneurs who plan to expand internationally to seek funding from financiers who understand both the opportunities and challenges of international activity. For ventures likely to stay local, on the other hand, purely local resources might suffice. Nevertheless, for any entrepreneur, even one who plans to be active only locally, a global perspective on access to resources can improve both venture performance and the quality of deal structures. Entrepreneurs need to understand the direct and indirect effects of the financing choices they make with respect to sources of funding, amounts raised, and other terms of a financing package. Especially in international ventures, entrepreneurs often place too little emphasis on the quality of sources of funding. This sometimes reflects ignorance of the extent of the spectrum of available funding sources.

The interaction of product-market strategy and financing is also important to later-stage entrepreneurial firms. For example, building on insights arrived at in this module, Module 5 examines the decision of a successful Indian software firm, Infosys, to list its shares on a stock exchange abroad. In the case of that firm a global perspective on access to resources helped to inform an optimal funding decision.

A Framework of Motives for International Expansion

Beyond suggesting that entrepreneurial opportunities range from purely local to global, cases in this book address the all-important questions of when and how international ventures should expand abroad. My earlier research suggests that firms expand abroad either to make better use of existing firm-specific capabilities or to enhance their stock of capabilities.[3] The former motive, which might be called home-base-exploiting (HBE), comprises any activity that enables a firm to offer its products and services in other countries, the latter motive, which might be called home-base-augmenting (HBA), any activity that helps a firm improve its products and service, including the sourcing of product ideas, business model know-how, and capital. **Exhibit 1** illustrates these activities and the direction of knowledge flows. The framework in **Exhibit 1** can be used to plan, communicate and monitor the international expansion of start-up firms.[4]

[2] In some cases, an entrepreneur might pursue an opportunity with local scope and expand to global scope over time, adjusting the financing strategy accordingly.

[3] Kuemmerle, Walter. 1999. The Drivers of Foreign Direct Investment into Research and Development. *Journal of International Business Studies* 30 (1): 1–24.

[4] For further reading on the framework depicted in **Exhibit 1** see: Kuemmerle, W. 2002. Home Base and Knowledge Management in International Ventures. *Journal of Business Venturing* 17: 99–122.

EXHIBIT 1
Direction of Knowledge Flows Between Home Base and Geographically Separate Sites in Start-up Firms

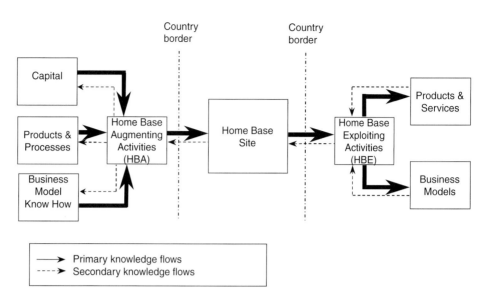

About two thirds of all the entrepreneurial firms studied in this book carried out both home-base-augmenting and home-base-exploiting activities within the first few years of their existence. Most of the firms studied made these geographic expansion decisions after the mid-1990s, suggesting that entrepreneurial ventures expand internationally much faster than in earlier periods. It is also remarkable that the sequence of international expansion in start-up firms often differs considerably from that in established firms. The literature describes how established multinational firms first expand with home-base-exploiting activities and only much later, if at all, engage in home-base-augmenting activities. In start-up firms, by contrast, home-base-augmenting investments often occur before home-base-exploiting investments or both types of investments occur around the same time. This suggests that lessons learned from the management of established multinational companies are not always directly applicable in start-up firms.

The cases on Spotfire and Mobilecom Tokyo in this module are vehicles for discussing motives for and the sequencing of international expansion, topics reinforced in later cases in this book, including Promise (Module 4) and TelePizza and Vacationspot (Module 5). The discussion about international expansion can also be linked back to two cases in the first module of this book, namely, @Hoc and Internet Securities.

Cases in This Module

This module consists of six cases. The first case of this module focuses on the reorganization of the largest mineral water bottling operation in Georgia. This country context is tricky to navigate, property rights and the legal system being extremely weak. The company is seeking to raise approximately $14 million in its third round of financing. Potential sources of capital include two supra-governmental organizations, the International Finance Corporation and the European Bank for Reconstruction and Development. The case promotes discussion of the benefits and drawbacks of this class of investor.[5]

[5] The case has interesting parallels with other cases set in countries in which property rights are weak (e.g., Officenet (Module 1) and QI-Tech, and Capital Alliance (this module)). It also has interesting parallels with Telewizja Wisla (Module 4) with respect to entrepreneurs interacting with government officials in countries that have recently transitioned from planned to market economies.

The second case addresses challenges to entrepreneurial managers who seek to mobilize resources in joint ventures. Additional capital was needed by a joint venture (QI-Tech) to manufacture and market precision-measurement machines undertaken by a small U.S. firm that wanted to reduce its stake and a state-owned enterprise in China. A previous attempt to attract a strategic investor had failed primarily because of lack of cultural sensitivity by the U.S. firm to negotiating processes in China. The case also accommodates discussion of how China as a context for entrepreneurship compares to other countries studied in this book, notably Georgia and Nigeria.[6]

The third case of the module revolves around Spotfire, a Swedish software company that has accepted a $3 million investment offer from a U.S. venture capitalist and the venture capitalist's condition that the firm relocate all activity except software development from Sweden to the United States. Analysis of the terms that were part of the offer reveals that they make sense even though they provide considerable downside protection for the venture capitalist.[7] Analysis of the company's evolution to date and its business model leads to questions about the accuracy of cash-flow forecasts. This case also facilitates a comprehensive review of motives for and the sequence of international expansion of start-ups. The CEO and COO are featured in a published video that complements the case.[8,9]

The fourth case of the module elucidates the notion that a global perspective on mobilizing resources improves deal structures and the likelihood of venture survival. The case, "Mobile Communications Tokyo, Inc.," portrays a somewhat rare species: an entrepreneur in Japan. After eight years of growing the company by reinvesting profits, with almost no external equity, the entrepreneur is considering whether an initial public offering might be a good way to raise capital. Among other things, case analysis must focus on a comparison of the contexts for entrepreneurship in Japan and the United States, highlighting the point that not just private equity, but also debt, is difficult for smaller firms to obtain in Japan. A detailed analysis of where a company might list its shares can then be made. Overall, the case permits a discussion of the interaction between product-market and financing strategies.[10]

The fifth case of Module 3 treats the challenge of mobilizing resources on two levels. Capital Alliance, the first private equity fund in Nigeria, plans to make its first investment in a telecommunications firm, GS Telecom, that caters to multinational firms. The founders of Capital Alliance do not want to go wrong with their first investment lest they undermine the confidence of investors in their fund. GS Telecom has operated with little

---

[6] The QI-Tech case has interesting parallels with the cases on Cityspace (Module 1) and Absolute Sensors (Module 2) with respect to entrepreneurs who must negotiate with larger firms' managers to mobilize resources. To succeed, such entrepreneurs must first analyze the objectives of those managers.

[7] The case builds on the Term Sheet Negotiations for Trendsetter case (Module 1) that analyzes venture capitalists' use of term sheets.

[8] Kuemmerle, Walter. 2002. *Spotfire Update: Reflections by Chris Ahlberg, CEO and Rock Gnatovich, President (HBS Case Video 802–804).* Boston: Harvard Business School Publishing.

[9] Spotfire is closely linked to @Hoc and Internet Securities (Module 1), Mobile Communications Tokyo (this module), and Vacationspot (Module 5) with regard to international expansion issues of start-ups. This also ties the case to the international expansion of more established firms such as TelePizza (Module 5) and Promise (Module 4).

[10] The case has close links to the Jafco and Promise cases (Module 4), which share its geographic focus on Japan. The case also has interesting parallels with Vacationspot (Module 5), in which a company that did not take a global perspective on access to resources lost its independence. Finally, international expansion considerations link the case to the cases on Internet Securities and @Hoc (Module 1) and TelePizza (Module 5).

equity for several years. It needs capital badly in order to exploit a significant opportunity. In providing an example of entrepreneurship in Africa, this case adds to the range of country contexts analyzed in this book. Nigeria is positioned towards the low end of the world spectrum in terms of transparency and quality of corporate governance. The case acknowledges the temptation for start-ups to engage in corruption and examines the pitfalls of doing so. Desiring to avoid these practices, Capital Alliance seeks capital from investors such as the African Development Bank. The case suggests that there are interesting opportunities in volatile contexts.[11]

The sixth case, Silicon Valley start-up TixToGo has developed an Internet service that enables on-line sign-ups and payments for events and conferences. A serial entrepreneur and his partner started the company in San Francisco in 1997. Although the business model seems quite attractive, TixToGo has had difficulty gaining momentum and the founders have decided to hire a manager with considerable start-up experience. The company is almost out of cash. The case provides an opportunity to assess the link between the company's financing strategy and its rapidly changing product-market strategy. The newly hired CEO also faces a range of other resource mobilization and crisis management challenges.[12]

---

[11] The topic of corruption also comes up in Officenet (Module 1) and Georgia Glass and Mineral Water (this module). The case has geographic links to Gray Security (Module 4), which deals with an entrepreneurial company in South Africa, and conceptual links to Telewizja Wisla (Module 4) with which it shares scenario analysis as a potentially useful tool.

[12] The case has parallels with Spotfire (this module) and with @Hoc and Internet Securities (Module 1) with respect to funding decisions. The case can also be contrasted with the only other dot-com case in this book, Vacationspot (Module 5), which, owing to a number of financing and product market decisions, fared differently than TixToGo.

Case

13

Georgian Glass
and Mineral Water

Jacques Fleury, CEO of Georgian Glass and Mineral Water (GGMW), stared thoughtfully into his wineglass. Georgian tradition called for a series of brief toasts to be made at the end of a good meal with friends, and it was Fleury's turn. His last toast had been to the health of the man who had hired him, Mamouka Khazaradze, and to that of his other colleagues at the long table. His next one, he felt, should be to the future of the company he had only heard of four months ago and had joined in early March. It was now April 13, 1997, and Fleury knew there were many things to wish for on behalf of his company.

Khazaradze, a 31-year-old Tbilisi-born entrepreneur, had founded GGMW in order to capture and grow the value of one of Georgia's most famous intangible assets—the popularity of mineral water from the springs of the Borjomi Valley. (See **Exhibit 1** for a map of the Republic of Georgia and **Exhibit 2** for macroeconomic data on Georgia.) Fleury had been recruited when Khazaradze and the other investors in GGMW had realized that the firm required dedicated professional management. Although he had never been to Georgia before, Fleury found the former Soviet republic charming, and had been excited about the prospect of revitalizing a brand with such wide and favorable recognition. The challenges facing him, however, were daunting.

When Fleury had joined, GGMW was nearly out of money and he had been told that the company would need to raise at least $3 million to cover necessary investments. Fleury's own investigations suggested that the capital needs of the company might be substantially higher if GGMW were to produce a consistent product of high quality and to truly establish GGMW's position in the market. While the company's shareholders were supportive, Fleury knew he would have to consider carefully what investments were necessary and when they would have to be made before he could argue his case successfully.

Moreover, even if the investments were made, GGMW faced a considerable series of challenges. Competition came not only from other bottled waters and soft drinks, but

Charles M. Williams Fellow Chad Ellis (MBA '98) prepared this case under the supervision of Professor Walter Kuemmerle. HBS cases are developed solely as the basis for class discussion. Cases are not intended to serve as endorsements, sources of primary data, or illustrations of effective or ineffective management.

EXHIBIT 1 Map of the Republic of Georgia

Source: Martin Greenwald Associates. 1998. *Maps on File, Georgia.* New York: Facts on File, p. 3. 10.

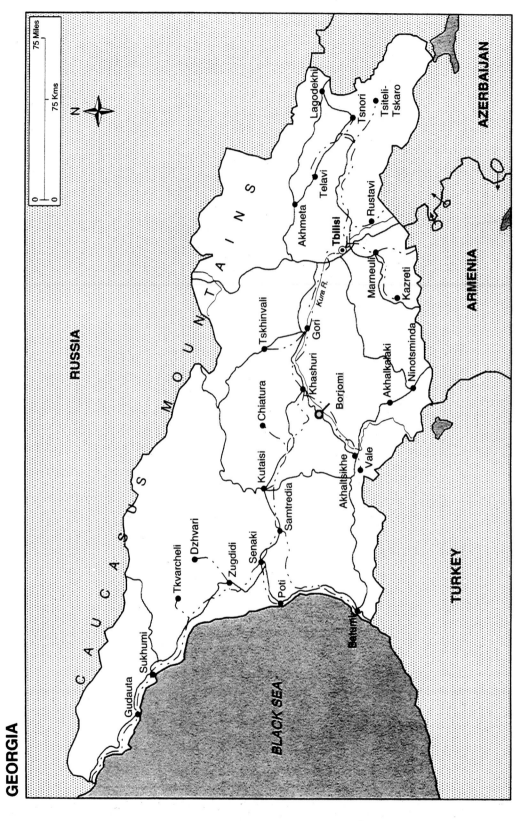

EXHIBIT 1 (Continued)

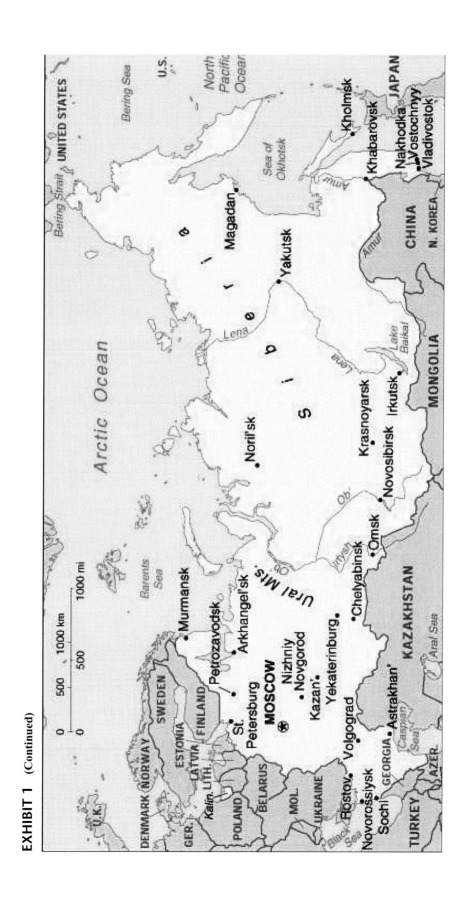

EXHIBIT 2 Georgian Economic Data

Source: Compiled from The World Bank. *World Development Report.* 1998/99. New York: Oxford University Press, pp. 190–232.

Poverty and Social	Georgia	Russian Federation
1997		
Population, mid-year (*millions*)	5.4	147
GNP per capita (*Atlas method, US$*)	840	2,740
GNP (*Atlas method, US$ billions*)	4.5	404
Average annual growth, 1991–1997		
Population (%)	−0.2	−0.2
Labor force (%)	−0.1	0.1
Most recent estimate (latest year available, 1991–1997)		
Poverty (*% of population below national poverty line*)	30	31
Urban population (*% of total population*)	58	77
Life expectancy at birth (*years*)	73	67
Infant mortality (*per 1,000 live births*)	18	17
Illiteracy (*% of population age 15+*)	1	—
Gross primary enrollment (*% of school-age population*)	86	91

Key Economic Ratios and Long-Term Trends (Georgia)	1996
GDP (*US$ billions*)	4.6
Gross domestic investment/GDP(%)	6.0
Exports of goods and services/GDP(%)	11.2
Gross domestic savings/GDP(%)	−1.8
Gross national savings/GDP(%)	2.3
Current account balance/GDP(%)	−9.1
Interest payments/GDP(%)	1.4
Total debt/GDP(%)	30.1
Total debt service/exports(%)	15.3
Present value of debt/GDP(%)	23.9
Present value of debt/exports(%)	213.4

	1996	1997
(*% average annual growth*)		
GDP	10.5	10.9
GNP per capita	12.7	12.8
Exports of goods and services	17.8	18.4

Structure of the Economy	1986	1996	1997
(*% of GDP*)			
Agriculture	26.8	33.4	31.6
Industry	37.0	25.1	23.4
Manufacturing	27.8	18.8	17.5
Services	36.2	41.5	45.0
Private consumption	57.4	92.7	95.2
General government consumption	12.8	9.1	9.0
Imports of goods and services	—	18.9	22.7

(continued)

EXHIBIT 2 (Continued)

(% annual growth)	1976–86	1987–97	1996	1997
Agriculture	—	—	3.0	3.5
Industry	—	—	2.0	2.0
Manufacturing	—	—	2.0	2.0
Services	—	—	16.8	17.2
Private consumption	—	—	2.2	15.4
General government consumption	—	—	40.0	10.9
Gross domestic investment	—	—	57.0	90.9
Imports of goods and services	—	—	9.7	39.2
Gross national product (annual % growth)	4.4	−16.5	12.7	11.2

Prices and Government Finance			1996	1997
Domestic prices				
(% change)				
Consumer prices			39.4	7.1
Implicit GDP deflator			40.2	7.1
Government finance				
(% of GDP, includes current grants)				
Current revenue			8.1	9.9
Current budget balance			−4.6	−3.5
Overall surplus/deficit			−5.8	−4.6

Trade			1996	1997
(US$ millions)				
Total exports (fob)			463	559
Black metal			80	101
Tea			19	24
Manufactures			231	236
Total imports (cif)			766	947
Food			213	154
Fuel and energy			184	196
Capital goods			129	330

Balance of Payments			1996	1997
(US$ millions)				
Exports of goods and services			511	623
Imports of goods and services			867	1,192
Resource balance			−356	−569
Net income			−62	34
Net current transfers			141	188
Current account balance			−418	−535
Financing items (net)			339	474
Changes in net reserves			70	61
Memo:				
Reserves including gold (US$ millions)			159	175
Conversion rate (DEC, local/US$)			1,263.0	—

(continued)

EXHIBIT 2 (Continued)

External Debt and Resource Flows	1996	1997
(US$ millions)		
Total debt outstanding and disbursed	1,378	1,550
IBRD	0	0
IDA	157	212
Total debt service	49	53
IBRD	0	0
IDA	1	1
Composition of net resource flows		
Official grants	141	84
Official creditors	186	192
Private creditors	0	0
Foreign direct investment	54	189
Portfolio equity	0	0
World Bank program		
Commitments	91	155
Disbursements	76	64
Principal repayments	0	0
Net flows	76	64
Interest payments	1	1
Net transfers	76	63

Note: 1997 data are preliminary estimates.

also from counterfeiters claiming to sell Borjomi water. In some cases their claims were real, but the water was often bottled under unsanitary conditions; in other cases it was simply tap water with some additives to create the characteristic Borjomi taste. Complicating matters further, although GGMW did have exclusive rights to the Borjomi brand, some of their competitors had a virtually identical product! Fleury knew it would be difficult to establish a successful branding strategy under these conditions.

Fleury also knew that he would have to manage the Georgian company without some of the tools he had previously taken for granted. The factories' financial records consisted of incomplete handwritten entries, many of which were unclear. It would be months, perhaps years before GGMW could have reliable financial statements and a true picture of its assets and liabilities.

Operating in a former Soviet republic also meant working without a clear legal framework. Although Georgia had made progress toward establishing a market-based economy, it lacked the legal institutions and experience necessary to establish a solid legal framework in which to operate. Mismanagement in the former State factories was high, and GGMW had become accustomed to losing some of its product to "leakage" at various points along the value chain. Fleury spent much of his time, as well as GGMW's money, fighting fires that would not exist in his native France. Could GGMW survive and thrive under these conditions, or would the allure of a powerful brand prove chimeric in an environment where value was so difficult to capture?

The Republic of Georgia

The Republic of Georgia, part of the former Soviet Union (FSU), was situated in the Caucasus Mountains between the Black and Caspian seas. Georgia had a landmass of 69,700 square kilometers (slightly smaller than South Carolina), and 310 kilometers of coastline. The climate was warm and pleasant, and tourism around the Black Sea had long been an important factor in its economy. Khazaradze recalled a Georgian fable about the country's origin:

> God was handing out land to all the peoples of the world. Each group waited in line and was given a nation to call their home. When God had finished, and all the land had been given away, the Georgians came running up. God told them they were late, and asked them why they had not come with everyone else. The Georgians replied that they had been drinking to God's health. God was so moved by this that he decided to give them the land he had set aside for himself.

Despite the pleasant geographical conditions, Georgia's recent history had been difficult. The economy suffered significantly following the collapse of the Soviet Union, and Georgia suffered civil war in the following years, only beginning to stabilize in 1994. The economic collapse was severe even by FSU standards, with GDP in 1994 standing at only 30% of 1990 levels. Private sector wages fell nearly 90% to about $40 per month—government workers earned less than half that much.

Following the end of Georgia's civil war, the country's fortunes began to improve. Free elections were held in 1995, with former Soviet Foreign Minister Eduard Shevardnadze re-elected as President. IMF and World Bank assistance, plus a commitment to reform helped improve Georgia's economy. A new currency introduced in 1995, helped stem hyperinflation, and GDP growth reached double-digit levels in 1996. Nevertheless, in 1997 Georgia still had roughly 250,000 internally displaced people (as a result of the civil war) and unemployment estimated at 21%. Ongoing unrest in northern Georgia often meant that trade between Georgia and Russia had to travel through Azerbaijan, adding time and expense. Net migration was nearly negative one per cent, and per capita GDP was estimated at $840. Short-term interest rates had declined somewhat, but remained above 30% in local currency.

An Old Brand in New Hands

Borjormi Spring Water

Borjomi mineral water was extracted from natural springs in the Borjomi Valley two hours drive from Tbilisi. At the height of the Soviet Union's power, Borjomi water was one of Georgia's leading exports, with over 450 million half-liter bottles of Borjomi water consumed each year. Since then, however, the equipment for extracting and bottling the water had deteriorated, production had declined sharply and counterfeiting had increased. By 1994, less than five million bottles were sold by the government-owned mineral water company and by 1995, production had fallen to an annualized rate of roughly one million. Nevertheless, the brand was well-known throughout the FSU, with recognition levels comparable to those commanded in the West by Coca-Cola.

Borjomi water was widely believed within the FSU to have almost magical curative properties, serving as a remedy for ills ranging from upset stomachs to the most severe hangovers. High levels of minerals gave it a very distinctive taste quite different from the mineral waters of the West, but which its customers believed indicated its medicinal value.

Mamouka Khazaradze

Mamouka Khazaradze was born in Tbilisi in 1966. As a young man he became the leader of Georgia's Young Communists at his university, which enabled him to mobilize resources for planning events and community activities. Khazaradze had always been full of energy. With the collapse of the Soviet Union he began looking for opportunities outside of politics. In 1991, he decided to go into business for himself, buying 1.2 million cans of American beer and trying to sell them in Russia.

In St. Petersburg Khazaradze met Bob Meijer, a Dutch venture capitalist who was known for his love of antique cars. Meijer, who spent a lot of time touring Europe in his old Bugatti, was visiting Russia and heard about Khazaradze from some business partners who had bought Khazaradze's beer. The enthusiastic young Georgian intrigued Meijer, and the two men became friends. Meijer promised to visit him in Georgia. In 1993, Meijer kept his promise, and decided to invest in two of Khazaradze's Georgian ventures, an outdoor advertising company and a small supermarket chain.

In 1995, Khazaradze, Meijer and other European partners, including Paul Thomas who had substantial experience in the mineral water business in the US and Europe, formed GGMW. Raising $2.6 million, in part from groups of French and Dutch investors, they bought a glass bottle manufacturing plant for $1 million in addition to assuming plant liabilities of $1.5 million. A further $900,000 of investment was required to repair and update the plant's equipment. GGMW hoped to work in partnership with two recently privatized bottlers, providing bottles and some equity in exchange for use of bottling capacity.

Shortly thereafter, however, the Georgian government renationalized the bottling plants, citing illegalities in the original privatization as well as evidence that the factory owners were violating the laws of Georgia. The bottling factory owners were arrested, and GGMW had to enter into a new agreement with the state-owned factories.

In October 1995, GGMW signed a contract with the bottling operation, but there were serious problems. Up to 13% of all empty bottles were lost due to "breakage." GGMW believed that much of this breakage actually reflected theft. Mamouka explained the extent of the corruption problem:

> For example, a Soviet-era director whom we fired had originally paid a substantial amount of money in bribes to become a director earning sixty dollars a month. He made back his money by withholding from employees or stealing from the company. This system was ingrained during the Soviet era. Theft isn't difficult to fight when all the companies are under private ownership, but when one is State-owned it is almost impossible to fight.

GGMW knew that it would always struggle to become profitable under current conditions, and lobbied the government for control of the bottling factories. Eventually the government decided to offer a limited privatization of the bottling factories by international tender, including exclusive rights to use the Borjomi name. While the factories would remain state-owned, the management rights would be sold in what was effectively a several-year concession. GGMW won the tender. Mamouka stated:

> It was not a perfect deal, but we had no choice. We needed the bottling facilities and the Borjomi brand. Unfortunately, several local and Russian financial investors and international mineral water operators also bid for them. If they had won they would have had a lot of leverage against us, and might have shut us out completely, preventing us from using our bottling plant.

GGMW resolved to reorganize the operation so that as much as possible remained under their control. Bottling would be done at the plant, but shipping, marketing and distribution would be arranged centrally by GGMW.

GGMW had needed to raise additional capital to improve the bottling operation. They turned to ING Barings, a Dutch investment bank, which had recently raised a dedicated fund for investing in Eastern Europe. ING invested $2.5 million in 1996, but made it clear they would not invest more unless GGMW committed to bring in a professional management team, including a CEO and CFO. Mamouka explained:

> Up to that point, we had tried to run the company among the four of us [Mamouka, Meijer, Thomas and Jean Patrick, one of the French investors], with each of us in different cities across Europe, trying to agree on things on our cell phones. By the time we took over management of the bottling factories, we realized we couldn't run the company like that.

GGMW began looking for an outside CEO who could lead the company forward. In February 1997, they brought to Georgia their leading candidate for the position: Jacques Fleury. Fleury had established a strong track record in managing businesses in the Middle East and Western Europe (see **Exhibit 3** for Jacques Fleury's resume), but had never been to Georgia. He recalled his initial experience:

> I found myself captivated by this beautiful country and its sense of history. On my second day here, we went to visit the Djvari Church (Church of the Cross) which lies between Tbilisi and Borjomi. It is from the 5th century, one of the oldest remaining Christian churches, and it stands atop a hillside overlooking the countryside.
>
> Of course, there are drawbacks to living here, too. My family lives in Paris, so I don't see them as often as I would like. Also, in the West we take certain things for granted, like saving food in our freezers. Freezers are available in Georgia, but the electricity fails almost daily, so you can't really store food for long with any reliability. So, you have to learn to live without some basic amenities.

The Opportunity—the Perrier of Eastern Europe?

Fleury's excitement for the business opportunity, however, even exceeded his excitement for the country. To chart the course of a brand which, despite its many problems, was recognized throughout the FSU was a rare opportunity. While the challenges might prove daunting, the prize for success was high. Fleury explained the potential:

> At its peak, Borjomi sold over 400 million bottles per year. We can cover our fixed costs at 40 million bottles, and probably less as our costs come down. Each bottle generates thirty cents [of ex-factory revenues] for us with a gross margin of 50%. Shipping costs are added on to our price, so that doesn't come out of the thirty cents. If we can solve the company's problems we could be profitable in 1998 and very profitable by the end of the century.

Historic behavior and some limited market research suggested that the brand had retained a high degree of loyalty. Despite the much lower living standards in Georgia compared with the West, Borjomi was priced at a level comparable to Western brands such as Evian, Vichy and Poland Springs. (See **Exhibit 4**.) Moreover, during recent economic crises, consumption of Borjomi in Georgia and Russia fell less than that of well-known soft drink brands such as Coca-Cola. Fleury saw no reason that Borjomi could not ultimately reclaim its former position and sales level. About a month after his arrival in Tbilisi Airport, Fleury agreed to become GGMW's CEO.

Some Unconventional Challenges
Building a brand without operational consistency

Despite his enthusiasm about Borjomi's potential, Fleury knew his task would not be easy. The company's newly acquired bottling operation needed upgrading, not just to increase volume but also to ensure product quality. Fleury was blunt about the company's starting point: "Our capacity to produce garbage was high, but our capacity to produce a consistent product was low. Without a stable, quality product, we could not hope to reestablish the Borjomi brand."

EXHIBIT 3 Resume of Jacques Fleury

Source: GGMW.

Professional Experience

1991–1996 Thomson-Csf Finance-TCI Compensation
Based in Athens, Greece

- AGROINVEST S.A.—**Chairman and Managing Director**. Private port and 4 agro-industries on the same site—Sales 90 M US$ (total capital invested from 1978 to 1981: $140 million)
- Management of a private port (capacity 1 M tons) and 3 factories—Animal feed plant-flour mill-oil mill (soja-sunflower-cotton). Trading of cereals and Soya (2 main brands)
- GREEK OIL MILLS S.A.—**Chairman.** Company formed in 1993 by merging Agroinvest oil business with the main local competitor (leader in the Greek market). One of the main world purchasers of Russian and Ukrainian sunflower seeds—Sales $41 million (annual growth 30%).
- AGROEFODIA—Chairman. New concept of self-service warehouses for farmers under license of POINT VERT-MAGASIN VERT (France). Company formed in 1994 as a 50-50 joint venture with the leading Greek fertilizer company. Sales $8 million (annual growth 100%)

1988–1991 Thomson-Csf Finance
Based in Cairo, Egypt
Project manager for Nadco-Les Jardins du Nil

- Responsible for the creation of a large agricultural project which was partially financed by a debt/equity swap by THOMPSON-CSF (28% of share capital) following an agreement with the Egyptian authorities. Development of 2,500ha of desert land for agriculture. Produced and exported (by air and sea) the following: potatoes, green beans, citrus, bananas, strawberries and table grapes. Total capital invested: $32 million.
- In charge of the complete design and implementation of the project in cooperation with two leading Saudi investors (Rolaco and AlMabani), from negotiations with Egyptian authorities to the selection of local partners from the Egyptian private sector (El Maghraby). Also presented the project to foreign development banks and institutions (European Investment Bank for risk capital 2M E.C.U. and long-term loan 8 M E.C.U.).

This project is one of the rare success stories in such an environment. Besides its technical and economical achievements it also had the following features:

- Contributed to the reduction of Egypt's foreign debt and improved balance of payments (specialization in the exportation of fresh fruit and vegetables).
- First agricultural land privatization since Nasser, with partial ownership by foreign investors.
- Close commercial and technical cooperation with Israel (the project has now CARMEL as an available brand name), Europe and the United States.

1983–1987 Thomson Csf Sodeteg
Based in Paris
Export Manager for the Cooperation and Development Division

- In charge of international development for a division specializing in the sales of engineering services and technical assistance, financed by international funds or banks (World Bank, European Development Fund, Asian and African Development Banks, etc.).
- Contracts negotiated and supervised in many countries: Malaysia, Guinea, Guinea-Bissau, Senegal Mauritania, Cameroon, Lebanon and Angola.

1980–1982 Zanzi Vivai-Italy
Based in Morocco
Export Manager

- In charge of identification and promotion of agro-industrial projects in the field of fruits and vegetables in the Mediterranean and Middle East areas. The projects were based upon the new technologies from Davis University, California. Activities were concentrated in Libya, Saudi Arabia, Abu-Dhabi, Jordan, Egypt, etc.
- In parallel Managing Director Zanzi-Morocco (local agricultural production).
- Sales and construction in Morocco of two factories (vegetable freezing and dehydration).

1975–1981 Zanai Vivai-Iran
Based in Tehran
Managing Director of the Iranian subsidiary of an Italian engineering group specialized in the food industry and in agriculture. Negotiations sale and execution of turn-key projects (500 employees and annual sales of $23 million).

(continued)

EXHIBIT 3   (Continued)

1972–1975 Bossard Consultant—France—Iran
Based in Paris and Tehran
Management Consultant
Responsible for the restructuring of ailing industries in France and Tunisia

- Starter and Managing director of the subsidiary in Iran (1974).
- Agent for Iran until 1980 for the Canadian group IRCAN, for the account of BOSSARD CONSULTANTS.
- Negotiations, construction and supply of equipment on a turnkey basis for 15 vocational training centers with a value of $50 million. The project was interrupted during execution by the Iranian revolution.

Achievements
Nomination as Chairman of Agroinvest in 1991. Company was in a state of liquidation with sales of $12 million but losses greater than sales. Spectacular growth accomplished with a return to operating profit in 1993 and regular progression since then.

- Responsible for the international development of the group (export sales: 40% to Arab and East European countries)

In parallel: Board member and technical advisor to the Chairman of Nadco-Les Jardins du Nil—Egypt

Studies

- Civil Engineer, Ecole Spéciale des Travaux Publics—Paris.
- Post Graduate diploma in Management, Institut d'Administration des Entreprises, Paris Dauphine University.
- M.Sc Economics—London School of Economics, London (specialization in Operational Research).

EXHIBIT 4
Price Comparison of Mineral Water Brands

	Borjomi	Vichy (France)	Poland Springs (U.S.)	Evian (France)
US$/liter	1.40[1]	1.50	1.29	1.70

[1]includes 20% VAT.

Source: GGMW.

Competition

Building brand value was further complicated by the fact that GGMW's competitors included both counterfeiters, who claimed to be selling Borjomi water, and other companies who were also temporarily authorized to bottle the water. Khazaradze explained how GGMW's exclusivity had been eroded:

> When GGMW won exclusivity for the Borjomi name, we developed a plan that would have gradually increased production. Sources had been over exploited in the 1980s, and this had reduced quality. So, our plan didn't use all of the capacity available at first in order to ensure product quality so we could build the brand. But the government ministers don't understand marketing or quality or even the notion of a brand—to them it was just a question of unused capacity. So even though we had been awarded exclusivity, they authorized fifteen other companies to bottle the Borjomi water for a temporary period of one year, leaving us the responsibility to sub-license the use of the name.

Counterfeiters came in two forms. Some small operators, often individuals, used recycled bottles to hold genuine Borjomi water, which they siphoned illegally from one of the water pipelines. Often this water was bottled under unsanitary conditions. Other, larger counterfeiters, especially in far away metropolitan areas of Russia, simply used tap water to fill bottles, which they then claimed to contain Borjomi water. Stores had an incentive to stock counterfeit Borjomi as it was considerably cheaper but could be sold at the same price as GGMW's product. GGMW had estimated that up to 90% of water sold as Borjomi in Russia during 1996 was counterfeit.

Both counterfeiters and legitimate rivals presented Borjomi with challenges Western brand managers seldom had to face. How could they build loyalty to a brand that they could not control and which often represented an inferior or even dangerous product? And, if they succeeded in reestablishing Borjomi as a premium product, how could they capture the value they had created? Consumers in Russia and Georgia knew that a lot of "fake" Borjomi was on the market, but the company needed a way to establish their product as "real" Borjomi as well as to make it difficult to copy.

Legitimate competition in Russia for "Health water" came from rival mineral water brands Narzan and Essentuki. GGMW believed Borjomi water was still the number one brand, with coverage of 80% of retail outlets in Moscow compared to 70% and 30%, respectively, for Narzan and Essentuki. Borjomi had, by far, the highest brand awareness rate (90%) of all mineral waters in Russia[1] and was still showing gains in consumption and awareness. Nevertheless, heavy counterfeiting had somewhat damaged the value of all famous traditional mineral waters including Borjomi, Narzan and Essentuki. At the other end of the market (low mineralised waters) new comers were appearing, challenging the positions of the traditional brands. St. Springs was a brand that Fleury classified in the "tap water substitution" category. He explained:

> St. Springs is just purified well water, but a Bishop in the Russian Orthodox Church somehow blessed it. Consumers may feel they are drinking a "Holy water." It's not really spring water, but since "Spring" is part of the commercial name customers infer that it is. This is a very smart marketing move.

In Georgia, GGMW's most significant rival was B.I.G., one of the firms with a temporary license to bottle the Borjomi water that had exploited the demand for plastic containers left unfulfilled by GGMW's initial strategy to restore the product image in glass containers. Other legitimate producers included GMW, Murgoni and Peritsixe, very minor operators, the rest of the 15 companies with temporary licenses not having really started to operate at all. GGMW believed it had a larger market share than any of its rivals, as well as superior financial resources and longer-term strategy. Counterfeiters had smaller market shares and were problematic, more for their potential to erode the value of "real" Borjomi water than for their market positions.

"Leakage" and Legal Issues

Theft and corruption had been a normal, even a necessary way of life for many under Soviet rule and remained a constant challenge for the managers of GGMW. Security costs at the two factories ran as high as $200,000 per year, despite low labor costs, and GGMW still had a substantial problem with what they referred to as product "leakage." In some instances, theft was not limited to pilfered bottles or small pieces of equipment. Khazaradze recalled an incident from late 1996:

> The manager of the glass bottle plant called me and said that our container of heavy fuel was nearly empty and that there was a risk of shutting down the glass furnace with all consequences. He had contacted a black market operator that could deliver the fuel providing he could be paid by undeclared cash. We needed the fuel, but we suspected that the manager himself was behind the story, and the unexpected level of fuel consumption surprised us, so we told him that if he delivered it we would pay and waited to see what happened.
>
> He told us he had arranged to have the fuel delivered. The morning after the fuel was scheduled to be returned he described how it had arrived in the early morning hours by train and had been unloaded into our container before the first shift arrived for work. We congratulated him and asked him to come into the office to meet with us. When he arrived, thinking we were going to hand him a sack of money, we told him he had a choice—sign the resignation letter we had typed up for him or face the police.

[1] Gallup Media Russia 1996.

You have to understand that to unload the fuel would take maybe twelve hours—certainly much longer than he had described. We had also taken care to mobilize surveillance during the whole night but of course they did not even hear the noise of a train. The whole story was preposterous. Later we found out that he had simply pumped the fuel into an adjacent storage tank that was generally unused. I can only think that he was used to dealing with people who knew nothing and didn't care so he thought he could get away with it.

As unusual as such incidents seemed to Fleury, they were perhaps less serious than claims made by old creditors—claims with little or no legal basis, but which consumed considerable resources. Fleury explained:

When GGMW won the management rights to the bottling plant, our contract stipulated that we would not be liable for any debts or obligations arising prior to our taking over. We had to have this guarantee because we knew that the previous owners had not paid a lot of people what they owed them and it would be impossible for us to be profitable or even to estimate how much we had to pay.

Suddenly, after I arrive and we have some investor money, a line of people appears at our door, each of them with some old claim. Legally, they have nothing, but unfortunately sometimes justice is a question of what someone is willing to pay the judge! Georgia's legal system is improving rapidly, but it is still young. The quality and integrity of judges is much better than it used to be but there are still some corrupt judges who will ignore the law if someone promises to share their claim.

Fleury soon found that nearly half of his time was taken up dealing with past creditors of the bottling plants. It quickly became clear that these claims were going to be costly to GGMW financially as well, either through settling with claimants or through high court costs.

The Russian Winter

Russia was GGMW's single largest market, accounting for 70% of sales. However, harsh winter conditions caused transportation costs per bottle to increase from $0.08 per bottle in the warmer months to $0.20 per bottle between the months of January and April because they would have to use expensive, insulated railroad equipment. By comparison, bottles shipped during the warmer months could be stored in Russia for roughly $0.04 per bottle, keeping Borjomi on the market year-round. Fleury estimated that ten to fifteen million bottles could be sold in Russia during the winter if they were shipped early.

Looking for Answers

Fleury knew he would have to address these challenges quickly if GGMW was to get back onto a successful path. Nor did he think he could deal with the issues in isolation, since they were interconnected; any impact on quality or volume through renovation of the lines would have consequences for GGMW's options for building brand awareness or shipping to Russia.

When Fleury had been recruited, GGMW's management had indicated that at least $3 million would need to be spent renovating the bottling lines. Much of the existing equipment was unreliable and expensive to maintain. The company's shareholders were aware of the need and would undoubtedly support the investment. However, Fleury felt that a somewhat larger investment might be needed. As part of his efforts to distinguish between GGMW's real Borjomi water and "fake" Borjomi, Fleury thought it might be effective to "brand" the glass bottles GGMW sold its water in. This would require buying new molds for the bottle manufacturing plant. Fleury also wanted to shrink-wrap cases of bottles (both empty and full ones) as soon as possible in the production process—not only for ease of shipping but also to reduce the ease with which employees could take "loose" bottles home with them. All told, the necessary investment could run almost as high as $4 million.

Another possibility that had to be considered was offering Borjomi in plastic bottles. Doing so would require additional capital investment of perhaps $1–2 million, but would offer some long-term cost savings. Fleury worried that producing Borjomi in plastic bottles might confuse their efforts to brand their Borjomi as the only "real" Borjomi by introducing a new format into the market. However, rival bottler B.I.G. was already serving this niche and Fleury was reluctant to leave an important segment of the market unchallenged.

Fleury also believed that GGMW had to be realistic about the claims being made against them. Although they had no legal basis, in Georgia's relatively undeveloped legal environment they were still likely to cost the company a good deal of money. Moreover, the longer GGMW avoided dealing with the issue, the longer its senior managers would spend half their time meeting and arguing with bogus "creditors." Fleury believed it would require another $3 to $4 million to settle the various claims against the company, even though some of these claims could be settled with product or even empty bottles. In addition, GGMW had incurred legitimate debts of roughly $1 million during 1995 and 1996 that would have to be covered.

Addressing the Russian market would require a significant investment in working capital. GGMW's marginal cost per bottle was fifteen cents. GGMW would also have to pay the normal shipping rates, although this would later be recovered from distributors. Building up stock to be held in Russia for the winter months would therefore require up to $3 million in order to cover costs that would be incurred before the bottles could be sold. Fleury described the descision:

> We knew that making such an investment in working capital was risky. Russian counterfeiters were aggressively expanding in the market. It was possible that GGMW could spend six months shipping water to Russia that would not have a market because of unfair competition. I felt, however, that the risk could be greater if GGMW was absent during the Russian winter, leaving distributors and retailers in the hands of its "competitors." Doing so might erode what remaining strength the brand had, as well as, the confidence of GGMW's distributors.

An alternative to shipping to Russia was to concentrate on the domestic market. GGMW estimated Georgian consumption of Borjomi water, real and fake, at 36 million bottles, more than GGMW was likely to produce in all of 1997. GGMW had de-emphasized the local market because it would only support an ex-factory price of twenty cents. Even with GGMW having to absorb the four cents storage cost, the Russian market was more profitable. Fleury wondered, though, if GGMW's Borjomi might command a premium price if the company were able to establish its own product as the only "real" Borjomi in the eyes of its customers and the only heir to the famous traditional Soviet mineral water Borjomi. Furthermore, GGMW's efforts to persuade Russian authorities to crack down on counterfeiters had often been met by arguments that counterfeiting was even more prevalent in Georgia. Stories of Georgian counterfeiting also provided much of the ammunition used by Russian competitors to discredit the brand. Fleury wondered if it would be possible to maintain Borjomi as a leading brand in Russia until it had improved the situation at home.

Fleury knew GGMW would have to set its strategic priorities quickly in order to raise the necessary capital to carry them out. Complicating the issue of how much capital to raise was the short visibility of GGMW's business conditions. All of Fleury's estimates of GGMW's capital needs were for 1997, but the company was unlikely to do much better than break even in 1998. Additional capital beyond what was needed for the current year might well prove necessary, and Fleury suspected it would be prudent to ask for it now rather than waiting for trouble to hit.

Sources of Capital

Based on discussions with GGMW's original investors, Fleury believed they were prepared to invest at least an additional $2 million. ING, whose insistence on outside management had been a driving force behind Fleury's recruitment, would probably invest another $5–6 million. If Fleury wanted to raise more capital than that, he would probably have to bring in new investors. See **Exhibit 5** for valuation comparisons and **Exhibit 6** for GGMW's financing history.

Fleury was reluctant to bring in new financial investors. With so much of the money being used to pay off old debts and with the visibility of the business uncertain, he suspected that new investors might want too large an equity stake. Furthermore, GGMW needed the money quickly in order to begin renovating the bottling plants; Fleury knew that a financial investor would either be alarmed by the rush or would take advantage of it.

There was, however, an alternative to financial investors. GGMW had already made contact with two international financial institutions, the European Bank for Reconstruction and Development (EBRD)[2] and the International Finance Corporation (IFC).[3] Both organizations could provide capital to a promising company in a developing nation.

Khazaradze and Meijer had first approached the EBRD in 1995, shortly before the company was formerly incorporated. At the time they did not actively seek a loan, although the Bank had been interested in the Borjomi story. There had been little further contact between GGMW and the EBRD since then. Fleury believed the odds were good that the EBRD would provide a loan as part of a financing deal, but he didn't know under what terms or how much could be borrowed.

The IFC, by contrast, had already done a fair amount of due diligence on GGMW. In 1996, Meijer and Khazaradze had spoken at an ING Barings breakfast on investment opportunities in the FSU. There they met Richard Zobol, managing director of Barings' first NIS fund, as well as Maria Thomas, an investment officer with the IFC. Intrigued by the idea of restoring the brand to its former glory, and the favorable consequences such a development would have on the Georgian economy, she decided to investigate whether GGMW would make a good candidate for an IFC investment. With $133,000 of grant money from the UK and Dutch governments, the IFC hired consultants to research

[2] The EBRD was a multi-national bank established in 1990 with the purpose of fostering the transition towards open market-oriented economies and promoting private and entrepreneurial initiative in central and eastern Europe.

[3] The IFC, a member of the World Bank Group, was the largest multi-national source of loan and equity capital for private sector projects in the developing world.

EXHIBIT 5   **Valuation Comparisons**

Source: FirstCall, Company Reports, ISI International, Datastream.

Company Name	Country	Business	Share Price (4/97)	Earnings per Share		
				1997	1998	1999
Coke Femsa (KOF) ADR	Mexico	Coke Bottler	$15.00	0.59	0.47	0.64
Brahma ADR	Brazil	Beer & Soft Drinks	$7.10	1.00	0.85	0.90
Zywiec	Poland	Brewing	206	16.3	24.2	—
Zwack Unicom	Hungary	Spirits & Liquers	3,650	359	444	518
Coca Cola	USA	Soft Drinks	55	1.42	1.40	1.58
Seagram	Canada	Beverages	51	0.59	0.58	0.52
Nestle	Switzerland	Food & Beverage	1740	102	109	121

Coke Femsa, Brahma and Coca Cola in US$. Other company data in local currency.

EXHIBIT 6   Financing History

Source: GGMW.

Original Financing 1995			Convertible Loans[a]	
Shareholder	Capital Contribution	CommonShares	Long-Term	Short Term '95
Cristal Clear Inc.	99,450	1,326		216,300
Singing Leaves Investments	99,450	1,326		216,300
Safebottler International	99,450	1,326		216,300
Uzori	34,200	456		
Georgian Development BV	99,450	1,326	1,005,550	216,300
Sasha Fund	18,000	240	182,000	39,150
	450,000	6,000	1,187,550	904,350

Next Financing 1996			Convertible Loans	
Shareholder	Capital Contribution	Common Shares	Long-Term	Short Term '95
Cristal Clear Inc.	315,750	217,626		250,000
Singing Leaves Investments	315,750	217,626		250,000
Safebottler International	315,750	217,626		215,000
Uzori[b]	—	—		
Georgian Development BV	315,750	217,626	1,005,550	250,000
Sasha Fund	57,150	39,390	182,000	45,250
	1,354,350	910,350	1,187,550	1,010,250

December 31, 1996			Convertible Loans	
Shareholder	Capital Contribution	Common Shares	Convertible	Preference Conv.
Cristal Clear Inc.	565,750	467,626		
Singing Leaves Investments	565,750	467,626		
Safebottler International	530,750	432,626		
Uzori	—	—		
Georgian Development BV	565,750	467,626	1,005,550	
Sasha Fund	102,400	84,640	182,000	
ING Barings				2,500,000
	2,364,600	1,920,600	1,187,550	2,500,000

(a)Financing structured with short term loans that would convert within one year on a $1 per share basis. Convertible loans bore interest at LIBOR +1% and were convertible into preferred convertible stock, with a final conversion into common shares at between $1.50 and $1.75 per share. All currency figures are US$.
(b)Uzori shares were repurchased by GGMW and cancelled.
Names of some shareholders have been disguised.

the market, legal and environmental issues and the company's financial statements. The IFC also met with government officials to discuss issues such as trademark protection and private-sector management of state-owned assets (such as the Borjomi springs).

The IFC had a long due diligence process, in part because although they looked for a financial return on their investments their mandate required them to examine the impact on overall development as well. Fleury knew that the IFC investment committee that had to approve an equity investment in GGMW would be concerned about the lack of a clear exit strategy. Georgia had no IPO market and while a trade sale was certainly possible it would be impossible to say with confidence when the company would be ready for sale.

There were other concerns as well. Even with a thorough review of GGMW's books it was impossible to determine the factories' true financial position. Many entries were written by hand and it wasn't clear whether or not all of the company's potential liabilities were yet known. Fleury suspected it might be another year before a "true" balance sheet could be constructed.

Nevertheless, Fleury knew that part of the IFC's charter was to invest in promising companies in developing countries that did not yet have easy access to the world capital markets, provided other partners were also investing. The IFC's due diligence had confirmed the underlying strength of the brand, and GGMW had the potential to be one of Georgia's leading exporters. With no substantial problems being raised during the due diligence, Fleury thought the chances the IFC would want to invest were good.

What Fleury was less confident of were the terms of the new investment. The original partners had invested $3.5 million to date. ING Barings had invested $2.5 million. Both would hopefully invest more, but the newer investors would naturally prefer a relatively low valuation while the original shareholders would emphasize the potential of the business. Fleury hoped an agreement could be reached smoothly.

A Toast to the Future

As he raised his glass and looked at Khazaradze, Fleury knew that choosing the right toast was the smallest of his challenges. Over the next month or two, he had to oversee the refurbishment of GGMW's bottling operation, set a marketing program that would distinguish GGMW as the only "real" Borjomi in the minds of consumers and decide what emphasis to place on the Russian and Georgian markets. At the same time, he had to persuade both new and existing investors to finance his plans, even if that meant providing considerably more capital than they expected.

Fleury wondered what his priorities should be. The Russian market was more profitable, but could GGMW hope to be known as the only real Borjomi abroad before it had conquered the domestic market? Was that even possible, considering that some of its competitors even if temporary were selling essentially an identical product with full government authority? Fleury knew that if GGMW failed, business students would look back on their effort and proclaim it doomed from the start.

The risks, however, were worth it. If he restored Borjomi to its former sales level, GGMW would be one of the leading companies in the FSU. It was hard to imagine a more exciting challenge. How many Westerners had the opportunity to turn around a former Soviet enterprise with a great brand name in the unpredictable "Wild East"?

Case

14

QI-TECH: A Chinese Technology Company for Sale

It was 6:00 p.m. on Wednesday, October 23rd, 1998. Roger Kollbrunner, Business Development Manager at Indivers BV, a Dutch holding company, was sitting at his desk in a suite at the Shangri-La Hotel in Qingdao, a city of 4 million people on the East Coast of China (see **Exhibit 1** for a map of China). From his window he could see the sun set over the silhouette of Qingdao's rapidly growing business district. In the distance he could also make out the urban sprawl of new housing developments. Qingdao's economic situation could hardly be better and somehow the combination of urban expansion, the mild climate and the port location reminded Kollbrunner of Amsterdam. However, as he looked at some of the business documents in Chinese on his desk he was reminded how far away from Europe he was. Some of the negotiations ahead would be much easier if there was no cultural barrier and, more importantly, if all the parties at the negotiation table were familiar with Western business practices.

The following day was going to be very important for the future of QI-TECH, in which Indivers owned a 50% share. QI-TECH developed and manufactured high-precision coordinate measurement machines (CMM) that were used in a wide variety of technologically intensive manufacturing industries (**Exhibit 2**). On October 24th, 1998 Kollbrunner and the President of QI-TECH, Li Hong Quan ("Li"), were expecting three senior managers from the U.S. CMM firm Brown & Sharpe for cooperation negotiations. Brown & Sharpe had completed due diligence on QI-TECH between August and October 1998. Kollbrunner knew that the two managers, Charles Junkunc, CFO of Brown & Sharpe, and Phil James, Vice President of Brown & Sharpe's CMM division had recently been given authorization by their company's board to acquire a majority stake in QI-TECH if the conditions were right.

Professor Walter Kuemmerle and Charles M. Williams Fellow Chad Ellis prepared this case. HBS cases are developed solely as the basis for class discussion. Cases are not intended to serve as endorsements, sources of primary data, or illustrations of effective or ineffective management.

EXHIBIT 1 Map of China

Source: *CIA World Factbook—China*. Accessed online at www.cia.gov/cia/publications/factbook. Accessed online on February 19, 1999.

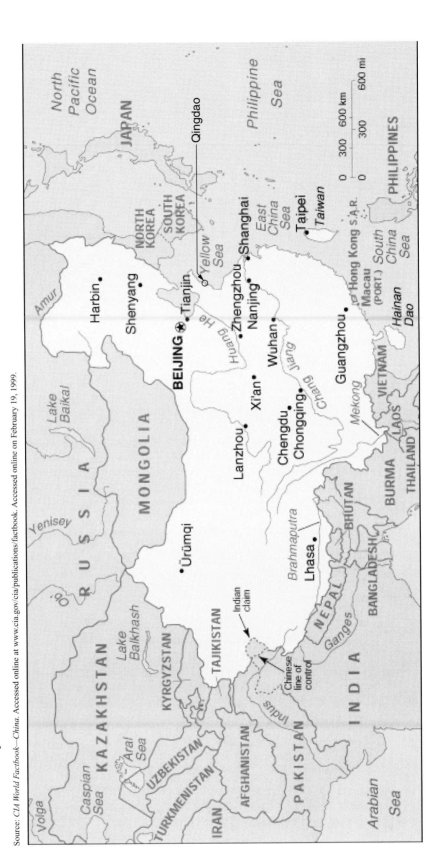

EXHIBIT 2
Some of QI-TECH's Coordinate Measuring Machines

Source: QI-TECH company documents.

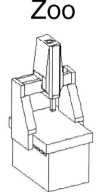 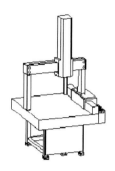 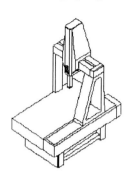

Kollbrunner felt that Brown & Sharpe was a good fit, but he also thought that there were several other interesting alternatives for the future of QI-TECH:

> In many ways it will come down to the price and conditions offered. During the due diligence we did not talk about price at all. It could easily be that our asking price and Brown & Sharpe's offer differ substantially. And then what? Li and I really have to come up with a feasible negotiation strategy over the next couple of hours. We need good answers for any of Brown & Sharpe's suggestions. And then there is QQMF, the other 50% shareholder in QI-TECH. We should talk to them again. They will be at the negotiation table on our side. But they are still a state-owned enterprise that needs approval from several government agencies to proceed with a deal.

As he was looking at the QI-TECH valuation spreadsheet on his laptop again, Kollbrunner was suddenly reminded of his business school days. Fifteen months before he had still been an MBA student at INSEAD, a business school in Fontainebleau, France. When he built spreadsheets at business school, the stakes were rarely very high, but now things were serious. He had to deliver results to his boss, Bert Twaalfhoven, HBS '54, the majority owner of Indivers BV (Indivers). Twaalfhoven had made it clear that he expected at least a 20% annualized return on his investment in QI-TECH.

Indivers and CMM Technology

Indivers BV was a Dutch holding company that had been established by Twaalfhoven who had built a business around the manufacture of aircraft engine parts in the 1970s. Interturbine, the core company in the Indivers BV portfolio, had built up high barriers to entry through high investments in R&D and smart contracts with aircraft engine manufacturers. Over time, Twaalfhoven had made several investments in high-tech start-ups to participate in the exciting growth opportunities for high technology companies and support entrepreneurship. All of these investments (10 in 1998) were targeted at high-technology industries and were grouped together under the Indivers umbrella.

Coordinate Measurement Machines (CMMs) were used widely in the aerospace industry and other industries such as automotive and electronics for quality control purposes. CMMs represented about 25% (US$600 million) of the world market for measurement instruments. CMMs cost between US$ 50,000 and US$ 500,000 depending on size of parts they could measure, speed of measurement and precision.

A CMM generally consisted of four elements: stationery devices, including a massive granite worktable; moving elements (a moving bridge that moved horizontally in one direction, a measurement head holder that moved sideways and vertically); electrical parts (motors and measurement head); and a controller (computer and software). In order to measure a part the operator would fixate the part on the table and program the controller to move the measurement head to different locations on the part. That way the coordinates of various locations on the part could be determined, and a three-dimensional image could be generated. The measurement accuracy of a QI-TECH's most popular "Zoo3" CMM machine was 2.5 μm (1 micron = 1 millionth of a meter), accurate enough to determine the thickness of a single hair (see **Exhibit 3** for a photograph of a "Zoo3" machine).

In 1984 Indivers co-funded Fanamation, Inc., which was a start-up in the CMM industry. Fanamation introduced new advanced technology and quickly gained a reputation for top accuracy and quality CMMs. Among its customers were Boeing and General Dynamics. By 1992 Fanamation revenues had reached $6.2 million. Between 1984 and 1992, Fanamation had outsourced electrical parts and the CMM controller. In 1992, however, Indivers purchased Kemco, a U.K.-based company that specialized in CMM software and controllers with 1992 revenues of $2.5 million. Kemco had been a supplier to a Chinese CMM company called QQMF. The CMM industry was highly cyclical and fluctuated roughly with the airline and automotive industries; it was hard hit by recession in 1993. Combined revenues of Fanamation and Kemco dropped to $6.5 million and in 1994 the combined company was on the brink of bankruptcy.

QQMF

Qingdao Qianshao Precision Machinery Company (QQMF) in Qingdao, China, was a division of a state-owned enterprise AVIC (the Aviation Industries in China), formerly known as the Ministry of Aviation. AVIC, based in Beijing employed over 560,000 people in over 500 divisions. QQMF with its 1,116 employees had produced pneumatic tools as well as high-quality granite surface plates for CMMs and other applications. Most of the value-added of CMMs stemmed from non-granite parts. By 1980, QQMF was selling complete granite sets to German CMM manufacturer Zeiss for US$ 4,000 while Zeiss sold the final CMM for US$ 150,000. After the top technical director of QQMF, professor Zhu Xijing (Zhu) completed some R&D studies in Europe, QQMF started manufacturing its own CMMs but purchased controllers from Kemco and other Western manufacturers. In 1992, QQMF sold 18 CMMs and enjoyed extraordinary profit margins in a Chinese market that was still highly protected. During 1992, QQMF started to increase its staffing in anticipation of higher domestic demand for CMMs.

At that point it became increasingly clear to QQMF managers that the company needed better access to foreign technology for further expansion of its market share in China. Existing ties with Kemco as well as Bert Twaalfhoven's assessment of the Chinese market led to discussions about a joint venture between Indivers BV and QQMF in 1993. According to Twaalfhoven's estimates, the domestic CMM market in China would grow at an annual rate of 15% over the next 10 years. (See **Exhibit 4** for 1998 growth rates.) Furthermore, China had very low labor costs and a growing pool of qualified engineers. Monthly salaries for technical workers averaged $130 and for engineers $180. Twaalfhoven figured that CMMs could also be exported from China, especially to other Asian countries. Indivers would contribute all the technology of Fanamation and Kemco and QQMF would contribute a dedicated workforce as well as physical facilities. The joint venture's operation would be concentrated in Qingdao.

QI-TECH's Start

By mid-1993 negotiations had reached a final stage. One of the issues still open was joint venture ownership. Indivers BV was pushing for majority ownership to avoid stalemate decision situations in the management of the joint venture. QQMF, on the other hand,

EXHIBIT 3   **QI-TECH "Zoo3" Coordinate Measurement Machine**

Source: QI-TECH company documents.

Zoo3
Affordable Performance

EXHIBIT 4
**1998 Market Growth
Rate for CMMs
in Major World
Markets**

Source: QI-TECH company
documents.

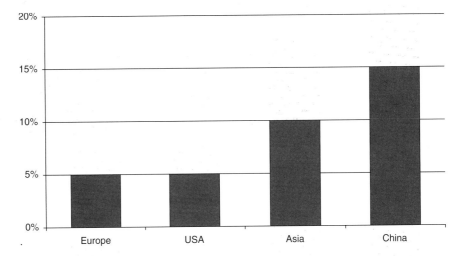

resisted primarily because employees of the state-owned enterprise were concerned that erratic management decisions by Indivers could "harm" the well-being of former QQMF employees. Eventually, the partners agreed on a 50/50 joint venture in which each side would be allowed to appoint the President of QI-TECH for two years at a time. Indivers BV appointed the son of Bert Twaalfhoven, Mark Twaalfhoven (Masters in Engineering, Stanford) as first President. Mark was also the President of Fanamation. Kollbrunner commented:

> In hindsight, Indivers BV should have pushed more strongly towards obtaining majority ownership. Although even majority ownership does not give you real control over a joint venture in China, 60% is psychologically much more than 50%, even in China.

QI-TECH started operations on January 1, 1994 with 127 QQMF employees. Fanamation and Kemco ended their operations in the United States and the United Kingdom respectively in Fall of 1993 and all the physical assets of the two firms were shipped to Qingdao in 14 large containers. Indivers BV also contributed expertise by dispatching three experts from Fanamation to Qingdao for a number of months. The enthusiasm among Indivers BV's management that had accompanied the joint venture's start was drastically reduced by two sobering events. First, the Chinese government revoked a rule that Fanamation and Kemco assets could be imported duty free when the containers with assets were already on their way. This meant additional expenditures of the new venture of $150,000. Second, QQMF had booked a number of 17 units as sales in 1993 that still needed to be installed in 1994. These installations absorbed manpower at QI-TECH. Mark Twaalfhoven noted:

> The first six months were very difficult because [QI-TECH] suddenly had to operate under a much more aggressive business plan . . . during the initial months of operation three separate employee boycotts took place. Employees were simply tired from overwork in 1993 and also demanded a pay increase.

But things only got worse from there: While the joint venture partners had agreed that QI-TECH would design a new CMM for the Chinese market combining the expertise of both parent companies, it became clear that redesign would take much longer than originally planned. Furthermore, Indivers realized that QI-TECH's marketing organization was second class at best. A much more concerted marketing effort would be needed to achieve sales targets. The combination of an installation backlog, lack of new products and an inefficient marketing organization lead to a dismal sales performance in 1994: only 12 CMMs were installed.

Laying New Foundations in Administration, Marketing and Product Development

In spite of this disappointing start of QI-TECH, Mark Twaalfhoven and his team of Chinese managers worked hard on several issues facing the company. During 1994 and 1995 management's primary focus was on getting administration and marketing of QI-TECH up to speed. Also, steps were taken to develop new products. Many management initiatives took much longer to implement than comparable measures would have taken in an industrialized country.

Sometimes, the obstacle to change was the lack of adequate service providers. When QI-TECH sought to implement a reliable monthly reporting system, for example, management quickly realized that the idea of management accounting was somewhat of a mystery to employees. Eventually, a number of employees were temporarily transferred to Interturbine's subsidiary in Singapore, where they received training and could experience a functioning reporting system first-hand. At other times, however, the main obstacle to change was the lack of communication and the different management styles of the QI-TECH/QQMF managers and the expatriates, as well as QQMF's lackluster support for any measures proposed by QI-TECH's President.

The creation of a sophisticated, air-conditioned demonstration room was one example. A demonstration room where products can be displayed and tested by potential customers was a key requirement for the sale of complex industrial equipment such as CMMs. QQMF did not have such a facility and it was agreed verbally in October 1993 that a demo room would be created as soon as possible after QI-TECH's start on the company's premises. It took more than one year and a lot of pushing from QI-TECH before QQMF finally agreed to convert some of QI-TECH's designated premises into a showroom. All of QI-TECH's 127 employees, except for the first President and two temporary expatriates from Indivers BV with technical expertise, came from QQMF. This was a problem. Some of the employees had been "imposed" on QI-TECH by QQMF. Some of these employees were not very enthusiastic about joining QI-TECH and were quite unwilling to change their working style. Mark Twaalfhoven estimated that only 20% of the employees were really willing to learn new ways and management systems.

The coordination of industrial marketing was another problem. At QQMF, sales staff had kept their customer contacts confidential. As is typical in China, sales representatives did not share data out of fear of losing control over the customer relationship. Thus, information regarding demand trends was difficult to aggregate. In a major effort, QI-TECH established a database of 1,345 CMM installations in China and of 1,500 potential customers. The database included not only installations by QI-TECH but also by major competitors such as Zeiss, LK Tools and Brown & Sharpe. QI-TECH created a CMM newsletter that was mailed to customers regularly. Over time the database proved to be very useful and sales staff started actively contributing to the maintenance of the database (see **Exhibit 5** for a database screen). In June 1995 QI-TECH also hired a new head of operations, Chao Tian Kong (from Singapore with an expatriate level salary), who had extensive international precision manufacturing experience.

Development of new products was of great importance if QI-TECH wanted to gain market share in China. QQMF had brought its basic "Zoo" machine to the joint venture. Technology from Kemco was used to fit "Zoo" with an advanced Microsoft Windows-based

EXHIBIT 5
Sample Screen of Customer Database

Source: QI-TECH company documents.

controller. It was clear, however, that QI-TECH needed more versatile, fast and precise CMMs. Versatility was determined by the width of the arch that covered the measurement table (called bridge). Furthermore, it was important for maximum versatility that the bridge was movable. Speed was determined by the amount of time that it took to measure one designated point on a part. Precision was determined by the level of accuracy with which the moving parts of a CMM moved. "Zoo2" represented a major improvement over "Zoo" in terms of precision and "Zoo3" combined additional precision over "Zoo2" with a significantly wider bridge. Upgrading of the controller of "Zoo" and development of "Zoo2" started in 1994. It became clear very quickly to QI-TECH's management that the development capabilities of QI-TECH's engineers could not be compared to the engineering departments of Zeiss or Brown & Sharpe with several hundred engineers. Therefore, three engineers spent 10 weeks at the Technical University of Eindhoven in the Netherlands (a leading technical university for metrology) to learn new design techniques and to get exposure to other CMM design. This training was made possible through Indivers BV's network of contacts and was partially funded by the European Community.

The development of "Zoo3" was risky because this machine would compete with the newest CMM systems offered by Western manufacturers. In order to achieve the targeted level of precision and measurement speed a new type of aluminum guide rails for the moving parts had to be manufactured. Seven additional engineers completed technical training in Europe while working on "Zoo3." **Exhibit 6** summarizes QI-TECH's product range in 1998.

While Mark Twaalfhoven and his team at QI-TECH made progress regarding the firm's administration, marketing and product development functions, most things happened more slowly than planned. Also, the China market for CMMs was relatively flat after QI-TECH's start and expanded from 60 (1994) to 80 (1996) units, which was much less than expected (**Exhibit 7**). Also, other "surprises" occurred. In January 1995, the Chinese government increased the value-added tax from 5.9% to 17% for QI-TECH's products and requested that the company "should" not raise prices as a result of this tax hike so as not to spur inflation. The QI-TECH team knew well that "should" translated as "may not."

As a result of slow change and surprising changes regarding conditions of competition, QI-TECH sold only 18 machines in 1995 instead of the planned 44 and QI-TECH reported a loss of $432,000. In 1996 only 18 units were sold and QI-TECH lost $376,000. But there was good news, too. Based on the improved quality of its products and competitive prices, the firm was able to make a number of sales to subsidiaries of blue chip firms

EXHIBIT 6   **QI-TECH Product Range**

Source: QI-TECH company documents.

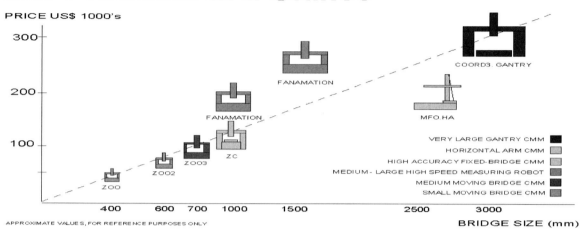

Our Products at a Glance

EXHIBIT 7   **Historic and Future Unit Sales, Market Share and Employment Data for QI-TECH**

Source: Company documents (1998 and onward: company predictions).

	1994	1995	1996	1997	1998	1999	2000	2001	2002
Size of Chinese CMM market (units)	60	70	80	140	200	240	288	346	415
Number of units sold by QI-TECH	5	17	18	32	52	75	100	150	200
Of which exported	0	4	2	3	2	5	15	30	45
QI-TECH market share in China	8%	19%	20%	21%	25%	29%	30%	35%	37%
QI-TECH world market share	Not significant (somewhere between 1% and 3%)								
Orders booked	5	17	18	29	55	89	110	150	200
Number of price quotes issued	25	53	140	160	280	NA	NA	NA	NA
Number of employees	127	110	106	103	99	90	85	85	85

in China, Singapore and South Korea, including IBM, Siemens, Peugeot and Daewoo. Furthermore, QI-TECH was able to export six machines (1995 and 1996 combined) to other Asian countries. Also, the market for CMM machines in China was forecasted to double from 1996 to 1999 (**Exhibit 7**) and QI-TECH intended to benefit from its investments in marketing and product development. Mark Twaalfhoven stated in late 1996: "The support from technical experts of [now defunct] Fanamation and Kemco was invaluable. We would not be where we are today without their technology. . . . Also, QQMF's connections (guanxi) helped a lot to improve our image. In October 1995, for example, Mr. Liu Hua Qing, the highest ranked military commander of the P.R. of China, toured our facilities. This gave us great press coverage. We are now ready to compete against other foreign CMM manufacturers."

The Mahr Deal—A Missed Opportunity?

In late 1995 Indivers considered selling its share in QI-TECH. Although the company still needed restructuring work there was a sense among managers that QI-TECH's situation was improving. A consultant was retained for the sale. One of the companies interested was Mahr GmbH from Germany, a hydraulic pump manufacturer with a metrology division. Mahr seemed like a good fit for two reasons. First, QI-TECH would complement the firm's product range of form and surface measurement equipment. Second, Mahr wanted to establish a stronger presence in China where it sold some equipment but had no manufacturing facility. In November 1995 Mahr completed its initial due diligence and signed a letter of intent with Indivers to acquire a majority stake in QI-TECH subject to approval by QQMF. To QI-TECH's surprise, QQMF rejected Mahr's proposal for one single reason. QQMF refused to have its ownership position in QI-TECH reduced to less than 50%. The reasoning was that Mahr had metrology experience, but almost no CMM market experience, which made QQMF feel uneasy about Mahr gaining control. QQMF also wanted to be recognized as the leader of the "successful" high-technology JV QI-TECH, which would give them a strong image within AVIC. Kollbrunner felt that the relationship with QQMF had improved since 1995. He stated:

> We missed the Mahr deal, but things have changed since 1995. QQMF now understands that QI-TECH simply does not have the technological depth to develop revolutionary CMMs on its own. Second, QQMF is more comfortable in working with a majority owner now.

From Business School to Business Development Manager

Kollbrunner joined Indivers in September 1997 after graduating from INSEAD. By that time, Mark Twaalfhoven had assumed another responsibility with a U.S. high-tech company as Director Asia Pacific Operations. Li Hong Quan, a former QQMF employee who had been with QI-TECH from inception and who was Vice President of Operations prior to becoming President, headed QI-TECH. 1997 proved to be much better than previous years. QI-TECH was about to increase sales from $1.4 million to $2.3 million. Losses were $185,000 and QI-TECH planned to achieve a net profit of about $400,000 in 1998. Also, QI-TECH reached the leading market share in China (23%), although Brown & Sharpe who had recently acquired Italian manufacturer DEA held a comparable combined market share (**Exhibit 8**).

EXHIBIT 8
China CMM Market Share (1997)

Source: QI-TECH company documents.

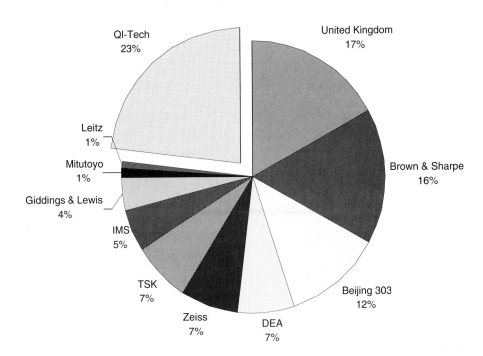

Kollbrunner held a master's degree in mechanical engineering from the Technical University in Zurich (ETHZ) and had worked for 2 years as a U.S. marketing manager for measuring equipment manufacturer Mettler-Toledo. At INSEAD Kollbrunner already had several job opportunities when he met Bert Twaalfhoven who had come to Fontainebleau to give a speech about entrepreneurship. The charisma and experience of Twaalfhoven as an entrepreneur intrigued Kollbrunner. He stated:

> At INSEAD I played the recruiting game pretty intensively. I had an offer to become CEO of an injection molding company in South Africa, but thought it was too risky considering the political climate in Johannesburg. Among some consulting offers I also had an offer to take over a small precision manufacturer in Switzerland, but found the location too remote. Finally, I also had an offer from my former employer for a regional marketing manager for South East Asia. I knew that I wanted to be an entrepreneur sooner rather than later and I thought that I could learn a lot from Bert, who had started over 40 companies. I approached him with my idea to work for him until I found my own start-up opportunity.

At Indivers BV Kollbrunner was given the assignment to manage six of the smaller portfolio companies and "to do what seemed right in order to achieve a 20% ROI for Indivers." After a quick analysis Kollbrunner had determined that four of the six companies represented different challenges. One portfolio company in the telecommunications sector was doing very well and the issue was how to best help this company grow further. Another company in the CAD/CAM software industry was in trouble and required turnaround management. A third company in the U.S. CMM service market was quite profitable and a trade sale should be considered. And finally there was QI-TECH. To date, Kollbrunner had spent about 35% of his time on QI-TECH. He had made four extensive trips to China since September 1997. First he sought to understand the company and establish a good relationship with management. He recalled:

> When I was put in charge, the company had already improved a lot. The marketing department had accumulated more knowledge about the Chinese market than had any competitor. Management received ISO 9001 certification and the quality of the products had improved significantly. But I also realized that there was still a lot of room for improvement, particularly in the area of machine assembly and quality control. When I arrived, teams of five specialized workers were assembling a machine at a time. While one of them was working, the others were basically standing around and looking on. This problem has not been remedied completely. We should be able to increase to about 100 units with the same number of employees. I also determined that QI-TECH had finally achieved a level of product quality that made attempts to export worthwhile. By 2002 QI-TECH should be able to export at least 25% its output. Also, the company had just received its ISO 9001 certification, somewhat of a reassurance for foreign customers[1] (see **Exhibits 7** and **9**).

Kollbrunner knew that his first challenge would be to gain the trust of QI-TECH's management, particularly the trust of Mr. Li, the President. Kollbrunner stated:

> In the beginning, everybody was suspicious. The general thinking was here comes another expatriate that wants to tell us how to run a business in China. Over time I gained their trust, and although I was in China only every four months we worked well together as a team. Today we communicate very efficiently through email and I gained important knowledge of who is making the decisions. I am surprised how well employees accepted me. Maybe this has something to do with the low average age of employees (34 years) which compares favorably with QQMF (42 years).

As a recent business school graduate, Kollbrunner was enthusiastic about introducing a new bonus system for the senior management. To his surprise, Mr. Li politely opposed the idea, saying, "I cannot accept a bonus until the company is continuously profitable.

[1] ISO 9001 was a certification of outstanding manufacturing operating procedures awarded by an independent institute.

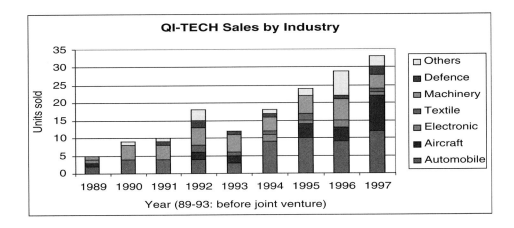

If I do, everybody will feel I have taken advantage of my position as President of QI-TECH. You know, in China everything is discussed very openly and the whole community knows about salaries, profits of companies, etc."

One of the most critical challenges, in Kollbrunner's opinion, was to get QI-TECH and QQMF committed to the idea of getting a new investor on board that would take Indivers's share over time. Kollbrunner recalled:

> After a couple of months I knew that a strong CMM partner was needed. QI-TECH was simply too small and needed a stronger CMM technology base and marketing network. I knew that I wanted to exit but I wanted to hear this from Mr. Li. In December 1997, we had a board meeting where we talked about the long-term future of QI-TECH and the intentions of its shareholders. It became clear that QQMF did not intend to exit the CCM business and were still committed to building QI-TECH further, although they were unwilling to inject additional capital. Indivers explained its viewpoint that in the medium term we were looking for an exit since QI-TECH had little in common with our core business. We had also learned through other channels that QQMF had to improve the efficiency of its core operations. Otherwise, according to the guidelines of the Communist Party's latest 5-year plan, Beijing could force a major restructuring or shutdown. QQMF also lowered their expectations regarding the payoff of their investment into the joint venture. They realized that a minority position in a successful JV was worth more than the majority of an unsuccessful one. This was the background of their decision to support a majority sale.

Options for Selling QI-TECH

There were basically four options for selling QI-TECH: a buy-out by QI-TECH's management, an IPO, a sale to a financial investor or a sale to a strategic buyer. Kollbrunner quickly ruled out the first option. Most of the top five managers had no cash available and could not obtain personal loans. However, Kollbrunner did not rule out allocating some shares to management during the sale process. Also, the second option would be very difficult because equity markets in China were not very well developed and QI-TECH was too small and would thrive more with an investor that provided more than just capital.

The third option was a sale to a financial buyer. Even as a stand-alone company, QI-TECH was interesting. Asia was the only rapidly growing market for CMMs and QI-TECH was the only company available for sale in Asia that had local manufacturing facilities and a competent local service organization. A QI-TECH study had determined that installation and maintenance services were considered the most important features of CMMs (**Exhibit 10**). A financial buyer, especially one with industry experience, might

EXHIBIT 10
CMM Customer
Demand Profile

Source: QI-TECH company
documents.

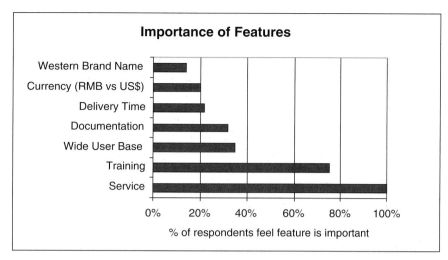

(Survey among 200 potential CMM customers in China. Conducted in 1995 by a European research student.)

find it very attractive to acquire Indivers BV's share and hold it for a number of years. Kollbrunner figured that private equity funds as well as firms in the broad industrial equipment industry with an interest in diversification should be interested.

Kollbrunner had used some of his INSEAD contacts to find the right intermediary for a sale to a financial buyer. In September 1998 he was in contact with two small investment banks. At this point neither Indivers nor QI-TECH had signed a retainer. One of the two banks had just informed Kollbrunner that they were in touch with a U.S. firm in the machine tool industry that was looking to acquire other small firms in the industry, particularly in China. At this point, the investment banker was asking to be put on an exclusive retainer to sell Indivers BV's share. Kollbrunner was currently negotiating the retainer fee and preparing the offering prospectus. The potential buyer seemed to be quite interested, although there were no negotiations at the time.

In July 1998, Kollbrunner had also been contacted by a private equity fund with a focus on Asia. People at the fund seemed quite interested and were very familiar with investing in emerging markets. However, Kollbrunner felt that a partner from the precision machine industry would add more value to QI-TECH.

To date, Kollbrunner had not pursued financial buyers aggressively, for two reasons. First, QI-TECH was almost too small for a typical Venture Capital firm and QQMF also favored a partner with extensive technology experience. Second, there were currently a number of interesting strategic buyers. It would be easier to get QQMF's agreement for a deal with a firm that could contribute to QI-TECH's success with technology and marketing know-how. Kollbrunner had contacted 12 major players in the CMM and machine tool industries. Kollbrunner had also contacted Mahr GmbH again. In principle the firm was still interested but they had just started a joint venture in another sector of the machine tool industry in China and did not have the management capacity to integrate QI-TECH over the next year or so. Three other firms were seriously interested in QI-TECH because of its superior marketing channels and professional management.

First, there was Zeiss, the German precision instruments firm that held a 7% CMM market share in China. Zeiss was the world technology leader and had pioneered many CMM innovations but suffered from high manufacturing costs in Germany. Zeiss managers visited QI-TECH in December 1997. The company envisioned producing its low-end machines in China thereby realizing significant cost savings. During further discussions in February 1998 it became clear, however, that the decision making process at Zeiss was quite slow. Zeiss could not make a decision before October 1998 because of a number of constraining factors inside the firm. Also, Kollbrunner was concerned that Zeiss managers might crush the enthusiasm of QI-TECH's management and reduce the capabilities inherent in QI-TECH through the imposition of the rigorous Zeiss management style. Still, Zeiss was a very interesting candidate.

Second, there was Excell, a medium-sized machine tool firm based in Singapore. A dynamic entrepreneur who knew the Chinese market quite well ran Excell. Excell did not have a CMM business but thought QI-TECH would complement its existing machine tool business quite well. Also, Excell was keen on gaining access to a manufacturing base in China. Discussions with Excell had not gone beyond the preliminary stage, but Kollbrunner had heard rumors that the company had been affected by the Asian financial crisis. Still, Excell seemed to have very deep pockets and Kollbrunner imagined that QQMF would get along well with Excell.

EXHIBIT 11   **Financial Comparison Brown & Sharpe vs. QI-TECH (Kollbrunner's Analysis)**

Source: BNS. Industry, Market: 1997 year end data.

Profitability Ratios	BNS 96	BNS 97	QI-TECH[e]	Industry[a]	Market[b]
Gross profit margin	35%	36%	58%	32%	45%
Pre-tax profit margin	3	−2	17	12	8
Net profit margin	2	−3	17	7	6
Return on equity	6	—	12	17	15
Return on assets	3	−3	7	8	3
Return on invested capital	15	−5	11	12	8

Valuation Ratios	BNS	BNS	QI-TECH[c]	Industry	Market
Price/sales ratio	5.3	0.5	$4.3	1.4	1.4
Price/earnings ratio	23.7	—	$8.9	19.0	28.8
Price/book ratio	1.3	1.4	$10.1	3.1	3.6
Price/cash flow ratio	13.3	38.1	$8.4	12.7	12.5

Operating Ratio	BNS	BNS	QI-TECH[d]	Industry	Market
Days of sales outstanding	126	114	119	63	49
Inventory turnover	2.9	2.8	0.7	4.3	7.8
Days cost of goods sold in inventory	126	130	497	84	46
Asset turnover	1.1	1.1	0.4	1.2	0.6
Net receivables turnover flow	2.9	3.3	2.9	6.2	8.2
Effective tax rate	11%	—	—	36%	51%

Financial Ratio	BNS	BNS	QI-TECH[e]	Industry	Market
Current ratio	1.9	2.2	1.4	2.0	1.4
Quick ratio	1.2	1.4	0.7	1.0	0.8
Leverage ratio	2.2	2.6	1.7	2.0	5.1
Total debt/equity	0.5	0.6	0.4	0.5	1.3
Interest coverage	2.1	−0.1	5.2	8.7	2.4

Financial Ratio	BNS	BNS	QI-TECH	Industry	Market
12-Month revenue growth	7.5%	−0.5%	48%	7.1%	12.3%
12-Month net income growth	410%	NA	NA	14.0%	14.2%
36-Month revenue growth	219%	7.60%	50%	27.3%	9.4%
36-Month net income growth	NA	NA	200%	52.9%	13.8%

[a]Industry: Industrial Equipment and Components, according to media General Financial Services Inc.
[b]Market: Approximately 8,000 public companies trading on the New York Stock Exchange, the American Stock Exchange, and the Nasdaq National Market.
[c]QI-TECH valuation in million US$ based on industry ratios and 1998 estimates for QI-TECH.
[d]Based on 1998 estimates for QI-TECH.
[e]Based on June 30, 1998, management accounts.

Third, there was Brown & Sharpe, the CMM world market leader with $320 million in sales. Brown & Sharpe had recently acquired several smaller CMM companies including DEA (Italy), Leitz (Germany), TESA (Switzerland) and Mauser (Germany) in order to establish a global presence. QI-TECH would give Brown & Sharpe a solid manufacturing base in China where the firm so far only had a network of sales agents. Brown & Sharpe had completed its preliminary due diligence.

Valuation

During the preliminary due diligence process Charles Junkunc (CFO) had almost jokingly asked Kollbrunner: "So Roger, how much do you think QI-TECH is worth?" Both of them laughed, but the question had remained unanswered at that point. Kollbrunner knew valuation would come up again on the following day. In preparation for the negotiations Kollbrunner had prepared a table with financial ratios of Brown & Sharpe, QI-TECH and comparable companies (**Exhibit 11**). Kollbrunner had also prepared historic balance sheets, P&L statements and projections for QI-TECH (**Exhibit 12**). Kollbrunner knew that companies could be valued as a multiple of sales, of earnings and

EXHIBIT 12A   QI-TECH—Historical Balance Sheets ($000)

Source: QI-TECH company documents.

	Dec-95	Dec-96	Dec-97	Aug-98
Cash	$ 198	$ 215	$ 164	$ 655
Accounts receivable	438	618	852	919
Other receivables	144	160	123	280
Prepaid expenses	94	71	43	42
Inventories	1,151	1,181	1,280	1,138
Current Assets	**$2,025**	**$2,246**	**$2,461**	**$3,034**
Fixed assets—gross	$2,430	$2,454	$2,217	$2,246
Accumulated depreciation	(396)	(557)	(640)	(747)
Fixed Assets	**$2,034**	**$1,897**	**$1,576**	**$1,499**
Know how—gross	$ 925	$ 926	$ 928	$ 928
Accumulated amortization	—	—	—	—
Know How	**$ 925**	**$ 926**	**$ 928**	**$ 928**
Other Assets	**$ 525**	**$ 491**	**$ 438**	**$ 431**
Total Debits	**$5,509**	**$5,560**	**$5,404**	**$5,893**
Short-term loans (foreign RMB)	$ 280	$ 250	$ 220	$ 220
Short-term loans (yuan RMB)	602	699	701	700
Accounts payable	218	131	262	152
Accrued liabilities	294	432	412	705
Customer advances	256	600	449	542
Current Liabilities	**$1,650**	**$2,112**	**$2,043**	**$2,321**
Long Term Debt	**$ 162**	**$ 162**	**$ 306**	**$ 306**
Other Liabilities	**$ —**	**$ —**	**$ —**	**$ —**
Capital	$4,313	$4,320	$4,330	$4,330
Retained earnings	(528)	(617)	(1,036)	(1,271)
Translation difference	(1)	(1)	(2)	2
Net income current year	(88)	(416)	(237)	205
Shareholders' Equity	**$3,697**	**$3,286**	**$3,055**	**$3,266**
Total Credits	**$5,509**	**$5,560**	**$5,404**	**$5,893**

Any calculation discrepancies are due to rounding.

EXHIBIT 12B   QI-TECH—P&L Statements ($000)

Source: QI-TECH company documents.

	1995	1996	1997	Jan–Aug 98	E1998
Domestic	$1,453	$1,322	$2,276	$1,648	$2,944
Export	316	99	59	5	40
Sales	**$1,769**	**$1,422**	**$2,336**	**$1,654**	**$2,984**
Materials	$ 858	$ 737	$1,127	$ 665	$1,338
Sales commissions	23	8	62	39	66
Total	$ 881	$ 746	$1,189	$ 704	$1,404
Gross Margin	**$ 888**	**$ 676**	**$1,147**	**$ 950**	**$1,580**
Personnel	$ 526	$ 513	$ 523	$ 332	$ 497
Facilities	130	135	131	88	132
Depreciation/amortization	276	198	206	134	201
Know how	—	—	—	—	—
Other	266	109	375	160	239
Total Operating Expenses	**$1,199**	**$ 956**	**$1,235**	**$ 713**	**$1,069**
Operating Income	**$(311)**	**$(280)**	**$ (88)**	**$ 249**	**$ 511**
Interest	$ 124	$ 119	$ 101	$ 62	$ 93
Other P & L	(2)	(24)	(3)	(71)	(50)
Profit before Tax	**$(432)**	**$(376)**	**$(185)**	**$ 257**	**$ 467**
Income tax	—	—	—	—	—
Net Income	**$(432)**	**$(376)**	**$(185)**	**$ 257**	**$ 467**

EXHIBIT 12C   QI-TECH—Projections ($000)

Source: QI-TECH company documents.

	1995	1996	1997	E1998	P1999	P2000	P2001
Domestic sales growth rate		−9%	72%	29%	30%	30%	25%
Domestic sales	$1,453	$1,322	$2,276	$2,944	$3,827	$4,975	$6,219
Export sales growth rate		−69%	−40%	−33%	500%	200%	150%
Export sales	$ 316	$ 99	$ 59	$ 40	$ 240	$ 720	$1,800
Sales	**$1,769**	**$1,422**	**$2,336**	**$2,984**	**$4,067**	**$5,695**	**$8,019**
Materials	858	737	1,127	1,338	1,830	2,563	3,609
Sales commissions	23	8	62	66	70	90	130
Total	$ 881	$ 746	$1,189	$1,404	$1,900	$2,653	$3,739
Gross Margin	**$ 888**	**$ 676**	**$1,147**	**$1,580**	**$2,167**	**$3,042**	**$4,281**
Personnel	$ 526	$ 513	$ 523	$ 497	$ 520	$ 550	$ 600
Facilities	130	135	131	132	140	150	160
Depreciation/amortization	276	198	206	201	210	220	230
Know how	—	—	—	—	—	—	—
Other	266	109	375	239	250	250	250
Total Operating Expenses	**$1,199**	**$ 956**	**$1,235**	**$1,069**	**$1,120**	**$1,170**	**$1,240**
Operating Income	**$ (311)**	**$(280)**	**$ (88)**	**$ 511**	**$1,047**	**$1,872**	**$3,041**
Interest	$ 124	$ 119	$ 101	$ 93	$ 100	$ 100	$ 120
Other P&L	(2)	(24)	(3)	(50)	—	—	—
Profit before Tax	(432)	(376)	(185)	467	947	1,772	2,921
Income tax	—	—	—	—	—	—	876
Net Income	**$ (432)**	**$ (376)**	**$ (185)**	**$ 467**	**$ 947**	**$1,772**	**$2,921**

Material costs: 45% of sales revenue (actual figures of 1998).

EXHIBIT 13   QI-TECH—Changes in Four Years

Source: QI-TECH company documents.

Criteria		QQMF CMM Dec. 1993	QI-TECH Dec. 1997
Market	China Market Share	11%	23%
	China Position	2	1
Sales	Number of Contracts—Orders Per Year	13	35
	Contract Value (RMB Million)	10.5	23.8
	Number of Total Installations	38	50
	Number of Products	2	7
	Demo Room	None	Top in China
Technology	Top Speed (mm/s)	100	500
	Time to Measure 100 Points Part	8 Minutes	70 Seconds
	Controller	Point to Point	Continuous
	Software	DOS	Windows 95
	Materials	Granite, Steel	Ceramic, Aluminum, Castings
	Accuracy	Basic	S/W Compensated
Work Tools	Computers	12	60
	FAX	None	4
	Phones	8	36
	IDD Lines	None	8
	Accounting	Abacus	5 PC's with Network Windows S/W

S/W = Software.

of book value. He was wondering which approach would be appropriate for a firm like QI-TECH that had just managed a turnaround (**Exhibit 13**) and held a unique position in the Chinese market.

Also, the buyers would certainly take into consideration that QI-TECH was quite dependent on QQMF. Over 30% of 1997 sales had been to affiliate firms of QQMF and AVIC. Kollbrunner was wondering whether Brown & Sharpe would be willing to acquire Indivers BV's entire share immediately or whether they would insist on a gradual transfer of ownership. Also, Kollbrunner was neither sure how much of its share QQMF was willing to sell, nor how much QQMF should sell for the benefit of QI-TECH. At least Kollbrunner knew that QQMF was in principle willing to accept a new partner under the condition that this partner would contribute significant capital and technology. QQMF's management had been "in the loop" when Brown & Sharpe was conducting due diligence in Summer 1998. Also, QQMF itself might soon be privatized and Kollbrunner knew that QQMF's President was currently looking to improve the company's financial position.

Long discussions took place between Kollbrunner and QQMF and often the different approach to valuation and share transactions caused misunderstandings. In general, QQMF and Indivers wanted Brown & Sharpe as a partner but for different reasons and with different motivations. For example, the Chinese government would not approve a transaction in which new shares were issued at or below the original book value. This would affect the image of the QQMF management in the Chinese business community and make them "lose face." CMM companies were often valued with 1-2x book value; therefore Kollbrunner had to expect Brown & Sharpe to pay no more than twice book value. On the other hand, the potential for market growth in China seemed much higher than in other countries where some of the recent CMM Company M&A transactions had taken place (**Exhibit 4**). This should influence the valuation.

As he was pondering these questions his phone rang. QI-TECH's President Li had just arrived in the hotel lobby. He and Kollbrunner planned to go over valuation and negotiation issues again over dinner.

15

Spotfire: Managing a Multinational Start-up

As he prepared to leave for another trip to Sweden, Chris Ahlberg, co-founder and CEO of Spotfire, stopped briefly by Rock Gnatovich's desk. As Gnatovich looked up, the two men smiled briefly, thinking back to all that had happened in the few months since Gnatovich joined Spotfire as President. The 29-year old Swede and the 45-year old American were working together well and the results were clear to everyone. Each knew, however, that there was a great deal more left to be done. It was June 24, 1998, and Spotfire had just moved from temporary offices in a posh downtown Boston highrise to a more modest permanent location in Cambridge across the road from MIT.

Ahlberg and Gnatovich chatted about recent progress in getting clients to adopt Spotfire throughout their R&D operations, and Gnatovich told him of a $50,000 purchase order they'd received that day. After reviewing their plans for the coming week, Ahlberg slipped a Discman and the latest Beastie Boys CD into his suitcase, and got ready to leave for Göteborg, where Spotfire's development team was based and where the company had been born.

"Don't forget," teased Gnatovich, as Ahlberg walked away, "we need you on this side of the Atlantic, too."

As Ahlberg waited for the elevator to arrive, Gnatovich's words stuck with him. Roughly half of Spotfire's current sales were in the United States, and over the longer term the United States would remain its most important market. Maintaining product development in Sweden had its advantages, but was it the best way forward? Spotfire would need additional funding within a year, and he and Gnatovich had a lot to accomplish if they were to position the firm in a way that would command the valuation they sought. Was the Swedish operation a hindrance to those tasks, or could it be used to Spotfire's advantage?

Charles M. Williams Fellow Chad Ellis, MBA '98, prepared this case under the supervision of Professor Walter Kuemmerle. HBS cases are developed solely as the basis for class discussion. Cases are not intended to serve as endorsements, sources of primary data, or illustrations of effective or ineffective management.

Ahlberg knew his business challenges were more than enough to keep him occupied, but on this particular trip the business would have to come second. After a brief visit with the development team in Sweden, Ahlberg would fly to Bermuda. His fiancée, who was soon to begin her MBA studies, was working in Bermuda for the Swedish construction company Skanska. Both would put their work aside for the moment—with their wedding just three days away, Chris knew he was not likely to have much time to look out a window and ponder the company's strategy!

From Ph.D. to CEO

Spotfire's core products were based on Ahlberg's doctoral research, along with the data visualization research of co-founders Staffan Truvé and Erik Wistrand. (See **Exhibit 1** for resumes of Spotfire's senior managers and **Exhibit 2** for Spotfire's organization chart.) Ahlberg received his Ph.D. in 1996 from Chalmers University of Technology in Sweden. Much of the most important thesis work, however, was done at the University of Maryland, which had excellent facilities and support for the type of research Ahlberg wanted to pursue. Ahlberg's motivation for pursuing a doctorate was largely intellectual curiosity, rather than any specific academic or entrepreneurial career path. "The Ph.D. allowed me to pursue some of the early ideas behind Spotfire that would have been hard to go after otherwise," he explained.

During his studies at Chalmers, Ahlberg participated in an entrepreneurship program in which he gave a brief presentation of the visualization technology he was developing. Innovations Kapital, one of the few Swedish venture capital (VC) firms operating at the time, saw the presentation and expressed interest. By the time Ahlberg earned his Ph.D., he had written a basic business plan and planned to turn his technology into a venture. Despite this rather unusual development from a Ph.D., Ahlberg did not consider himself the typical entrepreneur: "I was never the guy who had four different jobs to make money everywhere, but I've always done lots of entrepreneurial stuff. It's just so much fun with the somewhat crazy environment it creates!"

In April 1996, with seed financing from Innovations Kapital, Ahlberg, Truvé and Wistrand formed IVEE Development AB, later renamed Spotfire after the Company's core product. Although Spotfire recorded some income that year (see **Exhibit 3** for Spotfire's historic and projected P&L statements and **Exhibit 4** for Spotfire's historic and projected Cash Flow statements) from consulting, the focus of the firm was developing a commercial product.

In the first year of operations, Spotfire sought business from a wide variety of firms with data visualization needs. "We were far too all over the place," recalled Ahlberg. "The idea was to get out there and learn what we had, see what we could do with it." Spotfire sold its software to clients in packaged goods for consumers, manufacturing, banking, telecommunications and a range of other industries. Such a broad approach allowed Spotfire to learn from a variety of customers, but made it impossible to develop a more complete product which would add more value for a particular customer base.

In early 1997, Ahlberg sought out Atlas Ventures, which would later provide the bulk of Spotfire's $3 million first round financing. Atlas urged Spotfire to adopt a "vertical" strategy, focusing on one specific market where it could provide real solutions software by tailoring the product's data visualization capabilities to specific user needs. Ahlberg recalled:

> Picking a specific market was really difficult, as our technology was appealing to so many customers. Financial services companies had money, but also highly developed in-house tools. Technology companies had money but less satisfactory in-house tools. In the end our decision was partly driven by our early successes at Astra and Unilever.

EXHIBIT 1   Resumes of Spotfire's Senior Managers

Source: Spotfire.

Christopher Ahlberg, President

Employment History

1996–	CEO, IVEE Development AB (IVEE),[1] a venture capital backed company developing products for visual data mining. Member of the board of IVEE.
1993–96	Independent consultant (training and software design) for seven companies including Microsoft Corp. and Ericsson.
1993–97	Teaching assistant & Ph.D. student at Department of Computer Sciences, Chalmers University of Technology.
1991, 1993	Visiting research at Human-computer Interaction Laboratory, University of Maryland
1992	Human Factors engineering in building surveillance project for Byggforskningsradet, Sweden.
1990	Computer programmer at Akelius Skatt AB.

Miscellaneous

- Reviewed academic and professional publications on data visualization and computing.
- Military service at Arctic Ranger/Special Forces unit.
- Regularly organizes local workshops and seminars on human computer interaction with large attendance from industry and academia.
- On the program committee for several international workshops/conferences in the areas of human-computer interaction, visualization and database interfaces.
- More than 50 talks at universities, industry laboratories, companies and conferences such as Xerox PARC, Microsoft, Swedish Royal academy of Engineering Sciences, Ericsson, Swedish National Defence Research Establishment, etc.
- Winner of Innovation cup (with Staffian Truvé and Erik Wistrand) in Western Sweden with Spotfire product/research.

Staffan Truvé, Chief Technology Officer

Employment

1996–	Vice President Research, IVEE Development AB
1994–	Managing Director and Research, Carlstedt Research & Technology AB
1984–	Managing Director Research, Kigol Konsult AB
1992–94	Computer Architecture Research, Carstedt Elektronik AB
1986	Research Assistant, MIT
1985	Teaching Assistant, Chalmers University of Technology
1984	Amanuens at Chalmers University of Technology
1984	IBM Nordic Laboratories (internship)
1978–83	Systems programmer, Scan Vast Göteborg (summers)
1985–95	Software application consultant to 6 companies

Education

1995	Chalmers Advanced Management Program "LUST"
1992	Doctor of Technology (Ph.D.) in Computer Science, Chalmers University of Technology
1988	Bachelor of Business Administration, University of Göteborg
1987	Licentiate of Science in Computer Science, Chalmers University of Technology
1985–86	Fulbright scholarship for visiting Massachusetts Institute of Technology Master of Science in Engineering Physics, special branch of Computer Science Chalmers University of Technology

Miscellaneous

1995	13 publications on software
1985	Grants from The Fulbright Commission, The Swedish Institute, The Marcus Wallenberg Foundation and The Royal Swedish Academy of Science for studies in the USA
1985	Business Enterprise Award

---

[1] IVEE Development AB was later renamed Spotfire.

(continued)

EXHIBIT 1 (Continued)

1985	John Ericsson Award for Excellent Study Results from Chalmers University of Technology
1987–88	Military Service as Radar Technician, Royal Swedish Artillery Member of the NUTEK program committee for Program Development

Jonas Lagerblad, Vice President Software Development

Employment

1996–	VP Software Development, IVEE Development AB
1993–94	Carlstedt Elektronik AB Managed development environment in 50-person computer development firm.
1988–93	Swedish Institute for Software Development (SISU) SISU is a research institute with the purpose to introduce research results from the software engineering field, in industrial applications.
1984–88	MYAB Mikrokonsult AB. Project manager for UNIX computer development in ten-person startup firm.
1984–85	Military service
1983–84	SwedeCad AB Tasks: Porting of a very large CAD system, written in Fortran, from IBM mainframe computers to Hewlett Packard.
1983	Ericsson Radar Tasks: Test of PASCAL compiler.

Education

1990–91	MBA in International business administration, Chalmers University of Technology and Handelshogskolan in Göteborg.
1989	Ph.D. studies with Department for Computer Engineering, Chalmers University of Technology (discontinued due to lack of time)
1980–84	Master of Science in Electrical engineering and Computer Science, Chalmers University of Technology

Rock Steven Gnatovich

Employment

1996–1997	Co-founder, President and CEO, Windchill Technology (Bedford, MA) Recruited 31 employees within a year, developed a detailed product strategy and business plan, delivered a developer's release of the product, engaged a group of early adopters to include Airbus, Peugeot, Lockheed Martin, Nortel, ABB and CSC. Received commitments from three venture capital firms for $9M in first round funding. The company was recently acquired by Parametric Technology. Internet start up positioned to be the source for Web-native information management applications for discrete manufactures.
1995–1996	Vice President, Marketing, Computervision (Bedford, MA) $500M annual revenue industry leader in engineering and manufacturing software. Member of company's operating and strategy committees, chair of the product management committee.
1990–1995	VP, Product Data Management Operations, VP Marketing, SDRC (Cincinnati, Ohio) $200M annual revenue design automation software firm.
1985–1990	VP North American Operations, VP Marketing and Far East, CIMLINC, Inc. (Itasca, IL) $38M annual revenue (1990) UNIX based software developer.
1981–1985	Director, Corporate Accounts and Sales Planning, Appilcon, Inc. (Burlington, MA)
1979–1981	VP Marketing, Framingham Casting Co., Inc. (Framingham, MA)

Education

	B.A. from Wesleyan University post graduate work at both Vanderbilt University and at Florida State University as an Earhart Fellow in Economics from 1976 to 1978.

EXHIBIT 2 Spotfire Organizational Chart

Source: Spotfire.

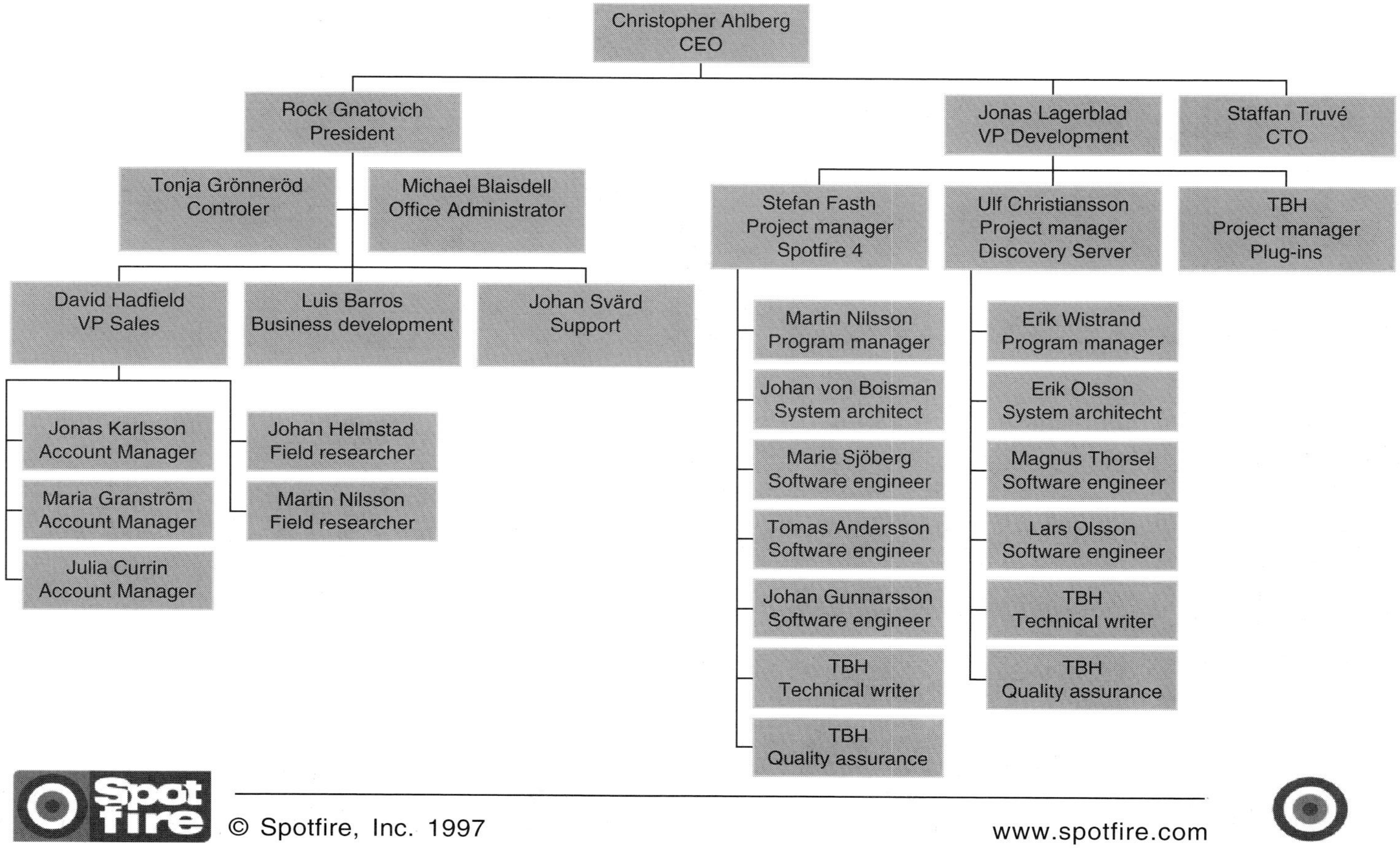

Christopher Ahlberg
CEO

Rock Gnatovich
President

Staffan Truvé
CTO

Jonas Lagerblad
VP Development

TBH
Project manager
Plug-ins

Ulf Christiansson
Project manager
Discovery Server

Stefan Fasth
Project manager
Spotfire 4

Erik Wistrand
Program manager

Erik Olsson
System architecht

Magnus Thorsel
Software engineer

Lars Olsson
Software engineer

TBH
Technical writer

TBH
Quality assurance

Martin Nilsson
Program manager

Johan von Boisman
System architect

Marie Sjöberg
Software engineer

Tomas Andersson
Software engineer

Johan Gunnarsson
Software engineer

TBH
Technical writer

TBH
Quality assurance

Tonja Grönneröd
Controler

Michael Blaisdell
Office Administrator

Luis Barros
Business development

Johan Svärd
Support

David Hadfield
VP Sales

Jonas Karlsson
Account Manager

Maria Granström
Account Manager

Julia Currin
Account Manager

Johan Helmstad
Field researcher

Martin Nilsson
Field researcher

www.spotfire.com

© Spotfire, Inc. 1997

287

EXHIBIT 3 **Spotfire Historic and Projected Profit and Loss Statement**

Source: Spotfire.

| 000s of $ | 1997 | | | | | 1998E | 1999E | 2000E |
	Q1	Q2	Q3	Q4	Year	Year	Year	Year
Sales	80	126	224	328	758	3,050	7,800	20,000
Cost of Sales	(2)	(4)	(7)	(10)	(23)	(153)	(390)	(1,000)
Gross Margin	78	122	217	318	735	2,897	7,410	19,000
Gross Margin (%)	98%	97%	97%	97%	97%	95%	95%	95%
Development Expense	(97)	(104)	(118)	(138)	(457)	(809)	(1,079)	(1,798)
Direct Customer Service	0	(14)	(14)	(19)	(47)	(186)	(247)	(495)
Marketing	(51)	(42)	(51)	(70)	(214)	(1,869)	(3,092)	(6,784)
SG&A	(76)	(121)	(152)	(209)	(558)	(2,014)	(3,457)	(5,683)
Operating Income	(146)	(158)	(118)	(118)	(539)	(1,981)	(465)	4,240
Interest Income/(Expense)	1	0	(1)	(1)	(0)	(79)	(19)	170
Net Income	(145)	(158)	(118)	(118)	(539)	(2,059)	(484)	4,410

Figures may not balance due to rounding. Estimates based on report to the Board on 1/98.

EXHIBIT 4 **Spotfire Historic and Projected Statement of Cash Flows**

Source: Spotfire.

| 000s of $ | 1997 | | | | | 1998E | 1999E | 2000E |
	Q1	Q2	Q3	Q4	Year	Year	Year	Year
Opening Balance	255	128	3,257	3,091	255	2,984	3,034	2,376
Net Income	(145)	(158)	(118)	(118)	(539)	(2,059)	(484)	4,409
Depreciation	9	11	12	12	44	72	85	123
Cash from Operations	(136)	(147)	(106)	(106)	(495)	(1,987)	(399)	4,532
Change in Working Capital	9	43	(60)	13	4	131	(146)	(443)
Purchase of Fixed Assets	—	(28)	—	(14)	(42)	(72)	(91)	(182)
Change in Borrowings	—	261	—	—	261	(22)	(22)	(22)
Other Sources/Uses	—	3,000	—	—	3,000	2,000	—	—
Closing Balance	128	3,257	3,091	2,984	2,984	3,034	2,376	6,261

Spotfire decided to focus on the related fields of chemistry and biology, in general, and the pharmaceutical industry in particular. (See **Exhibit 5** for a list of Spotfire's key customers as of early 1998.)

In November 1997, Ahlberg flew to the United States with Jonas Karlsson, a sales representative. "Jonas had the right American mindset for the trip," explained Ahlberg, "because he'd worked for American companies like Kodak and Parametric Technology." The two men visited a dozen companies, and convinced eight of them to become customers. "It was our first real sales trip in the United States," he recalled, "and we had no idea what to expect." Within the first two months of selling, they had generated $100,000 in revenues for Spotfire and, of equal importance, had gained positive response from many of their customers, giving Spotfire a base of external credibility for further sales efforts and for raising capital.

Adding Professional Management

In addition to recommending a vertical product/marketing strategy, Atlas felt that Spotfire had reached a stage where Chris needed to bring on a professional manager. Meanwhile, Gnatovich, who had managed an Internet start-up through its acquisition by

EXHIBIT 5
Key Pharmaceutical/
Chemical Spotfire
Customers

Source: Spotfire.

	U.S.-based	European-based
Pharmaceutical		
Glaxo Wellcome		✔
Novartis		✔
Hoechst Marion Roussel		✔
Pfizer	✔	
American Home Products	✔	
Smithkline Beecham	✔	
Lilly	✔	
Abbott	✔	
Astra		✔
Pharmacia & Upjohn		✔
Rhône-Poulenc Rorer		✔
Zeneca		✔
Warner Lambert	✔	
Du Pont	✔	
Specialty Chemical		
Unilever		✔
3M	✔	

Parametric Technology, was looking for a new challenge. Between January and May of 1998 he helped Atlas evaluate business plans and carry out due diligence on potential portfolio firms, while keeping an eye out for a company he could get involved with. When Spotfire was suggested, Gnatovich was intrigued:

> I liked Chris's early customer orientation. When you sit in on a lot of VC presentations, you get used to entrepreneurs who think their product or technology will carry the day all on its own. They have no customer validation, just their own conviction. Even though I had no direct experience in the pharmaceutical/biotech business, I called up several customers and had a very good feel for how this company could succeed . . . and knew I could sell people with the necessary experience on joining this business.

Gnatovich joined Spotfire in May as President, with Ahlberg remaining as CEO.

Ahlberg and Gnatovich offered quite a contrast. Ahlberg, 29, was the very image of a young entrepreneur—a passion for his product, infectious enthusiasm and marketing flair, but with little management experience. Gnatovich, 45, was a seasoned manager, who had run and grown several small companies in addition to his work with VC firms, and had strong opinions about what a company like Spotfire had to do to succeed.

From the start, the two men split the responsibilities of the U.S. operation while Ahlberg continued to manage Europe through his co-founders. Ahlberg was in charge of product development, linking customer feedback with the development team in Göteborg, as well as product marketing. Gnatovich was to develop and implement the sales strategy.

Both men were comfortable with the relationship, despite the difference in age and experience. "You have to hire people who are better than you are at whatever they are going to do," said Ahlberg. "I agreed with Atlas that we needed someone like Rock to come on board, and my only regret is that it took us too long to find him."

Visual Discovery

Many modern business endeavors involved gathering and using large, complex data sets. Firms wishing to analyze the data they had collected typically turned to dedicated statisticians and data analysts, using advanced statistics and algorithmic tools, such as SAS and DataMind. In many cases, however, these dedicated analysts lacked the skills or insights to interpret the data appropriately, just as those best able to interpret the data lacked the extensive training needed to use statistical analysis software.

Spotfire's technology was designed to enable individual researchers to visualize data in an intuitive and interactive format. By displaying data in a wide range of graphic formats, an experienced researcher could identify patterns or trends that could enable her quickly to develop leads or to eliminate unpromising lines of study. In drug discovery, for example, Spotfire software enabled researchers to mine data from extensive warehouses of chemical compound structure and behavior, looking for desired characteristics or interactions. This could dramatically reduce the early search process for candidate compounds and therefore reduce overall discovery time and time to market. (See **Exhibit 6** for a summary of Spotfire's usage potential at various stages in the drug discovery process.) Early successes at Swedish-based Astra and Anglo-Dutch Unilever had convinced Ahlberg and his co-founders that the huge potential revenues that came from discovering new patentable drugs/compounds offered Spotfire a tremendous opportunity.

Dr. Greg Tucker-Kellogg, of the Genetics Institute,[2] one of Spotfire's early U.S. customers, explained the value of Spotfire software to the Institute's genetic research:

> Due to technological advances, we can now measure the activity levels of hundreds or thousands of genes under particular conditions in a single measurement. Interpreting the vast data generated by such an experiment is a key step in early drug discovery. Spotfire offers visual data filtering; it's intuitive in a way very few products are.[3]
>
> Before Spotfire, a researcher had to go through a large number of steps, undoing and redoing different analyses. The process typically took anywhere from two hours to two days. Spotfire easily cuts that time in half.

Spotfire offered customers two basic product types, Spotfire Pro and plug-in programs. Spotfire Pro was the company's flagship data visualization tool. Spotfire Pro was applicable to any industry or broad category of data analysis. Spotfire Pro customers included manufacturing firms, financial services companies, and a wide range of other industries.

[2] Genetics Institute, a subsidiary of American Home Products Corporation, was a leading biopharmaceutical company specializing in recombinant DNA and related technologies.

[3] Casewriter interview.

EXHIBIT 6
Usage Potential for Spotfire Software in Pharmaceutical Industry by R&D Stage

Source: Spotfire.

R&D Stage	R&D Activity	Usage Potential for Spotfire Pro Software
1. Need identification	Identifying need for a new drug	Low
2. Receptor identification	Identifying receptors that need to be influenced in order to achieve therapeutic goal	High
3. Chemical compound development	Develop compound(s) likely to influence receptor(s)	High
4. Chemical compound modification	Modifying existing compounds in order to enhance therapeutic effectiveness	High
5. Pre-clinical testing	Testing new drug in laboratory setting	Medium
6. Clinical testing	Testing new drug in clinical setting (human subjects)	Low

Note: Development of a new drug until regulatory approval was estimated to cost about $400 million in 1999.

Spotfire also developed plug-in products designed for use with Spotfire Pro and which offered added value to a particular subset of customers, with more tailored forms of analysis. In Chemistry, for example, Spotfire developed Structure Visualizer, a plug-in product that linked Spotfire Pro with ISIS, the dominant chemical analysis database software operated by MDL.[4] The plug-in allowed researchers to visualize the compound structures, reactions and other data ISIS makes available. Kathleen Mensler of MDL explained, "The use of Spotfire Pro as the visual front end to ISIS will significantly increase the effective use of the chemical compound database."[5] Ahlberg elaborated, "The Structure Visualizer provides visual access to the compound database that is so critical to scientists in pre-clinical discovery."

Competition

As a new and somewhat revolutionary product, Spotfire faced not only conventional competition from similar products (discussed below), but also the need to persuade customers that "data visualization" was something they should spend money on in the first place. "So far we haven't walked into a situation where there's money budgeted for data visualization," said Ahlberg. "What we have are companies who have a problem but who haven't thought of this approach as a solution."

This need to persuade often drove the structure of early deals. Rather than attempt to sell an entire organization, Spotfire concentrated on getting the product in the door and in use, trusting that once researchers saw what it could do for them they would be able to move up the management chain and pursue an order for the larger organization. Ahlberg explained:

> We often based our proposal on how much money we thought the particular department head could spend without seeking outside approval. This meant that first-stage deals were typically $30,000 or less. In the early stage deals, our biggest competition isn't from other data visualization products, but simply from alternate demands on departmental budgets.

On some new products Spotfire had decided to introduce a quarterly payment plan, instead of their traditional annual fee, as a further inducement to get potential customers to give the software a trial run.

After gaining bottom-up support, Spotfire faced both direct and indirect competition to winning a larger order. Oxford Molecular, a competitor to MDL, offered a directly competing product in DIVA.[6] Rather than being a core business itself, DIVA served primarily as a competitive tool in the chemical database business, and did not allow the full interactivity offered by Spotfire. Ahlberg hoped that with the introduction of Spotfire's plug-in for MDL, which now gave full data mining and visualization capability to MDL users, Oxford would allow Spotfire to develop a plug-in product for their own database as well.

Another form of competition came from companies like Netgenics,[7] whose SYNERGY software integrated incompatible databases and analysis algorithms into a single format, for research in the biotechnology and pharmaceutical industries. "While our product is most attractive to the researchers, Netgenics goes straight to the CIO and says, 'We can build your entire IT structure,'" explained Gnatovich. "They're top down, while we're bottom up. In our view, their products are poor (in terms of data visualization), but their story is compelling to a CIO worried about system control."

---

[4] ISIS was the core product of MDL, a $53 million revenue subsidiary of Reed Elsevier, the Dutch publishing conglomerate.

[5] Spotfire press release.

[6] "DIVA" stands for Diverse Information Visualization and Analysis.

[7] Netgenics was incorporated in 1996 and had raised $8.1 million in VC funding.

Market Size

Spotfire's estimate of the market potential in Chemistry, Pharmaceutical and Biotechnology was as follows:

Chemistry

MDL had sold its core database product for roughly 25,000 seats, representing a dominant market share of about 90%. MDL believed the potential market for ISIS was closer to 75,000, but growth had been very slow in recent years, suggesting that the "true" market might be closer to around 30,000 seats. Spotfire felt that almost every MDL user was a potential customer for Spotfire Pro and the MDL Plug-in.

Pharmaceutical and Biotechnology

The combined *Fortune* 1000 and *Fortune Global* 1000 pharmaceutical and biotech companies employed a total of 1.2 to 1.3 million people at the end of 1997. While many of these firms did not disclose exact R&D employment, Spotfire estimated that 12% of these employees were in R&D.[8] Based on experience with Pharmaceutical and Biotechnology companies who had already adopted Spotfire the company further estimated that full adoption would imply one seat for every two R&D employees.

A House Divided?

With its origins in Sweden and its main market in the United States, Spotfire had to wrestle with early identity questions. The development team of Swedish engineers, fueled by national pride, felt that identifying Spotfire as a Swedish firm could be an asset, given the country's strong technical reputation. Gnatovich strongly disagreed:

> In my early meetings with the team in Sweden it became clear that this was going to be a problem. We already had challenges associated with being a small company with a young and only partially proven product. I told them flat-out, "This has to be an international company. If you present yourself as a Swedish firm, you've lost."

An early indicator of the perception problems Spotfire could face in the United States occurred during the move to its Cambridge offices. The new office required about $25,000 of general office equipment, and Gnatovich wanted to arrange lease financing to preserve the company's cash.

> I assumed that with $2 million in the bank and solid VC backing, this would be a simple deal. Then they [the finance company] asked me the name of our bank. When I told them it was Svenska Handelsbanken, their eyes glazed over, and they didn't want to offer us any financing. Never mind the two million, never mind that this is an international bank and we could put them in touch with the account manager in New York. They didn't want to know.

Spotfire was eventually offered financing, but on such unfavorable terms that Ahlberg and Gnatovich realized they needed to establish a relationship with a U.S. bank. "They wanted personal guarantees, they wanted to give us the money in stages, and they wanted a very high interest rate," said Gnatovich. "For a $25,000 lease I'd have offered the company better terms out of my own pocket!"

Spotfire established dual headquarters: the European headquarters and development center in Göteborg, Sweden, and U.S. headquarters in Cambridge, Massachusetts. Both Ahlberg and Gnatovich were based in the United States, to signal the firm's commitment to its U.S. customer base.

[8] Estimate came from extrapolation from firms that did disclose the number of employees in R&D.

Getting lease financing and demonstrating commitment weren't the only challenges to running an international start-up. Coordinating development in Sweden and marketing in the United States was a significant task, both in terms of information flow and morale. Ahlberg explained, "We have to make sure that the developers in Sweden feel connected to the U.S. marketing efforts, and that they are getting the best possible market feedback."

Spotfire addressed this challenge with regular meetings, both in Göteborg and Cambridge, and by having Ahlberg divide his time between the two offices. Members of the development team were also rotated through the Cambridge office, allowing them to spend time with customers and with the sales team. Despite the considerable expense and time investment, Ahlberg felt that the Göteborg/Cambridge division had its advantages as well.

> "One of the key problems of any software company," Ahlberg explained, "is setting up an effective information feedback loop between marketing and development. It's hard work, it's often not a lot of fun, and it's not necessarily the strength of the entrepreneur. So, many companies fail to do it and are unable to update their products effectively as a result. We don't have the luxury of hoping that our marketing and development teams will talk to each other without a lot of effort on our part, so we are forced to do a better job than we might have otherwise."

Ahlberg felt that developing the formal feedback loop between the two offices would be one of his most important responsibilities over the next six months, and he had several specific programs in mind to accomplish it. Software developers would be rotated from Sweden to the United States to serve as sales consultants for six months at a time, giving them client access and building closer relationships between sales and development personnel. Ahlberg also developed a computerized system for reporting problems and ideas in a structured way. Already in place for a year, the system had facilitated communication between the two offices. The U.S. office would also employ research and product marketing people whose job would be to be a bridge between customers in the United States and the development team in Sweden. The final ingredient to building links between the two offices would be Ahlberg, "traveling like crazy back and forth."

In addition to creating urgency behind the drive to build communications between marketing and development, there were tangible benefits to locating the development team in Sweden. Even after allowing for more generous benefits, Swedish programmers cost roughly $5,000 per month, compared to $8,000 per month for a comparable programmer in Cambridge, and were less costly to recruit. Retention was also much easier, since headhunters trying to lure them to other jobs heavily targeted programmers in the United States. "I would hate to try to manage a development team in Cambridge right now," said Gnatovich.

Gnatovich had his own concerns about having product development in Sweden: "Basically it came down to two things: talent pool and work ethic. If we need a hundred programmers can we get them in Göteborg? And would they have the drive you need to support an entrepreneurial venture?"

Since joining, Gnatovich had been pleased with Göteborg's performance, but some of his concerns remained.

> Sweden clearly has a large enough talent pool, but there aren't enough programmers with experience in product marketing or as end-users as we'd like—most have just been product developers. That makes communications with marketing harder. Also, while the work ethic has proven to be quite strong, there is still less of an entrepreneurial feel that sometimes makes me a little nervous. This will be the first summer I watch as the entire Göteborg office goes on August vacation.

It was not at all atypical for a middle-to-upper income Swede to own or have access to a Summer house and a boat, far away from Göteborg, so it would be difficult indeed to get programmers to return to work if anything urgent developed.

Financing

Spotfire's original funding consisted of $300,000 in seed money from Innovations Kapital (IK) in April 1996, followed by another $350,000 later that Fall. IK was a Swedish VC firm with approximately $40 million under management from a first fund and plans to raise a second, larger fund. Most of IK's investments were early stage and concentrated on Information Technology and Biotechnology. For its investment, IK received 46% of Spotfire's equity. The Spotfire team had given away a considerable piece of equity to get IK backing—in part because there weren't many alternatives and in part because they trusted IK's skills in building Swedish ventures. (See **Exhibit 7** for details on Spotfire's financing and equity ownership structure.) Carlstedt Research & Technology (CR&T), a high tech consulting firm which co-founder Truvé was involved with, also provided $40,000 in early financing, as well as technical support.

With relatively low overhead and some income from consulting projects, this was enough to get Spotfire through its first year of operations, and to establish its credibility to a point where it could approach a first round of financing with a substantially more favorable valuation. In August 1997, Spotfire completed its first round, raising $2,465,944 from Atlas Ventures and a further $616,486 from Innovations Kapital. The second round of financing also set aside stock options, which would, upon exercise, amount to 20% of the company's equity. Atlas had been the first of a half-dozen VC firms Spotfire met with, and they expressed the highest level of interest. Ahlberg reflected on the negotiations:

> It was hard to convince people on the West Coast to invest in Sweden, but otherwise I think we had a pretty good case. We met Atlas Ventures through IK, when one of the partners sat next to an Atlas guy at an EVCA (European Venture Capital Association) dinner and talked with him about Spotfire. He was interested and suggested that IK have me call Philippe Claude in the Paris office, which I did. With more than $500 million invested, Atlas was pretty unique in the venture community both in size and in that they were truly trans-Atlantic with partners in both the U.S. and in Europe. The fact that Atlas was global probably made it easier for them to evaluate us. Besides, they invested primarily in IT and in biotech, which helped them see Spotfire's potential clearly. I knew they could add a lot. Atlas wanted to buy

EXHIBIT 7 **Share Ownership and Financing Details**

Source: Spotfire.

	Shares at July 10, 1997		First Round, August 1, 1997		Ownership After First Round		
Share Holder	**Total**	**%**	**New Money ($000s)**	**Convertibles Issued**	**Shares Issued**	**Options**	**%**
Innovations Kapital	828,000	46%	$616	271,580	1,099,580		28.0%
C. Ahlberg	256,000	14%			256,000		6.5%
CR&T	181,000	10%			181,000		4.6%
Other Employees	521,000	29%			521,000		13.3%
Atlas Ventures			$2,466	1,086,319	1,086,319		27.6%
Options						785,975	20.0%
Total	1,786,000	100%			3, 929,874 (incl. options)		100.0%

roughly one-third of the company, so the negotiations on valuation had as much to do with how much we would raise as how much we would have to give away to get $3 million. We offered to sell at $3.40 per share, and Atlas offered $1.65. We agreed on $2.27.

Ahlberg's estimate of Spotfire's funding needs were headcount-driven: "Once you start laying out who you have to hire to achieve your goals you have to make sure you won't run out of money."

Atlas did considerable due diligence on the young firm. They spoke at length with several customers, making sure the product had the potential Ahlberg claimed, and also sought extensive personal references on each of the founders.

To protect their investment, Atlas insisted on three additional conditions common to VC investments. The first was an anti-dilution clause: if Spotfire did a follow-up financing at a lower valuation, Atlas would automatically be issued shares so as to protect their investment. (See **Exhibit 8** for a sample of software companies and VC financing details.) The second clause, commonly used to avoid being stuck in a "family business," stated that if no exit strategy had been carried out after five years, the VCs would have the option to withdraw their money with interest. In order to offer this and be consistent with Swedish law, the investment was done as a zero-coupon convertible bond with a term of five years. Finally, if Spotfire was acquired at a valuation that gave Atlas less than a 3x return, they would get their investment returned before dividing the rest pro-rata.

Atlas would have been willing to do without the first and third clauses in exchange for a lower valuation (Ahlberg estimated $2 per share instead of $2.27), but this had little appeal for the entrepreneur. "If we succeed in our plans, there is little risk that

EXHIBIT 8   **Sample of Software Companies and Most Recent VC Financings**

Source: Compiled from VentureSource database.

Company	Business Brief	Founded	Employees	Amount Raised	Date Raised	Post-Money Valuation
Success Factor Systems	Provider of integrated skill-based and competency-based HR management software products	10/95	15	$6.3	6/97	$26.5
Pavilion Technologies	Developer of data mining and real-time, online analytical processing software for process optimization and control.	1/92	100	10.0	9/97	N/A
Wisdom Ware	Developer of knowledge transfer solutions for sales, marketing and customer service.	7/96	16	4.0	12/97	7.5
Conduit Software	Developer of Software designed for human resource professionals	1/85	38	1.8	11/97	9.0
Digital Tools	Developer of enterprise-wide project management software solutions	1/89	115	6.5	4/98	23.5
Seeker Software	Producer of innovative employee self-use HR applications for the Web	1/96	90	7.5	N/A	25.7

All dollar amounts are in millions.

any future funding will be done at a lower valuation, and the likelihood of an acquisition taking place that does not return well over three times the VC's investment is remote."

Moving Forward—from Start-Up to Strategic Partner

Spotfire's challenge over the following twelve months was to establish itself as a strategic partner for its client companies, with Spotfire software forming a key element in their research processes. While the company had made strong progress in selling small orders, ranging from one to a few dozen seats, few clients had converted to large-scale use. While this was consistent with the long selling cycle for large research houses, Spotfire's management knew that large-scale adoption was key both to the company's long term viability and the upcoming second round of financing. "In order to get the valuation we want," explained Rock, "we need to show that customers will buy in a big way."

In addition to the long selling cycle, the shift from trial to strategic use of Spotfire raised pricing issues as well. One of Spotfire's early sales was to Unilever, a U.K./Netherlands consumer products company with £30 billion in revenues. Gnatovich explained:

> To get in Chris had to offer them 50% off on a twenty-seat deal. After trying the product out, Unilever was interested in going "research wide" with Spotfire, which means over a thousand seats. This is like a dream—they're saying they like our product and the benefit they get is directly proportional to the number of seats they have. But now that they've got $1,500 a seat as the price at twenty, how can we avoid lowering the price even further as part of a global deal? At the end of this, what should be a multi-million dollar deal will probably be less than one million. We'll end up yielding on price, but will hopefully get good terms, with most of the cash up front.

Spotfire was now sufficiently well established that entry discounts were no longer necessary, but setting prices remained tricky. Gnatovich's goal was to sell Spotfire Pro for an annual fee of $3,000 per seat. What the ultimate pricing structure would look like, and what discounts might have to be offered when customers scaled up their number of seats in use, remained unclear. Gnatovich knew it would be impossible to charge full list price for large adopters, but at least any future discounting would be done from $3,000 per seat rather than $1,500. How to price the appropriate Plug-in was more complicated.

> "The plug-in represents a lot of the value of the overall product," said Gnatovich. "It's what transforms Spotfire Pro from a generic data visualization tool to a real solutions product, by linking the general data-mining capability with specific intelligence on tasks the user will want to use regularly. But from a software perspective, it's clearly a less complicated product, so we can't try to sell it at a comparable price."

Spotfire hoped to solve this problem by pricing the plug-ins with a different structure. A customer would be charged a flat subscription fee, somewhere between $25,000 and $50,000 per year, for the plug-in, which would cover up to 25 Spotfire Pro users. The argument behind the pricing structure would be that, because they have to integrate with third party software, the plug-ins involve ongoing costs associated with upgrades.

Fortunately, Ahlberg believed that Spotfire did not have to worry about customers paying for one or a few seats and then trying to pirate or otherwise gain free use of the software. "These companies are naturally very careful about intellectual property," he explained. "They don't fool around here."

The proposed timing for the second round of financing, in the second quarter of 1999, fit not only with Spotfire's cash needs, but with the strategic development of the firm as well. "By that time," said Gnatovich, "we hope to be at the point where we know we can execute. That's when you don't want to bootstrap anymore, you want to go big and to go

EXHIBIT 9

Spotfire Headcount Projections

Source: Spotfire.

	Employed at Year-End			
	1997	**1998E**	**1999E**	**2000E**
Management	2	4	6	6
Administration	1	2	4	8
Sales	5	10	18	34
Marketing	1	3	4	8
Customer Service	2	3	4	8
Development	7	9	12	20
Total	18	31	48	84

EXHIBIT 10

Valuation Comparisons of Publicly Listed Software Firms (dollars in millions)

Source: Compiled from Standard & Poor's *Compustat,* Datastream International data.

Company Name	Net Income/ (Loss) 1997	Net Sales 1997	Market Value June 24, 1998
Sterling Software	(133.0)	489.0	2,282
Award Software Intl., Inc.	4.7	23.4	78
Parametric Technology	219.2	808.8	9,418

worldwide." (See **Exhibit 9** for Spotfire's headcount projections.) Gnatovich had put together a table with information on three publicly listed software firms. (See **Exhibit 10.**) He was not sure, however, how useful this table was going to be for the valuation of Spotfire.

Looking to the Future

As Ahlberg stepped into the elevator to head for Boston's Logan airport, he reflected on the challenges that lay ahead. Discussions had already begun with Spotfire's VCs on the second round of financing. For Spotfire to have the valuation he wanted, it would have to both increase its breadth and depth of market penetration and strengthen its internal infrastructure. Like any entrepreneur, he wore several hats in the company, selling software, managing relations between the two offices, and hiring key staff. But which tasks had priority now?

Ahlberg felt that Spotfire had given up too much equity in its seed round of financing. To avoid having that happen again, the firm needed both to expand its customer base and to convince some of its customers to adopt Spotfire on a much larger scale than they had to date. Meanwhile, they needed to introduce new products, such as a plug-in for biology databases, and continue to develop their existing product line so that new versions would be even more in-line with the needs of their customers.

Meanwhile, Spotfire also needed to develop its internal infrastructure. In addition to developing a formal feedback process to link development with marketing, Ahlberg knew Spotfire also needed to make some more key hires, such as a CFO, before the next financing round took place. He couldn't help thinking that arranging the final details of his wedding might prove a relaxing change of pace!

Case 16

Mobile Communications Tokyo, Inc.

"Yes, we should start thinking about going public. But there are so many other issues I am thinking about right now. Can you call me back on Monday?" Hatsuhiro Inoue, founder and president of Mobile Communications Tokyo, Inc. (MCT) hung up the phone. It was Friday, June 19, 1998 and he had just spent a couple of minutes fending off another sales pitch from an investment banker. Several bankers had called over the last months, all of them eager to take MCT public. MCT was still more than two years away from a potential initial public offering (IPO), but successful entrepreneurs were rare in Japan. An IPO of an entrepreneurial telecommunications company was mouthwatering even if the company was small.

Inoue picked up the phone to call the manufacturer of a new line of pagers for children that his company planned to sell. As he waited to be connected, Inoue looked out of his office window onto a backyard in Tokyo's upscale Aoyama neighborhood. This Saturday he would spend in the office again, but maybe there would be time to spend with his wife and son on Sunday.

A couple of minutes later he placed down the receiver again. Everything was on track with the manufacturing schedule for the Kids Pagers. (See **Exhibit 1** for a picture of the Kids Pager.) They would hit the market in 1998 and Inoue hoped that they would account for ¥204 million in revenues in 1999. At this point, Inoue was more concerned with the overall strategy of MCT. There were so many interesting avenues to pursue and he and his team had decided to focus not only on the traditional paging business but also on the cellular market and on Internet software. Was that too much at a time? Should Inoue try to refocus MCT just on paging? Or shift completely to becoming a niche Internet software provider?

Professor Walter Kuemmerle prepared this case with support from Professor Kiichiro Kobayashi, Keio Business School, Japan, and Charles M. Williams Fellow Chad Ellis, MBA '98, as the basis for class discussion rather than to illustrate either effective or ineffective handling of an administrative situation.

EXHIBIT 1
Kid's Pager

Source: MCT.

He would need to discuss these issues with his board and financiers, as well as his management team over the next couple of months. (See **Exhibit 2** for resumes of key MCT employees and **Exhibit 3** for MCT's organization chart.) Inoue thought: "It is ironic that while all these bankers are bullish about MCT's prospects, I am much more concerned about our future."

A True Start-up in Japan

Hatsuhiro Inoue was born in 1944, the only son of an electrical engineer. His father was a Hitachi employee and a very successful developer of electric motors. Hatsuhiro followed in his father's footsteps and studied electrical engineering at Waseda University in Tokyo. Following his father's recommendation he focused on telecommunications. After graduation in 1968 he joined Hitachi as a development engineer working on a wide range of

EXHIBIT 2   **Resumes of Key MCT Employees**

Source: MCT.

Hatsuhiro Inoue

PROFESSIONAL EXPERIENCE

Mobile Communications Tokyo, Inc., 1990 to Present

Founded Mobile Communications Tokyo Inc., establishing a new business in the development and sales of land mobile communication equipment.

- Hardware development of land mobile radio such as NTT (Nippon Telephone and Telegraph) pager, TACS cellular radio and the infrastructure, Japan digital cellular radio, personal handy phone system, and DSP (digital signal processing applications).
- Software development of above land mobile communication radio and the system.
- Consultation of above equipment and the infrastructure.
- Sales representative of NTT (paging/cellular), Tokyo Telemessage (paging) and IDO (cellular).

Nippon Motorola Ltd., 1980–1989

Implementation of paging/cellular/trunking as the director of communication division.

(1) NTT Paging and Cellular: Total sales reached 50M$/yr.
(2) New Common Carrier Paging
   - Introduction of MOTOROLA world standard pager to Japanese market.
   - Lobbying to MOPT (Ministry of Posts and Telecommunications), MITI (Ministry of International Trade and Industry), U.S. Embassy and LDP (Liberal Democratic Party) to liberalize the telecommunication business monopolized by NTT.
   - Sales amount of NCC paging (pager and system) reached 60M$/yr.
(3) New Common Carrier Cellular
   - Introduction of MOTOROLA cellular (TACS systems) to Japanese market.
   - Sales amount of NCC Cellular reached 140M$/yr.

Hitachi America Ltd. (New York office), 1974–1977

- Sales manager of communication department
- Key accounts: Hughes, Bell Lab, Western Electric, TRW, NASA, Raytheon, GE, HP, NBS, Motorola, MIT, NRAO, Philco-Ford, Scientific Atlanta, JPL.

Hitachi Ltd., 1968–1974 and 1977–1980

1968–1974 Development engineer of microwave components for satellite communication such as amplifier using GaAsFET, switches using pin diode, oscillators using gunn diode/impatt diode, SAW filter for radar such as tunnel diode and of land mobile communication equipment.
1977–1980 Sales Engineer

EDUCATION

Waseda University, 1968
(Majored in electronics and telecommunications)

DATE OF BIRTH
August 28, 1944

Takeshi Imai

PROFESSIONAL EXPERIENCE

Tokyo Mobile Communication, Inc., 1995
Engineer and Director

Nippon Motorola Ltd., 1984–1995
Engineering Manager in charge of
- NTT Cellular Radio
- Pager for NTT and other paging carrier
- Paging infrastructure for Tokyo Telemessage
- Standardization of New Paging ALR Interface (FLEX-TD) at ARIB

(continued)

EXHIBIT 2 (Continued)

The General Corporation, 1957–1984
Developed and designed two-way land mobile radios, trunk radio (MCA), pager, etc including systems for such as law enforcement, fire fighting, electric power company, press, etc.
EDUCATION
University of Telecommunications, BS (Radio Wave Engineering), 1957

Shoshichi Fukuda
PROFESSIONAL EXPERIENCE
Hitachi Denshi (Electronics) Co. Ltd., 1961–1967
Managing Director in charge with Telecommunication
EDUCATION
Waseda University
1959–1961, MBS
1955–1959, BS

Kazuya Miyakawa
Hitachi Denshi (Electronics) System Service Co., Ltd., 1961–1988
Director
Hitachi Denshi (Electronics) Co. Ltd., 1961–1988
Accounting Manager
EDUCATION
Yokohama University, 1957–1961, BA

Takumi Nishi
Born 1961; BA in electrical engineering; 1982–1990: Motorola Japan, sales engineer pager sales to NTT and NTT's new competitors), worked with Hatsuhiro Inoue; since 1992: sales planning manager, MCT; married.

K. Watanabe
Born 1945; 1967–1994; Fujitsu Corp., development engineer (21 years), computer sales engineer (6 years); 1995–1997: EMC Japan Corp.; since 1997: head of sales, MCT (recruited through headhunter).

communication devices including microwave components for satellites. Following a typical pattern in large Japanese manufacturing firms Inoue moved from development to sales after a number of years. In 1974 he was transferred to Hitachi America where he was involved with key accounts such as NASA, General Electric and Motorola. In 1977 he was transferred back to Japan to continue his work as a sales engineer.

At Hitachi Inoue was successful but felt that he did not face enough challenges. In 1980 he deviated from the typical Japanese career pattern. He quit Hitachi and joined Motorola Japan as employee #16. As a sales engineer, he first worked in the paging division and then in the cellular division. By 1988 he was managing 300 employees (about 7.5% of Motorola's total workforce in Japan) and had responsibility for more than $600 million in revenues. Once again, Inoue became dissatisfied. In hindsight he reasoned:

At Motorola I learned a lot, but over time the job became monotonous. I realized that I could develop pagers and cellular phones on my own. And I felt that in some niches in Japan I could do a better job than Motorola. In 1988 I started thinking about starting my own firm, but I was so busy in my day-to-day job that I did not really have time to reflect enough. In 1989 alone I made 20 business trips to the United States. There was really not time to flesh out a business plan.

EXHIBIT 3
Organization Chart

Source: MCT.

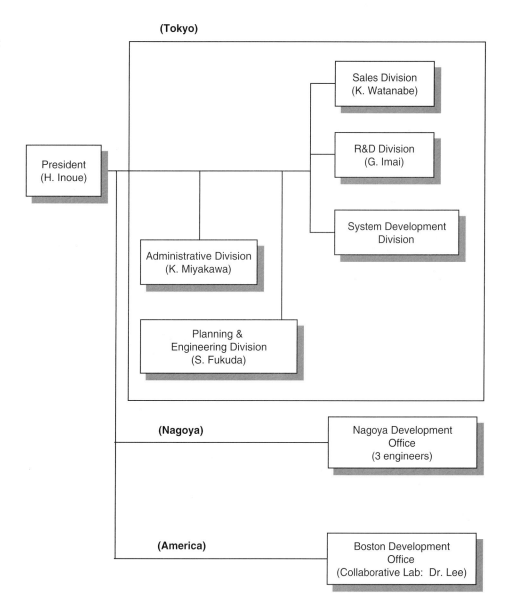

In December 1989 Inoue quit Motorola with the vision of starting a company on his own and with ¥30 million (approximately $220,000; US$ = ¥137 at 12/89). Inoue left Motorola on amicable terms: "My boss understood that I would be happier on my own. And my work at Motorola had been accomplished. In fact, I kept in touch with many employees at Motorola after I left." Inoue did not have a clear business plan but was confident that his extensive network of contacts would lead to revenues one way or the other. For the first couple of years, Inoue intended to provide software and hardware development services to paging service providers.

Inoue started out on his own as a one-person firm. MCT was incorporated in January 1990 and in February his former secretary at Hitachi joined him. Inoue reflected on 1990:

> Although it might seem crazy to start out without a detailed business plan, it worked for me. I knew a lot about paging hardware and software, at least I knew a lot more than most people in Japan at that time. And I knew that there were paging service providers who would be interested in my services.

As a first step Inoue got in touch with Shintaro Okazaki, Executive Managing Director of Tokyo Telemessage. Inoue and Okazaki had been working together while Inoue was still at Motorola and Okazaki was his customer. Tokyo Telemessage was the leading independent provider of paging services in the Tokyo metropolitan area. Inoue offered to develop electronic circuit boards and components for pagers distributed by Tokyo Telemessage. At the same time, Inoue contacted his former colleagues at Hitachi's communication equipment group, offering his development services.

Both sales pitches were successful and in July 1990 MobilCom booked its first sale. At first, Inoue worked out of a small office in Kita Aoyama. During his first year of operations he hired two engineers from Motorola Japan Inc. Inoue reasoned: "Motorola was a terrific labor pool for my firm and during the first four years of operations I hired six engineers from there. Motorola's engineers were typically about five years ahead compared to engineers working in Japanese firms with regards to their telecommunications equipment knowledge." (See **Exhibits 4** and **5** for an overview of MCT's financial statements over time.)

The Core Business: Innovative Paging and Cellular Hardware

In the early 1990s the Japanese market for mobile telecommunications was just emerging on a big scale and no business model had been finalized yet. The obvious role for MCT was to support design activities of some of the major manufacturers. Another possible strategy was to sell ready-made products to mobile telecommunications service providers such as TTM for narrowly defined niche markets. Finally, MCT could develop its own line of pagers or mobile telephones and sell them to communications retailers and electronics stores that also sold regular telephones. This strategy would be increasingly feasible as the market matured and as package deals by telecommunication providers (free phone combined with the obligation to subscribe to the provider for a certain period of time) became less likely since customers already owned mobile phones. (See **Exhibit 6** for a comparison of Japan vs. the United States. See **Exhibits 7** and **8** for an overview of the development of the cellular and pager markets in Japan.)

During 1990 Inoue developed a vision for MCT:

> After a couple of months my vision for MCT gradually emerged. I thought that MCT could become a preeminent provider of electronic circuits and circuit boards for mobile communications equipment, particularly for cellular telephone and for pagers. Eventually, I hoped that we could also develop our own line of telephones and pagers. For a specialist it is not that difficult to design and develop communications hardware. And there are so many excellent manufacturing companies in Japan and throughout Asia who can manufacture almost anything. I had a number of contacts to these manufacturers and I knew how to work with them based on my experience at Hitachi and Motorola. The bottleneck to developing our own range of phones and pagers was capital. We did not have any venture funding available, so we had no choice but to grow slowly.

In spite of these limits to independent development, MCT aspired to be more than a subcontractor for circuit design to large mobile communications equipment manufacturers. Already during its first year, MCT came up with innovative design proposals for circuit boards. Over time, an increasing share of MCT's products resulted from MCT's design initiatives and MCT established itself as a "technology push" design shop.

Also, MCT started working more intensively directly with paging service providers. Inoue reasoned:

> Mobile telecommunications is all about clever design and clever marketing. Manufacturing is relatively straightforward, at least if you have some experience in working with subcontractors who manufacture your design. We are very good at designing innovative products

EXHIBIT 4 **MCT Profit and Loss Statement/Ownership Structure/Employees (Amounts are in 000 US$) (1998 and later: forecasts)**

Source: Mobile Communications Tokyo, Inc.

	1990	1991	1992	1993	1994	1995	1996	1997	1998	1999	2000	2001	2002	2003
Revenues	16	600	1,056	1,384	1,776	1,848	2,448	3,736	6,560	10,080	16,120	22,520	28,000	34,960
Paging	[—]	[320]	[528]	[640]	[800]	[792]	[1,160]	[2,000]	[1,600]	[1,760]	[1,760]	[1,760]	[1,840]	[1,920]
Cellular(Hardware)	[—]	[280]	[528]	[744]	[792]	[88]	[240]	[936]	[2,240]	[4,880]	[10,000]	[15,440]	[20,160]	[26,240]
Cellular(Software)	[—]	[—]	[—]	[—]	[184]	[—]	[128]	[0]	[0]	[0]	[0]	[0]	[0]	[0]
Internet Software	[—]	[—]	[—]	[—]	[—]	[120]	[—]	[0]	[1,280]	[1,520]	[2,080]	[2,400]	[2,800]	[3,200]
Others(Hardware)	[—]	[—]	[—]	[—]	[—]	[448]	[560]	[800]	[1,320]	[1,600]	[1,760]	[2,000]	[2,160]	[2,400]
Others(Software)	[16]	[—]	[—]	[—]	[—]	[400]	[360]	[—]	[120]	[320]	[520]	[920]	[1,040]	[1,200]
Expenses	144	560	960	1,376	1,744	1,792	2,192	3,456	6,016	8,520	13,560	18,920	23,200	28,560
(Materials)	8	320	456	728	1,072	984	1,224	2,176	4,432	6,424	10,760	15,352	18,920	23,680
(SGA)	136	240	504	648	672	808	968	1,280	1,584	2,096	2,800	3,568	4,280	4,880
[Office Rent]	[64]	[64]	[88]	[104]	[96]	[80]	[120]	[160]	[160]	[240]	[280]	[400]	[440]	[480]
[Personal]	[32]	[120]	[296]	[392]	[392]	[432]	[536]	[800]	[960]	[1,160]	[1,400]	[1,600]	[1,880]	[2,160]
[R&D]	[—]	[—]	[—]	[—]	[—]	[—]	[—]	[—]	[—]	[—]	[—]	[—]	[—]	[—]
[Others]	[40]	[56]	[120]	[152]	[184]	[296]	[312]	[320]	[464]	[696]	[1,120]	[1,568]	[1,960]	[2,240]
Recurring Profit	-128	40	96	8	32	56	256	280	544	1,560	2,560	3,600	4,800	6,400
Profit before Tax	-128	40	96	8	32	64	88	128	544	1,560	2,560	3,600	4,800	6,400
Depreciation	4.0	4.0	4.0	2.4	12.0	12.8	12.0	22.4	24.0	40.0	56.0	64.0	64.0	64.0
Tax									264	720	1,120	1,600	2,160	3,136
Profit after Tax	-128	40	96	8	24	24	40	48	280	840	1,440	2,000	2,640	3,200
# of Shares	200	800	1,000	1,000	1,000	1,200	2,200	3,800	5,000	5,000	5,000	9,600	9,600	9,600
Paid in Capital ('000 US$)	80	320	400	400	400	480	880	920	1,440	1,440	1,440	3,840	3,840	3,840
Ownership(%)														
[Inoue]	100	50	40	40	40	33	30	57	56	56	56	45	45	45
[TaiyoKogyoGroup]	—	50	60	60	60	67	52	30	23	23	23	12	12	12
[Venture Capital]	—	—	—	—	—	—	9	8	13	13	13	8	8	8
[Venture Business]	—	—	—	—	—	—	9	5	3	3	3	3	3	3
[Others]	—	—	—	—	—	—	—	—	5	5	5	32	32	32
Employees #	2	5	8	10	13	14	18	21	26	31	36	38	41	44
[Permanent]	[2]	[4]	[6]	[7]	[9]	[10]	[12]	[13]	[16]	[21]	[26]	[28]	[31]	[34]
[Contract workers]	[0]	[1]	[2]	[3]	[4]	[4]	[6]	[8]	[10]	[10]	[10]	[10]	[10]	[10]
R&D¹														
(including Materials)	—	—	64	96	160	144	184	360	520	880	1,520	1,760	2,000	2,400

Note: All figures have been converted to $US at a rate of 1$US = 125 yen.

¹R&D expenses are included in SGA expenses above.

EXHIBIT 5 Balance Sheet (thousands of US$)

Source: MCT.

	1993	1994	1995	1996	1997
Quick Assets	$580	$715	$1,424	$1,920	$3,073
Cash & deposits	262	319	201	360	168
Accounts receivable	279	233	1,129	1,385	2,509
Goods in process	28	62	103	154	282
Short term loans	0	0	0	24	125
Suspense payments	7	99	0	6	0
Prepaid expenses	2	1	1	1	0
Reserve for uncollectible account	2	1	−10	−10	−11
Fixed Assets	219	171	161	279	$316
Furniture and fixtures	10	45	34	35	86
Telephone subscription right	3	3	3	4	4
Invested securities	4	0	0	20	20
Invested capital	1	1	1	1	1
Long-term loans	0	0	0	80	65
Security deposit	200	107	107	125	125
Insurance reserve	1	1	2	2	3
Membership right	0	14	14	12	12
Total assets	$799	$886	$1,585	$2,199	$3,389
Current liabilities	$175	$266	$417	$538	$454
Notes payable	0	113	0	122	0
Accounts payable	99	101	326	300	296
Short-term debt	21	21	1	1	9
Tax payable	0	0	37	33	64
Deposit received	20	19	20	32	30
Reserve for bonus	35	12	43	50	55
Fixed liabilities	214	189	627	692	$1,876
Long-term debt	214	189	627	692	1,236
Debenture	—	—	—	—	640
Total liabilities	$389	$455	$1,054	$1,230	$2,330
Capital	$400	$400	$480	$880	$920
Capital surplus	10	31	51	89	139
Stockholder's equity	$410	$431	$531	$969	$1,059

Financial data were converted at 1$=125¥.

but we have to move closer to the final customer, i.e. the paging or telecommunications firm, and away from large telecommunications hardware manufacturers if we want to capture a larger part of the pie.

In 1991 there were five large manufacturers of mobile telecommunications equipment: NEC, Matsushita, Fujitsu, Hitachi and Mitsubishi. MCT was the only small manufacturer with superior expertise. Particularly in the pager business, large manufacturers were not used to dealing with small lots of pagers that some of the paging service providers desired. This created an interesting niche for MCT. MCT could design and coordinate the manufacturing of lots of 10,000 components while a larger manufacturer would generally not accept any order below 100,000 components. In 1990 there were 4.2 million pagers in use in Japan. While NTT controlled the largest share of the market there were also a number of independent paging service providers with less than 250,000 subscribers. MCT could provide customized products and components for these firms. (See **Exhibit 9** for a comparison of design manufacturing capabilities.)

EXHIBIT 6   **U.S.-Japan Statistical Comparison**

Source: Compiled from Economist Intelligence Unit data.

	United States	Japan
Population (1,000:1995)	260,651	124,961
Population density (square kilometer:1995)	28	331
Area (1,000 square kilometer)	9,364	378
Average life expectancy (male:1995)	72.3	76.6
Average life expectancy (female:1995)	79.1	83.0
Persons aged over 65 (1994)	12.7%	14.0%
Persons aged over 65 (2025)	18.1%	25.8%
GDP (nominal/$billion:1995)	7,246	5,111
GDP (per capital/$:1995)	27,799	40,900
Real growth rate (1991–1995)	1.9%	1.3%
Real growth rate (1995)	2.0%	0.9%
Long-term interest rate (1995)	6.6%	3.4%
Short-term interest rate (1995)	5.5%	1.2%
Car production (1,000 unit:1995)	6,601	7,611
Car exports (1,000 unit:1995)	522	2,896
Car imports (1,000 unit:1995)	4,114	362
Personal computer possession (unit per 100 persons)	29.8	12.0
Total labor force (1,000 unit:1995)	132,474	66,450
No. of televisions (1,000 unit:1995)	210,500	77,000
No. of cellular telephones (1,000 unit:1997)	—	—
No. of pagers in service (1,000 unit:1996	—	—

EXHIBIT 7
Cellular Market in Japan (units)

Source: MCT.

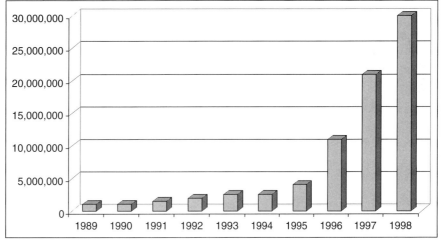

Notes: 1998 based on industry forecasts.

In 1998 the market for pagers had clearly peaked while the market for cellular phones was still growing. Paging hardware still represented the largest share of MCT's business (31%). This created new challenges for MCT, but also additional opportunities. Shintaro Okazaki, executive managing director of Tokyo Telemessage (TTM) which served 45% of the two million pagers in the Tokyo area and was an important customer of MCT, stated:

> The market for pagers is clearly maturing but it is also shifting. In 1990 maintenance workers and salaried employees were the fastest growing user group of pagers; in 1994 the fastest growing group were senior high school students, now it's elementary school students. In two

EXHIBIT 8
Pager Market in Japan (units)

Source: MCT.

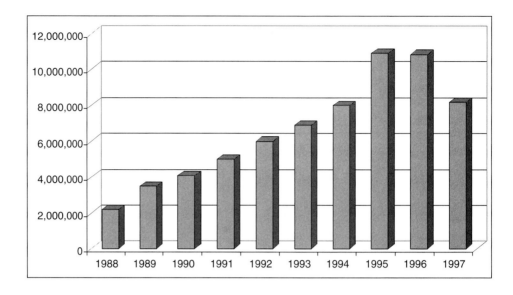

EXHIBIT 9

Comparison of Design and Manufacturing Capability of Large Telecommunications Equipment Manufacturing and MCT

Source: MCT.

	Large Manufacturer	MCT
Lot size	>100,000 units	>10,000 units
Order lead time	4 months	2 months
Design capabilities	Medium to high	Very high
Quality of manufacturing	High	Medium
Location of manufacturing	In-house	Outsourced

years the fastest growing customer group will be kids in kindergarten as well as new applications such as maintenance pagers in pieces of heavy equipment or pagers that report electricity consumption in households. Now the average monthly revenue per pager is ¥2,000 but this figure will most likely decline. With each shift we have to rethink our marketing approach. MCT is quite good in working with us in this regard. Not only has MCT maintained a technological edge over large firms since its inception but it is also more creative.

Indeed, in August 1996 MCT had introduced a relatively simple innovation in paging called Q-Call. The principle was one-touch paging that would deliver a certain message to a designated recipient. This product was targeted at senior citizens and small children; the sender would just press a button on a device adjacent to the phone and the care provider or parent would receive a page. The Q-call device could be attached to any regular phone. Its price ranged from ¥3,800 to ¥5,500. The profit margin was approximately 15%. To date MCT had sold 20,000 units. Sales of another 50,000 units were expected over the next two years.

Furthermore MCT had just designed a "speaking pager" for children aged four to six that was capable of transmitting and announcing a number of messages. This product was scheduled for market introduction in fall 1998. TTM had just signed a $3m order for these pagers and other products to be delivered over the next year.

The mobile telephone market in Japan was still growing (in terms of subscribers) but saturation was in sight. Japan had a population of 120 million and there were now 30 million cellular telephones plus 10 million mobile telephones that operated under the personal handyphone system (PHS). PHS was a Japanese technology, which consisted of a semi-mobile network grafted on the backbone of the fixed network. PHS technology was inferior to conventional cellular technology in certain respects; for example, PHS handsets could not be used in moving vehicles.

While prices of PHS services had remained stable over the last four years, prices for cellular services had declined by 60% and were now at par with PHS service prices. Industry analysts expected that the PHS network would rapidly lose customers. Competition in mobile telephone services was fierce and an industry consolidation was expected. In 1998 there were five cellular phone service providers and three PHS providers in the Tokyo area (25 million people) alone. Intense competition also affected manufacturers of mobile telephones as service providers were increasingly seeking to share market risks with phone manufacturers.

For future growth in its cellular business MCT relied on its superior development expertise. (See **Exhibit 9** for an assessment of MCT's design and manufacturing capabilities.) Over the years Inoue had succeeded in hiring a number of qualified engineers. The chief engineer, Takeshi Imai, and his team had just succeeded in miniaturizing a key chip for cellular phones. This achievement provided an almost instant contribution to MCT's 1998 revenues. In addition, Imai and his team were working intensively on CDMA technology, a digital cellular technology under development in the United States. It claimed superior quality, capacity and security over the status quo (called TDMA). Inoue felt confident that MCT's understanding of CDMA was as good as it could get for a firm of MCT's size. In 2003 Inoue expected 78% of revenues from the cellular business, most of which would be CDMA technology-based. (See **Exhibit 10** for a description of CDMA technology, **Exhibit 11** for a picture of MCT's CDMA RF module, **Exhibit 12** for CDMA sales forecasts in Japan and **Exhibit 13** for MCT CDMA sales forecasts.)

In June 1998, MCT prepared a bid for a PCS (personal communications network) for the Indian states of Maharashtra and Karnataka. This bid was prepared in cooperation with Hughes Network System in Germantown, MD. Hughes would provide the stationary investment in transmitters and switches. MCT planned to design the handsets and to subcontract manufacturing to another firm. The initial bid was for 20,000 mobile telephones. At a sales price of about ¥50,000 this represented revenues of ¥1,000,000,000 (about $8 million; at 1$ = ¥125) over two years.

In addition to its indigenous product development capabilities, MCT worked with an independent Lexington, Massachusetts-based engineering shop, Lee Laboratories, Inc. Inoue had known its boss, Dr. Chong W. Lee, for many years. Since 1993 Lee had provided focused support for MCT's Japan-based development, particularly in the area of circuit design. MCT had also secured some of its intellectual property. By 1998, MCT had 10 patents pending or approved in Japan.

The telecommunications market in Japan was developing rapidly, and Inoue knew that the precise future of the market was impossible to predict. However, he took comfort in knowing that in addition to his own experience he had access to the knowledge of his customers. In cellular these included Hitachi, Kokusai Denki, Hughes and Motorola, although not NTT. In paging, MCT's only major customer was Tokyo Telemessage.

A New Division: Internet Software

Between 1990 and 1994 MCT grew, but more slowly than Inoue had hoped. Inoue realized that selling his services and products to new customers was more difficult than expected. Inoue also became concerned that the company was too dependent on its two main customers, Hitachi and Tokyo Telemessage. In 1996 Inoue was approached by his uncle, Nobuyoshi Fukuyama, who was managing director of the Japan Amateur

EXHIBIT 10   Description of CDMA (Code Division Multiple Access)

Source: MCT.

What is Code Division Multiple Access?

One of the most important concepts of any cellular telephone system is that of "multiple access," meaning that multiple, simultaneous users can be supported. In other words, a large number of users share a common pool of radio channels and any user can gain access to any channel (each user is not always assigned to the same channel). A channel can be thought of as merely a portion of the limited radio resource which is temporarily allocated for a specific purpose, such as someone's phone call. A multiple access method is a definition of how the radio spectrum is divided into channels and how channels are allocated to the many users of the system.

Current Cellular Standards

Different types of cellular systems employ various methods of multiple access. The traditional analog cellular systems, such as those based on the Advanced Mobile Phone Service (AMPS) and Total Access Communications System (TACS) standards, use Frequency Division Multiple Access (FDMA). FDMA channels are defined by a range of radio frequencies, usually expressed in a number of kilohertz (kHz), out of the radio spectrum.

For example, AMPS systems use 30 kHz "slices" of spectrum for each channel. Narrowband AMPS (NAMPS) requires only 10 kHz per channel. TACS channels are 25 kHz wide. With FDMA, only one subscriber at a time is assigned a channel. No other conversations can access this channel until the subscriber's call is finished, or until that original call is handed off to a different channel by the system. A common multiple access method employed in new digital cellular systems is the Time Division Multiple Access (TDMA). TDMA digital standards include North American Digital Cellular (known by its standard number IS-54), Global System for Mobil Communications (GSM), and Personal Digital Cellular (PDC).

TDMA systems commonly start with a slice of spectrum, referred to as one "carrier." Each carrier is then divided into time slots. Only one subscriber at a time is assigned to each time slot, or channel. No other conversations can access this channel until the subscriber's call is finished, or until that original call is handed off to a different channel by the system.

For example, IS-54 systems, designed to coexist with AMPS systems, divide 30 kHz of spectrum into three channels. PDC divides 25 kHz slices of spectrum into three channels. GMS systems create eight time-division channels in 200 kHz wide carriers.

The CDMA Cellular Standard

With CDMA, unique digital codes, rather than separate RF frequencies or channels, are used to differentiate subscribers. The codes are shared by both the mobile station (cellular phone) and the base station, and are called "pseudo-Random Code Sequences." All users share the same range of radio spectrum.

For cellular telephony, CDMA is a digital multiple access technique specified by the Telecommunications Industry Association (TIA) as "IS-95."

In March 1992, the TIA established the TR-45.5 subcommittee with the charter of developing a spread-spectrum digital cellular standard. In July of 1993, the TIA gave its approval of the CDMA IS-95 standard.

IS-95 systems divided the radio spectrum into carriers which are 1,250 kHz (1.25 MHz) wide. One of the unique aspects of CDMA is that while there are certainly limits to the number of phone calls that can be handled by a carrier this is not a fixed number. Rather, the capacity of the systems will be dependent on a number of different factors. This will be discussed in later sections.

CDMA Technology

Though CDMA's application in cellular telephony is relatively new, it is not a new technology. CDMA has been used in many military applications, such as anti-jamming (because of the spread signal, it is difficult to jam or interfere with a CDMA signal), ranging (measuring the distance of the transmission to know when it will be received), and secure communications (the spread spectrum signal is very hard to detect).

Spread Spectrum

CDMA is a "spread spectrum" technology, which means that it spreads the information contained in a particular signal of interest over a much greater bandwidth than the original signal.

A CDMA call starts with a standard rate of 9,600 bits per second (9.6 kilobits per second). This is then spread to a transmitted rate of about 1.23 Megabits per second. Spreading means that digital codes are applied to the data bits associated with users in a cell. These data bits are transmitted along with the signals of all the other users in that cell. When the signal is received the codes are removed from the desired signal, separating the users and returning the call to a rate of 9,600 bps.

(continued)

EXHIBIT 10   (Continued)

Traditional uses of spread spectrum are in military operations. Because of the wide bandwidth of a spread spectrum signal, it is very difficult to jam, difficult to interfere with, and difficult to identify. This is in contrast to technologies using a narrower bandwidth of frequencies. Since a wideband spread spectrum signal is very hard to detect, it appears as nothing more than a slight rise in the "noise floor" or interference level. With other technologies, the power of the signal is concentrated in a narrower band, which makes it easier to detect.

Increased privacy is inherent in CDMA technology. CDMA phone calls will be secure from the casual eavesdropper since, unlike an analog conversation, a simple radio receiver will not be able to pick individual digital conversations out of the overall RF radiation in a frequency band.

Synchronization

In the final stages of encoding of the radio link from the base station to the mobile, CDMA adds a special "pseudo-random code" to the signal that repeats itself after a finite amount of time. Base stations in the system distinguish themselves from each other by transmitting different portions of the code at a given time. In other words, the base stations transmit time offset versions of the same pseudo-random code. In order to assure that the time offsets used remain unique from each other, CDMA stations must remain synchronized to a common time reference.

The Global Positioning System (GPS) provides this precise common time reference. GPS is a satellite based, radio navigation system capable of providing a practical and affordable means of determining continuous position, velocity, and time to an unlimited number of users.

"The Balancing Act"

CDMA cell coverage is dependent upon the way the system is designed. In fact, three primary system characteristics—Coverage, Quality, and Capacity—must be balanced off of each other to arrive at the desired level of system performance. In a CDMA system these three characteristics are tightly interrelated. Even higher capacity might be achieved through some degree of degradation in coverage and/or quality. Since these parameters are all intertwined, operators cannot have the best of all worlds: three times wider coverage, 40 times capacity, and "CD" quality sound. For example, the 13 kbps vocoder provides better sound quality, but reduces system capacity as compared to an 8 kbps vocoder.

CDMA Benefits

When implemented in a cellular telephone system, CDMA technology offers numerous benefits to the cellular operators and their subscribers. The following is an overview of the benefits of CDMA:
1. Capacity increases of 8 to 10 times that of an AMPS analog system and 4 to 5 times that of a GSM system.
2. Improved call quality, with better and more consistent sound as compared to AMPS.
3. Simplified system planning through the use of the same frequency in every sector of every cell.
4. Enhanced privacy.
5. Improved coverage characteristics, allowing for the possibility of fewer cell sites.
6. Increased talk time for portables.
7. Bandwidth on demand.

Sports Association (JASA), one of Japan's largest associations with over two million members. JASA was tendering the development of a secure website over which members could carry out a variety of transactions, including membership renewals and purchases of merchandise.

Engineers at MCT had recently spent some time investigating different encryption technologies as part of the development effort for the CDMA cellular technology. Inoue felt that the website project would make use of the knowledge that MCT had accumulated. MCT bid for the contract and won it. The contract ran until the year 2002. In 1997 Internet software development represented about 30% of revenues. While Internet software for JASA represented predictable revenues and income, MCT did not want to shift its focus entirely. According to forecasts, software development would represent only 13% of revenues by 2003.

EXHIBIT 11
RF Module for
W-CDMA Handset

Source: MCT.

EXHIBIT 12 **Cellular Market Forecast in Japan**

Source: MCT.

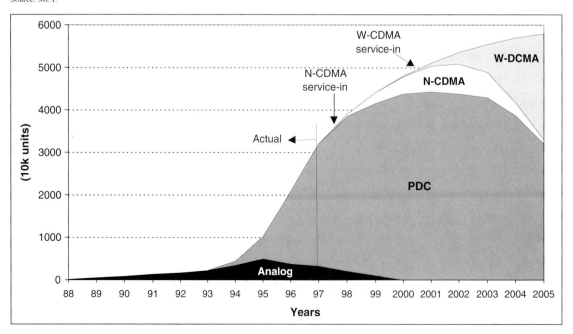

EXHIBIT 13   **Sales Forecast of RF Module for W-CDMA**

Source: MCT.

	1999	2000	2001	2002	2003	2004
Sales quantity (K units)	—	12	40	140	280	600
Unit price (K¥)	—[a]	25	10	8	7	5
Sales amount (M¥)	30	300	600	1,120	1,960	3,000
Profit (M¥)	6	75	150	224	294	450

[a]Delivery for trial use.

Note: Sales forecasts for the RF module for W-CDMA are included in the comprehensive sales forecast (**Exhibit 4**).

Financing Growth

During its first five years, MCT expanded rather cautiously. Inoue had started the firm with $300,000 of his own money. He briefly considered venture capital backing but realized quickly that the few Japanese "venture capitalists" generally backed firms that needed another round of financing before going public. In 1991 Inoue invited the owner and CEO of Taiyo Kogyo Industries, Kuniyasa Sakai, to invest in MCT. Inoue had known Sakai since 1984 when Inoue was looking (on behalf of Motorola) for a telecom factory in Japan—one of Sakai's factories was a lead candidate.

Taiyo Kogyo was a diversified electrical equipment manufacturer, which consisted of 30 companies that operated fairly independently. Overall sales were about ¥100 billion ($800 million) and employment was around 3000 employees. Sakai acquired 50% of the company (400 shares at ¥50,000 per share). By 1995 Sakai had increased his share to 67%, paying ¥50,000 per share for 200 shares each in 1992 and 1995. (See **Exhibit 14** for details of MCT share ownership over time.)

In many ways 1995 was a watershed year for MCT. The firm had finally built up a reputation as a reliable design shop and had developed its first proprietary paging products. Imai joined as chief engineer after 11 years at Motorola. At the same time, other sources of financing than Taiyo Kogyo became available. These included venture capitalists as well as strategic investors. In 1996 MCT invited a number of financial investors as well as a number of strategic investors to purchase 1,000 newly issued shares. Nissei Life Insurance, Sanwa Bank, Shin-Nippon Shoken, MVC, Hikari Tsushin, Kan Design, Asahi Life Insurance, and Nissho Inter Life all invested.

Two of the investors, MVC and Hikari Tsushin, were true venture capital firms modeled after their U.S. counterparts. MVC had been created in November 1996 as a subsidiary of the Japanese trading house Mitsui Corporation. (See **Exhibit 15** for an overview of MVC.) Its president, Hitoshi Suga, HBS 1985, had raised a ¥2.1 billion fund ($16.8 million) to invest primarily in high-technology and high growth companies. Mr. Suga stated:

> MCT was one of our first investments and I think it will be a very successful one. The deal came to us through our parent company that is affiliated with TokyoTelemessage. The management team is very strong. And they have learned how to play as a team. As an investor we are fortunate that the company had already been around for a while before we invested. This company will not fall apart because of chemistry problems.

In 1998 Inoue decided it was finally time to implement a plan he had been thinking about for quite some time: giving key employees the opportunity to participate in MCT's success through stock. He was not sure, however, how much equity to allocate to employees, or how it should be awarded. Employees could receive options or could simply be allowed to buy equity at an attractive valuation. Inoue wasn't sure which method was best.

EXHIBIT 14 Details of Share Ownership (000 US$)

Source: MCT.

	1990	1991	1992	1993	1994	1995	1996	1997	1998F	1999F	2000F	2001F	2002F	2003F
No. of shares	200	800	1,000	1,000	1,000	1,200	2,200	3,800	5,000	5,000	5,000	9,600	9,600	9,600
Paid in capital	80	320	400	400	400	480	880	920	1,440	1,440	1,440	3,840	3,840	3,840
Ownership (%)														
Inoue	100	50	40	40	40	33	30	57	56	56	56	45	45	45
Taiyo Kogyo G.	—	50	60	60	60	67	52	30	23	23	23	12	12	12
MVC Corp.	—	—	—	—	—	—	—	3	4	4	4	2	2	2
Nissei Capital	—	—	—	—	—	—	5	3	4	4	4	2	2	2
Nihon Saiken Bank Capital	—	—	—	—	—	—	—	—	2	2	2	1	1	1
Sanwa Capital	—	—	—	—	—	—	2	1	1	1	1	1	1	1
Shinnihon Finance	—	—	—	—	—	—	2	1	1	1	1	1	1	1
Asahi Seimei Capital	—	—	—	—	—	—	—	1	1	1	1	1	1	1
Nissho Inter Life	—	—	—	—	—	—	2	1	1	1	1	1	1	1
Hikari Tsushin	—	—	—	—	—	—	2	1	1	1	1	1	1	1
Kan Design	—	—	—	—	—	—	2	1	1	1	1	1	1	1
Others	—	—	—	—	—	—	3	2	5	5	5	32	32	32

EXHIBIT 15
MVC (Mitsui Venture Capital) Corporation

Source: Casewriter interviews.

MVC Corporation

MVC Corporation is Mitsui Group's newly-established global venture capital/private equity investment arm based in Tokyo, Japan, which is 62% owned by Mitsui & Co., Ltd., a giant Japanese trading company, and 38% owned by 11 other Mitsui Group companies including Sakura Bank, Toshiba, Mitsui Fire & Marine Casualties Insurance, Mitsukoshi Department Stores, etc. MVC Corp.'s total paid-in-capital is 450 million yen (US $3.6 million) and its initial venture capital fund under management in the form of Japanese Investment Partnership is 2.0 billion yen (US $16 million) with about 230 million yen (US $1.86 million) already invested in eight companies since April 1998. Its investors include not only Mitsui group companies but other well-known companies such as Suntory, Bridgestone, Nippon Life Insurance, Nihon Tobacco, Ssang Yong Group (Korea through its Japanese subsidiary), Nihon Soda, JAFCO, and Yamaichi Finance.

MVC focuses its investment in such areas as financial services, health care, retail and service, and information technologies. Its geographic coverage is diverse, given its parent company's extensive global presence with more than 170 offices worldwide, but investments are made mostly in North America (50%), Singapore (20%), Japan (20%), and Europe (10%), and are subject to review every three months.

Hitoshi Suga: President and Chief Executive Officer of MVC Corporation

Mr. Suga presently served as president and chief executive officer of MVC Corporation. Born in Tokyo in 1952, Mr. Suga obtained his BA from the School of Political Science and Economics, Waseda University, Tokyo and an MBA from Harvard Business School. He joined Mitsui & Co., Ltd. in 1976 and worked in the area of feed materials business both in Tokyo and Osaka for seven years followed by his successful completion of Harvard's MBA program in 1985 under Mitsui's sponsorship.

Since his graduation, he has worked in various private equity departments of the Corporate Planning Divisions of Mitsui, both in New York and Tokyo, being responsible for successfully initiating, negotiating and closing its first U.S. venture capital participation, LBO finances, and extensive cross-border mergers and acquisitions for Mitsui and its clients totaling more than $900 million as sub-manager, assistant manager, manager, and assistant general manager respectively over the last 11 years.

As executive vice president of MCD Capital Corporation, Mitsui's private equity investment vehicle in Delaware, U.S., Mr. Suga made MCD participate at private equity investment funds in India and the Philippines, to both of which Mitsui sends its regional general mangers as fund advisors. Mr. Suga now lives in Setagaya, Tokyo, and is married with two children.

Inoue estimated that MCT would need only modest additional financing before its planned IPO in early 2001. However, he was well aware of the fact that his revenue projections were somewhat ambitious. If these projections did not come true, an additional infusion of cash might be necessary. Borrowing in Japan was proving extremely difficult, so any significant expansion would almost certainly have to be financed through equity.

In 1998, Inoue wanted to raise roughly ¥50 million to meet short term capital needs. Due to the banking crisis in Japan, it had proved impossible to borrow even such a modest amount from Japanese banks. Inoue spoke with foreign banks but found that they were limiting their activities to loans above ¥10 billion as they lacked the personnel and local expertise to evaluate and offer small business loans. Inoue even turned to Citibank, one of the few banks that offered small loans of any kind, but was told that they only offered consumer loans. Inoue knew he might have to turn to VC investors for the needed funds.

Organizing Growth and Keeping the Firm Together

In 1996 MCT had 26 employees, of which 16 were regular employees and 10 were long term contract workers. Contract workers were a rather common phenomenon in Japan. Particularly in smaller firms, contract workers were beneficial since they represented a flexible labor pool that did not require large pension contributions. Most of MCT's operations were based in the Aoyama district of Tokyo. But MCT had opened an office with 4 engineers in Nagoya, two hours by train from Tokyo. The office in Nagoya was scheduled to grow to 10 employees over the next years. It focused on development of new cellular telephone software (CDMA technology). Thus, Inoue needed to manage not only an increasing number of employees but also two geographically separate sites.

Eventually, Inoue wanted to establish a U.S. subsidiary as well. This would help gain access to U.S. expertise as well as potentially generating overseas sales—currently MCT's sales were exclusively in Japan. Inoue believed that it was feasible to set up a U.S. subsidiary, but knew that doing so would require a great deal of personal attention. He explained:

> Twenty-six sounds like a small number but it is large when you try to manage everything yourself. Managing growth has been a very educational experience for me. I realized that I really had to delegate. At Motorola I grew a group from 0 to 300 employees but that was different. There was always a "net," somebody who could support you if you ran into trouble. That's different at MCT. During the first years our sales efforts did not work so well and I had to be heavily involved. Also, we did not have a chief engineer until 1995 and I had to be deeply involved in product development. Now that we have hired Yoshinori Watanabe as a director of sales and Takeshi Imai as chief engineer, I can focus more on building the MCT organization as a whole. And it is late enough for me to do that. So far, I did not have to fire anybody. Three people left MCT at their own discretion. But as we grow larger, there will invariably be more friction.

Employees and managers enjoyed the rather informal atmosphere at MCT. Watanabe stated, "This company is low on paperwork and that is great. At Fujitsu I did 30% of the work I do here, but I spent the same amount of time at the office." And Syoshichi Fukuda, chairman, stated, "Many Japanese firms call themselves families. In many cases that's lip service, but we are a family." Most employees were motivated not only by the atmosphere among employees but also by MCT's growth prospects. It was as a result of informal discussions with employees and at the strong suggestion of venture capital investors that Inoue had ultimately decided to provide key employees with some form of equity incentive. Inoue stated:

> I realized that employees who hold an equity stake in the company are much more motivated. Our real challenges at this point are sales and new product development, in that order. Over the first couple of years we did not do a very good job in sales. Of course, we had to build up goodwill. But maybe key employees did not try as hard as they could have. This should be different in the future.

MCT had set an ambitious plan of increasing revenues per employee by almost five times from 1996 to 2003. This increase was deemed possible partially through a higher component of outsourced goods and services but also through stronger and more focused sales efforts.

Building MCT's organization also meant recruiting the right people. As Inoue had almost used up his network of Motorola and Hitachi contacts to recruit new employees, he now had to go to the open job market. And that was difficult because potential employees did not know MCT and because they had to fit into the MCT culture. Inoue stated:

"It's hard to find experienced managers who can think in small company terms." MCT's financial controller had left in late 1997 because the transition from his former employer to MCT was difficult for him. It had taken MCT several months to find and hire Kazuya Myakawa, an experienced professional.

Finally, building MCT also meant delegation of day-to-day operations. Inoue reasoned: "I have to make myself more replaceable; when we go public the stock market will value the fact that this company is not just dependent on one person."

An IPO in 2001?

Inoue hoped to take MCT public in 2001. He felt that in an industry as dynamic as mobile communications MCT could only succeed if employees were exceptionally motivated and focused. And stock ownership in a successful, publicly listed firm was clearly attractive to employees. And the market was clearly interested in companies like MCT. There were relatively few independent companies in Japan and only some of them were suitable for an IPO (**Exhibit 16**). Already, Inoue had been invited to present his company to three investment banks: Nomura, ShinNippon, and Merrill-Lynch. The response from bankers had been favorable. However, as Inoue thought about an IPO, a number of questions remained. When was the best time for an IPO? Clearly it was too early at this point. MCT was just beginning to book substantial orders. But was it too early to think about positioning the company the right way? Was the firm's strategy appropriate? Should management focus on earnings rather than growth or vice versa?

At first, Inoue had assumed that he would list on the Tokyo over-the-counter (OTC) market, which had been developed for small Japanese companies. However, some investment bankers had also mentioned the possibility of an IPO in the United States on

EXHIBIT 16   **Types of Enterprise in Japan**

Source: *Survey of Business Activity of Small and Medium Enterprises.* December 1996. Tokyo: Small and Medium Enterprise Agency, p. 126.

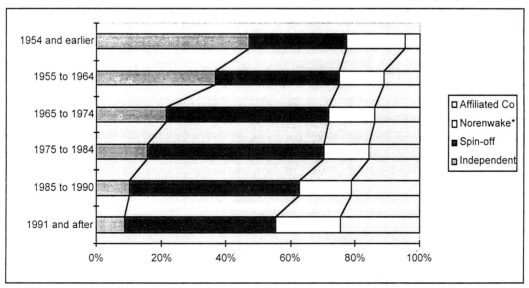

Note: Norenwake type (in which the entrepreneur parts company with his existing employer and sets up an independent business of the same type with his previous employer's blessing).

EXHIBIT 17 **General Japanese IPO Requirements**

Source: Morgan Stanley Dean Witter document compiled on January 10, 1998.

	TSE Second Section Listing	OTC Registration
Shares outstanding: (¥50 par value)	Over 4 million shares (for ¥50,000 face value shares: 4,000 shares) at latest year-end	Over 2 million shares (for ¥50,000 face value shares: 2,000 shares) at registration date and the average of 1 million shares (for ¥50,000 face value shares: 1,000 shares) during latest fiscal year
Number of shareholders:	Over 800–3,000 at listing date depending on the number of shares outstanding	Over 200 at registration date[3]
Distribution of shares:	10 largest shareholders, directors and special interest parties hold less than 80% at listing date and expected to be less than 75% at the first year end after the listing	(No criteria)
Years since incorporation:	Over 3 years	(No criteria)
Earnings before taxes:[1]	During the latest 3 years: Year 1 over ¥100 million Year 2 over ¥100 million Year 3 over ¥400 million	
Earnings per share:[1]	Over ¥15 (for ¥50,000 face value shares; ¥15,000) for Year 1 to Year 3 based on the average number of shares outstanding, over ¥20 (for ¥50,000 face value shares; ¥20,000) for Year 3 based on the number of shares at the fiscal year-end	Over ¥10 (for ¥50,000 face value shares: ¥10,000) for the latest year based on the average number of shares outstanding[4]
Net assets:	Over ¥1 billion and over ¥100 (for ¥50,000 face value shares; ¥100,000) per share at latest year-end	Over ¥200 million at latest year-end
Dividends:	Dividends paid during the latest year and expected to be over ¥5 (for ¥50,000 face values shares, ¥5,000) per share after listing	(No criteria)
Audited financial statements[2]	Unqualified statements for the latest year and auditor's report for the latest 3 years	Unqualified statements for the latest year and auditor's report for the latest 2 years
Share transfer:	Prohibited during the latest 2 years except for those in permitted forms	Prohibited during the latest 2 years except for those in permitted forms
Third party allotment:	Prohibited during the latest year and restricted during the year preceding the latest year	Prohibited during the latest 6 months and restricted during the 18 months preceding the latest 6 months
Form of Share Certificates:	In conformance with TSE requirements	In conformation with JSDA[5] requirements
Shareholder service agent	Approved by TSE	Located in an area designated by JSDA
Unit Share System[6]	Compliance required	Compliance required
Advertising:	Required in daily publication	Required in daily publication
Mergers and Acquisitions of Major Business Lines:	Prohibited during the latest year	Prohibited during the latest year
Other:		Not listed on any stock exchange At least 2 managing securities firms
Application submitted by:	Company	JSDA
Submitted to:	TSE	1. Managing securities firms 2. JSDA
Inspection:	TSE	JSDA
Final approval:	Minister of Finance	

Notes:

[1]"Earnings;" defined as the lower of "current profit" and "net income before taxes."

[2]Audit under Securities Exchange Law required.

[3]Over 400 at registration date for a company with over 20 million shares outstanding.

[4]Not required for a company designated by JSDA as essential for the growth of the national economy.

[5]Japan Securities Dealers Association.

[6]A system in which one unit equals the number of shares representing ¥50,000 in par value. For example, if a share has a ¥50 par value, 1,000 shares comprise one unit and if a share has a ¥500 par value, 100 shares comprise one unit.

EXHIBIT 18 NASDAQ Listing Requirements

Source: Compiled from NASDAQ website www.nasdaq.com/about/FeeStruc.stm and www.nasdaq.com/about/nmml.stm and www.nasdaq.com/about/scm.stm accessed on 9/30/98.

| | NASDAQ/National Market | | | | | NASDAQ/SmallCap Market | |
| | Initial Listing | | | Continued Listing[2] | | | |
	Alternative 1	Alternative 2	Alternative 3	Alternative 1&2	Alternative 3	Initial	Continued
Net Tangible Assets[1]	$6MM	$18MM		$4MM		$4MM	$2MM
Market Capitalization[3]			$75MM		—$50MM	or $50MM	or $35MM
Total Assets			$75MM		—$50MM	or	or
Net Income						$750,000	$500,000
Total Revenue			$75MM		—$50MM	—	—
Pre-tax Income (last fiscal year or 2 of last 3 fiscal years)	$1MM					—	—
Public Float[4]	1.1MM	1.1MM	1.1MM	750,000	1.1MM	1MM	500,000
Operating History		2 Years				1 year[6]	
Market Value of Public Float	$8MM	$18MM	$20MM	$5MM	$15MM	$5MM	$1MM
Minimum Bid Price	$5	$5	$5	$1	$5	$4	$1
Shareholders (round of lot holders)[5]	400	400	400	400	400	300	300
Market Makers	3	3	4	2	4	3	2

Note:
[1] Net tangible assets means total assets (excluding goodwill) less total liabilities.
[2] The numbers of initial listing alternatives corresponds to the numbers of continued listing alternatives.
[3] For initial or continued listing under option 3, a company must satisfy one of the following to be in compliance; the market capitalization requirement or the total assets and the total revenue.
[4] Public float is defined as shares that are not held directly or indirectly by any officer or director of the issuer and by any other person who is the beneficial owner of more than 10% of the total.
[5] Round lot holders are considered holders of 100 shares or more.
[6] If operating history is less than 1 year, initial listing requires market capitalization of at least $50 million.

EXHIBIT 19 **Japan's OTC Market: Problems and Prospects**

Source: Sakurada, Koichi, and Thierry Porte. 1998. *Japan's Over-the-Counter Market: Problems and Prospects* (paper prepared for "Symposium on Building the Financial System of the 21st Century—an Agenda for Japan and the United States"). Tokyo: Morgan Stanley Dean Witter, pp. 26–27.

Introduction

The Japanese over-the-counter ("OTC") stock market is currently suffering from a lack of liquidity and low valuation. By every measure—as witnessed in **Exhibit 20**—the OTC market is outpaced by its U.S. counterpart, NASDAQ. The OTC market in Japan does not provide an effective outlet for growth-oriented new ventures, technology or otherwise. Indeed, the OTC is dominated by non-bank financial, retail, wholesale, and other service companies that are often offshoots of established corporations (**Exhibit 21**).

The Japan Securities Dealers Association ("JSDA") recognizes these problems and has proposed a series of measures to reinvigorate the OTC market. However, while moving in the right direction, fundamental change in all aspects of listing and trading OTC stocks is needed.

Shortcomings of the OTC Market

There is a long list of shortcomings in the functioning of the OTC market. Among the most serious issues are the following:

Market Making: There are currently no active market makers for most ITC stocks, due largely to a shortage of experienced traders at Japanese brokers, and limited profit-making opportunities, resulting from the limit on daily price changes. Liquidity is available only through a broker's broker, Japan OTC Securities. The JSDA publishes price quotations twice weekly.

Quality of Companies: To stay ahead of competitors, Japanese securities companies have tried to retain as many companies as possible for which they can serve as "lead manager." Subsequently, they have tended to take companies public on the OTC market without thorough due diligence.

Types of Companies: The Japanese OTC market does not, counter-intuitively, contain many growth-type businesses such as technology and health care; rather, the majority of OTC companies are stable owner-founder type businesses such as retail and consumer finance companies. Many large-cap businesses are either taken public directly on the TSE, or just use OTC as a steppingstone for TSE listing.

Net Profit Requirements: OTC registration rules require positive earnings of at least ¥10 per share for companies going public. As a result, venture firms are effectively blocked from the market. The recent JSDA proposals to revitalize the market propose easing this requirement.

Ownership Structure: Due to auction pricing and allocation limitation rules—which were abolished in September 1997—distribution of OTC shares had been heavily skewed toward retail investors. Under the old rules, 50% of IPO shares had to be sold through auction; then the weighted average price in that auction would be the fixed offering price for the remaining half of the offered shares, with a maximum allocation of 5,000 shares to each beneficial owner. The OTC has also been regarded as an easier market for Japanese and foreign companies' subsidiary IPO's, because of the less strict rules of OTC registration compared to those of the TSE. These two factors have made the ownership structure of OTC shares divergent from the normal model.

Lack of Institutional Investors: Because of this ownership structure, there is little participation by institutional investors in OTC IPOs. Even in the secondary market, many Japanese institutional investors still have internal investment criteria that preclude the holding of OTC stocks. No index of the Japanese OTC market is traded on the exchange.

JSDA Proposals to Bolster the OTC Market: The JSDA has just started discussions on ways to activate the Japanese OTC market, for implementation by the end of 1998. The topics are reported to include:
- The creation of an OTC 1st Section, which will contain only issues with adequate liquidity;
- The introduction of a trading system with active market makers;
- Changes in OTC registration rules to accept a wider variety of companies;
- Stricter standards for "de-registration" of OTC companies; and
- Encouragement of companies' quarterly financial reporting and timely disclosure.

Further Action Needed

Although the JSDA's proposals are a step in the right direction, further action is needed. With only one-seventh the number of companies registered on NASDAQ, and only one-hundredth the amount of daily turnover (**Exhibit 22**), the Japanese OTC must take bold and dramatic steps to change the position and psychology of the market.

(continued)

EXHIBIT 19 (Continued)

Multiple Market Maker Structure: A stock needs to be traded by multiple active market makers to create a deep market and to produce fair valuation. A company listed on NASDAQ is traded by an average of ten market makers. Co-managers of each IPO may have to be forced to provide active secondary market-making at least for a certain period.

Institution Holdings: Institutional investors' support is critical for both IPO's and secondary market trading. Japanese institutions have to be educated for their own valuation and trading skills of OTC shares. Japanese brokers' IPO allocation policy will also have to change toward a more institution-only oriented approach.

Research Analysts: To stimulate growth in the OTC market, it is imperative that both sell-side and buy-side research analysts focus and deepen their knowledge to be able to produce improved research material.

Due Diligence: Japanese lead managers' bankers have to improve their diligence capability and establish higher professional standards in underwriting judgment. Analysts, lawyers, and accountants should assist in this process.

Disclosure: Honest, transparent, and timely disclosure is a prerequisite for a healthy equity market. Accounting standards closer to global standards, with consolidation and marking-to-the-market, should be deployed in Japan as soon as possible. A bolder proposal would be to have disclosure in English as well as Japanese. With almost 14% of OTC stocks currently held by foreigners, this does not seem an unreasonable request. Note that the Neuer Market in Germany requires English and German disclosure.

EXHIBIT 20 Comparison of Japanese OTC and other Equity Markets

Source: Sakurada, Koichi, and Thierry Porte. 1998. Op.cit. Exhibit 1.

	Japanese OTC	TSE[1]	NASDAQ[2]	NYSE	EASDAQ
Number of companies	835[5]	1,813[5]	5,400[5]	3,080[6]	26
Market value (US$ BN)[3]	68[7]	2,101[5]	2,214[5]	10,792[5]	12
Average daily trading volume (US$ MM)[3] [4] [5]	865	2,590	11,176[9]	30,975	0.48
Number of IPOs in 1998 to date[5]	10	5	122	20	4
Average price/earnings ratio[5] [8]	22.2	57.2 (1st Sec.) 37.9 (2nd Sec.)	71.8	38.0	n.a.

Notes:
[1] Including 1st and 2nd Sections
[2] Including National Markets and Small Cap
[3] $1 = ¥140
[4] Over a period of 1 month
[5] As of 4/30/98
[6] As of 5/31/98
[7] As of 3/31/98
[8] Based on actual earnings
[9] After adjustments to avoid double counting

NASDAQ. Paul Slawson, an American banker with Morgan Stanley Dean Witter in Tokyo explained:

> MCT is clearly on to something with regards to its RF technology for the upcoming W-CDMA standard. The market for MCT's products is potentially huge and spans not only cell phones but a variety of electronic devices—and sales could occur not only in Japan but abroad as well. My gut is that MCT will do better on the NASDAQ than in Japan. The U.S. market better understands this type of growth story. We clearly need to look at MCT's numbers to get a better sense of whether there is enough meat there to list the company and provide sufficient float. In general, however, I am sanguine about the opportunity.

EXHIBIT 21 Japanese OTC Market—Five Largest Industry Groups in TSE 1st Section and OTC

Source: Sakurada, Koichi, and Thierry Porte. 1998. Op.cit. Exhibit 2.

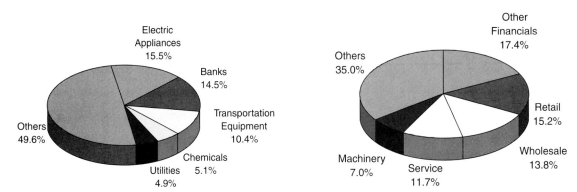

TSE Ist Section

OTC

EXHIBIT 22 Japanese OTC Market—Trading Volume, 1990–1998 YTD

Source: Sakurada, Koichi, and Thierry Porte. 1998. Op.cit. Exhibit 3.

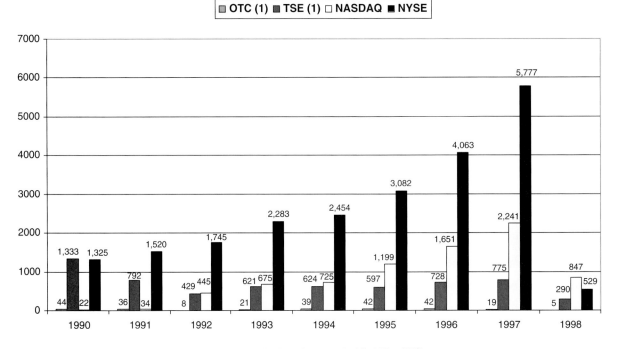

Numbers represent value of domestic and foreign shares traded (in billion US$)

Note: (1) Exchange Rate used for conversion: ¥140/US$.

Inoue had recently received a comparison of requirements for going public on the OTC in Tokyo and NASDAQ (see **Exhibits 17** through **22**). NASDAQ would give MCT a high level of visibility in the U.S., the world's most competitive telecommunications market, and potentially offered more liquidity than the OTC market in Tokyo. But, although 16 Japanese firms were listed on NASDAQ, no Japanese firm had ever done its IPO there. The NASDAQ also had stricter requirements for listing. Would MCT fulfill

EXHIBIT 23   **Financial Data On Japanese Telecommunications Companies, USD mils**

Source: OneSource Business Browser, Bloomberg.

Firm	FYE March 31 1998 Sales	FYE March 31 1998 Net Inc	1997 Sales	1997 Net Inc	6/15/98 Price	6/15/98 P/E	Yen/US$ 6/15/98 Exch. Rate	Yen 6/15/98 Price
DDI Corp	9,556.4	67.4	8,996.0	−231.5	3,079.2	39.995	146.14	450,000
Japan TeleCom	3,339.4	65.8	3,326.6	225.2	7,869.2	31.457		1,150,000
Kokusai Denshin Denwa*	2,959.0	40.0	3,551.1	113.8	32.2	33.840		4,700
Nippon Broadcasting System	889.4	29.3	1,025.4	44.5	39.5	25.090		5,770
Nippon Telegraph & Telephone**	76,639.6	2,350.8	82,091.0	1,326.2	6,979.6	98.190		1,020,000
NTT Data Corp	5,487.1	126.6	5,413.2	126.0	3,181.9	75.560		465,000

Note: Tokyo Telemessage Inc. (an MCT customer) is privately held.
Official name:
* KDD Co Ltd
** NTT Corp.

the criteria? If not at this point, what could be done? What companies on NASDAQ were comparable to MCT? Inoue made a note to push the U.S. investment bankers who kept calling him on this question. In the meantime he had prepared a short table with data on Japan's leading telecommunications providers (**Exhibit 23**).

Turning Back to Strategy

Before leaving the office on this Friday evening, Inoue stopped by the office of Takeshi Imai. Imai said:

> CDMA is increasingly likely as the next standard in cellular phones, and we are well positioned to grab a large share of the pie created by this technology in Japan. You know, I am not sure to what degree we should push our Internet software business. It's a nice source of revenue, but how much does this really contribute to the advancement of our position in paging and cellular systems?

"In some ways you are right," Inoue replied, "But the cellular business is not off the ground yet and I do not want to run out of cash. In any case, our challenge is to convert the work we have done over the last couple of years into actual revenues." As he walked out into the muggy June weather, Inoue made a mental note to examine once more his business forecasts until 2003. Maybe these forecasts were too low?

Case 17

Capital Alliance Private Equity: Creating a Private Equity Leader in Nigeria

Okey Enelamah, HBS MBA '94, and Dick Kramer, HBS MBA '58, CEO and Chairman, respectively, of Capital Alliance Private Equity (CAPE),[1] looked at each other across the small conference table in their office. It was a pleasant day in tropical Lagos,[2] where the weather changed very little over the course of the year. Outside of the conference room were several empty desks, testimony to CAPE's hopes for growth over the coming years. Kramer looked out of the window at the Lagos skyline for a moment before turning back to his younger partner. "So, Okey, what do you think?" Kramer and Enelamah had just reviewed the latest news from GS Telecom (GST). GST was a small firm within Nigeria's nascent telecommunications market and was a candidate to become CAPE's first equity investment. It was Friday, November 20, 1998, and Steve Chapman, GST's managing director, had just called with news that GST had been slightly less profitable in the first quarter of 1998 than had previously been estimated. (See **Exhibits 1A–C** for GST's summary financial statements and projections.) GST's low level of financial and accounting control had been a concern in the early stages of the deal. While the latest adjustments were modest and did not materially affect the assessment of GST's long-term

---

[1] Capital Alliance Private Equity is technically the name of the private equity fund. The investment firm (fund manager) is called African Capital Alliance, offshore and Capital Alliance Nigeria (CAN), in Nigeria.

[2] Although the official capital of Nigeria was changed from Lagos to Abuja in 1991, Lagos remained the dominant economic center of the country.

Charles M. Williams Fellow Chad Ellis, MBA '98 and Dean's Fellow William J. Coughlin, MBA '99 prepared this case under the supervision of Professor Walter Kuemmerle as the basis for class discussion rather than to illustrate either effective or ineffective handling of an administrative situation.

EXHIBIT 1 GST Financial Statements and Projections

Source: CAPE.

EXHIBIT 1A Summary Income Statements ($000)

	Actual		Projected		
	1996	**1997**	**1998**	**1999**	**2000**
Turnover	5,819	5,197	9,591	17,503	25,800
% Growth	*15.2%*	*−10.7%*	*84.5%*	*82.5%*	*47.4%*
Gross profit	2,132	2,619	3,462	5,846	8,173
Gross profit margin	*36.6%*	*50.4%*	*36.1%*	*33.4%*	*31.7%*
PBITD	884	508	1,214	2,601	4,128
PBITD margin	*15.2%*	*9.8%*	*12.7%*	*14.9%*	*16.0%*
PBIT	800	368	1,025	2,179	3,535
PBIT margin	*13.7%*	*7.1%*	*10.7%*	*12.4%*	*13.7%*
Tax	133	125	210	272	354
Profit after tax	667	243	815	1,907	3,182
Profit after tax margin	*11.5%*	*4.7%*	*8.5%*	*10.9%*	*12.3%*

Note: While the regular corporate income tax rate in Nigeria was 34%, GST's effective tax rate was considerably lower at times because the company conducted part of its business off-shore and was tax-exempt for these revenues.

EXHIBIT 1B Summary Balance Sheet ($000s)

	Actual December 31, 1997	Projected December 31, 1998
Capital Employed		
Shareholders' equity	1,425	4,500
Shareholders' loans	—	500
	1,425	5,000
Employment of Capital		
Fixed assets	475	1,036
Goodwill	—	809
Net current assets	950	3,155
Current assets	2,149	4,153
Stock	160	368
Accounts receivable	1,550	1,971
Other debtors	210	192
Cash/bank	229	1,622
Current liabilities	1,199	998
Creditors	1,169	788
Taxation	30	210
	1,425	5,000

future, it was yet another reminder that GST's books were not really in order. The two partners knew they would have to consider whether and how this latest surprise should change their thinking on GST as a potential portfolio investment.

GST, founded by Chapman and John Neville, had been operating in Nigeria for four years, was profitable, had established some valuable customer relationships and seemed well positioned to thrive in Nigeria's uncertain telecom environment. Moreover, it seemed like an ideal opportunity for a private equity firm to establish a value-adding partnership with an entrepreneurial firm. CAPE offered financial expertise and discipline, along with an extensive network of contacts in Nigeria, both of which would be quite valuable to the

EXHIBIT 1   (Continued)

EXHIBIT 1C   Forecast Financial Performance ($000s)

Year End December 31,	1999	2000	2001	2002	2003
Turnover	17,503	25,800	31,000	37,200	44,640
% Growth	*82.5%*	*47.4%*	*20.2%*	*20.0%*	*20.0%*
PBITD	2,601	4,128	4,650	5,580	6,696
% of Revenue	*14.9%*	*16.0%*	*15.0%*	*15.0%*	*15.0%*
Depreciation	423	593	799	1,047	1,345
PBIT	2,179	3,535	3,852	4,535	5,353
% Margin	*12.4%*	*13.7%*	*12.4%*	*12.2%*	*12.0%*
PAT	1,907	3,182	3,369	3,966	4,682
% Margin	*10.9%*	*12.2%*	*10.9%*	*10.7%*	*10.5%*
Income Statement Extracts:					
PBIT	2,179	3,535	3,852	4,535	5,353
Interest charge	53	50	45	37	26
PAT	1,907	3,182	3,369	3,966	4,682
Balance Sheet Extracts:					
Equity	6,823	9,894	13,186	17,161	21,783
Interest bearing loans	475	425	350	250	0
Cash balance (after payment of interest)	332	1,432	4,035	6,527	9,529
Working capital cycle (days of turnover)[a]	58	58	58	58	58
Stock (days of turnover)	13	13	13	13	13
Debtors (days of turnover)	75	75	75	75	75
Creditors (days of turnover)	30	30	30	30	30
Capex	2,000	1,020	1,240	1,488	1,786

[a]Excluding cash.

entrepreneurs at GST. Enelamah and Kramer also knew that GST was in serious need of equity capital and was unlikely to find many alternative sources, which should strengthen CAPE's negotiating position. Enelamah and Kramer realized, however, that this deal was of particular importance for CAPE as it represented the fund's first investment in a country where the concept of closed private equity funds was virtually unknown.

CAPE had already done substantial due diligence work on the company, and Enelamah and Kramer believed that GST's founders had the qualities CAPE was looking for in portfolio company management. (See **Exhibit 2** for a summary of CAPE's investment criteria.) Moreover, while GST's exact financials were in doubt due to lax controls and complex accounting requirements, the due diligence had provided a fairly high degree of confidence in the underlying projections of revenue and direct and operating costs. At this point, it was the financial details that were under question rather than the fundamental cash flows of the business.

There were, however, still some other underlying concerns about the business itself. GST had suffered a considerable level of staff turnover, both among middle management and newly trained engineers, which had contributed to a decline in profitability in 1997. Some steps had been taken to improve the situation, but it remained a problem. GST was also highly dependent on Nitel, the Nigerian public telecom monopoly, whose possible privatization represented a significant unknown factor in GST's future. Finally, although GST planned to benefit from hoped for deregulation in Nigeria's telecom market, and the growth expected as a result, Enelamah and Kramer knew that GST could also prove vulnerable if the market changed in a direction it did not anticipate.

EXHIBIT 2
CAPE Investment
Criteria

Source: CAPE.

- Strong and capable management committed to outstanding success and significantly invested relative to their net worth.
- Control or significant minority ownership with strong governance rights (range: 20% → >50%).
- Target investment size of under USD 5 million per investment (aim for USD 2 million on average per investment).
- Complete 3–5 investments per year.
- Investments that can achieve 30%–40% IRR in U.S. dollar terms, using conservative assumptions.
- Businesses that can achieve a leadership position in their respective niches.
- Pre-identified liquidity and exit strategies for each investment.

Investing in private equity would be more complicated in Nigeria than it was in most of the developed world. Many of the institutions, networks and legal and social customs that facilitated deal flow, negotiations and exit strategies in Boston, Silicon Valley or London did not exist in Lagos. Although proud of the team of domestic advisors and investors they had assembled, CAPE would eventually need to attract foreign capital as well. To do so, CAPE would need to establish a track record of successful investments and create sustainable deal flow. Enelamah and Kramer knew that the longer term future of CAPE would be heavily influenced by their early decisions, and that few would be more important than choosing which early bets to make with the fund's capital.

Nigeria

Overview and Political Environment

Located in Western Africa (see **Exhibit 3** for maps of Nigeria and Africa), Nigeria had the largest population in Africa (estimated 1998 population of approximately 110 to 120 million people). The country was composed of about 250 ethnic groups, making it one of the world's most ethnically diverse societies. The three main ethnic groups (Hausa-Fulani, Yoruba, and Ibo), together with the six next largest groups, comprised approximately 80% of the country's population. This ethnic diversity led to internal conflict and contributed to considerable political instability since Nigeria's independence from Britain in 1960. After a bloody civil war with an estimated 1 million deaths in the late 1960s, the 1970s and 1980s saw a succession of military coups interrupted by one brief period of civilian rule. In the 1990s it became increasingly clear to the military rulers, however, that a return to civilian rule was necessary to lead Nigeria out of its deep crisis. In June 1998 the military ruler, General Abdulsalami Abubakar announced a new democratization program and free elections with the goal of ending military rule by May 1999. (See **Exhibit 4** for a summary of Nigeria's political development.) Despite the more promising political situation, allegations of irregularities resurfaced at the end of 1998 during voter registration in October sending signals that politicians might not have learned lessons from the turbulent past. Ethnic discontent in the oil-producing Niger Delta exploded into violent unrest, which cut crude output by 28%. The tragic death of more than 700 villagers in a fuel pipeline explosion added to tension in the region.

Economic Environment

Nigeria was a country of profound economic contrasts, which resulted from weak institutions and inadequate economic policies. Expensive Italian sports cars were a common sight in certain neighborhoods of Lagos. At the same time, rush hour witnessed millions

EXHIBIT 3 Maps of Nigeria and Africa.

Source: 1997 Facts on File, Inc.

Nigeria

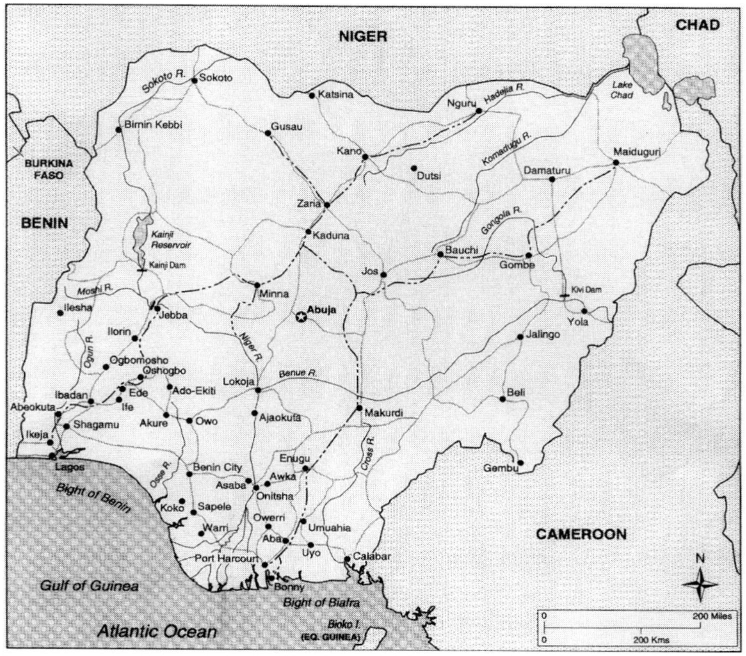

Africa

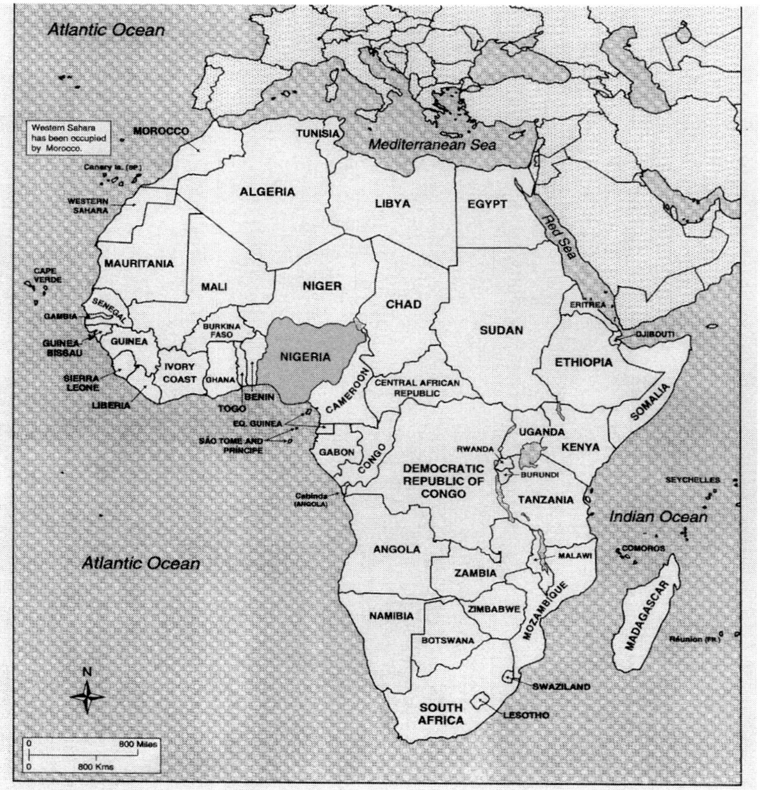

EXHIBIT 4 Nigeria's Political Development since Independence

Source: Compiled from *EIU Country Profile Nigeria.* London: Economist Intelligence Unit, 1999, pp. 4–6.

1960	Independence from Great Britain
1967	Military governor of Nigeria's eastern region declares independent Republic of Biafra. Resulting civil war lasts almost 3 years with over 1 million casualties.
1970–1985	Series of military coups (interrupted by period of civilian rule from 1979 to 1983). Considerable political instability. Principle causes of instability: – Disputes over allocation of Nigeria's rapidly growing oil revenues – Persistent demand for greater autonomy of regions – Growing power of military forces
August 1985	General Babangida assumes power in bloodless coup.
1986	IMF-style structural adjustment program launched. Babangida announces that Nigeria will return to civilian rule by October 1990.
1989	Return to civilian rule postponed to 1992. Administration's credibility undermined. Mounting unrest.
June 1993	Babangida annuls June 1993 presidential election when Chief Abiola, a businessman from the southwest, seems poised for victory.
August 1993	Babangida surrenders power under mounting pressure. Interim government takes office and promises new free elections for February 1994.
November 1993	Interim government is "encouraged" to resign by military forces. General Abacha assumes power.
June 1994	Chief Abiola proclaims himself president of Nigeria (one year after annulled elections). Abiola is arrested and detained. Street protests break out.
1994–1998	General Abacha relies increasingly on repression to engineer his own election as constitutional president.
June 1998	General Abacha dies from an apparent heart attack. General Abubakar takes office. He promises restoration of civilian rule by July 1999 and release of many political prisoners.
July 1998	Shortly before his release from prison, Chief Abiola also dies from an apparent heart attack. Anti-government demonstrations break out, but opposition politicians accept General Abacha's transition program.
November 1998	Voter registration for general elections.

of Nigerians making long commutes in overcrowded minibuses with bus drivers carefully navigating crater-like potholes in the streets. Over 95% of Nigeria's exports consisted of oil, yet there were often long lines at gas stations around the country.

In 1960, at the time of Nigeria's independence, agricultural exports accounted for more than 50% of GDP.[1] Over the years Nigeria had not succeeded in using its oil revenues to build a significant manufacturing and service sector. By 1997 its economy still relied mainly on agriculture (33% of GDP) and oil (37% of GDP). Oil revenue, controlled through the state-owned Nigerian National Petroleum Corporation, represented more than 66% of federal government revenue.[2] While foreign direct investment was high (4.3% of GDP) relative to some other African countries (for example, Ghana at 1.9%), the overwhelming part of this investment occurred by foreign companies investing in oil and gas exploration assets. (See **Exhibit 5** for macroeconomic data on Nigeria.) Thus, this investment did not lead to the development of indigenous manufacturing industries. Overall, Nigeria's oil revenues appeared to be far from a blessing. Adult literacy in 1997 stood at 53% (**Exhibit 5**) and was comparable to that of other African countries. Nigeria's underground economy accounted for 77% of Nigeria's official GDP, one of the world's highest percentages.[3]

[1] *EIU Country Profile Nigeria.* London: Economist Intelligence Unit, 1999, p. 17.

[2] *EIU Country Profile Nigeria.* London: Economist Intelligence Unit, 1999, p. 17.

[3] *The Statesman's Year-book.* 2004. 140th edition. New York: St. Martin's Press, p. 1233.

EXHIBIT 5 Comparative Economic Indicators (1997 unless otherwise indicated)

Source: Compiled from Economist Intelligence Unit data and from World Bank, *1999 World Development Indicators and 1998 Atlas.*

	Nigeria	Angola	Ghana	Côte d'Ivoire	South Africa	United States
Gross domestic product ($ billion)	37.5[a]	5.7	6.9	10.6	129.3	8,110.9
GDP per capita ($)	356	491	372	743	3,340	30,263
Consumer price inflation (%)	8.5	64.0	27.9	5.0	8.5	2.4
Foreign direct investment (% GDP 1996)	4.3	4.5	1.9	0.2	0.1	1.0
Net aid flows (% GDP 1996)	0.6	15.8	10.5	9.9	0.3	[b]
Electrical power						
Per capita (KwH 1996)	85	61	275	174	3,719	11,796
Production CAGR (% 1980–1996)	5.6	2.4	4.2	(0.1)	3.9	3.0
Paved roads (% total 1996)	18.8	25.0	24.1	9.7	41.5	60.8
Adult illiteracy (%)	43.0	58.0[c]	35.5[d]	59.9[d]	16.0	—
Life expectancy (years 1996)	53	46	59	54	65	77
Population (millions)	111.7	10.8	17.3	13.7	41.5	267.1
Population growth (% 1990–1996)	2.9	3.1	2.7	3.0	1.7	1.0
Telephone mainlines						
Per 1,000 people	4	5	6	9	107	644
In largest city (per 1,000 people)	—	—	28	40	415	—
Waiting list (000s)	98.1	—	28.3	82.4	116.0	NM
Waiting time (years)	4.2	—	1.5	6.3	0.4	0.0
Per employee	28	29	30	40	80	187
Revenue per line ($)	1,929	1,811	1,260	1,413	942	1,280
Cost of local call ($ per 3-minute call)	0.26	0.09	0.08	0.11	0.07	0.09
Outgoing international traffic (minute/subscriber)	121	351	208	282	88	134
Mobile telephones (per 1,000 people)	0	1	1	2	37	206

NM = Not meaningful.

[a] At the autonomous exchange rate (₦83.5:$1).

[b] Net aid donor.

[c] 1996.

[d] 1995.

EXHIBIT 5 (Continued) Economic Indicators

Source: Compiled from Economist Intelligence Unit data.

	1993	1994	1995	1996	1997
GDP at market prices (₦bn)	697.1	911.4	1,977.4	2,833.2	3,127.9
Real GDP growth (%)	2.3	1.3	2.2	3.3	3.8
Consumer price inflation (year-end %)	57.2	57.0	72.8	29.3	8.5
Current account ($ bn)	(0.78)	(2.13)	(3.12)	3.09	2.17
Total external debt ($ bn)	30.70	33.12	34.13	31.42	32.02
External debt-service ratio, paid (%)	12.5	17.9	14.8	12.9	13.0
Exchange rate (avg. ₦:$)[a]	22.07	22.00	82.3	81.0	83.5

[a]Autonomous rate. The official rate, applicable to selected government transactions, has remained at ₦21.9:$1.

Oil revenues were controlled by a small number of bureaucrats and managers. Lack of transparency and oversight led to squandering of foreign currency reserves. This occurred through direct bribes as well as through vast mismanagement. Investments into a domestic steel and petrochemical industry, for example, were not successful—one reason being that many of these new enterprises were state-controlled or state-owned and did not operate efficiently. There had also been periods of outright hostility to foreign business ownership. In 1977, for example, many foreign businesses were brought under local ownership. Although a partial liberalization of economic policy under General Abacha in 1995 contributed to some recovery, economic performance still fell short of expectations. Several governments had also accumulated large deficits, particularly in times when oil prices were low. (See **Exhibit 6** for a history of oil prices.) In order to fund these deficits, monetary expansion policies were put into place. This contributed to periods of high inflation. Inflation averaged 23% per year in the 1980s. It slowed down in 1990 and 1991, and shot up to 72.8% in 1995.[4] The yield of the Nigerian treasury bills had dropped from a high of 24.5% in December 1993 to 12.1% in September 1998. (See **Exhibit 7** for treasury bill and bond yields in Nigeria and the United States.)

Despite the fact that by 1998 the economic outlook had improved somewhat relative to 1995, there was considerable uncertainty regarding longer-term trends. Foreign and domestic investors were cautious. In 1997, gross fixed capital formation was concentrated in the oil industry and accounted for only 15% of GDP[5] (compared to approximately 20% in the G7 economies[6]).

Corruption

Coincident with the rise in political repression and centralization of power in the hands of the military elite came an increase in corruption, which reduced transparency in Nigerian business. In addition to the need for direct payments in order to compete for government-controlled contracts, businesses were vulnerable to tax "inspections" by task forces comprised of military personnel. One Nigerian businessman recalled an attempt:

> This task force arrived and demanded to audit our books on PAYE (pay as you earn). We showed them our books and our tax receipts, which were all in order and showed we were up to date. They then claimed that we owed something like $2 million. They wanted us to pay them a few hundred thousand to go away, but we took the risk and took them to court instead. It looked for a while like we might lose, but in the end they dropped it, presumably hoping to find people more willing to "do business" with them.

[4] *EIU Country Profile Nigeria.* London: Economist Intelligence Unit, 1999, p. 22.

[5] *EIU Country Profile Nigeria.* London: Economist Intelligence Unit, 1999, p. 18.

[6] Casewriter calculation based on data from IMF, *International Financial Statistics.* Accessed online at http://ifs.apdi.net/imf. Accessed on February 17, 2004.

EXHIBIT 6 Nigerian Oil Spot Prices

Sources: Platt's *Oil Price Handbook* and Oilmanac; Platt's *Oilgram Price Report*, Lexis-Nexis.

As of 12/31	1980	1981	1982	1983	1984	1985	1986	1987	1988	1989	1990	1991	1992	1993	1994	1995	1996	1997	1998
Bonny Light 37 API	37.00	36.50	30.23	28.80	27.25	27.28	15.83	16.49	15.44	19.95	28.85	18.89	18.69	14.14	16.09	18.60	24.50	15.50	9.85
Medium 25 API	35.73	35.20	29.43	28.70	27.15	27.10	15.81	16.35	15.17	19.60	27.86	18.60	18.40	13.93	15.92	18.58	24.45	N/A	N/A
Forcados 30 API	36.83	36.30	30.02	28.80	27.40	27.32	15.73	16.31	15.36	20.03	28.24	18.87	18.22	14.04	16.07	19.11	24.65	N/A	N/A
UK Brent 38 API	36.25	36.60	29.62	29.30	26.90	26.45	15.79	16.43	15.19	19.61	28.16	18.29	18.13	13.54	15.84	19.06	23.09	15.33	10.02

EXHIBIT 7 Treasury Bill and Bond Yields in Nigeria and the United States

Source: Datastream, *International Financial Statistics*. Bloomberg.

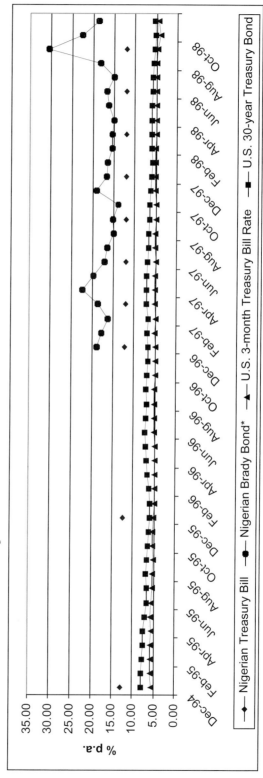

*The bond was issued by the Central Bank of Nigeria in January 1992. Coupon: 6.25%. Maturity: November 2020.

333

Capital Alliance Private Equity

Prior to 1998 the private equity market in Nigeria was virtually nonexistent. Although substantial wealth had accumulated within the hands of a small number of private individuals, this had not, for the most part, become a source of available capital for entrepreneurs. Kramer explained:

> There were several problems. Much of the wealth had been acquired illegitimately. This, and the lack of developed capital markets, meant that even people with money tended not to invest it in Nigeria. This, in turn, meant that there were few domestic projects worth investing in. Finally, when Nigerians have invested domestically it has tended to be with a very short-term focus, which doesn't lend itself to establishing healthy companies for the longer term.

To the extent that private equity was available at all in Nigeria, it tended to be on a small scale and solely between individuals. "A man might want to start a store," Enelamah explained, "so he would go to some contact that he or a family member had and ask for money. It was all very informal and unsophisticated, and limited to small ventures."

Kramer had first come to Nigeria in 1978 to establish Arthur Andersen's office there and had remained in the country since then. He had believed for some time that Nigeria needed to establish a more effective system for channeling its substantial wealth into long-term economic growth. Kramer and Enelamah met in 1988, when Enelamah came to work for Arthur Andersen in Nigeria. Enelamah then worked briefly for Arthur Andersen in London before beginning his MBA studies at Harvard in 1992. In 1993, Enelamah spent his summer working for Goldman Sachs in New York and London, and became interested in pursuing a career in private equity. Back at HBS he was introduced to Tom Barry, MBA '69, who was helping to form a private equity fund that would invest in South Africa. Enelamah went to work for Barry after graduation, raising funds for the South Africa Capital Growth Fund (SACGF) and getting involved in partnership negotiations with the other principals. Enelamah recalled:

> Tom offered me a good deal, with a decent salary and twenty per cent of the profits attributable to us, along with a promise to review the situation every six months. That meant that I had enough money to live on and a lot of potential upside and control over my own destiny. Tom was a good partner and mentor.

In August 1995 Enelamah moved to South Africa to focus on deal making in the media sector. Although excited about the opportunity to become more directly involved in SACGF's investments, he also had his concerns about the South African partners and their commitment to mentoring Enelamah. In April 1996, Kramer visited South Africa and met briefly with Enelamah to discuss the potential for a private equity fund in Nigeria. At the time Enelamah had no intentions of leaving SACGF, but later that year he had a small conflict with one of the fund partners and the two men talked again. He recalled:

> Dick is a big picture guy. His question was "How do you build an institution in Nigeria that will drive growth?" I knew that he was very good at adding value to businesses, and he had very strong connections in Nigeria and a great reputation. He had already lined up a strong team that could serve as a board of directors for a fund. They were all successful businessmen and represented all of Nigeria's major religious and ethnic groups, which meant the fund could count on a very broad network of contacts as it developed.

Kramer's team (see **Exhibit 8** for resumes of CAPE's managers and Board) consisted of a number of senior Nigerian business leaders who had developed a strong working friendship through their efforts to modernize Nigeria's economic and political systems.

EXHIBIT 8   Resumes of CAN Management and Board Members

Source: CAPE.

Richard Kramer, MBA (Harvard), CPA
Chairman, Executive Committee and Board of Directors
- American, graduate of Kansas University
- Founder and Principal of Strategic Research and Investments (Nigeria) Limited
- Founder and Managing Partner of Arthur Andersen Nigeria (1978–1994)
- Former Managing Partner of Arthur Andersen practices in Benelux and Argentina/Uruguay
- Pioneer Vice Chairman of the Nigerian Economic Summit Group and Technical Advisor for Vision 2010
- Taught at Lagos Business School (1991–1997) and Member of Board of Advisors
- CPA (State of Colorado) and Chartered Accountant (Nigeria)

Okechukwu Enelamah, MBA (Harvard), CFA
Chief Executive Officer
- Nigerian (South Eastern), graduate of University of Nigeria
- Former Principal of Capital Zephyr in South Africa
- Former Investment Manager at Zephyr Management LP New York
- Four years in various positions at Arthur Andersen in Nigeria and the United Kingdom
- Qualified as a Chartered Accountant in Nigeria

Thomas Barry, MBA (Harvard)
Director
- American, graduate of Yale University
- Over 25 years of investment management experience
- Founder and Chairman of the South Africa Capital Growth Fund
- Founder and Chief Executive Officer of Zephyr Management, L.P.
- 13 years at T. Rowe Price, in various senior capacities
- 11 years as CEO of Rockefeller & Co.

Chief Ernest Shonekan, AMP (Harvard)
Director
- Nigerian (Southwestern), law degree from University of London
- Chairman of the Vision 2010 Committee
- Former Head of State and Commander-in-Chief of the Armed Forces of the Federal Republic of Nigeria
- Former Head of the Nigerian federal Government and Chairman of the Transition Council
- Former Chairman and Managing Director of UAC Nigeria Ltd. (Unilever)
- Board member of Coca-Cola International and Maersk Shipping Line (Nigeria)
- Awarded "Commander of the Most Excellent Order of British Empire" by Queen Elizabeth II of the United Kingdom
- Called to the English and Nigerian Bars
- Member of Lagos Business School Board of Advisors

Mohammed Hayatu-Deen, PMD (Harvard)
Director
- Nigerian (Northern), graduate of Ahmadu Bello University in Nigeria
- Managing Director and CEO of FSB International Bank p.l.c. Nigeria
- Former Group Managing Director and CEO of New Nigeria Development Company
- Pioneer Board Member of the Nigerian Economic Summit Group and a key member of Vision 2010
- Board member of Northern Nigeria Investments Ltd.
- Director of the Nigerian Stock Exchange and Vice President of the Association of Nigerian Development Finance Institutions

Pascal Dozie, M.Sc. (City University, London)
Director
- Nigerian (South Eastern), graduate of the London School of Economics
- Chairman and CEO of Diamond Bank Limited Nigeria
- Founded Africa Development Consulting Group
- Former Senior Consultant to and Representative in Nigeria for Business International, S.A., Geneva
- Former Chairman of the Nigerian Stock Exchange
- Pioneer Chairman of the Nigerian Economic Summit Group and key member of Vision 2010
- Advisory Board member of the Lagos Business School

Many of them had served together on the Vision 2010 Committee, which had been established by General Sani Abacha with a mission to set a strategy for national development and modernization of Nigeria. As a result, the group enjoyed a high level of mutual respect and commitment as well as a shared purpose. Mohammed Hayatu-Deen, HBS PMD '98, explained:

> We knew each other well. Each of us had a strong commitment to moving Nigeria forward and we felt it was important for us to set an example. There is somewhat of a herd mentality in this country, so if we do this and are successful others will copy us, but without leadership this type of market may never develop. We want to make long-term profits, but whatever we do should be in the interest of the country, too.

Enelamah consulted with Barry, who had seen numerous private equity funds succeed and fail in both emerging and developed markets. Barry was impressed with the overall quality of the people involved, but nevertheless had some concerns about the new fund. On the other hand, Barry was concerned about the group's lack of private equity experience. Also he wondered whether the group was too patriotic and visionary rather than hands-on and profit driven. As Enelamah spent more time with the prospective team, he reassured himself over their focus and motivation:

> They are very profit driven. These are not incredibly rich people who have too much money to throw around and want to start a fund as a purely patriotic gesture, or for some other purpose like political gain. These are self-made businessmen who have maintained high ethical standards but who have nevertheless had the drive and discipline to build profitable businesses in an often-difficult economic environment.

Although Enelamah was less able to answer Barry's concern over the team's lack of private equity experience, he did not see this issue as insurmountable. The Partner's broad range of contacts and business expertise would be highly valuable for creating deal flow, identifying opportunities and adding value to portfolio companies. With his experience in South Africa and Barry as a sounding board, Enelamah felt he was up to the challenge of managing the fund with Kramer.

Kramer was particularly excited about Nigeria's potential to enter a period of rapid economic growth, which CAPE would be able to take advantage of. Kramer believed that recent political changes had contributed to a strong entrepreneurial spirit in a country with a highly educated population.

Despite his optimism, however, Kramer knew that Nigeria's future was still highly uncertain. "I think the next ten years are going to be boom years for Nigeria," he said, "but ten years ago I would have told you the same thing, and it sure wasn't. My one consolation is that no matter what happens it would be hard for things to get worse."

Enelamah and Kramer ultimately decided to go ahead, despite the difficulties. For Enelamah, this decision included moving back to Nigeria. He explained:

> When I first started talking with Dick, I hoped that I could help get this started but not actually have to come back and run it. As we moved forward I realized both that there was no one else who was going to do it and that I really believed in the idea and was very intrigued by the huge upside. Here there is a lot of potential to add value but also to have exit multiples that are significantly higher than our entry costs, both because of overall improvement in investor sentiment towards Nigeria and our negotiating strength as the only major source of private equity.

In addition to setting out the formal structure of the fund, including the incentives for its principals, they agreed on some fundamental criteria for how CAPE would be established. Enelamah explained, "We decided it was necessary to build a firm with a stellar reputation. Our investors are carefully selected. We know how they made their money."

Kramer elaborated, "This is a country where over the years people have plundered billions of dollars. Some of them are *seriously* wealthy. We can't completely shun these people—for example, we are close with a lot of people in the military and government. We just don't want their money." The same philosophy would apply to potential CAPE investments. "We will look at opportunities where you have to earn it in order to have it."

CAPE decided to raise $30 million for its initial fund. "We wanted to raise enough money to invest over three years," explained Kramer, "and we thought we would be able to do roughly four deals a year at $2.5 million each."

Enelamah added, "This is a pilot in Nigeria that should demonstrate whether or not private equity can work here. Assuming we are successful, and that nothing terrible happens on the macro level, we will be in a much better position to raise a sizeable fund internationally later on." During the second half of 1998, CAPE raised just over $20 million from local investors. Enelamah and Kramer were hopeful of raising the rest either from Nigerian investors or from institutions such as the Africa Development Bank, IFC (private sector affiliate of the World Bank), or Commonwealth Development Corporation (CDC). Barry had a long history with both the IFC, who was his lead investor in South Africa, and CDC, with whom he had started a business in Thailand. The presence of an offshore partner in CAPE and Barry specifically would be a positive factor in attracting those multilateral agencies which were not active in Nigeria due to political concerns.

GS Telecom

John Neville had worked as a McKinsey & Co consultant on a 1976 project to reorganize the Central Bank of Nigeria. Neville was subsequently a Senior Vice President of the Aviation Group at Spar, a leading aviation services company based in Canada, but had left Spar in 1989 to form his own venture capital company. Knowing his familiarity with the region, Spar Aerospace Canada asked him to resolve some major issues on a satellite sales project early in 1990. Even though Neville advised closing down the satellite project, he identified a major opportunity for Spar to sell its ground telecommunications equipment to the major oil companies in Nigeria. It took Neville over two years to get the requisite approvals and bring together Nitel and five international oil companies to build a $12 million private TDMA satellite network which would come to be called BIZNET. Two years later, Spar, a satellite technology provider with roughly $500 million in sales decided to divest its Nigerian operations. Neville and Steve Chapman, an engineer, who had been brought in to help establish the original network, spotted an opportunity and founded GS Telecom, which bought Spar Nigeria and its related service contracts for $750,000. (See **Exhibit 9** for resumes of senior management and key staff at GST.) Neville remained in Canada as group chairman, while Chapman was on the ground as managing director in Lagos.

Chapman and Neville had a shared vision of building GST into a niche leader in providing private satellite and wireless services within Nigeria and western Africa. To this end, they grew the business primarily in Nigeria, but also with operations in neighboring Ghana and in Tanzania, with further geographic expansion planned. Operationally, GST concentrated on three core business segments, Operation and Maintenance, Project Sales and Services and Network Services. (See **Exhibit 10** for GST's organization chart and **Exhibit 11** for a glossary of telecom-related terms.)

Operation and Maintenance (O&M) primarily referred to BIZNET, although it had expanded gradually into other networks. Although Nitel owned the BIZNET network, GST operated and maintained it under a set of contracts that provided the company with over

EXHIBIT 9
Resumes of GS Telecom Management

Source: GS Telecom.

John Neville, BA, MBA (Stanford)

Chairman
☐ Twenty-five years experience in shipping, aerospace and telecommunications
☐ Background in finance, business development and marketing
☐ Chairman of Quester Tangent Corporation
☐ Former
— Senior Vice President of SPAR Aerospace Limited
— Director of MDA Ltd.
— Chairman of MIL Industries Ltd.
— Vice President Melville Shipping Company Ltd.
— Treasurer of Fednav Limited
— Consultant with McKinsey & Co. Inc.
☐ Founding partner of GS Telecom in 1994

Steve Chapman, B.Sc. (Eng.)
Managing Director
☐ Canadian, graduate of Queen's University in Electrical Engineering
☐ Twenty years in International Oil Field Services and telecommunications
☐ Background in engineering, business development and marketing
☐ Worked for 10 years in Europe and 10 years in Africa
☐ Former Business Development Manager for Schlumberger (Europe, Africa, South America)
☐ Founding partner of GS Telecom in 1994

Peter Sinnott
General Manager Operations—Nigeria
☐ British, graduate City & Guilds Telecommunications
☐ Former Engineering instructor at British Telecom (BT)
☐ Management positions in Saudi Telephone and Electroman LLC (5 years)
☐ Former Managing Director Total Telecom Ltd. (U.K.)
☐ Former Managing Director Zircon Technology Ltd. (U.K.)
☐ Projects Manager Shell Petroleum Development Company of Nigeria
☐ Joined GS Telecom in April 1998

Adeyinka Adedayo
General Manager—Business Development
☐ Nigerian, graduate of University of Ife, Electrical and Electronics Engineering
☐ Trained at Nigerian Telecommunications Ltd.
☐ Twelve years with SITA
☐ Former Technical Manager Africa SITA based in Paris
☐ Former Regional Manager, West Africa based in Lagos
☐ GS Telecom in Lagos over two years

$1 million per year in fees. O&M represented a stable source of cash flow for GST as well as a competitive advantage in its Network Services business, as GST could offer customers one-stop shopping by building a custom network and then operating it for them.

Project Sales and Services referred to the development of private (i.e. closed) networks for large corporate customers. GST would design and install networks integrating multiple computer protocols and LAN technologies to VSAT and point-to-point radio technologies, depending on customer needs. Chapman described the Nigerian market's needs:

> This business is very different here than in the United States. For one thing, the overall telecom market in Nigeria is being driven by data communication rather than by voice. Businesses, for example in the oil producing region, are generating huge amounts of information that they need to be able to transmit to their central offices for processing. Moreover, the public networks are

EXHIBIT 10   GS Telecom Organization Charts

Source: GS Telecom.

GS Telecom Group Organization

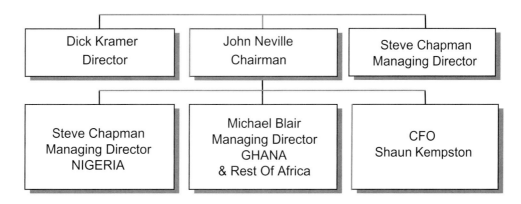

GS Telecom Operations

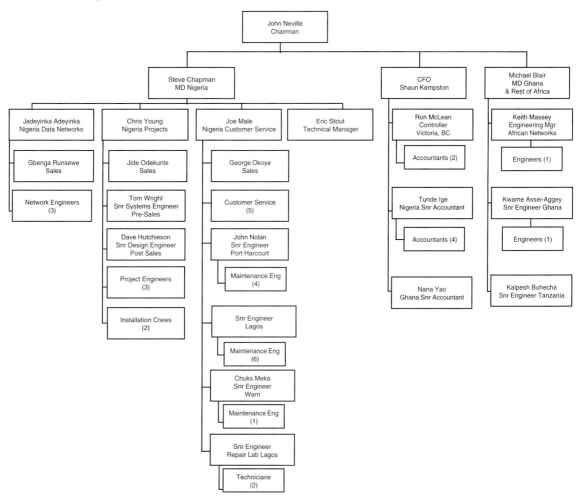

EXHIBIT 11 **Telecommunication Terms**

Source: GS Telecom.

Term	Definition
BIZNET	A private TDMA satellite network developed by GS Telecom.
Frame Relay	Form of packet switching that uses smaller packets (frames) and requires less error checking than other forms of packet switching. It is designed for data transfer only, so it's not well suited to videoconferencing or any other voice application. Frame relay is very good at efficiently handling high-speed, bursty data over wide area networks.
INTELSAT	International Telecommunications Satellite Organization. A nonprofit cooperative of about 120 countries that jointly own and operate a global communications satellite system serving the world. The system is used primarily for international communications, and by many countries for domestic communications.
LAN	Local Area Network. A local area network is a short-distance network used to link a group of computers together within a building. 10BaseT Ethernet is the most commonly used form of LAN.
Nitel	Nigerian Telecommunications Ltd. Nigeria's state owned telecom company.
TDMA	Time Division Multiple Access. A method of digital wireless communications transmissions allowing a number of users to access a single radio-frequency channel without interference. Each user is given a unique time slot within each channel.
VSAT	Very Small Aperture Terminal. A kind of ground station (or small satellite dish) used to contact a communications satellite.

highly unreliable, so being able to put forward a track record of reliable service makes a big difference. We've run BIZNET with 99.5% availability for over four years, which gives potential network customers a lot of confidence that we can deliver.

GST's local expertise had also enabled it to win contracts from major international telecom companies. GST installed medium and large earth stations for the INTELSAT business on behalf of Ericsson and Global One, which were used to provide international connectivity between Nigeria and Europe.

In addition to providing turnkey systems, GST could offer "virtual networks" to customers who did not want or need to develop an exclusive physical telecommunications network. In the Network Services business, GST leased network space and provided access to its clients on a self-contained basis such that two companies using the same actual network did not have any overlap or shared access. GST provided customers with circuits connecting Lagos to North America or Europe as well as providing full connectivity within Lagos through its owned and operated system, which extended 40km outside of the city.

Despite building a successful niche business, Chapman and Neville ran into some problems in GST's early days. Chapman recalled:

In 1996 we began serious expansion into other African countries, both to reduce our absolute dependence on Nigeria and with the hope of leveraging success with international customers to win their business outside of Nigeria. Our idea was to go for the big multinational accounts, but it was a complete flop. We were just too small, and on any contract that had to be approved by someone up the management chain we would always lose to someone like MCI.

After their initial difficulties, GST expanded more gradually into Ghana and Tanzania. Although large international contracts had proven nearly impossible to win, GST was able to leverage their reputation in Nigeria in winning more modest contracts. "Our service record over the past three years was very good," Chapman explained, "so customers were willing to trust us." (See **Exhibit 12** for a list of key customers of GS Telecom.)

EXHIBIT 12 **GS Telecom Key Customer List**

Source: GS Telecom.

- Chevron Nigeria Limited
- Elf Petroleum Nigeria Limited
- Mobil Producing Nigeria Ultd
- Mobil Oil Nigeria Plc
- Nigerian Agip Oil Company
- Shell Petroleum Development Company of Nigeria
- Texaco Overseas Petroleum Company of Nigeria
- Texaco Nigeria Plc
- Ashland Oil
- Diamond Bank Limited
- Central Bank of Nigeria
- Citibank Nigeria (NIB)
- Africa Online (Ghana) ISP
- SITA
- Ericsson Telecommuniczione SpA Nigeria LNG
- Sabena
- Coca-Cola Nigeria Limited
- Amansie Resources (Ghana) Limited/Resolute (Australia)
- Range Minerals (Ghana-Australia)
- Halliburton West Africa
- Teleglobe International
- Unisource (Dutch embassy VSAT Network)
- Global One (TSKJ Nigeria)
- Nigeria Online Limited (ISP)
- Link Serve Limited (ISP)

A more serious operational difficulty involved retaining key employees. Chapman explained the dilemma companies faced in trying to develop and maintain an engineering staff:

> We hire a trainee engineer for $400 per month and spend between $40,000 and $50,000 to train him over a period of three years. This generally includes three paid trips to the United States for training there. After that, he can command a salary of $1,000 per month and there is a lot of poaching of good people. It is very hard to keep people after you've sunk a lot of money into their training. In 1998 we lost three out of ten newly trained engineers as well as two others who had been with us for a while. For a company with a total headcount of around 80 people, that's pretty disruptive.

GST also had particular trouble filling the position of Project Manager, which partially caused a material shortfall in 1997 profits. Chapman recalled:

> We made a policy mistake in hiring for that spot. It costs a lot to bring in an expatriate with a family, so we concentrated our search on bachelors. That's still not cheap—the package is around $7,500 per month plus a car, residence with a staff and six weeks vacation including two paid trips home. The problem is that without roots these guys got drawn into the Lagos nightlife and weren't committed to the company. Add to that the fact that our Project Manager position is probably the toughest job in the building. The result is that we lost four managers over 18 months. Now we're looking for candidates with a family who will hopefully be more stable, but it won't be easy.

A more serious threat than GST's operational difficulties, however, was the cash crunch that came in 1997. Chapman recalled, "1996 was a good year in terms of cash flow, and we were able to finance our growth internally. We thought 1997 would be an improvement, which was probably naïve given the natural cycles of the oil business."

As oil prices declined, the Nigerian government reduced its 1997 budget in March. As a result, the national oil company was forced to extend its payment schedule by an average of 30 days as well as canceling some business. "A lot of small suppliers went bankrupt," Chapman recalled. "We kept afloat, but John had to mortgage his house."

Chapman and Neville agreed that they could not leave GST so vulnerable and had to look for external financing, rather than depending exclusively on internal cash flow and their own personal savings. They decided to look for both debt and equity financing, first approaching Barclays and Citibank either for a conventional business loan or for the factoring of GST's receivables. Their search for equity investors, which began outside of Nigeria, eventually led them to CAPE.

"We had not yet come across any serious VC firm who would invest in Nigeria," Chapman explained. "Then we met with Freddie Scott, a former [British] Royal Air Force pilot who stayed in Nigeria and started a local newsletter. Freddie is very well connected and aware of what's going on in Nigeria." Scott knew Kramer well, heard of the planned private equity fund and thought they might be interested in GST.

The Opportunity

The introduction of BIZNET into the Nigerian domestic telecommunications scene had enabled GST to snare all of the large customers in one move and in 1994/1996 GST/Nitel enjoyed 100% market share of the domestic VSAT business. However, the advent of deregulation and the entrance of a number of lower price competitors into the VSAT business led to considerable erosion of market share in the late nineties. In view of its higher service levels and expensive expatriate structure GST chose not to compete on price but rather on quality, reliability and technology.

In 1998, at a GST strategic marketing retreat, the plan to establish a domestic and international frame relay service was endorsed by all management. A frame service would enable GST to offer customers high-speed data links between designated offices at a much lower cost when compared with a comparable VSAT service. The cost effectiveness of a frame's use of bandwidth also meant that GST could expect very attractive margins providing that at least 10–20 customers bought the service in 70 or more locations.

Introduction of the frame service would cost upwards of US$2,000,000 and GST perceived that there was a window of opportunity to be the first carrier to offer such a service and tie up all the larger users. This window may last only into early 1999 before other competitors were attracted into the market.

Chapman and Neville first met with Kramer and Enelamah in February 1998. Chapman knew Kramer by reputation and was interested in Enelamah's experience in South Africa. "Dick had built Arthur Andersen up from nothing in Nigeria," Chapman recalled, "and if he was worth anything it was the contacts he had made. We knew he would be helpful. Enelamah knew about Africa and seemed very capable. At that point they didn't have funding yet, but we got to meet with prospective investors and felt reasonably confident they would put the fund together. We were also reassured that Dick and Enelamah had worked together before, and they obviously had a strong behind-the-scenes network."

Neville began the discussion by pointing out that recent public telecom mergers and acquisitions transactions were valued on a multiple of three to five times revenues, and that despite the need for a Nigeria discount the quality of GST's client base argued for a high valuation. With growth in the sector estimated at 25%–30% per annum (see **Exhibit 13** for data on the telecom equipment market in Nigeria) and deregulation expected to accelerate that growth, Neville felt that the upside fully compensated for the higher risk.

Enelamah and Kramer were quick to set expectations at a more modest level. "I told them I get very uncomfortable if I'm paying more than 3x EBITDA for a Nigerian business," Enelamah explained. "Besides, telecom companies in the same line of business as GST have been sold at around one times revenues and that was in the United States; there are specifics to GST that would call for a discount to that. We also made it clear that we were going to value the business based on the domestic [Nigerian] operations. The businesses they had elsewhere in western Africa were interesting, but were also small and relatively undeveloped."

EXHIBIT 13   **Telecommunication Equipment Market in Nigeria**

Source: GS Telecom.

	1996	1997	1998
Total market size $US (millions)	120	150	200
Total local production	0	0	0
Imports from United States	25	30	40
Other imports	95	120	160
Total imports	120	150	200

Neville and Chapman were also aware that they faced some significant hurdles in terms of raising equity funding. They had up until that point concentrated almost solely on the operations side, with the result that they had no real business plan or even significant financial data to offer. Poor financial controls and a rising number of transactions being completed in local Naira instead of dollars complicated issues. The end result was that GST could not put forward reliable numbers on profitability, cash flow or the company's financial position.

Despite the problems, Enelamah and Kramer saw a definite opportunity in GST. Kramer recalled:

> The problems were fairly obvious. Their financial controls and accounting were a mess, and they didn't yet have a CFO. John was first class, but based in Canada, just coming to Nigeria three to four times a year, which raised some questions about how committed he was to the business.
>
> On the upside, these were good guys, and they had good people working for them. We felt they had some considerable strength on both the management and technical side. Equally important was that they had good reputations as ethical businessmen. So we knew we could work with them.

In June 1998 GST hired an MBA based in Canada to write a business plan for the company. "He didn't do a great job with the numbers," Chapman recalled, "but he did a good job of putting forward the basic business case and our strengths. By July, despite receiving an offer for the factoring of receivables, GST decided to pursue equity capital and to talk exclusively with CAPE, although no formal exclusivity deal agreement was signed.

In order to address the severe shortage of reliable numbers, CAPE hired Arthur Andersen to conduct extensive due diligence on GST. "They had a team of three to four people in here for six weeks," Chapman recalled. "At the end of that they were able to make pretty solid estimates about GST's basic profitability. They also made some useful suggestions for us moving forward."

As the discussions moved forward, Neville was the first to broach the valuation issue directly, suggesting a pre-money valuation for GST of $6 million. GST hoped to raise roughly $2 million, implying a 25% stake for CAPE. Enelamah responded with a valuation of $2 million pre-money. Beyond the difference in firm valuation, one major sticking point was whether there would be a guarantee clause that would reduce the final valuation in the event that GST failed to meet its financial projections. Enelamah argued that the lack of reliable numbers made a guarantee clause a necessary safety measure for CAPE. Chapman and Neville, however, were adamantly opposed. They felt that the financial projections they had offered CAPE were sufficiently conservative that no additional protection should be needed and did not want to build in the possibility of further dilution of their stake.

EXHIBIT 14   Data on the Nigerian Stock Exchange

Sources: *The Salomon Smith Barney Guide to World Equity Markets* 1998; *The LGT Guide to World Equity Markets* 1997; *The Guide to Securities Market Indices; World Directory of Stock Exchanges; The IFR Handbook of World Stock & Commodity Exchanges;* Lagos Stock Exchange, www.mbendi.co.za/exng.htm

	1990	1991	1992	1993	1994	1995	1996	1997	1998
Number of companies listed	131	142	153	174	177	181	184	182	188
Total market capitalization (US$ billion)	1.242	1.606	1.280	1.030	0.770	1.740	3.570	3.760	3.512
Nigerian stock exchange all-share index 1/3/84 = 100	513.60	784.00	1,107.60	1,543.80	2,205.00	5,092.15	6,992.01	6,440.51	5,672.16
Total market P/E multiple	NA	NA	8.0	5.6	5.5	9.2	11.2	11.9	NA[a]

[a]1998 P/E multiple not available.

Exit Strategy

Enelamah and Kramer also had to consider how they would exit their investment in GST, and whether they were likely to do so at a favorable valuation. Nigeria did not offer as wide a range of likely exit vehicles as would be available in the developed world. The country's stock market had very low volumes and was not a meaningful source of capital. (See **Exhibit 14** for data on the Nigerian stock exchange.) While a domestic listing at some point in the future could not be ruled out, the prospect was fairly remote.

Nor was an IPO on a foreign exchange something CAPE wanted to rely on. Foreign investment sentiment towards Nigeria was heavily affected by political concerns and was currently at a very low level. "Many fund managers wouldn't even look at an investment in Nigeria," explained Enelamah. "Hopefully that will change with time, but for now we can't count on institutional investors bringing new money in."

CAPE was quite optimistic, however, that an exit could be realized through a trade sale. GST seemed well-positioned to be acquired by one of the large international telecom companies that would be likely to enter Nigeria over the next few years as demand for services rose. Chapman explained:

> Nigeria's telecom business will continue on a path of deregulation, regardless of what happens on the political scene, because everyone agrees it needs to happen. On the demand side, you have both major multi-nationals and one of the most underdeveloped national services in the world. Lots of major players are looking at this market.
>
> We've seen this pattern repeat itself in emerging markets all over the world. The first entrants are the small players, entrepreneurs who can afford to concentrate on a market when it is still very small and chaotic. Then, when the market reaches a point where it makes sense for the larger players to enter, they buy up the best of the smaller companies.
>
> John has got other business concerns in Canada, and I'm not planning on staying in GST for another 10 years. We have positioned ourselves from the beginning with a view towards being bought by a larger carrier who would view us as a nice little bit of feeder network. We don't make every business decision in the context of "how will this help us get taken out," but we have been consistently building the business with that exit in mind.

Enelamah did retain one concern about exiting the GST investment through a trade sale. "Assuming they continue to grow each of their business segments," he pointed out, "it may be difficult to find a single buyer who is interested in all of them. If we have to break the company up first that could delay the process."

What to Do Next

As they concluded their review meeting, both men agreed that they needed to do two things. First, they needed to do some more due diligence with regards to the financial figures, customer base and employee stability. These were tricky topics and maybe there was some information they had overlooked. Second, they needed to develop a viable negotiation strategy including a contingency plan if valuation proved to be a difficult topic. Enelamah and Kramer had to decide how much CAPE should be willing to pay for 25% of GST, whether 25% was the right stake, and whether a $2 million equity injection was sufficient to secure GST's future. They also needed to agree on whether any side issues in the negotiations could become deal breakers, or whether they could be factored into the base valuations or deal structure.

Case

18

TixToGo: Financing a Silicon Valley Start-up

"Raising funding is kind of like learning how to ride a bike: the experiences are the same but all generalities are false."

—*Lee Taylor, Co-Founder, TixToGo*

"And so how will we pay the bills?" asked Lu Cordova. Cordova had been an advisor to TixToGo, an on-line marketplace for ticketing activities, for almost six months and had been hired as chairman and CEO of the company. That day, May 18, 1999, was her first day on the job in her new role. The company had a very low monthly burn rate of $30,000, but Cordova had just been told that her new company had only $12,000 in the bank—not nearly enough money to cover payroll expenses. "I don't know," replied Ralph Marx, co-founder and president of TixToGo. "What do you think we should do?"

TixToGo was the creation of Marx and Co-Founder and VP of Operations, Lee Taylor, and had existed since 1997. The company name was a little of a misnomer as TixToGo did much more than just on-line ticketing. The company offered an on-line solution to individuals and organizations that wanted to offer the collection of registration fees, ticket purchases, donations, or sign-ups for activities (or "EVAs"—Events, Venues,[1] and Activities) over the Internet (see **Exhibit 1** for a sample list of services offered). TixToGo generated revenues primarily through commissions on payments made through its website, but also through advertising and souvenir sales (see **Exhibit 7C**).

---

[1] A venue is a facility that hosts events (e.g., a concert hall or a stadium).

Professor Walter Kuemmerle and Dean's Fellow William J. Coughlin prepared this case. HBS cases are developed solely as the basis for class discussion. Cases are not intended to serve as endorsements, sources of primary data, or illustrations of effective or ineffective management.

EXHIBIT 1
Description of
Services Offered

Source: TixToGo.

Organizing or Sponsoring an Activity?

Market Your Activity	Take Payments
Take Reservations	Register Members
Book Tickets	Collect RSVPs

TixToGo's free service allows organizers to bring the convenience of online registration and electronic payment to their constituents in a matter of minutes.

TixToGo uses the power of the Web to help organizations and individuals reach millions of people who will register, buy tickets, donate or sign up for activities. We increase the activity community's marketing presence while reducing its administrative load.

Sell reservations, book tickets, register members or receive donations 24 hours a day, without the hassle of transcribing faxes, voicemails or dealing with checks. TixTo-Go's comprehensive service provides activity coordinators with real-time, up-to-the-minute membership, donation or event "will-call" lists which can be viewed with any browser, printed or downloaded at any time. Additionally, our service transforms this will-call list into a powerful marketing tool for future activities. There is no software installation and we combine state-of-the-art security with absolute privacy. Information will not be sold to any third party. All this at no cost!

If you or your organization is responsible for …

Alumni Events	Dinners	Parties	Shows
Charities	Donation drives	Performances	Theater
Classes	Exhibitions	Races	Tours
Clubs	Expos	Raves	Training
Concerts	Festivals	Receptions	Workshops …
Conferences	Fund-raisers	Reunions	
Dance	Meetings	Seminars	

… then TixToGo is your complete online solution for increasing activity participation while dramatically reducing administrative and processing costs.

TixToGo was first created so event organizers could offer on-line ticketing for their events. (See **Exhibit 2** for a sample page from their website.) But soon customers started using TixToGo and the company's commercial engine in many different ways and for a much wider assortment of activities than the founders had first imagined. Customers were using TixToGo for everything from large conferences and festivals to Bar Mitzvahs and bachelor parties. Based on this newly discovered market demand, TixToGo became an Internet service that enabled on-line sign-ups and payments for registrations, admissions, memberships, sponsorships and donations. "We are really a self-service marketplace for activities where sellers can list their activities and buyers can come by to sign up and pay via credit card," explained Cordova.

Although the company had been in existence for some time, it had been having trouble raising outside funding. In order to address potential concerns about the management team, Marx and Taylor had hired Cordova and other managers chosen by Cordova, including a VP of marketing and a VP of Sales, to strengthen the management team ahead of raising money from venture capitalists. Although she had worked closely with the company before taking the job and knew there were some problems to fix, Cordova was nevertheless surprised by the cash situation when she arrived at the company. Cordova explained:

> When I walked in, I saw a situation where the company had a web site that was amateurish and had infrastructure problems, only had four people working at the company, and was about to run out of cash. What a crazy first day! However, TixToGo was built on a really good idea; the founders could see where they wanted to go but just not the path. And even though the web site was ugly, it worked and they already had customers despite the fact they had not had a formal sales or marketing effort.

EXHIBIT 2   Sample Screen Shot of TixToGo's Website

Source: TixToGo.

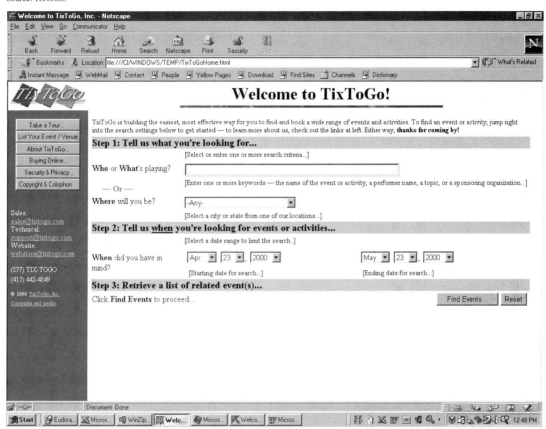

The question became what to do first? I knew the company was running out of cash, but there were a few, key things we could fix rather quickly with the product that would definitely give us a boost. Plus, we needed to get some more people on board to get sales pumping in order to support a reasonable valuation from investors. Because of all this, maybe VC funding would need to take a back seat for a bit. I said to myself: Maybe we can come up with some other sources of financing, like a bridge loan, before we go to the VCs. Or maybe we should just "bite the bullet" and go to the VCs before it is too late.

As noon approached on that foggy day in San Francisco, Cordova sat in her red brick office in Francisco's business-trendy Multimedia Gulch in the South of Market district, an "old economy" warehouse district that had recently been re-gentrified by "new economy" start-ups. Marx and Taylor came in and Marx suddenly repeated his earlier question to Cordova. "What should we do, Lu?" he asked. "I have a couple of ideas," Cordova replied.

The Gold Rush of '99—The U.S. Venture Community Heats Up

The first half of 1999 was a very active period in the venture capital community in the United States. According to the *Venture Capital Journal* (VCJ) and Venture Economics Information Services (VEIS), venture capitalists invested $12.6 billion in 1,763 companies during the first six months of 1999, a record both in terms of dollar amount and number of deals. The lion's share ($6.1 billion) of that money went into Internet companies, mostly content, e-commerce and service enterprises. Following suit, the venture industry hit new highs in deal sizes during the same period. The average venture investment in a company by any one VC fund grew to $7.87 million and the average amount of capital per round increased to $7.13 million (see **Exhibit 3** for comparable data). With California taking in 42% of that funding, the state consumed more capital than any other state.[2]

According to John Walecka, a partner at Brentwood Venture Capital, and Shawn Neidorf at the *Venture Capital Journal,* the trends reflected a shift in belief of both investors and entrepreneurs. Based on a conversation with Walecka, Neidorf wrote the following in an article for the VCJ:[3]

> The growing deal sizes simply reflect the reality of the current environment and the fevered pace required to get a portfolio company's product or service to market quickly. "You move slowly in this market, [and you've] missed it," [Walecka] says, recalling deals ranging from $2 million to $3 million a decade ago. Today, Walecka sees $7 million to $10 million deals. Although he has witnessed [venture capital] firms writing $60 million checks, Brentwood will not invest more than about $15 million in a single company from its current fund, a $300 million vehicle that will be fully invested within a few months.

Much of that investment in new funds was also the result of new records set for fund raising. 1998 saw a record year when $26.1 billion was raised in the VC industry. Following upon this trend, the first half of 1999 was also a big period for fund raising as 112 VC firms raised $10.4 billion in new capital according to VEIS (see **Exhibit 4**

[2] California accounted for 40% of 1998 venture activity. Massachusetts was second in the first half of 1999 with a 12% share.

[3] Shawn Neidorf, "VCs Engage in a First Half Spending Spree," *Venture Capital Journal*, September 1, 1999.

EXHIBIT 3 Venture Investment Data

Source: National Venture Capital Association, *Venture Economics Information Services.* Database accessed in January 2000.

Average Venture Investment in a Company ($mm)

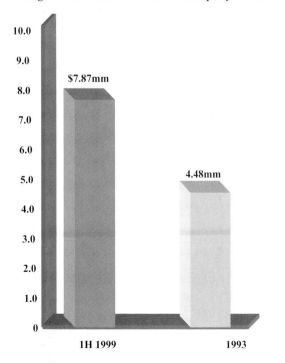

Average Capital Invested Per Round ($mm)

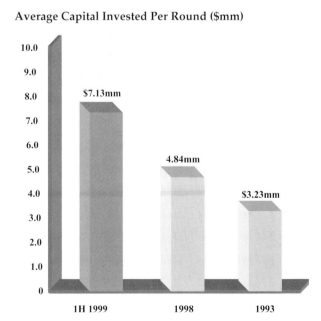

EXHIBIT 4   **Venture Capital Fundraising—1990–1999 (in $billions)**

Source: National Venture Capital Association, *Venture Economics Information Services.* Database accessed in January 2000.

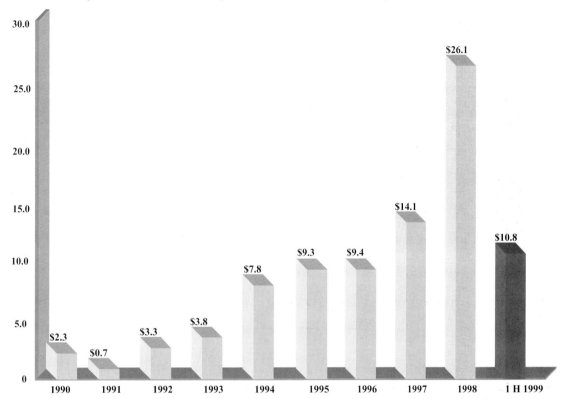

for fund-raising data). The bylaws of most funds required that the capital be invested within three to five years. If venture capitalists did not invest at high speeds their limited partners (investors) grew impatient since they needed to hold the capital committed to a VC fund in cash or other assets that could be liquidated within two weeks.

An Unlikely Beginning—The Genesis of TixToGo

Founders' Background

After graduating from the University of Massachusetts with an Engineering degree, Ralph Marx worked as a paralegal for Morrison & Forrester for four years before co-founding a software services company called Deets & Associates that served the legal market (see **Exhibit 5** for the biographies of key management at TixToGo). After working there for three more years, Marx split off from the company in 1987 to start his own software services firm called Advocate Systems. This firm focused on automation and computer consulting for the legal profession. Over time, Advocates operations grew to become one of the leaders in software solutions for the legal market.

Sometime around 1996, Marx got interested in the Internet. After spending the next year on legal software projects that were Internet focused, Marx decided he wanted to shift away from the legal market. "Ralph is a serial entrepreneur at heart," explained Taylor. "He is always looking to pursue that next great idea." Marx explained:

EXHIBIT 5   Biographies of Key Management

Source: TixToGo.

Lu Cordova, CEO and Chairman

Lu has over 20 years experience in marketing and strategic planning, with 6 years in operations and 5 years working with Internet start-ups. Lu establishes the vision, strategy, and goals of the company and spearheads TixToGo's financing efforts. Cordova originally served on TixToGo's Board of Directors as Chief Development Officer before becoming the CEO and Chairman of the Board. Formerly, Cordova was CEO of Corlund Industries—a consulting firm that guided high-tech companies through start-up to maturity and international scope by providing hands-on operations management, strategic planning, business development, and marketing experience. Cordova was also part of the original team at @Home Network, where Cordova co-founded their @Work Division, which accounted for 45% of total sales its first year. She then created @Home's Online Services department, which supported all P&L divisions of @Home Network. Before leaving, Cordova initiated and served as architect for @Home's business portal design and strategy with Excite and AT&T.

Ralph Marx, Co-founder and President

Founding his second technology company, Ralph Marx now serves as President and is a member of the Board of Directors. Drawing from 13 years of experience running his own software business, Ralph manages TixToGo's internal operations, including the Finance, Administration, Legal, and HR departments. Before TixToGo, Marx founded and served as CEO of Advocate Systems, Inc. The company quickly became the recognized leader of automation and computer consulting for the legal market. Advocate's clientele included some of America's largest law firms and corporate legal departments. In addition to generating custom solutions, Advocate Systems developed and marketed commercial products, including a $20 million joint venture with a British software development group backed by Guinness PLC, British Petroleum, OCE, and Syseca (a subsidiary of Thompson CSF).

Lee Taylor, Co-founder and VP of Operations

Lee Taylor supplied the technical expertise to provide the backbone powering the online TixToGo service. As co-founder and VP of Operations, Lee manages product development, engineering, and operations, including customer service and success efforts. A well-respected IT guru for over two decades, Taylor co-authored four books on Web design and development tools: *The Java Studio Blue Book* (Coriolis Press, 1999); *NetObjects Fusion: 3 Days to Effective Web Design* (International Thomson Computer Press, 1997); *FutureTense Texture* (International Thomson Computer Press, 1997); and *The Web Page Design Cookbook* (John Wiley & Sons, 1995). Taylor spent 12 years as an information design and development consultant in the technology sector. His private consultancy firm, Telluride Wordcraft, provided IT services to a clientele that included International Paper Corporation, Alcoa Corporation, John Deere Manufacturing, and IBM.

Mark Keyworth, VP of Marketing and Corporate Development

Engineer turned online marketing and business development expert, with particular strength in the payments industry, Keyworth is responsible for the strategy and execution of all of TixToGo's marketing efforts as well as technology partnerships. Previously, Keyworth headed up the Micropayments division of Cybergold, where he spearheaded its Earn & Spend strategy and product, as well as managed revenue-producing partnerships. Also, within a month of his joining Cybergold to advise on their strategic marketing and membership plans, he boosted account holders by 230% and transaction levels by 125%. At the same time, he consulted on the design and implementation of @Home Network's sales tracking procedure for their business affiliate and VAR channels, before eventually brokering a marketing agreement between Cybergold and @Home. Prior to @Home and Cybergold, Keyworth served as Senior Marketing Director for Applied Signal Technology and was responsible for tripling revenues and establishing an international marketing presence.

Phil Battat, VP Sales and Business Development

Phil Battat has been helping companies to build their businesses for over 15 years. Battat was with USWeb/CKS for five years as VP/GM of CKS Pictures and VP Business Development. As one of the founding members of CKS Pictures, Phil helped devise and execute the strategy to build the new division into a fast-growing, profitable unit in the broadcast, video and multimedia production area and ran the operation for over three years. As VP Business Development at USWeb/CKS, Battat led new business development for CKS's west coast offices. He developed a new business strategy and process for working with multiple CKS divisions. His efforts led to business from ten new clients in 15 months totaling over $11 million in revenue. Prior to USWeb/CKS, Battat was VP/GM of Jack Morton Productions where he helped build their event marketing business with major Silicon Valley companies and ran the company's San Francisco operation.

I really wanted to get into the Internet because I could see all of its possibilities but I was not sure about how to break in or what part of the market I wanted to attack. So I began networking around the Valley—going to meetings, meeting entrepreneurs, finding out what ideas were being pursued. I have to admit, it was all a bit clumsy because I still had a whole company to run with Advocate.

Then in January 1997, Marx had an idea. Fed up with the way Bass (a Bay-area company similar to TicketMaster) ran its operations and the prices they charged, Marx decided to focus on on-line ticketing. "I was trying to get a Christmas present for a friend," Marx recalled. "She wanted me to get her two tickets to a concert for the two of us. I hadn't used Bass or TicketMaster for something like five years and I forgot about how bad it was. Boy was that a nightmare!" As he began investigating the market, the idea looked increasingly attractive and Marx knew he had to begin formalizing the venture. Yet, he did not want to start up the business on his own, so he contacted an old friend, Lee Taylor, to see if he would be interested in joining Marx.

Taylor had a BA in Political Science from the University of the South (Sewanee) and an MA in creative writing from San Francisco State University, but was a self-taught technologist. Taylor met Marx while the two worked at Morrison & Forrester and Taylor was the purchasing and facilities manager there. Taylor explained his transition into technology:

I am what I would call a technically inclined liberal arts guy. At Morrison & Forrester, I got an Apple II computer and had all of these questions about how to use it for my job in purchasing. After a while…and since the MIS guys were always "too busy," I figured out I could learn and do everything on my own. That's where my real interest in technology began.

Taylor held several jobs in technology related functions (see **Exhibit 5**) including PDR Information Services, a technical documentation services firm. In addition, Taylor started his own technology consulting firm in Colorado called Telluride Worldcraft and co-authored several books on web design, including *The Web Design Cookbook*. Knowing that Taylor knew much more about the Internet than he, Marx wrote a half-page memorandum and called Taylor to pitch the idea to him. After asking for a night to think it over, Taylor called Marx the following morning and accepted his offer to investigate the idea further.

Networking: Laying the Groundwork for the Future

Between February and March 1997 Taylor and Marx separately investigated various aspects of their venture. The two met at the Bluegrass Festival in Telluride, Colorado, during the spring of 1997 to harvest their ideas. When looking at potential competition, the two big ticketing companies, Bass and Ticketmaster, immediately came to mind. The founders understood the web would present new challenges to these companies but they did not want to take the two leaders on head-to-head. After some analysis, Marx and Taylor discovered there were a vast amount of other opportunities as a consequence for ticketing that the big players never wanted to focus on because of the size of the venue was too small and the cost to serve those venues was too high. So the two decided to focus on venues with less than 200 seats, segmented this type of venue into 25–30 different markets, and assessed the size of each market. (See **Exhibit 6** for the list of the markets.) "We really believed that the Web could enable any size player to become an e-commerce player," explained Taylor, "and that the dynamics of the Internet would allow us to serve these markets profitably."

Although the two were convinced that consumers would adopt the new ticket distribution channel created by the Internet, they were a little less certain about how to go about pursuing the idea. "We really needed a book that would tell us 'How to Do a Start-up Internet

EXHIBIT 6 List of Initial Target Markets

Source: TixToGo.

Number of Cities in Category / Event Type	Share Factor	15 Large U.S. Cities	30 Medium U.S. Cities	100 Small U.S. Cities	150 Other U.S. Locations	Total Seats/Month	Potential Market Share**
Large convention (Moscone)	1	100,000	50,000			3,000,000	990,000
Small conventions (Squaw Valley)	2	—	50,000	10,000	5,000	3,250,000	2,145,000
Local sports events (bike rides, marathons, races)	3	10,000	6,000	2,000	2,000	830,000	821,700
Museums, aquariums, planetariums, zoo	2	20,000	9,000	2,000		770,000	508,200
Minor league sports	2	50,000	30,000	10,000	1,000	2,800,000	1,848,000
College sports	2	50,000	40,000	20,000	2,000	4,250,000	2,805,000
Movies	1	800,000	400,000	30,000	5,000	27,750,000	9,157,500
Small music/theatre clubs	3	40,000	13,000	1,000		1,090,000	1,079,100
Elks lodge-rotary club special events	1	5,000	3,000	1,000		265,000	87,450
Special events (bay to beakers, King Tut)	3	80,000	40,000	5,000	5,000	3,650,000	3,613,500
State & county fairs	2	5,000	5,000	5,000	1,000	875,000	577,500
Golf courses	1	100,000	600,000	400,000	200,000	89,500,000	29,535,000
Local park	1	5,000	3,000	1,000	1,000	415,000	136,950
State park	1	3,000	3,000	5,000	10,000	2,135,000	704,550
National park	1	5,000	5,000	10,000	50,000	8,725,000	2,879,250
Ski areas	1			2,000	10,000	1,700,000	561,000
Seminars & workshops (CLE, CPR, real estate)	1	30,000	10,000	5,000	4,000	1,850,000	610,500
Evangelical/religious	2	20,000	10,000	4,000	1,000	1,150,000	759,000
Weekend retreats	1	2,000	5,000	5,000	8,000	1,880,000	620,400
Campgrounds	1	—	2,000	5,000	8,000	1,760,000	580,800
Total Seat Count		1,325,000	1,284,000	523,000	313,000	157,645,000	60,020,400
Total Revenue *		$2,650,000	$2,568,000	$1,046,000	$626,000	$315,290,000	$120,040,800

Notes:

Share Factor is a weighting factor: The higher the number the better the penetration expected. Higher numbered markets were attacked first.

Potential Market Share: Assumed that one third of the market for these events would buy online as opposed to other channels.

*Unit Price: $2.00 ($2.00 was the commission that TixToGo hoped to achieve per ticket).

**Potential market share for TixToGo and its on-line competitors.

Style' or 'Silicon Valley Style'," Marx recollected. But that book did not exist. So Marx began networking again and got an introduction to Karen Skjverrem, of then-Coopers & Lybrand (C&L) in Silicon Valley. Skjverrem worked in a little-known group for C&L called the Emerging Companies Program. If C&L agreed to accept an entrepreneur into this program, C&L experts would help the entrepreneur prepare five-year financial projections (including a market analysis and determination of the cost structure of the business), assistance in writing their business plan, and would give them an introduction to VCs. Marx explained the experience:

> The Emerging Companies Program consisted of a few senior people at C&L that were chartered to give free or low cost services to promising people with a good idea. This was a way for C&L to get in early with promising companies and a way for promising companies to get in with the VCs since C&L was the auditor for most of the big venture capital firms. The program was great—kind of the earliest form of an incubator. And I just kind of heard about it from a couple of people. No one really knew about it at the time; that's where connections in the Valley really help.
>
> In August 1997, we got 20 minutes with Karen and she really fell in love with the idea. She saw that it was a huge market space but that it was crucial that we didn't go after the Ticketmaster market. At that point in time, we really liked the idea but were still not completely committed to it. It was Karen who pushed us to do it, committing to do tons of stuff for us at virtually no cost [$2,000]; but we had to promise her we would follow through with it.

After asking for 24 hours to think about it, Marx and Taylor decided to take Skjvierm up on her offer and TixToGo was born.

The Long Road Forward—Funding TixToGo

After agreeing to move forward, Marx and Taylor began working on the business plan for TixToGo in the fall of 1997. Taylor stayed in Telluride and began working full time on TixToGo out of his house while Marx worked part time on the new company and part time on Advocate. The plan was to have Marx work at Advocate, essentially funneling all of the profits from the company to TixToGo until the new company had raised outside financing. Once an initial plan had been put together, Marx hit the pavement to get meetings with venture capitalists.

Their first meeting with a venture capitalist came at the end of 1997 and the VC was quite critical of the idea. "It was our first meeting," explained Marx, "and we really weren't ready. We really wanted to use the meeting as a benchmark for where we were, get an idea of the weak spots in our plan, and prepare ourselves for future meetings with VCs." In March 1998, the founders had refined the business plan so that the plan was presentable to VCs, but they found the VCs to be unresponsive to their idea. Taylor explained:

> There was a lot of skepticism from venture capitalists whether there would be a market. It was really a common element amongst all of them that surprised Ralph and me. We assumed the average VC could jump at any good business idea but in the Valley that was becoming less and less frequent. Part of the reason is that VCs are in many ways entrepreneurs themselves. They see your idea and come up with their own solutions—and your solution had better jive with theirs. But the real reason seemed to be that they were reluctant investing in new, unproven markets. It probably had to do with the limited hours that they could spend on any idea and the increasing amount of deal flow they were seeing. Regardless, it seemed like there was a lot of "me too" out there in the venture community as if there was safety in numbers. It almost seemed like the most sophisticated investors were turning into lemmings.
>
> Since the VCs were not interested in investing in an unproven market, we had to go out and prove there was a market before we went back to them. I figured building the website wouldn't take all that much time or money so why not go out and give it a shot?

Relying on the profits generated by Marx at Advocate, Taylor created the TixToGo web site and in June 1998, the company signed up its first customer with the soft launch of the web site—The Telluride Jazz Festival. After using a total of $150,000 of their own money, Marx and Taylor decided to raise a seed round of capital from "friends and family" in order to get the site fully operational with an on-line commerce engine to process the transactions. The hope was to get the site up and generate enough traffic to convince the VCs they had a real market to pursue. But there were still some growing pains in the seed round of financing as well. Marx elaborated on the issues that surrounded the initial fund raising.

> Being naïve again, we weren't really sure about how to handle the legal work. For example, we weren't quite sure what a private placement document should look like. The key was we needed someone to pay attention but at a price we could afford. So I used my Advocate connections to sign up Hank Barry at Wilson, Sonsini, Goodrich & Rosati to prepare the legal documentation. Hank was great, but, given how busy he was and the cut-rate price we were paying, things moved pretty slow and it took us a couple of months to close the round.

Once they did close the $98,000 round of financing, however, they were soon able to launch their site and generate traffic.

Going Live—A Couple of Pleasant Surprises

Even though the company had some initial problems, Marx and Taylor did a number of things that benefited the company. Coming from a service background, the founders wanted to build a company that offered a true service to consumers, not just a software product like some of the big players like Ticketmaster and Bass offered. As a result, they designed the site in a way that it would be a true self-service tool for consumers, with elements that included an on-line commerce engine that allowed EVA organizers to collect funds on-line from the consumers. The founders believed that this ease of service assisted in attracting early users of the website.

Other fortuitous events also happened—but not all by design. When the site did go live, the founders discovered that the market was a little different from what they expected. Not only were they able to get people to use the site to sell tickets for things like smaller concert venues, but people were using the site to book other events—everything from Bar Mitzvahs to college fund raising. As a result, the market seemed to be much larger than the founders had first thought. This also presented the founders with an opportunity to focus first on some vertical markets that were outside of Ticketmaster's "radar." The one area TixToGo really focused on was the technology community. Marx recounted the genesis of their strategy:

> Since we were in the Valley and we had been working from the onset to make connections there, we decided to focus our early marketing efforts on the technology community. For example, one of our first big events was for a software development conference in San Jose. We chose the segment because we knew that the users were not afraid of the Internet and were familiar with e-commerce. Also, this was part of a community in which we were relatively known and in which we wanted to increase our presence. Perhaps most importantly, it was interconnected with the venture capital community. That way, in the next round of financing, the VCs would be calling us rather than we calling them. What better way of proving a market or a product than by telling the VCs that they had used it already?

Even though sales were starting to come along, the founders did not feel that they were moving fast enough. By October 1998, the company only had a couple of people on the payroll and they were getting low on funds. They were not sure of the genesis of the problem, so they decided to take a new plan of action. In December 1998, they hired Bob Boemer, an experienced tourism marketing executive, to re-examine their sales model and they were introduced to Lu Cordova who joined as an advisor. With Cordova's active assistance, things started to pick up. By the end of January 1999, Taylor and Marx decided to re-think their projections, put together a new business plan, and revisit the VCs (see **Exhibit 7A, 7B, 7C, 7D** and **7E** for the company's historical and projected financial information). In March, they were close to completing the business plan and were contacted by a venture capital firm. Scrambling to finish the plan, the founders visited venture capital funds in April and May. Marx described the events:

> Unlike before, we started to get a huge amount of interest. What I think happened was the industry shifted and people began to become interested in the market. The reception from the funds was much more encouraging, but the message was clear: You have proven the market and have met all criteria but one—you do not have a top-notch management team. We knew then that we had to solve the management problem.

With that in mind, they turned to their advisor Cordova to see if she could provide them with her biggest contribution yet: to join TixToGo as their new CEO.

A New Beginning and a New CEO

Life Before TixToGo—Lu Cordova's Background

Cordova completed BS degrees in political science and economics and a Ph.D.-A.B.D. in economics from the University of California at Berkeley. While in graduate school, she worked as a reporter at a start-up electronic news agency, Market News, then as a director at MMS International, which was sold to McGraw-Hill. She spun off a research institute, became its president, and came back to McGraw-Hill's Standard & Poor's as a VP Corporate Development working on emerging data technologies, Cordova decided to leave S&P for @Home. Cordova explained the move from S&P:

> While at S&P, I became very interested in the Internet and the way it would change the business world. I decided to join @Home as an original member because I really knew that broadband was the wave of the future. But even before I went to @Home, I became interested in the idea of on-line ticketing. I had worked for Bay Area concert promoter Bill Graham Presents and began talking with them about a ticketing service on the Web. I was interested in the space but abandoned the idea because my model was like a Ticketmaster Online, or Tickets.com, which is central box-office software that doesn't scale well. Every new customer needed to be configured and managed. I knew it was a poor model, and a smaller market, but at the time did not yet know enough about the Internet to know how to fix it. As a result, I decided to help start @Home.

@Home was a provider of high-speed Internet access and other on-line services over cable television lines. As part of a joint venture with TCI, Cox Communications, and Comcast, @Home's service allowed cable television lines to be plugged in to personal computers, dramatically improving the connection speed to the Internet, improving access speeds that were 1,000 times faster than a 28,800-bit modem.

While Working with @Home, Cordova co-founded their @Work Division, created @Home's Online Services and spearheaded @Home's Work.com business portal strategy with Excite and AT&T. On the side, she wanted to keep her hand in the entrepreneurial market and started Corlund Industries where she would consult with start-ups and organize workshops for entrepreneurs. While presenting at an e-commerce "Think Tank" in October 1998, Cordova met Marx who was also presenting. Cordova explained the meeting:

EXHIBIT 7A
Historic Profit and
Loss Statements

Source: TixTo Go.

	Jan–Dec '98	Jan–Apr '99
Ordinary Income/Expense		
Income		
4100 · Ticket Revenue	19,761.93	125,966.70
Total Income	**19,761.93**	**125,966.70**
Cost of Goods Sold		
5000 · Cost of Goods Sold		
5100 · Cost of Goods Sold	18,909.76	115,803.77
5800 · Merchant Fees	1,136.60	4,968.11
Total 5000 · Cost of Goods Sold	20,046.36	120,771.88
Total COGS	**20,046.36**	**120,771.88**
Gross Profit	**−284.43**	**5,194.82**
Expense		
6100 · Marketing		
6103 · Brochures	249.55	1,922.65
6100 · Marketing—Other	487.55	0.00
Total 6100 · Marketing	**737.10**	**1,922.65**
6120 · Advertising		
6121 · Media		3,000.00
6122 · Tech Shows		775.59
6124 · Publication		500.00
6125 · Advertising—Other	194.12	675.00
Total 6120 · Advertising	**194.12**	**4,950.59**
6180 · Marketing Salaries		1,000.00
6190 · Marketing Consulting	12,087.30	548.07
6280 · Sales Salaries		
6281 · Sales Compensation	5,480.77	40,485.81
6283 · Bonuses		8,270.00
6284 · Commissions		1,158.41
Total 6280 · Sales Salaries	**5,480.77**	**49,914.22**
6400 · Research & Development		
6402 · Technical	9,627.13	24,171.62
6490 · R&D Consulting	525.00	
Total 6400 · R&D/Consulting	**10,152.13**	**24,171.62**
6500 · General/Admin Salaries		
6501 · Executive Compensation	125,000.00	85,472.27
6502 · Administrative Compensation	17,793.50	14,772.24
Total 6500 · General/Admin Salaries	**142,793.50**	**100,244.51**
6505 · Payroll Taxes		
6505 · Payroll Taxes—Other	7,973.93	7,761.47
6506 · Payroll Taxes—Penalty	—	81.55
Total 6505 · Payroll Taxes	**7,973.93**	**7,843.02**
6510 · General Administrative		
6510 · Rent	7,400.00	5,550.00
6511 · Janitorial	1,840.00	1,340.00
6512 · Telephone	4,289.91	4,198.78
6513 · Security Services	190.00	108.00
6518 · Workers Comp Insurance	367.49	705.23
Total 6510 · General Administrative	**14,087.40**	**11,902.01**
6520 · Office Supplies/Equipment		
6520 · Office Supplies	6,381.43	4,536.67
6522 · Computer	96.57	
6523 · Furniture/Equipment	1,858.54	
6524 · Postage and Delivery	542.89	531.20
6525 · Printing and Reproduction	141.82	142.04

(continued)

EXHIBIT 7A
(Continued)

	Jan–Dec '98	Jan–Apr '99
6527 · Licenses and Permits	385.00	
6529 · Internet	618.50	4,034.79
Total 6520 · Office Supplies/Equipment	**10,024.75**	**9,244.70**
6530 · Publications/Subscriptions	861.32	70.00
6531 · Dues/Membership Fees		
6531 · Dues/Membership-Other	165.00	
6532 · Internet	559.65	
6533 · General Dues	240.00	288.00
Total 6531 · Dues/Membership Fees	**964.65**	**288.00**
6545 · Donations/Gifts		
6547 · Gifts	371.07	
Total 6545 · Donations/Gifts	**371.07**	**0.00**
6540 · Equipment Lease/Rental		
6548 · Leased Equipment	2,129.44	698.18
6549 · Equipment Rental	53.70	
Total 6540 · Equipment Lease/Rental	**2,183.14**	**698.18**
6550 · Repairs & Maintenance		
6552· Office Equipment	109.97	76.00
Total 6550 · Repairs & Maintenance	**109.97**	**76.00**
6556 · Automobile Expenses-Fuel	133.51	218.12
6560 · Tools/Parking	14.50	183.50
6565 · Bank Service Charge	−13.00	20.00
6570 · Professional Fees		
6570 · Professional Fees-Other		1,400.00
6571 · Accounting Fees	7,065.00	9,968.75
6572 · Legal Fees	7,511.41	1,247.00
6576 · Consulting Fees	15,042.00	37,883.00
6577 · Professional Development	441.75	537.27
Total 6570 · Professional Fees	**30,060.16**	**51,036.02**
6580 · Recruiting	65.00	180.00
6585 · Travel & Entertainment		
6587 · Entertainment	1,478.70	1,431.98
6588 · Meals	446.88	177.51
6589 · Travel	2,006.93	1,607.00
Total 6585 · Travel & Ent	**3,932.51**	**3,216.49**
6590 · Bad Debt	27.36	
6800 · Depreciation Expense	606.57	1,806.90
6805 · Amortization Expense	180.00	60.00
6900 · Penalties	36.89	
Total Expense	**230,116.03**	**267,374.91**
Net Ordinary Income	**−230,400.46**	**−262,180.09**
Other Income		
7010 · Interest Income	11.30	12.86
7030 · Other Income	3.41	
Total Other Income	**14.71**	**12.86**
Other Expense		
8010 · Other Expenses		
8012 · Interest Expense		
8012 · Interest Expense-Other	2,233.11	44.00
801210 · Officers Notes		3,888.00
801211 · Credit Cards		178.32
Total 8012 Interest Expense	**2233.11**	**3,610.32**
8030 · Income Taxes	600.00	800.00
Total Other Expense	**2,833.11**	**4,410.32**
Net Other Income	−2,818.40	−4,397.46
Net Income	**−233,218.86**	**−266,577.55**

EXHIBIT 7B
Historic Balance Sheets

Source: TixToGo.

	12/31/98	4/30/99
ASSETS		
Current Assets		
Checking/Savings		
1100 · Bank-Check (WFB)	13,371.09	–11,098.68
1102 · Bank-MMA (WFB)		31,558.31
Total Checking/Savings	13,371.09	20,459.63
Accounts Receivable		
1200 · Accounts Receivable	1,078.62	4,964.51
Total Accounts Receivable	1,078.62	4,964.51
Other Current Assets		
1140 · Employee Advances	52.51	—
1400 · Prepaid Expenses		
1402 · Maintenance		836.00
1500 · Deposits		
1501 · Workers Comp	883.00	883.00
Total 1500 · Deposits	883.00	883.00
Total Other Current Assets	935.51	883.00
Total Current Assets	15,385.22	27,143.14
Fixed Assets		
1600 · Computer		
1600 · Computer Equipment—Other	10,289.16	17,358.67
1601 · Acc Depreciation-Computer Equip	–372.34	–1,292.94
1602 · F/F/E	2,920.00	4,981.38
1603 · Acc Depreciation-F/F/E	–103.90	–284.64
1604 · Computer Developed Software	2,642.12	7,046.75
1605 · Acc Depreciation-Computer Develop	–130.33	–835.89
Total 1600 · Computer	15,244.71	26,973.33
Total Fixed Assets	15,244.71	26,973.33
Other Assets		
1800 · Organizational Costs		
1800 · Organizational Costs—Other	900.00	900.00
1801 · Acc Amortization	–195.00	–255.00
Total 1800 · Organizational Costs	705.00	645.00
1860 · Stock Offering Cost	9,716.85	9,716.85
Total Other Assets	10,421.85	10,361.85
TOTAL ASSETS	41,051.78	64,478.32
LIABILITIES & EQUITY		
Liabilities		
Current Liabilities		
Accounts Payable		
2000 · Accounts Payable	30,185.87	94,912.85
2011 · Accounts Payable-EVA's	456.90	456.90
2060 · Credit Card		
02070 · WFB-LT	192.61	144.68
02071 · WFB-RM	266.83	1,212.93
2072 · HRM-Pitneyworks		8,676.57
2074 · LT-American Express		1,681.09
2075 · RM American Express		373.83
Total Credit Cards	459.44	12,089.10
Total Accounts Payable	31,102.21	107,458.85

(continued)

EXHIBIT 7B
(Continued)

	12/31/98	4/30/99
2013 · Accrued Payroll	63,666.68	144,775.12
Payroll Liabilities		
2015 · FWH	3,048.94	3,014.00
2016 · FICA	2,854.22	2,711.90
2017 · Mcare	667.52	634.24
2018 · SWH-Ca	822.27	537.67
2019 · SDI-Ca	87.59	63.53
2020 · SUI-Ca	318.11	85.61
2021 · ETT-Ca	9.36	8.31
2022 · FUI	289.57	76.15
2023 · SWH-CO	749.40	431.00
2024 · SUI-CO		183.33
Total 2014 · Payroll Liabilities	**8,846.98**	**7,745.74**
2026 · Accrued Workers Comp	367.49	49.01
2029 · Other Accrued Expenses	203.25	203.25
2101 · Notes Payable-Convertible		50,000.00
Promissory Notes		
Total Current Liabilities	**104,186.61**	**310,231.97**
Long Term Liabilities		
Loans Payable		
2301 · Ralph Marx	60,595.10	150,595.10
230101 · Interest-Ralph Marx	1,423.46	4,529.30
2302 · Lee Taylor	9,920.43	9,920.43
230202 · Interest-Lee Taylor	668.13	950.29
Total Loans Payable	**72,607.12**	**165,995.12**
Total Long Term Liabilities	**72,607.12**	**165,995.12**
Total Liabilites	**176,793.73**	**476,227.09**
Equity		
3012 · Series A Preferred Stock	98,996.26	98,996.26
3014 · Common Stock	2,000.00	2,000.00
3900 · Retained Earnings	−3,519.35	−246,167.48
Net Income	−233,218.86	−266,577.55
Total Equity	**−135,741.95**	**−411,748.77**
TOTAL LIABILITIES & EQUITY	**41,051.78**	**64,478.32**

When Ralph presented TixToGo, my ears perked and that old entrepreneurial spirit revived as I listened to him explain his model. I realized that they had gotten it right: TixToGo was a Web-based, self-service application that had infinite scalability. Organizers could sign up their events, and participants would come and buy tickets, all automated. You make money while you sleep, and the customers do all the publishing work. I went up to Ralph after the meeting and told him about my background and about Corlund and asked if I could work with him a while for free just to see how he was doing and see if I could help.

With that, Cordova started to serve as an advisor to TixToGo. Between February and May Cordova helped devise a sales and marketing strategy that she felt would give TixToGo an edge in the market.

Cordova's strategy was dependent on hitting the market early before competition would really heat up. As of May 1999, there were several companies that were beginning to operate in similar markets, but none that had any critical mass in its space. One company, Enteronline.com, had a commerce engine like TixToGo, but was still a fledgling company targeted towards sports and had not reached significant levels of sales or traffic. In addition, there were the event planning companies, represented most prominently by Evite, a

EXHIBIT 7C   Income Statement Proforma ($)

Source: TixToGo.

	FY 1999	FY 2000	FY 2001	FY 2002	FY 2003
REVENUE					
Ticket Revenue	$25,294	$20,888,660	$52,221,651	$104,443,302	$156,664,954
Advertising Revenue	$1,913	$563,400	$2,400,000	$9,450,000	$17,280,000
Souvenir Revenue	$2,325	$528,300	$2,700,000	$7,560,000	$13,440,000
Other	$0	$0	$0	$0	$0
Total Revenue	$29,532	$21,980,360	$57,321,651	$121,453,302	$187,384,954
Cost of Goods Sold	$53,648	$700,583	$1,489,297	$1,966,935	$2,447,963
Gross Margin	($24,116)	$21,279,777	$55,832,355	$119,486,368	$184,936,991
% of Revenue	(82%)	97%	97%	98%	99%
Operating Expenses					
Engineering	$242,488	$1,516,908	$4,744,882	$6,757,424	$9,514,074
% of Revenue	821%	7%	8%	6%	5%
Marketing/Sales	$242,161	$12,480,918	$31,730,291	$64,226,275	$97,598,730
% of Revenue	820%	57%	55%	53%	52%
Administration	$441,457	$3,048,307	$5,416,983	$8,050,761	$10,076,694
% of Revenue	1495%	14%	9%	7%	5%
Total Operating Expenses	$926,106	$17,046,133	$41,914,156	$79,034,460	$117,189,498
% of Revenue	3136%	78%	73%	65%	63%
Income Before Interest & Taxes	($950,222)	$4,233,644	$13,918,199	$40,451,908	$67,747,493
% of Revenue	(3218%)	19%	24%	33%	36%
Interest Expense	$0	$0	$0	$0	$0
Interest Revenue	$0	$0	$0	$0	$0
Income Before Taxes	($950,222)	$4,233,644	$13,918,199	$40,451,908	$67,747,493
Tax Exp	$0	$1,313,369	$5,567,280	$16,180,763	$27,098,997
Net Income	($950,222)	$2,920,275	$8,350,919	$24,271,145	$40,648,496
% of Revenue	(3218%)	14%	15%	20%	22%

company that had recently made a move in the event planning space and had started generating consumer traffic. But none of the event planning companies, including Evite, had developed a method of accepting credit card payments over the Web. Other companies provided some similar ticketing services, but focused only on a specific vertical market, such as RaceGate.com that was a portal for race enthusiasts. The company and Cordova felt that the real competition would come from new start-ups or existing players that were not direct competitors as of yet but would be if they developed a commerce engine. As with all start-ups, it was a little unclear as to what these company's real plans were and how long it would take them to develop a similar product. (See **Exhibits 8** and **9** for recent investments in comparable companies and comparable company descriptions.)

Cordova had not planned on leaving @Home where she had six months of vesting left, but she felt compelled to join TixToGo:

> If it were just online ticketing I don't think I would have left @Home, but when I saw how people were using the service, the vast demand for a multitude of uses, I realized it was far more than ticketing. This commerce and reporting engine could handle payments of any kind, including registration, RSVPs, collection of membership dues, donations, sponsorships, anything. Everything from a PricewaterhouseCoopers conference to Zamora the Torture King's Houdini-like performance. I realized it was a marketplace for any type of activity, and

EXHIBIT 7D **Balance Sheet Proforma ($)**

Source: TixToGo.

	FY 1999	FY 2000	FY 2001	FY 2002	FY 2003
ASSETS					
Current Assets					
Cash	$1,382,316	$9,311,884	$17,701,981	$46,507,907	$91,768,480
Net Accounts Rec	$0	$0	$0	$0	$0
Inventory (0 days)	$0	$0	$0	$0	$0
Total Current Assets	$1,382,316	$9,311,884	$17,701,981	$46,507,907	$91,768,480
Gross Fixed Assets	**$122,600**	**$426,000**	**$700,600**	**$957,400**	**$1,228,100**
Less Accum. Depreciation	$14,214	$111,092	$344,625	$622,892	$890,258
Net Fixed Assets	**$108,386**	**$314,908**	**$355,975**	**$334,508**	**$337,842**
TOTAL ASSETS	**$1,490,702**	**$9,626,792**	**$18,057,956**	**$46,842,416**	**$92,106,322**
LIABILITIES					
Short Term Liabilities					
Accounts Payable (30 days)	$67,841	$1,814,933	$1,658,395	$3,366,906	$5,075,726
Salaries Payable (15 days)	$62,083	$217,438	$375,769	$527,202	$704,234
Taxes Payable (90 days)	$0	$1,313,369	$1,391,820	$4,045,191	$6,774,749
Line of Credit (0% net A/R)	$0	$0	$0	$0	$0
Current Portion of Capital Equipment Lease	$0	$0	$0	$0	$0
Current Portion of Long Term Debt	$0	$0	$0	$0	$0
Total Short Term Liabilities	**$129,924**	**$3,345,739**	**$3,425,983**	**$7,939,298**	**$12,554,709**
Long Term Liabilities					
Capital Equipment Lease (3 years)	$0	$0	$0	$0	$0
Long Term Debt (5 years)	$0	$0	$0	$0	$0
Total Long Term Liabilities	**$0**	**$0**	**$0**	**$0**	**$0**
TOTAL LIABILITIES	**$129,924**	**$3,345,739**	**$3,425,983**	**$7,939,298**	**$12,554,709**
Equity					
Preferred Stock	$2,099,000	$4,099,000	$4,099,000	$4,099.000	$4,099,000
Common Stock	$212,000	$212,000	$212,000	$212,000	$212,000
Retained Earnings	($950,222)	$1,970,053	$10,320,972	$34,592,117	$75,240,613
Total Equity	**$1,360,778**	**$6,281,053**	**$14,631,972**	**$38,903,117**	**$79,551,613**
LIABILITIES & EQUITY	**$1,490,702**	**$9,626,792**	**$18,057,956**	**$46,842,416**	**$92,106,322**

the market size was enormous. I also realized that we had about six months to create this marketplace and establish a leadership position. And I guess I felt that they needed my full time commitment, not a part-time interest to make it happen.

But Cordova knew she couldn't do it alone. After she convinced a couple of colleagues to join the firm with her, Cordova took the plunge and accepted the position as CEO of TixToGo, flanked by a new VP of Marketing and a new VP of Sales (See **Exhibit 5**). Taylor left Telluride behind and moved his family out to San Francisco, and Marx set Advocate aside and turned his focus full time to TixToGo.

The First Day on the Job

Cordova knew going in that there would be lots of work to do. Amongst other things, she knew that she needed to build a management team quickly in order to execute her strategy. Additionally, even though the site was up and working, it still needed some changes,

EXHIBIT 7E   **Cash Flow Statement Proforma**

Source: TixToGo.

	FY 1999	FY 2000	FY 2001	FY 2002	FY 2003
BEGINNING CASH	$0	$1,382,316	$9,311,884	$17,701,981	$46,507,907
Sources of Cash					
Net Income	($950,222)	$2,920,275	$8,350,919	$24,271,145	$40,648,496
Add Depreciation/Amortization	$14,214	$96,878	$233,533	$278,267	$267,367
Issuance of Preferred Stock	$2,099,000	$2,000,000	$0	$0	$0
Issuance of Common Stock	$212,000	$0	$0	$0	$0
Plus Changes in:					
Accounts Payable (30 days)	$67,841	$1,747,092	($156,538)	$1,708,511	$1,708,820
Salaries Payable (15 days)	$62,083	$155,354	$158,331	$151,433	$177,032
Taxes Payable (90 days)	$0	$1,313,369	$78,451	$2,653,371	$2,279,558
Additions to Line of Credit (0% of net A/R)	$0	$0	$0	$0	$0
Additions to Capital Equipment Lease (3 years)	$0	$0	$0	$0	$0
Additions to Long Term Debt (5 years)	$0	$0	$0	$0	$0
Total Sources of Cash	$1,504,916	$8,232,968	$8,664,697	$29,062,727	$45,531,273
Uses of Cash					
Less Changes in:					
Net Accounts Receivable	$0	$0	$0	$0	$0
Inventory (0 days)	$0	$0	$0	$0	$0
Gross Fixed Assets	$122,600	$303,400	$274,600	$256,800	$270,700
Reductions to Credit Line	$0	$0	$0	$0	$0
Reductions to Capital Equipment Lease	$0	$0	$0	$0	$0
Reductions to Long Term Debt	$0	$0	$0	$0	$0
Total Uses	$122,600	$303,400	$274,600	$256,800	$270,700
CHANGES IN CASH	$1,382,316	$7,929,569	$8,390,097	$28,805,927	$45,260,573
ENDING CASH	$1,382,316	$9,311,884	$17,701,981	$46,507,907	$91,768,480

EXHIBIT 8   **Recent Investment in Comparable Companies**

Source: VentureSource.

Company	Founded	Selected Investors	Amount Raised	Post-Money Valuation	Date Raised
ECircles.com	1998	Interactive Minds	$1.0 million	N/A	4Q 1998
eGroups	1998	CMGI	$6.2 million	N/A	4Q 1998
EventSource.com	1995	Sequoia, Angel Investors, LP	$3.7 million	$10.0 million	2Q 1999
Evite	1997	August Capital	$8.0 million	N/A	2Q 1999
Mambo.com	1998	Seed, Individuals	$0.02 million	N/A	4Q 1998
SeeUThere.com	1998	Draper Fisher	$3.7 million	$7.6 million	1Q 1999

EXHIBIT 9   **Description of Competitors**

Source: VentureSource.

ECircles.com

Developer and marketer of a consumer Web service that allowed circles of people to communicate online, plan group activities, and share information on products and services. Through this service, a user created or participated in any number of "circles" with family members, friends, or people in a club, team, or organization. These private circles offered features such as discussion boards, photo albums, a shared group calendar file storage, gift registries, and recommendation lists.

eGroups

Provider of e-mail group services. The company's service allows people to e-mail a group of people using just one e-mail address, create a customized group home page, and share a group events calendar. eGroup's clearly classified affinity groups offer targeted advertising opportunities through banners on eGroup Web pages, targeted sponsorships, opt-in offers in specific interest categories and ad banners embedded within group messages delivered via e-mail.

EventSource.com

Provider of a trading network used by corporate and association professionals to plan conferences, meetings, training, tradeshows, and sales and incentive programs. The company's trading network connected the group travel markets' meeting planners with suppliers such as hotels, cities, and event services. The company's BookIt! e-commerce service offered a way for users to research and book with more than 12,000 meeting hotels, convention centers, resorts, venues, and suppliers.

Evite

Provider of consumer group coordination and communication services using e-mail and the Web. The company allowed the user to "evite" an entire group in one step. The company would then tally the RSVPs, and display group feedback and decisions on a private, personalized group event Web page, created just for the user's group. A poll let guests vote for their preferred day and date and question fields could also be created.

Mambo.com

Provider of online invitation and group payment service that offers the broadest range of activities and events. The company brought consumers together for everyday activities, parties and events, utilizing the Web to build communities and commerce opportunities around these social gatherings. Had only received seed funding and was expected to raise venture capital.

SeeUThere.com

Provider of Web-based event coordination service. The company integrated Internet and traditional communications methods to allow event organizers to reach their membership. Metered services such as printed invites, faxes, telephone RSVPs, and pager notifications were available in addition to e-mail notices and Web forms. For example, invitations could be sent out in mass via e-mail, print or fax. Attendees could also RSVP through a touch-tone phone.

both cosmetically and technically, for it to work the way she thought it needed. She also thought that the name, TixToGo, might be a little bit of a misnomer. "We were a provider of e-commerce solutions for events and activities," Cordova explained, "not simply a ticketing company." Cordova was wondering what the best name would be. Finally, she knew that they would need to raise venture money, both to fund the firm's expansion and to lend it credibility in the marketplace.

What she didn't realize was how cash-strapped the company was. When she arrived on May 18, 1999, the company had a relatively low burn rate, but had only $12,000 in the bank. Although the company was generating some sales, this would not be nearly enough to cover expenses—most notably the payroll expenses. Cordova explained the predicament:

I knew that we needed to raise some funding soon, but I wasn't aware of the dire situation the company was in. There are really three things a company needs to operate: money, product, and people. When I arrived at TixToGo, all three needed some improving. The question was about priorities and maximizing the value of the firm. But one thing was clear: we needed cash—fast.

Cordova reasoned that the company really had three options to resolve its funding crisis.

Venture Capital Financing

The first option was venture funding. With an immediate funding need of around $5 million for the next six months, Cordova believed that VC funding was preferable over angel investors as VCs were much more capable of writing a large check. Moreover, she believed that VC funding was essential because of the stamp of approval a company would get from receiving money from a top VC. That stamp would not only help with future capital raising exercises, including an IPO, but would also help with recruiting new employees, attracting new customers and forming joint venture relationships. She also knew that if they chose the right VC, the VC could get actively involved in the business and could help sort out some of the issues the company would face in the future. However, she also had some concerns. Cordova elaborated on this option:

> Although VC funding would be beneficial, there are some concerns about heading into VC funding right away. First, our valuation would take a big hit if we were to approach a VC today. There are a lot of things that we know need fixing and we know how to fix. With a little more time, we could hire a couple of people, fix the web site and generate more revenue, which would provide an incredible boost to our valuation. In addition, VC funding usually takes quite some time to put together. We are going to have to find some way around this crunch, whether we approach VCs immediately or not. So perhaps we should first solve some of the big problems and then get a better valuation from our VC round later.

Bridge Financing

Another option would be to secure funding from angel investors or small venture capital funds. The benefit from this option would be that funding could be raised much more quickly than if TixToGo approached the top VCs. Moreover, Cordova felt that they could secure some much-needed attention from this source of financing. "We would be the star of their portfolio," Cordova explained. "Therefore, they would be much more amenable to providing us with some hands-on assistance in the business.

There were some risks with this strategy, however. The structuring of this type of deal could become quite tricky—especially if the company chose to fund the entire round with this source. At between $100,000 and $300,000 per investor, this would require a large number of investors, which in turn could cause investor relations nightmares and complications for future rounds of financing. Moreover, if the company were to take some bridge funding, there could also be a valuation problem with the subsequent VC round if the VC round was too close to the bridge round. The VCs not only wanted to make sure they would get a specific amount of control, return and absolute dollar exposure, but they also wanted to ensure that the founders and other employees, like Cordova, were given proper incentives. As a result, there could be an issue surrounding the optimization of both the proper size of the pie and the value of each party's piece. Finally there could be some issues regarding the structure of the deal that could cause complications for future rounds. Although it was not always the case, often times the structure and documentation of these deals could become overly burdensome. "You have to be careful," warned Cordova. "If things get too messy with the structure and the documentation, that could be enough 'hair' for the VCs to politely decline even before doing due diligence."

Exit

A final, though less appealing option, would be to find an immediate exit for the business. There were several players that were tangentially involved in TixToGo's space, like eGroups, that see a real value to adding the company's commerce engine capabilities to their existing product. Moreover, there were the horizontal portals, like Yahoo, or portals that focused on vertical markets that could be interested in the company's product. The big problem with this solution was that everyone at TixToGo really believed that they could build something great. Cordova also had some other concerns:

> I have a responsibility to the employees, especially to the ones who just joined with me, to ensure they are taken care of, both professionally and financially. It is one thing if a deal would benefit everyone tremendously and another thing if a deal provides a huge return to the founders, seed investors and myself, but only a modest return for the other employees, especially the ones who just joined us. I do not want to abandon those people or build up a reputation for being someone who just flips companies. I do not want to be a CEO that doesn't look out for the employees, who are shareholders, too, or does not have what it takes to build a company.

Decisions, Decisions

With those things in mind, Cordova looked at Marx from her new desk. She really believed that the company had a great idea and felt she had devised a strategy that would provide the road map to a successful company. But the cash constraints were real and severe. Could they even survive through a bridge round? Even though it was not optimal, would it still be best to sell out to a strategic player? Could one even be found in time? Cordova reminded herself that the NASDAQ had just had another of its increasingly frequent hick-ups with the composite index dropping 9.21% percent between April 13 and April 19, 1999.

Marx and Taylor turned to Cordova and asked, "So you said you had a couple of ideas?"

Module

Managing Contingencies and Changing Contexts

As indicated by the heading, this module has a dual focus. Unexpected changes in entrepreneurial ventures, typically for the worse, occur quite often. Courses of action for keeping ailing entrepreneurial ventures from failing are analyzed and tools for anticipating the likelihood of contingencies examined. Analysis of cases in this module suggests that causes of crises can be external or internal to ventures. The module's other focus is changes of context that occur over time in the wake of fundamental shifts such as industry sector restructurings or transitions from planned to market economies. Changes studied include the transition of Eastern Europe beginning in the 1990s, the end of the apartheid regime in South Africa, the Asian financial crisis, and Japan's ailing financial system. These kinds of externally induced shifts often offer entrepreneurs attractive opportunities for starting or restructuring companies.

The preface of this book argued that the structure of a venture determines its performance. Ventures do well if they are structured such that the opportunity effectively matches the available resources. The nature of this match is clearly dependent on the local context. This module illustrates how rapid context or other unforeseen changes can suddenly and drastically alter this match. Case analysis identifies patterns of entrepreneurial responses that sustain the quality of the match between opportunity at hand and resources available.

Several learning points and insights emerge from this module. The first, overarching learning point is that in times of crisis there is a need for rapid action. Entrepreneurial ventures rarely possess the excess cash or other types of insurance that enable them to survive a crisis simply by continuing their prior strategy and riding out the storm. Their strength lies instead in their ability to adapt to change quickly. Case analysis suggests that rapid action implies not just speed but also a refocusing of resources on the few big battles that matter.[1] The case of Jafco is an example of this.

[1] The argument that firms with higher levels of absorptive capacity (i.e., the ability to exploit new technological developments) will perform better than other firms in the face of rapid (technological) change is in line with the argument made in this module for entrepreneurial firms. Cohen, Wesley M., and Daniel A. Levinthal. "Fortune Favors the Prepared Firm." *Management Science* 40, no. 2 (1994): 227–252.

The second learning point is that it makes sense to think in terms of likelihood distribution curves of possible outcomes. This way of thinking is particularly relevant to cross-border ventures that are affected by more variables than ventures established in domestic settings. Although simulation software such as Crystal Ball® can support the relevant analysis, it is important to think carefully about the inputs to the simulation and their underlying distribution.

The third learning point is that differences in national cultures are too often blamed for crises in cross-border ventures. This module suggests that one needs to examine the degree to which a crisis is driven by firm culture rather than national culture. In many cross-border ventures firm culture exerts a greater impact than national culture on performance. This suggests that one start by analyzing what different national cultures have in common rather than what makes them different.

The fourth learning point is that it makes sense for entrepreneurs with nimble organizations to think of rapid context changes as opportunities for entrepreneurial ventures. For example, the Promise case, about a Japanese consumer finance firm, examines how an industry that enjoyed implicit government protection from failure offered unique opportunities for entrepreneurial start-ups and underdogs when that government protection was withdrawn.

The fifth learning point is that entrepreneurs should consider the concept of modularity in the design of ventures because it yields a higher level of flexibility, often at relatively low cost. This kind of flexibility is particularly useful if an external crisis affects a venture. It can also be helpful in the case of a crisis internal to a venture, because the part of the organization in crisis can be identified and thereby dealt with more easily. Finally, modularity is useful because it can help entrepreneurs pursue opportunities that result from contextual changes.

Cases in This Module

This module consists of five cases. "Jafco America Ventures, Inc.: Building a Venture Capital Firm" is the first case of this module. The parent firm, Jafco, is Japan's largest private equity firm, with more than 400 employees. Jafco America Ventures is making a second attempt to enter the U.S. venture capital market after all the principals involved in the first attempt quit the firm. The newly hired managing director is facing a range of challenges and wonders how he should cope with the crisis. Case analysis must tackle the question of which issues the managing director should focus on. Analysis should also examine whether the firm's problems vis-à-vis its Japanese parent are related more to the firm itself or to national culture. The newly hired managing director must also figure out how to make Jafco America Ventures more independent without losing the parent firm's support. A published video offers reflections on how he set priorities and dealt with the challenges.[2] Two scholarly articles provide useful background reading for this case.[3,4]

[2] Kuemmerle, Walter. *JAFCO America Ventures: Reflections by Barry Schiffman, President (HBS Video 9-802-805)*. Boston: Harvard Business School Publishing, 2002.

[3] Gompers, Paul A., and Josh Lerner. "What Drives Venture Capital Fund Raising." *Brookings Papers on Economic Activity* (1998): 149–192. Kuemmerle, W. "Comparing Catalysts of Change: Evolution and Institutional Differences in the Venture Capital Industries in the U.S., Japan and Germany." In *Research on Technological Innovation, Management and Policy*, edited by Robert Burgelman and Henry Chesbrough, 227–261. Greenwich, CT: JAI Press, 2001.

[4] The case has geographic ties to Mobile Communications Tokyo (Module 3) and Promise (this module) and has interesting parallels with Ducati (Module 2) inasmuch as both cases focus on private equity managers in their role as entrepreneurs.

The second case, Jinwoong, deals with an entrepreneurial venture that faces a severe crisis and potential bankruptcy. This case supports the central idea that a global perspective on access to resources is essential to the survival of a venture. The Korean firm Jinwoong did not have such a perspective. This 19-year-old company had grown into the world's largest manufacturer of camping tents. Jinwoong's main customers were large U.S. and European retailers. The firm's successful global expansion notwithstanding, all of its external financing was still debt provided by Korean banks. Due to the Asian (and Korean) financial crisis of 1997–1998, Jinwoong's banks began calling their loans. The entrepreneur, facing illiquidity, had to rethink his firm's financing plans. Case analysis should focus on whether the crisis, albeit painful in the short term, might act as a catalyst to configure the company differently with a stronger footing outside of Korea.[5]

The third case considers an entrepreneurial firm in crisis in a country that has recently undergone significant change. Unable to raise capital from seasoned venture capitalists during their initial search, the entrepreneurs behind Telewizja Wisla, a newly created TV station in Poland, sought funds from two medium-sized Polish service and construction firms. Now that the entrepreneurs are looking for a major strategic investor, these original investors have become a major roadblock. The case allows for a discussion how during a transition from a planned to a market economy, some contextual changes occur more slowly than others. For example, privatization of certain industries might occur early but the sophistication of local investors might improve only over time. Case analysis can also examine outcome variables (for example, an internal rate of return to investors) in terms of a likelihood distribution curve. Developing such a curve is useful not only for analytical purposes but also for communicating with business partners or investors. The case also lends itself well to a simulation analysis.[6]

The fourth case in this module focuses on the oldest company in this case book, Promise, a Japanese consumer finance company founded by an entrepreneur in 1963 and now run by the founder's nephew. A provider of unsecured loans, the company went public in 1996 and is doing quite well. The case illustrates how consumer finance companies in Japan have always had a somewhat shabby image and never received any active support from Japan's mighty ministry of finance. Banks in Japan, on the other hand, often operated under the assumption that the government would bail them out under any circumstances. As a result, some of the best consumer finance companies developed efficient structures for providing loans and assessing credit risk. When widespread mismanagement in the banking sector reduced government support, Japanese consumer finance companies emerged as darlings of foreign investors. Analysis of this case should focus on the advantages and disadvantages of being the underdog. Specifically, being an underdog can lead to radical innovation. This advantage over incumbents generally increases in industries that undergo fundamental change.

[5] Jinwoong has interesting parallels with Internet Securities (Module 1) and TelePizza (Module 5), with which it shares international expansion issues. Internet Securities has just begun its international expansion, TelePizza is further along, and Jinwoong has created a full-blown entrepreneurial multinational firm. Jinwoong can also be tied to Ducati (Module 2), as both involve private equity firms that benefited from entrepreneurial firms in a liquidity crisis, then helped their financing and product-market strategies. Finally, the case can be contrasted with TixToGo (Module 3) in that both firms had to raise cash quickly, albeit in quite different settings.

[6] Telewizja Wisla can be tied to Georgia Glass and Mineral Water and QI-Tech (Module 3), as all three involve country contexts that are in transition or have recently transitioned from planned economies. The case can also be linked to Capital Alliance (Module 3), as both cases lend themselves well to scenario analysis.

Case analysis should also examine whether Promise's business model might work outside of Japan. If not, international expansion must be approached with caution. In that case, Promise should probably make home-base-augmenting investments first as a way to understand how its business model needs to be adapted locally in other countries. In other words, a global perspective on opportunities is likely to improve Promise's performance. Finally, Promise is considering listing its shares in London or New York. Case analysis should examine whether this is a good decision. The case reinforces the notion that a global perspective on access to resources likely improves a firm's performance.[7]

The module's final case is concerned with an African company still run by its founders who have recently raised capital from a leading South African private equity firm. Gray Security provides building security services to commercial clients. The case suggests that the end of apartheid created considerable opportunity even as it occasioned uncertainty. Private enterprises were pressured by the South African government to make previously disadvantaged groups shareholders. Gray does not have such a shareholder group yet and is considering whether and how to build one. Case analysis should focus on how Gray can take advantage of recent changes. Its business model is that of a subscription firm with negative working capital. Although in public opinion entrepreneurship is often associated with high-tech ventures, this case suggests that prospective entrepreneurs should not overlook some quite attractive businesses simply because they seem too plain.[8]

---

[7] Promise has in common with the cases on @Hoc and Internet Securities (Module 1), Spotfire (Module 3), and TelePizza (Module 5) international expansion issues. Promise can be contrasted with Infosys (Module 5), which is also considering a listing on a U.S. exchange. Finally, Promise is tied to Mobile Communications Tokyo (Module 3) and Jafco (this module) by virtue of being set in Japan.

[8] Gray is linked to Capital Alliance (Module 3) by virtue of being located in Africa, a continent in dire need of more entrepreneurial activity. Gray also shares with Signature Security (Module 2), Jinwoong (this module), and TelePizza (Module 5) international expansion issues of more mature entrepreneurial firms.

Case

19

JAFCO America Ventures, Inc.: Building a Venture Capital Firm

"Par!" Barry Schiffman, president and chief investment officer of JAFCO America Ventures, Inc. (JAV), was delighted about his performance in JAV's golf tournament. The tournament was part of JAV's first strategy retreat meeting held in Applewood, California, two hours north of Palo Alto. If he got par on the last three holes of the Applewood golf course, he had a chance of winning the $600 prize money at stake. It was Friday, August 22, 1997, and Schiffman and all 14 employees and partners of JAV, including spouses, were enjoying the pleasant natural surroundings of Northern California's hills.

As Schiffman took a stance for his next tee shot, Hitoshi Imuta, chairman and chief operating officer of JAV, looked on. They exchanged a friendly smile. Imuta had recruited Schiffman to JAV in October 1996 from the renowned Silicon Valley venture capital firm Weiss, Peck and Greer Venture Partners where Schiffman had been a general partner. Since October 1996, Imuta had worked closely with Schiffman in rebuilding JAV after three of JAV's previous investment principals had left between April and August 1996 in a sweeping blow to JAV's parent company Japan Associated Finance Co., Ltd. (JAFCO).

Schiffman reminded himself that the challenges that lay ahead of him at JAV were more formidable than the task of scoring par on four successive golf holes. Schiffman reflected on his opening words for the strategy retreat on the previous day:

> We have come a long way since October 1996 and I would like to thank all of you for your efforts over the last months. But let's be clear about this: some of the biggest obstacles in making JAFCO America Ventures an outstanding venture capital firm are still ahead of us.

Professor Walter Kuemmerle, Professor Kiichiro Kobayashi of Keio Business School in Japan, and Charles M. Williams Fellow Chad Ellis, MBA '98 prepared this case as the basis for class discussion rather than to illustrate either effective or ineffective handling of an administrative situation. The assistance of the HBS California Research Center is gratefully acknowledged.

This retreat will lay the foundation for our efforts over the next year. This meeting is not only about developing an investment strategy but also about improving our execution capabilities. JAFCO America Ventures has access to unique resources. We must cultivate and use these resources more productively than we did in the past.

Schiffman felt he had done a good job in acknowledging his team's past efforts as well as in creating an increased sense of urgency among team members. However, numerous questions went through his mind: How should he go about recruiting an enterprise software partner to round out JAFCO's investment team? What was the best way to expand JAV's investment activities into life sciences? How could JAV improve the value-added activities provided to JAV's portfolio companies by JAFCO, JAV's parent company? Schiffman was particularly worried that JAFCO's flat compensation structure in Japan would trigger some of JAFCO's employees who were most valuable to JAV to leave the company. Schiffman summarized his challenge:

I have been recruited to manage a turnaround in a venture capital firm that has been drained of its principals. But beyond managing the turnaround there is a more fundamental question: How can we create one of the most uniquely positioned venture capital firms in the industry? How can we get into the best deals, achieve impressive returns and create a brand equity that rivals the best firms in Silicon Valley and Boston?

JAFCO and JAFCO America Ventures: The Origins

Japan Associated Finance Co., Ltd. (JAFCO) was established in 1973 as a joint venture between Nomura Securities Co., Ltd., Nippon Life Insurance Co., and the Sanwa Bank, Ltd. as the pioneering venture capital firm in Japan. The principal activities of JAFCO and its Japanese consolidated subsidiaries were investing in and offering consulting and information services to private companies with high potential for future growth. From its inception through March 31, 1997, JAFCO made investments in 1,656 venture businesses, backed initial public offerings (IPOs) of 423 companies, and managed 49 partnership funds with a cumulative ¥251.2 billion ($2.13 billion; US$1 = ¥118 in 8/97) in committed capital. JAFCO and its subsidiaries employed 406 people. (See **Exhibit 1** for JAFCO's organization chart.) In its fiscal year 1997, JAFCO achieved an operating profit of $102 million on total assets of $2,197 million. (See **Exhibit 2** and **3** for balance sheets and income statements.)

Unlike most U.S. venture capital firms, JAFCO was publicly held and traded on the Japanese OTC (see **Exhibit 4**). JAFCO's senior managers owned only a negligible share of the firm's equity and did not participate in its profits beyond an annual bonus not exceeding the base salary. JAFCO's investments were focused mainly on manufacturing and service industries and not solely on high technology sectors. In contrast to the United States, most technology development and commercialization in Japan is conducted in-house by large Japanese electronics, engineering, and pharmaceutical firms. JAFCO, with its 371 employees (not counting employees in subsidiaries) and 6 branch offices, was very large when compared to U.S. venture capital firms with an average of 3.5 partners. JAFCO used a highly structured process of screening a large number of potential portfolio companies, evaluating a smaller number of them in detail and eventually acquiring up to 10% of a portfolio firm's equity (see **Exhibit 5**). Over the years, JAFCO's performance had been quite good by Japanese standards. Generally, JAFCO's portfolio companies were taken public by Nomura's investment banking division. In Japan it took more than five years from the investment of a firm to its IPO for about 60% of all firms that went public. In the United States, by contrast about 60% of the firms went public in less than five years (see **Exhibit 6**).

EXHIBIT 1   **JAFCO (Japan), Inc. Organization Chart as of August 1997**

Source: JAFCO.

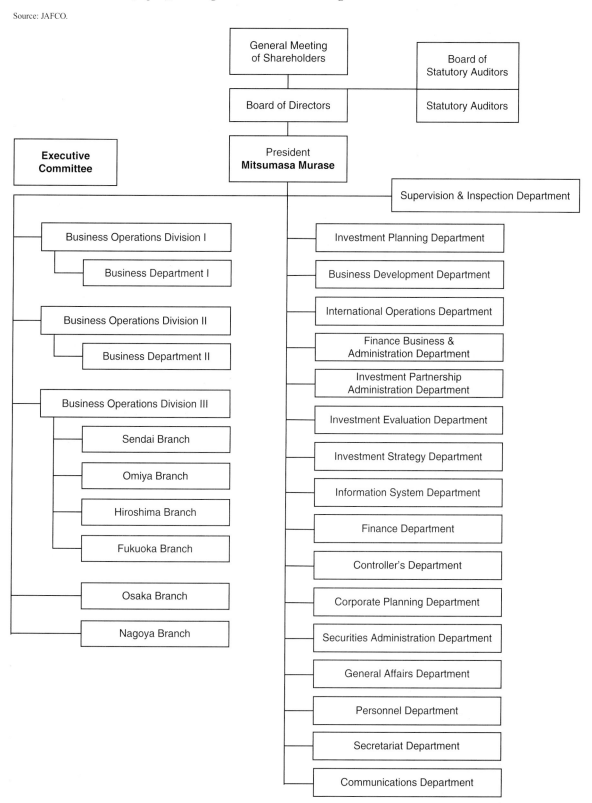

JAFCO's international expansion started in March 1983 with the establishment of JAFCO International (Asia) Ltd. in Hong Kong. In July 1984, JAV was established in Menlo Park, CA, and in February 1986, a representative office for Europe was established in London. JAFCO wanted to achieve two objectives by going abroad: first, the firm wanted to gain access to additional sources of capital for investments in Japan. Second, JAFCO's leaders wanted to learn more about the venture capital industry in the United States. In order to create deal flow, JAV had invited a number of partners at renowned VC firms, including such firms as Kleiner-Perkins, to join its advisory board. The former president, Mr. Yoshida, commented:

EXHIBIT 2
JAFCO Consolidated Income Statements

Source: JAFCO.

000s of US$ Except Per-Share Amounts	1996	1997
Revenues from operational investment securities	165,718	166,129
Investment management fees	58,032	69,887
Consulting fees	9,411	10,581
Interest on operational loans	31,597	23,186
Other	5,774	7,282
Net revenues	270,532	277,065
Cost of operational investment securities	81,030	62,266
Financial costs, net	18,935	18,936
Other	14,672	8,371
Cost of revenues	114,637	89,573
Gross profit	155,895	187,492
Selling, general and administrative expenses	84,379	85,379
Operating profit	71,516	102,113
Income from interest and dividends	6,411	7,419
Interest expense	8,742	5,742
Other, net	1,992	(10,089)
Income before tax	71,177	93,701
Income tax	53,411	58,685
Equity in net losses of affiliated companies	4,250	8,395
Net income	13,516	26,621
Net income per share	0.28	0.55
Cash dividends per share	0.20	0.20

EXHIBIT 3
JAFCO Consolidated Balance Sheets

Source: JAFCO.

000s of US$	1996	1997
ASSETS:		
Cash and time deposits	47,484	36,670
Marketable securities	106,089	110,669
Short-term loans receivable	87,847	58,516
Operational loans, net	750,960	653,710
Operational investment securities, net	730,710	727,113
Prepaid expenses and other assets	32,355	41,693
Property, plant and equipment, net	158,097	160,992
Investments in affiliated companies	44,879	36,782
Other investments and other assets, net	288,565	367,000
Intangible assets and deferred charges	8,847	4,694
Total Assets	2,255,831	2,197,839

(continued)

EXHIBIT 3
(Continued)

000s of US$	1996	1997
LIABILITIES:		
Short-term borrowings	804,234	660,419
Accrued income taxes	25,395	33,677
Accrued expenses and other liabilities	20,565	21,492
Long-term debt	652,444	711,186
Accrued retirement benefits	8,556	9,436
Total Liabilities	1,511,194	1,436,210
SHAREHOLDERS' EQUITY:		
Common Stock (80,000,000 shares authorized, 48,079,713 issued and outstanding)	264,444	264,444
Additional paid-in capital	260,371	260,371
Legal reserve	5,508	6,532
Retained earnings	214,855	230,395
Less—Treasury stock, at cost	(504)	(113)
Total Shareholders' Equity	744,637	761,629
Total Liabilities and Shareholders' Equity	2,255,831	2,197,839

EXHIBIT 4
**JAFCO's
Performance
(Financial and Share
Price)**

Source: Compiled from
JAFCO, Thomson Financial
Datastream data.

Financial Performance (figures in millions of ¥)

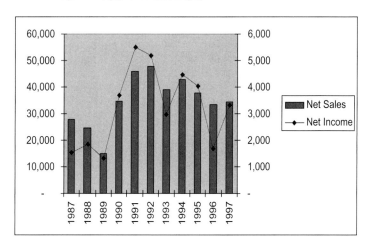

Share Price Performance

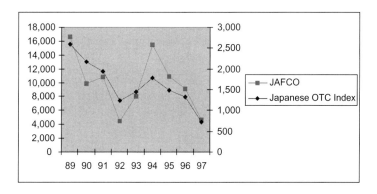

EXHIBIT 5   **JAFCO's Japan Investment Decision-making Process (August 1997)**

Source: JAFCO.

Roles of the Investment Department Staff	Roles of Back-up Teams	Reports	Investment Committee	Date
				X = Investment Date
Finding (# of Finding Team Members120) Meeting with Top Management	Investment Strategy Dep -Market Research -Teamwork with Industry and Academia	Development Report Preference List		X-90
Due Diligence 1	Investment Planning Dep -Recommendations for Financial Strategy	Financial Policy Report Business Plan		
Due Diligence 2	Investment Evaluation Dep -Evaluation of Business Plan -Evaluation of Technology -Appraisal of Marketability -Evaluation of Top Management -Grading			X-45
		Evaluation Memo (4~5 pages)		X-15
Investment Decisions NO (10%) YES (90%of proposals that reach this stage)			JAFCO Investment Committee (15 Directors) (Meets Each Friday)	X
Follow-up Value Added	Business Development Dep JAFCO Consulting JAFCO Asia Investment Service Other JAFCO Subsidiaries			
IPO Liquidation				

It was our main goal to source additional capital, but at the same time we were intrigued by the evolving venture capital industry in the United States and venture capital funded success stories like Lotus and Compaq. We thought that a couple of years down the road there might be something that JAFCO could learn from the venture capital (VC) system in the U.S.

Between 1984 and 1994, JAV focused on raising capital from U.S. investors. For that purpose, JAV opened an office in New York City in 1985, which became JAV's headquarters in 1988. JAFCO also moved its Menlo Park office to San Francisco in 1987. (See **Exhibits 7** and **8** for a list of investors in JAV's funds raised in the United States and invested in Japan.)

Between 1987 and 1996, JAV was successively headed by Shunsuke Fukuda, Shouichi Fujikawa, and Masahiko Saitoh, all Japanese nationals who had been temporarily transferred from Japan. In 1986, Bob Shell was hired as a fund manager. Shell's main role

EXHIBIT 6
Period of Time Elapsed from Company Creation to IPO (U.S. vs. Japan)

Source: *White Paper on Small and Medium Enterprises in Japan.* 1997. Tokyo: Small and Medium Enterprise Agency (MITI), p. 375.

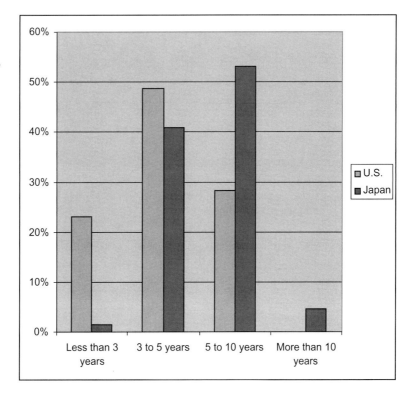

EXHIBIT 7
Investors in JAFCO America Venture Partners I (Fund raised in 9/1988)

Source: JAFCO.

Investor	US$ Invested
Leeway & Co.	8,000,000
General Electric	5,000,000
HLM Management	5,000,000
Chemical Equity	3,000,000
Exxon	2,000,000
Hoechst Celanese	2,000,000
Stanford University	2,000,000
Caisse des Depots	1,500,000
Shingetsu II	1,200,000
Hewlett Packard	1,000,000
Westinghouse	1,000,000
Raytheon	1,000,000
MSVC Japan	1,000,000
Marrion Merrell Dow	1,000,000
Hancock International	1,000,000
Greylock	500,000
JAFCO America	365,657
Total	36,565,657

was to act as an administrative head for JAV and to manage the relationship with investors to give JAV increased access to capital. In 1994, JAFCO's president, Mr. Yoshida, decided to push JAV to enter the U.S. VC market. While he suspected that the densely networked U.S. VC industry would represent considerable barriers to entry for a foreign firm, he felt that JAV could provide unique services to prospective portfolio firms. Yoshida stated:

EXHIBIT 8
Investors in JAFCO America Venture Partners II (Fund raised in 1994)

Source: JAFCO.

Investor	US$ Invested
Leeway & Co.	17,000,000
Exxon	10,000,000
IBM	10,000,000
NYNEX	10,000,000
Allstate Insurance	4,500,000
Allstate Life Insurance	2,500,000
Allstate Retirement	1,700,000
Allstate Agent	1,300,000
Hancock International	5,500,000
Hancock International Asia	900,000
Hancock Venture	750,000
Hewlett Packard	2,000,000
Johnson & Johnson	1,000,000
JAFCO America	678,283
Total	67,828,283

Between 1984 and 1990, we realized that you can only learn about VC in the U.S. by actually participating in investments and sweating through difficult situations in portfolio companies. We felt that we had a unique advantage over U.S. VC firms. We could provide potential portfolio companies with access to important distributors and customers in the world's second largest economy. Also, we could help portfolio companies find competent manufacturers. Finally, JAFCO had an excellent network within Asia. We decided to concentrate on information technology for three reasons. First, Japanese electronics and telecommunications firms were large and could be important lead customers and strategic partners for U.S. start-up firms. Second, Japanese electronics firms were reliable original equipment manufacturers (OEM) capable of producing large volumes of products at high quality levels. Third, other Asian countries where JAFCO had a dense network of contacts, such as Taiwan and Singapore, represented additional markets that were not immediately accessible for U.S. entrepreneurs.

In November 1994, JAFCO raised a ¥7 billion (U.S. $70 million; US$1 = ¥100 in 11/94) U.S. Information Technology Fund I from Japanese corporate investors, which included both operating and trading companies. The focus of this fund was balanced, including both early and late-stage investments in information technology firms in a broad sense (see **Exhibit 9**). Yoshida realized that in order to execute his investment philosophy of investing in U.S. companies, to whom JAFCO could provide unique value-added service, a team of qualified investment professionals would be needed. This team would bridge the geographical and cultural gap between Japan and the United States.

As a first step, in November 1994, Yoshida asked Jim Lu, a JAFCO employee, to transfer to JAV. Lu, of Chinese background, had been educated in Canada before joining JAFCO in Tokyo. He was fluent in Mandarin, English, and Japanese. At JAFCO, Lu had distinguished himself through a high level of analytical and coordination skills and a strong interest in Asian venture capital markets outside Japan. He knew many key employees at JAFCO well. As a second measure, Yoshida hired Marc Marsan to join Lu at JAV. Finally, Yoshida assigned Tanigawa as a key person within JAFCO's International Operations Department to provide value-added services to JAV's portfolio companies. While Shell, Lu and Marsan were based in San Francisco, Tanigawa continued to be based in Japan.

The compensation of Shell, Marsan, Lu, and Tanigawa was not comparable to that of partners of a U.S. VC firm, not even to one that, like JAFCO, did not have to raise its own funds. Shell had been hired for a representative and administrative role, and even after November 1994, his compensation structure did not change. Lu, who had just

EXHIBIT 9 USIT 1 Portfolio (August 1997)

Source: JAFCO.

Company	Shares	Avg. Cost Per Share	Total Cost	Liquidated to date (LTD)	Value of Unliquidated Securities	Total Market Value (LTD + Current Market)
AT/Comm	1,411	$567.00	$ 800,037	$ —	$ 800,037	$ 800,037
Advanced Fibre Communications	585,879	$ 6.83	$ 3,999,996	$ 25,890,720	$ —	$ 25,890,720
Brocade Communications Systems	637,139	$ 3.45	$ 2,199,998	$ —	$ 2,199,998	$ 2,199,998
Cielo Communications	1,119,398	$ 1.30	$ 1,453,044	$ —	$ 1,453,044	$ 1,453,044
Ciena	4,685,715	$ 0.46	$ 2,162,515	$223,504,018	$ —	$223,504,018
CISCO/LightSpeed	973,913	$ 1.64	$ 1,600,000	$ 11,120,000	$ 3,582,811	$ 14,702,811
Clear Communications	225,670	$ 7.09	$ 1,600,000	$ —	$ 1,600,000	$ 1,600,000
Com21	333,857	$ 2.52	$ 840,260	$ —	$ 6,677,140	$ 6,677,140
CommQuest Technologies	1,325,713	$ 1.81	$ 2,399,999	$ 9,119,996	$ 0	$ 9,119,996
DynaChip	825,491	$ 1.45	$ 1,196,962	$ —	$ 1,196,962	$ 1,196,962
Equator Technologies	620,104	$ 3.40	$ 2,110,676	$ —	$ 2,110,676	$ 2,110,676
Etec Systems	541,599	$ 4.88	$ 2,643,003	$ 15,104,381	$ —	$ 15,104,381
FlexiInternational Software	199,999	$ 4.00	$ 799,998	$ —	$ 799,998	$ 799,998
IWC Holdings	74,920	$ 6.67	$ 499,750	$ —	$ 499,750	$ 499,750
MMC Networks	422,640	$ 2.65	$ 1,119,996	$ 9,513,840	$ 1,252,800	$ 10,766,640
NeoMagic	175,439	$ 2.85	$ 500,001	$ 2,889,106	$ 0	$ 2,889,106
Network Integrity	579,852	$ 2.95	$ 1,711,645	$ —	$ 1,711,645	$ 1,711,645
NVidia	944,889	$ 2.01	$ 1,894,560	$ —	$ 1,894,560	$ 1,894,560
Objective System Integrators	636,363	$ 11.00	$ 6,999,993	$ —	$ 6,999,993	$ 6,999,993
PSINet	240,965	$ 4.15	$ 1,000,005	$ 2,262,302	$ —	$ 2,262,302
Pacific Monolithics	1,141,276	$ 2.21	$ 2,519,999	$ —	$ 2,519,999	$ 2,519,999
PocketScience Inc.	1,280,486	$ 1.63	$ 2,092,309	$ —	$ 2,092,309	$ 2,092,309
Sentient Networks, Inc.	456,491	$ 7.01	$ 3,200,002	$ —	$ 3,200,002	$ 3,200,002
SmartMaps International	343,992	$ 7.90	$ 2,719,200	$ —	$ 2,719,200	$ 2,719,200
Teleos Communication	350,000	$ 3.22	$ 1,126,385	$ 1,251,512	$ —	$ 1,251,512
The Lightspan Partnership	851,062	$ 3.76	$ 3,199,993	$ —	$ 3,199,993	$ 3,199,993
Vivid Semiconductor	890,380	$ 2.25	$ 2,000,097	$ —	$ 2,000,097	$ 2,000,097
Vixel Corporation	888,888	$ 4.50	$ 3,999,996	$ —	$ 3,999,996	$ 3,999,996
	21,353,531		$58,390,418	$300,655,875	$52,511,010	$353,166,886

transferred from JAFCO Tokyo, was not in a position to negotiate a substantial carry in deals as he did not have an individual deal-making record. Tanigawa continued to be paid a fixed salary, as were all of JAFCO's employees in Japan. Marsan, Lee, and Shell were compensated through a limited carry structure.

The team started working immediately. Between November 1994 and April 1996 they invested in 12 companies. By April 1, 1996, about $21,715,000 (¥2,823,000,000: 130¥ = 1$) would be invested, 7 companies were to go public and about $49,850,000 (¥6,480,000,000: 130¥ = 1$) would be realized. Among those portfolio companies was Ciena (February 1997) (see **Exhibit 10**), which had the largest market capitalization of any venture-backed IPO in history ($2.7 billion at the IPO). Tivoli Systems went public and was later acquired by IBM in 1996.

JAV's value-added investment proposition proved to be successful with portfolio companies and gave JAV access to considerable deal flow. Todd Brooks, Principal, HBS '93, who joined JAFCO on April 10, 1995, from Franklin Templeton Funds where he worked as a telecommunications analyst stated: "Often U.S. startup firms have very little, if any, ability to tap into the overseas markets which often represent enormous revenue opportunities. If a startup firm inks a substantial contract with NTT or NEC, for example, that lends substantial credibility to U.S. customers and members of the U.S. financial community." In the case of Ciena, JAFCO's introduction led to the first large contract outside the United States. JAV not only picked up the tab for the U.S. entrepreneurs' trip to Japan and provided introductions, but also followed up with potential business partners in Japan after the visit. Andy Goldfarb, HBS '93 and Managing Principal at JAFCO stated: "Entering the Japanese market is complicated. Evaluating potential entry strategies, such as joint ventures versus exclusive or non-exclusive distributors, requires a lot of management time and detailed market knowledge. JAFCO, by leveraging our Japan connections, can accelerate this decision making process by getting direct feedback from potential Japanese partners. We also leverage our portfolio companies' management time by helping in the process. Our ability to deliver on the value-added proposition is critical to our future success."

The Shakeout

While JAV's entry into the U.S. VC market proved to be successful from an investor's point of view, there were two major problems: compensation and decision making. Standard industry compensation for fund managers who did not raise capital on their own was a 2.5% management fee plus 10–15% of the realized profits of the whole fund. By contrast, Lu and Marsan earned much lower compensation. In the beginning, Marsan and Lu were content with their compensation, as they did not have any independent investment track record. As JAV's first investments showed signs of a highly positive payoff, however, Lu and Marsan in particular started to question JAV's flat compensation structure. They approached management about this issue in 1995 but received a negative response.

Decision-making routines were a second problem for JAV's local management. All the investment decisions for JAV were made by JAFCO in Japan. JAFCO sought to apply the same decision making process that it used for its investment decisions in Japan and Europe to JAV. The investment committee consisted exclusively of JAFCO board members. This meant that Japanese managers with a limited understanding of the U.S. venture market had to make decisions on investments in potential portfolio companies. Furthermore, decision making in Japan implied a longer time lag between the time a deal

EXHIBIT 10 Capital Gains of Investments in USIT 1 (August 1997)

Source: JAFCO America Ventures.

Company	Sales Proceeds	Cost Basis	Cap Gain/Loss	Multiple	Time of Investment	Time of Exit	Holding Period
Advanced Fibre Communications	25,890,720	$ 3,999,996	$ 21,890,724	6.5x	3Q95	2Q97	1.75 years
Ciena*	223,504,018	$ 2,162,515	$221,341,503	103.4x	1Q95	2Q97	2.25 years
CISCO/LightSpeed	14,702,811	$ 1,600,000	$ 13,102,811	9.2x	1Q96	2Q98	2.25 years
CommQuest Technologies	9,119,996	$ 2,399,999	$ 6,719,998	3.8x	3Q95	2Q98	2.75 years
Etec Systems	15,104,381	$ 2,643,003	$ 12,461,378	5.7x	3Q95	4Q96	1.25 years
MMC Networks	10,766,640	$ 1,119,996	$ 9,646,644	9.6x	4Q95	2Q98	2.25 years
NeoMagic	2,889,106	$ 500,001	$ 2,389,105	5.8x	3Q96	4Q97	1.25 years
PSINet	2,262,302	$ 1,000,005	$ 1,262,297	2.3x	1Q95	3Q97	2.75 years
Teleos Communication	1,251,512	$ 1,126,385	$ 125,127	1.1x	2Q95	1Q97	1.75 years
Total Return	305,491,486	$16,551,900	$288,939,587	18.5x			2.00 years

*Approximately 105 million of Ciena's sales proceeds were still held as marketable securities and had not been liquidated yet.

surfaced and a decision could be made. During this highly competitive period in the U.S. venture market, it took JAV eight weeks under optimal conditions to reach an investment decision while it took a local VC firm about two weeks.

Brooks stated: "The investment decision process at JAFCO would take three to four months from the point the deal showed up on JAFCO's radar screen. Furthermore, the JAFCO investment committee in Japan did not understand our deals and hardly ever met the entrepreneurs. In an increasingly competitive U.S. VC market, fast decision making is a competitive advantage that we lacked."

Lu and Marsan pushed for localized decision making but were turned down by JAFCO. While Mr. Saitoh (JAV president) acknowledged the importance of local decision making, he felt that JAV's investment professionals did not have the appropriate track record yet. Lu and Marsan's dissatisfaction led them to contemplate leaving the firm. Todd Brooks observed: "The first week after I joined it was fairly clear to me that the people who had hired me were not too hopeful that things at JAV would change. I guess they were contemplating leaving the firm and they were just waiting for the right time."

In early April 1996, Lu and Marsan announced their decision to quit JAV. JAFCO's management was stunned. While aware of Lu and Marsan's dissatisfaction, managers had perceived it as highly improbable that they would leave. Around the end of April, Tanigawa quit JAFCO in Tokyo. In some ways this was an even bigger shock, as Tanigawa, a member of JAFCO's board, had been employed under a quasi-lifetime employment. In late April, Lu and Marsan started GlobalVentures, their own venture capital firm. GlobalVentures's strategy was to compete directly against JAV. The company opened an office in Palo Alto and quickly raised $100M. In May 1996, Tanigawa and two of his JAFCO staff members joined GlobalVentures and the company established an office in Tokyo.

Starting Over: Imuta-san's Challenge

JAFCO's president, Yoshida, knew he had to act quickly to stop the bleeding at JAV. On May 5, 1996, he called one of his most capable managers, Hitoshi Imuta, into his office. Imuta had been with Nomura Securities for 23 years before joining JAFCO in 1993. At Nomura, Imuta had worked for four years in New York City and three years in Singapore as president of Nomura Singapore, Ltd. At JAFCO he had most recently been a director in charge of the investment partnership administration and personnel departments. "We have to take action quickly," Yoshida said to Imuta. "I want you to join JAV as its new president. This is our second attempt at entering the U.S. VC market. Let's make sure we do things right this time."

While he was on the plane from Tokyo to San Francisco, Imuta considered the challenges ahead of him. In the short run, it was important to create a sense of security at current portfolio companies. Also, he would have to take a close look at the remaining JAV employees and identify those who could help him rebuild JAV. Beyond these immediate steps, however, Imuta knew that he needed to develop and communicate a vision for JAV and take critical first steps towards execution of this vision. Imuta knew that he had Yoshida's backing for radical changes at JAV.

Soon after arriving in the United States, Imuta concluded: "JAV's strategy to provide capital and added value for entrepreneurs seeking market entry and manufacturing in Japan and Asia was right. However, the incentives for execution of this strategy were not well aligned. JAV needs the best local decision makers who are adequately compensated."

In May 1996 Imuta decided to move JAFCO's U.S. headquarters office from San Francisco to Palo Alto and the East Coast office from New York City to Boston. "We have to be as close as possible to where the action is, and for information technology that is Palo Alto and Boston." In addition, Imuta and Todd Brooks focused on monitoring existing portfolio companies. Imuta also hired a headhunter to find a new president. The headhunter "screened" 60 candidates and Imuta eventually met 6 of them; JAFCO's president Yoshida met the final three candidates. Imuta also involved JAFCO's current staff in his search. Imuta knew that the new leader would be crucial for JAV's success. In late August 1996, Schiffman signed a contract to start as the new president of JAV. Bob Shell left JAV that same month. Schiffman had spent his entire career in high-tech growth companies and venture capital. In the mid-1980s, Schiffman joined Apple Computer as one of two partners who managed Apple's corporate venture program. Notable investments included Sybase, ON Technology and NetFrame. In 1993, Schiffman joined Weiss, Peck and Greer Venture Partners as a general partner, where he focused on early-stage investments in information and communication technologies.

On October 18, 1996, Barry Schiffman became president and Chief Investment Officer of JAV and Imuta moved to become chairman of JAV. (See **Exhibit 11,** "JAFCO America Organization Chart.") Imuta reflected on his future challenges:

> From May to October 1996, JAV made no new investments. We effectively lost a seven-month opportunity window. Now we are back on track. My role at JAV will be to keep associates and partners happy. Furthermore, I have to make sure that the communication flow between Japan and the U.S. is improved. Otherwise we cannot deliver on our value-added promise. Finally, I hope that I can transfer some of the knowledge I gained about managing a U.S. VC firm back to Japan. With the changes in Japan's financial markets and corporate governance system, JAFCO will have to change, too. The question is to what degree the U.S. is an appropriate role model for JAFCO in Japan.

Brooks decided to stay provided JAFCO made whole on its promises to change. Hiring Schiffman, he explained: "Was a clear sign that JAFCO was serious about making the right kind of change and provided me the confidence to stay."

For learning purposes, JAFCO would rotate one employee at a time, having them spend six months at JAV before returning to Japan.

Barry Schiffman Takes Charge

Immediately after taking over in October 1996, Schiffman made a number of important changes. First, Todd Brooks became a Managing Principal, then Schiffman introduced a tighter control system of internal operations and a monitoring system for portfolio companies. Previously, updates about portfolio companies had been reviewed and added to portfolio company files. Schiffman introduced a routine where new data were entered into financial planning models to update previous estimates. Schiffman also negotiated a simplification of the biannual reports to JAFCO. This saved JAV overhead.

Second, Schiffman made a number of hiring decisions. Andy Goldfarb, HBS '93, joined JAV as a Managing Principal to open the Boston office in April 1997. Goldfarb had previously worked for Trans National Group in Boston where he had set up Trans National's venture capital business. Phil Wickham joined JAV in March 1997 as an associate. Phil had previously been a Kauffman Fellow at OneLiberty Ventures in Boston. Goldfarb, Brooks and Wickham received carried interest in proportion to their VC experience. JAV's other employees received salaries plus performance bonuses.

Third, Schiffman instituted a new investment process. Whenever one of JAV's managers came across an interesting investment opportunity, they would write and circulate a one-page memo. If the investment prospects in the deal improved, this would be followed by a two-page memo and eventually by a final investment memo (usually 10 pages plus appendices). The investment committee consisted of Barry Schiffman, Andrew

EXHIBIT 11   JAFCO America Ventures, Inc. Organization Chart

Source: JAFCO America Ventures.

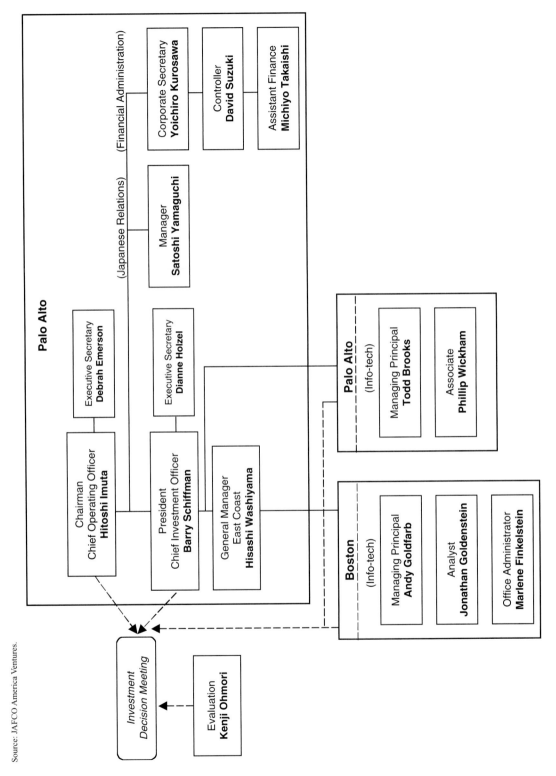

Goldfarb, Todd Brooks, Hitoshi Imuta and one JAFCO employee from Japan who acted primarily as an observer. The small and localized investment committee enabled JAV to make decisions on very short notice. If required, JAV could now reach an investment decision 14 days after a deal showed up on its radar screen (see **Exhibit 12** for the investment decision making process at JAV).

Schiffman and Imuta also introduced a number of reporting routines including a weekly Monday morning (Pacific Time) meeting for which the Boston and Palo Alto offices were linked by video conferencing. This meeting was used to discuss all current

EXHIBIT 12   **JAFCO America Ventures, Inc. Investment Decision Process**

Source: JAFCO America Ventures.

Process	Action Involved in US	Reports Sent to Tokyo	Action Involved in Tokyo	Date
				X = Investment Date
Finding	- Log in Business Plan - Review Deal Log at Weekly Staff Meeting	Prospective Deal List		X-15
Due Diligence Level 1	- Evaluate Business Plan - Meet with Company Management - Technology/Market Analysis	One Page		X-12
Due Diligence	- Ongoing Discussion with Company Management - Reference Check from 3rd Parties - Deal Negotiation			
Investment Recommendation	- Formal Recommendation by Investment Principal	- Business Plan - Product Profile		
Investment Decision Meeting	- Meeting (Imuta, Schiffman, Investment Principal & Evaluation Dept. Staff)	- Investment Outline Report - Investment Recommendation	Deal Summary for Board of Directors	X-8
NO YES			Present to Board of Directors Meeting in Tokyo (every Friday)	X-5
		Investment Decision Report signed by Imuta & Schiffman	Portfolio Allocation Meeting (Wednesday)	X-2
	- Deal Closing		Signing on Legal Document	X

issues, including the "investment funnel" of deals in early and late stages of evaluation. They also put one of JAFCO's employees, Satoshi Yamaguchi, in charge of systematically establishing relationships with the U.S. subsidiaries of Japanese companies that could potentially add value to JAFCO's portfolio companies. Schiffman reasoned that while key decisions about purchasing products from JAV's portfolio companies were made in Japan, the Japanese firms' U.S. subsidiaries could provide valuable direct contacts independent of JAFCO's designated employees in Japan.

Reflecting on his first months at JAV, Schiffman stated:

> I expected that I would have to perform all the tasks of somebody who starts over and that proved to be true. One big challenge I had not expected, though, was the issue of communications with JAFCO and with Japanese employees. I realized that I have to be very specific and clear in my communication with my Japanese counterparts. In the beginning I sometimes assumed that things were clear while they were not. I have made it a habit in our Monday meetings to proceed slowly and to make sure that everybody understands what we are talking about. That takes time but avoids trouble later.

Between October 1996 and July 1997, Schiffman refocused JAFCO's investment activities to second- or third-round investments in information technology, namely software and communications companies. Venture-funded companies generally went through two to four successive rounds of financing before an initial public offering or a sale of the company to a strategic investor. Among other companies, JAV invested in Lightspan, Equator, Brocade and Vixel (see **Exhibit 13A** for a list of JAV investments). While he was busy changing the internal processes at JAV, Schiffman also focused on creating deal flow. In July 1997, JAV raised a $100M fund to be invested across all stages.

VC firms co-invested in deals not only in order to share risk but also in order to get access to future deal flow. Board meetings of portfolio firms were the most important meeting platform for venture capitalists. The reputation of VC firm partners mattered a great deal and was easily tarnished by a number of under-performing investments. Information traveled quickly in the VC industry. Despite its economic importance, the industry consisted of only 610 firms in 1995.[1] Often, a VC firm that had invested in a promising portfolio company in the first round would invite selected other VC firms to invest in the second round not only because of the business expertise that these VC firms brought to the table but also in order to create goodwill among these VC firms and in order to get invited to co-invest in future deals. Also, VC firms sometimes invested in other VC firms' funds in order to establish and strengthen relationships (see **Exhibit 13B**).

Schiffman reflected: "Creating a deal flow of high quality is crucial in this business. You do not want to waste your time on evaluating mediocre deals. But top VC firms generally use their top early-stage deals as bargaining chips, especially where the VCs have good information about the quality of the management team."

Schiffman found that JAV's value-added proposition of providing various forms of access to Japan and Asia was credible. There was, however, competition from GlobalVentures, the VC firm founded by Lu and Marsan. GlobalVenture's principals had a good track record and they could point to Tanigawa, their partner in Japan, as a credible provider of value-added activities. In the case of Sentient, a developer of multiservice switches for telecommunications carriers, JAFCO America initially competed with several other firms including GlobalVentures. In its third round of financing in March 1997, Sentient was looking to raise $5–$6 million; however, the firm was offered $22 million from potential investors. The CEO of Sentient, Nimish Shah, knew Jim Lu of GlobalVentures very well. JAV had been invited to look at the deal by both Sequoia Capital and Sevin-Rosen, a VC firm that co-invested in the second-round financing. After careful consideration, Sentient decided to raise $14 million. Sentient chose JAFCO as the lead

[1]Source: Venture Economics Investor Services.

EXHIBIT 13A
List of all Past and Present JAFCO AV Portfolio Companies

Source: JAFCO.

Company Name	Date Invested	Company Name	Date Invested
Calgene	1/9/85	Nvidia	12/16/94
Foothill Research, Inc.	4/18/86	Ciena	2/3/95
Empress Foods	7/7/86	Thesis	3/31/95
Attain	8/25/87	First Medical	6/21/95
Microgenics	9/24/87	ComQuest Technologies	6/30/95
Novellus Systems	1/29/88	AT/Comm	7/8/95
Biomagnetic Technologies	8/23/88	ParcPlace Systems	8/4/95
C-Cube Microsystems	1/20/89	Wireless Access	8/16/95
Synergy Semiconductor	7/25/89	Etec Systems	8/30/95
Circle C Trucking	9/26/89	VTEL	9/7/95
Metalaser Technologies	11/17/89	Objective Systems	9/22/95
INMET	1/11/90	Integrators	
EMC	1/30/90	Advanced Fibre Communications	9/29/95
Aehr Test Systems	2/26/90	MMC Networks	11/14/95
Endosonics	3/20/90	AIT Delaware	12/15/95
Cephalon	5/17/90	Slate	12/29/95
Netrix	5/31/90	Network Integrity	2/20/96
FileNet Corp.	7/5/90	LightSpeed International	2/29/96
KVA Holding Corp.	11/15/90	Citrix Systems	3/13/96
Liant Software	1/24/91	Teleos Communications	4/2/96
Isis Pharmaceuticals	3/15/91	Sega Gameworks	4/5/96
Oclassen Pharmaceuticals	3/15/91	Cyberonics	4/8/96
United Biomedical	5/2/91	Ribozyme Pharmaceuticals	4/11/96
IGEN	6/13/91	Clear Channel Communications	4/26/96
Gensym	7/30/91	Pacific Monolithics	5/28/96
BMC West	9/30/91	Vivid Semiconductor	7/12/96
Alton Geoscience	10/9/91	International Wireless	8/9/96
ADAPTEC	2/7/92	Communications Holdings	
Advanced Computer	2/7/92	BENCHMARQ MICROELECTRONICS	9/9/96
Communications		Chromagen	10/4/96
Gliatech	2/24/92	Vixel Corporation	10/11/96
Immunopharmaceutics	4/30/92	CombiChem	11/7/96
Netwise	7/22/92	Brocade Communications	12/6/96
NPS Pharmaceuticals	8/10/92	Systems	
Network Computing Devices	11/6/92	Texas Biotechnology	12/17/96
Tivoly Systems	12/1/92	Aurora Biosciences	12/20/96
SyQuest Technology	12/16/92	Kinetix Pharmaceuticals	2/7/97
Retix	4/7/93	Fibermark	2/17/97
AntiCancer	5/31/93	TriQuint Semiconductor	2/24/97
Avigen	6/30/93	FlexiInternational Software	2/26/97
Synernetics	1/24/94	PocketScience Inc.	2/26/97
Cyrix	1/26/94	Micronics Computers	2/27/97
Crystalline Materials	1/26/94	SmartMaps International	3/21/97
Metatools	1/26/94	Sentient Networks	3/26/97
OsteoArthritis Sciences	3/25/94	Sepracor	5/16/97
PSINet	6/17/94	Spectrian	5/30/97
Micronix	6/26/94	DynaChip	6/13/97
NeoMagic	7/6/94	Lucent Medical Systems	6/23/97
Com21	9/9/94	The Lightspan Partnership	6/24/97
International Wireless	10/7/94	Equator Technologies	6/27/97
Communications		Calimetrics	8/6/97

EXHIBIT 13B
**JAFCO Investments
in Other VC Funds**

Source: JAFCO.

Company Name	Date[a]
Weiss, Peck & Greer Venture Associates, L.P.	11/30/84
Sevin Rosen Fund III	08/27/87
Philadelphia Venture Japan I	10/08/87
MDC/JAFCO Ventures	12/07/87
Philadelphia Venture Japan II	01/18/89
Hummer Winblad Venture Partners II	08/12/93
North Bridge Venture Partners	07/13/94
Sevin Rosen Fund V	10/23/95
Sequoia Capital VII	10/28/95
Vanguard Ventures V	02/29/96
Doll Technology Investment Fund	10/28/96
Forward Venture Partners	02/18/97

[a]Date of first capital call.

investor for this round with Ameritech and AT&T as co-investors. Shah observed: "JAFCO was best situated to provide introductions to potential customers in Japan. They had the better reputation."

In March 1997, another JAFCO employee, Shinohara, who had provided value-added activities for JAV, left because of compensation and organizational issues. This once again raised Schiffman's concerns about JAFCO's ability to maintain JAV's value proposition. As his successor, JAFCO succeeded in recruiting Hiro Ikegaya, a very seasoned and experienced technology executive from Mitsubishi Corporation. At Mitsubishi, Ikegaya had been heavily involved with CISCO's early penetration of the Japanese market through a series of joint ventures with Mitsubishi subsidiaries. Ikegaya turned out to be an important resource, but he was very thinly stretched with an increasing demand for value-added activities.

Looking Forward: How to Compete?

Barry Schiffman knew that while JAV had made a promising start, there were important challenges ahead. First, there was the issue of competitive positioning of JAV. Over the last months JAV had focused on late-stage investments in information technology. As more money was flowing into the venture capital industry, it became expensive to invest in later stages. Schiffman was wondering to what degree JAV should push into first-stage investing, also called seed investing. He knew that seed investing required a better understanding of information technology than most of his professionals had. Furthermore, seed investing demanded very good people skills, time-intensive handholding of stressed-out entrepreneurs and sometimes drastic replacement decisions. Finally, he had to be careful not to position JAFCO as directly competing with the top-tier firms that historically provided JAFCO with its later-stage deal flow.

JAFCO had just announced that it had raised a second U.S. Information Technology Fund (USIT II), and Schiffman thought that this might be the right point in time to start seed-stage investing.

At this point, JAV was looking to hire one more partner with a good understanding of software technology. With the right person, Schiffman figured, the move into seed-stage investing would be easier. Another open question about seed-stage investing by JAV was whether JAV's value-added proposition would work as well for seed-stage investments as it did for later-stage investments. Did entrepreneurs who had just started their company really need to be introduced to Japanese customers and manufacturers? Schiffman could think of several examples among JAV's portfolio companies where earlier access to the Japanese market would have helped.

Second, there were new markets to be developed. Schiffman thought that Venture Leasing could be an interesting area for JAFCO. Venture leasing was a leasing contract where the lessee provided favorable leasing rates to the lessor against a certain stake in the lessor's entrepreneurial start-up. Schiffman had recently had a closer look at venture leasing and had assigned a summer intern to collect more data. Also, JAFCO's new president, Mitsumasa Murase, had mentioned to Schiffman that he would like to see JAV move into management buyouts and leveraged buyouts (MBOs and LBOs).

Third, there was the large life sciences market. So far, all of JAFCO's life science investments, even those in the United States, were still handled by JAFCO in Japan. JAFCO had a group of life science experts that was headed by Dr. Otaki, who was well connected to the pharmaceutical industry in Japan. JAV was currently looking to hire a senior person in the life sciences area. Schiffman envisioned this person to be responsible for making JAV rather than JAFCO the vehicle for life science investments in the United States. Once an appropriate partner had been identified, however, the question was how much control over life science investing Dr. Otaki and his group would relinquish. Schiffman wanted to avoid an internal fight since it was highly detrimental to JAV's value-added proposition. If the new partner was in conflict with Dr. Otaki, Otaki's group would probably be unwilling to provide introductions to JAV's life science portfolio companies. Schiffman made a note to talk to Imuta about this issue.

Then there was the burning issue of compensation of Japanese employees. Schiffman and Imuta knew that Tanigawa and Shinohara left JAFCO over issues of compensation and decision making. It was only a question of time until other Japan-based JAFCO staff would become restless. A radical change in JAFCO's compensation structure for all of JAFCO's employees was not an option at this point. JAFCO acquired only small chunks of equity of its Japanese portfolio companies and employees bore virtually no risk. It would have been counterproductive to provide these employees with a windfall profit. But something had to be done about those employees who provided value-added activities to JAV. Schiffman knew that there was a system of a compensating highly qualified specialists outside of the general seniority system, particularly if they had been recruited from outside. Dr. Otaki was compensated under this system called "nenposei" and Schiffman was wondering whether it could be applied for Japanese staff in Tokyo, too.

Schiffman knew that the road ahead for JAV was challenging. At this point, only some of the internal management issues had been resolved. Also, there were a number of competitive challenges for JAV that needed to be addressed. As competition for the best deals in the VC market was heating up in 1997, JAV needed to continue building on its strengths. By this time, the bleeding at JAV had been stopped and things seemed to be moving in the right direction. But were they moving fast enough? Also, as the Japanese financial system was about to undergo a major deregulation in 1998, more opportunities for VC firms might open up in Japan and JAV's knowledge base about the U.S. VC industry was potentially very useful to JAFCO. The question was how to best transfer knowledge and skills to Japan. As Schiffman walked down the 16th fairway, he wondered how he should address all these challenges. These thoughts were definitely taking a toll on his golf score.

Case

20

Case

Jinwoong: Financing an Entrepreneurial Firm in the Wake of the Korean Financial Crisis

T.P. Lee sat in his office in Seoul, Korea, studying the letter of intent (LOI) that he had just received that day, October 1, 1998. The past year had been tumultuous for Korea and his company, Jinwoong, which he had started almost 20 years earlier and built into the largest tent manufacturer in the world (see **Exhibit 1** for Jinwoong product-line information). The recent Asian financial crisis had forced his country to turn to the International Monetary Fund (IMF) for a bailout of the economy. After the crisis, Jinwoong's creditors were calling in their loans, and the company desperately needed a lifeline to avoid a liquidity crisis. The LOI, from Warburg Pincus and Fidelity Capital (two well-known investment houses), outlined their proposed terms of investment in Jinwoong. Among other things, they were requesting three months of due diligence!

Lee had already received a bid from another consortium (International Investors) comprising a major insurance group and a prominent buyout firm. In addition, Korean government had just announced the establishment of a restructuring fund that would provide financial support to promising small and medium-sized companies like Jinwoong. By turning to the government for support, Jinwoong could potentially survive the current difficulties without a foreign investor. On the other hand, investors such as Pincus and International Investors could help Jinwoong clean up its overleveraged balance sheet and achieve its next goal: to become the leading outdoor travel equipment maker in the world, with a diverse product line that included tents, soft luggage, and mobile furniture.

Professor Walter Kuemmerle, James Lee (MBA '02), and Bokeun Jin (MBA '02) prepared this case. HBS cases are developed solely as the basis for class discussion. Cases are not intended to serve as endorsements, sources of primary data, or illustrations of effective or ineffective management.

EXHIBIT 1A
Jinwoong Product Line Information

Source: Jinwoong.

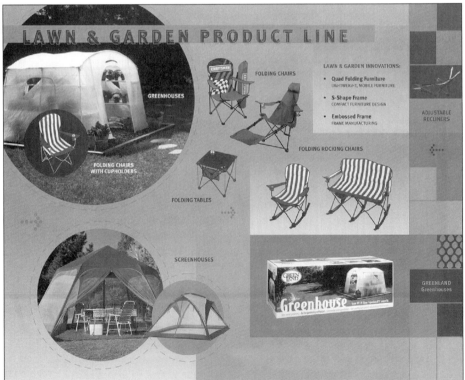

EXHIBIT 1B **Jinwoong Product Breakdown**

Source: Jinwoong.

Total Sales (in US$ millions)	1996		1997		1998	
Tents	115.8	80.2%	118.3	74.5%	101.8	61.4%
Luggage	9.3	6.4%	18.4	11.6%	41.4	25.0%
Backpacks	16.8	11.6%	16.6	10.5%	13.0	7.8%
Mobile furniture	—	—	—	—	1.6	1.0%
Other camping-related products	2.5	1.7%	5.5	3.5%	8.1	4.9%
Total	144.4	100.0%	158.8	100.0%	165.9	100.0%

EXHIBIT 2 **Korea Macroeconomic Data**

Source: Compiled from Bank of Korea data (accessed online at www.bok.or.kr).

	1991	1992	1993	1994	1995	1996	1997	1998
GDP growth rate (%)	9.2	5.4	5.5	8.3	8.9	6.8	5.0	−6.7
GDP per capita (US$)	6,792	7,162	7,787	9,012	10,856	11,402	10,360	6,913
Population (million)	43.3	43.7	44.1	44.5	45.1	45.5	46.0	46.6
Gross domestic savings rate (%)	37.3	36.4	36.2	35.5	35.5	33.8	33.4	34.0
Private savings rate (%)	30.6	29.1	28.5	26.9	25.8	23.5	22.8	25.1
Unemployment rate (%)	2.3	2.4	2.8	2.4	2	2	2.6	6.8
Current account (US$ million)	(8,317)	(3,943)	0.989	(3,867)	(8,508)	(23,005)	(8,167)	40,365
Capital account (US$ million)	6,412	6,587	2,741	10,295	16,786	23,327	1,314	(3,197)
Exchange rate (end of year, US$)	759.5	786.5	807.2	788.5	775.7	844.9	1,695.0	1,204.0

Which option should he choose? As a successful, independent entrepreneur, did he really want to risk giving up control of his company to foreign investors when the government was willing to step in and save the company?

Korea: The Economic Miracle

After the devastation of the Korean War (1950–1953), the Korean government adopted an export-oriented economic development strategy in the 1960s based on the Japanese development model. As a result, the nation rapidly industrialized. The Korean conglomerates, commonly known as chaebols, played an important role in the nation's industrialization. Backed by generous government-directed loans from banks and protected from foreign competition in the domestic market, the chaebols such as Samsung, Hyundai, LG, and Daewoo built the cars, ships, electronics goods, and semiconductors that were the cornerstone of Korea's tremendous economic growth. Between 1961 and 1979, gross domestic product (GDP) averaged a stunning 10% annual growth rate.[1] The GDP growth rate was also impressive during the 1980s, at an average of 8%. In a manifestation of its new prosperity to the rest of the world, Korea successfully hosted the 1988 Summer Olympics.

As the strong economic growth continued into the 1990s, Korea slowly but steadily enacted liberalization measures (see **Exhibit 2** for Korea macroeconomic data). Foreign investors were allowed to invest directly into the Korean Stock Market in 1992. And by 1996, Korea joined the Organization for Economic Cooperation and Development

[1] Yasheng Huang, "Korea: On the Back of a Tiger," HBS No. 700-097 (Boston: Harvard Business School Publishing, 2000). p. 4.

(OECD) and could boast the 11th-largest economy in the world. Membership into this rich-nations' club required greater opening of the economy to imports and capital flows such as foreign direct investment (FDI).

Entrepreneurial Environment in Korea

The Founding of the Chaebols

The mighty chaebols were founded by strong-willed, fiercely patriotic entrepreneurs who had lived through the harsh Japanese colonial occupation of Korea (1910–1945), the tragic division of the nation into North and South Korea following the Second World War, and then the savage Korean War. These bold entrepreneurs were determined to re-build Korea into a nation that would someday rival Japan in economic might; working closely with the government, they built the vast, diversified, family-controlled empires[2] that propelled the nation's export-driven economic success.

The next generation of entrepreneurs, like Lee, echoed the patriotic industriousness of their chaebol-founding predecessors. They too wanted to build strong companies that would contribute to their nation's economic success story. However, while the govern-ment spurred the chaebols' growth by granting preferential access to cheap loans, it was very difficult for this next generation of entrepreneurs to get favorable bank financing. With their loans concentrated on the chaebols, banks were reluctant lenders to small and medium-sized businesses (see **Exhibit 3** for leverage ratios of top chaebols and small and medium-sized companies). These entrepreneurs were further hindered by the lack of Western-style venture capital funding in Korea. Moreover, the domestic stock market was underdeveloped, volatile, and dominated by large-cap chaebol stocks (see **Exhibit 4** for information on KSE and KOSDAQ). Thus, these entrepreneurs were forced to rely on capital from family and friends to start their ventures.

As the nation rapidly developed during the 1970s and 1980s, some of the past entrepre-neurial fervor seemed to lessen. No longer a war-torn economy that manufactured cheap shoes and plastic toys, the standard of living and wages soared in the 1980s. The best and the brightest of Korea's university graduates coveted jobs as "salarymen" with one of the now well-established chaebols. Indeed, working for a small company or even starting one's

---

[2] The founding families typically retained control over the chaebols (through preferred shares or factual control of shares held by banks), despite the fact that the average equity stake of founders' families in the various group companies was just over 5%.

EXHIBIT 3 **Leverage Ratios of Top Chaebols and Small and Medium-Sized Companies**

Source: Compiled from Korea Federation of Small and Medium Business data (accessed online at www.kfsb.or.kr) and from Korean Ministry of Finance and the Economy data (accessed online at http://english/mofe.go.kr).

Year	Share of Credit to Top 30 Chaebols (%)	Debt/Equity Ratios of Top 30 Chaebols (%)	Debt/Equity Ratios of SMEs[a](%)
1991	41.2	403	262
1992	42.9	426	288
1993	36.8	400	255
1994	22.2	405	265
1995	23.0	390	285
1996	38.5	450	296
1997	40.3	519	305
1998	n/a	458	264

[a]SME = Small and medium-sized enterprises.

EXHIBIT 4 **Data on Korea Stock Exchange**

Source: Compiled from Korea Stock Exchange data, KOSDAQ data.

	December 1997		September 1998[a]	
	KOSDAQ	KSE	KOSDAQ	KSE
Index	97.25	376.31	61.03	310.32
Total market capitalization (won billion)	7,069	70,989	4,512	65,049
Number of companies listed	359	776	335	760
Total market P/E multiple	8	9.8	5.8	13.34

[a]As of end of September 1998.

own business was now perceived to be less prestigious and much riskier than a stable "job for life" with one of the chaebols. Additionally, the lack of a well-developed pension fund and unemployment insurance deterred many would-be entrepreneurs.

Structural Change and Entrepreneurial Spirit in the 1990s

The entrepreneurial spirit in Korea enjoyed resurgence in the mid-1990s. Western-educated Koreans, armed with MBAs and Ph.D.s in engineering and the sciences, returned to their homeland in droves and dreamt of starting their own businesses. The salarymen grew increasingly disenchanted with the principles of lifetime employment and seniority-based promotion so prevalent at the chaebols. In the aftermath of the financial crisis in 1997, the chaebols broke with the implicit promise of lifetime employment and fired thousands of employees; some of the highest-leveraged midsized chaebols went bankrupt, adding to the burgeoning unemployment lines. Banks cut off loans to small and medium-sized enterprises, and starved of capital, many of these businesses perished. The unemployment rate jumped from 2.6% in 1997 to a staggering 6.8% just a year later,[3] and more than 1 million jobs were lost after the onset of the crisis.

After the 1997 financial crisis, the promise of the Internet and new technologies spurred many would-be entrepreneurs to quit their jobs at the chaebols and venture out on their own. These start-ups were financed by a rapid surge in venture capital in Korea, led by strong local players such as Korea Technology Bank and Korea Technology Investment Corporation. Furthermore, the government, worried about the severe economic imbalance between the chaebols and small and medium-sized businesses, enacted new measures to help spur the entrepreneurial fervor. The KOSDAQ, based on the NASDAQ model, was established in July 1996 as a stock market where budding companies and technology ventures could source equity financing.[4] The government allowed Western-style stock options so that companies could attract and retain talented staff. Many of the venture capitalists were found in an area of Seoul called Yoido, akin to Palo Alto's Sand Hill Road, and start-ups were located on or near Teheran Street, a prosperous district in Seoul heralded as Korea's Silicon Valley.

The Korean Financial Crisis in 1997–1998

The Korean financial crisis was but one part of the overall Asian financial crisis that began in Thailand in the summer of 1997 and quickly spread throughout the rest of Asia as investors grew anxious about the region's weak, troubled financial systems and high corporate debt levels; Korea had not faced such a dire economic crisis since the Korean War. Foreign banks refused to roll over their loans to Korean companies, and foreign

[3] Huang, p. 18.

[4] Information is from the KOSDAQ Listed Companies Association Web site, <www.kosdaqca.or.kr>.

fund managers fled the stock market en masse and repatriated their capital. More than $30 billion in capital left the nation between September and December 1997.[5,6] The Korean won rapidly depreciated by more than 50%, and by December 1997, the nation's foreign exchange reserves reached dangerously low levels, totaling less than $4 billion. Incredibly, this newly minted member of the OECD was on the verge of defaulting on its foreign loans. Hat in hand, the Korean government was forced to turn to the IMF, the World Bank, and the Asia Development Bank for a $55 billion bailout.

The "IMF crisis"[7] revealed the fundamental weaknesses of Korea's economic development model. The chaebols, after years of reckless expansion and overdiversification, were bloated with exorbitantly high debt levels. By 1997, the average debt to equity ratio for the 30 largest chaebols stood at more than 500%. Healthy companies within the chaebols had typically made cross-guarantees on their weaker affiliates' debts.[8] Managers in many chaebols had assumed that they could always turn to the government for assistance. Productivity increases did not keep pace with the rising wage levels, and strikes by Korea's militant unions were frequent on the streets of Seoul. Foreign investors also complained of a lack of transparency, inconsistent accounting standards, and poor corporate governance.[9]

The financial sector, heavily burdened by a legacy of bad loans to the lumbering chaebols, was weak and in danger of collapse. For decades the banks had ignored Western-style credit-risk analysis and instead allowed the government to direct their lending policies to the chaebols. After all, there was an implicit understanding that the government would never let the chaebols fail. Yet, the government did allow some of the highly leveraged chaebols to fail, notably Kia Motors and Hanbo Steel; both chaebols went bankrupt in 1997, even before the financial crisis took its toll.

Jinwoong: A Korean Entrepreneur's Dream

Not Just Another Salaryman

T.P. Lee (his real name was Youn-jae Lee; T.P. was his nickname and stood for "Tent Pole"[10]) graduated from Yonsei University, one of Korea's best universities, in 1975 with a degree in political science. He also studied at International Christian University in Tokyo, Japan, for one year as an exchange student. This experience whetted his appetite for international business (see **Exhibit 5** for biographies of Lee and the senior management team of Jinwoong). After graduation, he joined the governmental organization Korea Trade-Investment Promotion Agency (KOTRA) because it was one of the few companies in Korea at that time that provided opportunities for employees to travel and work overseas. Lee worked at KOTRA for two years but grew restless of life as a government bureaucrat.

---

[5] Korea's Ministry of Finance and the Economy. *Beyond the Financial Crisis, A Resilient Korean Economy.* 2002. Seoul.

[6] For comparison purposes: $30 billion was equivalent to about 35% of the total market capitalization of the Korea Stock Exchange at the December 31, 1996 won/U.S. dollar exchange rate.

[7] The Korean press quickly dubbed this financial crisis the "IMF crisis" due to the structural reforms demanded by the IMF as a condition of its bailout. The reforms included higher interest rates, greater foreign ownership in listed companies, and more flexible labor laws that would facilitate large-scale layoffs.

[8] Huang, p. 12.

[9] For instance, there were no laws requiring boards of directors to have outside directors or companies to report consolidated financial statements.

[10] One of Lee's early overseas business contacts anointed this nickname because he found Lee's Korean name difficult to pronounce and because tent poles were an important value component of Jinwoong's products.

EXHIBIT 5

Resumes of CEO T.P. Lee and Senior Management Team

Source: Jinwoong.

YOUN JAE LEE (ENGLISH NAME: T.P. LEE)	
Experience	1979–present: Founder and CEO, Jinwoong
	1978: Hyodong
	1977–1978: Samhwa International
	1975–1977: Korea Trade-Investment Promotion Agency (KOTRA)
Education	Completed an executive education program at Seoul National University (1990)
	Exchange student at International Christian University, Tokyo, Japan (1973–1974)
	Yonsei University, Seoul, Korea
	1975: Political Science
HA BONG SUNG	
Experience	1986–present: President of Xiamen Jinwoong Enterprise Co., Ltd. (China operation)
	1982–1986: Gu Pung Enterprise Co., Ltd.
	1979–1981: Kumho Enterprise Co., Ltd.
Education	Yonsei University, Seoul, Korea
	1979: Political Science
CHANG RO AHN	
Experience	1994–present: CFO, Jinwoong
	1983–1994: Bank of Montreal, Seoul Branch
	1981–1983: American Express Bank, Seoul Branch
	1979–1981: The Export–Import Bank of Korea
Education	Sogang University, Seoul, Korea
	1979: Business Administration
SCOTT P. REEVES	
Experience	1987–present: President, Jinwoong, United States
	1983–1987: President, Duraflex, San Jose, United States
	1979–1983: Executive Vice President, Lunastran, San Jose, United States
Education	University of Colorado
	1977: Marketing

Lee then joined a Korean general trading company called Samhwa International but lasted just one year. He found out quickly that he did not enjoy life at a big Korean company as a typical salaryman either. His next career move was to work as a sales executive at Hyodong, a small Korean tent manufacturer. Lee hoped that he could gain more responsibility at a smaller company. However, to his disappointment, he soon clashed with his senior managers and was fired after just four months because they thought he was pushing sales too aggressively. Lee recalled, "On my own initiative, I brought in a new $500,000 order, but my boss was angry because he believed that I was undermining his authority. The next morning, I went to work and found that my desk was gone." Facing financial difficulties, Lee and his wife then opened a small leather handbag shop in a busy shopping district in Seoul, but it promptly failed.

Instead of joining another company again, Lee decided to venture out on his own as a general trading company working with contract manufacturers. With just $2,000 (approximately $7,000 in 1997 terms)[11] in seed capital and one secretary, at 31 years of age, he established Jinwoong in March 1979 in Seoul (in the Korean language, Jinwoong means "Moving forward in a great way"). Lee won orders to supply backpacks, handbags, and tents to Korean trading companies thanks to contacts he had made at his prior job; at first, he outsourced manufacturing to subcontractors. He relied on borrowings from his

---

[11] Calculated using the Korean Consumer Price Index.

family, friends, and loan sharks to grow his business. In 1981, Lee hired half a dozen engineers from the subcontractors and built his own production facility. By 1982, Jinwoong had 50 employees and sales topped 4 billion won (equivalent to US$5.5 million). (See **Exhibit 6** for historical sales and net income figures.)

In the 1960s, U.S. and European companies such as Coleman, Wenzel, Outdoor Ventures, and Eureka dominated the global tent market. In the early 1970s, Japanese manufacturers took over leadership of the market but were toppled by Taiwanese and Korean manufacturers in the late 1970s. Lee's main goal was to penetrate the U.S. market—the largest market in the world. Lee contacted a number of U.S. importers and wholesalers who were impressed by the high quality of his products. They began to purchase Jinwoong's tents but put on their own product labels and sold to retailers with a markup of 25%–30%. In the 1970s, large U.S. and European retailers purchased tents almost exclusively through these specialized importers. At the peak, there were 42 such firms.[12]

A Close Brush with Bankruptcy

In 1984, after winning a number of fiercely contested U.S. tent orders, Jinwoong was hit by an unexpected 40% increase in the price of nylon (due to the oil crisis), a key raw material. Instead of canceling the orders, Lee risked bankruptcy by completing them and in

[12] By 1998 the number of importers had dwindled to fewer than five firms.

EXHIBIT 6
Historical Sales and Net Income

Source: Jinwoong.

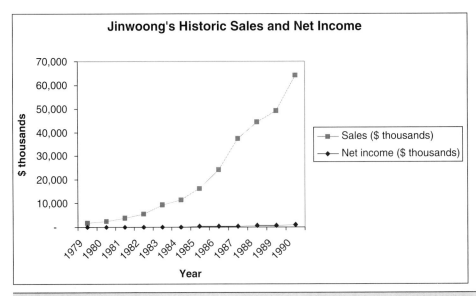

($ thousands)	Sales	Net Income
1979	1,647	2
1980	2,303	24
1981	3,732	7
1982	5,518	41
1983	9,521	77
1984	11,365	77
1985	16,340	186
1986	24,265	356
1987	37,519	381
1988	44,425	803
1989	49,076	687
1990	64,190	1,043

turn losing $3 million. According to Lee, "These were hard times for the company, but I was glad that I fulfilled my commitment to my customers. I considered the $3 million as an investment to build customer trust and Jinwoong's reputation." Jinwoong quickly rebounded the following year when it won a lucrative $6 million order to make the popular Cabbage Patch children's bed tent for the U.S. market.

Aggressive Overseas Expansion

At the beginning, all of Jinwoong's manufacturing was based in Korea, but rising labor costs forced Lee to shift all manufacturing overseas; he set up plants in the Dominican Republic in 1987, China in 1988, and Sri Lanka in 1992 and acquired an existing plant in Bangladesh starting in 1999. He also opened sales offices in the United States (1987), Japan (1990), Canada (1990), and Hong Kong (1992).[13] (See **Exhibit 7** for a map of Jinwoong's overseas operations.)

In addition to cost issues, there were other reasons for Jinwoong's move to the Dominican Republic and China. In 1985, the U.S. government imposed a special duty on finished tents imported from Korea. Lee experimented with importing tent parts (which were free of the special duty) and assembling them in the United States. However, he soon found that the Dominican Republic was an interesting alternative location for the manufacture of tents. Wages there were very low, no special duty was applied for tent imports from the Dominican Republic, and there was even an incentive scheme for exports from the Dominican Republic to Europe. On the other hand, Lee quickly realized that managing quality across large distances was a challenge and that costs in the Dominican Republic would not stay low enough forever. As a result, he started manufacturing in the south of China in 1988, at a time when few Western firms dared to tackle the bureaucratic hurdles and uncertainty in that country. The south of China was relatively close to Korea and had a

[13] In an effort to build sales in Europe, Jinwoong planned to establish a sales office in Copenhagen, Denmark in 1999.

EXHIBIT 7 **Map of Jinwoong's Overseas Operations**

Source: Jinwoong.

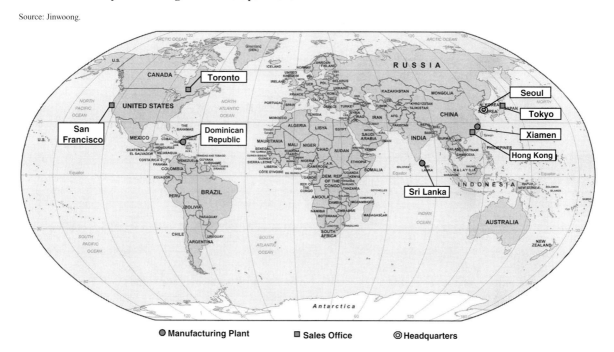

vast labor force. By 1998, most of Jinwoong's employees (close to 3,000) were located in China, with the remainder working in Sri Lanka (close to 2,000), Korea, the United States, Europe, and Bangladesh (about 1,000.)

In 1983, Lee had a meeting with Scott Reeves, whom he had known for several years in Reeves's role as a sales representative for a U.S. manufacturer of protruded fiberglass, the material an increasing share of tent poles were made of. During a discussion about market trends, Lee and Reeves agreed that the days of importers were limited and that large retailers would eventually buy directly from manufacturers. Lee offered Reeves a job as head of the newly created Jinwoong subsidiary in the United States. Reeves was a bit hesitant at first but eventually accepted. Reeves reflected: "Several of my colleagues in sales were pretty pessimistic. They said: 'You don't know him and you will be taken advantage of by Lee. There is a culture problem here.' However, I had a good feeling and accepted the job." By 1998 Reeves was still head of Jinwoong's U.S. operations. He commented: "Over time I found T.P. Lee to be very reliable and trusting. He is also very action oriented. He understands that in business you often have to *try* an idea in order to find out more about it. And, probably most importantly, he is an excellent listener."

In addition to keeping costs low, Lee focused on research and development, quality control, and customer service. Unlike other small manufacturers, Jinwoong built an in-house design facility and conducted market and consumer research in the U.S. market. The company set up a small customer service center in the U.S. office in Fremont, California.

From the mid-1980s, leading international retailers such as Wal-Mart, K-Mart, and Sears had established buying offices in east Asia to bypass importers and wholesalers. Lee cultivated relationships with these retailers and cut ties to the middlemen, selling directly to these retailers on a private-label basis. Reeves recalled: "In 1984 we made our first direct sales call to Wal-Mart. It was tough, but we were successful. That was a huge deal for us." From 1989, Lee also sold under the Jinwoong-owned brand "Quest." (See **Exhibit 8** for sales breakdown by top customers.) By 1994, Jinwoong had severed all ties with importers and wholesalers.

The company won many awards and accolades for its high-quality, well-designed products and fast, reliable delivery. By 1998, Jinwoong had a proprietary repository of over 2,000 tent designs. It won Wal-Mart's International Supplier of the Year Award from 1996–1999; K-Mart's Sporting Goods Strategic Vendor of the Year Award in 1996 and 1999; CTC's Vendor of the Year Award in 1992, 1993, 1997, and 1999; and Sears' Partner in Progress Award in 1999. In addition, Jinwoong held many patents in tent design, fabrics, pole assembly, and other aspects of its tent manufacture business. Lee observed: "Tent technology has come a long way since the days when tents were made of sail cloth and metal pipes and looked like roofs of regular houses. Nylon dyeing and printing alone is really a high-tech area now, and design of fiberglass poles for dome tents is also very sophisticated."

EXHIBIT 8   Sales Breakdown by Top Customers (US$ millions)

Source: Jinwoong.

Customer	1996		1997		1998	
Retailer A	42.4	56.1%	57.4	62.0%	67.5	59.0%
Retailer B	14.9	19.7%	13.9	15.0%	14.6	12.8%
Retailer C	7.4	9.8%	10.8	11.7%	9.1	8.0%
Retailer D	7.9	10.4%	5.4	5.8%	16.1	14.1%
Retailer E	3.0	4.0%	5.1	5.5%	4.7	4.1%
Retailer F	—	—	—	—	2.4	2.1%
Total	75.6	100.0%	92.6	100.0%	114.4	100.0%

Note: Retailer names disguised. All six top customers are U.S. retailers.

Regarding the concentration of retailers' purchasing power, Reeves observed:

> Being the market leader in your industry is key these days. The key question is how much re-
> tail shelf space in your category you control. It is almost like large retailers are renting this
> shelf space to you, and you better sell a lot per square foot allocated to you. Also, even
> though large retailers push every vendor hard, they like dealing with leading vendors because
> it generally means less hassle for them than dealing with several of the smaller guys.

"One of the Most Promising Entrepreneurs in Asia"

Between 1979 and 1990, Jinwoong's revenue soared at a compound annual growth rate
(CAGR) of 45%, mostly due to exports. The strong growth continued into the 1990s. In
1995, the company reached an important milestone when revenue reached 100 billion
won (equivalent to US$140 million; 1$ = 776 won). (See **Exhibit 9** for Jinwoong's historical financials.) Jinwoong truly boasted a globalized production base and sales force.
It had also diversified its product lines into soft luggage (1992) and mobile furniture
(1998), such as foldable chairs and tables. In 1993, *Fortune* magazine named Lee "one of
the most promising entrepreneurs in Asia."[14] By 1997, Jinwoong employed more than
5,000 people worldwide and controlled an estimated 60% and 35% of the U.S. and global
tent markets, respectively, besting competitors such as Coleman, North Face, ARP
(owned by Kellwood), Johnson Worldwide, and Brunswick (see **Exhibit 12E** for information on competitors).

In 1988 Jinwoong also created its own tent brand, Quest, and was moderately successful with it. Observed Reeves: "Building a brand is clearly an expensive undertaking.
In 1992 Quest represented about 10% of sales but absorbed 36% of overhead costs,
mostly due to advertising and promotion." While Jinwoong kept the Quest brand alive,
the company focused mostly on manufacturing on a private-label basis.

Lee observed:

> The key is consistent and high quality at low cost. We feel that our tents are as good as those
> of our branded competitors, if not better. Few consumers know who Jinwoong is, but all the
> major retailers know. Also, most people are not willing to spend more than $20 to $50 for a
> camping tent and not more than $80 to $100 for a family tent, and these are the price ranges
> we target. As a rule of thumb, only 8%–10% of sales in the tent industry are in the premium
> segment, where North Face is positioned. By the way, I am convinced that soft luggage,
> where brand still plays a major role in purchasing decisions, will evolve the same way tents
> did. Consumers will increasingly rely on the retailers' brands and watch their dollars.

In less than 20 years, Lee had built the largest tent maker in the world. In parallel with
his diversification moves, Lee gradually formed his new vision for Jinwoong: to become
the leading global outdoor travel equipment maker. Already with a leading position in
the U.S. market, Lee saw Europe and Asia as the company's next big growth markets.

The Impact of the IMF Crisis on Jinwoong

Jinwoong suffered from many of the same problems that led to the IMF crisis in Korea.
Lee was forced to rely on bank loans to finance his company's aggressive global expansion in plants and sales offices. In an attempt to secure equity financing and improve the
company's profile among Korean institutional investors, Jinwoong listed on the Korea
Stock Exchange in 1989. The stock started on a promising note but within a few months
fell below the 20,000 won level, never to breach it again. It was hurt by the small-cap
sector's low liquidity, as the large chaebol stocks and other blue chips dominated trading

[14] "Young Stars of Asia," Fortune International, November 1, 1993, p. 98.

EXHIBIT 9 Historical Financials (1991–1998)—Balance Sheet

Source: Jinwoong.

(Unit : US$ thousands)	December 1991	December 1992	December 1993	December 1994	December 1995	December 1996	December 1997	December 1998[a]
Total Assets	76,439	72,673	84,899	88,919	100,750	88,674	67,713	117,838
Current Assets	54,016	49,260	58,429	53,292	63,657	54,952	46,275	80,929
Quick Assets	17,538	13,109	31,685	27,915	44,809	39,605	41,459	73,696
Cash Equivalents & Financial Goods	5,402	1,485	15,858	10,561	23,492	29,465	12,084	31,200
Marketable Securities	306	294	430	445	443	280	91	122
Accounts Receivable	6,683	5,753	9,005	8,760	6,052	1,792	1,138	158
Inventory	36,479	36,151	26,744	25,377	18,848	15,347	4,816	7,233
Merchandise	9,847	7,671	7,186	5,505	4,084	1,575	106	52
Finished Goods	5,583	7,760	2,834	2,766	1,096	985	28	480
Work in Process	10,600	9,457	6,899	6,449	4,962	3,831	653	
Raw Materials	10,424	11,139	9,790	10,609	8,658	8,929	4,026	6,128
Fixed Assets	22,422	23,413	26,470	35,627	37,093	33,722	21,439	36,910
Total Liabilities	53,804	52,015	63,894	63,871	79,658	69,557	55,833	89,491
Current Liabilities	30,368	39,516	34,647	27,187	67,267	46,629	40,419	77,079
Accounts Payable	11,628	14,143	8,682	14,419	16,654	20,284	15,701	17,972
St. Debt	12,516	12,290	15,262	10,865	15,646	13,433	9,813	32,068
Current Portion of Debt	4,354	11,739	8,888	621	33,054	12,144	5,218	19,006
Long-term Liabilities	23,436	12,499	29,247	36,684	12,391	22,928	15,414	12,413
Bonds	20,540	8,392	8,053	9,004	773	18,345	9,145	11,628
Convertible Bonds			17,344	23,462	7,735			
Long-term Debt	2,319	2,577	4,340	5,182	3,383	3,830	5,667	1,733
Total Stockholders' Equity	22,634	20,657	21,005	25,048	21,092	19,117	11,881	28,347
Paid-in Capital	15,142	15,076	15,262	16,328	16,598	15,238	7,596	10,693
Capital Surplus	3,892	3,758	3,662	4,966	5,048	4,634	2,166	8,807
Retained Earnings	3,130	1,236	391	888	-3,466	-1,821	2,231	6,931

(continued)

[a] Expected figures for 1998.

Note that these are unconsolidated figures. All figures were converted from Korean won using year-end exchange rates.

EXHIBIT 9 (Continued) Historical Financials (1991–1998)—Income Statement

Source: Jinwoong.

(Unit : US$ thousands)	December 1991	December 1992	December 1993	December 1994	December 1995	December 1996	December 1997	December 1998[a]
Net Sales	70,051	85,074	94,105	120,030	139,958	144,585	121,269	154,789
Total Export Sales[a]	63,467	75,035	86,646	118,020			121,196	154,353
Total Domestic Sales[a]	6,585	10,039	7,459	2,010			74	436
Cost of Sales	55,162	72,897	79,562	103,209	118,454	123,161	107,945	122,697
Gross Profit	14,890	12,176	14,542	16,820	21,504	21,424	13,324	32,092
Selling, General & Administrative Expenses	7,835	9,080	9,634	11,509	14,691	12,047	7,269	15,903
Depreciation	264	261	384	522	664	551	262	406
Operating Profit	7,055	3,097	4,908	5,311	6,813	9,377	6,055	16,188
Non-operating Income	927	1,696	3,175	2,382	3,058	3,493	4,552	7,322
Interest Income	856	791	1,279	1,422	2,325	2,347	908	1,397
Non-operating Expenses	6,422	5,801	8,759	7,208	14,106	9,361	7,010	17,929
Interest Expenses	5,348	4,966	6,343	6,583	7,502	7,836	3,629	8,184
Amortization	805	674	451	189	207	81	30	48
Recurring Profit	1,560	−1,008	−676	485	−4,235	3,509	3,596	5,581
Pre-tax Profit	1,537	−1,026	−720	488	−4,193	3,505	3,596	5,581
Income Taxes	206		93		118	631	563	1,147
Net Profit	1,331	−1,026	−813	488	−4,311	2,874	3,034	4,434

(continued)

[a]Expected figures for 1998.
Note that these are unconsolidated figures. All figures were converted from Korean won using year-end exchange rates.

EXHIBIT 9 (Continued) Historical Financials (1991–1998)—Cash Flow Statement

Source: Jinwoong.

(Unit : US$ thousands)	December 1991	December 1992	December 1993	December 1994	December 1995	December 1996	December 1997	December 1998[a]
Cash Flows from Operating	−2,049	2,468	−42	8,252	8,085	15,297	−2,402	7,215
Net Profit	1,331	−1,026	−813	488	−4,311	2,874	3,034	4,434
Additions to Net Profit	2,168	2,651	1,908	2,025	8,857	3,510	2,045	4,830
Depreciation	462	451	441	477	615	497	262	406
Amortization	843	715	492	234	256	136	416	785
Others	863	1,486	975	1,314	8,044	2,877	1,367	3,639
Deductions from Net Profit	72	544	243	78	207	1,622	1,520	29
Changes in Assets/Liabilities from Operating	−5,477	1,387	−894	5,817	3,745	10,535	−5,961	−2,020
Decrease (Increase) in Assets from Operating	−2,914	−1,157	3,699	1,198	550	7,175	−20,529	8,990
Decrease in Accounts Receivable	−14	200	−3,996	843	2,852	3,764	−22,550	10,185
Decrease in Inventory	−2,623	−925	8,480	2,001	903	1,957	2,834	−454
Others	−277	−432	−785	−1,645	−3,205	1,453	−813	−742
Increase (Decrease) in Liabilities from Operating	−2,563	2,543	−4,593	4,618	3,195	3,360	14,568	−11,010
Increase in Accounts Payable	−1,746	2,915	−5,098	5,531	1,997	4,994	14,340	−10,755
Others	−817	−371	505	−912	1,198	−1,634	228	−255
Cash Flows from Investing	−7,393	−3,033	−4,871	−9,585	−5,477	3,217	−3,811	−16,154
Cash Flows from Financing	13,405	−3,218	19,324	−4,340	10,148	−10,617	3,610	23,126
Cash Inflows from Financing	16,866	3,405	31,657	9,775	10,823	96,002	50,318	119,722
Increase in St. Debt	873	1,434	3,905		4,601	75,741	38,573	97,487
Increase in Bond	8,690		25,262	8,345		17,525	3,540	15,365
Increase in Long-Term Debt	2,052	1,120	2,478	1,424	6,221	2,367	3,913	
Others	5,251	851	12	6		369	4,293	6,870
Cash Outflows from Financing	3,461	6,622	12,333	14,115	674	106,618	46,709	96,596
Decrease in St. Debt	1,128	1,231	617	4,759		76,672	35,456	79,234
Decrease in Current Portion of Long-Term Debt	948	4,205	11,421	9,099	631	28,075	6,787	7,345
Decrease in Bond								3,425
Decrease in Long-Term Debt	296	567	295	257	43	284	106	
Others	1,089	620				1,588	4,361	6,591
Increase in Cash	3,962	−3,782	14,411	−5,673	12,756	7,897	−2,603	14,188
Cash at the Beginning	1,440	5,216	1,447	16,234	10,735	21,568	14,687	17,012
Cash at the End	5,402	1,485	15,858	10,561	23,492	29,465	12,084	31,200

[a] Expected figures for 1998. Note that these are unconsolidated figures. All figures are converted from Korean won using year-end exchange rates.

on the bourse. In fact, Jinwoong did not draw much attention from institutional investors at all. After the start of the IMF crisis, the stock fell to its lowest level ever (see **Exhibit 10** for Jinwoong's stock price history).

Jinwoong was also plagued by other problems common to Korean companies: a lack of transparency and poor financial reporting standards. Despite having many overseas operations, Jinwoong did not publish consolidated financial statements. Inventory management was poor. Although the core management team was strong, there were some personal ties to Lee. His younger brother was the head of purchasing in Korea, and a high school friend was the manager of the Sri Lanka operations.

But the biggest problem was that Jinwoong, much like the chaebols, was highly leveraged and owed 79 billion won (equivalent to US$46 million; 1$ = 1,695 won) in debt in 1997. After the crisis, domestic interest rates soared above 30%,[15] and its creditors started to call in its loans. In addition, approximately US$153 million in liabilities, of which only $9.8 million were long-term debt, burdened the company and its overseas

---

[15] As mandated by the IMF-prescribed structural reforms mentioned above.

EXHIBIT 10A
Stock Price History

Source: Jinwoong.

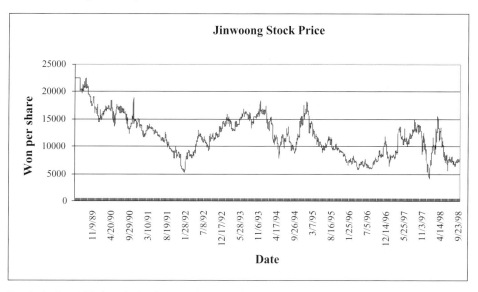

Note: On October 1, 1998, the total value of all outstanding shares of Jinwoong (i.e., 100% of common stock) was 20.4 billion won (US$14.7 million).

EXHIBIT 10B
Jinwoong's Stock Performance vs. KOSPI Index

Source: Jinwoong, Korea Stock Exchange.

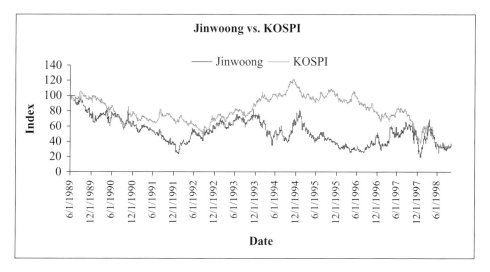

subsidiaries. The company was also not able to cash about $34 million in letters of credit, since Korean banks lacked adequate foreign exchange reserves. These two figures were not reflected in Jinwoong's unconsolidated financial statements (see **Exhibit 9** for the historical financials). In fact, Korean accounting laws did not require companies to re-port consolidated figures. Lee realized that "this liquidity crisis was the toughest chal-lenge the company had ever faced, and we needed some kind of a white knight."

The Decision to Seek Investors

Indeed, much like the IMF-led bailout of the Korean government, Jinwoong needed an investor to rescue it from its financial difficulties. But Lee also thought that Jinwoong needed a sizable working-capital injection so that it could aggressively expand in the soft-luggage segment and enter other similar businesses. Lee and his management team began their search for foreign investors that could provide both long-term capital and a strong stamp of credibility on the company. The domestic equity market was devastated by the IMF crisis, and debt financing (both domestic and international) did not seem like a feasible option for Jinwoong.

Through personal references, Lee met representatives of a company called SouthQuay, a financial services subsidiary of Singapore Technologies, a state-controlled conglomer-ate based in Singapore. Lee signed an exclusive memorandum of understanding (MOU) with SouthQuay in April 1998, by which it would act as Jinwoong's financial advisor. Moreover, it reserved the right to co-invest with the ultimate investors in Jinwoong. SouthQuay prepared an information memorandum and distributed it to various potential investors throughout Asia.

International Investors Is Introduced by SouthQuay

Over the next several months, a number of investors expressed interest and met with the management team, but none submitted formal bids. Then, in September 1998, SouthQuay introduced a consortium of a major insurance group and a private equity firm to Jinwoong. After some preliminary due diligence, this consortium showed strong interest in the company; it believed in the company's potential and concluded that the stock was severely undervalued due to the liquidity problems in the wake of the IMF crisis. Indeed, between September 1997 and September 1998, Jinwoong's stock price had plummeted by more than 40%.

SouthQuay joined the International Investors consortium as the lead investor. To-gether, they submitted a bid in September 1998 whereby they would purchase between $20 million and $24 million in newly issued convertible bonds. The conversion ratio would be some discount on Jinwoong's stock price in one or two years. They requested one month of due diligence. Upon successful completion of due diligence, SouthQuay and International Investors would inject capital into the company immediately. Further-more, Lee would maintain control of his company.

Enter Fidelity Capital and Warburg Pincus

Fidelity Capital was interested after receiving the South Quay information memorandum in June 1998. However, Fidelity wanted a coinvestor, and so it invited Warburg Pincus, with which it had worked before, to form an investment consortium. Chang Sun, a manag-ing director at Warburg Pincus, met with Lee and was impressed with his entrepreneurial skills and management team. Sun thought that Jinwoong probably had a good deal of potential and that its highly leveraged balance sheet could be remedied with help from sophisticated investors. However, Sun insisted on excluding SouthQuay as a coinvestor due to what he perceived to be a conflict of interest by its dual involvement as both Jinwoong's financial advisor and a potential investor.

After some preliminary due diligence, the Fidelity/Warburg Pincus consortium decided that it would invest between $35 million and $50 million and formally submitted an LOI on October 1, 1998 (see **Exhibit 11A** for the Fidelity/Warburg Pincus LOI). All operations of Jinwoong would be consolidated under a newly incorporated company; the consortium proposed to locate the headquarters of this new company outside Korea, such as in Hong Kong. It believed that this new offshore entity would have better access to international financing, at a much lower cost, and also better reflect the global nature of Jinwoong's business to investors. However, Fidelity/Warburg Pincus requested three months of intensive due diligence on the company before making a decision.

A Government Bailout?

On September 30, 1998, the Korean government announced the creation of the 1.6 trillion won (equivalent to US$1.3 billion; 1$ = 1,204 won) Corporate Restructuring Fund, which would finance promising small and medium-sized companies experiencing financial difficulties after the IMF crisis.[16] This plan was reminiscent of the government's traditional, implicit promise not to let the chaebols fail. Lee learned that Jinwoong was one of the

[16] "Corporate Debt Restructuring: The Missing Link in Financial Stabilization," Wondong Cho, deputy director general of the Ministry of Finance and Economy, Korea, and Michael Pomerleano, lead financial specialist of the World Bank, p. 30.

EXHIBIT 11A   **Preliminary LOI from Fidelity/Warburg Pincus**

Source: Jinwoong.

Summary of Key LOI Terms

- Investment Amount: $35 million–$50 million (probably a combination of equity [preferred stock] and loan from investors)
- Proposed Restructuring Guidelines
  - Put all operating entities under new holding company based outside of Korea.
  - Reduce the capital intensity of the business by rationalizing working capital in the parent company and subsidiaries.
  - Inject equity to reduce debt level and provide a cushion against any future downturns in the business.
- Exclusivity
  - Jinwoong not to enter into any agreements with any other potential investors. Upon signing the term sheet, Jinwoong agrees not to discuss or negotiate with any other investors up to the period ending December 15, 1998. This period may be further extended with consent of all three parties.
- Due Diligence: 3 months
- Fees and Expenses
  - If the investment is consummated, Jinwoong to pay 100% of the professional and out-of-pocket fees and expenses of lawyers, accountants, and other consultants.
  - If the investment is not consummated, Jinwoong to pay
    - Up to October 15, 0%
    - From October 16 to November 15, 15%
    - After November 15, 50%

EXHIBIT 11B
Current Ownership Structure

Source: Jinwoong.

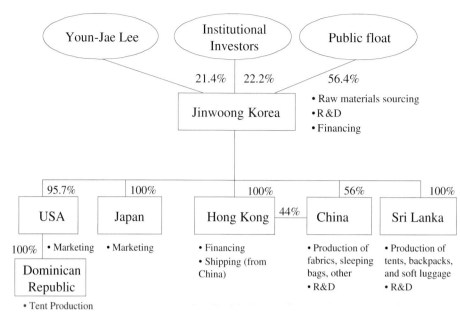

EXHIBIT 11C
Possible Future Ownership Structure

Source: Jinwoong.

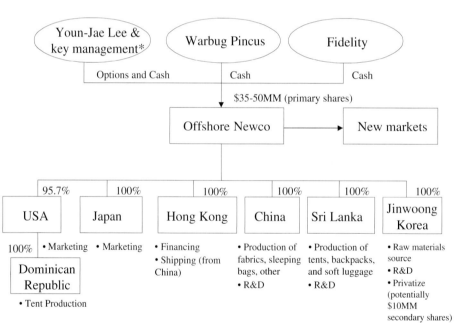

*Shares in Newco paid for at discount to investors' cost. Lee may roll up old shares in Newco once regulations permit.

companies selected by the government for support under the Corporate Restructuring Fund. Given Jinwoong's leading market share in the U.S. and global tent markets, the government was willing to bail out the company.

The Corporate Restructuring Fund could inject either debt or equity into the company. Moreover, Lee realized that the government "would not require much, if any, due diligence on Jinwoong and its operations. It looked as if we could carry on our business as usual." By choosing this option, Lee could close the door on both the International Investors and the Warbug Pincus/Fidelity bids. However, Lee was not sure how much and at what valuation the government would provide the financing.

EXHIBIT 11D Due Diligence Timetable

Source: Warburg Pincus.

	9/14	9/21	9/28	10/5	10/12	10/19	10/26	11/2	11/9	11/16	11/23	11/30	12/7	12/14
BUSINESS DUE DILIGENCE		Discussions with Korea mgmt. (finance, sourcing)		Discuss Term sheet		Discuss preliminary view of business	Agree on open business issues			Discuss acctg./legal issues				
	Draft/discuss conceptual financial structure			Revise financial model				Revise financial structure			Finalize financial structure			
		Review existing financials	Prepare financial model	▲	▲	▲	Draft financial model			Final financial model				
	Visit Xiamen facility		Visit U.S. retailers	▲	Visit Sri Lanka		(Visit DR facility)							
			Inventory review	▲	▲	▲								
			Sourcing review (price trends, geography)	▲	▲	▲								
			Manufacturing review (cost position, quality systems, etc.)	▲	▲	▲	▲	Address open issues						
		Tent market study	▲	▲	▲	▲								
		Luggage market study	▲	▲	▲	▲								
ACCOUNTING DUE DILIGENCE		Review key accounting issues with management					Interview/appoint accounting firm	Review accounts	▲	▲	▲	Accounting firm draft report		Accounting firm final report
LEGAL DUE DILIGENCE	Interviews/appoint law firm	Law firm review of financial restructuring (legality, tax)	▲					▲	▲	Law firm draft report		Law firm final report		
							Review incorp. documents, licenses, contracts							
DOCUMENTATION	Discuss and sign off LOI				Sign term sheet (earlier if possible)				Begin drafting documentation	(Purch. Agreement, s'holder agreement)	Review documentation	▲	▲	Closing

411

EXHIBIT 12A   Projected Financials of Jinwoong and Market Financial Data—Income Statement

Source: Warburg Pincus.

($ in thousands)	1998[a]	1999	2000	2001	2002	2003
Sales	180,906	201,037	217,429	235,586	255,836	278,477
Cost of Goods Sold	123,184	161,825	161,099	168,157	181,937	197,560
Distribution	—	5,698	5,381	5,524	5,799	6,127
Gross Profit	57,722	33,513	50,950	61,905	68,099	74,791
SG&A	23,242	21,380	24,475	25,878	27,411	29,092
EBIT	34,480	12,134	26,474	36,028	40,688	45,698
Amortization of intangibles & transaction fees	—	468	468	468	468	468
Net Interest Expense	21,819	10,542	6,647	5,378	4,349	3,339
Adjustments	152	(1,202)	(600)	(150)	(150)	(150)
Pre-tax Income	12,509	2,326	19,960	30,332	36,021	42,041
Taxes (20%)		465	3,992	6,066	7,204	8,408
Net Income		1,861	15,968	24,266	28,817	33,633

EXHIBIT 12B   Projected Financials of Jinwoong and Market Financial Data—Balance Sheet

Source: Warburg Pincus.

($ in thousands)	1998[a]	1999	2000	2001	2002	2003
ASSETS						
Cash and Deposits	445	5,000.0	5,000.0	5,000.0	5,000.0	9,064.3
Accounts Receivable	10,833	4,716	7,341	7,934	8,595	9,333
Inventories	92,755	63,633	53,902	56,560	61,361	66,785
Other Current Assets	22,902	19,777	12,777	12,777	12,777	12,777
Total Current Assets	126,935	93,126	79,020	82,271	87,733	97,959
PP&E	**19,260**	**24,783**	**24,084**	**23,025**	**21,817**	**20,533**
Investments and Other Non-Current	314	127	127	127	127	127
Transaction Fees and Expenses	—	1,600	1,200	800	400	—
Intangible Assets	2,704	2,636	2,569	2,501	2,434	2,366
Total Assets	149,213	122,272	107,000	108,725	112,510	120,985
LIABILITIES AND EQUITY						
Short-term Debt	34,312	25,142	—	—	—	—
Accounts Payable (using letter of credit)	54,167	53,207	53,902	51,014	25,622	—
Other Current Liabilities	54,660	30,467	23,767	4,129	4,503	4,932
Total Current Liabilities	143,139	108,816	77,669	55,142	30,125	4,932
Long-term Debt	9,846	—	—	—	—	—
Bond	—	27,000	27,000	27,000	27,000	27,000
Other Long-term Liabilities	160	160	160	160	160	160
Total Liabilities	153,145	135,976	104,829	82,302	57,285	32,092
Investor Preferred Equity	—	10,000	10,000	10,000	10,000	10,000
Common Equity	(3,932)	(23,704)	(7,830)	16,422	45,225	78,894
Total Equity	(3,932)	(13,704)	2,170	26,422	55,225	88,894
Total Liabilities and Sh. Equity	149,213	122,272	107,000	108,724	112,510	120,985

[a]Note that 1998 figures are prior to a possible transaction and are not directly comparable to 1999's. They represent a "best effort" by Warburg Pincus to produce comparable figures (to 1999's) from unconsolidated statements. Note that some figures may not add up due to rounding.

EXHIBIT 12C   **Projected Financials of Jinwoong and Market Financial Data—Cash Flow Statement**

Source: Warburg Pincus.

($ in thousands)	1998[a]	1999	2000	2001	2002	2003
Net Income		1,861	15,968	24,266	28,817	33,633
Depreciation		2,077	2,399	2,559	2,709	2,784
Amortization of Intangibles		68	68	68	68	68
Amortization of Transaction Fees and Expenses		400	400	400	400	400
Changes in Working Capital		12,264	7,179	(2,967)	(5,087)	(5,734)
Cash from Operations		16,670	26,013	24,325	26,906	31,151
Changes in Other Assets and Liabilities		187	—	—	—	—
Incremental Capex		2,000	—	—	—	—
Capital Expenditures		5,600	1,700	1,500	1,500	1,500
Free Cash Flow		9,257	24,313	22,825	25,406	29,651

[a]1998 figures not available.

Note: The financial information in **Exhibits 12a, 12b,** and **12c** was prepared by Warburg Pincus for purposes of evaluating a potential investment in Jinwoong in 1998. Such financial information is not indicative of results that were or will be obtained by Jinwoong. Such financial information is not current, has not been updated, and must not be relied upon for any purpose.

EXHIBIT 12D   **Interest Rate Information**

Source: Compiled from Bank of Korea, U.S. Treasury data.

	1996	1997	1998[a]
U.S. T-Bond (3 years)	5.91%	5.74%	4.62%
U.S. T-Bond (5 years)	6.07%	5.77%	4.62%
U.S. T-Bond (30 years)	6.55%	5.99%	5.20%
Republic of Korea U.S.$ bond[b]	—	—	11.89%
Korean T-Bond[c] (3 years)	12.91%	14.96%	11.84%
Korean T-Bond[c] (5 years)	12.12%	14.70%	11.87%
Korean Corporate Bond[c] (3 years)	12.57%	24.31%	12.51%

[a]As of September 30, 1998.
[b]Issued April 7, 1998; coupon: 8.75%; maturity: April 2003.
[c]Korean won denominated.

Which Investor Should Lee Choose?

Lee contemplated the three choices regarding his company. The government's Corporate Restructuring Fund would quickly inject much-needed capital into the company; the International Investors consortium was also promising and needed just one month of due diligence. On the other hand, although he somehow liked the Fidelity/Warburg Pincus idea of creating a new holding company outside Korea, Lee was not sure if his company could survive until the completion of their requested three months of due diligence. And what if at the end of their due diligence they decided to back out? In addition, what valuation should he expect from any of the potential investors? (See **Exhibit 12** for projections, comparables, and financial market data.) Lastly, from a long-term perspective, which investor would best help Jinwoong become the leading outdoor travel equipment maker in the world?

EXHIBIT 12E Comparables

Source: Compiled from Bloomberg, Datastream, SEC filings data.

	Sales		Net Income		Long-Term Debt		Market Capitalization		Equity Beta	Employees	EBITDA	EBITDA Multiple	P/E Ratio	EBIT	EBIT Multiple
	FY 1996	FY 1997	FY 1996	FY 1997	FY 1996	FY 1997	FY End 1997	10/01 1998	10/01 1998	10/01 1998	FY End 1997	FY 1997	10/01 1998	FY 1997	10/01 1998
Coleman[a]	1,220,216	1,154,294	−41,246	−2,536	583,613	477,799	856,838	480,096	0.98	6,000	71,066	6.76	n/m	33,089	14.51
Kellwood[b]	1,521,005	1,781,582	37,596	42,747	109,831	242,720	685,710	575,607	0.6	18,400	132,459	4.35	13.47	102,821	5.60
Johnson Worldwide[c]	344,373	303,121	11,355	2,056	61,501	88,753	113,487	57,571	0.74	1,366	24,688	2.33	28.00	12,739	4.52
Brunswick[d]	3,160,300	3,657,400	185,800	150,500	455,400	645,500	3,022,089	1,306,786	1.09	25,300	443,700	2.95	8.68	286,800	4.56
North Face[e]	158,226	208,403	4,801	11,107	135	5,177	253,044	162,318	1.63	713	25,725	6.31	14.61	20,595	7.88

Note: Equity betas are calculated as five years' monthly data with the exception of North Face (July 31, 1996–September 30, 1998).

[a]Coleman Company is a leading manufacturer and marketer of consumer products for outdoor recreation and home hardware use. It has two primary classes of products: outdoor recreation and hardware. The outdoor recreation products include a comprehensive line of lanterns/stoves, fuel-related products, coolers/jugs, sleeping bags, backpacks, tents, outdoor furniture, portable electric lights, spas, camping accessories, and other products. The home hardware products include portable generators, air compressors, smoke alarms, carbon monoxide detectors, and thermostats. In FY1997, outdoor recreation products accounted for 74% of revenues while hardware represented 26%.

[b]Kellwood Company is the seventh-largest publicly held apparel company in the United States. It is organized into five business segments: Better/Bridge branded apparel, Popular/Moderate branded apparel, Domestic Private label apparel, Smart Shirts (Far East private label), and American Recreation Products (ARP). The ARP division includes the following brands: Sierra Designs, Kelty, Wenzel (offering a full line of tents and sleeping bags), and Slumberjack. In FY1997, the ARP segment accounted for $138 million, or 7.7%, of Kellwood sales.

[c]Johnson Worldwide manufactures and markets a wide variety of outdoor recreation products. It is comprised of five divisions: Motors and Fishing Products, Motors and Marine Products, Fishing Products, Watercraft Products, and Outdoor Equipment Products (which includes Eureka | and Camp Trails camping tents and backpacks, Jack Wolfskin camping tents and backpacks, backpacks and outdoor clothing, and Silva field compasses). In 1997, the Outdoor Equipment Products division represented 25% of Johnson Worldwide revenues.

[d]Brunswick Corporation is a multinational, branded consumer products company serving the outdoor and indoor active recreation markets. It operates in two business segments: Recreation and Marine. In FY1997, the Recreation Group accounted for 34.7% of revenues and Marine Group sales represented 65.3%. The Recreation segment consists of the Brunswick Outdoor Recreation Group (BORG), the Life Fitness Division, and the Brunswick Indoor Recreation Group. BORG markets and manufactures fishing and camping equipment that include sleeping bags, tents, backpacks, canvas bags, foul-weather gear, waders, hunting apparel, propane lanterns and stoves, cookware, utensils, and shooting sports accessories. In 1996, the company invested $360.6 million to acquire various businesses including Roadmaster bicycles, American Camper (manufacturer of tents and camping equipment), and the Boston Whaler line of boats.

[e]The North Face is a leading consumer product company that has evolved into one of the world's premier brands of high-performance outdoor apparel and equipment. The company designs and distributes technical outerwear, sportswear, equipment, and outdoor accessories (including tents) under the North Face brand name.

Lee thought about all the hardships that he and his company had endured over the past 20 years: "We at Jinwoong became victims of Korea's outdated financial system. As a small, yet global company with no government ties, we should have seen the writing on the wall and lowered our leverage. This would probably have occurred at the expense of growth. But now we must look forward. We have always learned and grown from hardships, and this current crisis is no exception." Since the onset of the IMF crisis almost one year before, he had had many sleepless nights trying to save Jinwoong—renegotiating debt with his creditors, drastically cutting back on expenses, and keeping up the morale of his employees. As he prepared to make the biggest decision in the history of his company, it appeared that Lee had another long night ahead of him.

Case

21

Telewizja Wisla

Claire Hurley hung up the phone in her Newton, Massachusetts, home and stared out the window into the pre-dawn light of March 1996. Despite her best efforts over the last several months, Hurley was discouraged and frustrated by her inability to work with the current management of Telewizja Wisla (TVW; pronounced teh-leh-VEE-zya VEE-swah). She knew that time was running out in her quest to raise the capital needed to save the company.

Hurley, a 35-year-old U.S. citizen with a background in international finance and economic development, had co-founded TVW in 1991, with Wojtek Szczerba (VOY-tek sh-CHAR-bah), 41, a Polish freelance television producer living in London. In late 1994, Szczerba, with Hurley's help, secured the only private regional television broadcasting license for southern Poland. Soon thereafter, Szczerba was ousted from an operating position at TVW by its major investors, Realbud, a Polish construction firm, and Efekt, a Krakow-based real estate company. (See **Exhibit 1** for Szczerba's and Hurley's resumes.)

Since then, the company had been run by Roman Sztorc (sh-torts) and Jarek Potasz (POH-tash). Sztorc, a 56-year-old engineer, had spent most of his career managing multimillion-dollar construction projects for Realbud in the former Soviet Union and in Eastern Bloc and Middle East countries. Sztorc was very close to Realbud's chairman and principal decision maker, Ryszard Sciborowski (sh-chee-boh-ROFF-ski), and active in a number of other Realbud projects. Sztorc delegated responsibility for TVW's day-to-day operations to Potasz, whose abilities he trusted greatly. Potasz, a 33-year-old engineer, had managed several Polish print media concerns prior to working with TVW, and had held a senior position at a Krakow newspaper that a foreign media company acquired during his tenure.

Although Hurley, who moved back to the United States in late 1992, continued to work with Sztorc and Potasz to raise additional capital, she estimated that TVW still needed 18.5 million new Polish zloty ("PLN," equivalent to US $7.4 million; 1$ = 2.5 PLN) to fund start-up operating losses and complete its infrastructure build-out. Despite her best

President of Media Developments Ltd. Claire Hurley and Research Associate Andrew S. Janower prepared this case under the supervision of Professor Walter Kuemmerle as the basis for class discussion rather than to illustrate either effective or ineffective handling of an administrative situation.

EXHIBIT 1
Founder's Resumes

Source: TVW.

CLAIRE HURLEY

PROFESSIONAL EXPERIENCE
Inter-American Development Bank, Washington, D.C.
1992–1994: Debt financing officer (executed multi-currency debt financing strategies)

Security Pacific Merchant Bank, Hoare Govett Ltd. Corporate Advisory Group, London UK
1988–1992: Assistant Director
Performed extensive cross border acquisition, divestiture and leveraged buyout work. Advised clients active in UK broadcasting and media entertainment market.
1986-1988: Associate (MBA Rotational Training Program)
Worked in Corporate Finance, Mortgage Finance and Currency & Interest Rate Departments.

EDUCATION
The Wharton School
1984–1986: MBA

Princeton University
1978–1982: B.A. (History, Spanish)

WOJTEK SZCZERBA

PROFESSIONAL EXPERIENCE
Independent Television Producer, London
1986–1993: Produced television programming for European, American and Japanese networks. Devised and ran one of the first hands-on training courses for television producers from Eastern Europe with funding from the British Government's Know How Fund and the Thatcher Foundation.

Independent Film Company, Poland and UK
1979–1986: Managed an independent film production company which specialized in tourist and corporate promotion.

EDUCATION
Akademia Gornicz Hutnicza, Krakow, Poland
1974–1979: Degree course in geophysics

efforts to consummate a deal with one of several interested foreign media companies, including the Walt Disney Company, a combination of factors had hampered her progress. She recalled:

> I am constantly surprised by the difference in perspective between the Polish parties—the TV and Radio Council and our Polish investors—and potential foreign investors. The Polish parties seem content to allow more time to pass between key milestones—even the banks don't seem to be in a rush to get their loans repaid. By contrast, western investors understand the value of acting quickly in order to maximize the value of the franchise—they know that if we develop a great selection of programming and lock up key sports broadcasting rights, we will be well positioned to lead the supra-regional network or, better yet, convince the Council to grant TVW a national license with regional time slots.
>
> At the same time, despite their protests to the contrary, most large foreign companies are not truly prepared to do business with small start-up companies in developing countries like Poland, which has a business, legal and regulatory environment not yet fully adapted to a competitive free-market economy. When you compound this problem with significant cultural and language barriers, and the fact that Polish managers and government bureaucrats are not only often unfamiliar with capitalist concepts but also very wary of the motives of foreign investors, it becomes very hard to get things done.

By March 1996, the company faced an urgent liquidity crisis, with 5 million PLN (US $2 million) of TVW debt guaranteed by Realbud coming due in May. The company's primary bank, and several other local banks, were overextended to Realbud and unwilling to take an equity stake in TVW. The bank had, however, agreed to extend the loan and provide incremental debt capacity if TVW raised additional equity. With neither Realbud nor Efekt willing to invest further, TVW had to find a substantial new partner before it ran out of cash and had to shut down operations. (See **Exhibit 2** for TVW's ownership structure as of March 1996.)

In particular, the bank was encouraging Realbud to complete a deal with Bertelsmann AG, a large German media company that was closely related to one of the bank's major shareholders. While Hurley believed that Bertelsmann would be a good strategic partner for TVW because of its extensive programming library and strong financial condition, she was concerned about the political ramifications of such a deal. Even though Bertelsmann's voting equity interest would be limited to 33%, the National Council for Radio and Television had previously expressed concern with the increasing level of German influence in southern Polish media. Hurley worried that a TVW-Bertelsmann partnership could jeopardize TVW's ability to secure the Council's approval for several additional transmission sites needed to cover TVW's region adequately.

Hurley was also considering a proposal from a venture capital firm doing business in Eastern Europe, DBG Development Capital Eastern Europe, Ltd. ("DBG"). DBG's CEO was James O'Neill, Harvard Business School class of 1990. DBG was interested in taking over TVW by providing expansion capital that would buy out Efekt's position and dilute Realbud to a small shareholding, an ownership structure that would require Council approval. DBG would then recruit additional senior management talent to help grow the company, probably including Szczerba's return as president of TVW. Hurley commented on TVW's alternatives:

> Unlike many venture capitalists we have met with, DBG is savvy about Poland's legal and other operating constraints and has the explicit ability to pursue a media deal under its fund's investment mandate. While it clearly doesn't have the strategic advantages of Bertelsmann, we could always cut a deal with a strategic partner in a later financing round.
>
> From a personal perspective, DBG's offer would be preferable to Wojtek Szczerba and me; Wojtek would be able to return to an active management role and we would increase our combined ownership from 4% today to nearly 25% of the company. On the other hand, to the extent that our top priority is getting TVW back on track quickly, I am reluctant to introduce an alternative at this point in the process that may only distract Realbud and Efekt's attention from their consideration of Bertelsmann's offer and could possibly jeopardize this round of financing altogether.

Either way, the situation was urgent. If Hurley were unable to break through the current bottleneck over the next several weeks, TVW would default on its loans, run out of cash, and quite possibly lose its valuable broadcasting license. (See **Exhibit 3** for a timeline of events.)

The Polish Market

After the communist regime fell and the first Solidarity government took office in September 1989, Poland embarked on a radical market reform process that initially caused great distress to the Polish economy. Gross domestic product shrank 12% and inflation reached 680% in 1990. Since then, Poland experienced a dramatic economic rebound and, while the country's legal, regulatory and business environment were still not on a par with international free-market standards, by 1996 the country was widely considered one of the star economic performers of Central Europe (see **Exhibit 4A**). The government had

EXHIBIT 2 Telewizja Wisła's Shareholding History and Structure

Source: TVW.

Share Ownership as of

	September 5, 1994			February 15, 1995			July 1, 1995			August 1, 1995			October 15, 1995		
	Capital Contributed (NPLZ)	Shares Owned	% Owned	Capital Contributed (NPLZ)	Shares Owned	% Owned	Capital Contributed (NPLZ)	Shares Owned	% Owned	Capital Contributed (NPLZ)	Shares Owned	% Owned	Capital Contributed (NPLZ)	Shares Owned	% Owned
TVW Founders (a)	500,000	5,000	87.50%	500,000	5,000	10.00%	500,000	5,000	5.00%	500,000	5,000	5.00%	500,000	5,000	4.35%
Efekt (b)	35,700	357	6.25%	2,250,000	22,500	45.00%	4,750,000	47,500	47.50%	2,800,000	28,000	28.00%	2,800,000	28,000	24.35%
Realbud (c)	35,700	357	6.25%	2,250,000	22,500	45.00%	4,750,000	47,500	47.50%	6,700,000	67,000	67.00%	8,200,000	82,000	71.30%
Total	571,400	5,714	100.00%	5,000,000	50,000	100.00%	10,000,000	100,000	100.00%	10,000,000	100,000	100.00%	11,500,000	115,000	100.00%

Notes (a) Founders: Wojtek Szczerba, Bogdan Zięba and Claire Hurley. Claire will receive an additional 3000 shares when TVW closes a deal with a foreign investor.

(b) Efekt is a publicly traded company involved primarily in renting market stall space.

(c) Realbud is a privately held company involved in project construction and management.

EXHIBIT 3   TVW Historical Timeline

Source: Author.

1989	September	Solidarity government takes office
1991	Spring	Polish government starts working on private television franchise legislation
	Winter	Szczerba, Balinska, and Hurley begin exploring TVW idea
1992	Spring	Szczerba and Hurley approach foreign investors
		Szczerba begins lobbying Council for license
1993	March	Franchise legislation enacted
	September	Council asks for final applications for first franchise round (second round projected to be completed by June 1994)
		Szczerba and Zieba begin working full time on securing TVW franchise
1994	February	Polsat awarded national license, other franchise awards delayed
		Council asks TVW for firm evidence of Polish capital commitments
		Realbud and Efekt agree to become TVW's Polish capital providers
	May	Council announces TVW likely to receive license before end of August 1994
	June	Hurley starts working full time on securing a foreign partner for TVW
		Founders begin laying groundwork for entire business
	October	TVW begins focusing on securing Disney as TVW's partner
		TVW's equity capital increased 0.5 million PLN ($US 0.2 million)
	November	TVW receives license
	December	First franchise round complete (Council states now likely to complete second round by June 1995)
		TVW's capital increased to a total of 5 million PLN ($US 2 million)
1995	January	TVW's negotiations with Disney broken
	February	Polish shareholders' partnership expectations rise
		Founders stop partnership negotiations and focus exclusively on securing programming, advertising, and distribution network
	March	Efekt and Realbud search for partners independently
	April	Council starts second franchise round—applications due by June 1995
	June	Szczerba dismissed.
		TVW's capital increased to a total of 10 million PLN ($US 4 million)
	July	Efekt and Realbud falling out
		Realbud assumes majority control of business and completes distribution network and programming contracts begun under Szczerba
	August	Realbud and TVW hire Hurley to find partner for TVW
		Bertelsmann performs initial due diligence review
	September	Media companies uncomfortable with TVW shareholder and management situation
		Realbud and TVW concerned about Council's perception of Bertelsmann
	October	Second franchise awards delayed until early 1996
	December	TVW starts broadcasting
1996	February	Realbud begins serious negotiations with Bertelsmann
	March	Second franchise awards delayed until at least August 1996
	April	Realbud and Bertelsmann agree on letter of intent
		Bertelsmann begins detailed due diligence process
		DBG (venture capital firm) expresses interest in buyout of TVW

enacted reforms designed to attract foreign investment; these included the tax-free repatriation of profits and international standards governing the Warsaw Stock Exchange, which currently comprised some 60 companies (**Exhibit 4B**).

With a population of 38.8 million, Poland was by far the largest Central European market even though GDP per capita, an estimated $3,460 in 1996, lagged that of Hungary and the Czech Republic by roughly 25%. Since market reforms began, Poles had been voracious consumers, with the advertising market growing at a 79% annual growth rate, from $30 million in 1990 to over $550 million in 1995 (**Exhibit 5**).

EXHIBIT 4A   Data on the Polish, Czech and Hungarian Economy

Source: Compiled from EIU Country Report data (Poland, Hungary, Czech Republic) and the following other data sources: OECD Economic Surveys, IMF International Financial Statistics, Internet Securities, Lexis-Nexis, Datastream.

| | Poland | | | | | | | Hungary | Czech Republic | |
	1991	1992	1993	1994	1995	1996	1997 (e)	1996	1996	1997 (e)
Population (mil)	38.3	38.4	38.5	38.6	38.6	39.0	39.1	10.19	10.3	10.3
Nominal GDP (US$ bil)	76.4	84.3	85.9	92.7	117.5	135.1	142.8	44.1	52.7	58.4
Nominal GDP Growth p.a.	22.6%	10.3%	1.9%	7.9%	26.8%	14.9%	5.7%	0.8%	11.2%	10.8%
GDP/capita (US$)	1,995	2,195	2,230	2,402	3,044	3,500	3,652	4,328	5,117	5,670
Consumer Price Increase	60.4%	44.3%	37.6%	32.2%	27.8%	19.9%	16.8%	23.6%	8.9%	8.5%
Unemployment Rate	11.8%	13.6%	14.7%	16.0%	14.9%	13.2%	13.0%	9.5%	3.3%	4.0%
Prime Rate	54.6%	39.0%	35.3%	32.8%	33.5%	26.1%	22.0%	32.6%	12.8%	12.0%
Real GDP change (%)	−7.0%	2.6%	3.8%	5.0%	5.8%					

(e) = expected (forecast)

EXHIBIT 4B   Data on Warsaw Stock Exchange

Source: Compiled from EIU Country Report data (Poland, Hungary, Czech Republic) and the following other data sources: OECD Economic Surveys, IMF International Financial Statistics, Internet Securities, Lexis-Nexis, Datastream.

	1992	1993	1994	1995	1996
Number of Companies Listed	16	22	44	65	83
Total market capitalization (US$ million)	235	2,559	3,100	4,576	8,000
Index (WIG Index)	1,040	12,439	7,473	7,589	14,343
Total Market P/E Multiple	3.2	23.9	16.4	7.8	15.2

EXHIBIT 5   General Television Advertising-Related Statistics

Source: TVW based on (a)*New York Times,* based on Gazeta Wyborcza article on a January 1996 survey of 1,117 adults conducted by leading Polish public opinion polling organization. (b)Historic figures based on published reports in *Rzczechpolita, Media Polska* and *Gazeta Wyborcza* and *Amer Nielsen* research. Projected media share figures provided by Robinski & Associates. Projected total market figures based on conservative growth estimates.
(c)CME 1995 Share Offering Circular, based on advertising expenditure data from *Zenith Media, Media & Marketing Magazine, Mediapolis Praha* and *Advig-Bucharest.*

Polish Purchase of Consumer Goods Since 1989[a]

% Households Already Owning		% Households Planning to Buy Soon	
Refrigerator	95%	Mountain bicycle	14%
Color television	88%	Compact disk player	13%
Washing machine	62%	Video camera	12%
Videocassette recorder	53%	Home computer	12%
Stereo	27%	Washing machine	11%
Cable television service	20%	Stereo	11%
Mountain bicycle	15%	Satellite dish	11%
Home computer	13%	Microwave oven	11%
Compact disk player	13%	Videocassette recorder	9%

Polish Advertising Market Overview[b]

	Advertising Market by Media Share—(through December 31 of year listed)				
	1993	1994	1995	1996P	1997P
TV	62.1%	59.0%	55.1%	53.6%	52.0%
Magazines	9.5%	12.9%	14.1%	15.5%	15.6%
Newspapers	21.0%	16.0%	15.3%	14.9%	14.0%
Outdoors (billboards, etc.)	2.2%	4.5%	7.2%	7.8%	7.9%
Radio	5.3%	7.6%	8.4%	7.8%	7.5%
Other				0.5%	2.1%
Total %	100.0%	100.0%	100.0%	100.0%	100.0%
Total Market ($ millions)	300	450	600	750	900
Growth Rate (Year/Year)		50.00%	33.33%	25.00%	20.00%
TV Market ($ millions)	186	266	331	402	468

Comparison of Polish to Other Television Advertising Markets[c]

	Poland	Czech	Hungary	U.K.	Germany
Total TV Advertising Spend ($ million)	331	145	157	4,791	3,833
Population (million)	38.8	10.3	10.3	58.6	81.3
Per Capita ($)	9	14	15	82	47

P = projected (forecase)

Until 1989, both print and broadcast media in Poland had been state controlled. Employing 6,500 people, Public Television Poland (TVP) was a bureaucratic monopoly with a reputation for delivering drab content while treating advertisers and programming suppliers poorly. Advertising was limited to a maximum of 15% of air time and at least 60% of its output, exclusive of news, game-shows, and live sports, was allocated to domestically produced broadcast ("quota production").

Operating from 11 regional centers, TVP broadcast on four channels. TVP1 and TVP2, both national public channels, covered roughly 98% of the television viewing population and had average viewer shares of 50% and 21%, respectively. TVP1's national news programming generated viewer shares of 40% and was TVP's most consistently successful offering, while TVP2's content tended to be more intellectually oriented. By law, TVP1 and TVP2 had to maintain the same programming across all regions of the country except for one hour of daily local programs on TVP2. The individual service of each regional center, termed TVP3, covered approximately 53% of the population and provided a higher percentage of local content. Overall, TVP3 had an estimated 2.2% share of the total television market. The fourth channel, TV Polonia, which covered 32% of the population, was a satellite service designed for Poles living abroad and garnered an estimated 1.3% share of Poland's total television market **(Exhibit 6).**

Taking advantage of Poland's switch to a free market economy, independent entrepreneurs started land-based, illegal "pirate stations" in the early 1990s. By the time the government shut them down in early 1994, the most successful of these stations, Polonia One, had an estimated viewer share of over 25% in its markets, covering 21% of the population, and an impressive list of multinational advertisers as clients. Polonia One's output consisted mainly of inexpensive programming such as Brazilian soap operas, "MacGyver" and "The A-Team."

EXHIBIT 6 Television Viewer and Advertising Share Statistics

Source: TVW based on Robinski & Associates, based on January 1996 OBOP survey. Polsat and TVW figures based on adjusted March 1996 survey.

January 1996 Television Viewing Figures

TV Station	% Poland's Population Reached	Average Daily View Time per Person	% of Total Population's Viewing Time	% of Total Population Tuning into Station . . . at Least Once Daily	At Least Once Weekly
Total	99.0	4 hr. 30 min.	100.0	91.0	96.0
TVP1	98.0	2 hr. 16 min.	50.5	83.0	96.0
TVP2	97.0	0 hr. 57 min.	21.1	58.0	89.0
TVP3	53.0	0 hr. 06 min.	2.2	10.0	23.0
TV Polonia	32.0	0 hr. 03 min.	1.3	5.0	20.0
Polsat	75.0	0 hr. 46 min.	19.0	39.0	68.0
TVW (a)	10.0	0 hr. 01 min.	0.1	1.0	2.0
Others	30.0	0 hr. 14 min.	5.4	25.0	25.0
Video	53.0	0 hr. 05 min.	2.1	5.0	15.0

(a) TVW has only been on air for one month (January 1996).

TVP and Polsat Historic Viewer and Advertising Market Share

	12 Months Through December 31		
	1994	1995	1996
TVP			
1. % estimated coverage of TV advertising market	100.00%	100.00%	100.00%
2. % viewer share (% of Poles viewing station daily)	90.00%	80.00%	74.00%
3. Proportionate % share market (1 × 2)	90.00%	80.00%	74.00%
Actual share of TV ad market	87.00%	79.00%	68.00%
	1994	1995	1996
	(on air 8 months)		
POLSAT			
1. % estimated coverage of TV ad market	30.00%	60.00%	75.00%
2. % viewer share	3.00%	14.00%	20.00%
3. Proportionate % share market (1 × 2)	0.90%	8.40%	15.00%
Actual share of TV ad market	8.00%	18.00%	28.00%

The Origins of Telewizja Wisla

With historic changes taking place in early 1991, Wojtek Szczerba and his wife, Maria Balinska, dreamt about starting a television station in Szczerba's home city of Krakow. Szczerba, a London-based freelance cameraman, producer, and director, and Balinska, a senior news and current affairs producer at the BBC, were both intimately familiar with the industry and excited about bringing quality television to Poland. However, the cost of a station was well beyond their own resources so they sought the financial advice of Claire Hurley, a close friend of Balinska who worked in the cross-border financing group of Hoare Govett, a British investment bank. In their free time, Hurley and Szczerba put together a formal business plan and began approaching foreign media companies and venture capital firms. Szczerba recalled:

> While we had no trouble getting initial meetings with potential investors, we had no luck securing seed funding. Even the most excited candidates had a hard time getting their minds around the potential future value of a $4 million investment in a start-up private television station in a developing market with nascent advertising revenue, an uncertain and highly politicized licensing process, and strict foreign ownership restrictions.
>
> Additionally, many investors didn't fully understand the state of the Polish economy—they insisted on imputing Western pay scales to the venture, which totally devastated our proforma profits even though it was a time when, if you had $100 in your pocket, you were rich in Poland. Finally, it probably didn't help that we were completely unknown quantities with no direct operating experience in the broadcast industry, despite the fact that there were no executives in Poland with the kind of credentials that Western investors typically looked for.
>
> Despite our initial frustrations, we decided that the opportunity was too big to ignore; we decided to continue to fund the idea out of our own pockets and refocused on securing the broadcast license under the premise that once we controlled the asset, we would have an easier time attracting capital.

Securing the TVW License and Raising Start-up Capital

In 1993, the Polish government finally enacted legislation to allow independent operators to own commercial television and radio stations for the first time. This legislation gave the TV and Radio Council, a nine-member body of political appointments from Poland's various political parties, the responsibility for governing existing state-owned television and radio stations and awarding new commercial licenses (see **Exhibit 7**).

In September 1993, the Council invited official applications for television licenses. The Polish government planned to award an undetermined number of licenses throughout Poland subject to a set of requirements according to the newly created (but as yet untested) media law. The rest of each franchise proposal, including geographic areas to be covered, was up to the applicant.

Despite significant confusion about the licensing process, the Council ultimately received more than 80 applications for commercial television franchises, the majority filed by Polish companies seeking *local* broadcast rights. Ten applicants, primarily backed by major international media firms, sought *national* franchises, which would cover a substantial portion of the population and create effective competition to the government-owned channels. TVW, by contrast, submitted the only application for a *supra-regional* license; it argued that a private national network comprising three large regional services could tailor content to regional news, sports, and entertainment preferences while still benefiting from national economies of scale by buying programming and selling advertising air time together. Understanding that a tangled patchwork of existing spectrum users made TVW's plan technically unfeasible to implement in the short term, Szczerba

EXHIBIT 7   **Polish National Council for Radio and Television (as of March 1996)**

Source: TVW.

1) **Robert Kwiatkowski**—Member of the Democratic Left Alliance (SLD) political party, which has many members from the former communist party. Former adviser to Polish President Kwasniewski, responsible for his image in the presidential campaign.
2) **Michal Strak**—Member of the Peasants political party (PSL). Former Chief of Personnel for the Prime Minister's administration office.
3) **Ryszard Miazek**—PSL. Former senator; former spokesperson for head of the Peasants Party. Joined the Council in 1992. Trained as a journalist. Current president of TVP (Public Television Poland).
4) **Boleslaw Sulik**—Chairman of Council, appointed to the Council in 1992 by the first Solidarity party. Son of a WWII Polish general, brought up in the United Kingdom. Worked there as a television director for the BBC until moving to Poland after the changes of 1989.
5) **Andrzej Zarembski**—Council Secretary. Not politically aligned but linked to the old Solidarity party. Was in the opposition movement during communist times. Government spokesman in early Solidarity cabinet. Joined the Council at its inception in 1992.
6) **General Andracki**—Not politically aligned. Former general in the Army responsible for telecommunications. An expert in technical matters.
7) **Jan Szafraniec**—Member of ZehN (Christian–National Union), a right-wing Catholic party. Trained as a psychiatrist. Strong interest in protecting the mental health of children. A former senator. Member of the Council since 1992.
8) **Marek Jurek**—former Council Chairman. A conservative Catholic considered closely linked to ZehN. Worked as a journalist and history teacher. Joined the Council in 1995 as President Lech Walesa's representative.
9) **Witold Grabos**—Manager of a construction company. Former senator.

proposed that the Council initially grant TVW a broad regional mandate along with a modest actual coverage area. TVW's geographic reach could be extended to cover the rest of its region as additional transmission sites subsequently became available.

In addition to avoiding direct competition and providing the Council with additional licenses to award, Szczerba's concept enhanced his chance of success in other ways. Through his extended family, Szczerba had maintained a strong network of political and business contacts in the Krakow area. He believed that both Krakow, which in many ways was the cultural center of Poland, and the neighboring area of Katowice, which was densely populated with an educated work force, maintained a good supply of ambitious and creative yet low cost workers.

By September 1993, Szczerba and Hurley began working with Bogdan Zieba, an influential Krakow politician, lawyer, and businessman, to raise seed capital from reputable local investors. Szczerba explained:

> Once we decided to apply for a regional license, it was a logical next step to seek investors from within the region, especially given the economic and political climate at the time. With several nationalistic, right-wing parties playing an important role in parliament and on the Council, we knew that any venture with foreign participation would not be looked upon favorably. The challenge was finding Polish partners that were large enough and stable enough to support a long-term investment in a venture like TVW. It was a time when a lot of companies were growing very fast and then suddenly disappearing; we needed investors who would still be around at the end of the licensing process with enough money in the bank to be credible with the Council. Only a handful of companies or banks had the resources to back a venture like TVW. Of those that did, most had no conception of managing the risks associated with a start-up involving significant up-front capital investment and initial operating losses.

Ultimately, Realbud and Efekt agreed to back the company with a commitment to invest $4 million. Realbud, though privatized in 1991, still operated largely as a state-owned business under the communist regime: feudal in organization with a small cadre of people making all significant operating decisions. This group maintained close political ties with the ex-communist party. Headquartered in Krakow, Realbud's main business was managing large construction projects; it had also become a major shareholder in four banks and 15 other companies. It employed approximately 1,500 people, was owned by 159 individuals, and garnered sales of 73 million PLN in 1993 and 97 million PLN in 1994. Realbud was also one of Poland's most profitable companies, with profit before interest and tax (EBIT) of 25 million PLN and 23 million PLN in 1993 and 1994, respectively.

Efekt's main business activity was renting the stall and office space it owned to small businesses, focusing on short-term investment and arbitrage opportunities from Poland's hyper-inflationary environment. Efekt was established in 1989 and admitted to the Warsaw stock exchange in 1993. The company's sales and profit before interest and tax were 4.4 million PLN and 1.7 million PLN in 1993, and 5.9 million PLN and 1.4 million PLN in 1994.

In February 1994, the Council awarded a national license to Polsat, an all-Polish group that had recently received Poland's first satellite license. Then, in November, the Council unanimously voted to award TVW, with Realbud and Efekt's backing, a regional license for southern Poland. TVW was the only applicant besides Polsat to receive a land-based television license covering more than one million people. In addition to adhering to its proposed service, TVW was required to raise 5 million PLN ($US 2 million) of equity capital by December 1994, to raise an additional 5 million PLN by June 1995, and to start broadcasting by December 1995.

Under the terms of their 10-year licenses, both Polsat and TVW could use up to 15% of air time for advertising. Unlike TVP, which could only place ads in between shows, Polsat and TVW were allowed to place it within programs, a configuration significantly more desirable to advertisers. Both licenses were restricted to 33% foreign voting control (although investors could own a larger share of profits) and had to remain 51% owned by their original owners. The Council reserved the right to approve foreign investors. During each year of broadcasting, 40% and 30% of Polsat's and TVW's respective outputs were required to be quota (i.e., domestic) production. Finally, Polsat was required to broadcast the same programs across its entire broadcast area, thus precluding it from competing with TVW's regional focus.

For technical reasons, Polsat's license sites initially covered only 35% of the Polish population and TVW's only 20% of its 12.5 million-person region (see **Exhibit 8**). The broadcasters could expand their coverage by working with local Polish ministries and the

EXHIBIT 8
Map of Poland

Source: TVW.

Note: The shaded area is covered by TVW.

Council to maximize their signals' reach from their existing sites. However, the Council needed to award the licensees new transmission sites in order for them to cover their license areas fully.

Attracting Foreign Investors—The Disney Deal

While Realbud and Efekt's backing were crucial to TVW's success in securing its license, at the time of their commitment, the founders (Szczerba, Hurley and Zieba) were aware that $4 million of legitimate, liquid Polish capital was a truly scarce commodity. As such, they were not surprised when, shortly after TVW secured its broadcast license, Realbud and Efekt insisted that the founders find foreign investors who could sponsor the majority of TVW's equity financing. While both companies said they were willing to cede part of their claim on TVW's future profits in exchange for financing, neither would state more specific deal objectives in advance of finding a willing and able potential partner. Szczerba recalled:

> Despite their earlier commitment to fund the venture, Realbud and Efekt wanted to minimize the amount of cash they put into the company. Perhaps more importantly, over time it became clear to us how little they knew about this business and about business in general. At one point early in the fundraising process we made a presentation to Realbud's senior management about options for capitalizing TVW. They liked the fact that we had a multi-page spreadsheet, but clearly did not understand its contents. We explained that given cash flow projections the company could not borrow more than one to two times equity. At that point the financial director of Realbud stated, "Since there is no law in Poland against it, we should borrow much more."

In mid-1994, Hurley once again approached a number of potential foreign investors and identified several large media conglomerates interested in developing a partnership with TVW. By late 1994, several companies were in partnership discussions with TVW, including Disney, which was prepared to begin a detailed due diligence process. Szczerba and Hurley viewed Disney as an attractive partner on several accounts. Not only was its programming very popular, it was extremely strong in marketing and sales, expertise that was difficult to find in Poland.

On Szczerba and Hurley's instigation, Disney representatives and members of TVW's board met to negotiate the deal's key economic terms. Disney agreed to fund the majority of TVW's remaining equity requirement in exchange for a 30% voting equity interest and a larger share of the profits. The deal provided for certain super-majority governance provisions that allowed Disney to wield more control over TVW's economic performance without ceding legal control over the broadcasting license to foreign enterprises. Finally, Disney sought to tie the founders to TVW with employment agreements and non-recourse loans to purchase up to 26% voting control of the company; the remaining 44% of TVW would be split evenly between Realbud and Efekt.

With Realbud and Efekt's agreement to the basic terms, Hurley turned to negotiating the detailed deal provisions while helping Disney complete its diligence. She elaborated:

> Bridging the cultural gap between Disney and TVW's Polish shareholders during this period proved a continual hurdle. Whereas Disney sought to perform extensive due diligence, proposed complicated long-term agreements, and retained a number of outside advisers to review the transaction, the Polish parties expressed a more plodding negotiation style, seeking to enter a simple relationship where the details would be worked out as issues developed—"one step at a time." At the end of the day, we developed an agreement that provided Disney with sufficient control over the company's operations yet clearly protected the existing shareholder's interests.

With Disney's due diligence process substantially complete, the key parties set up a two-day meeting to finalize outstanding deal-related issues. Immediately before this meeting, however, Bogumil Adamek, Efekt's president and TVW's Supervisory Board chairman, changed the equity provisions of the deal from 44% for Realbud and Efekt to 51%, thus ensuring their continued voting control over the company's activities. At the meeting, he also proposed verbally that Realbud and Efekt put less money in the deal, and stated opposition to the level of equity ownership allocated to the founders. The deal came to a screeching halt at the meeting. Simon Kenny, Disney's lead representative on the TVW transaction, recalled:

> We negotiated a deal that had the potential of phenomenal returns for all investors. We had a nice amount of programming content that would have done well in the Polish market as well as a significant amount of experience in TV station management. The company had two strong entrepreneurial leaders in Wojtek and Claire, who were on the right learning curve to succeed as TVW's management. But the guys on the other side (Realbud and Efekt) posed a real problem and they succeeded in alienating us as potential business partners. They thought if Disney was interested in this deal, everybody would be interested; they thought rolling out a supra-regional television station was a trivial task.
>
> What killed the deal was the issue of control. It was hard for us at Disney to imagine investing in TVW if the majority of the votes—and day-to-day operating control—were to be held by entities who knew virtually nothing about the TV business. It's a pity that it didn't work out. We would have been on the air within six months and the station would have been profitable by Fall 1996.

Picking Up the Pieces

In early 1995, following the Disney fiasco, neither Realbud nor Efekt was willing to invest more money in TVW. Realbud's 1995 profits were projected to decline and its debt load had increased from 2 million PLN to well over 20.0 million PLN in the past two years. Efekt's 1994 profits were largely attributable to aggressive write-ups of its equity investments. TVW's board requested that Hurley find a new foreign partner willing to fund the business in a transaction that would pay a premium directly to the shareholders but not require Realbud and Efekt to cede operating control. In the interim, the board instructed Szczerba to make do with TVW's existing 5 million PLN of equity financing and whatever debt he could raise from local banks.

Despite its being undercapitalized, under Szczerba's leadership TVW made significant progress after receiving its license. The company had contracted for satellite access, completed construction of a state-of-the-art digital transmission network, secured the rights to high-quality foreign programming, and hired capable senior staff (see **Exhibit 9** for TVW's organization chart).

In Spring 1995, Efekt announced that it intended to write up its TVW shares to 3.5 times their nominal value and to transfer some of these shares to a newly created subsidiary. Szczerba suspected that Efekt was taking these steps to prepare a sale of its shares to a third party. It was unclear to Szczerba how Efekt had determined the multiple of 3.5 but he suspected that Efekt's managers had talked to some securities analysts or even a potential buyer. TVW's license stipulated that the original shareholders had to retain control of 51% of the shares and foreigners could own only 33% of the shares. Efekt could potentially sell all of its 22,500 shares (16,666 of which to foreigners) without violating this condition. Such a transaction, however, would make it impossible for Realbud and the Founders to sell any more shares to foreign owners and raise much needed capital. Therefore Szczerba refused to give his permission to the transfer. His fallout with Efekt led to his dismissal from TVW. In June 1995, TVW's capital was increased

EXHIBIT 9

Source: TVW.

Telewizja Wisla Organization Chart

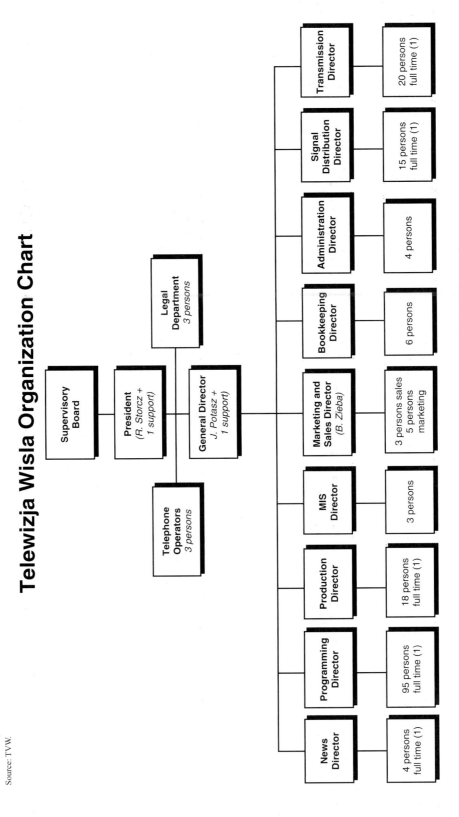

Note (1): Many station employees are on part-time contracts, the numbers listed are man-hours equivalent to full-time workers.

Supervisory Board

President
*(R. Storcz +
1 support)*

Legal Department
3 persons

Telephone Operators
3 persons

General Director
*J. Potasz +
1 support*

News Director — 4 persons full time (1)

Programming Director — 95 persons full time (1)

Production Director — 18 persons full time (1)

MIS Director — 3 persons

Marketing and Sales Director *(B. Zieba)* — 3 persons sales, 5 persons marketing

Bookkeeping Director — 6 persons

Administration Director — 4 persons

Signal Distribution Director — 15 persons full time (1)

Transmission Director — 20 persons full time (1)

430

from PLN 5 million to PLN 10 million ($4 million). Realbud and Efekt contributed PLN 2.5 million each. In July 1995 disagreements between Realbud and Efekt over TVW's strategy increased. Realbud realized that if it wanted to preserve the option of selling up to 33% of TVW's equity to a foreign party it would have to buy out Efekt. Realbud purchased 19,500 shares from Efekt and became majority shareholder of TVW. Sciborowski, Realbud's chairman, became TVW's chairman of the board and appointed Sztorc as TVW's new president.

At the same time, Sciborowski asked Hurley to help Realbud sell 30,000 of its shares to a legitimate foreign partner for TVW. Struck by the dramatic change in Realbud's attitude, Hurley agreed to return to the company if TVW would compensate her for her prior work on the Disney deal, for which she had never been paid. After some negotiation, she accepted Sciborowski's offer of $85,000 up front and 3,000 shares if she helped Realbud consummate a deal. Hurley explained:

> With Szczerba no longer involved, none of TVW's new senior managers had any experience in private television and, with the exception of TVW's new finance director, none were conversant in English. While I was generally able to communicate effectively with Sztorc and Potasz through a translator, the company was clearly handicapped in communicating with the outside world without Szczerba; without his charisma or passionate devotion to the success of the company, it was going to be difficult to sell new investors on TVW's potential. As a foreigner, I couldn't fulfill this role; it takes an entrepreneur with the right package of talents to clinch a sensible business deal on the best possible terms.
>
> Despite my best attempts to reconcile Realbud and Szczerba, Realbud held Szczerba responsible for failing to get TVW on the air to date and did not believe that his expertise was indispensable. Regardless, TVW needed my help, and, having spent much of the last four years of my life launching the company, I had a vested interested in seeing TVW succeed.

On Sciborowski's prodding, Hurley began by reopening discussions with Disney, which was still interested in investing in Polish broadcasting. But Disney was concerned that the station was not yet on the air and, without Szczerba, lacked compelling leadership. Approaching other media companies, Hurley found that while many of them were equally uncomfortable with TVW's situation, a small handful expressed interest in pursuing a deal. Specifically, after completing a preliminary due diligence review, the large German media company Bertelsmann remained interested.

The Polish Television Industry in 1996

By March 1996, Polsat and TVW remained the only two major private terrestrial broadcasters, and the Council was deeply mired in the second round franchise process. TVP's (Public Television Poland) content was over 70% domestic production, and TVP's president had recently announced that Polish output would increase by 2–3%. They also would no longer criticize politicians. At the same time, the television advertising market continued to develop rapidly, with surveys demonstrating that 97% of Poles owned a television, 85% of the population watched television at least once a day, with the average being 4.5 hours a day.

Leveraging its existing satellite service, Polsat had begun broadcasting within months of receiving its license in February 1994. By March 1996, it commanded a 21% share of its viewer market and a 28% share of the advertising market. For its part, TVW did not begin broadcasting until late December 1995, more than a year after receiving its license. In March 1996, the company's broadcasts still reached only 30% of its region, receiving a meager 1.1% average local viewer share. Under its current technical specifications,

EXHIBIT 10 **Earnings Sensitivity Analysis (US$ millions)**

Source: TVW.

A. TV Ad Market—all of Poland		12 months through March 31				
		1997	1998	1999	2000	2001
Total TV Ad Market (mil.$)		419	502	603	723	868
Growth Rate		26.59%	20.00%	20.00%	20.00%	20.00%

B. Technical equals % of coverage (millions)	total population	TV Advertising Market—in covered area (% covered × total market (A) listed above)				
6.98	18.00%	75	90	108	130	156
9.70	25.00%	105	126	151	181	217
12.80	33.00%	138	166	199	239	286

C. Coverage (mil. people)	TVW's Share of Covered Ad Market	Estimated Net Revenue (Covered market above (B) × % share × .82 (1))				
6.98	5.00%	3.1	3.7	4.4	5.3	6.4
9.70		4.3	5.1	6.2	7.4	8.9
12.80		5.7	6.8	8.2	9.8	11.7
6.98	12.00%	7.4	8.9	10.7	12.8	15.4
9.70		10.3	12.4	14.8	17.8	21.3
12.80		13.6	16.3	19.6	23.5	28.2
6.98	20.00%	12.4	14.8	17.8	21.3	25.6
9.70		17.2	20.6	24.7	29.6	35.6
12.80		22.6	27.2	32.6	39.1	47.0
6.98	25.00%	15.4	18.5	22.2	26.7	32.0
9.70		21.4	25.7	30.9	37.1	44.5
12.80		28.3	34.0	40.8	48.9	58.7

D. TVW Costs (see proforma)		10.4	13.4	14.3	15.3	16.4
(Note: national programming cost structure)						

E. Coverage (mil. people)	TVW's Share of Covered Ad Mkt.	Estimated TVW Profit Before Tax, excluding debt costs (Net of estimated gross revenues and TVW costs above (C–D))				
		1997	1998	1999	2000	2001
6.98	5.00%	(7.3)	(9.7)	(9.9)	(10.0)	(10.0)
9.70		(6.1)	(8.3)	(8.1)	(7.9)	(7.5)
12.80		(4.8)	(6.6)	(6.2)	(5.5)	(4.6)
6.98	12.00%	(3.0)	(4.5)	(3.6)	(2.5)	(1.0)
9.70		(0.1)	(1.1)	0.5	2.5	5.0
12.80		3.2	2.9	5.3	8.2	11.8
6.98	20.00%	1.9	1.4	3.5	6.1	9.3
9.70		6.7	7.2	10.4	14.4	19.2
12.80		12.2	13.8	18.3	23.9	30.6
6.98	25.00%	5.0	5.1	7.9	11.4	15.7
9.70		11.0	12.3	16.6	21.8	28.1
12.80		17.9	20.6	26.5	33.6	42.3

Note: (1) Net revenue equals % share × .82 (this assumes 15% ad agency commissions and an estimated 3% Polish copyright "zaix" charge (unavoidable cost))

TVW's maximum possible terrestrial reach within southern Poland was limited to about 6.25 million people, or 50% of its region. To further expand its terrestrial reach beyond this point, the Council would have to award it additional broadcast sites. Outside of its official coverage area, TVW had the potential to reach up to 8 million additional people by developing carriage arrangements with Polish cable operators.

TVW's Economics

Starting a completely new television station in Poland required making a significant up-front capital investment in broadcasting and production facilities as well as paying a license fee. Once the station was on the air, economics were largely driven by television ratings, which measured the number and demographics of people watching the station's programming. To date, TVW had primarily focused on meeting the technical requirements to get on air, and not on developing a strategy to maximize its share of its potential viewer and advertiser markets. However, Hurley believed that with proper marketing, promotion and a good advertising sales force, a station should capture at least its proportionate share of the advertising market.

While TVW had raised and spent nearly $9 million of capital to date, composed of $4.6 million of equity and $4.4 million of debt, the company still had a long way to go before it would achieve enough critical mass to generate attractive returns. Hurley estimated that the station could reach break-even within one year if it could capture an average ad market share of 12%. She further estimated it needed to expand its reach to at least 7.5 million people in its region, and generate a local advertising market share of over 20% in order to provide attractive long-term returns on equity (see **Exhibits 10, 11, and 12**).

While these targets seemed like a stretch based on TVW's current market position, Hurley believed that with the right strategic investor, TVW (and/or Polsat, for that matter) had the opportunity to dominate the Polish market and duplicate the financial success of Central European Media Enterprise's (CME) Czech station. In 1993, CME and a local partner had secured the right to run one of the Czech Republic's national channels. By 1995, CME's station commanded approximately a 70% market share. Hurley viewed CME as a close business comparable and useful role model for TVW's development (see **Exhibit 13**).

TVW's Decision

Recognizing that TVW was desperate for capital, in March 1996, Realbud decided to focus on Bertelsmann's interest. Bertelsmann's proposal was similar to Disney's, although Realbud would receive $2.5 million for 19,500 of its shares and instead of working with the founders, Bertelsmann would supply its own management team. Although Bertelsmann was not known for its marketing and sales expertise, it had a good programming and sports rights library and was used to dealing with TV councils in other countries. Furthermore, the company was close to merging its programming division with the television interests of one of the largest television operators in Europe, in a transaction that would create a powerful partner for TVW.

In April 1996, Hurley met with James O'Neill, HBS MBA '90, a venture capitalist from DBG, which had just raised a DM 100 million (US$65 million) fund for Central European investments. The fund was backed by multinational institutional investors and could invest in media deals. Although a U.S. citizen, the venture capitalist had lived in Poland for several years and dealt with different kinds of companies and Council-like bodies throughout Central Europe. After briefly reviewing TVW's business plan, the venture capitalist stated he was interested in pursuing a deal that involved buying out Efekt, reducing Realbud to a minority shareholder, and bringing in new management talent and the return of Szczerba as president. However, he would only actively focus on the deal after the Council agreed generally to his concept, and if Realbud and Efekt agreed to sell their shares at a price that would allow his return on investment to be at

EXHIBIT 11 Proforma Financial Statements (US$ millions)

Source: TVW.

Profit and Loss Statement (1)	12 Months Through March 31				
TVW Profit and Loss	1997	1998	1999	2000	2001
Net Revenue	7.41	20.59	40.77	48.92	58.71
assumes					
% reach of	18.00%	25.00%	33.00%	33.00%	33.00%
% ad market share of	12.00%	20.00%	25.00%	25.00%	25.00%
Fixed Costs (2)					
Transmission/Distribution	1.52	1.83	1.83	1.83	1.83
Salaries	0.70	0.77	0.85	0.93	1.02
General Overheads	0.60	0.60	0.60	0.60	0.60
Marketing	1.00	1.00	1.00	1.00	1.00
Depreciation	0.57	1.08	1.08	1.08	1.08
Subtotal	4.39	5.28	5.36	5.44	5.54
Variable Costs (3)					
TVW Programming	2.63	4.09	4.50	4.95	5.44
Purchased Programming	3.43	4.05	4.45	4.90	5.39
Subtotal	6.05	8.14	8.95	9.85	10.83
Total Costs	10.44	13.42	14.31	15.29	16.37
Net Profit before Tax	(3.03)	7.17	26.46	33.63	42.34
Interest Income/(Expense) (4)	(0.77)	(0.54)	0.65	2.24	4.07
(Tax)/Extraordinary Tax Credit	1.21	(2.87)	(10.58)	(13.45)	(16.94)
Net Profit after Tax	(2.58)	3.76	16.53	22.42	29.47

(continued)

Notes: (1) Projections in $US millions as most of TVW's costs and revenues are US$ linked.

(2) Transmission/distribution and general overhead mostly contracted for 10 years. Increase in the transmission/distribution cost between 1997 and 1998 due to increased TVW coverage.

Salary projections provide for $300,000 for 6 senior managers + board salaries and 40 staff members at an average salary of $850 per month (2.5 times the national average). This cost increases 10% p.a. after 1997.

Distribution expenses depreciated over 10 years. Equipment depreciated over five years.

(3) Projections assume 14 hours of programming/day in 1997 and 18 hours after that. Quota requirement: 30% of programming must be Polish. (TVW produces 50% of this and purchases the rest).

Cost of own production: $4,000/hour (can be repeated once).

Cost of purchased production: $1,500/hour. The budget also provides for 48 minutes daily non-quota production. 1997 Polish production budget assumes one additional hour of Polish quota production daily (50% repeat rate). Costs grow 10% p.a. after 1997.

(4) Interest on debt: 12% p.a. interest income on cash: 6% p.a.

least 30%. The venture capitalist argued that this required rate of return reflected the required return for a comparable project in Western Europe plus a country risk premium. Szczerba reflected:

> I would welcome the opportunity to run TVW again. If Bertelsmann comes in I will not have that chance. In any case, it is critical to resolve TVW's situation in the next few months in order for the company to be in a position to capture the lucrative fourth quarter advertising spend. Missing this cycle, which is booked by advertising agencies in September, could cost TVW up to $4 million of incremental profit, thus increasing the external financing need from $7.4 million to nearly $11 million.

Hurley commented on TVW's current situation:

> From my initial discussion of the idea with Wojtek back in 1991, TVW has come farther than I ever expected, yet not as far as I had hoped. Who could have guessed that such a seemingly simple idea would turn out to be so difficult to execute? We clearly underestimated the importance of a business environment with a developed capital base and rational economic incentives.

As Hurley pondered TVW's options, she watched the sunrise and poured herself another cup of coffee. While she remained frustrated about developments at TVW over the last year, she desperately wanted to help get the company back on track.

EXHIBIT 11   (Continued) Balance Sheet and Cash Flow (US$ millions)

Balance Sheet	12 Months Through March 31				
	1997	1998	1999	2000	2001
Tangible Assets					
Distribution	1.47	1.31	1.15	0.99	0.83
Production System	3.33	3.11	3.14	3.42	5.70
Adaptation of existing fixed assets	1.16	1.02	0.88	0.74	0.60
Intangible Assets					
One off License Fee	0.50	0.44	0.38	0.32	0.26
Payment-in-kind	0.20	0.20	0.20	0.20	0.20
Cash	2.05	7.76	20.68	40.28	67.83
Total Assets	8.71	13.84	26.43	45.95	75.42
Liabilities					
Creditors	0.50	0.50	0.50	0.50	0.50
Debt	8.40	6.90	2.90	0.00	0.00
Total Liabilities	8.90	7.40	3.40	0.50	0.50
Net Assets	(0.19)	6.44	23.03	45.45	74.92
Equity					
Paid-in Capital	8.00	8.00	8.00	8.00	8.00
Profit/(Losses)	(5.26)	(1.50)	15.03	37.45	66.92
Tax Loss Carryforward	(2.93)	(0.06)	0.00	0.00	0.00
Total	(0.19)	6.44	23.03	45.45	74.92

Cash Flow	12 Months Through March 31				
	1997	1998	1999	2000	2001
Operating					
Net Profit after Tax	(2.58)	3.76	16.53	22.42	29.47
Extraordinary Tax Credit Adjustment	(1.21)	2.87	0.06	0.00	0.00
Depreciation	0.57	1.08	1.08	1.08	1.08
Subtotal	(3.22)	7.71	17.67	23.50	30.55
Change in Working Capital	0.15	0.00	0.00	0.00	0.00
Capital Investment	(2.55)	(0.50)	(0.75)	(1.00)	(3.00)
License Fees	(0.30)	0.00	0.00	0.00	0.00
Subtotal	(2.70)	(0.50)	(0.75)	(1.00)	(3.00)
Total Cash	(5.92)	7.21	16.92	22.50	27.55
Opening Cash	0.57	2.05	7.76	20.68	40.28
Total Cash	(5.92)	7.21	16.92	22.50	27.55
Debt	4.00	(1.50)	(4.00)	(2.90)	0.00
Equity	3.40	0.00	0.00	0.00	0.00
Closing Cash	2.05	7.76	20.68	40.28	67.83

EXHIBIT 12

Total Capital Needs of TVW 1995–2001 (assessed in March 1996)

Source: TVW.

Distribution System:	$1.6 m
Production and Adaptation	$5.0 m
Licensing Fee	$0.5 m
Salaries, Insurance, Overhead	$1.3 m
Programming	
TVW	$2.63 m
Purchased (Polish and foreign)	$3.43 m
Short-term Cash for Taxes and VAT	$2.0 m
TOTAL	$16.46 m

Note: The difference between financing needs projected in 1994 and financing needs projected in 1997 is mainly due to TVW's delay in going on air.

EXHIBIT 13 Data on Central European Media Enterprises Ltd. (CME)

Source: CME 1995 Annual Report.

Television Operations	Country	Population Reach at Launch (millions)	CME Economic Interest
Current broadcast operations			
Nova TV	Czech Republic	10.3	66%
PULS (Berlin)	Germany	6	49%
Nuremberg Station	Germany	1.1	37%
POP TV	Slovenia	1.4	72%
PRO TV	Romania	8.1	78%
		26.9	
Operations under development			
STS	Slovak Republic	2.7	80%
2002 Kft	Hungary	26.9	95%
Leipzig and Dresden	Germany	1.8	16%
		31.4	

		Year Ended Dec. 31,			
		1992	1993	1994	1995
Operating Data	($000's)				
Gross revenues		0	0	64,389	121,113
Discounts and commissions		0	0	(10,823)	(22,194)
Net Revenues		0	0	53,566	98,919
Operating Expenses		191	5,321	52,609	76,611
Operating (loss) income		(191)	(5,321)	957	22,308
Equity in loss of affiliates		(141)	(3,671)	(13,677)	(14,816)
Interest & other income		0	64	179	1,238
Interest expense		0	(140)	(1,992)	(4,959)
Foreign currency loss (gain)		0	(176)	(245)	324
Provision of income taxes		0	0	(3,331)	(16,340)
Loss before interest in consolidated subsidiaries		(332)	(9,244)	(18,109)	(12,245)
Minority interest in (loss) income of consolidated subsidiaries		7	884	(2,396)	(6,491)
Net loss		(325)	(8,360)	(20,505)	(18,736)
Shares oustanding (000's)					14,678
Net loss per common share					(1.28)
Balance Sheet Data					
Current assets		0	4,773	71,447	116,728
Total assets		0	17,824	115,332	222,027
Total debt & advances fr. affiliates		0	6,178	32,592	20,285
Shareholder's equity		0	3,464	62,631	138,936

Note: The company's NASDAQ ticker symbol is "CETV."

Case 22

Promise: Building a Consumer Finance Company in Japan

It was July 5, 2000, and Hiroki Jinnai had a long night ahead of him. Not only was he heading to dinner at Kasuga, an upscale tempura[1] restaurant in Tokyo that only served 12 guests per night, but he also planned to think about the strategic future of his company with Shunji Kosugi, managing director of Corporate Planning, Isao Takeuchi, managing director of Finance, and Teruaki Watanabe, managing director of Operations and Systems at Promise. Promise was one of the three largest consumer finance companies (CFCs) in Japan and Jinnai was its president.[2] CFCs offered individuals unsecured revolving credit. Due to a Japanese law on maximum interest rates that had been passed in 1954, CFCs had been somewhat on the fringe of Japanese business and society for the larger part of that period of time. CFCs had gone through a difficult period until the early 1990s due to the Japanese cultural shame regarding personal debt and due to a booming economy. The burst of the Japanese "bubble" economy and the improved public perception of consumer finance had recently provided a period of unparalleled growth and prosperity for the large consumer finance companies like Promise (see **Exhibit 1**). Despite this success, however, Jinnai had many concerns that were shared by Ryoichi Jinnai, Hiroki's uncle, who had founded Promise. Although Hiroki Jinnai was president now he still consulted with Ryoichi Jinnai about strategic issues. Hiroki Jinnai stated his thoughts:

> We have done very well recently, but the environment is changing. Some changes are positive, like the new law allowing CFCs to issue corporate bonds and commercial paper (CP) for any use including as a source of funding for lending. Some changes are negative, like the new law lowering the maximum rate we can charge to our customers. And some changes in

[1] Tempura is a popular Japanese dish.

[2] Hiroki Jinnai (46) was the youngest among the presidents of the top four CFCs in Japan.

Dean's Fellow William J. Coughlan (MBA '99) prepared this case under the supervision of Professor Walter Kuemmerle. HBS cases are developed solely as the basis for class discussion. Cases are not intended to serve as endorsements, sources of primary data, or illustrations of effective or ineffective management. The authors would like to thank Professor Tomoaki Sakano of Waseda University, for his contributions to this case.

EXHIBIT 1
Trend in New Consumer Credit by Type of Lender

Source: Promise (from Japan Credit Industry Association).

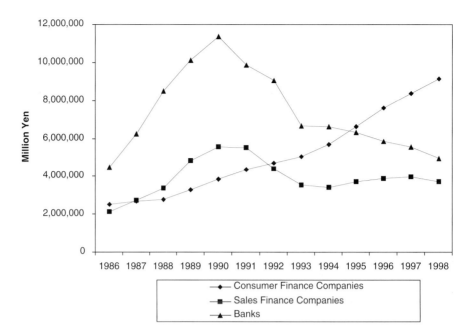

society will have an effect on Promise that is rather unclear. Promise and some of its competitors have done very well during the economic downturn in the 1990s, but the economy seems to have bottomed out and there are questions about the industry reaching a saturation point in its current customer base. How will we do in this new environment? And how will we continue to grow if our core business begins to slow?

Ryoichi and Hiroki Jinnai knew that Promise had several options to achieve future growth: the company could try to expand into new customer groups with a different risk profile through an acquisition or a joint venture. Promise could also look to develop new products for specific segments, like the growing number of professional women in Japan. Promise could even look to expand the relationship it had with its current customer base by consolidating loans or offering these customers new products. All of this would require Promise securing new capital and the good news was that there were now more financing options for the company to pursue. But, because of a 1980s crisis in the CFC sector that brought every company close to bankruptcy, Promise tended to be very conservative in its capital structure.

"We have a lot to think about tonight," Jinnai mused to his team as he stepped out of the hot July night and removed his shoes to enter the air-conditioned tempura house.

Japan's Economy and Financial Sector: The Bubble Had Burst

Japan was the world's second-largest economy and a powerhouse in consumer electronics and passenger vehicle manufacturing. During the 1980s Japan's economy grew at a remarkable 3.8% per annum.[3] Japanese firms broadly fell into two categories: On the one hand there were large firms with a multinational presence and close ties to specific banks and trading houses. They formed a number of so-called "keiretsu" or horizontally linked industrial groups. On the other hand, there were many small firms that supplied large firms or operated in industries with low export ratios such as textiles or food. After WW II, Japan's bureaucrats had focused primarily on fostering the success of export-oriented firms

[3] Economist Intelligence Unit. *EIU Country Data.* Accessed online at http://80-countrydata.bvdep.com on February 17, 2004.

that were part of a keiretsu. Currency receipts from exports were crucial for Japan since it depended on imports of many natural resources, most importantly, oil.

Japan's economic growth entailed a run-up in stock prices. Japan also had one of the highest population densities in the world and the rise in equity prices was followed by a rise in real estate prices. During the 1980s this did not go unnoticed by corporations. Many of them started making speculative investments in real estate, an activity that was outside of their core business. Banks were eager to lend to corporations for this purpose, particularly to corporations within the same industrial group. Real estate development projects were not always subjected to sufficient scrutiny. Banks assumed that corporations had done their due diligence on a project, while corporations assumed that bankers would not lend unless they had done their own homework.

With Japan's labor cost increasing and its population aging, economic growth suddenly stuttered. In 1990 the so-called asset bubble burst and stock prices started to decline precipitously. During the 1990s Japan suffered five technical recessions.[4] In 1998 GDP shrank by a shocking 2.5%. Real estate prices also started to decline. Japan's Economic Planning Agency estimated that the end of the bubble had led to cumulative losses of ¥1,117 trn[5] (nearly $ 10 trn). This figure represented about two full years of Japan's economic output.[6] The Japanese government sought to address Japan's problems through a series of fiscal stimulus packages that typically consisted of increased public spending and tax cuts. Also, the Bank of Japan lowered its discount rate to 0.5% in September 1995. (See **Exhibit 2** for economic performance and **Exhibit 3** for recent policy events.)

[4] *IMF Staff Country Report* No. 00/143. Washington, DC, 2000, p. 5.

[5] In early July 2000, US$1 = ¥106.1.

[6] *EIU Country Profile Japan.* London: Economist Intelligence Unit, 2000, p. 25.

EXHIBIT 2A

Comparative Economic Indicators, 1999

Source: Compiled from Economist Intelligence Unit data and from IMF, *International Financial Statistics* data.

	Japan	U.S.	Germany	China
GDP ($ bn)	4,353	9,255	2,108	976
GDP per head ($)	34,356	33,944	25,556	780
Consumer price inflation (av; %)	−0.3	2.2	0.6	−1.3
Current-account balance ($ bn)	105.9	−339.0	−17.8	18.9
Exports of goods fob ($ bn)	457.0	685.0	540.5	194.7
Imports of goods fob ($ bn)	317.1	1,030.2	472.6	159.0
Foreign trade[a] (% of GDP)	17.8	18.5	48.1	36.2

[a]Merchandise exports plus imports.

EXHIBIT 2B

Annual Economic Indicators

Source: Compiled from Economist Intelligence Unit Country Report, First Quarter 2000.

	1995	1996	1997	1998	1999
GDP at market prices (¥ trn)	483.1	500.8	509.8	498.5	498.2[a]
Real GDP growth (%)	1.4	5.2	1.6	−2.5	0.6[a]
Consumer price inflation (av; %)	−0.1	0.1	1.7	0.7	−0.3
Population (m; Oct 1st)	125.6	125.9	126.2	126.5	126.7
Exports fob ($ bn)	428.7	400.3	409.2	374.0	399.5[a]
Imports fob ($ bn)	296.9	316.7	307.6	251.7	272.0[a]
Current-account balance ($ bn)	111.1	65.9	94.4	120.7	115.0[a]
Reserves excluding gold ($ bn)	183.3	216.6	219.6	215.5	286.9
General government balance (% of GDP)	−3.6	−4.2	−3.3	−6.1	−7.9[a]
General government debt (% of GDP)	76.0	80.9	87.2	96.7	106.7[a]
Exchange rate (av; ¥:$)	94.1	108.8	121.0	130.9	113.9
February 8th 2000 ¥109.5:$1					

[a]EIU estimate.

EXHIBIT 2C
Economic Data

Source: Adapted from Bank of Japan, *Financial and Economic Data 2000.*

Year	Official Discount Rate End of Year — Interest per Annum (%)	Prime Rates End of Year — Short-term Prime Lending Rate Percent per Annum	10-Year Government Bonds Yield to Subscribers End of Year — Percent per Annum	TOPIX (TSE First Section Price Index) End of Year (January 4, 1968 = 100)
1970	6			148.35
1971	4.75	5.5		199.45
1972	4.25	4.5	6.717	401.7
1973	9	7.25	7.302	306.44
1974	9	9.25	8.414	278.34
1975	6.5	6.75	8.227	323.43
1976	6.5	6.75	8.227	383.88
1977	4.25	4.5	6.683	364.08
1978	3.5	3.75	6.18	449.55
1979	6.25	6.5	7.788	459.61
1980	7.25	7.5	8.227	494.1
1981	5.5	6	8.367	570.31
1982	5.5	6	7.969	593.72
1983	5	5.5	7.698	731.82
1984	5	5.5	6.969	913.37
1985	5	5.5	6.582	1,049.40
1986	3	3.75	5.454	1,556.37
1987	2.5	3.375	5	1,725.83
1988	2.5	3.375	4.811	2,357.03
1989	4.25	5.75	5.306	2,881.37
1990	6	8.25	6.799	1,733.83
1991	4.5	6.625	5.836	1,714.68
1992	3.25	4.5	4.763	1,307.66
1993	1.75	3	3.469	1,439.31
1994	1.75	3	4.55	1,559.09
1995	0.5	1.625	2.907	1,577.70
1996	0.5	1.625	2.751	1,470.94
1997	0.5	1.625	1.991	1,175.03
1998	0.5	1.5	0.972	1,086.99
1999	0.5	1.375	1.836	1,722.20

Impact on Financial Institutions

Since real estate was typically pledged as collateral for loans, the burst of the bubble had alarming consequences for the health of banks. In many instances real estate prices had dropped to 20% of the original value.[7] In 1999 the government estimated that 16% of loans outstanding were problematic. Unofficial estimates were much higher, at 30%.[8] The biggest problem of the real estate price collapse was the uncertainty around the true size of required write-offs. Individual banks and the government were not forthcoming with accurate data, fearing a crisis in investor confidence. Some observers argued that this behavior made the crisis worse. Banks reacted by limiting new credit. This affected primarily small and medium-sized enterprises that stood at the bottom of banks' preferred borrower lists.

[7] *EIU Country Profile Japan.* London: Economist Intelligence Unit, 2000, p. 25.

[8] *EIU Country Profile Japan.* London: Economist Intelligence Unit, 2000, p. 25.

EXHIBIT 3   Important Economic Policy Events in Japan

Source: *EIU Country Profile Japan.* London: Economist Intelligence Unit, 2000, pp. 28–29.

"**December 1997:** The Diet passes the Fiscal Structural Reform Law, which aims to reduce Japan's general budget deficit to 3% of GDP or less by 2003/04. The Diet passes the revised Deposit Insurance Law, which gives the Deposit Insurance Corporation the right to cover the loans losses of merging banks. The revised Anti-Monopoly Law takes effect.

January 1998: The Diet passes a bill for temporary tax cuts worth ¥2trn ($15bn). The so-called 5-3-3-2 rule, governing what proportion of pension funds could be invested in which instruments, is abolished.

April 1998: The revised Foreign Exchange Law and Bank of Japan Law both take effect. A fiscal stimulus package worth ¥16.7trn is announced [...]. The definition of non-performing loans held by financial institutions is broadened to include loans more than three months due and all restructured loans. [...]

May 1998: The Diet passes the revised Fiscal Structural Reform Act, postponing the target year for reducing the general government fiscal deficit to 3% or less to 2005/06.

June 1998: The Financial Supervisory Agency is launched.

September 1998: The BOJ says it will guide the overnight call rate down to around 0.25% from just under 0.5%.

October 1998: The Diet passes a package of bank reform bills, allowing it to nationalise unviable banks and to establish a bank recapitalisation fund. The government nationalises the Long Term Credit Bank, the first bank nationalisation since the second world war. The finance minister, Kiichi Miyazawa, announces a financial aid package for Asia worth $30bn, which becomes known as the Miyazawa Initiative.

November 1998: The government announces a fiscal stimulus package worth ¥23.9trn.

December 1998: The government nationalises the Nippon Credit Bank. [...] The Financial Reconstruction Commission (FRC) starts operations. The government announces a ¥9.3trn tax reform package for 1999/2000.

February 1999: The BOJ announces it will guide the overnight call rate down further, to around 0.15%.

March 1999: The FRC injects ¥7.5trn of public funds into 15 large banks. Nissan Motor announces a tie-up with Renault.

April 1999: The Diet passes a law allowing non-banks to issue corporate bonds.

June 1999: Cable & Wireless outbids Nippon Telephone and Telegraph (NTT) to buy most of the shares in a telecommunications company, IDC; NTT is reorganised into a holding company, two regional companies and one long-distance communications company.

August 1999: The Industrial Bank of Japan, Fuji Bank and Dai-ichi Kangyo Bank announce they will set up a holding company at end-2000 and merge operations from early 2002.

September 1999: The FRC decides to sell Long Term Credit Bank to a consortium led by Ripplewood Holdings of the US.

October 1999: Regulations on stock transaction commissions are completely lifted. Asahi Bank and Tokai Bank announce they will set up a holding company at end-2001. Sumitomo Bank and Sakura Bank announce they will merge by 2002/03."

In its policy decisions regarding the crisis of financial institutions, Japan's government was between a rock and a hard place. It could either let banks fail outright, nationalize them to protect depositors, or try to revive them. Reviving banks through capital injections, however, was tricky because a failed revival entailed a waste of government resources. By 2000 it appeared that the government had opted for a face-saving approach instead of letting banks fail outright. In 1998 it nationalized the venerable Long Term Credit Bank of Japan. Other nationalizations followed. In an interesting and innovative twist, the government agreed to some foreign participation in the restructuring. In September 1999, American-led buyout firm Ripplewood received permission to acquire the Long Term Credit Bank of Japan. The government also helped engineer mergers. For example, in August 1999, the Industrial Bank of Japan, Fuji Bank, and Dai-ichi

Kangyo Bank merged. These measures helped to restore confidence of investors to some degree, but the longer-term outlook for Japan's large banks was mixed because of the public's perception that the bad-loan problem had not been fully addressed. (See **Exhibit 4** for more information on the financial services sector.)

EXHIBIT 4   **Financial Services Sector**

Source: *EIU Country Profile Japan.* London: Economist Intelligence Unit, 2000, p. 37–38.

"The Big Bang

Although its financial markets are still highly regulated compared with those of the US or the UK, Japan has made considerable progress in recent years. Among the most significant deregulation initiatives to date is the Big Bang programme of financial reforms announced in 1996 by the then prime minister, Ryutaro Hashimoto. Designed to improve competition, transparency, and fairness in Japan's financial sector so that Tokyo can offer a range of financial services equal to that offered by New York or London, these reforms have had a profound impact on the country's financial industry. Three of the most important measures were implemented from April 1998; others, such as allowing cross-sectoral competition between banks and insurance companies, are due to be implemented over the coming years. [...] The short-term implications of these and other reforms are mixed. The deregulation of stock transaction commissions, for example, has hurt profit margins at small and medium-sized securities houses and threatens to put many such institutions out of business. The revisions to the Foreign Exchange Law also threaten to weaken some of Japan's most fragile banks further, particularly if significant numbers of Japanese take advantage of their new-found freedom and move their savings to large—and presumably safer—foreign financial institutions. [...]

The Stockmarket

Japan's stockmarket has been depressed since the collapse of the asset-price bubble at the beginning of the 1990s. Share prices stabilised in 1994–96 owing to a perception that Japan's economy would soon recover, despite the fact that share prices on the Nikkei average of 225 shares, listed on the Tokyo Stock Exchange's first section, were still 50–60% down on the peak recorded in 1989 of just under ¥40,000. The worsening economic outlook in 1997–98 caused share prices to fall further, and by the end of 1998 the Nikkei average had fallen below ¥14,000, a level only marginally higher than that recorded in 1985. The Nikkei average recovered some of the ground lost in 1999, ending the year at just under ¥19,000, on the back of renewed optimism on the part of foreign investors regarding Japan's short-term outlook, and renewed interest from individual investors looking for higher returns than were available from bank savings. [...]

Cross-shareholdings

The proportion of shares owned by individuals in Japan is significantly lower than in many other developed countries, while that owned by financial institutions and companies is markedly higher; in 1998/99, for example, individuals accounted for 22.4% of the total, financial institutions 39.3%, and companies 24.1%. This results mainly from the long-standing practice of Japan's financial institutions and companies holding shares in each other—cross-shareholding or mochiai kabu—in order to cement long-term business relationships and guard against hostile takeovers. One result of this has been to reduce the number of shares on the market at any one time, which has held back supply and helped keep Japan's share prices artificially high. Although financial institutions are starting to unwind these cross-shareholdings as part of their restructuring efforts, the process is likely to be a long one, ensuring that they remain a feature of Japan's stockmarket for some years to come.

Price-keeping Operations

A further factor artificially boosting share prices has been large government share purchases at key points in the financial year to keep prices from falling—called price-keeping operations. The main reason for the government's intervention is to prevent capital adequacy ratios at Japan's banks, as defined by the Bank for International Settlements (BIS), from falling. The BIS allows Japan's banks to count 45% of unrealised profits on shareholdings towards their Tier Two capital. It is widely accepted that the level of these unrealised profits becomes critical when the Nikkei average falls below ¥14,000. The unwinding of cross-shareholdings and the ending of government intervention are therefore prerequisites for ensuring that stock prices become an accurate measure for gauging the financial strength of many Japanese companies."

Consumer Finance Companies and Promise: From Sub-Prime to Primetime in Four Stages

Consumer finance companies were outside the mainstream regulatory system in Japan and were not afforded some of the conveniences offered to commercial banks. Commercial banks, as an acknowledged part of the finance system, were "guided" and often protected from severe losses by the Ministry of Finance (MoF). But with that protection came responsibility. Historically, banks did not get involved in unsecured loans to individuals. Part of the reason was that the maximum interest rate a bank could charge was between 15%–20%, a rate considered too low for the risk involved with unsecured loans. A more telling reason was the culture in the Japanese financial system. Shunji Kosugi, managing director of Corporate Planning at Promise, explained:

> The purpose of Japanese commercial banks after WWII was to financially support business and commercial activities of large Japanese corporations. Consumer loans were much smaller in size and were not deemed to be as important as commercial activities. Furthermore, in our society, it was shameful to incur personal debt except for mortgage loans. For the banks, not only was it embarrassing to be involved in loans of such small a scale, but it was very embarrassing to be a facilitator of such a "shameful" activity as consumer loans. Also, demand for commercial loans was high during that period, and banks focused on building a commercial loan business rather than a consumer loan business. That provided the consumer finance industry with an opportunity.

Since banks did not offer consumer loans, the industry was rather informal; and prior to 1954, the law regarding maximum interest rates was very vague. "Traditional [pre-consumer finance] companies were very aggressive in pursuing loans and payments," Kosugi said. "Some of them engaged in all types of collection activities, like taking away a debtor's furniture or even engaging in violence." Consumers had access to credit but in other forms through mortgages or other secured loans and credit from retailers. In 1954, the MoF set a maximum rate of interest of 109.5% for consumer credit through the Capital Subscription laws. The stage was then set for the CFCs to engage in business. Unlike the banks, CFCs were not governed by a specific law but were implicitly instructed to impose self-regulation.

Stage 1 (1963–1979): The Building Years

In 1963, Hiroki Jinnai's uncle, Ryoichi Jinnai, decided to found Promise. Ryoichi Jinnai had a strong vision and was talented at putting operating systems into place. He developed the first revolving loan programs that did not require collateral and also introduced a rapid credit examination process. The first customers were generally "salary men" (professionals at the top corporations in Japan) or civil servants. The loan was to provide these people with short-term liquidity for entertainment and other personal consumption. Teruaki Watanabe, Managing Director of Operations and Systems at Promise, explained:

> At that time Japan was in high economic growth mode. Consumers spent a considerable part of their income purchasing durable consumer goods such as fridge, TV, and furniture. Also, in Japan, on average, around 80% of a man's salary would go into the wife's bank account as she controlled the finances. These factors left very little salary to the husband. Promise's loans would provide the customer with some liquidity until payday or the big bonus.

To deal with the stigma of personal debt, Promise and other CFCs had to come up with a product that would make it easier for consumers to avoid shame. The CFCs accomplished this in several ways: First, they created a product that was initially small, paid out immediately and was not secured to any asset. Second, it was secret. A person could take out a loan and no one would need to know, not even the spouse. In addition, the locations of the CFC facilities were important. CFCs were always in areas of high visibility, so a customer could locate the company easily, but the entrances were discrete so that a customer could hardly be seen by others when entering the office. Promise went to great lengths to train their employees in how to handle and respect the customer. "The transaction is a personal promise between the customer and Promise—an equal partnership," Jinnai explained. "We did not want to engage in activities like the loan sharks that existed before Promise and we needed to make sure that the customer felt safe with us."

During these early years, Promise established the foundations for the system that was used throughout its history. Promise and the CFCs took several steps, from underwriting to collections, to ensure the consumer's privacy was kept. Promise devised various paper-based mechanisms so that the customer would not forget the due date.[9] In the process of collecting delinquent loans, Promise would never call the customer or send any information regarding payments to the customer at home without the customer's prior consent. Instead, Promise would call the customer at the workplace but would never disclose the company name. If that was not sufficient, the company would request an in-person visit from the borrower. These visits would be used to develop a repayment plan and to counsel customers with all aspects of their financial affairs, an area where Promise spent a lot of resources. If none of these measures worked, Promise would write off the bad loans, and wait for the customer's financial condition to recover. "That is why we place such an emphasis on counseling," Watanabe explained. "We are proud to have a positive relationship with our customers and we do not want to break our promise to the customer that we will keep the partnership a secret. Our company name 'Promise' was derived from this basic business philosophy."

One of the major constraints during this period was capital. Growth was quite slow in the early stages as many building owners did not want to rent to CFCs. As a result, CFCs remained clustered together, taking up every floor of a building in order to take advantage of "rentable" property. In other instances, CFCs were located in buildings that also housed restaurants and other entertainment venues (see **Exhibit 6** for photos). More importantly, banks and other institutions did not want to loan capital to the CFCs. Most of the capital came from the founders and top managers' personal assets as collateral for loans. In addition, until 1978, Promise would borrow money from its own employees at 8%–10% interest rates.[10]

One of the most important events during this early period was the establishment of the CFC credit information center. To lower risks, CFCs were encouraged to set up the credit information center to share credit information. CFCs would pool *all* the information, both positive and negative, about the customers to whom they lent money and update this information upon every transaction. This was an important distinction from other credit associations, such as the commercial bank association. Commercial banks did not report all transactions to their association, and shared only partial information of their customers. Their data was not updated in real time, only monthly. And their data was transaction-based and not customer-based, which meant it was very difficult for commercial banks to create complete customer files. In comparison to the United States,

---

[9] This was before modern technology. In 1999, the primary form of correspondence between Promise and the customer was through the receipt given at the ATM machine. There Promise would give the notice of the next payment due date, would inform the borrower of a delinquency and would often request the customer come in for consultation if he or she was seriously past due. (See **Exhibit 5** for a copy of an ATM receipt.)

[10] Ryoichi Jinnai owned 100% of the company during this period.

EXHIBIT 5   **ATM Receipt**

Source: Promise.

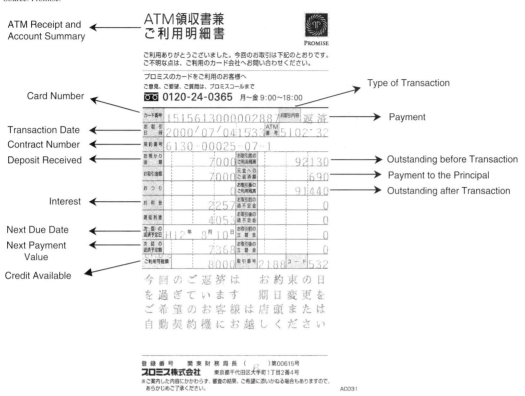

EXHIBIT 6
Promise Store Locations

Source: Promise.

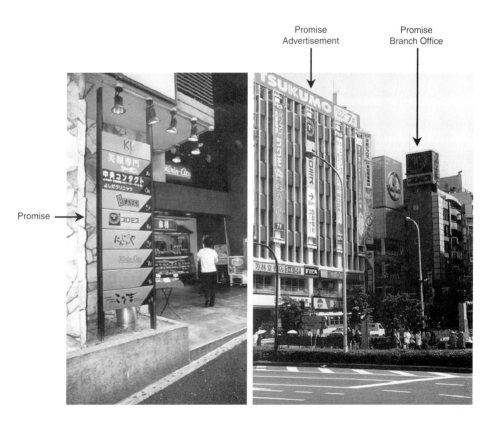

where the playing field was leveled because all financial companies could gain access to the full credit history of a potential customer, CFCs had an advantage in Japan since they were the only ones sharing all customer-based positive and negative information in real time.[11]

Stage 2 (1980–1983): The Growth Years

Access to capital became easier than ever before for CFCs and growth in the industry took off. Domestic banks began lending to the CFCs at rates of about 12% p.a. and the customer base began to expand. With this expansion of customers came a restructuring of the guidelines for a loan—not so much in the procedures used in the underwriting or collection process, but in identity of the target consumer. Originally, the target customer in the first stage was the salary man at a blue chip company. Promise and the CFCs lowered the criteria on the employers and would now lend to anyone who had a regular salary regardless of the company they worked at. Branch expansion ensued dramatically as capital started to pour into the industry. Jinnai recalled this period:

> This was a big period for the CFC industry. It became easier for us to collect capital—in many cases foreign capital as well—and we were able to expand dramatically. Since we had taken such great pains to develop a sound underwriting and collection process, we were encouraged by the fact we didn't have to make many alterations to the process to keep growing.

Stage 3 (1984–1990): A Period of Change and Restructuring

At the end of 1983, the fortunes for the CFC industry began to change. Some CFCs had expanded too quickly and engaged in "forceful" collection activities. The mass media reported extensively on these practices. As a result, the stigma that had stuck with the industry worsened. The government responded to the scandal by creating two laws. The Regulatory Law prohibited excessive lending and forceful collection activities. The amended Capital Subscription Law required a staged reduction of the maximum lending rate from 109.5% to 40.004%. The banks responded by ceasing lending to the industry. This had a fast impact as most of the loans were short-term facilities and liquidity dried up almost immediately. Therefore, several companies in the industry went bankrupt. Promise also had to write off a large number of bad loans and saw its customer base drop by one third.

Even though Promise was viewed as one of the better CFCs, the company still needed to undergo some changes. Promise began to de-lever its balance sheet and shifted its funding resources away from utilizing many institutions towards two banks and two life insurance companies. These banks and insurance companies took equity stakes in Promise. The company also went through some major managerial changes. All in all, it was a painful period for Promise and the CFC industry as a whole.

Amidst these negative changes, an important positive change for Promise was the centralization of the underwriting process. Where the branch manager had had almost complete authority to approve a loan in the past (see **Exhibit 7** for a list of some current rejection criteria), he now had become the bottleneck for growth. Changes in information technology and the growing significance of credit bureau information also made centralization appealing. The founder Ryoichi Jinnai developed an automated centralized loan approval system that set rather generous limits for loans. This was based on Ryoichi Jinnai's philosophy that customers would "keep the promise" and repay loans if they felt that Promise had some trust in them. Even though a loan's limit was set by headquarters, much of the qualitative aspects were still important in the process and the branch

---

[11] Members only had access to the information in their own credit association's records. For example, a bank did not have access to the CFC association even if they wished to engage in consumer lending. Starting in 1987, the three credit associations (started by the following three groups: banks, sales finance companies, CFCs) shared some negative information. Positive information was not shared.

EXHIBIT 7
Selected Loan
Rejection Criteria

Source: Promise.

Current Criteria for a Rejection

- Negative information within Promise's database
- Personal bankruptcy
- Applicants misrepresenting their identity
- Other personal issues:
- Problems at working/living place
- Inability to understand/operate Automatic Contract Machine
- Apparent gang membership
- Negative image of employer
- Negative information at the CFC credit information center
- Negative information from other credit sources
- Age, long leave from work, no job, part-time worker for a short duration only

Selected Personal Criteria Requiring Further Investigation

- Customer married and shirt sleeves dirty (signals trouble at home)
- Health Insurance Identification Card
  - Dirty (signals lack of care)[a]
  - The location of the local government which issued the card doesn't match the applicant's address.
- Customer says he is working for a big company as a white-collar employee and is wearing workman's clothes (need to check more thoroughly)
- Identification problems
- Problems reaching the applicant at his office. If co-workers say he is on holiday, ask if he has been on holiday a lot lately (probably means he has been terminated)

Five Most Frequent Reasons For Rejection[b]

1. More than four CFC accounts
2. Negative assessment by branch manager based on appearance and background
3. Negative information at the credit information center
4. No job (no stable income)
5. Negative information within Promise's database

[a]In the past, holes in all corners of the Health Insurance Identification Card were also a criterion requiring further investigation. CFCs used to put a notch in a corner of the health card when approving a loan. If all corners were punched, it meant that the customer had at least four loans outstanding which was too many for CFCs to lend more.
[b]Reasons 1 and 2 triggered half of all rejections. Overall rejection rate for Promise was 32% in 1999.

manager did have the authority to reject or lower the limit of a loan if he deemed it necessary. As a result, not only did the size of the portfolio eventually increase through centralization, but the quality of the portfolio was raised as well. Technological change also manifested itself in other ways, such as an alliance with banks for the use of their ATM machines for both withdrawals *and* for payments and 24-hour phone lines. This not only allowed the customer 24-hour access but also improved the image of Promise.

The profile of the target customer began to shift for Promise. During this period, Japan's economy was booming. As a result, the wealth of middle managers increased dramatically and there was not as great a need for loans as there were in the past. These customers began to gain more access to financing, especially through second home mortgages through one of the "main banks" affiliated with their blue chip employer.[12] In response, Promise began to focus more on lending to younger people at blue chip firms, even to people right out of college. The company believed that since young singles had high disposable incomes and enjoyed guaranteed employment at these blue chip firms,

[12] A blue chip Japanese company had a "main bank" through which it would conduct business. Company employees were encouraged to conduct business through this bank by having their bank accounts there and by securing the financing for their cars and homes from this bank.

this segment could be a good target if reviewed properly.[13] In some instances, Promise even began to shift away from salaried workers and towards hourly personnel as potential customers.

Stage 4 (1991–1999): The "Refounding" Period

In 1991, the Japanese bubble economy burst. As land prices collapsed and guaranteed employment ended, the mortgage loans taken out by middle management became a huge burden for the employees and the banks. As a result, Promise began an even stronger shift away from the blue chip middle manager. Its customer base became younger and consisted less and less of salaried workers (see **Exhibit 8** for an overview of Promise's customer base).

Promise began to introduce many new products. The issuance of cards and the use of ATM machines saw much broader acceptance due to another technological innovation: The Automatic Contract Machine (ACM). Promise had started development work on the ACM 10 years earlier. By creating the ACM, Promise and other CFCs were able to dramatically increase their loan base. (See **Exhibit 9** for Promise's customer base over time.) By sitting in a smoked-glass room, customers would feel like they were interacting with a machine, even though there was a person watching them via video at a centralized location. (See **Exhibit 10** for an overview of the automatic lending process.) This also allowed Promise to establish remote ACM sites that were monitored from a more fully staffed branch where the approval process would be completed. Jinnai explained the significance of the improvements and the increase in their business:

> The Automatic Contract Machines brought a new level of anonymity to the underwriting process. Also, being rejected by a machine rather than a human did not feel as bad to many potential customers. As a result applications increased. But the ACM was only one aspect of the increase in the loan portfolio. Other important events were the IPOs of Promise as well as the IPOs of Acom and Sanyo Simpan. Not only did this provide us, and the other CFCs that went public,[14] with a valuable source of capital, but it also dramatically improved the image of the industry. Now we had become legitimate in many people's eyes. The combination of these events dramatically improved our business.

With this new image came a new source of capital. In May 1999, the government created the Law on Bond Issuance for financial companies. While CFCs had not been able to use capital from the issuance of bonds for lending in the past, the new law enabled CFCs to do so. As a result, Promise's capital structure changed considerably (see **Exhibit 11** for Promise's capital structure and its change over time). In 2000, financing from corporate bonds represented more than 20% of long-term fund procurement; and Promise planned to expand this figure to 30% by March 2001. Promise also started to issue longer-term bonds with a maturity of 12 years. All of these were the result of the unparalleled growth of Promise and other CFCs.

Promise in 1999: The Market's Perspective

As the new millennium started, Promise and the CFC industry were in the midst of a renaissance of sorts. Promise had emerged from restructuring stronger than it had ever been (see **Exhibit 12** for Promise financial statements). According to Jinnai, public opinion of the company, and really the entire industry as a whole, had dramatically improved at the end of the 1990s (see **Exhibit 13** for a list of the top CFCs). Investors, especially

[13] The banks also targeted this segment but quickly exited unsecured lending to this customer due to high loss rates.

[14] Promise, Acom and Sanyo Shinpan all listed in the first section of the Tokyo Stock Exchange in September 1996. Takefuji listed in December 1998 and Aiful listed in March 2000.

EXHIBIT 8   Promise Customer Profile

Source: Promise.

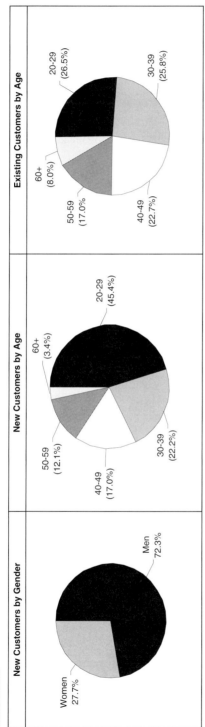

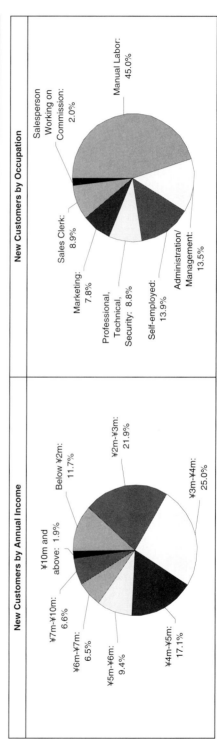

EXHIBIT 9A
Promise New Customer Profile (by Annual Income) (%)

Source: Promise.

	Below ¥2m	¥2m–¥3m	¥3m–¥4m	¥4m–¥5m	¥5m–¥6m	¥6m–¥7m	¥7m–¥10m	>¥10m	Total
Mar-1992	9.7	24.5	26.3	17.0	8.8	5.9	5.7	2.1	100%
Mar-1993	7.9	21.8	25.7	18.1	10.1	6.9	7.0	2.5	100%
Mar-1994	6.8	20.8	25.9	18.5	10.6	7.3	7.6	2.5	100%
Mar-1995	6.3	20.4	25.6	18.7	10.8	7.6	8.0	2.6	100%
Mar-1996	6.6	20.5	26.0	19.0	10.7	7.4	7.6	2.2	100%
Mar-1997	8.1	20.6	25.9	18.5	10.5	7.2	7.2	2.0	100%
Mar-1998	9.5	21.2	25.4	17.9	10.1	6.9	7.1	1.9	100%
Mar-1999	10.8	21.5	25.0	17.5	9.8	6.7	6.8	1.9	100%
Mar-2000	11.7	21.9	25.0	17.1	9.4	6.5	6.6	1.8	100%

EXHIBIT 9B
New Customers at Promise and Major Competitors

Source: Promise (data obtained from *Consumer Credit Monthly,* July 2000).

New Promise Customers over Time (in thousands)

1990	1991	1992	1993	1994	1995	1996	1997	1998	1999	2000
261	274	285	295	312	318	445	470	420	395	430

New Customers over Time (in thousands)

	Number of New Customers FY 2000 (in 000s)	Compared with the Previous Fiscal Year
Takefuji	423	−1.8%
Acom	427	−5.6%
Promise	430	+8.9%
Aiful	425	+4.7%

EXHIBIT 10 **Sample Layout of Promise Branch**

Source: Promise.

Typical Branch Layout (Our staffed branches consist of a staffed counter, an automated credit area and an ATM lobby.)

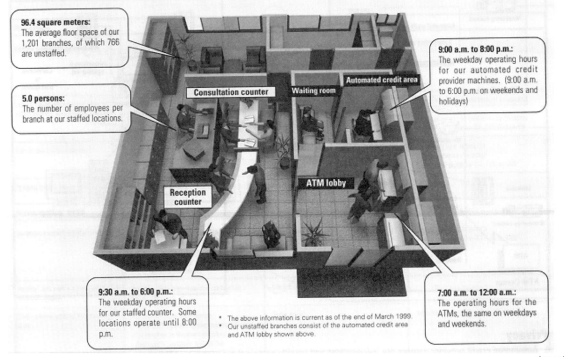

96.4 square meters: The average floor space of our 1,201 branches, of which 766 are unstaffed.

5.0 persons: The number of employees per branch at our staffed locations.

9:00 a.m. to 8:00 p.m.: The weekday operating hours for our automated credit provider machines. (9:00 a.m. to 6:00 p.m. on weekends and holidays)

Consultation counter

Waiting room

Automated credit area

Reception counter

ATM lobby

9:30 a.m. to 6:00 p.m.: The weekday operating hours for our staffed counter. Some locations operate until 8:00 p.m.

* The above information is current as of the end of March 1999.
* Our unstaffed branches consist of the automated credit area and ATM lobby shown above.

7:00 a.m. to 12:00 a.m.: The operating hours for the ATMs, the same on weekdays and weekends.

(continued)

EXHIBIT 10 (Continued) **Overview of the Automated Lending Process**

From Application to Completion of Loan Agreement
The main points in the loan application process are described below.
It usually takes 30 to 40 minutes from application to loan agreement.
Currently, the success rate of loan application stands at about 70%

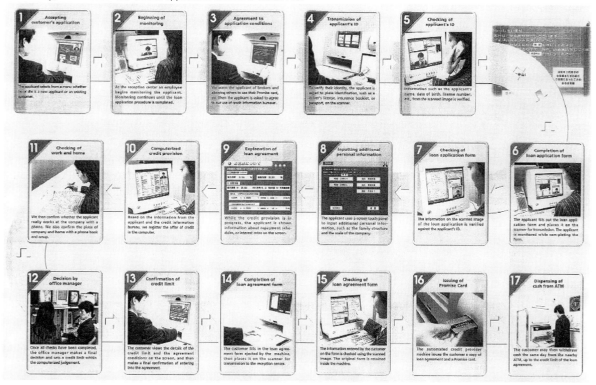

EXHIBIT 11 **Promise's Capital Structure (millions of yen)**

Source: Promise.

	1995	1996	1997	1998	1999	2000
Total fund procurement	573,078	641,728	706,110	772,472	834,047	869,675
Short-term fund procurement	34,546	51,731	53,000	64,800	22,800	6,400
Short-term borrowings	34,546	51,731	53,000	44,800	22,800	6,400
Commerce paper	0	0	0	20,000	0	0
Long-term fund procurement	538,532	589,997	653,110	727,672	811,247	863,275
Long-term borrowings	538,532	579,997	633,110	688,742	742,317	678,275
Ratio of long-term fund procurement to total fund procurement (%)	94.0	91.9	92.5	94.2	97.3	99.3
At fixed interest rate	100,818	224,092	349,594	438,826	474,206	426,504
At variable interest rate	437,714	355,905	283,516	249,916	268,111	251,771
of which interest rate swaps	150,000	100,000	45,000	0	12,840	141,720
Straight bonds	0	0	10,000	30,000	60,000	185,000
Convertible bonds	0	10,000	10,000	8,930	8,930	0
Actual fixed ratio (%)	43.8	52.1	58.7	61.8	66.7	86.6

Note: Actual fixed ratio = (long-term borrowings at fixed interest rate + long-term borrowings with interest rate swaps + straight bonds + convertible bonds) ÷ total fund procurement.
The company procured long-term borrowings at fixed interest rates, taking into account market interest rates. On March 31, 2000, the Company's actual fixed ratio stood at 86.6%, including corporate bonds.

(continued)

EXHIBIT 11
(Continued)

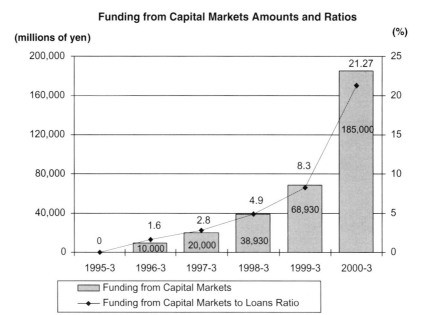

Funding from Capital Markets Amounts and Ratios

Note: Ratio of funding from capital markets = funding from capital markets ÷ (funding from capital markets + loans). The 2000 funding from capital markets to loans ratios for Promise, Takefuji, Acom and Aiful were 21.27%, 6.89%, 17.69% and 20.68%.

EXHIBIT 12
Promise Financial
Statements
Promise Co., Ltd.—
Consolidated
Balance Sheets,
March 31, 1999 and
1998

Source: Promise

	Million of Yen ¥		Thousands of US$
	1999	1998	1999
ASSETS			
Current assets:			
Cash and cash equivalents	171,599	136,283	$1,423,466
Receivables and consumer loans:			
Notes and accounts receivable	46,970	38,478	389,635
Consumer loans receivable			
Principal	1,025,452	913,564	8,506,449
Accrued interest income	9,692	9,627	80,395
Less: allowance for credit losses	(39,112)	(30,224)	(324,452)
	1,043,002	931,445	8,652,027
Short-term investments	3,566	8,002	29,583
Prepaid expenses	3,054	3,300	25,334
Other current assets	13,621	15,978	112,991
Total current assets	1,234,842	1,095,008	10,243,401
Investments and advances:			
Investments in securities	11,418	10,254	94,714
Investments in and advances to unconsolidated subsidiaries and affiliates	5,780	7,502	47,943
Investment in equity other than capital stock	5,188	5,229	43,035
Long-term prepaid expenses	9,747	3,783	80,856
Other investments and advances	7,623	6,765	63,237
Less: allowance for credit losses	(859)	(870)	(7,126)
Total investments and advances	38,897	32,663	322,659
Property and equipment, net	61,042	60,131	506,363
Fixed leasehold deposits	13,509	13,247	112,066

(continued)

EXHIBIT 12
(Continued)

	Million of Yen ¥		Thousands of US$
	1999	**1998**	**1999**
Deferred charge	1,926	0	15,978
Adjustments on foreign currency statement translation	280	26	2,319
Total assets	1,350,496	1,201,075	11,202,786
LIABILITIES AND SHAREHOLDERS' EQUITY	¥	¥	$
Current liabilities:			
Short-term borrowings	48,425	83,305	401,695
Current portion of long-term debt	268,528	211,210	2,227,524
Accounts payable:			
Trade	430	567	3,571
Other	8,798	7,770	72,978
	9,228	8,337	76,549
Accrued income taxes	25,386	26,713	210,588
Accrued expenses	5,639	5,213	46,780
Deferred unrealized profit on sales	1,448	1,791	12,012
Other current liabilities	6,381	5,257	52,933
Total current liabilities	365,035	341,826	3,028,081
Long-term liabilities:			
Long-term debt	599,635	568,666	$4,974,158
Noncurrent accounts payable	7,846	8,590	65,081
Accrued severance indemnities	7,418	6,910	61,533
Excess investment cost under net assets of consolidated subsidiaries acquired	0	48	0
Other long-term debt	1,950	1,981	16,184
Total long-term liabilities	616,849	586,195	5,116,956
Minority interest	4,297	4,186	35,648
Contingent liabilities			
Shareholders' equity			
Common stock, ¥50 par value:			
Authorized—300,000,000 shares			
Issued:			
—119,615,061 shares at March 31, 1999	44,446	0	368,692
—108,615,061 shares at March 31, 1988	0	13,558	0
Additional paid-in capital	54,240	23,363	449,937
Retained earnings	265,630	231,949	2,203,478
Less: treasury stock	0	0	0
Total shareholders' equity	364,316	268,870	3,022,107
Total liabilities and shareholders' equity	1,350,497	1,201,077	11,202,792

Note: US$ figures in **Exhibit 12** are based on the March 31, 1999 exchange rate of US$1 = ¥120.5.

(continued)

foreign investors, had taken a real interest in the sector as the rest of the Japanese financial sector struggled. David Richards, a research analyst covering Japanese CFCs at Goldman Sachs, offered his opinion of the industry and of Promise:

> By 1999, the consumer finance companies were at an inflection point in their collective histories. The industry as a whole had seen tremendous growth during 1997 through 1999—periods when the economy as a whole was at its worst. The IPOs brought improved public

EXHIBIT 12
(Continued)
Promise Co., Ltd.—
Consolidated
Statements of
Income for the Years
Ended March 31,
1999 and 1998

Source: Promise

	Million of Yen ¥		Thousands of US$
	1999	**1998**	**1999**
Operating Income			
Interest on consumer loans	244,570	224,079	$2,028,784
Sales	14,971	19,046	124,188
Other operating income	11,513	9,961	95,504
Total operating income	271,054	253,086	2,248,476
Operating expenses:			
Financial expenses	23,108	23,752	191,686
Cost of sales	12,914	16,985	107,128
General and administrative expenses	106,914	95,204	886,887
Credit losses including provision for uncollectible loans	40,764	28,751	338,145
Total operating expenses	183,700	164,692	1,523,846
Operating profit	87,354	88,394	724,630
Other income (expenses):			
Interest and dividend income on investments	321	376	2,661
Amortization of deferred charge	(963)	0	(7,989)
Bond issue expenses	(163)	(120)	(1,350)
Insurance money received and insurance dividend	140	173	1,164
Interest expense	(933)	(832)	(7,735)
Equity in earnings of Tokumei Kumiai	979	579	8,118
Net loss on sales of short-term investments and investments in securities	(160)	(962)	(1,326)
Loss on valuation of investments in securities	(44)	(1,784)	(368)
Net loss on sales or disposal of property and equipment	(2,366)	(2,871)	(19,628)
Gain on liquidation of Tokumei Kumiai	0	1,151	0
Amortization of excess of cost under net assets acquired, net	49	48	404
Other, net	347	(300)	2,876
Total other expenses, net	(2,793)	(4,542)	(23,173)
Income before income taxes	84,561	83,852	701,457
Income taxes	43,764	44,858	363,032
Minority interest	165	43	1,367
Net income	40,632	38,951	337,058
	Yen ¥		**US$**
Amount per share:			
Net income:			
Basic	346.59	359.40	2.88
Diluted	340.81	352.28	2.83
Cash dividends	65.00	63.00	0.54
Weighted average number of shares (000s):			
Basic	117,234	108,378	117,234
Diluted	119,222	110,568	119,222

EXHIBIT 12 (Continued) Preliminary Data for 2000 and Projections for 2001

Source: Promise.

Consolidated		March-1997	YOY (%)	March-1998	YOY (%)	March-1999	YOY (%)	March-2000	YOY (%)	March-2001	YOY (%)
Operating revenues	(Yen-million)	225,009	11.5	253,085	12.5	271,053	7.1	300,724	10.9	358,424	19.2
Operating income	(Yen-million)	70,334	13.3	78,872	12.1	87,354	10.8	106,027	21.4	124,127	17.1
Ordinary income	(Yen-million)	68,890	10.2	76,288	10.7	90,015	18.0	106,061	17.8	123,083	16.0
Net income	(Yen-million)	35,173	11.8	38,941	10.7	40,632	4.3	58,571	44.1	69,413	18.5
Total assets	(Yen-million)	1,059,872	11.4	1,201,075	13.3	1,350,495	12.4	1,477,849	9.4	1,728,739	17.0
Total shareholders' equity	(Yen-million)	235,299	14.1	268,867	14.3	364,314	35.5	438,090	20.3	513,002	17.1
Consumer loans outstanding	(Yen-million)	821,856	15.0	913,563	11.2	1,025,452	12.2	1,159,253	13.0	1,387,541	19.7
Interest-bearing debt	(Yen-million)	752,589	10.4	863,181	14.7	916,588	6.2	970,598	5.9	1,143,395	17.8
Net income per share	(Yen)	356.48	11.8	376.09	5.5	339.69	−9.7	486.92	43.3	570.84	17.2
Shareholders' equity per share	(Yen)	2,388.14	14.1	2,475.42	3.7	3,045.72	23.0	3,602.80	18.3	4,141.84	15.0
Ratio of consolidated/ nonconsolidated for operating revenue	(times)	1.13	0.01	1.14	0.01	1.13	−0.01	1.13	0.00	1.22	0.09
Ratio of consolidated/ nonconsolidated net income	(times)	1.01	−0.01	1.00	−0.01	1.01	0.01	1.02	0.01	1.02	0.00
Shareholders' equity ratio	(%)	22.20	0.52	2.38	0.18	26.97	4.59	29.64	2.67	29.67	0.03
ROE	(%)	15.90	−0.36	15.44	−0.46	12.83	−2.61	14.59	1.76	14.59	0.00
ROA	(%)	3.49	0.00	3.44	−0.05	3.18	−0.26	4.14	0.96	4.32	0.18

YOY = Year-on-Year Change.

EXHIBIT 13
The Top CFCs
(¥ millions)

Source: Promise (data
obtained from *Nihon Financial
News*.)

Company	Loans Outstanding[a]
1. Takefuji	¥1,492,202
2. Acom	1,347,757
3. Promise	1,100,546
4. Aiful	1,001,080
5. Lake	600,000
6. AIC	520,100
7. DIC Finance	263,102
8. Sanyo Shinpan	262,774
9. Shinki	186,980
10. Unimat Life	146,500
11. Hitachi Shinpan	130,730
12. Nissin	111,484
13. Sanwa Finance	103,089
14. Taihei	100,476
15. Shinwa	78,949
16. Credia	74,361
17. Marufuku	72,719
18. Rich	61,588
19. Koei Credit	60,000
20. Eiwa	57,051

[a]As of March 2000.

perception and innovations like the Automatic Contract Machines brought a new level of anonymity to the process and enabled a strong growth in new account activity. The new machines—small cubes with smoked windows—generated a huge press following. The entire process is really amazing when compared to the United States. The potential for fraud is so large that it could never be used in the United States, but in Japan it works.

Promise was a relatively conservative consumer finance company. The company never rushed into new businesses and, as a result, tended not to be a first mover. They were a leader in lowering rates proactively in order to gain share but this had not been very successful; the market was not that rate sensitive. Consumers looked more at the probability of approval than at rates. And since there should not be any further maximum rate cuts by the government aside from the one just announced, this is not much of an issue going forward. (See **Exhibit 14** for trends in maximum interest rates.) Even though Promise has a reputation for being a slow mover, it is still a solid number three in the market and is excellent at communicating with investors and the press. Yet if the company wants to stay in favor in this environment, it needs to move faster. (See **Exhibit 15** for comparable data of Japanese CFCs; Volatility of Japanese CFCs and banks; and **Exhibit 16** for U.S. comparables.)

According to Richards, investors had begun to shift away from the CFC sector and towards the Japanese banking sector by the end of the year. The CFC sector had performed well in a down market, but there were questions surrounding the long-term attractiveness of the market as banks completed their restructuring and started operating aggressively again.

A New Beginning: New Financing Challenges for Promise

Looking Ahead from a Position of Strength?

"We definitely have our work cut out for us," Kosugi explained. "But we do have a strong base to build off of." One of the greatest advantages the CFC industry had was the database of information generated by the CFC trade association. Unlike the banking sector, the industry as a whole shared a lot of positive and negative information on the

EXHIBIT 14   Trend in Maximum Interest Rates

Source: Promise.

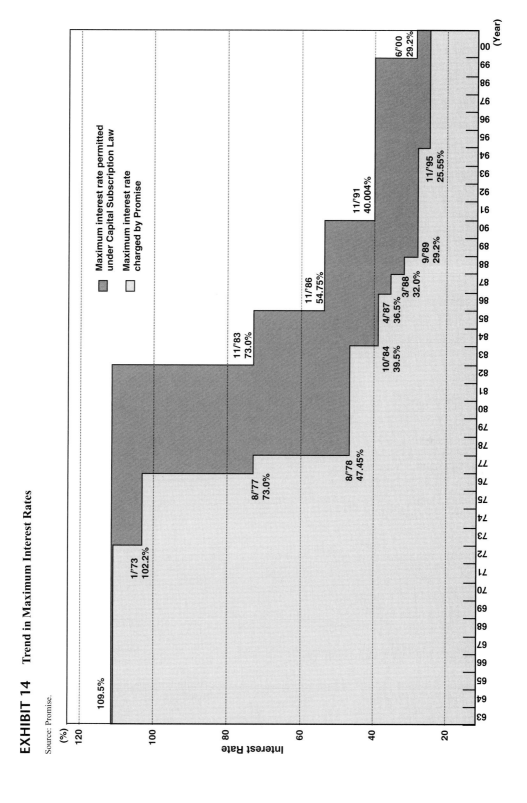

EXHIBIT 15A Financial and Valuation Data for Japanese CFCs

Source: Goldman, Sachs, 2000. Data compiled on April 12, 2000.

	Shohkoh Fund	Nichiei	Takefuji	Acom	Promise	Aiful	Credit Saison	Aeon Credit	Average
Fundamental Indicators (FY99E)									
Return on equity	9.3%	9.3%	21.0%	19.3%	15.0%	19.9%	8.7%	14.6%	14.6%
Return on assets	4.4	3.6	6.6	4.3	4.4	4.1	2.1	2.9	4.1
Equity/assets	51.1	42.8	33.1	25.2	30.0	20.2	24.0	20.3	30.8
SG&A (excluding credit costs)/loans	8.6	7.0	6.6	13.2	10.1	10.2	10.9	15.1	10.2
Write-offs/loans[a]	3.0	7.3	2.8	2.7	3.4	3.8	2.1	2.5	3.5
Reserves/loans	5.7	14.4	5.5	4.2	3.5	5.4	3.9	2.6	5.7
Valuations									
Market capitalization (¥ bn)	292	160	1,776	1,562	1,076	976	312	342	—
Share price (¥)	23,800	2,415	12,060	10,650	8,850	11,600	1,840	7,200	—
FY99 P/E (X)	13.6	8.2	15.9	21.5	18.7	21.9	17.8	44.1	20.2
FY00 P/E (X)	14.1	9.2	13.7	18.4	17.1	18.9	16.8	36.7	18.1
FY00 P/B (X)	1.2	0.7	3.2	4.1	2.6	4.0	1.5	6.0	3.4
3-year estimated operating profit growth	−3%	−17%	10%	10%	9%	15%	7%	23%	10%
P/E to growth	NM	NM	159%	215%	209%	145%	270%	188%	201%
Target P/E	15	10	17	20	17	21	21	25	18
Target share price	24,815	2,593	15,096	11,802	8,781	12,810	2,257	4,993	—
Versus current	4%	7%	25%	11%	−1%	10%	23%	−31%	—

Note: FY00 is the year ending March 31, 2000.

[a]Internal analysis by Promise led to the following ratios of write-offs/loans for March 2000: Promise 2.7%, Takefuji 2.7%, Acom 2.8%, Aiful 3%. For comparison purposes, write-offs for U.S. credit card firms were around 6% of loans.

EXHIBIT 15B
Equity Betas (Period: October 1, 1997- March 31, 2000) for Japanese CFCs and Banks

Source: Promise (data obtained from *TOPIX News Series*, vol. 9, June 2000).

CFCs	30-Month Equity Beta	Banks	30-Month Equity Beta
Takefuji	0.53	Industrial Bank of Japan	1.98
Acom	0.58	Dai-ichi Kangyo Bank	1.24
Promise	0.33	Sakura Bank	2.01
		Bank of Tokyo Mitsubishi	1.52
		Fuji Bank	2.53
		Sumitomo Bank	1.34
		Sanwa Bank	1.30

customers, thereby providing better information to the CFC industry participants. But Promise believed that it was better than the industry as a whole. Teruaki Watanabe highlighted Promise's strengths in data collection and in the underwriting process:

> Our data is much more accurate than our competitors' and our internal controls are much more rigorous. Also, due to our emphasis on technology and superior information, we have a centralized underwriting process and our branch managers have less authority than those at our competitors. Our computer-based scoring system allows us to grow quickly while keeping up the quality. Managers can only decrease but cannot increase the computer-generated limits. This way we are not throwing away our branch manager's experience or the value of personal observations. Another strength of Promise is in collections and much of this has been due to the strength of the underwriting process.

Even though there were things Promise could be proud of, there were many challenges ahead for the company and the industry as a whole.

The Changes of December 1999

December 1999 was an interesting time for Promise and Jinnai. For starters there were the concerns raised by market observers: slower growth due to a maturing market and the question of the effects of general economic prosperity on CFCs. Moreover, there was the threat of foreign competition, as seen most clearly by the purchase of Lake Corporation by GE Capital. Finally there were the changes to the regulatory environment. The government had recently announced that it was to lower the maximum interest rate to 29.2% from 40.004% and this was undoubtedly going to cause a shakeout in the industry. Promise had already lowered the maximum interest rate it charged to 25.55% in November 1995 and felt rather well prepared for the price war that was likely going to occur from July 2000 onwards. There were also the recent changes to the bond issue laws. CFCs could now issue longer-term bonds and use commercial paper programs for any corporate purpose. Jinnai stated: "The question becomes how these changes should influence our financing policies."

New Opportunities

The shakeout was bound to create opportunities. On one hand, Promise could hope to pick up many clients from second-tier companies that could fall on hard times. On the other, Promise could take a more proactive measure by acquiring some of the more inefficient companies. Jinnai explained:

> An acquisition program could have many benefits for Promise and the companies we purchase. For many of the smaller companies, access to capital is still quite limited. Since they do not have the scale we have, they do not have a publicly listed security, which in turn has limited their access to both the public and private debt markets. Many of these companies

EXHIBIT 16 United States versus Japan Valuation Comparison

Source: Richards, David. 2000. *Specialty Finance: We Remain Bullish*. Tokyo: Goldman Sachs, p. 5. Data on Estimated Three-year Growth, Debt/EV, Debt/Book Equity from Global Access database.

	Business Lines	Rating	P/E (X) FY99	P/E (X) FY00	Estimated Three-year Growth	P/B(X)	ROE (%)	ROA (%)	Equity/ Assets (%)	Debt/ EV	Debt/ Book Equity
United States											
Associates First Capital	Consumer Credit	RL	9.8	8.6	14.0%	2.3	17.6	1.8	10.0	82	7.01
American Express	Credit Cards, Asset Management, Travel Services	MO	23.1	20.4	16.0	6.8	22.3	3.2	7.0	37	3.46
Capital One Financial	Credit Cards	MO	20.8	16.7	20.0	7.9	25.0	1.7	14.5	33	2.59
FINOVA Group	Commercial Financing, Leasing	MO	3.6	3.2	15.0	0.7	14.5	2.2	6.6	94	6.43
Heller Financial	Commercial Finance	RL	9.0	8.1	15.0	1.2	11.6	1.6	7.3	90	5.87
Household International	Consumer Credit	RL	11.4	9.9	15.0	3.3	23.5	3.0	7.9	70	6.53
MBNA	Credit Cards	RL	18.0	15.0	20.0	9.7	25.0	4.3	5.9	24	1.61
Providian Financial	Credit Cards	RL	16.3	13.2	25.0	8.3	50.0	3.0	16.6	8	0.73
Average			**14.0**	**11.9**	**17.5%**	**5.0**	**23.7**	**2.6**	**9.5**	**55**	**4.28**
Japan											
Shohkoh Fund	Commercial Finance	MO	13.6	14.1	-2.7%	1.2	9.3	4.4	51.1	33	1.98
Nichiei	Commercial Finance	MP	8.2	9.2	-48.3	0.7	9.3	3.6	42.8	86	1.16
Takefuji	Commercial Finance	NR	15.9	13.7	10.0	3.2	21.0	6.6	33.1	39	1.85
Acom	Consumer Finance	MO	21.5	18.4	8.6	4.1	19.3	4.3	25.2	48	2.67
Promise	Consumer Finance	MP	18.7	17.1	8.7	2.6	15.0	4.4	30.0	47	2.02
Aiful	Consumer Finance	MO	21.9	18.9	12.5	4.0	19.9	4.1	20.2	53	3.53
Credit Saison	Credit Cards	MO	17.8	16.8	5.6	1.5	8.7	2.1	24.0	73	2.74
Aeon Credit Service	Credit Cards	MP	44.1	36.7	17.4	6.0	14.6	2.9	20.3	32	2.75
Average			**20.2**	**18.1**	**1.5%**	**2.9**	**14.6**	**4.0**	**30.9**	**54**	**2.34**

Note: U.S. P/B ratios are based on latest reported book value. U.S. ROA is for 4Q99. Equity to assets is estimated from ROE and ROA data. FY99 and FY00 are the regular calendar years.

have a higher cost structure than Promise and could be wiped out by the reduction in interest rates, so an alliance with Promise could be beneficial. (See **Exhibit 17** for a comparative cost structure of Promise and a typical CFC.) For Promise, it can give us access to a new risk class as we would probably continue to charge the highest allowable rate for these customers, as opposed to the Promise customer to which we charge a rate lower than the maximum (see **Exhibit 14**). Eventually, we could look into combining these entities under one brand name and one operating company, where the information on the customers could be shared throughout the Promise system. But right now, we cannot conduct a merger of this sort and each entity must be run separately. The government and the public would not stand for a U.S. style merger with large layoffs and restructuring measures.[15] The problem with mergers in this area would not only be cultural but would also have a broader business concern: you never know exactly what you are getting until you buy it.

Promise had already taken some first steps in the acquisition program and had recently committed to acquisitions of three smaller CFCs (see **Exhibit 18**). The big question was whether Promise should intensify its acquisition program. Another option for Jinnai was to target the other extreme: low-risk customers. In this scenario, Promise would look to expand its asset base by attracting customers of this lower risk class through lower interest rates. Promise was a little unsure about how to target this customer class. Attracting these customers through an independent green-field operation, whether or not it was under the Promise name, might be difficult as Promise had not

[15] According to Japanese law a CFC had to obtain written consent from each customer in the course of an acquisition in order to get access to the customer's information. The intention of this law was to protect customers from being acquired by criminal groups (Yakuza).

EXHIBIT 17A
Comparative Cost Structure versus Typical Medium-sized CFCs

Source: Promise.

	Promise	CFC "A"	CFC "B"	CFC "C"
Interest income (%)	24.8	27.4	35.1	29.4
Financial expenses (%)	2.0	5.1	2.7	6.1
Charge-off (%)	2.8	6.0	9.2	9.9
Operating costs (%)	10.1	13.0	13.3	14.1
Total costs (%)	14.9	24.1	25.2	30.1

All figures are % of loans outstanding.

EXHIBIT 17B
Comparative Cost Structure versus Major CFCs

Source: Promise.

Financial Expenses as % of Loans Outstanding				
	Promise	Takefuji	Acom	Aiful
1999	2.14%	2.44%	2.39%	2.68%
2000	1.93%	1.87%	2.17%	2.56%

EXHIBIT 18
Promise's Recent Acquisitions

Source: Promise.

Company Name	Rich	Shinko	Towa	Compare: Promise
Date	5/00	4/00	5/00	
Stake acquired	100%	100%	25.7%	
Number of employees	478	254	109	3,874
Number of branches	130	48	21	1,299
Loans outstanding (million yen)	¥61,588	¥31,773	¥22,265	¥1,100,546
Net profit (million yen)	(¥1,603)	¥1,650	¥378	¥57,237

pursued these customers for years. Since the banks were really the only ones who aimed at these customers, large numbers of acquisition targets were not available. One idea that Ryoichi and Hiroki Jinnai had come up with was to form a joint venture with an established bank to expand into this segment. Kosugi explained:

> By partnering with a bank, we will be able to establish a business with an institution that has experience in serving this customer base. Promise will bring to the relationship its underwriting process and entire technological expertise, which many of the banks are lacking. The banks, in turn, would provide credibility.

In May of 2000, Promise had made a first step towards the banking customer segment by establishing a joint venture called "MOBIT" with Sanwa Bank and Aplus, a sales finance company. Sanwa Bank held 50% in MOBIT; Promise, 40%; and Aplus, 10%. The plan was that MOBIT would offer unsecured loans at lower interest rates (15%–18%) to customers who earned higher incomes (5–8 million Yen p.a.). Just like the acquisition program however, MOBIT was still in its earliest stages. Also, due to the historic rivalry between banks and CFCs, the two groups had each set up their credit information organizations for exclusive use. Thus, MOBIT could not use existing customer data from Promise or from Sanwa Bank. Jinnai asked himself how aggressively Promise should get involved in expanding MOBIT.

A third option existed for the company within its existing customer base. The company could look to consolidate the loans of its existing clients. Often customers had loans with more than one CFC. Promise could look to consolidate all the loans for one customer. "We just have to be careful not to get into a price war," explained Jinnai. "We would want to use our superior information to target the customers that are not necessarily the best, but are overlooked. Everyone will try to consolidate the 'Platinum' accounts by competing on rates. We want to target the crowd just below the 'Platinum' accounts." Another area for growth would be to offer other products or services to existing customers, like credit cards (see **Exhibit 19** for a list of Promise's products). But this was not the easiest option. "This is still an industry that is not in the mainstream," Kosugi warned. "We should not look like we are stuffing products down unsuspecting customers throats." Another problem, especially with credit cards, was structural, not cultural. Richards explained:

> Cards in Japan have more of a convenience function than they are a source of credit. The issue of having a revolving credit card is less cultural than structural. There is no checking system in Japan. All "credit cards" are paid off with a direct debit at month's end. Since there is no payment flexibility in this direct debit system, there is a huge barrier to the acceptance of a credit card. Moreover, credit card payments show up on the monthly bank statement that is generally visible to the spouse.

Promise could target other segments of the consumer finance market, such as the growing number of professional women in the workforce. "This is easier said than done," warned Jinnai. "In the past, Promise tried to target this segment when the foreign exchange rules were lifted. We expected women to travel more—to say Hawaii—and created a new product for the segment. But it did not become a major product." Finally, other products, like small business loans, were a possibility. "We could enter this market through one of our sales finance subsidiaries. But the small business loan market could be even more dangerous," Kosugi warned, "as small business loan providers have a terrible reputation. The reason we have had the cuts in interest rates in the first place was due to scandals in this segment. If we want to enter this market, we need to devise a new type of small business loan."

EXHIBIT 19 **Promise Products Available (except for discontinued lines)**

Source: Promise.

Unsecured Loans					
Product Type	**Product Name**	**Features**	**Type of Interest Rate**	**Interest Rate**	**Maximum Credit Limit**
Revolving (1)	Free Cashing	Promise's main product	Fixed-rate	25.55%	¥2,000,000 *If an ordinary credit investigation is done: ¥500,000
				25.00%	
				24.50%	
				23.90%	
				23.50%	
				22.995%	
				21.90%	
				21.40%	
				19.80%	
				17.80%	
			Stepped (2)	25.55% if balance is less than ¥500,000 21.90% if balance is between ¥500,000 and ¥1,000,000	¥1,000,000
				25.55% if balance is less than ¥500,000 19.80% if balance is between ¥500,000 and ¥1,000,000	¥1,000,000
	Tsuki-wari (3)	Installment loan repaid as a lump-sum with borrower's bonus	Fixed-rate	25.55%	¥500,000
	1$ Cashy (4)	Exclusively for women; Lump-sum repayment	Fixed-rate	14.60%	¥100,000
Installment-payment	Flower Pack (5)	Exclusively for women; Repaid in equal payments by electronic funds transfer	Fixed-rate	16.50%	¥200,000
	Application-specific Loan (6)	Eligible uses include (1) travel, (2) moving, (3) childbirth, (4) education, etc	Fixed-rate	13.50%	¥500,000
				16.50%	
				19.50%	
	Nittsu Travel Loan	Nittsu's tie-up loans for travel	Fixed-rate	13.50%	¥500,000

(1) Allows free withdrawals and repayment up to the line of credit determined in advance.
(2) Under the stepped interest rate method, the rate applied varies by the balance of the loan outstanding as follows:
  a) an effective interest rate of 25.55% per annum is applied to the portion of ¥500,000 or less, and 19.80% is applied to the portion over ¥500,000 to ¥1,000,000.
  b) An effective interest rate of 25.55% per annum is applied to the portion of ¥500,000 or less, and 21.90% is applied to the portion over ¥500,000 to ¥1,000,000.
(3) *Tsuki-wari* provides installment finance, to which the borrower will make one or two-time repayment with bonuses. It is designed for customers with fixed monthly outgoings, such as those financing children living separately.
(4) 1$ Cashy is offered exclusively to female customers. In addition to the prime rate schemes, US$ exchange service (free of charge, available at limited branches) is also attached as special covenants, the first service of its kind within the industry.
(5) Flower Pack is also offered exclusively for women with a preferential interest rate. It is repaid in equal payments by electronic fund transfer.
(6) A lower-interest product whose application is limited to (1) travel, (2) moving, (3) childbirth, (4) education, etc.

(continued)

Secured Loans						
Loan Type	Product Name	Size of Loan	Interest Rate	Delinquent Charge	Term of Contract	Contract Type
Real estate card loan	Type 500	¥1.01–5 million	13.5%–16.5%	29.2%	Maximum 10 years	Mortgage creation agreement
	Type 300	¥1.01–3 million	17.0%	29.2%	Maximum 10 years	Contract creating a credit line

Financing Alternatives

Another key question was how to finance the company in the future. There were new sources of capital, such as the Commercial Paper product and corporate bonds, as well as other options like raising new equity. The company was very leery of debt. Isao Takeuchi, Promise's CFO, explained Promise's financial policy:

> Promise has had a conservative capital structure ever since the 1980s when the debt crisis hit the industry. Almost overnight all the liquidity was sucked out of the market as banks called back the loans they had given to us that had been used to fund all areas of the company's business. We never want to put ourselves in such a position again. As a result, we look to maintain our equity ratio of 30% and to increase the proportion of long-term debt. Even though debt is cheaper, this is true only up to a certain level of debt. So while we are fortunate enough to be one of the few CFCs with more options for debt instruments, we need to be very careful about how we utilize these new options.

With respect to equity, there were also new considerations for the company. Takefuji, a major competitor, had recently (March 22, 2000) listed on the London Stock Exchange. Since the proportion of foreigners holding Promise stock had increased, listing abroad could be an interesting move. Takeuchi was puzzled by recent delistings of Japanese banks on foreign exchanges. Daiichi Kangyo Bank, Fuji Bank, and others had once listed on various overseas capital markets but had recently drastically reduced the number of exchanges on which they appeared. "I am not sure if the option of listing abroad would be all that attractive for us," Takeuchi reasoned. "Also, should we list in London or New York?"

What to Do and Where to Raise Funds

Jinnai looked at the three managing directors. They had finished the main course of their dinner and the restaurant owner signaled that dessert, which was served in a separate room, was ready. Any decision could substantially affect the company's value.[16] The Tempura dinner would be over soon and Jinnai was scheduled to meet with Promise's senior management on the following day. What was he going to tell his team?

---

[16] By March 31, 2000, members of the Jinnai family still held 34.5% of Promise's shares. By March 31, 1999, Japanese financial institutions held about 32.6%. Foreign institutional shareholders held about 20.1%. These figures had changed little by March 2000.

Case

23

Gray Security: Building a South African Services Firm

Dick Aubin, cofounder and chairman of Gray Security, looked out across the harbor of Cape Town, South Africa. Several miles behind him, and 3,600 feet above him, tourists were looking over the same beach from the top of Table Mountain, but Aubin preferred to look from where he could hear and smell the ocean. Cape Town, he felt, was one of the world's loveliest cities and well worth experiencing from within. Taking a deep breath of the ocean air, Aubin turned and began walking back to Gray's head office on the waterfront. It was January 4, 1999, a pleasant summer day, and he would be meeting with his key management team over the next few days to outline Gray's strategy for the coming years. Aubin wondered what he should communicate as his top priorities at this meeting.

Aubin felt he had good reason to be proud of Gray's growth to date, as well as to be optimistic about the company's future. From a modest beginning financed through personal capital, Gray had grown at a consistent rate of 30% per annum to become the largest company offering complete security services to South African firms. A business strategy that produced healthy cash flows had enabled this growth to take place without need for outside funding. Indeed, Gray's owners had been able to capture much of the firm's value through a leveraged refinancing that the firm's cash flows had comfortably been able to support.

Gray had also developed an operations strategy that Aubin felt gave it an edge over its competitors. Few South African companies could offer the scope of services Gray brought to its clients, and Gray was often able to create value for its clients beyond the normal benefits of outsourcing. Moreover, Gray's approach to human resources management had resulted in relatively low employee turnover and overall labor relations well above the industry, or the South African, norm. Aubin had continuously emphasized the need to hire and to retain the best people at all levels of the company, and he believed Gray had been largely successful in doing so.

Professor Walter Kuemmerle and Charles M. Williams Fellow Chad Ellis (MBA '98) prepared this case. HBS cases are developed solely as the basis for class discussion. Cases are not intended to serve as endorsements, sources of primary data, or illustrations of effective or ineffective management.

Despite Gray's strong market position, however, Aubin knew there were some difficult challenges ahead. For one, South Africa was changing. The end of apartheid and the rise to power of the black majority African National Congress (ANC) Party was changing the face of South Africa. Gray had never relied heavily on government contracts, but the current changes went far beyond normal political shifts. Programs and pressure for redistribution of South Africa's wealth in favor of previously disadvantaged groups would continue to change the way business was conducted across many fronts.

South Africa's economic outlook had changed, too. The local currency, the rand ($1 = R5.860 in January 1999), had depreciated significantly in recent years (see **Exhibit 1** for exchange rate history) and was widely expected to continue to weaken against most foreign currencies. Successful expansion into other African nations and then into Western Europe had established Gray's international presence. With a weak currency and prospects for a lengthy recession at home, Aubin felt it was in Gray's best interests to accelerate its overseas growth.

Changes in the security industry itself also argued for building Gray into an international firm. The industry was globalizing as multinational companies tried to reduce the number of suppliers they relied on, whether for goods or services. Oil firms and other multinational players had been a key source of contracts for Gray, and early expansion into other African countries had been in part driven by the benefits of offering services across Africa. Now that trend was extending to global contracts. Moreover, where a pan-African approach had been a source of competitive advantage until now, in the future a global service might become a competitive necessity, without which even Gray's core South African business could come under threat. Transforming Gray into an international firm was not merely a way to reduce its shareholders' dependence on South African earnings; it might prove necessary for the firm's long-term survival.

But if becoming a global player was a strategic goal, the best path to take was by no means clear. Gray had expanded primarily through organic growth, supported by modest strategic acquisitions. This had enabled the company to maintain a corporate culture and vision that Aubin felt had served it well. Could Gray continue to base the core of its expansion on opening new offices in other countries, or would the company have to turn to more ambitious acquisitions?

Aubin knew there was another possibility to consider. Gray was not the only security firm considering acquisitions as part of a global consolidation. As the clear leader among African firms, Gray would make an attractive target for acquisition by one of the world's other major players. Was it better, in this case, to be the hunted rather than the hunter?

South Africa—A Story of Turbulent Political and Economic Development

Historical Background

South Africa, a country about twice the size of France, occupied the Southern tip of Africa. (See **Exhibit 2** for a map.) The indigenous people were gradually driven north by Dutch farmers who arrived after a trading post was established at the Cape in 1652.[1] The descendants of the Dutch came to be known as Afrikaners or Boers. They imported slave labor from a variety of countries including Mozambique and Madagascar.[2] British settlers who started arriving in the nineteenth century settled mostly along the coastline. In a series of conflicts between Afrikaners and British, the British eventually prevailed.

[1] *The Statesman's Year-book.* 2004. 140th edition. New York: St. Martin's Press, p. 1457.

[2] Byrnes, Rita M. 1996. *South Africa: A Country Study.* Washington, DC: Federal Division, Library of Congress, p. 13.

EXHIBIT 1 Interest and Exchange Rate Data

Source: Compiled from IMF, *International Financial Statistics* data.

	1994				1995				1996				1997				1998			
	Q1	Q2	Q3	Q4	Q1	Q2	Q3	Q4	Q1	Q2	Q3	Q4	Q1	Q2	Q3	Q4	Q1	Q2	Q3	Q4
South African Rand : U.S. dollar (end of quarter)	3.4795	3.6515	3.5645	3.5435	3.5905	3.6365	3.6495	3.6475	3.9805	4.3345	4.5300	4.6825	4.4225	4.5305	4.6615	4.8675	5.0345	5.8665	5.8725	5.8600
South African prime lending rate (repo)	15.25	15.25	15.58	16.25	17.08	17.50	18.50	18.50	18.50	20.17	19.50	19.92	20.25	20.25	20.25	19.25	18.92	19.58	25.00	23.67
South African Treasury bill rate	10.15	10.64	10.78	12.15	12.87	13.50	13.95	13.80	14.03	15.32	15.39	15.40	15.94	15.64	14.86	14.59	13.89	13.99	20.12	18.14
U.S. Treasury bill note	3.52	4.18	4.64	5.64	5.73	5.50	5.26	5.16	4.96	5.11	5.15	4.87	5.14	4.92	4.97	5.16	5.03	4.99	4.74	4.42

Note: At the time of the case, 20 year U.S. Government Bonds had a yield of 5.4%. A U.S. dollar bond issued by the South African government maturing in 2017 yielded 11.7%.

EXHIBIT 2 Map of South Africa

Source: *EIU Country Profile South Africa 1998–99*. London: Economist Intelligence Unit, 1998, preface.

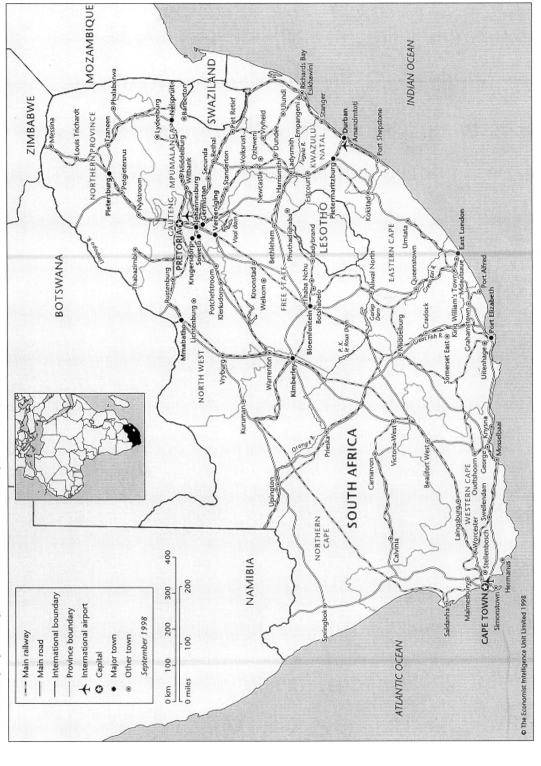

A strong level of resentment over this loss persisted within the Afrikaner community well into the twentieth century.[3] South Africa started to exist as a state in 1910 with the establishment of the Union of South Africa.

Rise and Fall of Apartheid

While there was ongoing tension between Afrikaners and the British, both sides were eager to keep joint control over a steady supply of cheap African labor. Many of the African workers were employed in diamond and gold mines. Exports of these two resources formed the basis of South Africa's wealth at the time and extracting these resources was labor-intensive. A number of laws restricted the mobility of African workers. Also, in 1913 a law was enacted that reserved 93% of South Africa's land for white ownership.[4] African workers lived in so-called "townships" under dismal conditions. By law, colored mining workers could hold only unskilled or semiskilled jobs.

Resistance to discrimination led to the formation of the predecessor-organization of the African National Congress (ANC) in 1912.[5] But this did little to stop the further cementing of segregation. In 1948 the ruling party officially introduced the system of apartheid—"in theory the separate, but equal, development of all racial groups, in practice leading to white, particularly Afrikaner, supremacy . . . ."[6] In 1964, Nelson Mandela, an important ANC leader, was jailed. Over the years it became increasingly clear to white South Africans that the system of apartheid was not sustainable, especially with South Africa being increasingly isolated by the international community. However, inertia kept the system going. Surprisingly, other countries imposed tough economic sanctions only after South Africa declared a state of emergency in 1986 to control increasing civil unrest.[7] White South Africans finally got serious about change. In February 1990 Nelson Mandela was released from prison and in 1992, a white-only referendum effectively ended apartheid. In the first general election, Nelson Mandela was elected president in March 1994. He was succeeded by Thabo Mbeki in the 1999 elections.

South Africa in 1999

Between 1994 and 1999, relations between Afrikaners and previously disadvantaged groups were characterized by a surprisingly constructive attitude. Both sides seemed eager to build a new South Africa. On the bright side, the country had a good infrastructure, especially by the standards of other African countries. For example, 41.5% of all roads were paved versus 18.8% in Nigeria and 9.3% in Brazil. However, by 1999 South Africa was still a country of huge contrasts. Whites were educated and were typically affluent, while most blacks were poor. Adult literacy stood at only 16%.[8] (See **Exhibit 3** for economic statistics.) Segregation now occurred by wealth rather than strictly by color. The Johannesburg suburb of Sandton, for example, was affluent and host to many new corporate headquarters buildings. Downtown Johannesburg, by contrast, had lost many of its corporate tenants. Squatters had taken over. Carjackings at traffic stops were common and whites sought to avoid the area.

Even though efforts were underway to improve general education and access to jobs, it would likely take at least one or two generations for previously disadvantaged groups to reach standards of living comparable to those of white South Africans.[9] The uncertainty

---

[3] Casewriter interview with Gray management.

[4] Byrnes, Rita M., op. cit., p. 45.

[5] Byrnes, Rita M., op. cit., p. 45.

[6] *The Europa World Year Book*. 2003. 44th edition. London: Europa Publications Limited, p. 3762.

[7] *The Statesman's Year-book*. 2004. 140th edition. New York: St. Martin's Press, p. 1458.

[8] Compared to Nigeria's literacy rate at 43%.

[9] Casewriter interview with Gray management.

around South Africa's future was reflected in the development of its currency, the rand, which had declined from 2.27R/\$ in 1988 to 3.48R/\$ in early 1994 and to 5.86R/\$ in late 1998. (See **Exhibit 4** for recent exchange rate history and **Exhibits 5** and **6** for capital flow and reserve information.)

EXHIBIT 3 Economic Statistics

Source: Compiled from Economist Intelligence Unit data.

South African Economic Data	1994	1995	1996	1997	1998[a]
GDP at market prices (R bn)	431.1	484.6	542.7	594.9	637.7[b]
Real GDP growth (%)	2.7	3.4	3.2	1.7	0.1[b]
Consumer price inflation (year-end %)	9.0	8.6	7.4	8.5	6.5
Current account ($ bn)	(0.32)	(2.76)	(1.71)	(1.93)	(2.36)
Total external debt ($ bn)	18.7	22.3	23.6	24.3	25.7
Debt-service ratio, paid (%)	8.9	8.7	10.6	10.7	10.5
Exchange rate (Avg. R:$)	3.549	3.627	4.271	4.603	5.530

[a]Actual.
[b]EIU estimates.

Source: "1999 World Development Indicators" and "1998 Atlas," World Bank; Economist Intelligence Unit; African Development Bank; U.S. National Center for Health Statistics, Vital Statistics; U.S. Bureau of Justice; Criminal Statistics, England and Wales 1997; the U.K. Home Office.

Comparative Economic Indicators (1997 unless otherwise indicated)	South Africa	Zimbabwe	Nigeria	Brazil	United Kingdom	United States
Gross domestic product ($ bn)	129.3	8.5	37.5[a]	806.4	1,288.2	8,110.9
GDP per capita ($)	3,340	733	356	5,048	21,848	30,263
Consumer price inflation (%)	8.5	18.9	8.5	6.4	2.8	2.4
Merchandise exports fob ($ bn)	30.4	2.3	15.6	53.0	279.3	680.3
Merchandise imports fob ($ bn)	28.4	2.4	8.2	61.4	299.8	877.3
Foreign direct investment (% GDP 1996)	0.1	0.1	4.3	1.3	2.8	1.0
Net aid flows (% GDP 1996)	0.3	5.2	0.6	0.1	(b)	(b)
Electrical power						
Per capita (KwH 1996)	3,719	765	85	1,660	5,198	11,796
Production CAGR (% 1980–1996)	3.9	6.0	5.6	4.6	1.3	3.0
Paved roads (% total 1996)	41.5	47.4	18.8	9.3	100.0	60.8
Adult illiteracy (%)	16.0	15.0[c]	43.0	16.7	—	—
Life expectancy (years 1996)	65	56	53	67	77	77
Population (m)	41.5	11.2	111.7	159.0	58.1	267.1
Population growth (% 1990–1996)	1.7	2.4	2.9	1.4	0.3	1.0
Telephone mainlines						
Per 1,000 people	107	17	4	107	540	644
In largest city (per 1,000 people)	415				—	—
Burglary (per 1,000 homes)	1.5[e]	—	—	—	23.1	44.6
Homicide (per 100,000 people)	59.2	—	—	—	1.4[d]	7.4

[a]At the 1997 average autonomous exchange rate (₦83.5:$1).
[b]Net aid donor.
[c]1995.
[d]England and Wales only.
[e]Statistics given come from the South African police. However, the vast majority of the population of South Africa live in squatter camps and tenement housing developments, and the probability that every break-in will be reported is extremely low. In addition, the deterioration of the level of service of the SAPS is so marked that unless there is an insurance claim possibility, it is also unlikely that the more affluent population will report every break-in.

EXHIBIT 4
Recent Exchange
Rate History

Source: *EIU Country Profile South Africa 1998–99.* London: Economist Intelligence Unit, 1998, pp. 40–41.

1995	"On March 10, the financial rand was abolished.[a]"
February 1996	"On February 16 [the] rand suffered its most turbulent day since the 1994 general election following unfounded rumors that the president, Nelson Mandela, was ill and that exchange controls were about to be eased further."
February–March 1996	"A sequence of other political and economic rumors, combined with concrete events such as the resignation of the finance minister, [...] buffeted the currency in the months that followed. From steady levels of around R3.65:$1 seen during most of 1995, the rand fell to R4:$1 in March 1996."
Late 1996	"Brief rallies were followed by fresh plunges; by mid-December 1996 the currency was trading at slightly over R4.7:$1 and lost nearly 30% of its value against the dollar in 1996."
1997	"The currency declined only slightly between November 1996 and March 1997 but experienced renewed volatility owing to contagion effects from the Southeast Asian markets crisis, to trade at close to R4.90:$1 in December 1997."
July 1998	"The value of the rand plummeted to its lowest level of R6.75:$1 on July 6, 1998 when the financial markets reacted negatively to the appointment of Tito Mboweni as the governor-designate of [...] the central bank."
September 1998	"[The rand] recovered to R6.05:$1 at the end of September. A 6-percentage-point rise in the prime lending rate to 24% in June and July helped to stabilize the rand. [...]"

"[a][The financial rand was] a second-tier currency, available only to foreigners, which traded at a discount to the commercial rand and was used for all conventional balance-of-payments transactions, thereby insulating the country's foreign reserves from politically inspired capital flight."

EXHIBIT 5
Recent Capital Flow
History

Source: *EIU Country Profile South Africa 1998–99.* London: Economist Intelligence Unit, 1998, p. 39.

1984–1993	Substantial short-term capital outflows—country net capital exporter. Reasons include international sanctions and related disinvestment, as well as the unilateral declaration by the central bank of a debt standstill in 1985 in response to a perceived external debt crisis.
1994–1995	Dramatic turnaround in flows after the 1994 election of Mandela. Net capital inflow of $1.8 billion in 1994 and $1.9 billion in 1995.
1996	"[Net capital inflows slow sharply] as much of this short-term investment left the country with the plunge of the rand."
1997	Capital inflows rise to record levels as the SARB lifts exchange rate controls for nonresidents in July, thus enabling the future repatriation of profits and capital.
1998	Capital inflows affected by the emerging-market crisis and the rand crisis in June.

The Roots of Gray Security

Aubin was born in 1946 to a Canadian father and South African mother. He grew up in Port Elizabeth, and in 1971 he graduated, with honors, from the University of Cape Town. He joined the engineering firm Hubert Davies and Co. in Johannesburg, where he rose to the level of director and had control of five subsidiary companies (see **Exhibit 7** for management résumés).

EXHIBIT 6 Foreign Reserve Information

Source: Compiled from Economist Intelligence Unit data and IMF, *International Financial Statistics* data.

($ millions; end-period)	1994	1995	1996	1997	1998
SDRs	1	5	1	7	132
Foreign exchange	1,684	2,815	940	4,790	4,171
Total reserves excluding gold	1,685	2,820	942	4,799	4,357
Gold[a]	1,212	1,229	1,261	1,048	1,034
Total reserves including gold	2,897	4,049	2,203	5,847	5,391

[a]Valued at 75% of the fourth-quarter London gold price.

In 1979, Aubin left Hubert Davies and moved to Cape Town as managing director of Consani Engineering, a heavy-engineering company that was part of a large conglomerate headed by South Africa's largest insurance company. Sabotage had begun to be a concern at Consani, and Aubin decided it would be best to hire a professional security firm to help safeguard the plant's production. He recalled:

> We looked for a quality security company, but we couldn't find one. Security was more of a luxury issue in the late '70s and early '80s, as there was not much crime in South Africa. While several large firms, particularly in mining and oil, had security, it was usually handled in-house. I hired Andy Gray through a headhunter to put together a team of 20 people over six months. From that point on, the idea of starting a professional security firm was always on our minds.

Aubin approached his superiors about forming a security company within the group, but there was little interest and no financial support. Deciding that the idea was worth pursuing, Aubin, together with Gray, Chris Convery, and Steve Woods, formed a new venture. In late 1980, financed with R25,000 in equity from an overdraft loan, Gray Security Service (Pty.) Ltd. was formed. Aubin recalled:

> The problem, initially, was credibility. We had an innovative idea for winning the confidence of new clients; we would assume full liability for losses up to an amount covered by a professional indemnity insurance policy we would take out. That reduced the risk a client might feel they were taking with a new firm, but we still needed that initial contract to let us show what we could do.

The initial contract came in 1982 from oil giant Mobil, which awarded Gray an annual contract of just under R1 million to take over seven of its facilities in South Africa including an oil refinery. Aubin explained that Mobil might not have realized how important its contract was for securing Gray's future:

> The Mobil contract was obviously very important to us. Here was a major multinational, working at a strategic asset for South Africa, hiring us to handle their security needs. They may have trusted us based on the names of our board of directors, which had a lot of overlap with our former parent company, Abercom Group. Those names appeared on our proposal letter,[10] and Mobil may have just assumed that Abercom was backing us financially.

Several other contracts followed Mobil's, and Aubin soon felt that his business instincts had been borne out. Three years later he left Consani to devote himself full time to the new company.

[10] As required by South African law.

EXHIBIT 7   **Management Résumés**

Source: Gray Security.

Chairman—Richard Aubin (52)

Aubin attained a B Bus Sc degree with Honors at the University of Cape Town. He joined the engineering industry and was employed by Hubert Davies and Co. where he was appointed the Director and Executive Chairman of five subsidiary companies. In 1980 he joined Abercom Group and became a director of Abercom Group and the Deputy Chairman and Managing Director of Constant Engineering. During 1984 he left Abercom Group to join Gray as the Chairman. Aubin is one of the founding shareholders of Gray.

Deputy Chairman—Chris Convery (53)

Convery initially obtained a B.Sc (Maths) degree at the University of the Witwatersrand. He spent a few years in the insurance industry before moving to Deloitte Haskins & Sells, and qualified as a Chartered Accountant in 1976. He served as a manager after qualifying and was involved with liquidation and judicial management work for two years. He spent a period in International Commodity Trading (Raphaely's) before joining Consani Engineering as the Financial Director.

   Convery is one of the founding shareholders of Gray and joined Gray on a full-time basis in 1983, with responsibility for its finance and administration. At different times he has acted in a wide spectrum of responsibilities. He was seconded to Imperial Security Services for four years in London (1991–1994).

Chief Executive Officer—David Plane (49)

Plane completed a Business Management Diploma and attended the Program for Management Development and Advancement Management Program at the University of Cape Town Graduate School of Business. While employed in the marketing and contracting field, Plane became a director of three companies in the Protea Holdings/Malbak group. As a citizen force soldier he attained the rank of Lieutenant-Colonel and commanded the Cape Town Highlanders Regiment from 1970 to 1983. Plane became involved in the contract security industry 12 years ago and has been with Gray for nine years.

Executive Director—Paul Bell (52)

Bell completed his BA (Maths/Economics) and BAI (Engineering) at Trinity College Dublin in 1971. The majority of Paul's working career has been spent in heavy engineering and construction, initially with the Dorbyl Group and subsequently with Genrec Holdings and Murray & Roberts. He served on the boards of Murray & Roberts Engineering Holdings and Genrec Holdings, and was Chairman of Elgin Engineering, Alloywheels International, Consani Engineering and Gentec.

   Bell joined Gray in June 1998 and became involved with setting up project management systems for the electronics division of the company. He is currently an executive director of the company with responsibility for the United Kingdom and European operations.

Executive Director—Alex De Witt (43)

De Witt has completed several management courses. He joined the South African Defense Force in 1978, leaving in 1991 with the rank of Lieutenant-Colonel. De Witt joined Gray in 1991, initially as regional manager and subsequently as the Managing Director of Gray Security Services (North) (Proprietary) Limited. He was a serving member of the Guarding Advisory Committee of the Security Officers' Board. He is currently an executive director of Gray, responsible for operations in Africa outside of South Africa's borders.

Executive Director—Fanie De Witt (42)

De Witt was the Commanding Officer of the Citizen Force Tank Regiment, Prince Alfred's Guard from 1987 to 1993 and holds the rank of Lieutenant-Colonel. De Witt joined Distillers Corporation in Port Elizabeth in June 1984 and was subsequently promoted to National Product Manager at Distillers Corporation head office. He has completed several management courses including the Programme for Management Development at the University of Stellenbosch. He joined Gray in November 1991 and established Gray in the Eastern Cape. De Witt became an executive director of Gray, with responsibility for the three coastal companies in the group. He currently is the Executive Director responsible for new business development in the Americas.

Early Growth

Gray spread rapidly through the Western Cape region. Aubin believed this growth was possible due to two key factors: a business model with healthy cash flows and minimal capital requirements, and a hiring policy that attracted entrepreneurs. He explained:

> The key is finding the right guy. We would look for someone with some experience in the security industry and who had proven himself as a businessman. We didn't want yes-men, or people who needed a lot of direction. That guy then had to go out and win some contracts before we would even begin operations. He would then be paid a base salary plus 10% of the pretax profits of his business. If he was very successful, and in several cases this happened, he could be getting paid more than I was.
>
> Because we only start spending money once we've already got some business, we have usually been able to achieve positive cash flow within the first year. Our billing system helps with this. We don't pay our staff until the 30th of the month, but our clients pay in advance; on average we receive payment on the seventh of each month for that month's service. This means that we have negative working capital in a business that requires very little in the way of long-term capital.
>
> Of course, not all of our clients like paying in advance, but we have usually been able to negotiate it into our contracts. We point out that we incur an up-front cost during our security audit, i.e., when we examine their facilities and determine with them what their needs are. When that fails, sometimes we can solve the problem with a bit of creativity. In one of our few government contracts, we were told that payment in advance was impossible. During the negotiations we agreed to accept payment at the end of the month, but in return they gave us a one-month deposit!

By 1985, Gray had expanded into three major areas: Cape Town, Durban, and Johannesburg. The company had reached sales of R2.63 million, with plans to expand further in South Africa and elsewhere, all without taking on any additional capital.

Managing Expansion

As Gray expanded, it became clear that the firm needed to develop and implement systems and values throughout the company in order to prevent decentralization from leading to a loss of control (see **Exhibit 8** for an organizational chart). "All our local units are highly autonomous," explained Aubin, "but that is a challenge in and of itself. You have to make sure that they perform well, in terms of cash flow and profitability, and also in terms of protecting and promoting Gray's reputation. We need to be able to tell them what to do, while letting them decide how best to do it." Gray's management concentrated on a number of core policies that could be instilled throughout the group: human resources, integrity, type of service, and financial performance.

Human Resources Management—A Core Process in a Service Company

Staff turnover in the South African security industry was notoriously high, with some industry firms reaching annual levels of 200%. "Most security firms in South Africa are run like paramilitary organizations," explained David Plane, who joined Gray in 1989 from one of its competitors and was appointed CEO in 1995. "I opened a small security firm in Cape Town for Coin Security (one of Gray's competitors) but didn't like the way they treated people." Most industry players saw security guards as plentiful, relatively unskilled, prone to quitting but easily replaced. Antagonistic labor relations therefore characterized much of the industry, with strikes, violence, and pay fraud being common.

EXHIBIT 8
Organizational Chart

Source: Gray Security

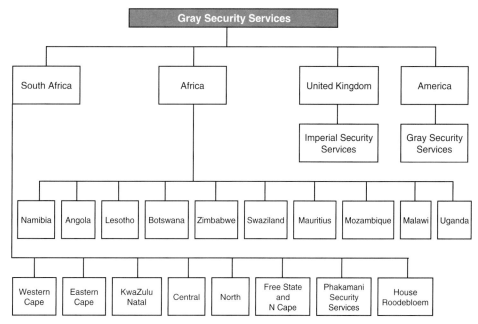

Note: Headcount—16,000 guards worldwide (including 1,000 at imperial Security).

Gray took a contrary approach to human resources. "From the start we wanted to hire, train, and retain the best people throughout the company," explained Jenny Ibbotson, director of human resources. "Although we know we will probably never quite reach that point, our philosophy has always been that we should be able to develop any security guard to become a local area manager." Whenever possible, Gray emphasized promotion from within, and several local managers had risen to a point where Gray sponsored them to open a new regional office.

The structure of promotions also appealed more to entry-level employees looking for longer-term employment. A new Gray guard earned between R1,200 and R1,500 per month. While this compared favorably with other security firms, it was below the level earned by a starting worker in the manufacturing sector and was not enough to live on. By the end of the first year, however, a Gray employee typically earned more than his counterpart in manufacturing did. "It's not unusual for a good employee to receive two or three promotions in his first year," commented Plane. "At that point he's better off with us than with most other employers, and he can see a real future with Gray."

A Gray security guard received more training than did those at any other South African security company. Gray's basic training started at 15 working days, as opposed to an average of five working days for a competitor's. In addition, Gray did between five and 10 working days of on-the-job training and additional class work during the first year of service of an employee. (See **Exhibit 9** for a list of areas in which Gray guards received training.) Training continued throughout an employee's career, including management courses at local business schools as well as industry-specific courses at Gray's own training centers.

Gray also strove to avoid the paramilitary feel of most of its competitors, believing this suited not only its corporate clients' desire for a professional, nonthreatening force but also its employees. Although some uniforms were somewhat military in appearance (see **Exhibit 10** for pictures of typical Gray Security uniforms), most guards wore uniforms more like suits than military garb.

EXHIBIT 9 **Training at Gray Security**

Source: Gray Security.

- The foundation for a successful career with Gray Securities Services rests on a balance between integrating new recruits within a team, whilst encouraging individual initiative.
- Gray has more training centres than any other security company in Africa. Furthermore, great emphasis is placed on ensuring that the training Gray personnel receive remains relevant to Clients' needs.
- All recruits undergo a basic training programme covering practical aspects of security. Prior to the commencement of duties, candidates are familiarised with the specific requirements of the site to which they will be assigned. Formal induction training is mandatory for all Security Officers arriving on site for the first time. On-the-job training is conducted by Supervisors and Managers.
- On site, Gray recruits display the confident, courteous but firm manner required to command respect and co-operation.

Basic Training Curriculum
- Access control
- Loss control
- Communications
- Emergency procedures
- Legal powers of arrest and search
- First-aid
- Safety
- Fires
- Records
- Reports
- Alarm systems
- Self-defence
- Criminal tactics
- Equipment identification
- Public relations
- Junior leadership

Industry Specific Training
- Hotel & Leisure
- Gaming
- Retail
- Mining
- Petro-chemical
- Aviation

Qualified instructors ensure that the highest standards of training are being maintained.

EXHIBIT 10   **Gray Security Uniforms**

Source: Gray Security.

- Gray Security Services' uniforms are designed in accordance with varying environments. Clients are consulted on their individual preferences. This varies from corporate apparel to utility uniforms.
- Gray is synonymous with smart, identifiable uniforms which portray a professional, rather than a militaristic, appearance.

Gray Security Services personnel in corporate uniform (left) and the utility uniform (right).

The result of these efforts was that Gray's annual staff turnover was just 38%, which Ibbotson believed to be the lowest of any major security firm. Gray also felt that it was able to hire and retain a higher caliber of workers.

Integrity—A Key Requirement in the Security Industry

Closely linked to Gray's determination to develop a high-quality workforce was its commitment to integrity on the job. Corruption or theft at one site could affect Gray's reputation throughout the organization. Gray therefore had a very strict policy on employee misconduct. As Plane explained, maintaining integrity in the organization was more complicated than it might seem:

> The temptation of corruption is only part of the challenge. Guards are being paid a small fraction of the value of what they protect, so the temptation is always there. It is fairly common in the industry to find that dishonest employees of the client firm will recruit guards to help them steal. Guards can also come under threat from employees if they won't cooperate and may be naturally reluctant to turn people in if they catch them. So the psychology is a complex problem.

> We try to deal with this in several ways. First, our hiring process screens out anyone with a criminal record. Then, our training includes ethics and measures to detect criminal behavior. Finally, when we design a security system for a client, we make it difficult for any individual guard to have too much control over a given area.
>
> Nothing is foolproof, however, and one of our challenges is often that our clients do not have as strict disciplinary policies as we do. In one case, some of our guards and our client's employees were caught stealing. The client was having some labor difficulties and did not want to press charges against their employees and asked us not to press charges either. We told them we would walk off the site before we would compromise our discipline. We aren't selling uniforms, we're selling honesty, and both our clients and our employees have to know we won't make exceptions.

Plane estimated that roughly 5% of the South African security workforce was fired each year for involvement in crime at the work site.

Segmentation of Security Services

Private security in South Africa consisted of a wide range of segments. Home-security companies offered a private equivalent to the local police force, with home monitors and armed response teams. Other firms concentrated on transporting valuables in armored vehicles. Gray avoided these areas, which were characterized by high levels of violence, and concentrated exclusively on providing integrated security services to commercial sites. Plane explained:

> Our sites vary a great deal in size, ranging from just one guard on duty at a time to over a hundred total staff. In general we aim for contracts involving over 20 of our guards, because those are the ones where we can offer the most added value. We emphasize full service, including handling technology aspects and finding ways to improve security beyond simply supplying a number of guards.

Gray believed that its strategic emphasis on full-service corporate contracts had positioned it as the leading firm for the most attractive contracts. As major companies outsourced activities like security, they were able to pay Gray quite attractive rates and still reduce costs. The vice president of security for a large South African insurance company explained the decision to retain Gray for its head office:

> They certainly aren't cheap. In fact, they may be the most expensive in the industry. But we have almost 8,000 people working here [at this site], and we need both to keep track of that flow and to prevent other security problems like theft. There are at most one or two other firms that could credibly meet our needs, and the costs of having the job done poorly don't stay hidden for long. I get calls every week from people wanting this contract, but when I ask them what their biggest contract is, they have never covered anything nearly this big.

Louis Rademerer, the project manager, explained some of the advantages Gray offered:

> There are 65 guards working on the site, and the [lobby] receptionists are also Gray. Our guards have the training it takes to fit in with an environment like this and to understand all of its security needs. We're also able to design and implement a security system that meets the client's needs better than most of our competitors. Security engineers are good in theory, but they haven't worked behind a desk, so if a client goes to an alarm or monitoring company they often design and implement a system that doesn't fit. We know what works and can integrate human guards and electronic security.

Aubin believed that Gray's commitment to high-quality service, and its strategic emphasis on contracts few other companies could compete for, had been key to the firm's rapid growth. Despite charging premium rates, Gray's annual client retention was 95%, and expansion was often supported by new business from clients who were Gray customers in other regions. Gray's customers clearly felt they were getting good value.

Financial Performance—Nothing to Worry About?

Gray monitored several key metrics to ensure that its various operating companies were meeting the necessary performance objectives (see **Exhibits 11** and **12** for Gray financial information). This enabled the company to detect any slippage in performance by a particular region or manager and to address the issue early without micromanaging a local operation. Plane explained the measurements he examined most carefully:

> First, there's growth in turnover. This is closely linked to growth in employees; although we sell services, not people, manpower is by far our greatest cost. Gross margin tells us how efficiently those people are being managed. We know margins will vary from region to region, but tracking a given region over time helps us keep track of performance. Staff turnover, which is running at about 38% per year, helps us track how satisfied our employees are. Sometimes we can take action to reduce staff turnover throughout the organization, which can save a lot of money. One problem has been a lot of employees wanting to quit just before Christmas and then hope to be rehired afterwards. We've recently implemented a policy not to rehire guards who quit before Christmas. Finally, cash collections are very important to our business model. We collect 70% of revenues for a given month's service by the seventh of the month.

Gray's careful strategic focus had enabled the firm to grow rapidly through the 1980s and 1990s. The company had not only done so without recourse to additional equity capital, it had built up a cash reserve of R8.8 million.

Brait Capital Partners—A Local Private Equity Player

Brait Capital Partners was one of a relatively small number of private equity firms in South Africa. Brait was currently investing its second private equity fund (Fund II). This fund had investor commitments of $150 million, 80% of which were from U.S. investors.

EXHIBIT 11   Profit History and Forecast (R'000)

Source: Gray Security.

	Profit Forecast for Year Ending 31 August 1999	Year Ended 31 August 1998	Years Ended Last Day of February			
			1997	1996	1995	1994
Turnover	517,063	425,917	304,434	215,353	163,490	128,860
Operating income before interest	46,289	32,927	16,655	6,747	6,636	4,312
Interest paid	15,771	25,509	1,778	1,807	1,292	719
Shareholders' loans[a]	12,671	23,202	—	—	—	—
Other	3,100	2,307	1,778	1,807	1,292	719
Net income before taxation	30,518	7,418	14,877	4,940	5,344	3,593
Taxation	(10,681)	(1,994)	(5,888)	(1,706)	(3,231)	(1,085)
Atttributable earnings	19,837	5,424	8,989	3,234	2,113	2,508

[a]The Gray group achieved significant growth in turnover and operating income before interest paid over the last three years. Despite this fact, the Gray group reported substantially lower attributable earnings for the year ended 31 August 1998. This was solely due to the financial restructuring which took place during August 1997 which resulted in an interest charge of R23,202 million on shareholders' loans for the year ended 31 August 1998 and results in an interest charge of R12,671 million on shareholders' loans for the year ending 31 August 1999. In terms of this restructuring, structured loan agreements were entered into on 1 September 1997 between Gray and certain of its shareholders, to the value of R124 million. In order to present comparable results, the attributable earnings for the year ended 31 August 1998 and the year ending 31 August 1999 have been adjusted to represent the earnings that would have been generated by the group (i.e., absent higher interest charges) had the restructuring not taken place.

EXHIBIT 12
Balance Sheet (R000)

Source: Gray Security.

	31 August 1998[a]
Capital Employed	
Share capital	54,104
Distributable reserves	4,993
Shareholders' equity	59,097
Long-term liabilities and loans	111,722
	170,819
Employment of Capital	
Property, plant and equipment	25,069
Goodwill[b]	159,066
Deferred taxation	4,345
Trademark	34,289
Net current liabilities	(51,950)
Current assets	31,886
Inventories	312
Accounts receivable	22,752
Funds on call	7,200
Bank balances and cash	1,622
Current liabilities	83,836
Accounts payable	73,077
Taxation	5,902
Bank overdraft	4,857
	170,819

[a]Due to massive restructuring, prior year balance sheets were not comparable.
[b]It was anticipated that goodwill would be depreciated over 30 years. This depreciation would have *no* tax effects.

EXHIBIT 12
(Continued) Cash Flow Statement for the Year Ended 31 August 1998 (R000)

Source: Gray Security.

	Group 1998
Cash Flows from Operating Activities	
Cash generated from operations	84,796
Interest received	2,067
Dividends received	—
Interest paid	(25,226)
Taxation paid	(83)
Cash Flows Expended on Investment Activities	(214,893)
Additions to property, plant and equipment	(20,369)
Acquisition of goodwill	(104,968)
Acquisition of trademarks	(34,289)
Proceeds on disposal of property, plant and equipment	1,714
Acquisition of subsidiaries	(58,103)
Increase in loans to subsidiary companies	—
Interest in joint ventures	1,122
Increase in loans from joint venture companies	—
Cash Flows from Financing Activities	157,304
Proceeds on issue of share capital and share premium	54,104
Increase in long-term liabilities	660
Increase in long-term portion of shareholders' loans	102,540
Cash and Cash Equivalents at End of Year	3,965
Total Cash and Cash Equivalents Comprise:	
Funds on call	7,200
Bank balances and cash	1,622
Bank overdrafts	(4,857)
Total Cash and Cash Equivalents	3,965

Eduardo Garcia, a partner in the Johannesburg office, had joined the firm in April 1997. He explained the firm's origin and strategy:

> Private equity has been, and remains, a neglected asset class in South Africa. Contrary to what you see in much of the developed world, in South Africa there isn't a lot of money chasing deals. On the other hand, the deal flow itself is much less developed, so you have to be more creative about finding opportunities. I think what we're best at is sitting down face-to-face with people and negotiating deals. Currently we're involved in fairly traditional venture capital investing, but we are planning on raising a larger fund which will seek to capture the hidden value in a lot of South Africa's conglomerates.

In April 1997, Gray hired Brait to help it identify a value-adding "black empowerment partner." Black empowerment partners (BEPs) were shareholder groups, often affiliated with trade unions, created as part of the effort to redistribute wealth in postapartheid South Africa. Such partners typically acquired stakes in white-owned companies at a discount to market value, and in some cases received board representation as well. Having a BEP shareholder was not a statutory requirement but was considered an advantage when doing business with the government or with companies with a significant dependence on government contracts.

Although Aubin believed that bringing in a BEP was important for Gray, there was no urgency behind the search. Aubin explained:

> We have almost no government business and aren't that eager to get more, as the government isn't the most reliable when it comes to paying on schedule. So, while we wanted a black empowerment partner as a significant shareholder, we felt we could be fairly selective. We didn't want to give away a board seat unnecessarily, and we didn't want anyone who would have to borrow money in order to buy our equity. That left us with about seven groups to look at.

The search for an appropriate BEP also served to develop a relationship between a leading South African operating company and one of its few true VCs. Gray wanted to develop a relationship with Brait with a view toward potential fund-raising abroad, while Brait was naturally interested in developing ties with a fast-growing firm with strong cash flows.

Financial Restructuring—Reshuffling the Deck

While working with Gray to identify BEP candidates, Garcia became interested in negotiating a buyout of the firm. He recalled the factors he felt formed a basis for such a deal:

> Gray was a simple, well-run business with fairly predictable cash flows and good prospects. Working capital was negative, and the business wasn't asset intensive. This suggested to us that the firm could support a good deal of leverage. Furthermore, Gray's record of very low levels of labor unrest reassured us that unpleasant surprises on that front were unlikely.

Aubin originally resisted the idea of a buyout. "The same factors that made Gray attractive from a buyout perspective meant that they didn't really need capital, and the owners were very jealous of the business," Garcia recalled. "I knew we would have to devise a deal structure that appealed to them if we were going to make this work."

Garcia looked carefully at other factors that might influence the deal. Experience with other South African entrepreneurs had taught him that a refinancing could prove attractive even when founders wanted to retain control of a business and there was little or no need for additional capital. Some shareholders inevitably wanted to achieve liquidity on at least part of their investment, and Garcia knew that some of Gray's original shareholders were now less involved with the business and might want to cash out.

Garcia also knew that Aubin wanted to increase Gray's international presence, which was complicated somewhat by South Africa's exchange controls. A local Gray entity in a foreign country would be able to access international capital markets in a way that Gray itself could not under its current structure, most obviously through a local listing in that country, but also simply by borrowing from local institutions that might not wish to lend money to a South African firm. Aubin had also expressed an interest in motivating Gray's managers with equity, either through grants or options, and Garcia knew a refinancing might facilitate such an incentive system.

Garcia approached Aubin with an innovative deal structure that he felt would meet the needs of Gray's various shareholders. (See **Exhibit 13** for a diagram of the refinancing structure.) A new company (Newco) would purchase Gray's business operations for R140 million,[11] of which R71 million would be cash with the remainder on loan account. Brait would provide R55 million to Newco, of which R24 million would be an equity investment in Newco, on shareholders' loan account, and the rest would be a conventional loan. Another 16 million of surplus cash would be put toward the purchase price of Gray.

The ownership of Newco would be structured in a way that would allow certain of Gray's existing shareholders to retain exposure to further upside and would also enable executives to acquire equity. There would also be an allocation of equity to employees for a nominal consideration. Fund II acquired an effective equity stake of 24.5% of Newco; employees received 15%, with the balance of 60.5% going to certain existing shareholders and the management team.

A significant component of Brait's Fund II was based offshore. Thus, if Gray wanted to expand overseas through acquisitions, it would be possible to raise capital from the offshore component of Fund II and through access to Fund II's offshore investor base. The transaction structure also proved to be tax effective due to a mismatch on the deductibility of interest paid on the loans by Gray and the taxation on the interest received by the providers of the loans.

[11] Details, such as the final purchase price and consequent shareholdings, would be finalized after negotiation between the parties.

EXHIBIT 13
Structure of the Gray Group after the Brait Investment

Source: Gray Security.

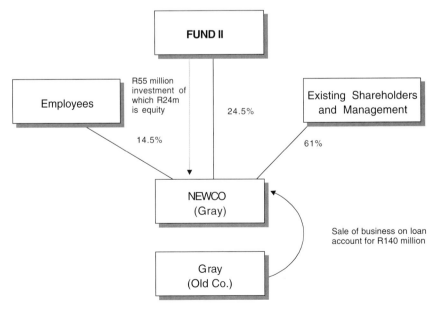

Note: The interest rate on the loan was 22%, the South African banking prime lending rate (the lowest interest rate charged to AAA corporate clients).

Aubin and Gray's other shareholders agreed to the restructuring, which was carried out on August 30, 1997. As anticipated, Gray's vigorous cash flows enabled it to service its debt obligations, and the company maintained its level of annual growth. Aubin felt, however, that the restructuring was only the first step necessary toward positioning Gray for the long-term future.

Looking to the Future

Despite his success to date, Aubin felt more needed to be done:

> I am concerned about globalization. International companies are trying to cut back on their number of suppliers, especially in noncore activities like security, so there is an increasing trend toward regional or global contracts. South African Breweries recently asked us if we could provide security for their brewery in Poland. The poor company [that had been providing security previously] didn't know what hit them. I don't want to find Gray in the reverse situation.
>
> If we manage it right, globalization can really work for us, because our reputation will help us compete for these big contracts and make us an attractive partner for other firms. In the aviation industry, for example, we have a reputation for being very reliable. Gray guards 97% of all foreign airlines flying into South Africa. That's a strong position to be in.

Gray had expanded outside South Africa with the acquisition of Imperial Security Services in the United Kingdom in September 1998, as well as organic ventures elsewhere in Europe. More recently, Gray had sent one of its senior managers to the United States to develop business there. "The guy who went to the United States prepared for nine months to go there," Aubin explained. Gray hoped through organic expansion or strategic acquisition to be able to transform itself from a regional power to a global competitor.

One step Aubin was considering was an initial public offering (IPO) of Gray Security shares on the South African stock exchange (see **Exhibit 14** for stock exchange data). There were several strategic advantages to doing so, he explained:

> An IPO would probably be a good idea even without the need to grow globally. It would provide our employee shareholders with liquidity and would also be an ideal opportunity to bring in a good black empowerment partner. But globalization is what makes it particularly attractive. Public companies are more transparent, which enhances their credibility with

EXHIBIT 14   **Data on the Johannesburg Stock Exchange**

Source: "Guide to World Equity Markets," Salomon Smith Barney, 1998; "World Stock Exchange Factbook," 1994/1995, 1998; Johannesburg Stock Exchange, <www.jse.co.za>.

	1990	1991	1992	1993	1994	1995	1996	1997	1998
Number of companies listed	781	740	683	647	639	638	626	642	668
Total Market Capitalization (US$ million), year-end	167,311	190,074	164,631	220,869	252,450	258,620	266,235	245,072	178,525
JSE All Share Index	2,719.74	3,440.30	3,258.80	4,893.00	5,866.90	6,228.40	6,657.53	6,202.31	5,433.22
Total Market P/E Multiple	9.35	12.64	12.61	18.28	18.90	16.60	15.00	16.90	n/a

certain clients. For example, their credibility would be enhanced with the central bank, which would improve Gray's prospects of getting central bank approval to acquire offshore entities.[12] As a public company we would also be in a position to acquire another public company abroad, through a share exchange, and might then be able to raise capital abroad.

Gray had retained the investment banker Merrill Lynch to examine the prospects of a local IPO. A Merrill Lynch analyst had prepared earnings estimates for Gray over the next few years and a table of comparable companies that investors might use to value Gray during an IPO (see **Exhibits 15** through **17**).

Aubin knew, however, that an IPO in and of itself would do only so much to position Gray as a global firm. It was not clear how strong a currency rand-denominated equity would be in acquiring firms with hard-currency earnings. Moreover, there were larger firms already beginning to acquire smaller players.

Aubin smiled as he completed the walk back to his office and closed the door behind him. Gray's journey over the past years had not been easy, but he and his team had succeeded through a clear strategic vision and hard work. The problems to come were of a somewhat different nature. The direction and financing of growth was going to be a bigger challenge than ever.

[12] In January 1999, the South African Central Bank maintained strict exchange controls. This meant that Gray had to seek approval for any investment abroad or any transfer of funds to offshore destinations. While a very small number of South African firms, including conglomerate Anglo American Corporation, were considering listing their shares on stock exchanges abroad, gaining approval for a similar move would have been very difficult for a small firm like Gray.

EXHIBIT 15
Analysis of Main Competitors

Source: Brait Capital Partners.

Gray has three significant competitors. They are Fidelity Guards, Coin Security and Springbok Patrols.

Fidelity Guards is a private equity investment of Corvest which is controlled by Rand Merchant Bank. It offers a range of security services from cash-in-transit protection through to contract guarding. They enjoy a solid reputation and are Gray's most serious competitor. Fidelity is diversified, offering security services such as cash-in-transit protection, armed response and contract security. Consequently, it is not considered by Gray to be a significant threat.

Coin Security is organized and run as a para-military organization. Many of its staff are housed in barrack-type accommodations, which has allowed labor dissatisfaction to foment. In December 1994 there was a violent incident of labor unrest at one of Coin's hostels. Coin has a high profile in the cash-in-transit market but is not able to effectively compete in high-quality service provision in the contract security market, as it is said to be losing focus. Coin appears to be losing market share in the contract security market.

Springbok Patrols are at the bottom end of the market. It has a poor reputation, particularly for its alleged abusive labor practices. It is able to offer guards at a low cost but with limited service. Gray does not consider Springbok to be a serious competitor at its end of the market. A substantial portion of Springbok Patrols has recently been sold to DLJ's South Africa fund.

There are no security companies listed on the Johannesburg Stock Exchange that are directly comparable to Gray. The sentry security/armed division of Klipton focuses primarily on the provision of domestic security.

EXHIBIT 16A   Valuation Comparisons: Local Firms

Source: Compiled from I-Net consensus estimates, Merrill Lynch estimates.

Company	Share Price (R)	Equity Beta	FY1998 EPS	FY1999 EPS	Historic P/E	Forward P/E	Market Cap ZARm	Long-Term Debt ZARm	D/(D+E)	Security Earnings	Guarding Earnings
Super Group	1,170	1.14	5.23	71	22.4x	16.5x	3,471	367.9	9.6%	15%	1%
Servest	250	0.73	9.6	15	26.0x	16.7x	280	6.9	2.4	40	15
Bidvest	4,640	0.99	185.6	270	25.0x	17.2x	13,019	35.0	0.3	1	1
Klipton	630	0.70	55.3	66	11.4x	9.5x	228	21.2	8.5	95	5
Paramed	325	NA	19.2	24	16.9x	13.5x	167	7.4	4.2	90	10
Average					20.3x	14.7x			5.0		
Gray Security										100%	100%

Note: Since there were no listed companies that were directly comparable to Gray, the companies above were used by Merrill Lynch. As a matter of reference, Super Group was a transportation company, Servest was a diversified services company, Bidvest was a conglomerate, and both Klipton and Paramed's operations were mainly in the personal security industry.

485

EXHIBIT 16B Valuation Comparison: European Firms

Source: Compiled from Merrill Lynch, Worldscope, Bloomberg data. EPS = Earnings per Share; EV = Enterprise Value Long-term debt on . . . [a]3/31/98 [b]12/31/98 [c]6/30/98.

	Market Cap £m (12/31/98) Price (p) (~12/31/98)	LT Debt £m 12/31/98	D/(D+E) 12/31/98	Equity Beta	Year End	Pretax £m	Tax %	EPS p	P/E	Net Div p	Yield	EPS Growth	EV/ Sales	EV/ EBITDA
AEA[a] (AEATF) B-4-3-7 Reduce/q/	581 673p	35.0	5.7%	1.06	31/03/98	29.0	31	23.5	28.6	9.6	1.40%	19.90%	2.0	15.7
					31/03/99E	33.7	32	26.9	25.0	10.75	1.6	14.5	1.7	13.5
					31/03/00E	38.2	32	31.1	21.6	12.0	1.8	15.6	1.6	11.4
					31/03/01E	42.7	32	34.0	19.8	13.2	2.0	9.3	1.4	10.6
Aggreko[b] (ARGKF) C-1-2-7 Buy/q/	480 184p	97.8	16.9%	0.71	31/03/97	33.4	39	7.9	23.3	3.5	1.9		3.4	7.8
					31/12/97	33.2	35	8.2	22.4	3.8	2.1	3.8	3.4	7.8
					31/12/98E	37.0	37	8.9	20.7	4.0	2.2	8.5	3.3	7.1
					31/12/99E	40.0	37	9.6	19.2	4.4	2.4	7.9	3.0	6.5
Atkins, W.S.[a] (WATKF) B-3-2-7 Neutral/q/	454 493p	3.0	0.7%	0.92	31/03/98	30.5	39	20.2	24.4	8.1	1.6	16.8	0.9	11.2
					31/03/99E	34.0	39	22.7	21.7	9.2	1.9	12.4	0.8	11.1
					31/03/00E	36.2	38	24.5	20.1	10.0	2.0	7.9	0.7	0.8
					31/03/01E	39.0	37	26.6	18.5	11.0	2.2	8.6	0.6	8.5
Bunzl 240[b] (BULNF) B-3-2-7 Neutral/q/	1,078 240p	117.3	9.8%	0.82	31/12/97	123.7	35	17.6	13.6	6.8	2.8	7.3	0.7	8.1
					31/12/98E	130.0	35	18.5	13.0	7.3	3.0	5.1	0.6	7.3
					31/12/99E	136.0	35	19.1	12.6	7.8	3.3	3.2	0.6	6.8
Capita[b] (CTAGF) B-2-1-7 Accumulate/q/	969 522p	0.2	0.0%	0.95	31/12/97	18.3	32	6.5	80.3	2.1	0.4	35.4	5.5	45.0
					31/12/98E	26.5	32	8.8	59.3	2.8	0.5	35.4	3.8	30.6
					31/12/99E	33.8	32	11.2	46.6	3.3	0.6	27.3	3.0	23.0
					31/12/00	38.9	32	12.9	40.5	3.9	0.7	15.2	2.5	19.8
Davis Service[b] (DVSVF) B-1-2-7 Buy/q/	500 361p	49.2	9.0%	0.91	31/12/97	44.3	32	21.9	16.5	11.3	3.11	15.5	1.4	4.5
					31/12/98E	53.0	32	26.0	13.9	12.5	3.5	18.6	1.4	4.2
					31/12/99E	56.0	32	27.5	13.1	13.7	3.8	5.8	1.4	3.9
					31/12/00E	60.0	32	29.5	12.2	14.7	4.1	7.3	1.3	3.6
Hays[c] (HAYPF) A-3-2-7 Neutral/q/	4,948 578p	217.7	4.2%	1.01	30/06/98	201.2	28	17.0	343.1	5.35	0.9	28.9	3.3	19.9
					30/06/99E	233.5	29	19.5	29.6	6.15	1.1	15.0	2.8	17.3
					30/06/00E	262.0	29	21.6	26.8	7.08	1.2	10.8	2.4	15.4
					30/06/01E	294.5	30	24.0	24.1	8.13	1.4	11.1	2.1	13.9
Mitie[a] (MTIGF) B-2-2-7 Accumulate/q/	195 147p	5.2	2.6%	0.69	31/03/97	8.2	34	4.0	36.8	1.0	0.7	24.8	0.9	17.2
					31/03/98	11.1	32	5.1	28.8	1.25	0.9	27.5	0.8	12.4
					31/03/99E	14.0	32	6.3	23.3	1.5	1.0	23.5	0.7	9.6
					31/03/00E	16.5	32	7.4	19.9	1.8	1.2	17.5	0.6	8.0

(continued)

EXHIBIT 16B (Continued)

	Market Cap £m (12/31/98) Price (p) (~12/31/98)	LT Debt £m 12/31/98	D/(D+E) 12/31/98	Equity Beta	Year End	Pretax £m	Tax %	EPS p	P/E	Net Div p	Yield	EPS Growth	EV/ Sales	EV/ EBITD
Rentokil[b]	13,499	342.1	2.5%	1.00	31/12/97	417.0	29	10.3	45.8	3.06	0.6	20.7	4.8	23.3
(RTOIF)					31/12/98E	496.0	30	12.2	38.9	3.64	0.8	17.9	4.6	20.0
B-2-2-7					31/12/99E	586.0	30	14.2	33.3	4.37	0.9	16.7	4.2	17.4
Accumulate/q/	473p				31/12/00E	661.0	31	15.9	29.8	5.24	1.1	11.8	3.8	15.6
Serco[b]	735	49.0	6.3%	1.01	31/12/97	22.0	343	23.9	50.9	6.4	0.5	27.1	1.6	30.6
(SRCPF)					31/12/98	26.5	31	28.8	42.3	7.4	0.6	20.5	1.3	26.9
B-3-2-7					31/12/99E	30.5	32	33.9	35.9	8.5	0.7	17.7	1.1	20.2
Neutral/q/	1,217p				31/12/00	34.0	32	39.1	31.1	9.7	0.8	15.3	1.0	17.4
Williams[b]	2,282	824.4	26.5%	0.73	31/12/96	243.0	34	23.5	13.4	15.1	4.8	11.0	1.4	8.0
(WIHGF)					31/12/97	285.1	34	22.4	14.1	15.8	5.0	-4.7	1.5	8.6
B-3-2-7					31/12/98E	306.0	34	23.2	13.6	16.5	5.2	3.6	1.4	7.3
Neutral/q/	316p				31/12/99E	306.0	34	24.5	12.9	17.2	5.4	5.6	1.4	7.3
Market Average			7.6%		31/12/97				22.0		2.20%	6.00%		
(FT Non-financials)					31/12/98E				22.0		2.4	0.0		
Estimates based on					31/12/99E				20.7		2.6	6.0		
ML Analysts Forecasts					31/12/00E				19.2		2.8	8.0		

EXHIBIT 17
Gray Earnings Forecast

Source: Merrill Lynch estimates.

	FY1998A	FY1999E	%Δ	FY2000E	%Δ	FY2001E	%Δ
Turnover	425	530	25	661	25	819	24
South Africa	350	412	18	494	20	593	20
Africa	23	53	130	69	30	90	30
United Kingdom/Other	52	65	25	98	50	137	40
Operating income before interest	33	47	42	60	28	76	26
South Africa	26	37	42	46	23	56	21
Africa	7	7	6	9	30	12	30
United Kingdom	0	2	NA	5	112	8	68
Interest paid/received	−26	−16	−37	1	NA	5	460
Net income before taxation	7	31	314	61	99	81	32
Taxation	2	11	428	18	74	24	32
Attributable earnings	5	20	272	43	112	56	32

Module

V

Growth, Harvesting and Exit

This module illuminates entrepreneurial financing challenges at a number of successful and not-so-successful later-stage international ventures. "Later stage" does not necessarily mean "old." Rather, it means that a venture's basic business model has been proven, in which case the questions become not so much whether, but in what form, the venture will survive and how its further expansion can be financed. The module examines initial public offerings and trade sales as well as such alternative ways of financing growth as franchising. It explores how a public offering affects the management challenges in an entrepreneurial firm and examines issues involved in timing the sale of part or all of a venture.

There are several reasons for including this module. First, aspiring entrepreneurs are often preoccupied with *starting* entrepreneurial ventures. They see the short-term opportunities and challenges clearly, but have only a vague idea of what will happen in the long run. In this module, entrepreneurship is shown to require a long breath and willingness to be involved in a venture for many years. Expansion and harvesting decisions might seem far out in the future to aspiring entrepreneurs, but there is much to be learned about successfully seeding trees from looking at fast-growing and more mature ones. Early choices about which opportunities to pursue and under what terms to assemble resources have a big impact on the likelihood of a venture's success.

Second, aspiring entrepreneurs should understand that an initial public offering is not itself an exit event. There is a new imperative for further growth combined with stability following an IPO. The module discusses how entrepreneurial firms try to achieve this and how they fail or succeed as publicly listed entities. Third, entrepreneurs need to know their limits. A time might come when it is best to harvest an investment either because the context and opportunity are changing or because the entrepreneur simply is not a great manager for a larger enterprise. Fourth, this module is also useful in tying International Entrepreneurship to the study of established firms. Two cases in the module, TelePizza and Infosys, are concerned with companies that are still managed by their founders but also large and publicly listed, making them comparable to the companies typically studied in finance, international management, and strategy.

The module reviews and deepens three central themes of *International Entrepreneurship:* the relevance of local context; the importance of a global perspective on opportunities; and the importance of a global perspective on resources. These central themes are shown to apply to mature as well as start-up firms. The module also introduces a number of extensions regarding access to resources in more mature entrepreneurial firms. This being the last module of the book, many of the cases have an integrative character and each focuses on a range of topics. Finally, the module seeks to instill two attitudinal objectives. The cases show that entrepreneurship is often a long-term endeavor that requires passion and persistence over many years. The case of Infosys is an example. Second, the module seeks to inspire by describing a number of entrepreneurs who were eventually successful, but only after they overcame a range of difficulties. Examples include VacationSpot, TelePizza, and TCS.

A global perspective on opportunities is particularly important for more mature entrepreneurial ventures that have proven their business models domestically. Local context is relevant not just to the frequency and form of entrepreneurship but also to harvesting decisions. Experience suggests that entrepreneurial firms' international expansion exhibits a strong overconfidence bias. This can be quite costly and even lead a firm to fail. A global perspective on resources also matters. Although more mature entrepreneurial firms might be generating rather than consuming cash, they are also large enough to raise substantial outside equity on public markets for further expansion or as a stepping-stone to harvesting by the founders.

This module introduces four extensions to the topic of access to resources. First, it examines how franchising can be used to accelerate growth and considers its drawbacks. Certain business models such as restaurants or other localized service operations permit a gradual rollout, site by site. These sites are capital intensive but offer relatively steady cash flows once customers have shown acceptance of the basic business model, making it attractive for the entrepreneur to accelerate growth by enabling local site operators to become site owners. Since capital outlays are limited because of franchising, the entrepreneur needs to raise less external financing and can typically retain a larger ownership than in a firm of comparable size that does not use franchising. The module shows that franchising can be a useful concept, particularly in country contexts in which the market for private equity is not well developed. The TelePizza case provides a powerful illustration.

Second, entrepreneurial firms' use of leasing is discussed. Apart from tax considerations, a lease might make sense if it is less costly and time-consuming to sign a standardized lease than to negotiate a long-term secured loan. One can argue that, particularly in volatile contexts, it is optimal for an entrepreneurial company to keep debt levels low. High levels of debt to equity might expose a firm to hold-up by banks, particularly in emerging markets. Also, it might be the case that at the same cost banks are less sophisticated at assessing the value of an asset to be financed than leasing companies are at assessing the value of an asset to be leased. In summary, the use of financial leases might enable more flexible and faster growth of a young company. The TCS case serves as an example.

Third, the module examines the reasons for an initial public offering (IPO) for an entrepreneurial firm. These can include raising equity, providing a stepping-stone towards partial or complete divestment by the entrepreneur, establishing a public market value for the firm to facilitate employee compensation, or simply to gain visibility. Aspiring entrepreneurs sometimes think of an IPO as a final goal of their entrepreneurial aspirations. The module shows that an IPO is typically just a stepping-stone towards liquidity for an entrepreneur. Also, an IPO often changes the nature of the opportunity set for an entrepreneurial firm. Predictability of earnings and steadiness of business model suddenly become more important than experimentation and freewheeling creativity. The pressure this shift puts on organizational culture is not to be underestimated, particularly in contexts with a relatively small and young public equity system.

Fourth, the motives for a U.S. listing (via depository receipts) and its impact on a firm domiciled in an emerging market are examined. Listing a firm in the United States or United Kingdom is typically perceived to signal the performance and quality of governance of the listing firm. The listing can also raise a firm's visibility with customers and suppliers in the country in which it lists. In addition, the listing can facilitate acquisitions of and by local firms as well as option-based employee compensation. These aspects can be particularly important for entrepreneurial firms that seek to accelerate growth. Listing is not without cost, however, and entrepreneurs need to make trade-off decisions. The Infosys case provides an interesting example.

Finally, the module looks at how entrepreneurs should approach the sale of their companies. Apart from the desire to cash out, a sale might be driven by a changing competitive context or a mismatch between the entrepreneur's capabilities and the nature of the growing firm. Case analysis will typically compare various possibilities such as an initial public offering, a trade sale, and a sale to a financial buyer. The module examines harvesting conflicts between venture capital investors and entrepreneurs as well as merger negotiations between entrepreneurial firms. Early planning of a harvesting decision improves the yield for the entrepreneur. The cases on TCS, VacationSpot, and Mandic provide useful insights in this regard. There is also an opportunity to establish links to cases in earlier modules that had associated with them possible harvesting decisions; Internet Securities (Module 1), Infox (Module 2), and QI-Tech (Module 3) come to mind.

Cases in this Module

This module consists of six cases. The first case focuses on TCS, a successful air-express company in Pakistan. The case provides an encouraging, yet realistic, look at Pakistan. It is the only case in this volume set in a predominantly Islamic country. The founder has succeeded in building a sizable company despite serious obstacles, including pressure from the public postal system, an environment prone to corruption, and a nonexistent market for venture capital. The firm has largely followed an internal financing strategy and made extensive use of leasing contracts. The case date is September 14, 2001. In the aftermath of the terrorist attacks in the United States on September 11, the founder is faced with considerable uncertainty. He also encounters a number of questions regarding further expansion and is beginning to think about diversifying his personal wealth, which is concentrated almost entirely in TCS. Analysis of the case must examine whether and how TCS should expand in Pakistan, whether geographic expansion into other countries makes sense and how these decisions are tied to harvesting considerations.[1,2]

[1] The insight from the TCS case is consistent with recent research that suggests that reinvestment of profits by entrepreneurs is influenced by the quality of local property rights. Johnson, Simon, John McMillan, and Christopher Woodruff. 2002. Property Rights and Finance. *American Economic Review* (5): 1335–1356.

[2] The case can be linked to other cases on countries in which property rights are weak and the context is volatile (e.g., Capital Alliance and Georgia Glass and Mineral Water (Module 3)). The case also has ties to other cases concerned with harvesting decisions (e.g., TelePizza and VacationSpot (this module)). Finally, the case has parallels with Mobilecom Tokyo (Module 3) and Gray (Module 4), both of which were financed primarily through reinvestment of profits during their early years.

The second case of the module focuses on an entrepreneurial success story, the creation of TelePizza, Spain's largest pizza chain. An initial equity investment of $100,000 in 1988 turned into a cash return of more than $300 million for the founder ten years later. As in the Gray Security case in the previous module, analysis shows that there are attractive opportunities in seemingly plain industries for entrepreneurs who are ingenious and disciplined. It also reveals that TelePizza achieved its impressive growth through a unique positioning of pizza as "home food" in the untapped Spanish market. The company used franchising to accelerate its growth.[3] The case also illustrates the new challenges that face an entrepreneurial company as it goes public. At the time of the case TelePizza has been public for about two years and sales growth and earnings management have clearly become issues for the entrepreneur. Case analysis must examine how TelePizza can expand to sustain its aggressive growth strategy. Options include further domestic expansion, international expansion and expansion through other fast-food concepts.[4]

In the third case the feasibility of a buy-out of a dental equipment manufacturer, Sirona, from conglomerate Siemens is considered. Sirona's home base is in Germany, but it also has manufacturing operations in the United States. This case serves two purposes. First, it provides a review of entrepreneurial buy-out transactions, which were covered earlier in this volume. Case analysis must examine how realistic certain growth assumptions in the case are and how costs can be reduced once an entrepreneurial leader takes over. Second, case analysis must focus on how to assemble a management team capable of leading the firm after the buy-out. There are questions about the ideal profiles of these managers and how such managers might be identified, hired, and compensated.[5]

The fourth case of the module presents another harvesting case, this one involving a merger. VacationSpot.com and Rent-A-Holiday, two firms active in the leisure-lodging rental market, were started at the same time but in different locations, VacationSpot.com in Seattle and Rent-A-Holiday in Brussels. Pairs of entrepreneurs lead both companies. Although Brussels-based Rent-A-Holiday has more listings, the most recent valuation of VacationSpot.com is nine times higher. Rent-A-Holiday is strong in Europe, VacationSpot.com in the United States.

At the time of the case the two companies are holding their first merger negotiations. The case demonstrates that differences in country context can lead to significantly different valuations. Both firms are similar in nature, but at the time of funding the venture capital market in the United States was more competitive and average valuations were higher. Also, the U.S. firm's forecasts were much rosier than the Belgian firm's modest forecasts. Case analysis should examine whether it would have made sense for the entrepreneurs at Rent-A-Holiday to pursue a different funding strategy early in the life of

---

[3] A technical note on franchising can be used in conjunction with the case. Gompers, Paul, and Catherine Coneely. 1997. *A Note on Franchising (9-297-108)*. Boston: Harvard Business School Publishing.

[4] The TelePizza case can be tied to Gray (Module 4) and Infosys (this module), which also examine highly successful entrepreneurial firms in service industries in which consistent and effective management of human resources is of great importance. Gray and TelePizza demonstrate that an entrepreneur with considerable prior management experience does particularly well in this type of business. The TelePizza case can also be linked to Signature Security (Module 2), Spotfire (Module 3), and Jinwoong (Module 4) with which it shares international expansion issues.

[5] The case can be tied to other cases on entrepreneurial buyouts (e.g., Butler Capital, Ducati, and Signature Security (Module 2)). The Sirona case also has parallels with the cases on Singulus (Module 1) and Absolute Sensors (Module 2), in which the entrepreneurs had to negotiate deals with established firms.

their venture. The case also lends itself well to negotiation analysis and simulation. Case analysis reveals that even though valuations of the two companies differ considerably, a merger might make sense. Thus, both sides need to understand each other's objectives and must look for common ground.[6]

The module's fifth case focuses once again on a public company. From humble beginnings, its founders grew Infosys, one of the most impressive software companies in India, to revenues of $70 million in 1998. Case analysis should examine the drivers of Infosys's performance. Overall, the case offers an encouraging perspective on entrepreneurial opportunities in emerging markets.

Infosys is already listed on the Bombay Stock Exchange and is now considering listing on either Nasdaq or the NYSE. Case analysis must examine whether it makes sense for Infosys to list in the U.S. and if yes, on which exchange. The case also permits discussion of how the U.S. listing will most likely affect Infosys's cost of capital. A technical note on depository receipts provides further reading on the subject of cross-border listings.[7] Finally, Infosys offers an interesting insight into how international expansion can almost break a company. Infosys almost failed under its old business model when it performed most of its services on site in industrialized countries. Only after the company developed a new approach to software development and performed most of its work in India did its fortunes improve. A published video offers reflections by CEO Narayana N. Murthy.[8,9]

Mandic, the sixth case in this module, also focuses on harvesting. The case describes an online access provider in São Paolo that has grown from humble beginnings to a sizable subscriber base. In 1998 GP, a private equity investor, wants to sell its entire stake in Mandic. The entrepreneur must decide what to do with his own stake: hold, sell part, or sell nothing. Overall, analysis suggests that a global perspective on alternative opportunities and on access to new resources should be considered in the entrepreneur's harvesting decision and that harvesting is rarely a single-step decision. The case also highlights the differences between local and national contexts. Mandic operates only in São Paolo and analysis reveals that economic factors in São Paolo are, on average, much more favorable than in Brazil. This suggests that sometimes it is not enough for an entrepreneur to examine just the national context; local context must also be considered.[10]

---

[6] The case can be tied to QI-Tech (Module 3), in which an initial negotiation between the entrepreneur and his Chinese joint venture partner failed because it was not well prepared. The case can also be tied to Spotfire (Module 3), which also involves differences in start-up valuations by venture capitalists in Europe and the United States. Case analysis suggests that these differences were caused by a much smaller supply of venture capital and by entrepreneurs' differing expectations.

[7] Kuemmerle, Walter. 2002. *A Note on Depository Receipts (803-026)*. Boston: Harvard Business School Publishing.

[8] Kuemmerle, Walter. 2001. *Narayana N. Murthy and Infosys: Reflections by the CEO of a Leading Indian Software Firm, Video (801-801)*. Boston: Harvard Business School Publishing.

[9] The case can be contrasted with Promise (Module 4), in which a global perspective on access to resources also increased the likelihood of venture survival. In Promise's case, however, this meant *not* listing its shares abroad. Infosys can also be tied to Gray (Module 4) and TelePizza (Module 5), two other entrepreneurial companies that succeeded because they managed people well. The case suggests that international expansion is rarely a smooth process, as can be seen as well in Internet Securities and AtHoc (Module 1) and Spotfire (Module 3).

[10] The case can be tied to other cases that involve harvesting decisions such as Infox (Module 2) and TCS (this module). It can also be tied to GP and Officenet (Module 1) for geographic reasons.

Case

24

TCS: An Entrepreneurial Air-Express Company in Pakistan

Khalid Awan (Awan), chairman of TCS, knew this was not going to be a typical conference call. He was sitting in his office in Mississauga, Canada, preparing for a phone conversation with his protégé Jamil Janjua, the chief operating officer (COO) of TCS in Karachi, Pakistan. It was September 14, 2001. The main topic of the phone conversation would be a comprehensive assessment of how the terrorist attacks of September 11 might affect the courier services industry in Pakistan. The phone started ringing, but Awan's thoughts wandered as he gazed into the bright early-morning sky of a late-summer day in Ontario. A number of issues were racing through his mind. First, there was a deep feeling of sadness about the attacks in the United States. As a Muslim, Awan was hurt that extremists would commit such heinous crimes in the name of his religion. Then, there were questions about TCS. Awan knew that the short-term challenges and the longer-term objectives for TCS and for his own life might be closely intertwined.

TCS had come a long way since Awan founded the company with his brother in 1983. The company was headquartered in Karachi, Pakistan, and had started operations in the United Arab Emirates (UAE) in 1996 and Canada in 1999. TCS operated in four principal business segments: domestic courier services, international courier services, overland shipping, and gift delivery. It commanded a remarkable 55% market share in the Pakistan domestic courier services business.

Awan recognized the challenges of expanding the business beyond Pakistan, particularly at a time when uncertainty was impacting all businesses with exposure to international transportation negatively. Additionally, he pondered the merits of two strategic alternatives discussed recently. First, his team had identified the potential for leveraging TCS's information technology expertise in order to provide supply-chain management solutions to large companies with assembly operations in Pakistan. Second, management

Professor Walter Kuemmerle and Zahid Ahmed, MBA '02, prepared this case. HBS cases are developed solely as the basis for class discussion. Cases are not intended to serve as endorsements, sources of primary data, or illustrations of effective or ineffective management.

was considering a proposal to start an intermediary that would link the numerous small exporters in Pakistan's major industries such as textiles and leather goods with their buyers in North America and Europe.

Pakistan

Pakistan, with a land area roughly twice the size of California, had a population of 138 million people, making it the world's seventh most populous country (see **Exhibit 1** for a map of Pakistan) after Russia (146 million). Carved out of British India, Pakistan gained its independence on August 14, 1947, and was a predominantly Muslim state.

Pakistan had a rocky history as an independent nation, having been under military dictatorships for 24 of the 54 years since independence. The current government of President Pervez Musharraf had seized power in a military coup on October 12, 1999. Although free provincial and national elections were scheduled for October 2002, a great deal of uncertainty existed about the future of the democratic tradition in Pakistan given the corruption and underachievement that had characterized previous civilian governments. The Musharraf government had undertaken a variety of economic reforms, including a concerted effort to accelerate the privatization of key state-owned enterprises. On September 14, a few days after the tragic terrorist attacks, it remained to be seen whether Pakistan would move closer to the United States or further away.

EXHIBIT 1
Map of Pakistan

Source: Adapted from
Maps.com.

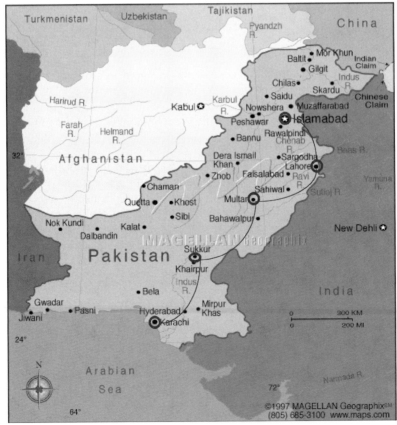

O TCS key hubs

EXHIBIT 2   Key Economic Indicators

Source: Compiled from State Bank of Pakistan data, World Bank data.

Indicator %	Annual Average for		
	1980s	1990/91–1994/95	1995/96–1999/00
Compound growth rate of real GDP	6.5	4.9	3.3
Poverty Incidence	46 (1985/86)	34	33
Inflation (period average)	7.2	11.5	7.9
Fiscal Deficit/GDP (excl. grants)	7.1	7.2	6.5
Fiscal Deficit/GDP (incl. grants)	6.4	6.7	6.4
Public Debt/GDP	66 (mid-1980)	94 (mid-1990)	101 (mid-2000)

Notes: Year 1999 GDP per capita: US$430; 1999 GDP per capita in purchasing power parity (U.S. = 100): 5.8.
Interest rate information for September 14, 2001:
Pakistan government bond (issued in US$; maturity: 2005) yielded 15.7%.
Five-year U.S. Treasury bond yielded 4.42%.

With a per capita gross domestic product (GDP) of only $440, Pakistan was a poor country with a wide income disparity; the top quintile of the population reportedly earned over 41% of the income in the country. Tax evasion was a chronic problem, with only a few salaried citizens paying income taxes while the agricultural landlords and industrialists who controlled the majority of the country's wealth remained untaxed. Agriculture and industry both accounted for approximately 25% of real GDP in fiscal 2000–2001, with the services sector responsible for the remaining 50%.[1] Pakistan had a relatively well-developed export sector, with total exports valued at $9.2 billion in 2000–2001. Textiles accounted for 63% of all exports in 2000–2001. (**Exhibit 2** presents some key economic indicators.)

The Karachi Stock Exchange (KSE) was the principal exchange in Pakistan, with listed companies representing a total market capitalization of only $4.5 billion.[2] (**Exhibit 3** shows the 10 largest publicly listed companies by market capitalization.) The low ratio of equity market capitalization to GDP was largely due to the predominantly private family-owned structure of Pakistani businesses, particularly in key sectors such as textiles. Large family groups dominated the industrial landscape, and commercial banks were the primary source of financing given the underdeveloped capital markets.

Periodic attempts had been made to introduce Islamic finance to Pakistan's banking system, most recently by the Nawaz Sharif government in 1998. One of the principal characteristics of an Islamic banking system was the absence of risk-free interest on the grounds that it promoted usury, which was against the principles of Islam.[3] This would have serious ramifications for the Pakistani banking system, which was styled along Western lines and thus relied heavily on interest for its proper functioning.

Pakistan suffered from endemic corruption, and it was notoriously difficult to maintain clean business dealings as of 2001. Five successive elected governments had been dismissed on charges of corruption and mismanagement since 1988. The Musharraf government had made the elimination of corruption one of its key goals when it came to

[1] From the State Bank of Pakistan Web site, <www.sbp.org>.

[2] Based on an exchange rate of 64.05 rupees (Rs) = US $1.00 as of September 14, 2001.

[3] Islamic scholars and clergymen differed widely in their interpretation of the relevant passages of the Koran. A small minority of scholars argued that the use of interest should only be prohibited if lending of the principal amount was actually *risk free* to the lender. On the other hand, the great majority of religious Shariah scholars considered any interest on a financial contract as "haram" (i.e., forbidden). Independent of these discussions, financial intermediaries in countries such as Yemen or Saudi Arabia where Islamic finance dominated daily life had often adopted a pragmatic approach by charging "loan arrangement fees," which effectively worked as up-front interest payments.

EXHIBIT 3   **Top 10 Listed Companies in Pakistan**

Source: Karachi Stock Exchange.

	Market Cap R millions (a)	Market Cap $ millions (b)	Sales (2001) R millions (a)	Sales (2001) $ millions (b)
1 Pakistan Telecommunications Ltd.	52,081	813	62,041	968
2 Hub Power	16,374	256	29,086	454
3 Pakistan State Oil	16,930	264	169,726	2,649
4 Fauji Fertilizer	8,157	127	11,982	187
5 Lever Brothers (c)	9,412	147	20,508	320
6 Engro Chemical	6,479	101	8,220	128
7 Pakistan Oilfields	8,213	128	5,408	84
8 Sui Southern Gas Company	5,940	93	24,317	379
9 Nestle Milkpack (c)	5,658	88	6,575	103
10 Shell Pakistan	7,124	111	65,725	1,026
Top 10 Firms	**136,368**	**2,128**		
Total Market	**290,189**	**4,531**		

(a) As of September 14, 2001.
(b) Based on interbank exchange rate of R64.05 = US $1.00 as of September 14, 2001.
(c) Sales figures are for 2000.
(d) Fauji Fertilizer, Lever Brothers, Nestle Milkpack, and Engro Chemical have June 30 fiscal year-ends.

power in 1999. The National Accountability Bureau, the military's anti-corruption arm, secured its first major conviction in July 2000 when a court sentenced ousted Prime Minister Nawaz Sharif to 14 years' imprisonment.

From Flight Engineer to Entrepreneur

Khalid Awan was an unlikely entrepreneur. As a young flight engineer with Pakistan International Airlines (PIA), he worried about the redundancy facing his profession as aircraft cockpits got progressively automated, and he left the airline in 1983 at age 35. Just about this time, his brother Sadiq Awan, who was 23 years older, entered into an agreement with DHL (the international courier services giant) to set up a joint venture in Pakistan designed to be 51% owned by DHL and 49% by the Awan brothers.

Pakistan was then under military rule, and the economy was tightly regulated. During negotiations for the joint venture, the government, while agreeing to profit repatriation by DHL, had two major concerns. First, it wished to narrow its foreign exchange liability by restricting DHL to international courier business only, that is, DHL could not transport documents within Pakistan. Secondly, the government demanded that the local joint venture partner be fully responsible for any security violations. Sadiq Awan argued with DHL that this meant that he should have operational control of the joint venture. DHL, worried about the upkeep of its operating standards, agreed to this under the condition that his brother Khalid Awan undergo thorough training in DHL's procedures. Awan was subsequently named DHL's country manager for Pakistan. With DHL's training, Awan got valuable insight into the business, and the company in Pakistan was soon outperforming other DHL companies in the region in terms of productivity, service standards, and customer endorsements.

As soon as Awan assumed control over DHL Pakistan, he recognized the large opportunity presented by the domestic market and the disadvantage of not being able to offer domestic courier service. He figured that in order to address the government's foreign exchange concern it would make sense to have a 100% locally owned company in the domestic courier business. The Awans already owned a local company whose abbreviations spelt TCS, a name that was eventually given to the new domestic courier services company. The challenge was to find a way around government regulations protecting the Pakistan Post Office, a state-owned postal service that enjoyed a monopoly on all domestic deliveries. The outdated Post Office Act of 1898, a legacy of the British Raj, actually made it illegal for any entity other than the Post Office to deliver "letters," although the definition of this term was vague (see **Exhibit 4** for the relevant excerpt from the act).

After lengthy negotiations, in which the Awan brothers argued that there was strong market demand for a domestic courier service, the government yielded an approval that restricted TCS to transmission of "business-related documents" only. While this agreement implicitly established that business-related documents were not letters in the sense of the Post Office Act of 1898, it still left TCS vulnerable to the Post Office's randomly disputing any shipment. These random disputes with the Post Office continued through 2001. However, the pressure eased somewhat when in 1989 TCS offered to pay 10% of revenues as a central excise duty. In 2000 this duty was renamed as general sales tax and increased to 15%.

EXHIBIT 4
Post Office Act of 1898

Source: TCS.

Privilege and Protection of the Government

4. - (1) Wherever within (Pakistan) posts or postal communications are established by the (Central Government), the (Central Government) shall have the exclusive privilege of conveying by post, from one place to another, all letters, except in the following cases, and shall also have the exclusive privilege of performing all the incidental services of receiving, collecting, sending, dispatching and delivering all letters, except in the following cases, that is to say: -

a) Letters sent by a private friend in his way, journey or travel, to be delivered by him to the person to whom they are directed, without hire, reward or other profit or advantage for receiving, carrying or delivering them;

b) Letters solely concerning the affairs of the sender or receiver thereof, sent by a messenger on purpose; and

c) Letters solely concerning goods or property, sent (by sea or by land or by air) to be delivered with the goods or property which the letters concern, without hire, reward or other profit or advantage for receiving carrying or delivering them:

Provided that nothing in the section shall authorize any person to make a collection of letters excepted as aforesaid for the purpose of sending them otherwise than by post.

(2) For the purposes of this section and section 5, the expression "letters" includes postcards.

5. Wherever within (Pakistan) posts or postal communications are established by the (Central Government), the following persons are expressly forbidden to collect, carry, tender or deliver letters, or to receive letters for the purpose of carrying or delivering them, although they obtain no hire, reward or other profit or advantage for so doing, that is to say: -

a) Common carriers of passengers or goods, and their servants or agents, except as regards letters solely concerning goods in their carts or carriages;

b) Owners and masters of vessels sailing or passing on any river or canal in (Pakistan), or between any ports or places in (Pakistan), and their servants or agents, excepts as regards letters solely concerning goods on board, and except as regards postal articles received for conveyance under Chapter VIII (; and)

c) Owners, pilots and other members of the crew of aircraft flying from or to any airports in Pakistan.

Parting of Ways and Evolution of TCS

In the initial years (1982–1991) the international and domestic businesses were operated jointly with Awan as chief executive of both companies and his brother Sadiq as chairman. The domestic business, which came to be known as TCS, initially relied heavily on DHL for all kinds of operational support. Awan, however, ensured meticulous separation of the respective costs of the two businesses. Domestic air transportation was subcontracted to PIA.

TCS got a strong "wind in its sails" when it won a major contract in 1985 from the Pakistan Banking Council to link 4,000 bank branches across the country with an overnight delivery service. Successful implementation of this project earned TCS nationwide recognition, and it was soon establishing its own branches across the country (which DHL could list in its worldwide directory). The joint venture between DHL and TCS was now on a fast-growth path. TCS was benefiting from DHL's systems, while TCS's countrywide penetration gave DHL a lead over foreign competitors that had arrived later in Pakistan.

As business thrived, Awan started thinking about family issues and succession planning. While the two Awan brothers enjoyed an excellent relationship, Sadiq's only son Salim was estranged from the family and lived in Abu-Dhabi in the UAE pursuing a career as a military officer. Under Pakistani law, based on Islamic "shariah,"[4] the son was legal heir to his father's assets, and so Salim would one day be entering the business. Both brothers agreed that any such transition should be managed rather than left to itself. After careful consideration, they decided in 1991 that Sadiq would keep the more profitable DHL joint venture while Khalid would assume the "younger man's job" and become full owner of TCS. Despite this process, a rift soon developed between Awan and his nephew Salim because Salim felt that TCS, while less profitable, was the more valuable of the two businesses. Also, with the separation DHL withdrew a major contract from TCS, and the first years after 1991 proved to be a real test for Awan.

At that time, TCS's managerial issues were considerable. TCS barely broke even because it handled 50 times more shipments and had 15 times more employees than DHL Pakistan with only about the same revenue level. The company had no financing lines and was geographically dispersed in over 100 remote locations, presenting a real challenge in terms of maintaining discipline, staff motivation, and service standards. Petty-cash control and monthly sales recovery from over 10,000 accounts across the country presented a daunting accounting challenge. Finally, complete dependence on PIA for air transportation made TCS very vulnerable.

Awan received offers for joint ventures from other international courier services but decided to remain independent. He said: "I really felt I had to address these challenges with my team at TCS. Anything else would have been an excuse." Having defined the company's mission to remain the leading domestic courier service, Awan started what he called "operation self-renewal." The effort was centered on customer satisfaction and human resources management. Among other initiatives, employees and management alike relinquished their titles for a year and suffixed themselves as "Khadim," that is, one who serves. Simultaneously, a management audit aimed at lowering costs.

During this period Awan also had to deal with a group of senior executives who left to start a competitor. A lot of bad press resulted. But Awan felt that the team that stuck with TCS emerged from the ordeal stronger than before. By 1994 TCS had established itself as the country's top courier service. It had acquired its own aircraft and operated them under its own airline license. It had also successfully linked its major stations with a wide-area network, a pioneering achievement for Pakistan in those days.

---

[4] "Shariah" was Islamic law, which supplemented Pakistan's legal system originally inherited from the British.

The impact of managerial defections and his interest in his family led Awan to bring another nephew, Naveed Awan (son of a late brother), into the firm in 1997. At that point he granted Naveed a 10% stake in TCS, basically for free. The idea was that Naveed would grow into Khalid's shoes. However, Naveed did not turn out to be as well suited for the business as Khalid had hoped. Even though Naveed left TCS in 2000, he still held a 10% stake as of September 2001.

Finally, in 1996, TCS entered the international courier services market, not in direct competition with DHL but through a different value-added model. Due to the downsizing in many state-owned enterprises and the trend toward outsourcing in large companies, opportunities arose for integrated services such as "mail room management." Typically, a big customer like a bank would have a large number of documents to dispatch both internationally and domestically. TCS could offer a one-stop solution for the customer's entire courier needs. While it would distribute the domestic shipments itself, it would find the most appropriate solution for international shipments; for example, for shipments to the United States, TCS might choose FedEx, and for shipments to Japan, TCS might choose DHL Far East. Also, because of its greater volumes TCS could negotiate lower rates with these firms. Furthermore, since courier service rates differed across countries depending on the competitive situation, TCS decided to carry documents to neighboring Dubai itself and feed them into international distribution from there.

Geographic expansion outside Pakistan had another important driver. Awan had always been wary of corruption, and the country's political elite would ask for "favors" that could sometimes not be met. In a particularly distressing episode that occurred in 1995 under Benazir Bhutto's government, Awan was asked to acquire an aircraft without proper documentation. His refusal to do so threatened TCS's very existence, and the incident was reported in the national press (see **Exhibit 5**). After this, Awan vowed to develop business outside Pakistan as well.

Business Units

Up until 1985, TCS focused on building its domestic services business. In 1985, Awan identified another business opportunity focused on gift delivery and started Sentiments Express (described below) in response. This venture focused on the consumer market and was based on a customer needs analysis by TCS. Similarly, in 1986, TCS started Overland Express (described below) to service customers that required "time-definite but not time-sensitive" door-to-door delivery of heavy packages. This opportunity was also identified through extensive market research.

By 2001, TCS operated in four principal business segments: domestic courier services, international courier services, overland shipping, and gift delivery. The company enjoyed an average operating margin of approximately 15% across the four business units.

Domestic Courier Services

Domestic Courier Services was the heart of TCS. This business unit offered a wide range of services including Same Day Express, Overnight Express, and Second Day Express throughout 350 cities in Pakistan. Additional options such as time-specific delivery, insurance coverage, and money-back guarantee were also offered. Customized products such as mailroom management, bulk-mail deliveries, and invoice distribution were available for business customers. TCS's market share in the domestic business was a remarkable 55% in 2001. Revenue was approximately R558 million in 2001, representing 75% of total revenues. Management expected 15% growth in this business unit for 2002.

EXHIBIT 5 Newspaper Article from Newsline Regarding Corruption Pressure on TCS

Source: *Newsline*, June 1996.

Newsbeat

Crash Landing?

The country's premier courier service paid 250,000 U.S. dollars to a PPP MNA to stay in business.

By Zahid Hussain

In the first week of June, TCS – the country's largest courier company – announced the closure of its aviation service which had been in operation for a few years. This decision came in response to the repeated suspension of the service by the Civil Aviation Authority (CAA) on one pretext or the other over the past one year.

The trouble began in July 1995 when TCS aviation services were suspended on direct orders from the Prime Minister's secretariat. The suspension orders remained in force until the company agreed to pay a substantial sum in extortion money to Shahid Nazir, a PPP MNA from Faisalabad. It was only allowed to resume operations in the following month when 250,000 dollars had changed hands. But, in spite of this massive payment made under duress, TCS's nightmare has not to come an end.

The TCS story is a glaring example of how the political leadership of the country uses spineless officials for purposes of intimidation and extortion. The predicament of

Pakistan's premier courier service began early last year when it terminated negotiations to buy a Cessna plane owned by the Nazir family when MNA Shahid Nazir could not furnish authentic documents for the plane. The cancellation of this deal was to cost TCS a great deal. Using his political clout and influence at the highest political level, Shahid Nazir got the CAA to suspend the TCS aviation service, a network that offered air charter and delivery services. TCS was eventually left with no other option but to comply with Shahid Nazir's demands and cough up a huge amount of money in the guise of compensation for the mental and physical strain he suffered as a result of the cancellation of the deal.

TCS entered into a business deal with the MNA from Faisalabad when it hired the Nazir family's Cessna Caravan aircraft for its Dubai-Saudi Arabia operations. Shahid Nazir, who was at the time in dire

financial straits after the death of his father, former MNA Chaudhry Nazir, had stationed the aircraft for sale at Dubai. The Nazir family had accumulated a huge debt from state-owned banks and could not afford to retain the Cessna. The hiring of the aircraft by TCS helped ease Nazir's financial problem but he tried to persuade the courier service to buy the plane outright. With a growing demand for chartered flights, TCS evinced interest in the deal but it could not be clinched as Nazir refused to provide proper documentation. The aircraft was shown as the property of Alpha company, registered in the United States. Initially, the MNA's brother, Zahid Nazir, was shown as the owner of the company, but the story kept on changing as the negotiations proceeded. The talks between the two parties stalled when the BRR Modaraba, through which TCS was arranging finance for the purchase, asked the Alpha company to fulfil certain requirements. It asked for Alpha's audit balance sheet, its tax record, details of bank accounts, sources of funds whereby the company purchased the aircraft and an indemnity from Shahid Nazir that would hold him responsible for any misrepresentation as to the true status of the company.

These were minimum requirements that had to be complied with as the plane was registered in the United States. BRR Modaraba was willing to finance the purchase as long as the requisite documents were supplied by the owners of the aircraft. Interestingly, the Cessna aircraft was the only asset the Alpha company had. In any case, Shahid Nazir flatly refused

EXHIBIT 5 (Continued)

Newsbeat

---

to supply the documents and threatened TCS with dire consequences if it did not purchase the aircraft. Placed under tremendous pressure, TCS officials approached Grindlays Bank for financing, but continued to insist on the provision of an indemnity bond and endorsement of the sales deed by the Pakistani Embassy in Washington. Shahid Nazir refused to meet even these basic conditions, leaving TCS with no other option but to cancel the deal. The courier service returned the aircraft to Shahid Nazir during that period and terminated its service to Saudi Arabia. At the time, TCS had also paid over 100,000 dollars as an advance to Nazir, which he later refused to refund.

On June 7, 1995, TCS informed Shahid Nazir through a letter that unless he could provide the required documentation the deal could not be concluded. The MNA

instructions to call the aircraft back were issued by the office of Air Marshal Hatif, then chief of the CAA. The objective behind the whole exercise soon became clear as a contingent of police surrounded the TCS office at the airport and searched it. No explanation was given for the raid on the TCS office which clearly constituted harassment to force the courier company to accede to Shahid Nazir's demand. It was also apparent that Air Marshal Hatif was involved in arm twisting on the instructions of a VVIP in Islamabad. Even in the chequered history of Pakistan, there seems to be no precedence of the use of the head of a government institution by high authority to force a reputable business organisation to pay extortion money to a legislator.

But the worst was yet to come. On July 12, 1995, an Operational Safety Audit

the Prime Minister's house. However, it is not clear who gave that order. The CAA might have been acting on the orders of political leaders, but the action also reflects poorly on the conduct of a former senior air force official.

The CAA was not the only government organisation that was used against TCS. The PIA chairman was also instructed to stop transportation of TCS packages, as this action would have totally destroyed TCS operations. In desperation, TCS executives contacted PPP senator Gulzar Ahmed to help resolve the issue. Gulzar persuaded TCS officials to agree to pay 250,000 dollars to Shahid Nazir in order to save their business. Succumbing to these pressures, TCS finally agreed to pay the ransom money. The payment was made in installments and the transactions were monitored by the CAA chairman. The Air

O n July 12, 1995, an Operational Safety Audit Team of the CAA barred the flight of all TCS aircraft on the pretext of the company's committing a breach of safety rules. However, officials of the team made it clear to TCS that there was another reason behind the action. Air Commodore Jamal Hussain, president of the Safety Inspection Board (SIB), reportedly told TCS officials before imposing the ban that it would continue until the courier service settled its dispute with Shahid Nazir: "Either settle your dispute with the MNA or forget about doing business in this country."

not only refused to comply with this requirement but stipulated that ransom money would have to be paid if the deal did not come through. He also threatened to destroy the courier service operation through the use of government machinery. Following this, TCS formally terminated the sales negotiations on June 22, 1995.

Shahid Nazir did not waste any time in acting upon his threat. Using political clout at the highest level, he started tightening the screws around TCS. On June 30, a TCS aircraft on a routine flight to Abu Dhabi for maintenance was called back to Karachi by the control tower on the basis of a dubious bomb threat call. The aircraft was thoroughly checked by the bomb squad and it soon transpired that the 'bomb threat' was just a pretext used to recall the aircraft. Significantly,

Team of the CAA barred the flight of all TCS aircraft on the pretext of the company's committing a breach of safety rules. However, officials of the team made it clear to TCS that there was another reason behind the action. Air Commodore Jamal Hussain, president of the Safety Inspection Board (SIB), reportedly told TCS officials before imposing the ban that it would continue until the courier service settled its dispute with Shahid Nazir: "Either settle your dispute with the MNA or forget about doing business in this country."

Obviously, the Air Commodore was only following the instructions of the CAA chief, who was a crucial pawn in the game. But whose orders was Air Marshal Hatif following? During a conversation with a top executive of TCS, Shahid Nazir claimed that the order came directly from

Marshal refused to lift the ban on TCS Aviation until the entire sum was paid to the PPP MNA.

The three-week long ban on TCS Aviation was finally lifted on August 6, 1995 after Air Marshal Hatif got confirmation from Shahid Nazir that the entire amount had been transferred into his foreign account. That brought the sordid saga to a close, but the harassment continued in different forms. The company which prided itself on its legitimate and professional operations could never recover from the shock. What happened with the company is perhaps one small example of how the political leadership of the country is brazenly involved in extortion. Will the superior courts of the country take notice of these criminal and unlawful acts being committed under the patronage of higher authorities? ■

International Courier Services

The International Courier Services business covered over 200 countries, providing the same breadth of services as Domestic Courier Services. TCS contracted actual delivery to all of these countries except the UAE and Canada to other major firms with strong, established networks. TCS held a 7% market share in this highly competitive segment in 2001. Revenue was approximately R82 million in 2001, representing 11% of total revenues. Management anticipated 15% growth in 2002.

Overland Express

Overland Express offered its clients fast bulk-cargo (over five kilograms) solutions. Services included door-to-door pickup and delivery, regular daily departures from all major cities to over 150 locations, shipment tracking with delivery confirmation, insurance coverage, refrigerated cargo handling, and customized transportation and project-handling capabilities. Overland Express had a 50% market share in 2001. Revenue was approximately R74 million in 2001, representing 10% of total revenues. This business unit was expected to grow by 20% in 2002.

Sentiments Express

Sentiments Express was a gift-delivery and greetings service that demonstrated TCS's innovative ability. TCS successfully created the local market for gift delivery, much like its pioneering concept of express courier services in 1983. It enjoyed a 60% share of this market segment in 2001. Revenue was approximately R30 million in 2001, representing 4% of total revenues. Management anticipated 35% growth in 2002.

Operations

TCS's business operations relied on a sophisticated hub-and-spoke system that was designed for maximum efficiency. Domestically, the company operated two planes that flew a unique route system covering five key hubs (see **Exhibit 1** for a map of Pakistan). The first plane took off from the southern port city of Karachi, the country's commercial center, at 11:30 p.m. every night and made half-hour stops to load and unload packages at the cities of Sukkur, Multan, and Lahore before arriving at the capital city of Islamabad, its final destination, at 5:30 a.m. The second plane followed the identical route in reverse during the same six-hour period, taking off from Islamabad and ending its flight in Karachi. This system effectively allowed TCS to cover most of the country, as the majority of its over 2,000 service locations were within a six-hour drive of one of the five hubs. Round-the-clock sorting facilities were located in each of the hub cities and ensured the timely departure of the planes. These sorting facilities were the nerve center of the company's operations, serving as the critical link between the aircraft and TCS's extensive ground transportation network. TCS relied on a fleet of 60 trucks, 20 minivans, and 600 motorcycles (mostly leased) that serviced these sorting facilities in addition to making customer deliveries (see **Exhibit 6** for pictures of the TCS fleet).

TCS handled an average of over 125,000 shipments on any given day. Its record volume was 190,000 shipments. The overall business was not particularly seasonal, and volume was fairly consistent throughout the year, although Sentiments Express typically experienced higher volumes around the major Muslim festivals of *Eid-ul-Azha* and *Eid-ul-Fitr*.[5] One somewhat simplistic way to assess the potential for growth in the Pakistan courier services market in general and TCS's core business in particular was to compare TCS annual

---

[5] Islam followed a lunar calendar. Thus, the dates for these holidays changed from year to year. *Eid-ul-Azha* celebrated Abraham's sacrifice of his son Ismail, while *Eid-ul-Fitr* celebrated the end of *Ramadan*, the month of fasting for Muslims across the world.

EXHIBIT 6   **TCS Fleet**

Source: TCS.

shipments on a per capita (of population) basis with those of a company like FedEx operating in the significantly more mature U.S. market. TCS delivered an average of 0.33 packages per capita on an annual basis, compared with 6.2 packages per capita for FedEx.[6]

Competitive Landscape

Despite its dominant market position, TCS had a host of aggressive competitors in Pakistan (**Exhibit 7** compares TCS's shipping rates with those of its principal competitors). The three biggest competitors were OCS, TNT, and Leopard. Each of these companies competed with TCS in at least three of its four principal business units. OCS Pakistan was the local licensee for the Japanese courier services company from which it took its name. It had grown out of a family business that had been involved in the automobile sector prior to obtaining the OCS license in 1987. In terms of market share, OCS Pakistan was second to TCS in both the overland and the gift-delivery segments, third behind TCS and Leopard in the domestic segment, and actually ahead of TCS in the international segment. TNT Pakistan was a subsidiary of the TNT Post Group, the giant European competitor in global express distribution, logistics, and international mail. In terms of market share, TNT Pakistan was fourth in the domestic segment, third in gift deliveries, and had equal market share with TCS in the international segment. Leopard was a 10-year-old local competitor with a highly successful low-cost strategy. In terms of market share, it was second to TCS

[6] FedEx data from company Web site, <www.fedex.com>. Casewriter calculations based on Pakistani population of 138 million and U.S. population of 280 million.

EXHIBIT 7   Comparison of Shipping Rates

Source: TCS.

Cash Tariff: Comparison Chart of TCS with Competitors

Service/Courier		TCS	Gerry's	TNT	OCS
Overnight Express		Rs	Rs	Rs	Rs
Within City	0 to 0.5 kg	25	22	25	20
	0.6 to 1 kg	40	25	35	40
	Each additional kg	40	25	35	30
Same Zone	0 to 0.5 kg	40	35	35	35
	0.6 to 1 kg	45	40	42	40
	Each additional kg	45	40	42	40
Different Zone	0 to 0.5 kg	80	70	70	70
	0.6 to 1 kg	90	80	80	80
	Each additional kg	90	80	80	80
Same Day Express					
Within City	0 to 0.5 kg	N/A	N/A	75	N/A
	0.6 to 1 kg	90	55	85	60
	Each additional kg	50	55	35	40
City to City	Up to 1 kg	350	350	N/A	N/A
	Each additional kg	120	100	N/A	N/A
Same Zone	0 to 0.5 kg	N/A	N/A	285	N/A
	0.6 to 1 kg	N/A	N/A	292	N/A
	Each additional kg	N/A	N/A	42	N/A
Different Zone	0 to 0.5 kg	N/A	N/A	325	N/A
	0.6 to 1 kg	N/A	N/A	335	N/A
	Each additional kg	N/A	N/A	80	N/A

(continued)

EXHIBIT 7   (Continued)

Service / Courier		TCS	Gerry's	TNT	OCS
Second Day Express		**Rs**	**Rs**	**Rs**	**Rs**
Within City	0 to 0.5 kg	N/A	N/A	18	N/A
	0.6 to 1 kg	N/A	N/A	25	N/A
	Each additional kg	N/A	N/A	25	N/A
Same Zone	Up to 3 kg	N/A	N/A	105	N/A
	Each additional kg	N/A	N/A	35	N/A
Different Zone	Up to 3 kg	135	120	120	N/A
	Each additional kg	45	40	40	N/A
Extra Special Express					
Within City	0 to 0.5 kg	N/A	N/A	35	N/A
	0.6 to 1 kg	65	50	50	N/A
	Each additional kg	65	50	35	N/A
City to City	Up to 1 kg	150	120	N/A	N/A
	Each additional kg	150	120	N/A	N/A
Same Zone	0 to 0.5 kg	N/A	N/A	100	N/A
	0.6 to 1 kg	N/A	N/A	120	N/A
	Each additional kg	N/A	N/A	42	N/A
Different Zone	0 to 0.5 kg	N/A	N/A	100	N/A
	0.6 to 1 kg	N/A	N/A	130	N/A
	Each additional kg	N/A	N/A	80	N/A
Sunday & Holiday Deliveries					
Additional Charges	1 kg	50	100	150	N/A
	Over 3 kg	N/A	N/A	N/A	50
Overland Express					
Same Zone	Up to 3 kg	N/A	N/A	N/A	75
	Each additional kg	N/A	N/A	N/A	25
Different Zone	Up to 3 kg	N/A	N/A	N/A	120
	Each additional kg	N/A	N/A	N/A	40
Overland Express					
Within City	Up to 1 kg	N/A	20	N/A	N/A
	Each additional kg	N/A	20	N/A	N/A
Same Zone	Up to 1 kg	N/A	35	N/A	N/A
	Each additional kg	N/A	35	N/A	N/A
Different Zone	Up to 1 kg	N/A	70	N/A	N/A
	Each additional kg	N/A	70	N/A	N/A

in the domestic segment, third behind TCS and OCS in the overland segment, and fourth in gift deliveries. (**Exhibit 8** gives the market share breakdown between TCS and its principal competitors in each of its four business segments.) All industry players benefited from Awan's successful battle against the Post Office, as the TCS agreement with the government had opened up the local courier services market for them.

TCS management considered the threat of competition from any new players to be small. There were significant barriers to entry for a new entrant. In particular, the cost of building a national network and installing an extensive fleet of vehicles and airplanes seemed prohibitive. Any serious competitor would also have to match TCS's highly trained workforce, advertise heavily to brand countrywide, and invest in sophisticated information technology to create a package-tracking system and logistical backbone.

EXHIBIT 8
Market Shares by
Business Segment

Source: TCS.

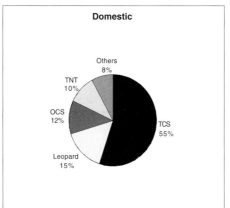

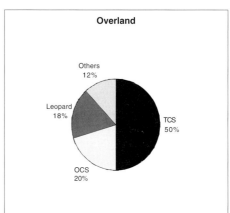

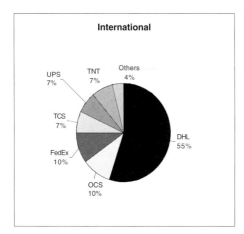

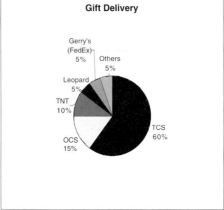

Financing

TCS had been self-funded since inception, although it did receive significant nonmonetary help in the form of management expertise, support services, and marketing services from DHL before the two companies were formally separated in 1984. That TCS had been able to internally generate sufficient cash flow for all of its past capital needs was quite remarkable, given the uphill battle the company faced against the Post Office in its early years when it struggled to establish itself and the tremendous subsequent growth of the business. The company had never taken on any long-term debt and relied on a working capital facility with its commercial bank for its short-term financing needs. TCS's cash balance, property assets, and receivables secured the existing facility of R20 million, which was available at an interest rate of 16% per annum.

As a key part of its overall financing and growth strategy, TCS had historically used leasing extensively to acquire assets. The primary reason for this approach was the tremendous tax benefit associated with leasing versus buying. All lease rental payments were admissible tax-deductible expenditures under Pakistan tax laws; hence, leasing assets allowed TCS to reduce its tax expenses. The leases used by TCS acted as a source of financing and eliminated the need for a large credit facility to finance purchases while preserving the firm's limited capital. This had minimized the company's balance sheet exposure while enabling rapid expansion. Due to certain financial-exposure restrictions under the Prudential Regulations of the State Bank of Pakistan (the central bank), TCS needed to use a number of leasing companies. Hence, TCS used seven big leasing companies that provided similar facilities on competitive terms. These were primarily local firms and included Orix Leasing, Askari Leasing, Saudi Pak Leasing, Crescent Leasing, First Grindlays Modaraba, National Development Leasing Corporation, and Dawood Leasing. The typical lease was for a three-year term and did not require any up-front payment, as all payments were built into the monthly lease rentals. At the end of the lease term, TCS usually had to pay 5% to 15% of the residual asset value to the lessor and then owned the asset outright.

(**Exhibit 9** details TCS's leasing history since 1993. **Exhibits 10–12** show TCS's income statements, balance sheets, and cash flow statements for the five years from 1997–2001. **Exhibits 13–15** show projected income statements, balance sheets, and cash

EXHIBIT 9
TCS Leasing History

Source: TCS.

Assets Acquired Through Lease: 1993–2002 (in Pakistani Rupees 000)				
	IT Equipment	Vehicles	Other Equipment	TOTAL
1993–94	2,617	1,192	970	4,778
1994–95	2,617	8,376	5,573	16,566
1995–96	—	4,501	18,368	22,870
1996–97	4,115	2,563	—	6,678
1997–98	544	1,769	895	3,208
1998–99	8,084	8,330	5,320	21,735
1999–00	4,541	13,134	2,150	19,826
2000–01	—	18,987	12,326	31,312
2001–02	1,905	20,438	4,342	26,686
Total	24,423	79,290	49,944	153,659

EXHIBIT 10 Historical Profit and Loss Account for Five Years from 1997 to 2001 (Pakistani Rupees 000)

Source: TCS.

	2001	2000	1999	1998	1997
Net Sales from Services Rendered	743,739	651,527	576,603	497,811	463,033
Operating Admin. & Marketing Expenses	730,067	620,125	525,334	443,740	435,975
Operating Profit	**13,672**	**31,402**	**51,269**	**54,071**	**27,058**
Financial Charges	7,955	6,974	5,440	5,405	6,539
	5,717	24,428	45,829	48,666	20,519
Other Income	5,245	3,041	2,466	3,192	4,276
Liability no longer payable written back			2,433	6,004	2,505
Profit before taxation	10,962	27,469	50,728	57,862	27,300
Provision for taxation —current	5,900	14,500	24,000	26,000	10,000
—prior	2,751	3,422	3,841	7,000	3,000
	8,651	17,922	27,841	33,000	13,000
Profit after taxation	2,311	9,547	22,887	24,862	14,300
Excess of liability over book value of aircrafts lease terminated					1,036
Accumulated profit brought forward	58,840	58,793	57,906	33,044	27,829
Profit available for appropriation	61,151	68,340	80,793	57,906	43,165
Appropriations: Interim dividend		9,500	22,000		10,121
Unappropriated profit carried over	61,151	58,840	58,793	57,906	33,044

EXHIBIT 11   **Historical Balance Sheet for Five Years from 1997 to 2001 (Pakistani Rupees 000)**

Source: TCS.

	2001	2000	1999	1998	1997
Share Capital Reserves					
Authorized capital					
200,000 (2000: 200,000) ordinary					
Shares of Rs 100/- each	20,000	20,000	20,000	20,000	20,000
Issued, subscribed and paid-up capital	10,000	10,000	10,000	10,000	10,000
Accumulated Profit	61,148	58,838	58,792	57,905	33,044
	71,148	68,838	68,792	67,905	43,044
Surplus on Revaluation of Fixed Assets	23,399	23,399	9,196	9,196	9,196
Liabilities against Assets subject to Finance Lease	24,748	18,181	14,491	2,162	5,463
Deferred Liabilities	43,459	44,125	36,210	25,630	21,903
Long-Term Liabilities	4,898	—	—	—	—
Current Liabilities					
Current portion of finance lease	21,227	13,362	7,439	5,317	10,922
Bank finance under markup arrangement secured	11,482	2,765	7,196	8,306	6,413
Security deposits	387	103	129	103	103
Creditors, accrued and other liabilities	61,553	56,200	61,343	59,364	65,657
	94,650	72,430	76,107	73,090	83,094
Contingencies and Commitments	—	—	—	—	—
Rupees	262,302	226,973	204,796	177,984	162,700
Fixed Assets	101,893	85,508	63,223	54,268	58,364
Long-Term Advances—unsecured, considered good	—	—	1,078	1,078	1,078
Long-Term Deposits	4,832	3,628	3,698	1,425	1,300
Current Assets					
Trade debts—unsecured, considered good	77,414	67,592	62,101	44,124	45,829
Advances, deposits, prepayments, and other receivables	53,998	54,191	47,642	41,571	40,925
Cash and bank balances	24,165	16,055	27,055	35,518	15,204
	155,577	137,838	136,798	121,213	101,959
Rupees	262,302	226,973	204,796	177,984	162,700

flow statements prepared by management assuming that TCS would stop its practice of leasing key assets. **Exhibits 16–18** show projected financial statements assuming that TCS will continue to lease its assets. The company's fiscal year end is June 30.)

Over the years, Awan had explored various offers to either merge or sell the business. Additionally, various investment banks approached him about undertaking an initial public offering on the KSE, but most of the interest came from local strategic players and investment banks. Instead of diluting his ownership, Awan chose to grow the company organically. He was convinced TCS had great growth potential and was unwilling to exit the business before realizing full value. Only recently had he decided to pursue geographic expansion. This was the reason he was planning to give Janjua (his protégé) the responsibility for day-to-day management in the near future, while he was probably going to spend more time focused on the international effort. He was also planning to soon begin the process of (at least partly) harvesting his substantial investment in the company. The question was when and how to best do this.

EXHIBIT 12   **Historical Cash Flow Statement for Five Years from 1997 to 2001 (Pakistani Rupees 000)**

Source: TCS.

	2001	2000	1999	1998	1997
Cash flow from operating activities					
Profit before taxation	10,962	27,469	50,728	57,862	27,300
Add: Adjustments from noncash items					
Depreciation	16,786	13,521	10,617	8,647	9,444
Amortization of intangible fixed assets	1,402				
Provision for gratuity	6,835	12,731	8,364	8,548	6,677
(Gain)/loss disposal of fixed assets	(1,098)	(380)	(809)	(468)	11
Financial charges on lease payments	6,111	5,281	2,018	2,423	4,592
	30,036	31,153	20,190	19,150	20,724
	40,998	58,622	70,918	77,012	48,024
Increase/Decrease in current assets					
Trade debts	(9,822)	(5,491)	(17,978)	1,706	(6,576)
Advances, deposits, prepayments and other receivables	18,257	3,038	(8,391)	(13,780)	(6,255)
	8,435	(2,453)	(26,369)	(12,074)	(12,831)
Increase/(decrease) in current liabilities					
Creditors, accrued and other liabilities	5,540	4,022	4,734	(11,967)	8,895
Security deposit	284	(26)	26		15
	5,824	3,996	4,760	(11,967)	8,910
	55,257	60,165	49,309	52,971	44,103
Income tax paid	(26,715)	(37,805)	(24,041)	(11,995)	(16,755)
Gratuity paid	(7,687)	(2,814)	(3,707)	(4,842)	(4,184)
Net cash flows from operating activities	20,855	19,546	21,561	36,134	23,164
Cash flow from investing activities					
Fixed capital expenditure	(17,069)	(4,452)	(4,710)	(3,052)	(2,613)
Sales proceeds of fixed assets	14,687	2,855	7,165	1,250	1,188
Long-term deposits	(1,203)	477	47	(2,445)	136
Net cash outflow	(3,585)	(1,120)	2,502	(4,247)	(1,289)
Cash flow from financing activities					
Lease rental paid	(22,772)	(15,495)	(9,292)	(13,590)	(16,852)
Acquisition of long-term deposits	4,898				
Dividend paid		(9,500)	(22,000)		(10,121)
Net cash outflow	(17,874)	(24,995)	(31,292)	(13,590)	(26,973)
Net decrease in cash and cash equivalents	(604)	(6,569)	(7,229)	18,297	(5,098)
Cash and cash equivalents at the beginning of the year	13,291	19,860	27,089	8,792	13,890
Cash and cash equivalents at the end of the year	12,687	13,291	19,860	27,089	8,792

The international operations in the UAE and Canada had been set up as joint ventures (in the UAE, TCS owned 49% of the venture but had total management control, whereas in Canada TCS had 100% ownership but had local partners without ownership stakes), in keeping with TCS's philosophy of risk management and the importance of local expertise. The local partner in the UAE, however, was a passive investor who primarily helped meet the strict legal requirement that all UAE-based businesses have a local partner. The UAE had been a logical first choice for international expansion for two reasons. First, Dubai (part of the UAE) had a central geographic location that made it a natural industrial hub in the region. Second, the UAE government was quite focused on industrial development and had put in place significant tax incentives for certain types of businesses.

EXHIBIT 13   Projected Profit and Loss Account for Five Years from 2002 to 2006 (Pakistani Rupees 000)

(Assumes that TCS will start purchasing, as opposed to leasing, key assets)

Source: TCS.

	2002	2003	2004	2005	2006
Gross Sales from services rendered	1,007,736	1,189,128	1,403,172	1,655,742	1,953,776
Less: General Sales Tax	(132,736)	(156,629)	(184,822)	(218,090)	(257,346)
NET SALES	875,000	1,032,499	1,218,350	1,437,652	1,696,430
Operating, Administrative & Marketing expenses	826,631	942,412	1,057,174	1,168,962	1,286,412
Operating Profit	48,369	90,087	161,176	268,690	410,018
Financial charges	14,343	1,300	1,080	675	
Profit before taxation	34,026	88,787	160,096	268,015	410,018
Provision for taxation	16,000	39,955	72,043	120,607	184,508
Profit after taxation	18,026	48,832	88,053	147,408	225,510
Accumulated profit brought forward	61,147	79,173	128,005	216,058	363,466
Profit available for appropriation	79,173	128,005	216,058	363,466	588,976
Appropriations: Interim dividend					
Unappropriated profit carried forward	79,173	128,005	216,058	363,466	588,976

EXHIBIT 14   Projected Balance Sheet (2002–2006) (Pakistani Rupees 000)

(Assumes that TCS will start purchasing, as opposed to leasing, key assets)

Source: TCS.

	2002	2003	2004	2005	2006
Share Capital and Reserves					
Authorized capital					
200,000 (2000: 200,000) ordinary shares of Rs 100/-each	20,000	20,000	20,000	20,000	20,000
Issued, subscribed and paid-up capital	10,000	10,000	10,000	10,000	10,000
Accumulated Profit	79,173	128,006	216,059	363,468	588,978
	89,173	138,006	226,059	373,468	598,978
Surplus on Revaluation of Fixed Assets	23,399	23,399	23,399	23,399	23,399
Liabilities against Assets Subject to Finance Lease		—	—	—	—
Deferred Liabilities	63,094	65,618	68,861	71,616	74,481
Long-Term Liabilities	4,996	4,247	7,856	14,534	26,888
Current Liabilities					
Current portion of finance lease	20,020	12,374	—	—	—
Bank finance under markup arrangement	10,000	5,000	—	—	—
Security deposits	387	387	387	387	387
Creditors, accrued and other liabilities	80,182	103,500	113,850	125,235	137,759
	110,589	121,261	114,237	125,622	138,146
	291,251	352,531	440,413	608,639	861,891
Fixed Assets	123,428	131,034	131,416	147,731	154,111
Long-Term Deposits	4,976	5,125	5,279	5,437	5,600

(continued)

EXHIBIT 14   (Continued)

	2002	2003	2004	2005	2006
Current Assets					
Trade debts—unsecured, considered good	86,914	104,297	125,156	150,187	180,225
Advances, deposits, prepayments and other receivables	58,317	64,149	70,564	77,620	85,382
Cash and bank balances	17,616	47,926	107,998	227,662	436,572
	162,847	216,372	303,718	455,470	702,179
	291,251	352,531	440,413	608,639	861,891

EXHIBIT 15   Projected Cash Flow Statement for Five Years from 2002 to 2006 (Pakistani Rupees 000)

(Assumes that TCS will start purchasing, as opposed to leasing, key assets)

Source: TCS.

	2002	2003	2004	2005	2006
Cash flow from operating activities					
Profit before taxation	**34,026**	**88,788**	**160,096**	**268,016**	**410,018**
Add: Adjustments for noncash items					
Depreciation	15,534	17,034	17,084	19,205	20,034
Amortization of intangible fixed assets	1,000	400	—	—	—
Provision for gratuity	6,972	7,111	7,253	7,398	7,546
(Gain)/Loss on disposal of fixed assets					
Financial charges on lease payments	2,000	1,500	—	—	—
	25,505	26,045	24,337	26,603	27,581
	59,531	114,833	184,433	294,620	437,599
(Increase)/decrease in current assets Trade debts	(9,500)	(17,383)	(20,859)	(25,031)	(30,037)
Advances, deposits, prepayments and other receivables	(4,320)	(5,832)	(6,415)	(7,056)	(7,762)
	(13,820)	(23,215)	(27,274)	(32,087)	(37,799)
Increase/(decrease) in current liabilities					
Creditors, accrued and other liabilities	18,629	23,318	10,350	11,385	12,524
Security deposit	—	—	—	—	—
	18,629	23,318	10,350	11,385	12,524
	64,340	114,937	167,509	273,917	412,323
Income tax paid	(16,000)	(39,955)	(72,043)	(120,607)	(184,508)
Gratuity paid	(7,077)	(8,000)	(8,240)	(8,487)	(8,742)
Net cash flows	41,263	66,982	87,226	144,823	219,073
Cash flow from investing activities					
Fixed capital expenditure	(21,535)	(19,000)	(22,000)	(25,000)	(10,000)
Sales proceeds of fixed assets					
Long-term deposits	(145)	(149)	(154)	(158)	(163)
Net cash flow	(21,680)	(19,149)	(22,154)	(25,158)	(10,163)
Cash flow from financing activities					
Lease rental paid	(24,748)	(12,374)	—	—	—
Acquisition of long-term deposits	98	(149)	—	—	—
Dividend paid	—	—	—	—	—
Net cash outflow	(24,650)	(12,523)	—	—	—
Net increase (decrease) in cash and cash equivalents	(5,067)	35,310	65,072	119,664	208,910

(continued)

EXHIBIT 15 (Continued)

	2002	2003	2004	2005	2006
Cash and cash equivalents at beginning of the year	12,683	7,616	42,926	107,998	227,662
Cash and cash equivalents at the end of the year	7,616	42,926	107,998	227,662	436,572

EXHIBIT 16 Projected P&L (2002–2006) (Pakistani Rupees 000)

(Assumes that TCS will keep leasing key assets)

Source: TCS.

	2001	2002	2003	2004	2005	2006
Gross income from services rendered	743,738	1,007,736	1,189,128	1,403,172	1,655,742	1,953,776
Less: General Sales Tax	—	(132,736)	(156,629)	(184,822)	(218,090)	(257,346)
NET SALES	743,738	875,000	1,032,500	1,218,350	1,437,653	1,696,430
Operating administrative and marketing expenses	730,067	826,631	942,412	1,057,174	1,168,962	1,286,412
Operating Profit	13,671	48,369	90,088	161,176	268,691	410,018
Financial charges	7,955	16,273	4,400	4,824	4,786	2,985
	5,716	32,096	85,688	156,352	263,905	407,033
Other income	5,245	0	0	0	0	0
Profit before taxation	10,961	32,096	85,688	156,352	263,905	407,033
Provision for taxation						
—current 45%	5,900	16,000	38,560	70,358	118,757	183,165
—prior	2,752	0	0	0	0	0
	8,652	16,000	38,560	70,358	118,757	183,165
Profit after taxation	2,309	16,096	47,128	85,993	145,148	223,868
Accumulated profit brought forward	58,838	61,147	77,243	124,371	210,365	355,513
Profit available for appropriation	61,147	77,243	124,371	210,365	355,513	579,381
Appropriations:						
Interim dividend	0	0	0	0	0	0
Unappropriated profit carried forward	61,147	77,243	124,371	210,365	355,513	579,381

EXHIBIT 17 Projected Balance Sheet (2002–2006) (Pakistani Rupees 000)

(Assumes that TCS will keep leasing key assets)

Source: TCS.

	2001	2002	2003	2004	2005	2006
Share Capital and Reserves						
Authorized capital						
200,000 (2000: 200,000) ordinary shares of Rs 100/-each	20,000	20,000	20,000	20,000	20,000	20,000
Issued, subscribed and paid-up capital	10,000	10,000	10,000	10,000	10,000	10,000
Accumulated profit	61,147	77,243	124,371	210,365	355,513	579,381
	71,147	87,243	134,371	220,365	365,513	589,381

(continued)

EXHIBIT 17   (Continued)

	2001	2002	2003	2004	2005	2006
Surplus on Revaluation of Fixed Assets	23,399	23,399	23,399	23,399	23,399	23,399
Liabilities against Assets Subject to Finance Lease	24,748	14,352	11,832	12,377	16,668	15,008
Deferred Liabilities	43,459	63,094	65,618	68,861	71,616	74,481
Long-Term Liabilities	4,898	4,996	4,247	7,856	14,534	26,888
Current Liabilities						
Current portion of finance lease	21,227	21,958	21,831	13,740	16,485	12,057
Bank finance under markup arrangement	11,482	10,000	5,000	0	0	0
Security deposits	387	387	387	387	387	387
Creditors, accrued and other liabilities	61,553	80,182	103,500	113,850	125,235	137,759
	94,649	112,527	130,718	127,977	142,107	150,203
Rupees	262,300	305,611	370,185	460,836	633,837	879,359
Fixed Assets	101,893	123,428	131,034	131,416	147,731	154,111
Long-Term Deposits	4,831	4,976	5,125	5,279	5,437	5,600
Current Assets						
Trade debts—unsecured, considered good	77,414	86,914	104,297	125,156	150,187	180,225
Advances, deposits, prepayments and other receivables	53,997	58,317	64,149	70,564	77,620	85,382
Cash and bank balances	24,165	31,976	65,580	128,421	252,861	454,040
	155,576	177,207	234,026	324,141	480,668	719,647
Rupees	262,300	305,611	370,185	460,836	633,837	879,359

EXHIBIT 18   **Projected Cash Flow Statement (2002–2006) (Pakistani Rupees 000)**

(Assumes that TCS will keep leasing key assets)

Source: TCS.

	2001	2002	2003	2004	2005	2006
Cash flow from operating activities						
Profit before taxation	**10,961**	**32,096**	**85,687**	**156,352**	**263,904**	**407,033**
Add: Adjustments for noncash items						
Depreciation	16,786	15,534	17,034	17,084	19,205	20,034
Amortization of intangible fixed assets	1,402	1,000	400			
Provision for gratuity	6,835	6,972	7,111	7,253	7,398	7,546
(Gain)/loss on disposal of fixed assets	(1,098)					
Financial charges on lease payments	6,111	3,930	4,600	3,744	4,111	2,985
	30,036	27,436	29,145	28,081	30,714	30,565
	40,997	59,532	114,832	184,433	294,618	437,598
(Increase)/decrease in current assets						
Trade debts	(9,822)	(9,500)	(17,383)	(20,859)	(25,031)	(30,037)
Advances, deposits, prepayments and other receivable	18,257	(4,320)	(5,832)	(6,415)	(7,056)	(7,762)
	8,435	(13,820)	(23,215)	(27,274)	(32,087)	(37,799)
Increase/(decrease) in current liabilities						
Creditors, accrued and other liabilities	5,540	18,629	23,318	10,350	11,385	12,524
Security deposit	284					

(continued)

EXHIBIT 18 (Continued)

	2001	2002	2003	2004	2005	2006
	5,824	18,629	23,318	10,350	11,385	12,524
	55,256	64,341	114,935	167,509	273,916	412,323
Income tax paid	(26,715)	(16,000)	(38,560)	(70,358)	(118,757)	(183,165)
Gratuity paid	(7,687)	(7,077)	(8,000)	(8,240)	(8,487)	(8,742)
Net cash flows from operating activities	20,854	41,264	68,377	88,911	146,672	220,417
Cash flow from investing activities						
Fixed capital expenditure	(17,069)					
Sales proceeds of fixed assets	14,687					
Long-term deposits	(1,203)	(145)	(149)	(154)	(158)	(163)
Net cash outflow from investing activities	(3,585)	(145)	(149)	(154)	(158)	(163)
Cash flow from financing activities						
Lease rental paid	(22,772)	(31,924)	(29,474)	(20,916)	(22,074)	(19,074)
Acquisition of long-term deposits	4,898	98	(149)			
Dividend paid						
Net cash outflow from financing activities	(17,874)	(31,826)	(29,623)	(20,916)	(22,074)	(19,074)
Net increase (decrease) in cash and cash equivalents	(605)	9,293	38,605	67,841	124,440	201,180
Cash and cash equivalents at the beginning of the year	13,290	12,685	21,978	60,583	128,424	252,864
Cash and cash equivalents at the end of the year	12,685	21,978	60,583	128,424	252,864	454,044

TCS Culture: Innovation, Openness, Collaboration

Awan firmly believed that TCS's strong corporate culture nurtured in the critical years following the separation from his brother's business was a key contributor to its success. In many ways, he was responsible for shaping this culture by personal example. For instance, the Awan brothers were well known as two of Pakistan's highest taxpayers. In a country where tax evasion at both the corporate and the individual level was rampant, this gave TCS a reputation for integrity. The TCS culture was characterized by innovation, openness, and collaboration and was fully geared to meeting the goal of being an outstanding service provider. TCS was one of the first (and few) South Asian companies with a stated set of corporate values that permeated the organization (see **Exhibit 19** for TCS core values).

Awan liked to cite several examples of innovation. TCS had recently struck a deal with a mobile phone company; it offered package-tracking services to customers through their mobile phones. Although local competitors did not offer such a service, world leaders such as FedEx and UPS offered comparable services. A simpler example was the manner in which TCS communicated critical information to its nearly 2,500 employees (see **Exhibit 20** for employee headcount). Such communications were included with employees' monthly paychecks, ensuring everyone read them. Another illustration of TCS's innovation was its self-employment scheme. TCS was one of the few Pakistani companies encouraging self-employment. Awan developed this scheme in response to what he called a "monitoring problem." It was hard for managers to keep track of productivity levels of individual delivery personnel, so Awan decided to

EXHIBIT 19
TCS Core Values

Source: TCS.

Excellence
To continually strive to achieve excellence—both on and off the job.

Quality
TCS people should direct every effort to deliver maximum value and satisfaction to our customers.

Profitability through Efficiency
Efficiency will be the hallmark of TCS people to optimize profitability and growth.

Justice
Justice is to be the guiding principle of TCS people.

Ethical Behavior
Nothing unethical shall ever be practiced by TCS people in relation to our customers and the world at large.

Exemplary Conduct
Inspirational and motivational in all that TCS people accomplish.

EXHIBIT 20
Headcount Summary

Source: TCS.

Year	Employees	Sales Solicitors	Total
2001	1,818	597	2,415
2000	1,839	554	2,393
1999	1,854	523	2,377
1998	1,664	530	2,194
1997	1,789	418	2,207

incentivize such workers by giving them a certain percentage of all income above an amount that covered all their expenses, including lease payments on motorbikes, fuel, and uniforms. This way, the need to monitor productivity was greatly reduced. Anyone who was willing to be trained had the opportunity to become a courier. Motorcycles or trucks were provided through a leasing company if needed. No formal employment contract existed between TCS and these workers. However, there was an agreement on territorial exclusivity. The attractiveness of the territory was inversely correlated with the variable component of compensation. This open-ended arrangement was attractive for the workers as it enabled them to set their own schedules and determine their own compensation.

Openness and collaboration were other important elements of the TCS culture. Management (see **Exhibit 21** for management resumes) had instituted a system whereby all officers of the company would post a log of their daily activities on an internal e-mail-based interface that 400 key employees could access directly. Printouts of this information were also displayed at major offices giving employees without the e-mail version easy access. This allowed each member of the team to be aware of developments in different functional or geographic areas in real time and made the coordination of effort easy where appropriate. A bimonthly newsletter called TCS Connect served to keep clients apprised of important developments at TCS.

TCS was also committed to giving back to the local community and donated generously to various organizations in addition to sponsoring workshops on a wide range of topics including human resource development. Human resource development was a key area of focus for Janjua, who left TCS after 11 years of service in 1996 to set up a management development center in collaboration with the British Council, before returning as COO in 2000. Janjua's return to the company was itself a tribute to the TCS culture, which he cited as the primary reason for his decision.

EXHIBIT 21 Management Resumes

Source: TCS.

Khalid Awan, Chairman. When the brothers founded TCS in 1993, Sadiq became its first Chairman and Khalid its first Chief Executive. Upon their "parting of ways" in 1991, Khalid also assumed the position of Chairman. Subsequent to his move to Canada in 2001, in pursuit of TCS's international expansion, Khalid nominated long-time associate and Chief Operating Officer Jamil Janjua as the Chief Executive, while himself retaining the Chairman's position. A mechanical-engineering graduate, Khalid spent his earlier years as a flight-engineer with Pakistan International Airlines (PIA).

Jamil Janjua, CEO. Their relationship going back to the days when he was a pilot with PIA, Jamil joined TCS as an Operations Manager in 1986. He held various positions, most notably as the Communications Coordinator during "Operation Self Renewal" in 1991, thereafter he headed Human Resource Development and Training. Left TCS in 1996 to join the British Council as Head of Management Services. He rejoined as Chief Operating Officer in May 2000. Appointed CEO in December 2000.

Saadia Awan, President. Saadia is Khalid Awan's wife. A director of the company since 1991, she played a major role in the crucial years of 1992 to 1995, filling in management gaps on a full time basis. She was named President in 1995.

Hafiz Siraj Muneer, Head of Finance. Associated with TCS since December 1999. Initially served as Head of Internal Audit. He is a Chartered Accountant and a Certified Internal Auditor by training. He has over 13 years of experience in the fields of Finance & Internal Audit and has worked in senior management positions with leading organizations. He is a member of the board of governors of IIA (Institute of Internal Audit). He is a frequent speaker on various professional and management topics at different institutes and business organizations.

Saqib Hamdani, Head of Operations. Joined TCS in mid-level position at a small station in 1987. His strong performance led to his induction in the company's "rising star" programme. Designed by Khalid this programme seeks to recognise potential high achievers and put them on a fast track to personal development. By 1995, he was Area Manager for Lahore, the company's second largest station and its main operational hub, where he implemented significant service improvements and cost reductions. Left TCS to further enhance experience in field of distribution, he rejoined after 4 years in 2000, as Head of Operations. His most recent achievement has been upgrading of TCS's aviation and road transportation capabilities, which led to increased capacity, lesser cost per unit, and enhanced profitability.

Najeeb Nayyer, Head of Marketing. Another graduate of the "rising star" programme, he too joined TCS at a small station, while still a student at age 19 in 1989. After a diversified experience both within and outside TCS, he was appointed Head of Marketing in 2000, and has since implemented major marketing initiatives.

Amir Hussain, Manager I.T. Responsible for networked data systems development, management and support, Amir has over 16 years experience in data warehousing, security, and web based applications. He brought to TCS previous experience with Fedex Pakistan, banking and communication companies.

Sohail Yaqoob, Head of Sales. Sohail joined TCS in July 2001. He has over 16 years of experience in sales having held key positions with leading multinationals and local companies. He obtained his B.S. degree from Karachi University and later got his MBA with a major in Marketing. He has lectured at various forums including Hamdard University, PCBA and Marketing Association of Pakistan. Sohail has served as Joint Secretary of Marketing Association of Pakistan, Lahore Chapter and also as Director of the Pakistan American Cultural Center.

Ali Leghari, Head Of Corporate Affairs. Ali is the most recent addition to the senior TCS team as Head of Corporate Affairs dealing with Public Relations, Legal and IT issues. Previously he served as an Executive Manager Special Projects, where he was a key player in the Marketing Department, and was instrumental in helping to update and improve the corporate and Sentiments Express websites. Prior to joining TCS he was a director in several family businesses.

Shahid Jaffery M.S., VP of Corporate Development. Experience with computer applications in banking industry. Joined TCS as Data Processing Manager in 1985. Responsible for developing relationship between TCS and Sun Microsystems and GE Information Systems. Shahid migrated to Canada in 1999 and continues his relationship with TCS as V.P. Corporate Development.

One measure of the strength of the TCS culture was that, although compensation was very competitive in local terms and hence helped attract substantial interest in the firm, employees often cited the firm culture as their principal reason for staying with the firm.

Key Challenges

Despite its success to date, both Awan and Janjua recognized that TCS faced many challenges in 2002. First and foremost, the government bureaucracy in Pakistan was a constant obstacle to business. In the words of Janjua, "legislative barriers like the Post Office Act of 1898 are like swords over our head." The Post Office periodically challenged TCS's right to deliver certain packages, alleging they were "letters" under the 1898 Act and hence could only be transported by the Post Office. This seriously restricted the types of parcels TCS could transport for its clients. A mitigating factor was that competitors such as OCS and TNT had to deal with similar problems. A second major concern was the uncertain macroeconomic direction of the Pakistan economy. Recent events had highlighted the precarious foreign debt position, and the country was still not fully integrated into the international trading system. This was due to a combination of factors. For example, major export sectors such as textiles and leather goods faced heavy tariff barriers in key Western markets, and Pakistan's nuclear program had resulted in trade sanctions from key trading partners like the United States. Furthermore, real GDP growth had slowed from 3.9% in 2000 to 2.6% in 2001, and a further slowdown could directly impact the growth of TCS. Finally, local competition had intensified. Management was particularly concerned about Leopard because of its focus on the low end of the courier services market. Leopard offered substantially cheaper prices because of its low overhead and minimal marketing expenditure. Management was concerned Leopard might be able to migrate to the high end of the market if organizations that used Leopard for their low-end needs were tempted by the lower cost to use them for their high-end needs.

Another key challenge was in human resource development. Janjua believed that although the company had come a long way in this regard, the biggest barrier to achieving information technology-based dominance was to transform the TCS culture into an information-based one populated with what he called "knowledge workers." This was difficult for a variety of reasons: Pakistan suffered from a high level of illiteracy;[7] creativity was not emphasized enough during schooling, as the majority of literate people had received their education at government schools that encouraged rote learning; and Pakistani society tended to be hierarchical in nature. For example, at Pakistan's founding in 1947, most of the new country's wealth was concentrated in the hands of only 22 families. Although the situation had since changed, there was still a strong hierarchy that governed control over the country's productive assets.[8]

TCS in Late 2001

Janjua articulated TCS's mission statement as follows:

> TCS is a service-driven company whose primary thrust is specializing in collecting, loading, unloading, clearing, storing, picking up, and delivering all types of carriageable goods and documents at the doorstep of its clients through the fastest, most reliable and secure means. Our mission is to provide service and value to customers which will contribute to their success while maintaining a decent profit.

[7] In 1997, only 40.9% of Pakistan's population was considered literate. Source: Economist. 2001. *Pocket World in Figures*. London, UK: The Economist, p. 182.

[8] A feudal system existed in the agricultural sector whereby large landlords exerted tremendous power over farm workers who depended on them for their livelihood.

A closely related goal was to be the "most outstanding service provider" in south Asia. Management acknowledged the relative maturity of the courier services business and saw the future growth of the company coming from new services. In the words of Janjua, "A logical extension of our services is to partner with companies and provide support in the areas of transportation, logistics, inventory control, and warehousing."

The Way Forward

Awan and Janjua had to evaluate the merits of the two principal strategic proposals, which were designed to achieve the corporate vision of the company's becoming a "total solution provider" for its clients while addressing the question of future growth (see **Exhibit 22** for TCS's strategy statement). This had to be done in the context of the new TCS with its international presence and exposure.

The first proposal was intended to leverage TCS's information technology infrastructure, one of its most valuable resources. The basic idea was to use TCS's IT expertise to provide supply-chain management solutions to large local manufacturers and multinationals with assembly operations in Pakistan. FedEx, arguably the best-in-class global competitor, had a similar business called FedEx Supply Chain Services. There were no supply-chain management businesses in Pakistan as of late 2001; hence, TCS would be a first mover if it went ahead with this proposal. Although this was a high-margin business with an attractive growth profile, there was concern that straying from TCS's core competency as a courier services company might be unwise. It was also not at all clear what the size of this opportunity was.

The second proposal was to take advantage of the growing export trade by creating an intermediary that would link the numerous small exporters in Pakistan's major industries such as textiles and leather goods with their buyers in North America and Europe. TCS thus hoped to earn a commission on each trade while facilitating exports. Management felt TCS was well suited to playing the intermediary role given its existing customer relationships with many small exporters who did not have the front-end capabilities needed to successfully market their products abroad. Also, the events of September 11 could make it much more difficult for small merchants to obtain visas to travel abroad to make sales calls and service their customers. While TCS would not make actual sales calls for these merchants, Awan imagined that TCS could create a virtual platform to bring buyers and sellers together. Also, TCS could handle a large part of the export paperwork and coordinate storage and shipping. Just as with the first proposal, the size of the opportunity was unclear.

EXHIBIT 22   **Statement of Strategy**

Source: TCS.

Statement of Strategy, 2001–2003

TCS during these years will remain the leading courier company of Pakistan in all aspects of quality and service. It will do so through a passion for excellence in customer care and imbued with the value of respect for all individuals, honesty, hard work, and an innovative spirit.

TCS will continue developing its services through strategic alliances and with a focus on broadening its range of customized services, while placing a high priority on profitability, internal development of IT systems and procedures and harmonized Human Resource development. While we will concentrate efforts in Pakistan we will actively develop new international markets for our core services. UAE and North America will be our initial targets where we will continue to expand wherever practical and profitable. We will utilize facilities of the international division to perform this function. In general TCS will establish a new service only if the return on investment is projected to exceed 30% before taxes within 3 years.

EXHIBIT 23   Financial Data on Global Air-Express Companies

(US $ millions, except beta, p/e and employee figures)

Source: Compiled from Bloomberg, Datastream, SEC filings, OneSource data.

		Federal Express[1]	Airborne[2]	Deutsche Post[3]	CNF[4]	UPS[5]
Sales	FY 1999	18,257	3,140	23,813	5,593	27,052
	FY 2000	19,629	3,276	30,169	5,572	29,771
Net Income	FY 1999	688	91	1,184	182	883
	FY 2000	584	28	1,395	127	2,399
Long-Term Debt	FY 1999	1,776	315	1,203	558	10,554
	FY 2000	1,900	322	41,183	660	11,927
Market Capitalization	FY end 2000	12,291	468	25,494	1,641	66,663
	9/10/2001	11,894	585	14,633	1,490	60,252
Equity Beta	9/10/2001	0.96	1.29	0.77	0.66	0.74
F/T Employees	FY end 2000	88,000	24,091	324,203	28,700	371,000
EBITDA	FY 2000	2,385	274	3,205	442	5,685
EBITDA multiple	9/10/2001	4.99	2.13	4.57	3.37	10.59
P/E Ratio	9/10/2001	20.35	20.53	10.49	11.75	20.54
EBIT	FY 2000	1,109	68	2,107	278	4,630
EBIT multiple	9/10/2001	10.72	8.65	6.95	5.37	13.01

[1]**FedEx Corporation (FedEx)** is a global provider of transportation, e-commerce, and supply-chain management services. Services offered by FedEx companies, through over 215,000 employees and contractors, include worldwide express delivery, ground small-parcel delivery, less-than-truckload freight delivery, supply-chain management, customs brokerage, and trade facilitation and electronic commerce solutions. FedEx offers its integrated business solutions through a portfolio of operating companies, including Federal Express Corporation, the company's largest subsidiary.

[2]**Airborne, Inc.** is a holding company operating through its subsidiaries as an air-express company and airfreight forwarder. Airborne expedites shipments of all sizes to destinations throughout the U.S. and most foreign countries. The company's wholly owned operating subsidiaries include Airborne Express, Inc. (AEI), ABX Air, Inc. (ABX), and Sky Courier, Inc. AEI provides domestic and international delivery services in addition to customer service, sales, and marketing activities. ABX provides domestic express cargo service and cargo service to Canada and Puerto Rico. Sky Courier provides delivery service on an expedited basis.

[3]**Deutsche Post AG.** The Group's principal activities are divided into four divisions: letters: the conveying and distribution of letters in Germany; express parcels: conveying and distribution of parcels; logistics: the distribution of freight worldwide; and financial services: banking. Mail accounted for 34% of 2001 revenues; logistics, 26%; financial services, 22%; and express parcels, 18%. Deutsche Post owns 46% of DHL Worldwide Express, a global market leader of the international air-express industry.

[4]**CNF, Inc.** is a management company of global supply-chain services. CNF's operations are represented primarily by four business segments: Con-Way Transportation Services (Con-Way), Emery Worldwide (Emery), Menlo Logistics (Menlo), and Other Con-Way. Con-Way provides regional next-day and second-day less-than-truckload freight trucking throughout the United States, Canada, and Mexico, as well as expedited transportation, logistics, airfreight forwarding, and truckload brokerage services. Emery provides expedited and deferred domestic and international heavy airfreight services, ocean delivery, and customs brokerage. Menlo provides integrated contract logistics services, including the development and management of complex distribution networks, and supply-chain engineering and consulting. The Other segment primarily includes the operating results of Road Systems, a trailer manufacturer, and Vector SCM.

[5]**United Parcel Service, Inc. (UPS)** is an express carrier package delivery company and global provider of specialized transportation and logistics services. In 2001, UPS delivered an average of more than 13.5 million pieces per day worldwide. UPS has established a vast global transportation infrastructure and developed a comprehensive portfolio of guaranteed delivery services for packages in over 200 countries, and it supports these services with advanced technology. The company provides logistics services, including integrated supply-chain management, for major companies worldwide. UPS is also engaged in the delivery of goods purchased over the Internet.

Notes:

Equity betas are calculated with five years of monthly data except Deutsche Post (December 2000-August 2001) and UPS (November 1999-August 2001).

UPS merged with Fritz Companies on May 24, 2001 and First International Bancorp on August 7, 2001.

Finally, Awan and Janjua needed to ascertain how well these two proposals fit with TCS's plans for continued geographic expansion. There was lots of room for growth in the UAE market, and the Canadian operations would need significant management attention and capital to gain a foothold in the brutally competitive North American market. TCS was also considering expanding into the central Asian republics (Kazakhstan, Kyrgyzstan, Tajikistan, Turkmenistan, and Uzbekistan) in the near future, and Awan had aspirations of eventually building a truly global company (see **Exhibit 23** for financial information on five global air-express companies).

Awan picked up the phone. There were a number of things he wanted to talk about. Above all there was the likely impact of September 11, 2001. Then there were the proposals for new businesses, and finally there were considerations about harvesting some part of his firm.

Case

25

TelePizza

As he walked towards the exit of a recently opened TeleGrill in Madrid, Leopoldo Fernández, founder and CEO of TelePizza, paused. It was Thursday, October 22, 1998, and the restaurant was quiet. Only three diners were seated at tables, and most of the delivery staff was waiting for orders. Fernández knew that it was too early in the evening to expect much activity, but the TeleGrill concept was still relatively new and untested.

Together with a project team, Fernández had spent many hours planning the TeleGrill concept, but he knew that planning wasn't everything in the restaurant business. What really mattered was the number and timing of improvement iterations early in the life of a concept. Fernández looked around. Was the food preparation area, which was visible to customers through a large window, attractive and clean? Were the color combinations of dining room interior and waiter's uniforms appealing? Was the room lighting too bright? After all, TeleGrill was not designed to be another fast-food restaurant. There were so many judgement calls to make over the coming months.

If TeleGrill was to form part of the aggressive growth plan the TelePizza company had set for itself, Fernandez had to be sure the concept was attractive. In any case, the sister chain would be hard-pressed to match TelePizza's success. From a single store in 1988, TelePizza had grown to become the largest pizza chain in Spain, ending 1997 with 399 stores in Spain and an estimated market share of 62% plus 68 stores internationally. (See **Exhibit 1** for a recent history of store growth.) Chain-wide sales, including owned and franchised stores, had grown to Ptas 39.6 billion ($1 = Ptas 143). (See **Exhibit 2** for TelePizza's financial statements.)

TelePizza's ability to set demanding targets and then achieve them had earned the company a high valuation on the Spanish IBEX 35 index,[1] enriching not only Fernández (who controlled 36% of the company) but many of his employees who owned stock or

[1] The IBEX 35 is the major Spanish stock market index. In 1998, its 35 companies represented approximately 80% of the total Spanish stock market capitalization. TelePizza, added in July 1998, was the most recent component of the index.

Charles M. Williams Fellow Chad Ellis (MBA '98) prepared this case under the supervision of Professor Walter Kuemmerle and Professor Juan Roure of IESE Barcelona, Spain. HBS cases are developed solely as the basis for class discussion. Cases are not intended to serve as endorsements, sources of primary data, or illustrations of effective or ineffective management.

EXHIBIT 1
Store Growth History

Source: TelePizza.

	1997	1996	1995	1994	1993
Spain	399	236	204	150	100
TelePizza	311	236	204	150	100
Pizza World	88	0	0	0	0
Other Countries	68	51	44	32	21
TelePizza					
Portugal	26	21	18	11	9
Mexico	24	16	14	11	8
Poland	8	6	4	3	1
Chile	10	8	8	7	3
Total number of stores	467	287	248	182	121

EXHIBIT 2
TelePizza Financial Statements

Sources: TelePizza Annual Report.

Consolidated Profit and Loss Account (at December 31)—(Figures in Millions of Pesetas)

	1997	1996
Turnover	26,876	17,993
Other revenues	2,081	1,373
Total revenues	**28,957**	**19,366**
Total consumables	**(9,276)**	**(6,207)**
Gross margin	**19,681**	**13,159**
Personnel costs	(8,383)	(5,572)
Depreciation and amortization	(1,219)	(746)
Other operating expenses	(6,139)	(3,867)
Total operating expenses	**(15,741)**	**(10,185)**
Operating profit	**3,940**	**2,974**
Financial income	83	66
Financial expenses	(141)	(147)
Financial result	**(58)**	**(81)**
Share in profits from companies consolidated under the equity method	90	54
Amortization of consolidated goodwill	(104)	(106)
Profit before extraordinary items	**3,868**	**2,841**
Extraordinary income	121	153
Extraordinary expenses	(282)	(381)
Extraordinary results	**(161)**	**(228)**
Profit before taxes	**3,707**	**2,613**
Corporation tax	(1,091)	(840)
Profit for the year	**2,616**	**1,773**
Profit allocated to minority interests	(105)	(71)
Profit allocated to the parent company	**2,511**	**1,702**

(continued)

had options on TelePizza shares. (See **Exhibit 3** for valuation comparisons, including analysts' consensus estimates for TelePizza.) Fernández knew that stumbling now could jeopardize some of that valuation, hampering the firm's ability to raise capital and reducing the value of the equity and options held by his employees.

Fernández took another look around and made a mental note to talk to his team about the brightness of the lighting. After a friendly nod to the store manager, he walked out onto the Madrid streets and remembered that refining the TeleGrill concept was only one of the challenges he and his management team faced. Growing rapidly off a small, domestic base had been difficult enough. Maintaining the same rate of growth now would

EXHIBIT 2
(Continued)

Consolidated Balance Sheet (at December 31)—(Figures in Millions of Pesetas)		
	1997	1996
Assets		
Fixed assets	9,673	5,359
Start-up expenses	28	27
Intangible assets	813	892
Tangible assets	7,742	3,964
Financial assets	434	226
Parent company shares	656	250
Merger goodwill	659	733
Consolidated goodwill	1,424	283
Deferred expenses	264	265
Current assets	3,843	2,944
Stocks	808	449
Debtors	1,896	1,216
Short-term investments	29	857
Cash and banks	1,001	377
Prepayments and accrued interest	109	45
Total assets	15,863	9,584
Liabilities		
Capital and reserves	5,913	3,279
Subscribed capital	1,073	1,073
Reserves	2,329	504
Profit and loss allocated to the parent company	2,511	1,702
Minority interests	292	205
Negative consolidation difference	233	236
Provisions for risks and liabilities	371	299
Long-term liabilities	2,369	1,119
Current liabilities	6,685	4,446
Total liabilities	15,863	9,584

require opening new stores more rapidly than the company had ever done before. Could TelePizza duplicate its success in other countries? How effective would the company's current structure and management philosophy be at handling that growth?

From Medical Instruments to Pizza

Fernández was born in Cuba in 1947 to a family descended from military Spaniards and other immigrants. From his earliest days he wanted to establish himself in business. "All my grandparents were entrepreneurs," he recalled. "My parents were professionals who had a comfortable life until 1959, but my mentality was always to be an entrepreneur."

Fernández's family left Cuba on July 18, 1960, and went into exile to the United States. In 1968, Fernández left college, entered the U.S. military and spent one year in Vietnam, during which time his mother died. After four years in the military, where he graduated number one in his class at Officer Candidate School, Fernández went back to college, keeping a promise he had made to his mother before going to Vietnam. He earned an undergraduate degree in accounting and finance from Stetson University in Florida. "Any entrepreneur must understand a P&L statement, balance sheet, cash-flow projections and the importance of each in order to evaluate a business," he explained.

After college, Fernández spent less than a year working in sales for Proctor & Gamble. "Within three months I had made my annual quota," he recalled. "They came to see me from Cincinnati." Despite tripling sales, he was given only a 10% salary increase, and seven months later Fernández left the company.

EXHIBIT 3 Valuation Comparisons

Source: Compiled from Thomson Financial Datastream, Firstcall data.

	Share Price (local) (10/22/98)	Market Capitalization (blns)	Earnings per Share			Total Sales 1997 (mlns)
			1997	1998E	1999E	
TelePizza	Ptas 1,150	227.8	11.7	17.2	23.0	28,975
High-Growth Spanish Cos.						
Aumar	3,170	195	90	95	100	32,129
Tabacalera	3,425	631	94	110	118	255,900
Vallehermoso	1,770	228	43	47	65	46,200
Fast food companies						
Tricon (Pizza Hut)	$46	7.2	−0.56	2.57	2.65	9,413
Papa John's	$36.25	1.1	0.93	1.25	1.64	509
Pizza Express (UK)	595p	0.4	26.4	34.1	42.6	100
Wendy's	$19	2.6	1.33	1.15	1.30	2,037
McDonalds	$67	47.3	2.29	2.52	2.85	11,408

Note: TelePizza and other Spanish company data in Ptas. Pizza Express share data in pence; market capitalization and sales in pounds sterling. Tricon, Papa John's, Wendy's and McDonald's data all in US$. The equity beta for TelePizza in October 1998 was 0.74.

In 1975, Fernández joined Johnson & Johnson (J&J), selling surgical instruments in New York City. In 1976 he was promoted to head of sales for the Latin American surgical instruments company. Despite his success, Fernández ran into difficulties with his boss. "I always went my own way, wanted to be my own boss. He told me he thought I was after his job." The following year Fernández was promoted and moved to Guatemala. He quickly changed the operation there, firing 90% of the sales force over 18 months and replacing them with bilingual college graduates.

Fernández moved several times over the next nine years, starting new ventures for J&J in Latin America and then in Spain. In December of 1986, however, he found himself facing another conflict with a supervisor. "I was totally gung-ho J&J," he explained. "I had moved five times in six years for J&J, and suddenly I was presented with a boss who saw the business differently."

Fernández felt he had two options, either to stay in Spain or to return to the United States. In addition to his career questions, Fernández was in the process of getting divorced. He decided to take the opportunity to indulge his entrepreneurial ambitions:

> I had only small savings, around $100,000, and was getting divorced in my late 30s. Nevertheless, I felt confident of my future. I decided it was time to go it on my own. The idea of pizza delivery service was in the air—U.S. chains were already doing well. I started a pizza store near my home because there was only one little store in my neighborhood.

Still working at J&J (he would not leave until December 1988), Fernández opened his first store, under the name Pizzaphone, in October 1987. Exactly one year later, he opened his second, this time under the name of TelePizza. In both cases, Fernández borrowed heavily from the fast-food practices of the major chains such as McDonald's and Domino's. He also decided to expand through franchises in order to gain the maximum benefit from expansion of the brand.

The results were highly profitable stores and rapid growth. TelePizza ended 1989 with eight stores and 1990 with eighteen. By 1993 there were 121 TelePizza stores, of which roughly 70% were franchised, and the chain had expanded into Latin America and other European countries. Moreover, this growth had come with only modest external financing. Initial equity of $100,000 in 1987 and $300,000 in 1988 had been provided by Fernández and his brother, Eduardo. In 1991, the brothers raised an additional $1.4 million from 30 different individual investors, who provided an additional $700,000 in 1994. Fernández, therefore, retained 40% of the equity in his company throughout its rapid expansion.

Despite this success, Fernández was forced out of the company in September 1995. Three years earlier, Eduardo, who held 32% of TelePizza's equity from his early investments, had come to work in the company. The two brothers had differences, particularly over the question of harvesting their investment. While Fernández was working on expanding the chain's presence in Mexico, Eduardo and other shareholders with an additional 20% of the equity forced him to step down as CEO.

Fernández returned as CEO in July 1996 because it became clear to the other shareholders that he was extremely difficult to replace. One employee stated, "Fernández is really the spirit behind TelePizza." TelePizza held an initial public offering of its shares in November of that year, at which point Eduardo sold his stake in the company.[2] Despite his successful return, Fernández did not look back upon his ouster fondly. "In my opinion, there were a number of people who committed treason," he stated. "I am not talking to my brother any more."

The TelePizza Concept

Management Philosophy

Although Fernández sought to learn from the successes and failures of other fast-food chains, he also developed TelePizza in line with his personal philosophy and the lessons he learned at P&G and J&J. TelePizza placed a high emphasis on hiring the best people, even for notoriously high-turnover positions such as food preparation and delivery, entrusting them with a relatively high degree of responsibility and providing them with the training, opportunity and incentives to succeed. (See **Exhibit 4** for resumes of senior management.) José Luis Vazquez, joint Managing Director, stated:

> When I joined in 1996, my biggest surprise was the commitment of TelePizza's people.
> I think this is because we hire people very young, often without experience, and give them
> opportunities for growth. This company is very different from any other company I know.

Most of TelePizza's store managers had started with the company as delivery people, and if an employee showed sufficient capabilities, TelePizza would often help them become franchisees. Entry-level employees could also rise to top management positions. Both Eduardo Hernandez, Director of International Operations, and Pedro Espanol, Director of Human Resources, began their TelePizza careers as a delivery boys.

TelePizza also maintained a strong commitment to organizational flexibility. Positions, responsibilities and strategy were frequently changed to respond to new information or changing market conditions. Vazquez explained:

> We change this organization constantly, whenever Leopoldo or Carlos[3] or I think something
> is not going well. For example, we used to have different supervisors for owned and fran-
> chised stores, but now we supervise stores on a geographic basis. For us, more than eight
> months with the same organization chart feels strange now.

The ability to react quickly and to push responsibility down the organization was supported by a commitment to measurement. "We measure everything," explained Vazquez. "Without that we would not have the tools to make good decisions."

Human Resources

Human resources (HR) management was central to TelePizza's approach. "Our biggest bottleneck," Fernández explained, "is human resources—finding and developing management talent." To improve its HR capabilities, TelePizza had recently replaced much

[2] No new capital was raised for TelePizza in the IPO.

[3] Carlos Lopez, joint managing director.

EXHIBIT 4
Management
Resumes

Source: TelePizza.

Jose Luis Vasquez

Personal
- Date of birth: October, 4 1953
- Married, two children

Education
- Universidad Complutense (Madrid), Graduated 1976 with degree in Mathematics
- Universidad Autonoma (Madrid), received Masters degree in Operational Research, 1976

Professional Experience
- Andersen Consulting (1977–1982), Marketing and Distribution Consultant
- Pond's Eliba Gibb (Unilever Group) (1982–1988), Director of Marketing and Sales
- Repsol, S.A. (1988–1996) General Manager of Retail Business
- TelePizza, S.A. (1996 to present) General Manager

Carlos López Casas

Personal
- Date of birth: November 19, 1960
- Married, two children

Education
- Universidad Pontificia de Comillas, received degrees in Law (1982) and Economics and Business Administration (1983)

Professional Experience
- Arthur Andersen (1989–1994), Team Chief (1987–1989) and Manager/Director (1989–1994)
- Cofir (1994–1996) Director of Investments
- TelePizza, S.A. (1996 to present) General Manager
- Since 1983: Professor of Finance at ICADE, Universidad Pontificia de Comillas

---

of its HR department. "We used to have psychologists in HR," said Espanol. "We dismissed them. Now the best store managers work for a year in HR and then go out as store supervisors."

Along with the staffing change came a revised approach to HR within TelePizza. Espanol explained the need for change:

> Human resources has three responsibilities: recruiting, training and evaluating. The old HR people didn't fully respect TelePizza's philosophy of hiring and growing the best young people, so they didn't invest enough effort in training them or in making sure managers have the right mentality to help their employees grow.

The new system centered around anonymous evaluations of each manager by up to 50 people who worked with him or her. This data enabled HR to determine where each manager needed to develop his or her capabilities. It also told them when a manager's "mentality" was incompatible with TelePizza's strategy. "When we implemented the new system," Espanol recalled, "we immediately found three managers we had to dismiss."

Store supervisors visited each store in their region twice per month. They monitored success and compliance with TelePizza operating procedures, but also sought to share the accumulated learning of the organization so each manager had the tools to improve. "Most store managers," explained Fernández, "need not only control, but coaching. In fact, good coaching makes the difference. Good control only gets you so far."

Fernández was pleased with TelePizza's HR capabilities. "I think we do a better job than Domino's or Pizza Hut at helping people to become managers," he stated. "Our system is also very selective, so we seldom have to fire people at the management level. However, the worst disease in management is not to be able to fire subordinates. If you can't do that, you develop parasites."

TelePizza's management approach required that senior managers maintain contact with line personnel. Espanol recalled a visit to a store with Fernández during which the CEO had stopped an assistant manager and asked about an illness he had been suffering from during the last visit. This level of close contact and communication was considered central to TelePizza's management philosophy, but the company's rapid growth had put strains on the system. "Each day it is harder for us to stay close with line management," admitted Vazquez, "but we do try."

Workforce Challenges

The most serious management challenge for TelePizza arose from the basic nature of the food delivery business. Delivery jobs offered fairly low wages, tended to attract younger workers and had high turnover. Managing a relatively unskilled and rapidly changing group could prove difficult. "I once had a franchisee who also owned a five-star hotel," Fernández recalled with a smile. "He said managing his TelePizza store was more challenging."

Most delivery chains responded to this by making the delivery job as simple as possible so that replacing a worker was a relatively smooth transition. TelePizza instead sought to upgrade both its entry-level employees and the responsibilities they handled. In return, employees were rewarded with incentives; over 20% of compensation for delivery staff came from performance bonuses.

TelePizza placed a strong emphasis on hiring college students and helping them build part-time work schedules that fit their studies. Seventy percent of the firm's part-time workers were in college. Another 15% were hoping to build a full-time career within TelePizza. Only 15% were in transition or between jobs and likely to leave on short notice. Thus, while turnover was still a challenge for management, TelePizza believed its turnover was lower than that of its competitors.

TelePizza also entrusted employees with more responsibility than did most competitors, as illustrated by the company's couponing system. A typical TelePizza store would map out the area it was responsible for and segment it into eighty-eight different sections. Each delivery person would be responsible for two sections. When the store opened, each delivery person would walk through his or her area and count all the mailboxes. Then, for two hours each week, they would revisit their sections, putting coupons in each mailbox.

This system was supported by TelePizza's passion for measurements. Whenever an order came in, the store's computer automatically recorded which section it was from. By aggregating the measures, the store could identify underperforming sections and reward employees whose section performed well.

Growing Sales Through Service

TelePizza's employees were also responsible for a variety of other activities to maximize sales. Each day employees at every TelePizza store would call every tenth customer who had visited the previous day to thank them for their order and to make sure they were satisfied. The store computer would also alert staff to previous customers who had not ordered a pizza within the past six months. Store employees would then call that customer with a special offer, such as two pizzas for the price of one or a discount on their next order.

Building a Brand

Part of TelePizza's efforts to build sales lay in the development of a distinct identity in the consumers' mind. "From the start," explained Fernández, "whenever we took an order we would ask, 'What TelePizza would you like?' We want our customers to think of pizza in terms of TelePizza." In order to raise awareness of the brand, TelePizza delivery people also wore standard uniforms and delivered pizzas on red mopeds. On-time delivery and customer service were stressed in personnel training.

TelePizza concentrated its efforts on families eating at home. "The fast food market in Spain only began growing when more women started working," explained Fernández. "They want convenience at an attractive price and with a variety of products." TelePizza sought to meet this need by offering salads, side dishes (such as gazpacho[4] in the summer) and ice cream, along with its variety of pizza toppings. Non-pizza items accounted for roughly 8% of sales. Modest pricing and regular coupon specials provided a sense of value to cost-conscious customers. (See **Exhibit 5** for a TelePizza menu.)

TelePizza also sought to be the preferred choice of young children, believing that when a family ordered pizza, it would likely be the children that decided whether to call for pizza. TelePizza, therefore, offered promotions such as their Magic Club. Children were offered a free videotape that explained 12 magic tricks. Through pizza purchases children could build up points towards the gadgets needed to perform the tricks described in the video. Buying two pizzas would be enough to earn one trick. In 1998, the Magic Club had an average of 3,000 members per store. TelePizza also offered specials for birthdays and used its computer database to mail birthday-party advertisements to Magic Club members when his or her birthday was approaching.

In order to create an even higher level of awareness among children, TelePizza had also created a program to familiarize classes of school children and their teachers to the closest TelePizza store. Store managers would regularly invite classes of kindergarten and elementary school children to their store during off-peak hours, typically in the morning. After a tour of the store and a pizza tasting, each child would be photographed with a TelePizza hat. In order to mail the developed picture to each child, the store manager would collect all the children's addresses. This data could later be used for marketing efforts.

As a result of TelePizza's efforts, the brand enjoyed almost universal recognition within Spain. "Talking about pizza in Spain means TelePizza," stated Mercedes Sanjuanbenito, Director of Marketing. Surveys TelePizza commissioned showed brand awareness of nearly 100% and a favorable perception of TelePizza's quality and value.

Competition

TelePizza's rise was helped by the less-developed state of the Spanish pizza market. Although both the Domino's and Pizza Hut chains were present in Spain, neither had reached the level of market presence achieved in the U.S. In recent years, in fact, both U.S. chains had been on the decline in Spain, and the acquisition by TelePizza of its major domestic rival, Pizza World (described below), had cemented the company's leading market-share position. (See **Exhibit 6** for the number of stores by chain.)

Growth through Franchising

Nearly half of TelePizza's stores were owned and operated by roughly 100 franchisees, the largest of whom owned 14 stores. Many franchisees had been managers in TelePizza stores, while others were simply entrepreneurs who wanted to run their own business but preferred to invest in a proven concept with relatively low risk.

A franchisee would be given exclusive delivery rights within a 400-meter radius from the store. In TelePizza's early years, exclusivity had been for a two-kilometer radius in year one and one kilometer in year two. If TelePizza planned on opening another store nearby, the franchisee would normally be given the first opportunity to open it. A typical franchise contract ran for ten years, and stipulated compliance with TelePizza's operating procedures, a royalty on sales, and required spending on promotions.

---

[4] A vegetable soup served cold, popular in Spain.

EXHIBIT 5 TelePizza and TeleGrill Menus

Source: TelePizza.

(continued)

EXHIBIT 5 (Continued)

TelePizza Menu (Inside View)

OFERTAS

2 x 1 — Local y Recoger
Llévese **2 PIZZAS PAGUE SOLO 1**
Pizzas Medianas y Familiares
(3 ó más ingredientes)
(de igual o menor valor la segunda)
No incluye la 3 PISOS

DESCUENTO 50% — Local y Domicilio
50% DE DESCUENTO en la compra de la **2ª PIZZA**
Medianas y Familiares
(de igual o menor valor la segunda)
3 o más ingredientes
No incluye la 3 PISOS

Válidas los 7 días de la semana

OFERTA DESCUENTO — Local y Domicilio
350 Pts. PIZZA MEDIANA Y 3 PISOS
500 Pts. PIZZA FAMILIAR
3 o más ingredientes

BEBIDAS GRATIS — Local y Domicilio
PIZZA FAMILIAR (5 ó más ingredientes)
GRATIS 4 BEBIDAS Y 6 ALITAS DE POLLO

MENU MEDIANA — Local y Domicilio
PIZZA MEDIANA (Hasta 3 ingredientes)
+ 2 BEBIDAS + 2 HELADOS 100 ml.
ó
+ 2 HELADOS 500 ml. +1 ENSALADA
SOLO 1.895 Pts. No incluye Especialidades

Válidas los 7 días de la semana
LAS OFERTAS NO SON ACUMULABLES ENTRE SI.

PIZZAS AL GUSTO

	Precio Pequeña (1 persona) 23 cm	Precio Mediana (2-3 pers.) 31 cm	Precio Familiar (4-6 pers.) 41 cm
TelePizza **Base** (Tomate, orégano y mozzarella)	750	1.045	1.675
TelePizza **Ingrediente adicional**	105	170	220
TelePizza **Base + 1 ingrediente**	855	1.215	1.895
TelePizza **Base + 2 ingredientes**	960	1.385	2.115
TelePizza **Base + 3 ingredientes**	1.065	1.555	2.335
TelePizza **Base + 4 ingredientes**	1.170	1.725	2.555
TelePizza **Base + 5 ingredientes**	1.275	1.895	2.775
Porción en local	255		

SUGERENCIAS

	Precio Pequeña	Precio Mediana	Precio Familiar
TelePizza **ESPECIAL DE LA CASA**	1.275	1.895	2.775
TelePizza **HAWAIANA**	1.065	1.555	2.335
TelePizza **SUPREMA**	1.275	1.895	2.775
TelePizza **JALISCO**	1.275	1.895	2.775

ESPECIALIDADES

	Precio Pequeña	Precio Mediana	Precio Familiar
TelePizza **AHUMADOS**	1.275	1.895	2.775
TelePizza **4 QUESOS**	1.205	1.780	2.650
TelePizza **3 PISOS**		1.635	
TelePizza **Ingrediente adicional**	105	170	220

COMPLEMENTOS

Alitas de Pollo 6 uds. 300 / 6 piezas 445
Salsa adicional 50

ENSALADAS

Ensalada Palomas 295
Ensalada Cangrejos 375
Ensalada Americana 295

BEBIDAS 33 cl.

Coca Cola / Fanta 145
Cerveza / Mahou 145
Agua mineral 100

GAZPACHO

100% NATURAL 245

HELADOS

VASO 100 ml. 275
VASO 500 ml. 725

SALSAS

12 uds. 450
10 piezas 655

INGREDIENTES:

Extra mozzarella, Pimiento verde, Pimiento morrón, Jamón, Bacon, Ternera, Cebolla, Champiñón, Anchoas, Atún, Piña, Pepperoni, Aceitunas verdes, Aceitunas negras, Alcaparras, Salsa Jalisco

TelePizza A SU GUSTO: Si lo desea, podemos hacer su pizza con una mitad de un gusto y la otra mitad de otro. PEDIDO MÍNIMO DE 1 PIZZA COMPLETA.

(continued)

EXHIBIT 5 (Continued)

TeleGrill Menu (Rear View)

TeleGrill Menu (Front View)

(continued)

EXHIBIT 5   (Continued)

TeleGrill Menu (Inside View)

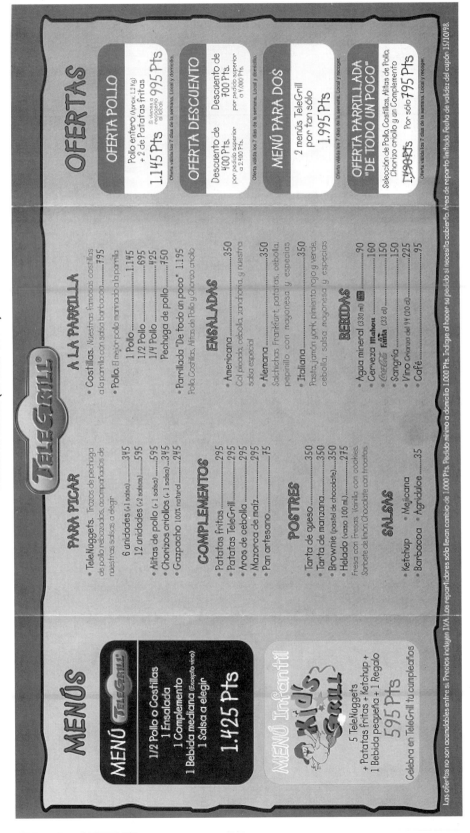

EXHIBIT 6
**Major Competitors
in Spain**

Source: TelePizza.

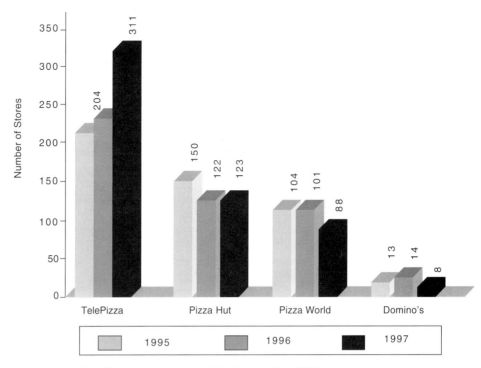

Pizza World was acquired by TelePizza in May 1997.

Pizza World was acquired by TelePizza in May 1997.

Ricardo Garrastazu became a franchisee after working in TelePizza. Garrastazu worked under Fernández at J&J and had always wanted to be an entrepreneur. When Fernández left J&J in 1988 to devote himself to TelePizza, Garrastazu joined him. "Leo was a good teacher of business," he recalled, "and I wanted to continue learning from him." Later Garrastazu would realize his ambitions of entrepreneurship:

> In 1989 we had eight stores, of which one was franchised. My first job was to write a manual on store operations so that each store would be run as efficiently as possible. Later I became marketing manager, but I really wanted my own business. When I joined, Leo gave me 1% of the company. In 1993 I exchanged that for two stores.

Garrastazu opened three additional stores over the next five years. Although financially he would have been better off holding on to his 1%, he was happy with his decision. "I have the satisfaction of running my own stores and the freedom of being self-employed. The only thing I miss is the opportunity to make really big decisions that affect the whole company."

Most franchisee relationships had worked out well. Fernández believed this was due largely to the profitability of running a TelePizza franchise; the company estimated the pre-tax return on investment for a franchisee at 40%. Nevertheless, conflicts could arise, and the franchise contract included an agreed-on exit price of five times trailing earnings before interest and depreciation. Fernández explained, "Our mentality is that a franchisee is like an employee. When we do the franchise contract, we already have an exit—five times earnings of the last twelve months."

Store Economics

A franchisee considering opening a TelePizza store had to make an up-front investment of roughly Ptas 30 million and pay TelePizza a one-time franchise fee of Ptas 2.5 million. Once established, a new store would typically generate monthly sales of at least Ptas 10 million, at which point it would have a monthly operating profit of Ptas 1 million. Successful stores often had monthly sales in excess of Ptas 12 million. Costs for a store broke down roughly as follows: 30% ingredients, 10% fixed wages, 20% variable wages, 2% special promotions, 15% rent & other fixed expenses, and 9% for the franchise royalty and advertising fee. The advertising fee supported TelePizza's advertising expenditures, which ran at roughly 4% of chain-wide sales.

Acquisition of Pizza World

In May 1997, TelePizza acquired Pizza World for Ptas 1.84 billion. Pizza World was Spain's number 3 competitor behind TelePizza and Pizza Hut, with 39 owned and 71 franchised stores concentrated in the state of Catalonia.

The acquisition served several strategic goals. Domino's, at that point only a marginal player in the Spanish pizza market, had expressed interest in buying Pizza World. TelePizza was therefore able to pre-empt a possible effort to establish critical mass in Spain. But Carlos Lopez, joint managing director for TelePizza, said that the acquisition offered TelePizza more than excluding a potential rival:

> Acquiring Pizza World was a positive experience for the group overall. We learned a lot about how to do an acquisition and how to integrate our management systems into an acquired store. This is important for us, because as we expand into other countries acquiring an existing chain is one way we can do it.

TelePizza originally intended to convert all Pizza World stores to the TelePizza brand, but ultimately decided to convert only 19 stores and maintain Pizza World as a separate brand. Sanjuanbenito explained the decision:

> TelePizza means family and friends together. It's enjoyment, sharing, warm food. The Pizza World brand appeals more to teenagers—there is a feeling of independence from your parents. We decided that it made sense to maintain a second brand that would compete in that market niche.

While the brand was left alone, substantial changes were made in Pizza World's management. TelePizza brought to Pizza World the operations techniques and management philosophy on which it had built its success. Roughly 90% of Pizza World's permanent employees left during the transition, but Lopez believed the transition had been successful. "Our processes are mostly in place and most Pizza World stores are on track to sell Ptas 10 million per month."

Support Operations

 In order to ensure consistent quality and taste throughout the chain, TelePizza centralized manufacturing of its dough in Guadalajara, Spain. Dough for Latin American stores or other stores too distant to be serviced from Spain was manufactured locally. Other ingredients were purchased from two to three suppliers of that material, which the company believed, gave it the maximum advantages in cost and consistency without excessive risk of disruption of supply.

Although TelePizza preferred to purchase most of its non-dough ingredients from independent suppliers, in May 1998, the company integrated vertically into cheese production by buying a cheese factory. Fernández explained the decision:

> Well, first we think it is a profitable investment. But strategically, there was only one domestic producer large enough to service the entire chain, which gave this producer too much bargaining power. We also do research and development on cheese, which we do not want spilling over to our competitors. If we develop a cheese that performs well but have to show an independent company how to manufacture it, it would be hard to keep it secret.

TelePizza also invested $4 million to establish its own fleet of 70 trucks. "There weren't any companies large enough to handle our requirements at the price we would desire," Fernández stated. "We also work on a just-in-time basis with very low inventories at the store level, so ensuring on-time delivery is crucial."

Although each of these expansions made strategic sense, Fernández knew that there were opportunity costs involved in vertical integration, both in terms of capital and management focus. It would be important to make sure TelePizza carefully considered any similar plans in the future.

The Mission: We Must Grow

Underlying all of TelePizza's efforts to support its brand and existing stores lay an almost obsessive commitment to growth. Fernández said:

> I realized in 1989 that our biggest cost was not growing sales because we have a high fixed cost. There are two ways you can manage in this business: to make money by investing for growth or to not lose money by holding back costs. The latter was Pizza World's way.

TelePizza's strategy for growth had three main elements: expansion within the domestic pizza market, international expansion and introducing new concepts such as TeleGrill.

Domestic Pizza Market

"Our core business in Spain is growing at 20% p.a. for at least the next three years," stated Vazquez. He explained his enthusiasm for the Spanish market:

> The opportunity for growth is there. If we look at the U.S. market, Domino's went from 200 stores to 2,000 stores because of growth in demand. This wasn't primarily new people deciding to eat pizza; it was an increase in repetition and an increase in the size of the average order.

Analysis by industry research group Euromonitor, showed how far Spanish pizza consumption would have to grow to reach U.S. per-capita levels. (See **Exhibit 7.**) Although pizza had a higher share of the overall fast food market in Spain than in the U.S., American per-capita spending on pizza was over thirteen times Spanish levels. (See **Exhibit 8** for macroeconomic data on Spain.)

TelePizza hoped to grow domestic sales not only by opening new stores, but also by increasing both the frequency and size of customer purchases. Couponing strategies and collectible promotions such as the Magic Club were designed to increase customer repetition, and staff training emphasized techniques to maximize orders, such as asking customers if they would like an additional side order or telling them of specials. "Our profits are closely correlated with sales," explained Garrastazu. "If we increase the average order size by Ptas 200 it would represent Ptas 1 million more in sales per store per month."

TelePizza's management knew that domestic expansion through new store openings would not be as easy in the future as it had been. Penetration was already high, with at least one TelePizza store in every Spanish city with more than 20,000 residents.

International Expansion

Hernandez described TelePizza's vision for international expansion:

> [We want to] be number one in fast food in all countries we go to. Our criteria for expansion are the size of the market, cultural proximity, language and geographic proximity. Our approach is to grow organically with owned and franchised stores, considering also the possibility of buying an existing business in the more developed markets.

TelePizza had entered Portugal, Mexico and Poland in 1992, Chile in 1993 and France in 1998. The United Kingdom, Morocco, Germany, Brazil and several smaller countries were targeted for 1999 and 2000. In each of these markets, TelePizza looked for possible

EXHIBIT 7 International Comparisons: Pizza Consumption

Source: Company documents.

Pizza Market Share in the Fast-Food Market

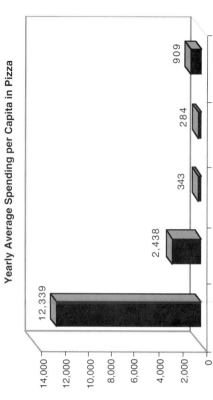

Yearly Average Spending per Capita in Pizza

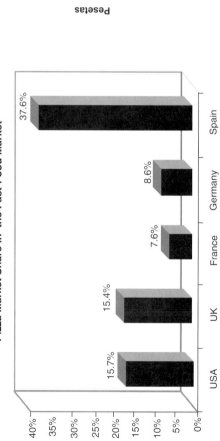

EXHIBIT 8

Macroeconomic Data on Spain

Source: Compiled from World Bank data.

	1976	1986	1996	1997
GDP ($ billions)	108.6	230.8	581.6	531.4
GDP Deflator (inflation %)	16.5	11.1	3.3	2.3
Population (millions)				39.3
Urban population (% of total)				77
Life expectancy at birth (years)				77
Illiteracy rate (%)				<5

EXHIBIT 9

Sales Breakdown by Country (in millions of pesetas)

Source: TelePizza.

	1997	1996	1995	1994	1993
Spain	**35,651**	**24,580**	**18,824**	**12,330**	**7,112**
TelePizza	33,178	24,580	18,824	12,330	7,112
Pizza World	2,473				
Other Countries	**3,992**	**2,727**	**1,950**	**1,298**	**670**
TelePizza					
Portugal	2,209	1,620	1,121	760	445
Mexico	356	210	120	45	20
Poland	256	210	120	45	20
Chile	657	476	450	248	68
Total chain sales	**39,643**	**27,307**	**20,774**	**13,628**	**7,782**

acquisition targets; where none were available (typically in less developed countries), the company grew organically. (See **Exhibit 9** for a sales breakdown by country.)

New Concepts

TelePizza also hoped to leverage its brand, franchise network, and operational and HR capabilities by introducing new fast-food concepts into the markets where TelePizza had proved successful. TeleGrill was the first such concept, with 16 stores expected to be opened by year-end. TeleGrill offered a similar service to TelePizza—some in-store dining with an emphasis on delivery plus good, modestly priced food—but TeleGrill offered chicken and ribs (along with salads and side orders) instead of pizza.

TeleGrill used identical lettering to TelePizza, which the company hoped would make people feel comfortable trying the new store. In a survey, 120 people in Madrid were shown the lettering of TeleGrill and were asked, "What do you think is the relation between TelePizza and TeleGrill?" Most of them believed that TeleGrill was part of TelePizza. The rest recognized the similarity but assumed it was another company trying to copy TelePizza.

TelePizza wanted existing franchisees to open new concepts in their regions when possible. Fernández knew, however, that it would not always be easy to convince them. "No franchise is as profitable as a TelePizza franchise," he claimed. "With TeleGrill, the ingredient cost will be 35–40% of sales, rather than 30% for TelePizza. I would be happy if TeleGrill had an ROI of 25–30%."

TelePizza hoped to introduce one new concept each year. The next concept launch was TeleOriental, offering Chinese and Japanese food. A trial store was scheduled to be opened in 1999.

The Dream

"At the end of this year we will have more than 500 stores," said Fernández. "My vision is that we will have 2,000 stores in five years, 6,000 stores in ten years and 30,000 stores in twenty years." Fernández knew it would be difficult to manage such rapid growth, but believed that TelePizza was in an excellent position to attract talented people. "We went

EXHIBIT 10
Summary of Bain Capital's Acquisition of Domino's Chain

Source: Compiled from Gibson, Richard. 1998. "Bain Capital Pays Estimated $1 Billion for 90%-Plus Stake in Domino's Pizza." *Wall Street Journal,* September 28, 1998, B5.

Date of Transaction	September 1998
Consideration	$1 billion
Stake acquired	90%
Total Domino's Outlets	6,100
Domino's Revenues (1997)	$3.2 billion

to Instituto d'Empresa[5] once and gave a presentation," he recalled. "We made it very clear that every new employee, independent of education or background, has to work for six months at a TelePizza store to learn the business. About a hundred MBAs applied to work at TelePizza afterwards."

Valuation

TelePizza's operational success had been matched by an impressive share price performance. From an IPO price of Ptas 150 per share, the stock had climbed to a high of Ptas 1,650 and now stood at Ptas 1,150. At this level, the stock was trading on a P/E ratio 67 times 1998 earnings per share and 50 times the consensus forecast for 1999. The high valuation made the possibility of a large acquisition financed through a share exchange possible, but also carried certain risks. "Lots of our employees own shares," explained Hernandez, "so they pay a lot of attention to the stock price. That's what happens when you become a public company."

TelePizza's management knew that companies with high valuations could see rapid declines in their stock price if they disappointed the market. They were not, however, too worried. "We are doing our forecasts very conservatively," explained Vazquez, "and we have outperformed our growth targets consistently."

Fernández concurred. "The average company in the IBEX [stock index] is growing at perhaps 15–20% per year. TelePizza is growing at 40%. I would be worried if our P/E was lower because we could be acquired." It had hardly escaped Fernandez's notice that the Domino's pizza chain had recently been acquired by Bain Capital. (See **Exhibit 10.**) "Once we are expanding internationally the way we have in Spain, our current P/E will seem low." He conceded, however, that TelePizza would have to continue carefully. "We have always done everything we said we would do. I think we would probably have some problems if we didn't."

Moving Forward—Setting Priorities for Growth

As he walked out onto the Madrid street, Fernández smiled. He believed the TeleGrill concept was sound; TelePizza had spent many months developing the concept and testing it with focus groups, and several franchisees had expressed enthusiasm about opening TeleGrill stores in their regions. Moreover, it was just one of many avenues of growth the company was pursuing towards his vision of more than tripling its size every five years. The company did not have all of its hopes resting on the success of any one strategy.

Fernández knew there were serious challenges ahead, however, and part of setting the company's strategy would be recognizing which were the most difficult and how each could be addressed. Could TelePizza's familial style of management, which had helped the company grow to 500 stores, be maintained as it grew to 2,000? To what extent, if any, should the TelePizza model be modified in countries where pizza tastes differed? What markets were the most appropriate for expansion? Fernández was confident that he and his team would find the answers.

[5] A well-known Spanish business school.

Case

26

Sirona

Thomas Jetter, a Partner of Schroder Ventures (SV), reflected on his recent meeting with his counterpart Richard Winckles as he tried again to get comfortable in the hard seat in front of gate 4 of London's Heathrow Airport. Jetter was grateful that the rest of their work on SV's acquisition of the dental systems businesses (known collectively as Sirona[1]) of German industrial conglomerate, Siemens AG, would take place in Germany. Due in part to the complexity of the due diligence required and the size of the deal, but mostly due to the extreme time pressure, the Sirona transaction had required different offices of SV to work together for the first time. As a result, the deal had involved a great deal of travel, often on short notice. Now the culmination of their efforts was close at hand. It was September 12, 1997. In three days Siemens would expect a binding offer letter from SV.

SV had been eager to participate in the Sirona acquisition ever since Siemens announced its intention to divest the business. Intuitively, the private equity community knew there would be scope to reduce costs and refocus management as an independent company, and this intuition had been supported by SV's extensive due diligence. Moreover, Jetter and his colleagues knew that deals of this nature were likely to become more common as Germany's industrial giants became more shareholder-driven and concentrated on a smaller number of core businesses. A successful completion of this deal would leave the firm well positioned to compete for further business. Similarly, while access to private equity deal flow was not as good in Germany as in Britain or the United States, the availability of investment professionals was an even more serious constraint. (See **Exhibit 1.**) Attracting the best financial and operational managers would be critical to SV's long-term success in the German private equity business.

[1] The process of incorporating Siemens's dental products businesses under a single holding company was not yet complete at September 12, but for the most part these businesses had already functioned as a division within the Siemens conglomerate. For simplicity, the case will refer to the dental products businesses as Sirona throughout.

Charles M. Williams Fellow Chad Ellis, MBA '98, prepared this case under the supervision of Professor Walter Kuemmerle. HBS cases are developed solely as the basis for class discussion. Cases are not intended to serve as endorsements, sources of primary data, or illustrations of effective or ineffective management.

EXHIBIT 1
**International
Comparison of
Access to Private
Equity Deal Flow
and Availability of
Investment
Professionals**

Source: Kuemmerle, Walter,
Frederick M. Paul, and Henrik
Freye. 1998. *Survey of Private
Equity in Germany—Summary
of Results and Analysis
(Working Paper 98–112).*
Boston: Harvard Business
School. Adapted from Figures 4
and 5 on pp. 8–9.

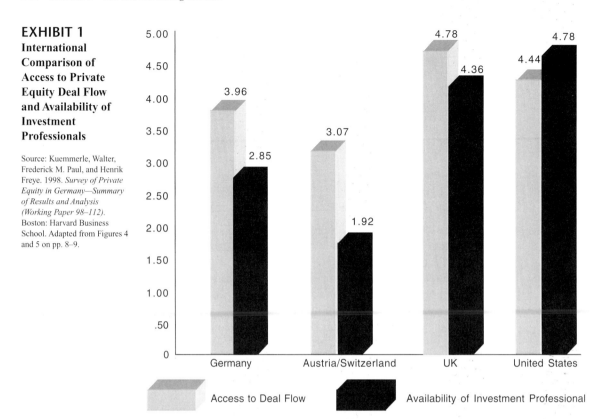

Some concerns remained, however. The due diligence had been complicated by the lack of reliable data provided by Siemens. Sirona represented less than 1% of the parent company's 1996 revenues of DM94.2 billion ($1 = DM1.77), and some financial details seemed to have fallen through the cracks within Siemens. This had proven especially true in the case of the U.S. operation, where further investigation showed greater than expected losses and the likelihood of a large inventory write-down. Jetter and Winckles knew that further surprises were possible, and that a full picture of the profitability as well as the assets and liabilities of Sirona would not be available until after the deal was completed. It was ironic to be buying such a substantial business from a major multinational parent and yet not have access to a balance sheet.

Management was another potential concern. Most of Sirona's managers had operated under the Siemens umbrella for many years. While replacing top management was probably inevitable, it would be difficult to replace more than a small percentage of middle managers, who held important market know-how and contacts. Could SV sufficiently change the corporate culture of Sirona within a short period of time, and how much would this cost?

Finally, there was the issue of price. SV had approached the deal aggressively, with a preliminary bid of DM800 million, higher than any rival's. Jetter knew, for example, that one private equity fund had dropped out with a final bid below DM500 million, considering the deal fully priced at that level. He and Winckles believed that no other bidder had offered more than DM700 million. They had agreed that in situations like this, "You either lead the auction or you bid low and wait for everyone else to drop out because problems develop in the deal. Anything in the middle ground is a waste of time." They knew, however, that the transaction would still have to earn a sufficient return if they were successful. Winning a high-profile deal where SV's investors did not make a good return or even lost money would be no victory.

These concerns had been magnified by the time constraints surrounding the deal. Siemens wanted the transaction completed quickly, but they also placed heavy restrictions on SV's access to management. "It was constantly, 'You have two days here' and, 'No, you may not,'" recalled Winckles. "We were constantly fighting for time and access."

Background on Siemens AG

With roughly 150 years of history and nearly DM100 billion in revenues, Siemens AG was one of the world's largest electrical engineering and electronics companies, with global market leadership in many of its businesses. Due both to increasing global competition by specialized and smaller competitors and the evolution of German capital markets, with a resulting shift in focus towards building shareholder value, Siemens had begun to refocus its energies on a number of core businesses, while divesting those which did not offer sufficient synergies with the rest of the group. In April 1997, Heinrich von Pierer, Siemens' CEO, announced the company's intention to sell all of its dental products businesses, part of its troubled Medical group. Siemens indicated that it hoped to close the deal by the following fall.

Siemens hired JP Morgan (Morgan) to write an information memorandum, outlining the businesses to be sold, their products, markets, technologies and assets. Rather than existing as one entity, the businesses that would comprise Sirona were divided among several Siemens holding companies, and had only recently been formally incorporated. (See **Exhibit 2.**) Nevertheless, the vast majority of the dental businesses had been operating with close links for several years; future integration was not seen as too much of a problem.

Based on the information provided in the Morgan memorandum, more than 50 potential financial and industrial buyers were invited to bid for Sirona. Of these, nine (including SV) were invited to the second stage, in which they were given access to internal data and management presentations. The SV team suspected that of the eight other bidders, four represented credible rivals for the deal.

Sirona—the Global Leader in Dental Equipment

With fiscal 1996 sales of DM878.4 million (see **Exhibit 3** for Sirona's consolidated sales and Sirona balance sheets), Sirona was the largest dental products company in the world, and had leading market shares in most of its product areas. (See **Exhibit 4.**) Sirona was the only global manufacturer of dental equipment with significant market shares in each major segment of the market (described in more detail below) and was also the only major producer with an owned dealer network.

Main Business Components

Although Sirona was comprised of several legal entities, there were three key business units: the main manufacturing center in Bensheim, Germany, a U.S. subsidiary, and owned dealerships. Founded in 1962, Bensheim produced Sirona's entire product range, and supplied most foreign markets as well as Germany. Bensheim also housed Sirona's global headquarters. Pelton & Crane (P&C), a Charlotte, NC subsidiary acquired in 1986, served the U.S. market. P&C produced treatment units, x-ray machines and sterilizers. Both the Bensheim and Pelton & Crane plants operated on a stand-alone basis within Siemens and provided no products or services to companies outside of the dental group.

EXHIBIT 2 **Organization Chart of Sirona under Siemens AG**

Source: Siemens AG.

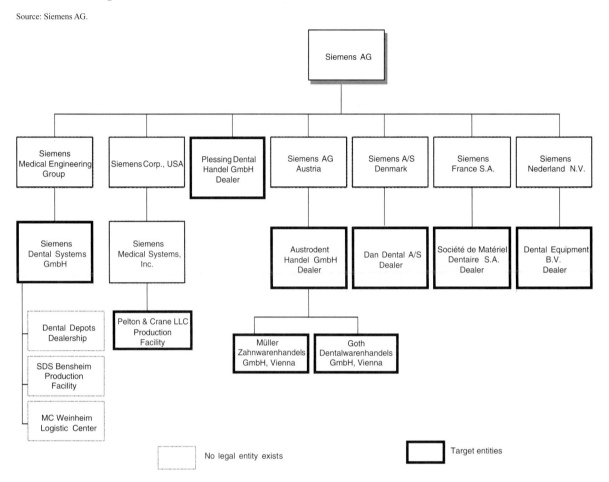

EXHIBIT 3A
Sirona Consolidated Sales by Source (in DM million German GAAP)

Source: Sirona management accounts.

September Year End	1995–1996 Sales	% of Total
Bensheim	406.8	
Pelton & Crane	88.0	
Consolidation	(29.3)	
Total "ex-factory" sales	465.4	53%
Dental depots	273.7	
Plessing Dental Handel	159.4	
Other	132.0	
Consolidation	(6.8)	
Total "dealer" sales	558.3	47%[a]
Consolidation	(145.3)	
Total consolidation sales	878.4	100%

[a]47% = (558.3 − 145.3)/878.4.

Finally, Sirona owned two German dental products dealerships, Dental Depots and Plessing Dental Handel, the latter having been acquired in 1979. Sirona also owned other, smaller dealers in other markets. All these dealerships combined, accounted for roughly one-third of the company's sales.

EXHIBIT 3B
Sirona Balance Sheet
(millions of DM)

Source: Siemens estimates
(preliminary).

	Historical 1996	Estimated 1997 (pre-transaction)
ASSETS		
Cash	6.7	6.7
Accounts Receivable	186.7	190.7
Inventory	206.2	194.2
Prepaid & Other Current Assets	—	—
	399.6	391.6
Net Fixed Assets	81.2	79.3
Real Estate	25.0	25.0
Patents and Licenses	—	—
Investments	3.2	3.8
Deferred Financing Fees	—	—
Deferred Taxes	—	—
Transaction Goodwill	—	—
Intangibles and Other LT Assets	—	—
	109.4	108.1
Total Assets	509.0	499.7
LIABILITIES AND EQUITY		
Accounts Payable	84.3	85.7
Other payables/accrued liabilities	40.5	40.2
Other Current Liabilities	—	—
	124.8	125.9
Pension Provision, net	73.6	81.5
Other LT Liabilities	—	—
Stockholder's Equity	310.6	292.3
Total Liabilities and Equity	509.0	499.7

Note: These balance sheets were constructed 'ex post' by Siemens when the company decided to divest Sirona.

Additional Data	
Corporate Tax Rate	50%
Sirona Yearly capital expenditures 1998–2002 (as % of sales) (Siemens estimate)	2.50%

EXHIBIT 4
Sirona's Worldwide
Competitive Position
by Product Area in
1995–1996

Source: Sirona management
estimates.

Product Area	% of Sales[a]	Ranking	Worldwide Market Share %
Dental units	49%	No. 1	13%
Dental X-ray	20	No. 1	19
Dental instruments	18	No. 3	10
CEREC (restoration)	10	No. 1	53
Dental sterilizers	3	No. 4	5
Total	100%	No. 1	14%

[a]Ex-factory sales of DM465 million.

Life as a Siemens Subsidiary

Sirona's history as part of the Siemens conglomerate had shaped its culture and strategies for competition. Jetter explained:

> Like many large companies, Siemens's philosophy is more to dominate markets through technology than to serve them. As a result, they engage in practices that increase market share but may hurt profits or cash flow and increase inefficiency. They also tend to be over-staffed and less flexible, with highly centralized decision-making and low accountability at the lower levels.

Interviews with Sirona personnel confirmed many of SV's concerns. Lower-level managers tended to pass decisions and responsibility up, and the decision-making process was slow. Dr. Harald Fett, a newly hired dentist and former McKinsey consultant, stated, "You couldn't just replace a part without filling out five forms. Time and money weren't that important, and people weren't proactive about solving problems."

It was also clear that Sirona's management had not emphasized cash flow. Salesmen regularly extended payment terms for clients; the average payment period in 1996 was nearly 75 days. This was typical of other areas of the organization, too. Jetter knew it would not be easy to change Sirona's corporate culture to one where cash flow was a priority.

There were, however, advantages to being a member of the Siemens group, of which the Siemens brand was probably the most important. "The Siemens name means quality all over the world," explained Fett. "In some markets like the United States, where Siemens [dental business] had problems, using the Sirona name will not change this instantly—some people will associate it with bad experiences they've had. In other markets, Sirona is just not known."

Products

The 1996 worldwide market for dental equipment was estimated to be roughly DM3.4 billion at the wholesale level. The dental equipment market was generally split into five product segments: treatment units/chairs, instruments, X-ray equipment, tooth restoration and sterilizers. (See **Exhibit 5** for a breakdown of Sirona's 1996 sales by region and product.) Other sales to dentists, such as office equipment and supplies, computers, wax, cement and polishing materials were not included in this figure. Annual growth over the

EXHIBIT 5   Sirona 1996 "Ex-Factory" Sales by Region and Product

Source: Sirona.

	Dental Units		Instruments		X-ray		Dental Sterilizers		CEREC		Total	
	DM Mio	%	DM Mio	%	DM Mio	%	DM Mio	%	DM Mio	%	DM Mio	%
Germany	101	45%	44	55%	32	35%	2	9%	28	61%	208	45%
Western Europe	44	19	21	27	14	15	2	11	4	9	86	18
United States	34	15	2	2	21	23	10	55	2	5	69	15
Japan	10	4	5	6	3	3	0	2	2	5	21	4
South East Asia	6	3	4	5	5	6	4	23	1	1	20	4
CIS	16	7	4	6	4	4	0	0	2	4	26	6
Rest of World	16	7	0	0	13	14	0	0	7	15	36	8
Total	227	100%	80	100%	92	100%	18	100%	45	100%	465	100%

coming five years was expected to be roughly 3.4% p.a., although this growth was likely to vary considerably between markets. (See **Exhibit 6** for a breakdown of the world dental equipment market and forecast five-year CAGR.)

By far, the largest market, representing nearly half of Sirona's ex-factory sales, was dental treatment units. Sirona estimated the global market for units at DM1.7 billion, or 94,000 units per year. A treatment unit included the patient chair, an instrument delivery system, an assistant's unit and an operating light. Dental units varied considerably in price and features; Sirona viewed the market as divided into four classes: Comfort, Standard, Basic and Sub-basic. Comfort units, as in the market for luxury cars, provided enhanced features, such as inter-oral video cameras and computer-controlled support systems, as well as enhanced status for the dentist. They were most popular in Germany, Austria, and Switzerland (the so-called DACH countries). Standard and Basic units were more practical, and were popular in areas of the developed world, such as the United States, where the profitability of the dentist's office was a higher priority than image. Sub-basic units were demanded only in lesser-developed countries and offered a minimum number of features.

Although the class segments were fairly consistent between regions in terms of functionality, prices varied considerably. The DACH countries, in addition to their preference for high-end chairs, supported a price premium compared with the rest of Europe, the United States, and even Japan. (See **Exhibit 7** for a breakdown of price by class and region.)

Sirona, with its proximity to the DACH market and its parent company's emphasis on high-end engineering, had leading market shares in the Comfort class and did fairly well in Standard, but had difficulty penetrating the Basic class, particularly in the large but relatively low-price U.S. market. The acquisition of P&C had been intended to address this problem, but without great success. Uwe Meyer, VP of Sales for Germany, recalled:

> The original attempt to export (to the United States) didn't meet market demands. We tried to have German standards but offer international prices, and were unsuccessful. We realized that we couldn't do it from Bensheim, so we acquired Pelton & Crane. But, the development team that worked on the new product line was still the German team, and the resulting products were still too expensive.

EXHIBIT 6   Worldwide Market Size and Growth 1996–2001 by Company and Segment

Source: Company documents.

DM Millions	Germany		in %[a]	Western EU (excl. Germany)		in %[a]	United States		in %[a]
Units/chairs	235	255	1.6%	275	319	3.0%	285	343	3.8%
Instruments	200	223	2.2%	163	194	3.5%	150	185	4.3%
X-ray	62	69	2.2%	100	119	3.5%	125	153	4.1%
Sterilizers	43	46	1.4%	64	74	2.9%	50	60	3.7%
Restoration	44	51	3.0%	15	19	4.8%	4	6	8.4%
Total	584	644	2.0%	617	725	3.3%	614	747	4.0%

	Japan		in %[a]	ROW		in %[a]	Total		in %[a]
Units/chairs	250	283	2.5%	655	788	3.8%	1,700	1,988	3.2%
Instruments	91	81	−2.3%	234	290	4.4%	838	973	3.0%
X-ray	72	84	3.1%	136	170	4.6%	495	595	3.7%
Sterilizers	28	31	2.1%	65	77	3.4%	250	288	2.9%
Restoration	5	7	7.0%	21	27	5.2%	89	110	4.3%
Total	446	513	2.8%	1,111	1,352	4.0%	3,372	3,954	3.2%

[a]Compound annual growth rate over five-year period.

EXHIBIT 7
**Comparison of
Dental Unit/Chair
Prices by Segment
and Region (000s of
DM)**

Source: Sirona.

• DACH:	– Comfort Class	60–100
	– Standard Class	30–60
	– Basic Class	15–30
	– Sub-Basic Class	Does not exist
• Europe:	– Comfort Class	50–80
	– Standard Class	20–40
	– Basic Class	15–20
	– Sub-Basic Class	Does not exist
• United States:	– Comfort Class	40–50
	– Standard Class	20–40
	– Basic Class	10–20
	– Sub-Basic Class	Hardly exists
• Japan:	– Comfort Class	50–80
	– Standard Class	25–50
	– Basic Class	Below 25
	– Sub-Basic Class	Does not exist
• Rest of the World:	– Comfort Class	> 30
	– Standard Class	20–40
	– Basic Class	10–20
	– Sub-Basic Class	Below 10

The DM500 million market for X-ray equipment was split evenly between two methods, intra-oral and panoramic.[2] Although the overall market was expected to grow at just 2% p.a., digital radiography systems were expected to grow at over 20% p.a., displacing the traditional use of film and film chemicals. Sirona offered a full range of X-ray equipment. Its low-end product offered a comparable price-point to its competitors with, management believed, superior functionality. At the high end, Sirona's price was slightly higher than its competition, but the company believed its product was demonstrably superior.

Dental instruments included drills, cleaners, syringes and hoses. Sirona estimated the total market at DM838 million and had the third largest market share, behind KaVo (31%) and Dentsply (12%). Tighter government health regulations, which required regular sterilization of instruments between patients, had increased the number of spare instruments dentists had to keep on hand and frequent sterilization had accelerated instrument wearing. As a result, the instrument market had shown annual growth rates of 4.5% over the past five years, and durability and ease of cleaning had become increasingly important product features. Sirona believed its new product lines, T1 Line and T1 Control, offered superior functionality and durability at a lower price to the end-user. As a result, the company expected to increase its market share in coming years, and had targeted an increase from 10% to 12% by fiscal year 2001.

Although smaller than other segments of the dental equipment market at DM 89 million, the restoration equipment segment offered Sirona an important avenue of growth. Sirona's CEREC (CEramic REConstruction) product, first introduced in 1987, enabled dentists to provide clients with bio-compatible, natural-looking restorations instead of the more traditional gold or metallic fillings. In 1994 Sirona introduced CEREC 2, which could manufacture crowns and offered improved features that made it attractive to dental laboratories. As a result of these products, Sirona expected to grow its market share from an already dominant 53% to 60% by the year 2001. In addition, the overall market was expected to grow at 6% p.a. during the same period.

[2] A panoramic X-ray took the picture from outside, using special film held inside the mouth.

Representing only 3% of Sirona's ex-factory sales, the sterilizer market was Sirona's weakest segment, with a market share of just 5% worldwide. Sirona planned to discontinue manufacturing of sterilizers over the next few years.

The Opportunity

While financial leverage could magnify any increase in Sirona's value achieved post acquisition, the returns SV needed could only be achieved if Sirona's enterprise value were substantially enhanced through increased earnings. There were essentially two ways this might be done—growth and cost cutting.

Growth

The Morgan memorandum strongly emphasized Sirona's potential for growth. It outlined a plan, developed alongside Sirona's senior management, which would increase Sirona's market share throughout the world and increase sales by 35% between fiscal years 1996 and 2001. (See **Exhibit 8.**)

Sirona hoped to grow its already high market-share in the DACH countries by presenting itself as a system supplier with a full range of high-end products. The company believed that dentists would have to market their services more actively than in the past, and that high-tech products like CEREC would enable Sirona to expand its already-leading position. A dentist using CEREC, for example, could show a patient exactly how a tooth was damaged and how CEREC would create a safe, natural-looking restoration.

In Western Europe, Sirona's market share varied considerably by country, with strong positions in France and Spain (15%–20%), but substantially weaker in the United Kingdom and Italy (5%). Unlike the DACH countries, demand in the rest of Europe focused on Standard and Basic products, and Sirona intended to attack these markets with new products targeting those segments. Low market share in the United Kingdom and Italy had been partly due to distribution problems, which the company felt it was close to solving.

EXHIBIT 8
International Market Share Plan (millions of DM)

Source: Sirona management accounts and estimates.

Year Ended September	Actual 1993	1996	Forecast 2001
Germany:			
Sales	211	205	234
Market share	32%	35%	39%
Western Europe (excl. Germany):			
Sales	84	96	125
Market share	13%	15%	18%
Japan:			
Sales	10	21	39
Market share	2%	5%	8%
United States:			
Sales	75	67	105
Market share	10%	10%	14%
Australia and New Zealand:			
Sales	7	7	11
Market share	15%	15%	22%
Rest of the World:			
Sales	68	73	116
Market share	7%	7%	10%

Note: Sales figures exclude cash discounts, amounting to approximately DM4 million worldwide in 1996.

Although Sirona's market share in Japan was just 5%, it had more than doubled in the past few years and Sirona was now larger than any other non-Japanese player. The Comfort and Standard segments were most important in the Japanese market, and Sirona believed it would continue to grow its market share in Japan over time due to its superior product offerings in these segments.

In the United States, the Morgan document outlined a two-pronged growth strategy. Most importantly, Sirona had just introduced its new Spirit line of treatment units, aimed at the Basic segment and manufactured at P&C. The Spirit line was intended to offer more features and better productivity for the dentist at a comparable price to other Basic units. Also important, cosmetic work, especially using lifelike ceramics, was gaining popularity in the United States, which Sirona believed created excellent opportunities for CEREC.

In less developed countries, Sirona had tended to operate in select niches, as the Basic and Sub-Basic segments were more significant than Comfort or Standard. The company had done well in the X-ray market in these countries, and hoped to increase its market share in the lower-end products with the Spirit line.

Although the growth scenarios spelled out by Morgan and Sirona's senior management looked attractive, the SV team had some concerns. It was not uncommon to see management plans that called for sales growth to come at least in part from increases in market share. With spreadsheet tools, simply projecting growth was temptingly easy compared with running a detailed analysis of cost and demand factors. Jetter and Winckles had known that evaluating Sirona's growth prospects would be one of the key tasks during due diligence.

Cost Cutting

An alternative to creating value by growing Sirona's business was to concentrate on reducing costs in the existing operations. Siemens had already begun a cost-cutting initiative ahead of the disposal, but SV believed there might be considerable scope for further cost reductions. In fiscal 1996, Sirona's EBIT[3] margin was just 4.7%. Analysis by an investment bank suggested that its manufacturing competitors had EBIT margins ranging from 18% to 22% in the same period, while distribution competitors had EBIT margins ranging from 3.9% to 7.5%. (See **Exhibit 9.**) Although somewhat cursory, this benchmarking suggested that Sirona's EBIT performance could be significantly improved.

Searching for Reality—The Due Diligence

After their preliminary bid won them access to Siemens documents and Sirona's management, SV began an intense due diligence effort to determine Sirona's true potential. In addition to their own team of fifteen, SV hired Bain & Co. (Bain), which provided ten consultants to do targeted research on Sirona.

Bain's consultants performed both qualitative and quantitative analysis. They interviewed all department[4] heads and purchasing managers within Sirona. They also performed detailed reviews of the personnel functions of each department, activity-based costing and cost per person by department. From this analysis, the consultants were able to estimate how much money could be saved by headcount reductions and through improved purchasing, and how much the savings would cost to achieve. SV analysts worked closely with Bain on most of these tasks.

Bain also conducted interviews with Sirona's competitors and customers. The data gleaned from these interviews enabled SV to get a clearer picture of Sirona's market image and outside perspectives on its strategy to date. The interviews also suggested

[3] Earnings before interest and tax.

[4] A department was defined as any unit of five people or more.

EXHIBIT 9 **EBIT** Comparison

Source: Company documents.

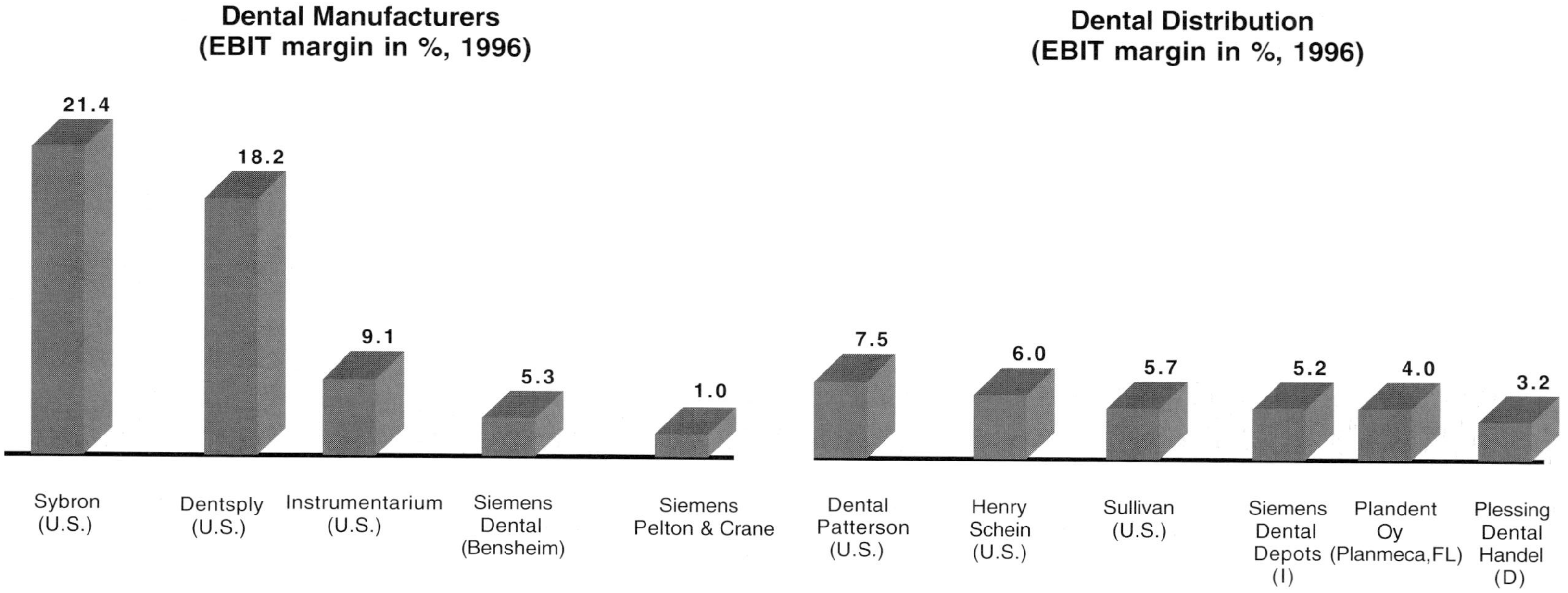

Dental Manufacturers
(EBIT margin in %, 1996)

Sybron (U.S.)	Dentsply (U.S.)	Instrumentarium (U.S.)	Siemens Dental (Bensheim)	Siemens Pelton & Crane
21.4	18.2	9.1	5.3	1.0

Dental Distribution
(EBIT margin in %, 1996)

Patterson Dental (U.S.)	Henry Schein (U.S.)	Sullivan (U.S.)	Siemens Dental Depots (I)	Plandent Oy (Planmeca,FL)	Plessing Dental Handel (D)
7.5	6.0	5.7	5.2	4.0	3.2

that while few of Sirona's competitors were interested in bidding for the entire company, there might be interest in acquiring either parts of the product line or the distribution centers.

The due diligence analysis resulted in estimates of the potential cost-savings in Sirona. In Bensheim, Bain estimated that total employment of 1,307 (470 direct labor, 837 indirect) could be reduced by 286. This reduction would come from reducing overmanning on certain functions (43% of total reduction), improving processes and reducing double-tasking (38%) and a net saving resulting in outsourcing some internal processes (19%). Bain believed this reduction could be completed by the end of fiscal 1999, resulting in ongoing savings of DM30.9 million, starting in fiscal 2000.

Bain also believed significant savings could be achieved in the owned distribution centers. The two centers employed 657 people in 17 depots and the logistics center in Bensheim. Each depot had not only its own dedicated sales force, but also an independent order processing and administrative groups. Bain believed that headcount reductions of 49 could be achieved by centralizing order processing and some administrative functions. Nearly all of the reduction would come in fiscal 1999, with ongoing savings of DM4.9 million from fiscal 2000 onward.

Based on an average of 14 years of service, and using Siemens's severance formula, Bain estimated the total cost of the headcount reduction at DM26.3 million, of which DM14.8 million would be incurred in fiscal 1998 and DM11.5 million in fiscal 1999.

Considerable scope for cost savings in purchasing were also identified. In addition to interviewing purchasing managers and reviewing existing practices, Bain analyzed suppliers representing 50% of current factory purchases. Several key levers for cost reduction were determined:

1. Managers had inadequate incentives and lacked certain skills, particularly in international purchasing. Training, better targets and improved incentives would enable them to reduce costs.
2. Reduction of the number of suppliers (currently at 1,000 for Bensheim).
3. Increase of the frequency of competitive tendering for supply contracts.
4. Sourcing components internationally.
5. Pooling of purchasing for different products to take advantage of buyer power.

Bain estimated that improved purchasing at Bensheim and in Distribution could represent an ongoing savings of DM16.4 million by fiscal 2000. In their experience, such savings would be achieved at a cost (typically incurred in the years before the savings were realized) of roughly 50% of the savings achieved. SV believed that Bain had done a good job in doing the cost reduction estimates, although SV was still unsure about the time frame of headcount reductions which would require cooperation from the Worker's Council.

Problems at Pelton & Crane

While the due diligence effort generated positive news on the cost-cutting potential at Bensheim and in Distribution, it also uncovered serious problems at P&C. Rather than representing the foundation of a "Convincing growth plan for North America," as described in the Morgan memorandum, it now appeared that P&C would not break even before the year 2000, and might have to be closed down.

Although some industry players considered the new Spirit treatment units to be of good quality, the launch had gone badly. In addition to delays caused by significant parts and manufacturing difficulties, the units proved difficult to operate and to install, making dealer technical reps and sales people reluctant to recommend it. Largely as a result of these problems, fiscal 1997 sales were estimated at $48.5 million vs. the company's plan of $55 million, and pre-tax losses were greater than expected at $14 million. Inventories rose to $31 million.

Sirona planned to educate dealer representatives and to relaunch the product, but there were serious concerns about the prospects for success. Sirona had priced the Spirit line competitively with the expectation that its costs would come down to a satisfactory level. Bain's analysis suggested that this might not be the case. P&C's suppliers' cost, quality, and delivery performance was poor, resulting in high cost of goods sold. P&C also had a low manufacturing scale relative to its competition and relied on some expensive parts from Bensheim, both of which suggested a structural cost disadvantage. Even if these problems could be addressed, the U.S. dealer network was alienated by the failed launch and might be skeptical of a second attempt.

Jetter knew that Siemens was only interested in bids for the entire dental group; a bid that did not include P&C would be equivalent to withdrawing from the auction. How to respond to the disturbing developments in Charlotte, however, was not clear.

Exit Options

In order to realize a satisfactory return on their investment, the SV team knew it had to consider not only how much improvement could be made in Sirona's EBIT performance, but how and when SV would be able to exit the business and harvest the increased value. SV engaged SBC Warburg (Warburgs) to help with the exit discussions and several options were identified.

The first issue to be considered was under what structure could the maximum value be obtained. The three possibilities were keeping the company in its current form, separating the manufacturing and distribution businesses, or a full break-up by product lines. The major exit options were a trade sale (or sales, if broken up), and/or an initial public offering (IPO).

Warburgs' recommendation was a separation of manufacturing and distribution, with a two-stage exit strategy. Warburgs had identified a number of potential trade buyers who might be interested in the distribution business—both non-German dental distributors seeking to enter the European market and German companies with dental interests. In addition to serving a possible exit strategy, there were many in the business who argued that separating distribution from manufacturing made simple business sense. "Having your own distribution is a Janus-headed thing," argued an executive from KaVo, Sirona's largest manufacturing competitor. "You control some parts of the distribution, but you offend the other (independent) dealers."[5]

Warburgs thought the distribution business could command a valuation of roughly 0.5 to 0.6 times sales or 12 to 14 times EBIT, and that a trade sale could be arranged within one to two years. Jetter, however, was unsure about the wisdom of selling the business before the restructuring was complete, and preferred to base his analysis on an exit in 2000.

Once the turnaround of the manufacturing business was complete, an IPO could be undertaken. It would be important to maintain Sirona's leadership position, but assuming that was done, an EBIT multiple of 11x to 12x looked like a reasonable target.

Warburgs did not think there would be trade interest in the manufacturing business, and felt that a break-up of the Bensheim operation would be too risky. There were, however, indications of interest in buying parts of the business, as well as suggestions that Sirona's "portfolio" approach was a poor strategy. One competitor said Sirona "made sense under the roof of a giant like Siemens, but as a stand-alone it should be broken up

---

[5] Bain interview summary, from SV documents.

into its specialized businesses."[6] Indeed, most of Sirona's competitors operated in only a few segments of the market at most. (See **Exhibit 10.**) See **Exhibit 11** for financial information on comparable companies and on short-term interest rates.

Financing the Deal

Jetter knew that the financing details could often add considerable value to a deal. Although the final details were yet to be worked out, the SV team had outlined the financing they expected to use to finance the deal. DM280 million of senior debt would be raised, bearing an interest rate of LIBOR[7] + 2%. Siemens had agreed in principal to provide a vendor note of DM100 million. This would be subordinate to the senior debt and would bear interest at 5%, increasing by 1% each year after the fifth. Interest on this loan would accrue, rather than being paid immediately, although the loan was payable upon exit by SV. The vendor note would have a term of 11 years.

A further DM170 million would be raised through a bridge loan to be repaid by the proceeds of a bond issued in the public high-yield debt market. Warburgs would both provide the bridge loan and underwrite the bond offering. Based on discussions with Warburgs and recent high-yield offerings (see **Exhibit 12**), SV believed they could issue a bond yielding between 9% and 10%. Although this was considerably higher than the cost of senior debt, Warburgs had advised that it would be difficult to make a smaller offering as the bond's liquidity would be too low.

The rest of the financing would be provided by SV's investors, with DM180 million in the form of a shareholder loan and the rest in equity. Providing capital in the form of a shareholder loan provided the investors with a mechanism to realize some of its investment in the event that a full exit took longer than expected to achieve and provided considerable tax benefits if SV exited through a refinancing rather than through an IPO or outright sale.

What Next?

As he walked forward to board his plane back to Frankfurt, Jetter knew that the next several days would be critical to the deal's success. He was reasonably confident SV's bid would be accepted, but would SV be able to generate a high enough return for its

[6] Bain interview summary, from SV documents.

[7] The London Inter-Bank Offer Rate, 4% at the time of the case.

EXHIBIT 10   **Activities of Dental Equipment Manufacturers**

Source: Sirona.

Segment Player	Units	X-rays	Instruments	Sterilizers	Restoration	Dental Supplies	Non-Dental
Sirona	✔	✔	✔	✔	✔		
Dentsply		✔	✔	—	—	✔	
A-Dec	✔		✔				
Planmeca	✔	✔					✔(X-rays)
Morita	✔	✔	✔	✔		✔	
KaVo	✔		✔				
Takara Belmont	✔	✔	✔				
Castellini	✔		✔				
Empress					✔		
Trophy		✔					✔(X-rays)
Melag				✔			
Aesculap				✔		✔	✔

EXHIBIT 11 Information on Some Comparable Companies[1]

Source: Compiled from Ward's Business Directory, Bloomberg, Thomson Financial Datastream, SEC filings data.

SIC Code 3843 (Dental Equipment & Supplies)
(U.S.$ thousands, except beta & employee figures)

	FY end date	Sales		Net Income		Long-Term Debt		Market Capitalization		Equity Beta	No. of Employees	
		FY 1995	FY 1996	FY 1995	FY 1996	FY 1995	FY 1996	FY end 1996	9/12/97	9/12/97	1996	1997
Sybron International	30-Sep	519,200	674,457	48,915	57,584	406,547	481,037	551,364	831,963	0.83	5,700	6,300
Dentsply	31-Dec	572,028	656,557	53,963	67,222	68,675	75,109	1,276,610	1,520,380	0.89	5,100	5,300
Henry Schein	31-Dec	616,209	829,962	(10,216)	19,340	30,381	24,569	759,580	935,030	0.84	3,200	5,000
Patterson Dental	30-Apr	532,598	581,893	24,180	28,747	3,188	3,024	726,680	847,010	0.89	2,500	2,913

[1]Note: Ward's Business Directory listed 53 companies with primary SIC code 3843, 9 of these were listed as public.
Equity beta reflects 5 years of monthly data.
U.S. T-Bill rate (8/97): 5.3% (1 year)

EXHIBIT 12
Sample of High-Yield Bond Offerings

Source: Compiled from Thomson Financial Datastream data.

	Proceeds ($ mil.)	Offer Yield (%)	S&P Rating	Date of Offering
Staples Inc. (USA)	199.6	7.155	BB+	8/7/97
Enerplus (Malaysia)	08.0	7.500	NR	8/13/97
OCI Holdings Corp (USA)	105.0	9.25	B–	8/12/97
YPF SA (Argentina)	297.6	7.868	BBB–	8/20/97
Bay View Capital (USA)	99.4	9.23	B+	8/22/97
Republic of Venezuela	467.5	10.179	B+	6/27/97
Esat Telecom Group (Ireland)	35.2	11.875	B+	8/14/97

investors? While the prospects for improving Sirona's EBIT performance were promising, Jetter knew SV needed insurance against any further surprises like those found at P&C.

Jetter was proud of the way the team had performed so far, and very much wanted to bring the Sirona deal to a happy conclusion. He also knew, however, that getting emotionally attached to a deal could carry serious consequences. The success of the coming days would depend on setting the right objectives for the team and knowing what they needed to do to achieve them.

Case 27

VacationSpot.com & Rent-A-Holiday: Negotiating a Trans-Atlantic Merger of Start-Ups

"I can't believe you asked us to come all the way to Seattle for this," exclaimed Karim Dhanani, one of the investors in Rent-A-Holiday. "This is not worth our time!" With that, the Rent-A-Holiday negotiating team stormed out of the VacationSpot.com offices, bringing an abrupt end to the one-day merger negotiations. It was April 23, 1999.

Rent-A-Holiday (RAH) and VacationSpot.com (VS) were both online travel companies that focused on the independent leisure lodging segment of the travel market (i.e., villas and bed & breakfasts (B&Bs) see **Exhibit 1** for a description of the market). Both companies not only focused on the same space, but had started at around the same time (RAH in January 1997, VS in September 1997) in locations half-way around the world from each other: VS was a Seattle, Washington-based company and RAH was a Brussels, Belgium-based company. The two companies had known of each other's existence for about a year before the two sides entered into formal merger negotiations in April 1999. As he stared at the door that had just closed behind Dhanani, Greg Slyngstad, co-founder and COO of VS, looked at Steve Murch, co-founder and CEO of VS.

> Steve, what in the world just happened? Did I see that right? The negotiations have been going really well; I mean this has been a *real* love-fest. We have just spent a couple of days discussing each company's vision and strategy and basically spent the time getting to know each other. Everything was going so smoothly up until the point we broached the subject of valuation. Both of us have recently completed a round of financing and all I did was say that we should

Dean's Fellow William J. Coughlin (MBA '99) prepared this case under the supervision of Professor Walter Kuemmerle. HBS cases are developed solely as the basis for class discussion. Cases are not intended to serve as endorsements, sources of primary data, or illustrations of effective or ineffective management.

EXHIBIT 1 Overview of the Travel Market and Independent Leisure Lodging Segment

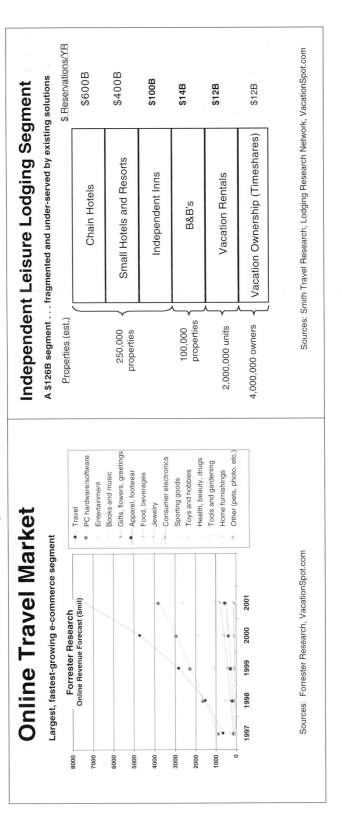

Online Travel Market

Largest, fastest-growing e-commerce segment

Forrester Research
Online Revenue Forecast ($mil)

- Travel
- PC hardware/software
- Entertainment
- Books and music
- Gifts, flowers, greetings
- Apparel, footwear
- Food, beverages
- Jewelry
- Consumer electronics
- Sporting goods
- Toys and hobbies
- Health, beauty, drugs
- Tools and gardening
- Home furnishings
- Other (pets, photo, etc.)

Sources: Forrester Research, VacationSpot.com

Independent Leisure Lodging Segment

A $126B segment . . . fragmented and under-served by existing solutions

Properties (est.)		$ Reservations/YR
	Chain Hotels	$600B
250,000 properties	Small Hotels and Resorts	$400B
	Independent Inns	**$100B**
100,000 properties	B&B's	**$14B**
2,000,000 units	Vacation Rentals	**$12B**
4,000,000 owners	Vacation Ownership (Timeshares)	$12B

Sources: Smith Travel Research, Lodging Research Network, VacationSpot.com

use that as a basis for valuation: a 9:1 ratio based on a $27 million valuation for us and a $2 to $3 million valuation for them. It seems very logical but these guys just exploded. Do you think we have reached a point of no return?

At the same time Laurent Coppieters, co-founder and co-CEO of RAH looked at Dhanani as they were walking back to their hotel in downtown Seattle and said:

> Karim, these guys are proposing a valuation of our company that is completely unfair. Rent-a-Holiday is worth more than that. I don't know where these guys learned to value companies. It's a pity, though; these two days of face-to-face meetings went well. After we spent all that time looking for fit, I think we really seemed to see many advantages in a merger. I just can't believe this is falling apart. I guess we'll be back in Brussels sooner than planned.

As dusk approached on this rainy day in Seattle, both companies were left trying to figure out what had just happened and what each should do next. Both sides were basically in the same quandary. Was this the end of the negotiations or was this a temporary set back? Was this just a cultural misunderstanding or was this a fundamental problem? Was there any common ground possible on the valuation front and how could the negotiations be restarted? There was a plane for Brussels leaving Seattle at noon the next day. "Should we take that plane?" Coppieters wondered. "Or should we give it one more day?"

Independent Leisure Lodging: A Fragmented Segment of a Large Market

By 1999, leisure travel was a very large market with an estimated worldwide size of over $3 trillion.[1] The market comprised anything from air travel and car rentals to hotel reservations and package vacations. Moreover, the market was expected to offer tremendous growth opportunities for Internet-based companies (see **Exhibit 1**). Forrester Research estimated that more than 8 million trips were booked online in 1998 generating over $3.1 billion in revenues. By 2003, Forrester estimated that consumers would book 65.5 million leisure trips online, generating $29.5 billion in revenues.[2]

Part of that larger market was the independent leisure travel lodging market. This broad market segment included condominiums, homes, ski cabins, chalets, villas, and timeshare property units and was estimated to have generated over $126 billion in revenues in 1998, but was quite fragmented and not well served by the existing reservation networks. The "traditional" channels—such as travel agents and tour planners—poorly covered these types of properties. Information was hard to find primarily because travel agents did not list the properties in any kind of computerized reservation system (CRS). CRS's, such as Sabre and Worldspan, were built primarily with large travel suppliers (airlines and chain hotels) in mind. Due to the ease of electronic reservation via CRS, consumers and travel agents chose to focus on selling lodging from the larger, less fragmented hotel chains and spent the rest of their time selling airline tickets and car rentals.

In addition, the independent leisure lodging segment was poorly marketed. There was no good source for print items on these properties (like brochures) and the owner, property manager, or rental agent was often unsophisticated. Marketing generally consisted of putting an advertisement in the local newspaper in the hopes that customers would see it. This lack of marketing sophistication was often due to the principal motives of the owner: Many independent leisure properties were purchased not as investments but for other reasons, such as weekend get-away destinations for the owners. This led to inconsistent pricing and massive under-utilization of the assets: estimates on average yearly vacancy rates were around 80% for these types of properties.

[1] VacationSpot.com estimate.

[2] Source: Forrester Research, *Online Leisure Travel Report*, September 1998.

Yet there was considerable consumer appeal for this segment, particularly for the vast baby boomer leisure travel segment. Vacation rentals such as villas and ski condos came with more room, more amenities, and lower cost than any other lodging segment. Americans took 33 million ski trips each year, with over half of the overnight stays using condos or cabins instead of hotels. And business travelers used to the standard fare at chain hotels increasingly found unique getaways such as inns and B&B's far more enjoyable for their vacation.

At the beginning of 1999, there were several companies looking to take advantage of this situation by offering online services for this segment. Steve Murch (HBS '91), co-founder and CEO of VacationSpot.com, commented on the nature of the online independent leisure lodging market.

> There were several sites that addressed the segment, but most of the web sites were similar to online classified advertisements, offering a few lines of text and perhaps a picture. Moreover, most of these sites had relatively unsophisticated search functions and very little marketing support. For example, nearly all the sites allowed you to browse via a simple hierarchy but none let you search by amenities, price, availability, or style. Even fewer web sites offered real-time online reservation capabilities and those that did, like WorldRes, really did not focus on the villa, condo, and B&B segment; they targeted the hotel chains, just like the online travel agents like Travelocity and Expedia did.

Given the fragmented and unsophisticated nature of the industry, the founders of both VS and RAH felt that this was a tremendous opportunity for their respective companies. By April 1999 no other player was as far along in their development as VS and RAH.

VacationSpot.com History: Growing from Seattle

The Genesis of VacationSpot.com: A Honeymoon

After graduating from Carnegie Mellon University with a degree in Computer Science, Murch spent three years at Bell Communications Research (Bellcore) working with the large Baby Bells on ISDN research. (See **Exhibit 15** for the biographies of VS founders.) Bellcore sent Murch to Stanford University for a Masters in Computer Science in 1987. In 1989, Murch left Bellcore and went to HBS, where he spent his summer working at the consulting firm Booz, Allen & Hamilton. After graduating as a Baker Scholar in 1991, while seeing most of his section choose consulting or investment banking jobs, Murch decided to join Microsoft, which was just beginning to ship Windows 3.0. Murch described his decision:

> While at HBS, I really wanted to start a company. I had worked on a business plan during my second year and had even received funding for it. But in the final lecture of his class, one of the professors gave a lecture that changed my thinking. He suggested that the best thing to do would be to pick an industry you are interested in and work for a moderately sized, rapidly growing company. From there you learn the ropes of your industry and eventually move on. The industry in which I was interested was this new phenomenon called interactive software and services. In fact, it was not a real industry yet, but I knew from my work at Bellcore that it could be huge. I chose to join Microsoft because at the time, it *was* a moderately sized rapidly growing company that focused at least somewhat on my industry.

Murch joined Microsoft and worked in several positions, including product manager for relational database products such as Microsoft Access and FoxPro, and later, he started the Internet Gaming Zone area within Microsoft. By 1999 this had become the largest games site on the Internet with over 10 million members. Murch had the VacationSpot idea when he was planning his honeymoon with his fiancée to the Tuscany region of Italy in 1996. Murch originally wanted to get a small villa for the trip but was unable to find one available, so he booked a hotel instead. When he arrived in Tuscany, he was shocked to see the high vacancy rates of villas there, so he decided to do some investigating and found the segment to be a great opportunity. During his stint in the Consumer Division at Microsoft, Murch met Slyngstad, who was then head of Expedia (an online travel service that Slyngstad changed from a CD-ROM product into an Internet site) and was formerly Group Program Manager of the Word group. After Murch had written a draft business plan, he turned to the retired Slyngstad for advice on the idea. Murch described his activities:

> The motivation of me joining Microsoft was to work with a small team of creative people who was trying to change the world. But over time the percentage of my time spent on doing that stuff decreased dramatically and I began to feel I was working at a *really* large company. Microsoft is the greatest 30,000+-person company anyone could work for, but it is still a 30,000+-person company. I wanted to start a company and a family but ideally a company first and a family later. That is why I jumped at the VacationSpot opportunity when I discovered it. It seemed like a perfect fit with the Internet: it was large enough to build a nice business but not so large as to attract immediate interest from established firms. Also, a reservation is a perfect virtual product to deliver. After working at Microsoft, I knew that Expedia and online offerings like it did not have enough time or resources to focus on the segment. They had to cater to the airlines and car rental companies and had barely enough time to seek out hotel chains to round out their product offering; there was no time for B&Bs. Yet it was still a $100 billion segment of a $3 trillion market where the average transaction size of $1,500-plus was high enough to make it worth our while.
>
> I wrote a pretty bad business plan at Microsoft on nights and weekends, and I sought out Greg, who was the guy who sold Bill Gates on online travel while he was general manager of Expedia. When I asked Greg for his comments he said he had two. His first comment was he thought it was a great opportunity, but would be perfect if I got an online, real-time reservation system in place. His second comment was more of a question: Was I looking for a partner?

The Early Years at VacationSpot.com: Acquiring Technology and Property Inventory

Murch and Slyngstad started VacationSpot.com in September 1997 with a three-pronged strategy. They wanted to have a comprehensive property offering, a superior reservation technology, and a strong distribution system. After using angel financing and their own money to get things started, they approached Microsoft in April 1998 for their first deal, but it wasn't for money. "We knew that asking Microsoft for cash would be a lengthy process," recalled Murch, "so we entered into a long-term distribution deal. This gave us a premier position on Expedia in the accommodations segment for two years and lots of banner advertising for a modest amount [20%] of equity that valued us at $3 million pre-money." The company did raise money from investors with a first-round private placement in July 1998 (see **Exhibit 2** for VacationSpot.com's financing history).

VacationSpot.com focused on executing its strategy through an aggressive acquisition program and through the execution of several distribution agreements (see **Exhibit 3** for a VacationSpot.com timeline of events). VS made a total of three acquisitions over a period of six months in an attempt to address weaknesses in its strategy (see **Exhibit 4** for a description of its acquisitions). One of the acquisitions was of a company that developed a Windows-based reservation software product for inns and B&Bs. VacationSpot eventually developed this software into a reservation database management product called Avail that served both the company and customer's database needs, connecting into the VacationSpot.com site via the Internet to process reservations. "While we started out with paid listings while building out our supply, we are now in a position to effectively take a commission on all transactions,"

EXHIBIT 2   VacationSpot.com Financing History

Source: VacationSpot.com.

Round	Investor	Amount Raised	Premoney Valuation
Seed (August 1997)	Steve Murch, Greg Slyngstad	$200,000	$200,000
Distribution agreement (April 1998)	Microsoft	$0[a]	$3 million
First round—Series A (July 1998)	Various Seattle and Bay-area technology executives	$2 million	$6.1 million
Second round—Series B (March 1999)	Technology Crossover Ventures, Madrona Group, first round investors	$7 million	$20 million

Approx. Ownership Structure as of 4/99	
TCV	21%
Management	47%
Microsoft	12%
Madrona	2%
Others	18%
	100%

[a]No money was raised but Microsoft received 20% of the equity in exchange for a long-term distribution agreement.

EXHIBIT 3   VacationSpot.com Timeline

Source: VacationSpot.com.

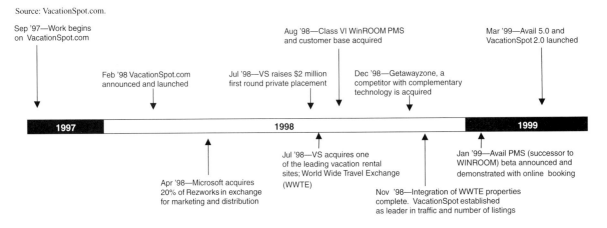

EXHIBIT 4   VacationSpot.com Acquisition History

Source: VacationSpot.com.

Company	Date	Description	Cost
World Wide Travel Exchange (www.wwte.com)	Apr-98	Leading vacation rental site 2,800 Properties	$700,000 (mostly cash; 0.5% equity)
Class VI WinROOM Property	Aug-98	Leading reservation software company 1,000 Customers	$70,000 (or 0.5% equity)
Management Software Getawayzone.com	Dec-98	Leading competitor in ski market with complementary technology and management team 1,400 Properties	$500,000 (plus options for six employees)

explained Slyngstad. "Eventually we will get a full commission [8% of sales] on reservations made through our site and a lower commission [4%] on reservations made off our site as a royalty for use of the database management program."

The other two acquisitions helped the company build its property offerings. "Starting out we felt it was a cheaper way of acquiring properties," explained Murch. "We figured it would cost us around $300 to acquire a supplier on our own and that the company acquisitions we made to get property listings would be cheaper."[3] In total, these acquisitions allowed the company to make progress on fulfilling all three elements of its strategy. Slyngstad explained the dynamics of the strategy:

> Although the initial distribution agreement with Microsoft hurt us with respect to entering into other distribution agreements, all that changed when we got some scale with the acquisitions, especially the first acquisition which was one of the leading vacation rental sites at the time. People like Travelocity simply could not ignore us any longer. Additionally, our acquisitions improved our position with both our "suppliers" [property owners or managers] and potential distribution partners by strengthening all three areas of our strategy.[4] Once the technology issue was addressed, we started a virtuous circle where the more properties we signed-up, the more attractive a distribution partner we became and vice versa.

VacationSpot.com in April 1999

By April 1999, the company had completed a second round of financing, raising $7 million at a pre-money valuation of $20 million. Murch recalled the company's strategy.

> In our Series B round, we received term sheets from many investors but chose Technology Crossover Ventures [www.tcv.com] and the Madrona Group [www.madronagroup.com] over everyone else. We not only chose them because of their success with companies like CNET, Evite, Ariba, MyPoints [TCV], Amazon.com, and HomeGrocer [Madrona], but because their business approach complemented our strategy. For example, we turned down a term sheet from Kleiner Perkins. KP is awesome at branding and PR, but our ideas on building our business were different from theirs. At the time, Kleiner wanted to spend big money on building a brand fast; that works well when you have a well-established distribution channel and fulfillment nailed. In our space, we needed to *build* the distribution network, and *build* the reservation platform; it didn't exist when we started. It has taken us until now [April 1999] to feel like we have the network in place to be willing to drive branding full-stream. By April 1999, we had a strong group of investors that we worked well with, and got very proactive support from them.

The company was still growing its listings and had recently changed its revenue model. In order to slow the burn rate, VS had started operations by charging a flat listing fee but switched to a commission-based system after the Avail 5.0 program was launched in March 1999 and was beginning to migrate its customers to this new model. (See **Exhibits 5 and 6** for an overview of the Avail 5.0 system and the VacationSpot.com site.) Under this new revenue system, VacationSpot.com effectively cut out the existing travel agents, charging a fee of around 8% compared to the average travel agent fee of around 10% (see **Exhibit 7** for an overview of the traditional vacation property value chain). The company was continuing to add listings and was getting more and more booking inquiries every day (see **Exhibit 8** for booking inquiries and property listings over time). While things were going well, the company was becoming somewhat concerned about the quality of the listings and the comprehensiveness of the offering. Murch explained:

> We really feel that our strategy is falling into place. We feel our distribution agreements and our proprietary software, and our upcoming Web-based reservation platform provide us with an edge over the competition and a way to scale our revenues rapidly with the number of

---

[3] At the outset, the RAH team estimated the cost of acquiring each property would be $500.

[4] Property owners, agents and the like will be referred to as suppliers throughout this case.

EXHIBIT 5 Avail 5.0 System Overview

Source: VacationSpot.com.

"I've looked at most of the alternative reservation management solutions and this is not only easy-to-use, but it solidly addresses the needs of specialized properties like inns and bed and breakfasts."
Dick Robinson, *president of the Washington State Bed and Breakfast Guild and owner of the Hillside House, in San Juan Islands, WA.*

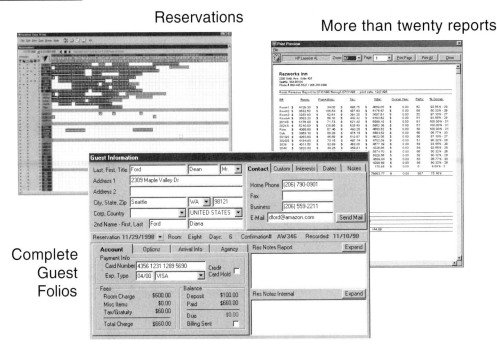

consumers using our network. Although 95% of our transactions are still email request based, we are beginning to automate the process. Moreover, we believe that our property offerings give us more listings than any other site. The only real area of our strategy that we still need to address is in the comprehensiveness of our listings. We have recently conducted a review of our customer request profile and we have found that we are relatively weak in our European offerings. We could address this by focusing our business development efforts on Europe but this really doesn't satisfy our needs fast enough. The relationships and an understanding of the customer in the market are key. As a result, we feel that an acquisition would suit us better than a green field effort: it is an easy way to get scale and expertise at the same time.

With that in mind, Murch and Slyngstad decided it was time to contact Rent-A-Holiday about a possible merger.

Rent-A-Holiday: Growing from Brussels

The Genesis of Rent-A-Holiday: Another Honeymoon

Peter Ingelbrecht graduated from the University of Gent in Belgium with a degree in economics. (See **Exhibit 15** for the biographies of RAH founders.) He first worked at Procter & Gamble as a Product Manager for brands such as Always, Ariel (detergent), and Punica (fruit drink). After eight years at P&G, Ingelbrecht enrolled at Stanford Business

EXHIBIT 6   **VacationSpot.com Site Overview**

Source: VacationSpot.com.

Easy Searching

"The slickest site yet for vacation rentals" -- *Online Traveler, Nov. '98*

…on Rent.Net

…onInfoSpace

…Results

EXHIBIT 7
Vacation Property Value Chain

Source: VacationSpot.com.

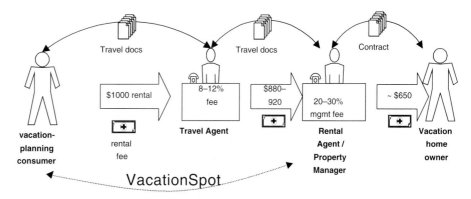

- Consumers want large selection, instant availability, market-efficient pricing, specials, reviews & more.

- Suppliers want improved distribution, more cost-effective marketing, easy-to-maintain electronic presence, yield management & more.

- No electronic reservation network yet exists for the vast majority of vacation property.

EXHIBIT 8 VacationSpot.com Booking Inquiries and Property Listings

Source: VacationSpot.com.

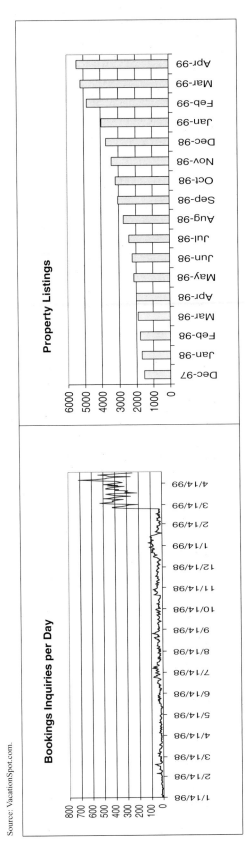

Property Listings

Bookings Inquiries per Day

School from which he graduated in 1995. Although he initially wanted to do a start-up he decided against the idea and returned to Europe to work for The Boston Consulting Group in Brussels, Belgium. Ingelbrecht explained his choice.

> I really wanted to start my own company, but the debts accumulated from Stanford made that impossible. So I decided to head back to Europe to work for BCG. I felt I needed to be in Europe because I felt I had an edge there and that I did not have one in the United States. I liked BCG because it was strong in consumer products and marketing, areas of interest and strength for me. Moreover, I liked the short, three to four month cases and the strategic nature of the business. I felt this would give me a good base knowledge and flexibility for the future.

On his first case, Ingelbrecht worked with Laurent Coppieters, a three-year BCG consultant who had graduated from the Free University of Brussels (ULB) with a commercial engineering degree. They shared their ideas about long-term career goals and found they had a mutual interest to start their own company. The two kept in touch over the next couple of years. Ingelbrecht then came up with the idea for RAH after having an experience similar to Murch while on his honeymoon in Spain in 1996. He had originally wanted to book a small villa and after spending a tremendous amount of time searching through the typical sources like agencies and newspapers, he found nothing was free so he booked a hotel instead. When he got to Spain, he was surprised to find there was plenty availability. Ingelbrecht explained what he found:

> Once I was there I saw *at least* 20% vacancy right off the bat and determined that this market must not be very efficient. So I visited some of the property managers to find out more about their business . . . and to find new lodging! . . . and found that marketing in the segment was very unprofessional, at least in Spain. They only advertised locally and had absolutely no clue about cross-border marketing. At the same time, property owners and tour operators granted substantial commissions to these people. So I knew there was an opportunity.

With this new knowledge, Ingelbrecht went to his colleague Coppieters and the two decided in January 1997, to quit their job at BCG and began Rent-A-Holiday. Coppieters explained the move:

> We did not have any funding at the time but we knew we had a good idea and we knew it needed our complete attention. So we quit BCG to create a rental company focused on Europe. We wrote a business plan and started in April 1997, with our own funds. The first capital round followed in June 1997.

The Early Years at Rent-a-Holiday: Building Property Inventory and Raising Capital

Rent-A-Holiday's strategy was to become a worldwide player by focusing first on Europe. According to the company's estimates, 90% of vacation rentals in Europe were to other European citizens. Moreover, RAH estimated that about 17% of all overnight stays in Europe were in B&Bs and another 17% were in vacation rentals; the corresponding figures were around 4% for both segments in the United States. By focusing on a "Fortress Europe" strategy, RAH felt that they could build up a solid business while protecting themselves from the threat of competition outside of Europe. The strategy was to be executed both through proprietary inventory development and through acquisitions, similar to VacationSpot.com. However, the RAH business was slightly different from VacationSpot.com in that not only did the entrepreneurs have to convince the suppliers to use their service, but they had to educate them about the Internet as well. Since only 5%–10% of the potential suppliers used the Internet, the company had to rely on more traditional means of communication, like fax machines, telephones, and direct country visits.[5]

---

[5] The Internet penetration amongst suppliers in the US was around 50% according to VS estimates.

As a result the acquisition of suppliers turned out to be more costly than planned. While RAH had originally budgeted 3 man-years to acquire a certain number of suppliers and listings it eventually took 10 man-years to achieve the target. On the positive side RAH benefited from the fact that many Belgian's spoke several languages and that there was a considerable multilingual foreign population in Brussels, which was also the location of many administrative offices of the European Union. In comparison to the United States it was fairly easy to hire a workforce with outstanding language skills at a low cost. This multilingual and multicultural workforce could effectively build inventory via phone calls or local visits. The added complexity of having an end-user and a supplier that often times spoke different languages also complicated development of the website. As a result of this, RAH focused their technology development efforts on creating a user interface that could switch between seven major European languages[6] and help the supplier and the end-user communicate with each other. The founders believed that the development of this translation engine provided RAH with a distinct edge over their competition.

Due to low Internet penetration among suppliers, RAH was unable to offer an interactive reservation engine to web visitors. Instead, the company relied on a listing-fee-based revenue model. If a supplier wanted to list a home, she would be charged a fixed annual listing fee on a sliding scale: BFr3000 (~$75) (in 1999, it went to BFr5000) per year if she wanted to list one home, BFr25000 (~$600) if she wanted to list 25 homes.[7] Once a customer had identified a property he liked, he would submit an inquiry via the RAH web page. This inquiry would translate automatically into the supplier's language. The supplier would then get back to the traveler, by email, fax or telephone, to confirm availability and ask for payment. Dates of availability for each site could be updated by the supplier via the web.

One major difficulty the RAH founders had throughout the course of building the business was in obtaining financing (see **Exhibit 9** for Rent-A-Holiday's financing history). Ingelbrecht explained:

> Although we had a similar vision and business model as VacationSpot.com, we had not been able to raise as much money. The venture capital community in Europe, and in Belgium in particular was not as developed as the VC market in the U.S. As a result, we had to spend a lot more time on capital raising than VS did, but got less money. Our first round of financing (completed in June 1997) took four, hard months to complete. We were finding ourselves spending the larger share of our time on such subjects as trying to convince investors that the Internet wasn't just for geeks![8]

[6] English, Spanish, German, Italian, Swedish, Dutch, and Portuguese.

[7] During the start-up phase, RAH offered a certain number of suppliers free listings in order to create an inventory of properties.

[8] VacationSpot had spent about 80% of their time on acquiring and generating property listings according to the VS founders.

EXHIBIT 9
Rent-A-Holiday Financing History

Source: Rent-A-Holiday.

Round	Investor	Amount Raised	Premoney Valuation
Seed (April 1997)	Founders	$100,000	$0
First round (June 1997)	Investors	$700,000	$600,000
Second round (July 1998)	Investors	$500,000	$1,800,000
Third Round	Investors	$400,000	$1,800,000

Ownership Structure as of 4/99

Investors	73%
Founders	27%

Also, as a small company in Europe, the RAH founders discovered it was tough to attract talent, both in terms of number and quality. Moreover, Belgian tax law made it difficult to use options as an incentive for potential employees as the employee would be taxed immediately upon the grant of the option, unlike in the United States where the employee would be taxed upon selling the security the option had been converted into.

Rent-A-Holiday in April 1999

While financing and hiring issues probably slowed the growth of RAH, by April 1999 the company was the largest European player in the market and they had roughly the same number of property listings as VacationSpot.com. (See **Exhibits 10–14** for booking inquiries and property listings over time, comparative statistics, company financials, and comparable company valuations.) RAH's founders felt that they were making good progress in terms of generating traffic and getting property listings. Also, the translation engine and user interface were unmatched by competitors. Financing had taken its time, however, and the founders were just getting started on the design of a European acquisition program to further increase their listings.

EXHIBIT 10   **Rent-A-Holiday Booking Inquiries and Property Listings**

Source: Rent-A-Holiday.

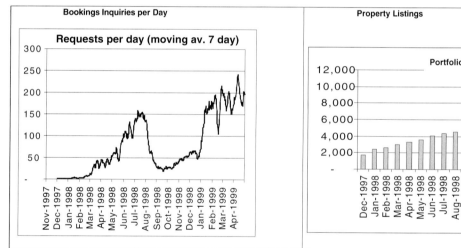
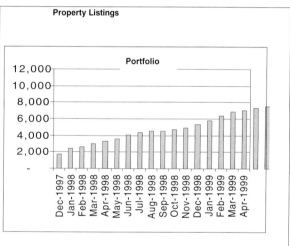

EXHIBIT 11
Comparative Statistics

Source: Rent-A-Holiday.

Key Figures	VacationSpot.com	Rent-A-Holiday
Visitors per day	8,000	2,000
Properties/ads	6,000	7,000
Rentable units	65,000	25,000
Customers	2,500	800
Sales per month (USD)	50,000	21,000
Managers	5	2
Full-time employees	23	5
Distribution deals	9	2
Supplier acquisition cost	$300	$500
Site visitor acquisition cost	$0.27/visitor	$.025
Cash raised (USD)	9,000,000	1,750,000
Cash available (USD) (in 4/99)	7,000,000	350,000

EXHIBIT 12 VacationSpot.com Historical and Projected Financials

Source: VacationSpot.com.

			Five Year Revenue Forecast			
	1998	1999	2000	2001	2002	2003
Advertising Revenue						
New Paid Property Listings	4,000	4,500	5,000	4,000	3,000	2,000
Cumulative Listings (with 80% renewal)	4,000	7,700	11,160	12,928	13,342	12,674
Avg Revenue per listing	80	85	90	100	105	110
Total Advertising Revenue	$320,000	$654,500	$1,004,400	$1,292,800	$1,400,952	$1,394,131
On-line booking revenue						
Bookable Properties Online (avg for year)		1,100	7,000	12,000	18,000	24,000
Average # units/property		10	10	10	11	11
Bookable Units (avg for year)		11,000	70,000	120,000	198,000	264,000
Commissionable bookings per unit/per year		1	2	3	5	7
Commissionable bookings		11,000	140,000	360,000	990,000	1,848,000
Avg Revenue per comm booking		$42	$39	$36	$34	$32
Commissionable booking revenue (Rezworks sales)		$462,000	$5,460,000	$12,960,000	$33,660,000	$59,136,000
Property Inet site bookings per unit/per year		2	4	5	6	6
Property managed bookings per year		22,000	280,000	600,000	1,188,000	1,584,000
Direct booking transaction fee		$7.00	$6.00	$5.50	$5.00	$5.00
Transaction Revenue from Direct Sales		$154,000	$1,680,000	$3,300,000	$5,940,000	$7,920,000
Total On-line booking revenue		$616,000	$7,140,000	$16,260,000	$39,600,000	$67,056,000
PMS Software revenue						
Avail/WinROOM systems sold	40	200	450	500	600	700
Revenue per system	$400	$400	$400	$400	$400	$400
Avail revenue	$16,000	$80,000	$180,000	$200,000	$240,000	$280,000
AvailPro systems sold		5	80	200	350	400
AvailPro revenue per system		$2,000	$2,000	$2,000	$2,000	$2,000
AvailPro Revenue		$10,000	$160,000	$400,000	$700,000	$800,000
Total PMS Software revenue	$16,000	$90,000	$340,000	$600,000	$940,000	$1,080,000
Grand Total Revenue	336,000	1,360,500	8,484,400	18,152,800	41,940,952	69,530,131

(continued)

1998: actual; 1999: expected; 2000–2003 forecast.

EXHIBIT 12 (Continued)

Source: VacationSpot.com.

			Five Year Revenue Forecast			
	1998	1999	2000	2001	2002	2003
Sales & Marketing						
PR Expenses	$37,000	$120,000	$150,000	$195,000	$253,500	$329,550
VacationSpot Marketing	$48,000	$400,000	$300,000	$300,000	$300,000	$300,000
Avail & AvailPro Marketing	$12,000	$360,000	$432,000	$518,400	$622,080	$746,496
Rezworks Network Marketing		$900,000	$1,350,000	$2,160,000	$3,672,000	$6,242,400
Rezworks Network Distribution costs		$92,400	$1,092,000	$2,592,000	$6,732,000	$11,827,200
Total Marketing Expense	**$97,000**	**$1,872,400**	**$3,324,000**	**$5,765,400**	**$11,579,580**	**$19,445,646**
Staffing Costs						
Avg number of employees	8	24	33	44	56	72
Salaries and Benefits per employee	$60,000	$66,000	$72,600	$79,860	$87,846	$96,631
Total Salaries	$480,000	$1,584,000	$2,395,800	$3,513,840	$4,919,376	$6,957,432
Contractors	$8,000	$24,000	$66,000	$88,000	$112,000	$144,000
Total Staffing Costs	**$488,000**	**$1,608,000**	**$2,461,800**	**$3,601,840**	**$5,031,376**	**$7,101,432**
Other Costs						
Office Lease	$48,000	$52,800	$61,776	$72,278	$84,565	$98,941
Communications (phones * Inet access)	$24,000	$28,800	$34,560	$41,472	$49,766	$59,720
Datacenter (servers, hosting & comm)	$18,000	$23,400	$30,420	$39,546	$51,410	$66,833
Furniture	$8,000	$24,000	$33,000	$44,000	$56,000	$72,000
Office supplies	$6,000	$7,800	$10,140	$13,182	$17,137	$22,278
Recruiting	$12,000	$14,400	$17,280	$20,736	$24,883	$29,860
Legal	$24,000	$28,800	$34,560	$41,472	$49,766	$59,720
Travel & Entertainment	$8,000	$24,000	$33,600	$47,040	$65,856	$92,198
Computer Equipment	$18,000	$28,800	$39,600	$52,800	$67,200	$86,400
Computer Software	$6,400	$14,400	$19,800	$26,400	$33,600	$43,200
Wash State Tax—3% revs	$10,080	$40,815	$254,532	$544,584	$1,258,229	$2,085,904
Total Other Costs	**$182,480**	**$288,015**	**$569,268**	**$943,510**	**$1,758,412**	**$2,717,054**
Total Revenue (from prev sheet)	**$336,000**	**$1,360,500**	**$8,484,400**	**$18,152,800**	**$41,940,952**	**$69,530,131**
Total Costs	**$767,480**	**$3,768,415**	**$6,355,068**	**$10,310,750**	**$18,369,368**	**$29,264,132**
Total Profit (Loss)	**($431,480)**	**($2,407,915)**	**$2,129,332**	**$7,842,050**	**$23,571,584**	**$40,265,999**

(continued)

EXHIBIT 12 (Continued) VacationSpot.com—Historical Financials (January–April 1999)

Source: VacationSpot.com.

Income Statement

	January	February	March	April	YTD April
Revenue					
Paid listings	29,977	32,223	33,955	43,435	139,590
Property management software sales	13,935	10,585	9,010	11,003	44,533
Banner advertisements/web development	450	150	700	900	2,200
Commissions	1,436	1,555	(485)	1,789	4,295
Gross revenue	45,798	44,513	43,180	57,127	190,618
Expenses					
Depreciation/amortization	110,000	110,000	110,000	110,000	440,000
Contract labor	14,178	17,720	18,412	27,112	77,422
Guaranteed payments	14,167	42,499	28,333	19,180	104,179
Marketing	18,520	18,705	34,134	31,262	102,621
Salaries	63,506	56,350	64,791	85,637	270,284
Other expenses	55,508	79,100	63,355	87,001	284,964
Total expenses	275,879	324,374	319,025	360,192	1,279,470
Interest Income	2,068	1,484	1,216	3,459	8,227
Net Loss	(228,013)	(278,377)	(274,629)	(299,606)	(1,080,625)

Statement of Cash Flows

	January	February	March	April	YTD April
Net Loss	(228,013)	(278,377)	(274,629)	(299,606)	(1,080,625)
Depreciation/Amortization	110,000	110,000	110,000	110,000	440,000
(Increase) decrease Working Capital	(1,606)	309	8,218	(5,432)	1,489
Purchase of fixed assets	(2,574)	(3,929)	(6,398)	(60,637)	(73,538)
Shareholder Contributions				5,725,000	5,725,000
Net Increase (Decrease) in Cash	(122,193)	(171,997)	(162,809)	5,469,325	5,012,326
Cash, Beginning of Period	727,032	604,839	432,842	270,033	727,032
Cash, End of Period	604,839	432,842	270,033	5,739,358	5,739,358

Balance Sheet

	January	February	March	April	
ASSETS					
Current Assets					
Checking/savings	604,840	432,843	270,033	5,739,358	
Other current assets	117,160	116,488	113,587	117,312	
Fixed Assets	102,303	106,231	112,630	173,267	
Less: Accumulated depreciation	(25,875)	(25,875)	(25,875)	(25,875)	
Net fixed assets	76,428	80,356	86,755	147,392	
Other Assets	1,246,669	1,136,669	1,026,669	916,669	
TOTAL ASSETS	2,045,097	1,766,356	1,497,044	6,920,731	
LIABILITIES & OWNERS' EQUITY					
Misc. liabilities	5,018	4,654	9,971	8,263	
Owners' equity	2,040,079	1,761,702	1,487,074	6,912,467	
TOTAL LIABILITIES & EQUITY	2,045,097	1,766,356	1,497,045	6,920,730	

EXHIBIT 13
Rent-A-Holiday
Historical and
Projected Financials

Source: Rent-A-Holiday.

Historical Financials		
Converted to USD	**1997**	**1998**
Revenues	14,276	139,573
Costs	246,798	765,841
Net Profit	−232,522	−626,269

Projected Figures

	Financial Summary				
	1999	**2000**	**2001**	**2002**	**2003**
Total customers	1,122	3,548	6,744	11,158	17,292
Total ads	12,440	38,129	61,405	82,886	103,642
Traffic (IP sessions)	961,849	3,774,951	5,658,012	8,061,335	10,986,329
Requests	75,865	316,975	508,892	773,166	1,119,483
Euros					
Revenues	334,086	1,219,560	2,364,064	3,878,766	5,395,487
Investments	194,553	424,498	460,127	532,117	591,918
Costs	1,175,510	1,758,440	2,073,500	2,436,330	2,821,180
Profit	(841,424)	(538,880)	290,564	1,442,436	2,574,307
Cash flow	(964,033)	(947,964)	(151,430)	943,470	2,088,581
Number of shares	9,247	9,247	9,247	9,247	9,247
Earnings per share	(90)	(58)	31	156	278

Note: All figures excluding online reservations.
1 Euro = 40.3399 BEF, 1, 95583 DEM, 6.55957 FRF, ~1.07 USD.

EXHIBIT 14   **Sample of Internet Travel Companies and Most Recent VC Financing**

Source: Compiled from VentureSource data.

Company	Business Brief	Founded	Employees	Amount Raised	Post-Money Valuation	Date Raised
Biztravel.com	Provider of Internet travel reservation services	1995	37	$10.0 million	$60.6 million	Dec. 1997
GetThere.com	Provider of Internet-based travel procurement, primarily for business and travel suppliers	1995	271	$6.5 million	$22.5 million	Aug. 1997
				$30.3 million	$100.0 million[a]	May 1998
Preview Travel	Marketer of travel and vacation packages via the Internet	1985	161	$27.5 million	$154.2 million[b]	Nov. 1997
WorldRes, Inc.	Real-time reservation network for chain hotels via the internet	1995	70	$12.0 million	$60.0 million	Mar 1999
Xtra On-line	Provider of Internet-based travel reservation software and related services for corporate travelers	1996	62	$15.0 million	$75.0 million	Jul. 1998

Note: The above information was the result of an extensive search on VentureSource. Only those companies where complete valuation data could be obtained were presented.
[a]Corporate investment by United Airlines.
[b]Initial Public Offering.

Up until the March 1999, RAH had followed a "Fortress Europe" strategy by building the best company in the space in Europe and by attracting as many European properties as possible. The question was whether and how a potential merger with a U.S. company would change that strategy.

Merger Discussions between RAH and VS

The Courtship Begins . . . and Ends?

The first contact between the two companies had actually occurred one year before, in March 1998, when Coppieters e-mailed Murch. Murch recalled this first contact:

> Laurent actually contacted us in 1998 to discuss the possibility of link exchanges, and potentially a joint venture between our two companies. The proposal was to share our property listings and to somehow share the revenues. They were actually a little bigger than we were at that time—about 4,000 listings to our 3,000—but we really didn't want to do a JV. Microsoft always preached the perils of joint ventures; it is extremely tough to align incentives in them. The history of JVs in high technology is littered with failures. So we decided to pass on the opportunity and we kind of lost sight of each other. Then when we completed the survey of our site and discovered that we were weak in Europe, I decided to give them a call.

Coppieters remembered that conversation:

> At the end of March, Steve called me out of the blue one day and asked me if we wanted to merge with them. That was really a crazy call! It took me completely by surprise. But we started talking, found that they were serious and decided it would be worth a trip out to Seattle. So I hopped on a plane to Seattle along with Karim, one of the investors.

From the initial telephone discussions through the first few hours of the face-to-face meetings in April, the two sides never discussed valuation. They spent their time instead trying to understand each company's business model and vision and simply trying to see if there was a "fit." "It almost seemed as if we were all avoiding the valuation issue in order not to lose sight of the fundamental issues," recalled Coppieters, "It seems both sides share the same long-term vision and strategy." As both sides became comfortable with the direction the combined entity would follow, Slyngstad decided to begin the discussion about valuation. Slyngstad said that since both companies had recently closed a round of financing, that the valuation from the round would be the best place to start. So he made an initial offer where VacationSpot.com would merge with Rent-A-Holiday at a 9-to-1 ratio, subject to Ingelbrecht and Coppieters signing a long-term employment contract. Upon hearing the offer, Dhanani exploded and the RAH team walked out.

VacationSpot.com Reaction: Picking Up the Pieces

Sitting in their offices after the meeting, Murch and Slyngstad looked at each other again. They believed that their offer was more of a starting point for negotiations and that since both companies had recently completed a round of financing, their approach was rather reasonable. Slyngstad turned to Murch and said:

> Since we both had just raised money, I thought that the prior rounds were a good starting point for the negotiations. We started with a zero premium and were preparing to move on from there. But I don't understand what just happened and I am not sure how to interpret it. Was this a cultural misunderstanding and they really feel we low-balled them? Or was this just a negotiating tactic to get us to increase our offer? What's really strange is that we do not know if the talks are over or they are only suspended. I am leaning towards this being a negotiating tactic, but regardless, this is quite strange.

EXHIBIT 15   Founders' Resumes

Source: VacationSpot.com and Rent-A-Holiday.

VacationSpot.com

Steven D. Murch, President and CEO

Prior to founding VacationSpot.com, Murch held several management, marketing and technical positions at Microsoft, including his last position as Product Unit Manager, Internet Gaming Zone, '95–'97. In this job, he led the strategy, technical design, and team for what became the Internet Gaming Zone (www.zone.com), now the largest gaming site on the Internet with over 10 million registered users. In this job, Murch led a team of 80, including development, testing, operations, marketing, and had full P&L responsibility. Murch also held other positions within Microsoft, most importantly as the marketing manager for relational database products (Microsoft Access and FoxPro). Here he led the database developer-relations effort and worked on building the developer community for Microsoft Access from its launch through Access 2.0. Previously, Murch worked at Bell Communications Research (Bellcore) in Livingston, New Jersey, where he was a member of Technical Staff focused on ISDN protocol planning and coordination with the Regional Bell Operating Companies. Murch earned an MBA from the Harvard Business School and graduated as a Baker Scholar in 1991. Murch also earned a Masters in Computer Science from Stanford University and a bachelor's degree in Business/Applied Mathematics from Carnegie Mellon University.

Greg Slyngstad, Chief Operating Officer

Greg Slyngstad is a recognized leading expert in the travel industry, particularly the exploding online sector. Slyngstad co-founded VacationSpot.com after spending 14 years in management positions at Microsoft. Slyngstad served as General Manager of Microsoft's Travel Group where he sold Bill Gates on the market potential for conducting on-line air and hotel bookings. As a result of this effort, he built the team that created Microsoft Expedia and the Microsoft Travel Technologies. In recognition of his Internet travel leadership, Slyngstad was named one of the 25 most influential executives in the travel industry by *Business Travel News* magazine in 1997. Prior to this position, Slyngstad was director of Far East Product Development in Microsoft's Tokyo office where he coordinated the development of Microsoft's Asian products, with a focus on assisting in the creation of Far East Windows 3.1 (Japanese, Chinese and Korean). Slyngstad was responsible for bringing the Redmond development methodology to the Japanese development organization, which included over 200 engineers at the time. He ultimately played a leading role in the restructuring of both the Redmond and Tokyo process that Microsoft used for developing its Asian language products. Slyngstad was program manager and group program manager in the Word group. In this role, he led the design and managed the project for several versions of DOS Word, culminating with the launch of Microsoft Word for Windows 1.0. As one of the earliest developers working on Windows, Slyngstad worked closely with the original Windows team, was on the original Windows UI task force and played a key role in shaping the user interface for not only Word, but many of the standards for Windows applications and Windows itself.

Rent-A-Holiday

Peter Ingelbrecht

Peter is co-founder and CEO of Rent-A-Holiday. Since 1995, Peter has worked as a consultant at the Brussels office of the Boston Consulting Group. During this time, he advised a broad group of clients across Europe on different types of strategic issues. The clients included a Belgian food retailer, a European broadcaster, the European division of an international credit card company, a Dutch based food company and the European division of a major food company. Prior to this Peter worked for 8 years at Procter & Gamble, first information systems manager of the Dutch subsidiary, followed by 5 years in the Belgian marketing department. During his period as an information systems manager, he led developments and supervised operations of a videotext based sales information system. In the marketing department Peter had brand management responsibilities in the laundry, paper, and beverage categories. Peter holds a Bachelors degree in Economics from the University of Gent and a Masters degree from Stanford Business School. He left BCG in January 1997 to found Rent-a-Holiday.

Laurent Coppieters

Laurent is co-founder and CEO of Rent-A-Holiday. From 1994 to January 1997 Laurent worked as a consultant with the Boston Consulting Group. Based in Brussels, London and Amsterdam, he worked on strategic and

(continued)

EXHIBIT 15   (Continued)

operational issues, including: new product development for a leading biotech company, defining the strategy of a European food manufacturer, reorganizing the duty free operations of a leading global producer and marketer of spirits and wine and the restructuring of call center operations. Prior to BCG he also worked in strategy and finance at Societe Generale de Belgique. Laurent holds a degree as a commercial engineer from Solvay Business School (ULB). He left BCG in January 1997 to start Rent-a-Holiday.

Murch was just as surprised as Slyngstad. However, Murch thought that there may have been a fundamental misunderstanding between the two parties and was somewhat more concerned than his partner about the status of their merger discussions with RAH. Murch responded to Slyngstad:

> We definitely want to resolve this misunderstanding with RAH. As a company, we need to get a stronger presence in Europe and although there are other companies out there, we like the fact they have a leadership position and we believe that their translation engine provides real value. What's more important is that we really liked Laurent and Peter. I think they are the *real* value in the business and that is why I want to get them into a long-term employment contract; we need to make sure the proper incentives are in place for them. The question is what kind of incentives do we need to offer them. We could also "conquer" Europe through a greenfield approach but this is the last thing we really want to do. There have been a number of U.S. companies that have gone to Europe, tried to use the same brand and tactics and have failed miserably. I think that proper business and cultural expertise is the most critical element of a foreign venture and I think that it is really difficult to develop internally. As a result, I really want to make an acquisition and I feel that these are the best guys out there.

Rent-A-Holiday Reaction: Take the Next Plane?

Back at the Sheraton Hotel, the Rent-A-Holiday team was trying to regroup. The low valuation offer was disappointing and RAH was just as unsure as to the direction of the negotiations. Coppieters had prepared for the negotiations by putting together a list of items that he thought could serve as a matrix for the valuation (see **Exhibit 11**). Since the VC market in the United States was so different from the VC market in Europe, they felt that these items rather than last-round valuations gave a much better indication of relative value than the prior rounds of financing. Coppieters outlined the RAH position:

> I put together a matrix that compared our companies according to several different operating and other statistics. In addition to this matrix, though, there are other considerations. For instance, the VS team is somewhat more advanced on the technological front. Although we realize that our translation engine provides a lot of value, their property management tool (Avail) is probably better than anything else out there and that holds a significant amount of value. In addition, they have much better financing sources than we do which would help us in several ways. For instance, it eliminates a lot of uncertainty potential European employees have regarding joining a small company like ours. Nevertheless, we do not *have* to continue with the negotiations. We could continue with our Fortress Europe strategy and compete against them effectively if they enter the European market without us. We have identified a couple of acquisition targets that would solidify our position in Europe and we could just as easily go that route if the deal is not fair. Also, the VC market in Europe is improving and we might be "overrun" by potential investors soon.

Another reaction of Coppieters was a result of the visit to Seattle rather than of the failed negotiation an hour before. Somehow the trip and the two-day search for fit made the entrepreneur realize that if a merger took place, the new home base of the firm would most likely be Seattle. This made sense: Seattle had better access to important inputs (such as capital and qualified employees) for the combined entity than Brussels. The merged company would keep offices in Brussels to develop the European market, but for how long and to what extent would Brussels become a subsidiary focused on strategy execution? And if Ingelbrecht and Coppieters wanted to co-lead would they need to move to Seattle? Despite their struggles in starting RAH Coppieters and Ingelbrecht really liked *their* company. Maybe it was better to continue alone.

Dhanani had some additional concerns. He not only felt that the offer for RAH was too low, but felt it was even more unfavorable to the investor group than it was to Ingelbrecht and Coppieters. He believed that the options that would be part of the potential employment contracts for Ingelbrecht and Coppieters were really a transfer of value from the investor group to the founders. Accordingly, he believed that the equity involved in the employment contracts was really part of the total consideration for the company and that the investors should get their pro rata share of these options.

What's Next?

As they reflected upon what happened, both sides were not sure what the next move should be. Should they be the ones to reinitiate contact or should they wait for the other party to make the first move? As they sat in the hotel lobby Coppieters looked at the phone and said, "I think this is worth another try, but we are not going to make the first move. They owe us." At the same time Murch looked at Slyngstad: "I really don't know whether this is a fundamental problem or just a cultural thing or smart tactics on their behalf. What do you think, Greg?"

Case 28

Infosys: Financing an Indian Software Start-Up

It was late afternoon rush hour on January 13, 1999, and N. R. Narayana Murthy and Nandan Nilekani had just arrived from another business trip to the United States. As he watched the heavy traffic in the crowded streets of downtown Bangalore, Murthy thought, "I must have made this trip several hundred times since founding the company back in 1981." Tiring as it might be, it was an essential element of his business. Murthy was CEO and chairman, and Nilekani was president and chief operating officer (COO), of Infosys Technologies Ltd., a company located in Bangalore, India, that developed software and provided information technology (IT) consulting services for international clients. But this time, Murthy and Nilekani were coming back from a visit not with customers but with U.S. investment bankers. Infosys had gone public on the Bombay Stock Exchange (BSE) in 1993 but was now considering an offering in the United States that would include a listing on one of the U.S. exchanges. As the driver of the EuropeCar dodged the traffic of the streets of Bangalore, several questions rushed through Murthy's head. Did it make sense to go ahead with the U.S. offering from a strategic standpoint? From a financial standpoint? If they completed the offering, which of their courtiers should they go with: the tech-laden NASDAQ or the more prestigious NYSE? What were their alternatives outside of an offering, and what were the relative merits of each?

On their way to the Infosys campus, Murthy and Nilekani passed the Indian subsidiaries of IBM, Hewlett-Packard, and Microsoft. Even though the offering was important, there was still business to attend to in terms of running Infosys's operations. Infosys was on the high of a run on the BSE (see **Exhibit 1**), but that was no cause for overexcitement. "We have a moral obligation to all of our shareholders—our employees and our financial investors—to keep posting results that will give adequate returns to them, and to run this company while keeping with the highest principles of corporate governance," Murthy often explained. "That is quite a task." With all of these concerns swimming

Professor Walter Kuemmerle and Dean's Fellow William J. Coughlin (MBA '99) prepared this case. HBS cases are developed solely as the basis for class discussion. Cases are not intended to serve as endorsements, sources of primary data, or illustrations of effective or ineffective management.

EXHIBIT 1
Stock Price Graph

Source: Infosys.

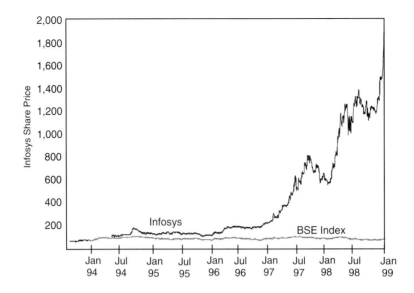

through Murthy's head, the car pulled up to the driveway of the Infosys campus. The security guard saluted as Murthy and Nilekani talked about the long night ahead.

India and Software—an Uncommon Match?

The culture of India dates back to two early civilizations. The Indus valley was first settled 7000 years ago by Dravidian peoples. Over time they expanded their settlements across India. Around 3500 years ago Aryan peoples migrated to the Ganges valley from Persia.[1] The caste system that remains intact in India to this date was developed at that time. Dravidian and Aryan cultures merged into a Hindu culture. The following centuries saw the rise and fall of many different regional empires. While no single ruler managed to unite India, Hindu culture and religion spread across the region. In 1498 Vasco da Gama reached India by ship, and trade with Europe started in earnest. In 1600 the English East India Company was created; by 1850 Britain controlled more than 50% of the Indian subcontinent and had a strong influence over much of the rest of the territory. (See **Exhibit 2** for a map of India.)

Britain's rule over India was largely exploitative in nature and there was rising pressure among Indians for independence, epitomized by Mahatma Ghandi's campaign of nonviolence (started in 1920). India eventually achieved independence in 1947 and was split into Pakistan, with an Islamic constitution, and India, with a secular one. Jawaharlal Nehru, leader of the Indian National Congress, became India's first prime minister. Nehru, educated at Oxford, was a socialist. He supported state ownership of major productive assets and protectionist policies. During the 1980s it became increasingly clear to many leading Indian thinkers that these policies were harmful rather than helpful for India's development. Significant change (liberalization of trade, currency fluctuation, enabling of foreign direct investment) was triggered by a 1991 financial crisis but also by the collapse of other planned economies around the world.[2] By 1999 India was still largely an agricultural society where about 75% of the workforce was employed. (See **Exhibit 3** for economic information on India.)

[1] *The Statesman's Year-book.* 2004. 140th edition. New York: St. Martin's Press. p. 810.

[2] *EIU Country Profile India 1999–00.* London: Economist Intelligence Unit. 1999. p. 20.

EXHIBIT 2   **Map of India**

Source: *EIU Country Profile India -Nepal 1999–00.* London: Economist Intelligence Unit, 1999, preface.

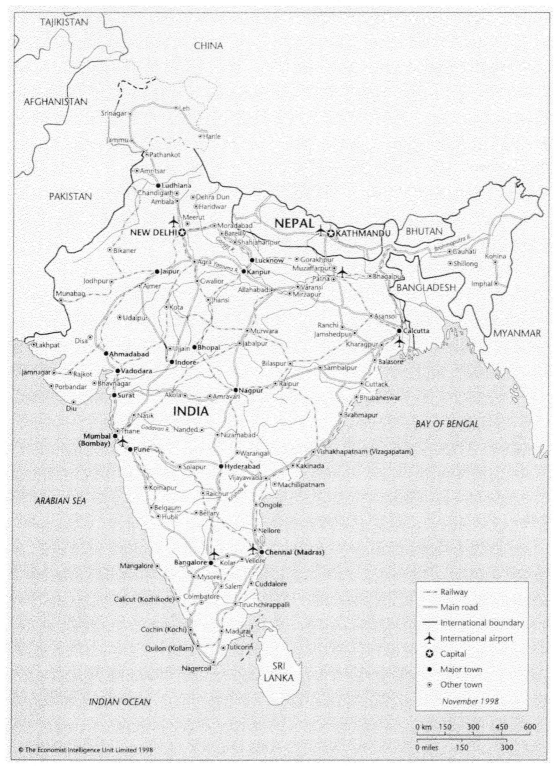

EXHIBIT 3 Comparable Economic Information

Source: Taran Khanna and Danielle Melito, "Modern India," HBS No. 797-108 (Boston: Harvard Business School Publishing, 1999), p. 11.

Indicators	1996			1991		
	India	UK	U.S.	India	UK	U.S.
Local currency : US$[a] (year average)	R35.43	£0.64	—	R22.74	£0.56	—
Population[a] (millions)	956.6[d]	58.8[d]	265.3	827	57.8	252.6
GDP[a] (market prices in local cur. bn)	12,619[d]	733.9[d]	7,580	5,420	575.7	5,917
Exports[a] (in local currency bn)	656.8[de]	164.0[d]	613.5[d]	413.9	102.3	416.9
Imports[a] (in local currency bn)	775.3[de]	175.6[d]	769.9[d]	461.6	112.5	491.0
GDP % real growth[a]	5.7%[d]	2.3%[d]	2.5%	5.4%	−2.0%	−1.0%
GDP % financial, bus. & other services[b]	11.1%[fh]	22.2%[f]	35.6%[gi]	10.2%[h]	24.6%	35.8%[i]
Capital Markets[c] (Jan. 31)						
Price index	172.9	183.5	192.3	100.0	100.0	100.0
Volume of shares traded (millions)	27,491	12,229	12,263	n/a	5,187	4,164
Market Value (in local currency bn)	2,584	857	5,658	736	403	2,583
Val. of volume (in local currency m)	5,552	43,613	508,923	n/a	12,309	134,425

Ratings Index (unless otherwise noted), 1995[j]

Ratings are on a scale of 0 to 10. Higher scores indicate more desirable situation.

	India	UK	U.S.
Finance Market			
No. of listed domestic companies (1994)	appr. 5,000[n]	2,070	7,770
No. of companies followed by at least one analyst[k]	347	n/a	n/a
No. of securities analysts (individuals)[k]	121	1,347	523,000
Ability of foreign investors to control domestic companies	6.57	9.38	8.46
Local capital markets accessible to domestic & foreign co.	5.66	8.72	8.22
Stock markets reflect real value of companies	4.32	6.35	6.91
Availability of venture capital	4.58	7.64	8.31
Adequate financial regulations	6.26	7.53	7.54
Accounting standards	5.70	7.80	7.10
Information & Infrastructure			
Urban population (%)	26.8%	89.5%	76.2%
No. of business students[l] (% of pop.)	0.1%	0.4%	0.9%
Radios per 1,000 pop.[l]	81	1,429	2,122
Phone lines in use per 1,000 pop. (1994)	9	477	576
TVs per 1,000[l] (1994)	40	439	817
Newspaper circulation per 1,000 pop. (1992)	31	383	240
Electricity generation (annual Kwh per capita, 1993)	363	5,533	11,158
Adequacy of power supply	2.76	8.40	9.00
Adequacy of roads	2.15	5.49	8.34
Adequacy of telecom infrastructure	4.00	8.26	9.09
Overall efficiency of distribution systems	5.14	7.54	8.78

(continued)

EXHIBIT 3   (Continued)

Political Risk Factors[m]			
Efficiency of judicial system	8.00	10.00	10.00
Rule of law	4.17	8.57	10.00
Corruption	4.58	9.10	8.63
Risk expropriation	7.75	9.71	9.98
Risk of contract repudiation by government	6.11	9.63	9.0

[a]As reported in *Economic Intelligence Unit (EIU) Country Reports*, various countries, 1st quarter, 1997 and 4th quarter, 1996. [b]As reported in *EIU Country Profiles*, various countries, 1996–1997 and 1993–1994. [c]Datastream International, 1997. Indian data from CRISIL 500 Equity Index, Bombay, India. [d]*EIU* estimate. [e]Merchandise exports and imports only. [f]1995 data. [g]1993 data. [h]Real estate and finance only. [i]Includes real estate and insurance. [j]Unless otherwise noted, data is from *World Competitiveness Report*, 1996. [k]*US Statistical Abstract*, Table 654, 1996 (US) and *Nelson's Directory of Investment Research*, Vol. II, 1996 (UK) and 1997 (India). [l]*UNESCO Statistical Yearbook*, 1996. [m]*Law and Finance*, by Raphael La Porta, Florencio Lopez-de-Silanes, Andrei Shleifer, and Robert W. Vishny, working paper #5661, The National Bureau of Economic Research, Inc., July 1996, Table 7. The ratings are an average of the months of April and October from the *International Country Risk's* monthly index between 1982 and 1995. The "Efficiency of judicial system" rating is a 1980–1983 average of raw numbers provided by the Business International Corporation. [n]Estimates vary widely.

The economic policy supported by the government prior to 1991 caused many problems for business, especially for those businesses that wanted to import goods from a foreign market. In 1981, it would take 18–24 months to import a computer. Furthermore, the infrastructure in India was very poor; a telecommunications facility was not simply costly but really not available. It was not until 1985 that the first satellite communications link was set up. In light of India's poorly developed technology infrastructure and import restrictions, it seemed somewhat unlikely in the 1980s that Indian software firms could grow rapidly. On the other hand, India's top universities produced a large pool of highly skilled engineers with sound mathematical and analytical training.

This labor pool was faced with a lack of employment opportunities in traditional manufacturing industries and at the same time particularly qualified to develop software. Computer software consisted of the programs, routines, and symbolic languages that controlled the functioning of computer hardware and directed its operations.[3] Estimates of the size of the global software industry in 1999 ranged from $300 billion to up to $750 billion if the software development performed by users in-house was included.[4] The industry was growing at 15%–20% rates and even faster than that in developing countries, although more than 80% of demand was in developed countries.

Based on a survey by the Indian software industry association, NASSCOM, India's software exports increased from $128 million in 1990–1991 to $2.65 billion in 1998–1999, representing a compound annual growth rate of 46%. In 1999 software accounted for approximately 5% of the country's total exports, and the industry was projected to grow to $3.9 billion in 1999–2000.[5] (See **Exhibit 4** for data on India's software industry.) North America (the United States and Canada) absorbed 61% of Indian software exports, Europe 23%, Japan 4%, and Southeast Asia 4%. The North American share was down from nearly 80% in the 1980s (see **Exhibit 5** for the top five Indian software exporters). Domestically, India was plagued by software piracy rates estimated at approximately 70%.

Indian exporters concentrated on support services, maintenance and the like (in which their share of world demand was estimated to be 10% or more)[6] rather than on higher-end services such as application solutions and software consulting or the development

[3] The remaining paragraphs in this section were adapted from Pankaj Ghemawat, "The Indian Software Industry at the Millennium," HBS No. 700-036 (Boston: Harvard Business School Publishing, 2000).

[4] Paul Taylor, "India's IT Mantra," Survey of Indian Information Technology, *Financial Times*, December 2, 1998.

[5] The NASSCOM data cited here are all drawn from that organization's website at www.nasscom.org accessed in October 1999.

[6] Paul Taylor, "Software Exports," Survey on Indian Information Technology, *Financial Times*, December 2, 1998.

EXHIBIT 4

India's Software Exports, Domestic Sales, and Imports (R. Billion/$ Million)

Source: Ghemawat, P. *The Software Industry in India.* 1999. HBS No. 700-036, p. 24. Compiled from NASSCOM (www.nasscom.org); R. Heeks. 1996. *India's Software Industry: State Policy, Liberalization and Development.* New Delhi: Sage Publications.

Year	Exports	Domestic Sales	Exports/ Total Sales (%)	Software Imports	Hardware Imports
1987–1988	R0.70 $52	R1.00	41	a	$154
1990–1991	R2.50 $128	R2.25	52	$25	$14
1991–1992	R4.30 $164	R3.20	57	a	$22.5
1992–1993	R6.70 $225	R4.90	57	$56	$18
1993–1994	R10.20 $330	R6.95	59	$60	$33
1994–1995	R15.30 $485	R10.70	59	$100	$7
1995–1996	R25.20 $735	R16.70	60	$133	a
1996–1997	R39.00 $1,110	R25.00	61	a	a
1997–1998	R65.3 $1,790	R35.8	64		
1998–1999	R109 $2,650	R49.5	68	$500 (estimate)	

ªFigures not available.

Note: The figures for the domestic software activity do not include in-house development of software by end users, which is presumed to be a considerable amount.

and marketing of packaged software. However, several successful Indian software firms had recently added IT consulting and related high-end services to their offering. Services performed on-site (at the client site) accounted for 59% of India's software exports in 1998–1999, compared with 95% in 1990. The shift from on-site toward offshore[7] (i.e., in India) business had been accompanied by significant changes in contractual form.[8] Lower-end work was typically governed by time-and-materials contracts and higher-end work by fixed-price contracts that were particularly subject to large overruns, a large fraction of which were typically borne by the Indian software vendor (see **Exhibit 6** for information on the "value chain" in software).

Issues of contractual form continued to be important because customized software continued to dominate India's software exports; standardized products and packages, which typically required large investments in research and development (R&D) and marketing, accounted for only about 10% of total exports. Once again, Indian exporters concentrated on the low end of this segment: on systems software and utilities and niche products for other developing countries rather than, for example, mass-market applications. The share of packaged software in Indian exports had actually slipped toward the end of the millennium because of the increasing focus on Y2K solutions (and the emergent demand for euro conversions). Y2K-related revenues accounted for about 20% of total exports.

[7] The offshore percentage includes packages developed in India that were sold overseas.

[8] The discussion in this paragraph is based on Abhijit V. Bannerjee and Esther Duflo, "Reputation Effects and the Limits of Contracting: A Study of the Indian Software Industry," unpublished working paper, MIT, June 9, 1999.

EXHIBIT 5 **Top Five Indian Software Exports**

Source: Compiled from: (1) Ghemawat, P. *The Software Industry in India.* 1999. HBS No. 700-036, p. 16–20. (2) NASSCOM data.

Company	R Million	Description
1 Tata Consultancy (TCS)	15,185	India's first software company and the largest software independent in Asia. Owned by the Tata industrial group. Revenues had grown at an annual rate of 40% over the past five years and were split 90:10 between exports and the domestic market.
2 Wipro	6,325	Diversified public company. Software 40% of sales; software exports 63% of operating profit. 75% of shares family controlled. CEO transformed company from sleepy manufacturer of hydrogenated oils to a leading Indian high-tech company.
3 Pentafour	5,118	Approximately 44% of revenues were accounted for by software exports, 49% by software multimedia, 4% by domestic software, and 3% by training. Family-controlled company that recently underwent governance changes (including divesting holdings in other family companies).
4 Infosys	5,002	Approximately 97% of its revenues were generated by software exports, with domestic software accounting for the remainder. Revenues and earnings had grown at 60%–80% rates over the past two years. Infosys was the first Indian IT services firm to achieve CMM level 4 certification. CMM level 5 certifications were relatively rare.
5 NIIT	3,949	Revenues spread across software exports (30%), software multimedia (17%, focused on educational packages), domestic software (16%), and training (37%). India's largest computer training firm. NIIT was considered part of the closely held HCL (Hindustan Computers Limited) group, which on a consolidated basis had been the largest IT group in India until overtaken by TCS in 1997–1998.
Top 5 Total	35,579	
India's total exports	109,400	
Share of top 5 firms	32.5%	

Infosys—the Beginning

Murthy was born the son of a schoolteacher in 1946. He grew up in a modest environment and graduated with master's degrees in electrical engineering and computer science from I.I.T. Kanpur in 1969. After graduation, he took a job in Paris instead of pursuing a higher degree:

> I was preparing to go to either the United States or Israel for a Ph.D. when the job in Paris was offered to me based on a paper I had presented in Italy. Professionally, it gave me a chance to be part of a team that was to design a huge new operating system. But, for me personally, the job was even more compelling. I was 23 years old and, like all good Indians at the time, I was something of a socialist who lived on a heavy diet of Nehru's socialist philosophy. So, for me, post-1968 Paris was a very interesting time.

EXHIBIT 6
IT Software Value-Added Chain for Software Service Providers

Source: Company documents.

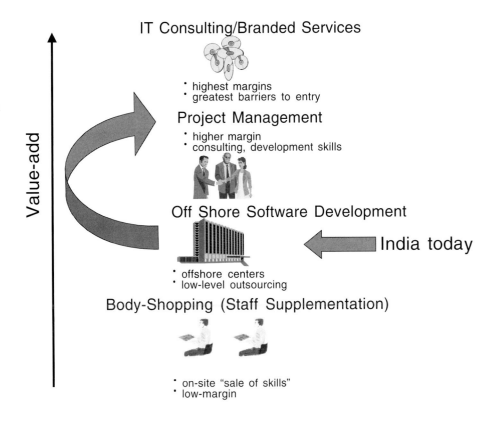

IT Consulting/Branded Services

· highest margins
· greatest barriers to entry

Project Management

· higher margin
· consulting, development skills

Off Shore Software Development

India today

· offshore centers
· low-level outsourcing

Body-Shopping (Staff Supplementation)

· on-site "sale of skills"
· low-margin

Value-add

The decision worked out to Murthy's expectations. In 1971, Murthy found himself in the midst of the post-1968 student revolution. During his time in Paris, he attended talks by existentialists and even met the head of the French Communist Party. These interactions and experiences gave him a chance to formulate his personal philosophy on life:

> With a reasonably active Communist Party, I was able to witness firsthand the maximum impression of socialism, and I came away with four observations. First, the only way a society can create wealth for people is not by distributing it but by actually fostering its creation. Second, after looking at business as a whole, I came to grudgingly acknowledge that there are relatively few people who are capable of leading the creation of wealth on a meaningful scale. Third, good people need the proper incentives—money, power . . . whatever, it can take many forms—to create that wealth. My greatest insight out of all of this was that it is not the job of the government to create wealth but to create the environment where the incentives for wealth creation exist.

When his tour in Paris was completed, Murthy hitchhiked back to India, over the course of the next year living on the $450 he had saved for himself. After a two-and-a-half-year stint with a public-sector think tank, he decided that the public sector was not for him. "I wanted to see firsthand how wealth was created and to see if I could make it," he said. So in 1977 he joined a start-up of a friend of his called PCS and became the head of the software group. But soon he wanted to create his own enterprise and, after four years at PCS, he left to start Infosys with six other PCS employees.

While the seven founders had complementary skills in finance, technology, human resources, and marketing, they shared the vision of creating wealth in a legal and ethical manner and going public in 10 years. But they were short on capital. Venture capital did not exist in India at that time, and banks did not provide funds without collateral. Furthermore, none of the founders had ties to significant family money or to one of the large Indian family-group companies. Thus, the founders started with just $1,000.

Because the domestic market held no real opportunity for the new company, Infosys focused on international markets for its software products. Indian-made computer hardware was not sufficient for development of software that could meet the demands of an international market, so Infosys had to use foreign equipment. However, because of the laws existing in India at the time, hardware was virtually impossible to import, even if the firm had the money to do so. As a result, the company had to perform the work on customers' equipment outside of India. Murthy recalled:

> We struck a deal with a company in New York that needed to upgrade its systems from a 16-bit to a 32-bit computer. So we went to the United States and met with them. We said, "Here are our strengths and here is how we can add value for you, but here are our constraints." And they said, "No problem. You can use our equipment." We entered into a six-year contract where they paid all of our expenses, let us use their equipment, and paid us a consulting fee.

With that, Murthy sent the founding members to New York to work on the project, and Infosys had officially begun operations.

Managing and Financing Growth

Weathering the Early Storms

Infosys slowly started to add new customers and to take on new projects over the next several years. From 1981 through 1989, the company grew from its original seven founders to a company with over 100 people. Despite some early cash-flow concerns, operations were running relatively smoothly until the crisis hit in 1989. Murthy offered the following summary:

> In 1989, we almost closed down business. The turning point was when one of the founders left the firm and migrated to the United States. Infosys had customers but was still fledgling. Because the factor conditions hadn't changed dramatically, we were forced to send people outside of India to complete the work. Ninety percent of the work was still being performed outside of India at the client site. This wasn't the vision we had for the company; we wanted to add maximum value *inside* of India.

Nilekani agreed with Murthy's assessment: "The departure of a founder brought the realization that we were executing a bad strategy. Steady growth with a low profile just didn't work. Some MNCs [multinational corporations] were already here, and we knew more would come. If we didn't do something, we knew we would get crushed, especially on the people side."

At that point, Murthy called a meeting and offered to buy out all the shares of the remaining founders. (See **Exhibit 7** for resumes of Infosys remaining founders.) Within half an hour, the other five founders rallied behind him and vowed to continue with Infosys. An external booster followed this new internal impetus—the liberalization of the Indian economy. There were five key reform measures that made a difference for the Indian software industry. These were a more responsive government, the establishment of software-development parks, current-account convertibility, the permission for 100% foreign ownership of any high-technology company, and the elimination of government-dictated pricing of new equity securities. In 1983 the company moved its headquarters from Bombay to Bangalore because of better access to engineering talent and better quality of life, which would help in attracting engineering talent from all over India.

EXHIBIT 7 Infosys Founders

(description of duties in January 1999)

Source: Infosys.

1. *N R Narayana Murthy:* Mr. Murthy is the Chairman of the board and Chief Executive Officer of Infosys Technologies Limited. He has varied experience in developing software products, project management. He also has extensive exposure to the international business environment. He is credited with designing the first BASIC INTERPRETER for an Indian computer manufacturer. Mr. Murthy has also served as the President of the National Association of Software and Service Companies (NASSCOM). He was given the "IT Man of the Year" award for 1996 by Dataquest, India and also the prestigious JRD Tata Corporate Leadership Award in 1998. He is a Fellow of the All India Management Association and the Computer Society of India. Mr. Murthy holds a Bachelors degree in Electrical Engineering from the University of Mysore and a Masters degree from the Indian Institute of Technology (I.I.T.), Kanpur.

2. *Nandan M Nilekani:* Mr. Nilekani is the Head of the Marketing and Sales functions of Infosys Technologies Limited. Before this, he has held various positions at the company including that of "Head of the Banking Business Unit" and 'Manager of International Marketing.' Mr. Nilekani is a co-founder of NASSCOM and has over 20 years of experience in the software industry. He holds a Bachelors degree in Electrical Engineering from IIT, Mumbai. Under the new reorganization announced in August 1998, Mr. Nilekani will assume the duties of Managing Director, President and Chief Operating Officer of the company.

3. *N S Raghavan:* Mr. Raghavan has served as a Director of Infosys Technologies Limited since 1981. He is also the head of Human Resources and Education at Infosys. Prior to this he held various senior management positions at the company. Mr. Raghavan is a veteran of the software services industry and has over 30 years of experience. Before starting Infosys in 1981, he worked at Patni Computers in India. He holds a Bachelors degree in Electrical Engineering from Andhra University.

4. *S Gopalakrishnan:* Mr. Gopalakrishnan has been the Head of Client Delivery and Technology at Infosys Technologies Limited since 1996. From 1994 to 1996, he served in the capacity of the Head of Technical Support Services at Infosys. From 1987 to 1994, he managed projects at the US based K SA/Infosys joint venture as the Technical Vice President. Before 1987, he guided the technical direction of the company as the Technical Director of Infosys. He has over 19 years of experience in the software technology industry. He holds a Masters degree in Physics and Computer Science from I.I.T. Chennai.

5. *K Dinesh:* Mr. Dinesh is the Head of Quality, Productivity and MIS at Infosys Technologies Limited. Prior to this he has held various senior project management positions at the company and was responsible for the worldwide software development efforts of the company. He is the author of DMAP, a large application package used by various distributors for inventory management. He has over 22 years of experience in the software industry and holds a Masters degree in Mathematics from Bangalore University.

6. *S D Shibulal:* Mr. Shibulal serves as the Head of Manufacturing, Distribution and Year 2000 business unit and also the Internet and Intranet business unit. Prior to that he worked on various software development projects for Infosys in the United States. From 1991 to 1996 Mr. Shibulal was on sabbatical from Infosys and served as Senior Information Resource Manager at Sun Microsystems. He holds a Masters degree in Physics from the University of Kerala and a Masters in Computer Science from Boston University.

Infosys's Financial History

Infosys had used little outside capital to fund its business. Beyond the initial $1,000 on which the company was founded and periodic working-capital funding, there had only been six outside-capital infusions prior to January 1999. These capital infusions took the form of four loans ($225,000 in fiscal year 1986, $250,000 in fiscal year 1989, $150,000 in fiscal year 1991, and $100,000 in fiscal year 1992) for purchasing hardware and other movable property, an IPO in 1993, and a private placement to international investors in fiscal 1995. Infosys's chief financial officer, Mohandas Pai, explained the company's financing philosophy:

> The financing history of Infosys is partially the history of the business and partially the culture instilled by Murthy. Service businesses generally have positive cash flow, and this helped shape our financial policy. But equally important is the company's reluctance to use

debt financing. The conservative, middle-class background of Murthy and the other founders has directly contributed to that reluctance. As a result, we are quite frugal and have avoided debt as much as possible. Financing has mainly been through profit retention, lower-than-market salaries for the founders, tight cost control [the founders always chose the low-cost option provided the quality of deliverables was not compromised], and relatively low capital expenditure [computer equipment was shared between employees and fully utilized].

In early 1994, we drew up a financing policy that had three main elements. First, we need to have liquidity of up to 25% of revenue in the form of cash and liquid assets. This is to ensure we can cover our next eight months of expenses—especially salaries—at any time. Next, we pay a dividend only if we have a cash surplus above that level and it will represent no more than 20% of a year's profits. Even though we are a high-growth company, Indian investors demand a dividend. Much of this stems from the old wealth tax of 2%—a tax that was levied because you owned something. Even though equity shares were made exempt from this wealth tax in 1993, Indians still look for yielding assets. We fund all capital expenditures and working-capital needs out of our cash flow. Borrowing, if at all, would only be a bridge to match cash flow and would always be fully collateralized by the cash balances. In those days banks were not willing to lend money to a people-intensive, as opposed to an asset-intensive, business. Even though debt financing is more accessible today, we still do not employ it.

Once the reforms were passed in 1991, we were able to take advantage of the capital markets with one of the first market-priced IPOs, in 1993. There were two motivations behind the IPO. The first was to realize the value of the investment by the employees and to contribute to the creation of wealth in India. The second was to take advantage of the tremendous growth opportunities in India through investment in the business. One of the first investments was in new facilities that could absorb the growth we anticipated in the business. We invested 130 million rupees in the new facilities even though our 1993 revenue level was only R145 million (1992 revenues were 95 million).[9] After the IPO, our business really took off—revenues doubled, and we had a stock split in 1994. We started making three- to five-year projections, and we realized we needed more resources. Since we didn't want to constrain liquidity, we decided to complete the private placement in fiscal 1995 to fuel our anticipated resource requirements.

Since that time, Infosys had seen tremendous growth in its business (see **Exhibit 8** for recent financial data). These initial investments allowed Infosys to expand the scope of its business, and the company had been able to generate sufficient cash flow for all of its past capital needs. During that time, Infosys had grown to become one of the largest and most successful companies in the Indian software industry. Moreover, the company achieved its goal of becoming a leader in Indian business. (See **Exhibit 9** for a full list of Infosys accomplishments.)

Infosys in 1999—the Star of India?

Putting People First

Between 1989 and 1999, Infosys dramatically transformed its business and image. Whereas in 1989 only 10%–20% of the work was being performed in India, operations had dramatically improved by the start of 1999. At that time, 75% of the work performed by Infosys was conducted domestically, yet only 2% of the company's sales were to Indian customers. It was estimated by industry insiders that Infosys's attrition rate was around 11%, well below the Indian average of 25%–30% in the software industry and dramatically below the 50%–60% levels found at software companies in Bombay.[10] In fact, Infosys was considered one of the most desirable places of employment among Indian students. Murthy explained the reason for the turnaround:

[9] In January 1999, the exchange rate between the rupee and the U.S. dollar was approximately R42.5: $1.

[10] Source: Casewriter interviews with Indian software experts outside Infosys.

EXHIBIT 8 Infosys Recent Financial Data

(R in millions, except per share data, other information and ratios)

Source: Infosys.

For the Years Ended March 31,	1982	1994	1995	1996	1997	1998
Particulars						
Revenue	1.2	300.8	577.0	934.1	1,438.1	2,603.7
Operating profit (PBIDT)	—	97.1	198.6	339.5	500.6	886.1
Interest	—	0.5	—	—	6.1	—
Depreciation	—	8.1	46.0	86.3	105.2	227.5
Provision for taxation	—	7.6	19.4	43.1	52.5	55.0
Profit after tax from ordinary activities	0.4	8.1	133.2	210.1	336.8	603.6
Dividend	—	11.7	23.1	36.3	39.9	70.3
Return on average net worth (%)	96.88	39.61	29.71	29.53	34.96	42.24
Return on average capital employed (PBIT/average capital employed) (%)	96.88	43.13	31.79	33.12	40.16	46.09
As at the end of the Year						
Share capital	0.01	33.5	72.6	72.6	72.6	160.2
Reserves and surplus	0.38	253.5	552.0	725.8	1,055.8	1,569.4
Loan funds	—	—	63.4	42.6	—	—
Gross block	0.002	82.7	253.2	468.6	712.9	1,051.4
Capital investment	0.002	71.3	252.3	155.5	273.1	344.1
Net current assets	0.63	139.4	324.7	411.7	542.0	972.3
Debt—equity ratio	—	—	0.10	0.05	—	—
Market capitalization	—	2,011.0	3,488.0	3,593.0	7,310.4	29,275.0
Per share data						
Earnings from ordinary activities (R)[a]	377.77	2.45	4.03	6.35	10.18	18.25
Dividend per share (R)	—	3.50	4.50	5.00	5.50	6.00
Book value (R)	383.10	9.00	19.00	24.00	34.00	52.00
Other information						
Number of shareholders	7	6,033	6,526	6,909	6,414	6,622
Credit rating from CRISIL[b]						
Commercial paper	—	—	"P1+"	"P1+"	"P1+"	"P1+"
Non-convertible debentures	—	—	"AA"	"AA"	"AA"	"AA"

Note: The above figures are based on Indian GAAP.

[a] On a fully diluted basis and adjusted for bonus issue of 1:1 during 1994–1995, 1997–1998, and 1998–1999.

[b] CRISIL = Credit Rating Information Services of India Limited.

The changes in government policy were a boon to our business, but they were certainly not going to make Infosys a success in and of themselves. We knew that it was up to us to create a sustainable business. But if the solutions to the problems were within Infosys, the question became, "How can we transform Infosys to get people to want to work here?" We needed to create an environment where people used speed and imagination in everything that they did, where people benchmarked themselves on a global scale, and where we recognized what our strategic resources were. We needed to become a globally respected firm and a leader in the Indian market.

EXHIBIT 9
List of Infosys Accomplishments

Source: Infosys.

Infosys Firsts

Infosys Technologies Ltd. was:

1. The first major Indian software company to obtain immediate certification to ISO 9001, an international software quality standard.
2. The first Indian software company to conceptualize, articulate, and implement the 24-hour productive day and the Offshore Software Development Center (OSDC) concepts.
3. The first Indian company to follow the U.S. GAAP system of accounting.
4. The first Indian company to value human resources and publish the valuation with its statement of accounts.
5. The first Indian company to value its brand and publish this information with its balance sheet.
6. The first Indian company to publish all mandatory and optional disclosures.
7. The first Indian company to distribute audited quarterly reports to its investors.
8. The first Indian company to guarantee publication of audited annual balance sheets by April 15 of each year. (Year-end closing is March 31.)
9. The first Indian company to provide audited balance sheets in soft copy format (floppy disks and CD ROM) to investors. Infosys was also the first Indian company to make its balance sheet available on the Internet.
10. The first Indian company to offer employee stock options to all qualified employees.
11. The first Indian company to have installed 1,400 nodes in one given location.
12. The first Indian company to have 160,000 sq. ft. of built-up software area in one location in India.

As a result, Infosys worked to create an environment that would enhance the overall experience for employees. With the funds from the IPO in 1993, Infosys began construction of the company's "campus," a number of multifloor buildings on a five-acre facility that included basketball and volleyball courts, shower rooms, banking and ATM facilities, and a fleet of 26 buses that ran to several different locations. "We even have sleeping facilities for the employees if a project requires them to work late into the evening," explained Senior Vice President of Human Resource Development Hema Ravichandar. She continued:

> There are three reasons why a person would stay with Infosys. People stay if there is learning value-added, if there is financial value-added, and if there is emotional value-added. We must address each of these needs if we are going to attract and retain employees.
>
> On the learning side, Infosys allows you to have a chance. We give you responsibility early and allow you to progress quickly in the organization due to the fact that we are growing so fast—both in terms of revenues and employees.
>
> On the financial side, it is not just salary. Infosys was the first company in India to institute a stock-option plan. In addition, as a compensation benefit, we created a series of loan programs for our employees. We offer low-interest and zero-interest loans while the current interest rates in the market are at 16%–18%. Depending on one's level and tenure, we even offer a home loan with a second lease on property, which means employees can take an Infosys home loan in addition to another loan for a house, something which has been virtually impossible to secure for most people in India. The home loan comes with a ballooning repayment facility that means the employee can pay more as time goes by and his or her salary increases. These initiatives are the embodiment of the company's philosophy of assisting in asset and wealth creation in India, but there are benefits to Infosys as well. For example, the plans are progressive in nature and are a function of level and salary; as one progresses, you first become eligible for a two-wheeler loan, then for a car loan, then a home loan, and so on. As a result, the attrition rate of people who participate in the housing loan program is much lower than the overall level of 11%.

The emotional side, however, is perhaps the most important element we have created in this organization. The culture at a company is hugely important and is a little more difficult to quantify. For example, if someone has just lost a close relative, Infosys really helps out and is always there to get people through tough times. The friendliness, openness, and transparency of the organization are really the key factors in our ability to attract and retain people.

Infosys as the Market Leader

In addition to the operating environment Infosys had created, there were several areas where Infosys had taken a leadership position in the Indian market. Much of that leadership was formalized in the Indian business environment, as Murthy and other employees held numerous leadership positions in Indian business associations. Murthy served as president of NASSCOM, the software trade association in India, from 1992 to 1994.

Aside from these formal positions, Infosys had been a leader in India mostly by example. In addition to being the first company to institute an employee stock plan, it was the first Indian company to file a 10K and the first to perform a full audit according to U.S. generally accepted accounting principles (GAAP). Nilekani explained the push for transparency:

Most of the large and successful companies in India have existed for some time and were run akin to personal empires, even if they are now public. In the old regime, there used to be the 2% wealth tax. Often this tax was higher than the yield the owner was receiving on the asset, which meant he would need to sell off some of this asset in order to pay the tax. What this did was create a perverse system where there was no incentive to increase the value of an asset; in fact, quite the opposite was true. People were only able to get value out of their businesses through other means, rather than through the creation of shareholder value.

As a result, there has been very little transparency in traditional Indian businesses. What we understood early on was that investors—especially foreign institutional investors—place a high value on transparency. One of the reasons why Infosys has been able to realize the value it has in the public market is its willingness to be transparent. We have won many awards, in India and throughout Asia, for the standards we have set in our reporting and disclosure policies.

Pai summarized Infosys's leadership position as follows:

Murthy has established the vision of creating maximum value in India in a legal and ethical manner, but this vision extends beyond Infosys itself. We have learned that you can create wealth in a legal and ethical manner. We have a huge competitive advantage by keeping management and ownership separate and a bigger competitive advantage through our transparency. But we do not want to just simply keep it for ourselves. We want to share all of our best practices with all Indian companies and will even help them implement it. That is how you create maximum value in all of India.

Growing Pains

Increasing Productivity

Although Infosys could look back on many accomplishments, the company faced several challenges in the months and years ahead. The major issue on the horizon was with regard to productivity. Although Infosys compared favorably to U.S. companies on a productivity basis when using operating profit as the measuring guideline, the company lagged far behind when looking at revenues per employee (see **Exhibit 10** for comparable productivity data). The cause for concern was in the wage differential between India and the United States. According to Infosys, Indian wages for software engineers were

EXHIBIT 10 Productivity Parameters, Indian vs. U.S. Software Companies

Source: "India Software: A Comparison of India's Top Software Exporters," Morgan Stanley Dean Witter, August 7, 1998.

Indian Software Sector: Key Productivity Parameters

(US$ 000s)[a]	DSQ Software	Infosys	NIIT	Pentafour Software	Satyam Computer	Tata Infotech	Wipro
Sales/Employee	31,551	32,014	30,037	67,366	27,775	33,081	30,270
Operating Cost/Employee	22,309	21,341	20,137	37,700	17,364	28,410	20,882
Operating Profit/Employee	9,242	10,674	9,900	29,666	10,411	4,671	9,388
PBIT/Employee	8,452	8,184	9,235	22,087	6,894	4,557	8,118
Net Profit/Employee	6,734	7,500	6,287	16,185	6,081	3,502	5,621
Capital/Employee	28,902	17,755	25,863	80,310	27,330	12,000	30,324
ROCE (%)	29.2	46.1	35.7	27.5	25.2	38.0	26.8

[a]Calculated based on an average exchange rate of R37.2/US$ for FY1998.

U.S. Software Sector: Key Productivity Parameters

(US$ 000s)	Cambridge Technology Partners	Complete Business Solutions	Computer Horizons Corp.	Information Management Resources	Keane Assoc.	Mastech Corp.	Sapient Corp.	Technology Solutions Company
Revenue/Employee	166,158	70,769	102,270	71,349	93,312	80,281	134,165	208,974
Operating Cost/Employee	139,837	63,628	89,681	54,370	79,204	69,218	103,826	177,198
Operating Profit/Employee	26,321	7,141	12,588	16,980	14,108	11,063	30,339	31,776
PBIT/Employee	23,781	6,688	12,277	14,987	11,511	10,864	29,786	28,012
Net Profit/Employee	13,454	4,289	6,918	10,157	6,552	6,393	18,349	16,157
Capital/Employee	51,597	27,023	39,193	66,575	31,893	36,686	111,385	100,535
ROCE (%)	46.1	24.7	31.3	22.5	36.1	29.6	26.7	27.9

Note: Cambridge Technology Partners' revenues were generated almost entirely through fixed-price contracts.

growing at approximately 25% per annum (see **Exhibit 11** for industry cost comparisons). With the wage differential closing, top-line productivity gains were a top priority at Infosys. Murthy explained Infosys's views on the challenge:

In order to remain competitive on a global basis, we need to close the gap in per capita revenue by moving up the "value chain" of software development. To do so, we must accomplish three objectives. First, we need to increase our customer penetration. Currently, our largest project is $7 million. In order to increase our revenue base, we are going to have to a) take on more projects, and b) take on bigger projects. Right now, about 80% of our revenues represent repeat business, which is on the high range of our target [70%–80% repeat business]. One tool we have used to acquire a new customer is to work on Y2K projects. Although this is relatively mundane work, it has acted as an inroad to the client and has allowed us to begin a partnership with the client—to begin a long-term relationship. Since this is a temporary phenomenon that is about to end, we have been very selective in the Y2K projects we have taken and have been working to decrease our exposure to the business. Our goal is to limit our Y2K exposure to 25% at its peak [see **Exhibit 12** for historical and projected Y2K exposure].

In order to take on bigger projects, we need to convince the customer of our ability to do so. That leads to our second objective—increase our brand equity. We need to create a buzz around the Infosys name, but we need to take a distinctive approach. Where Andersen

EXHIBIT 11
1994 Software Industry Cost Comparisons (indexed)

Sources: Table: Ghemawat, P. *The Software Industry in India.* 1999. HBS No. 700-036, p. 26. Based on "How Much is that Ant in the Window?" *The Economist.* July 30, 1994, p. 63. Information in footnote: Guha, K. 1998. Software Houses. *Financial Times,* October 26, 1998, p. 6.

Country	Programmer	Systems Analyst
United States	1,164	1,124
Japan	1,293	1,185
Germany	1,351	1,196
France	1,135	1,307
Britain	781	1,287
Mexico	652	658
India	100	100
Russia	80	84
China	75	80

According to estimates by Jardine Fleming, it cost $3,000 per month by the end of the 1990s to outsource work to an Indian programmer, compared with about $6,000 in basic salary for a U.S. programmer, or $9,000 per month including benefits. The costs of using Indian personnel were compounded by turnover rates that had reached 25%–30% per year.

EXHIBIT 12
Infosys Historical and Projected Y2K Exposure

Source: Infosys.

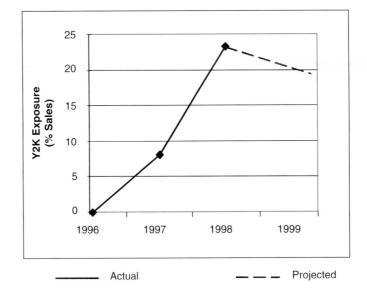

Consulting can enhance its brand through mass marketing, we are not in a position to do that. Our target audience is maybe 15,000 people worldwide—CIOs and executive directors. As a result, we need to focus more on seminars and direct marketing—one-on-one customer meetings. While we have made strong inroads on this effort, we still have our work cut out for us.

A third objective is to increase the amount of fixed price contracts we work on.[11] [See **Exhibit 13** for historical and projected fixed-price contracts.] There are three risks in increasing that figure. First, we are not able to appropriately define the scope of the project. Second, we do not know where we are going on a project because the customer has not figured out where he or she wants to go. Third, both the customer and Infosys are dependent on a third-party technology that neither of us can control. However, the customer is king, and if he or she prefers for us to take up a project on a time-and-materials basis, we will. So increasing the mix of fixed-price projects is an objective, but it will take some time to achieve. Better communication with the client can fix some of these problems but not all of them.

[11] The company was generally engaged on projects in two manners: on a fixed-price contract basis and on a time-and-material reimbursement basis. Fixed-price contracts were generally viewed as "higher-value-added" projects, as the software company took on increased risks (such as the length and complexity of the project, which directly affected the costs) and was compensated for managing those risks.

EXHIBIT 13
Infosys Historical and Projected Fixed Price Contracts

Source: Infosys.

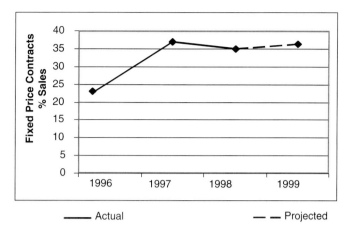

While there were numerous challenges, Infosys felt that several of its software development concepts were cutting edge. Its "Global Delivery Model," for example, was a distributed project-management methodology that divided projects into components to be executed independently and concurrently—part at the client site and the rest at remote development centers. Spreading development across time zones allowed for 24-hour workdays, and simultaneous processing of different modules accelerated delivery time of larger projects.

Cultural Concerns

In order for Infosys to accomplish many of the objectives with regard to productivity, the company believed that it would need to increase the number of foreign personnel working for the firm. As of the start of 1999, Infosys only had eight non-Indians working at the company. In order to accomplish its goal of high growth, Infosys believed that the company had to grow, both organically and, perhaps, through acquisition. "We are entering a new era where all companies want to be more global," explained K. Dinesh, director and head of Productivity, Quality, and Management Information Systems (MIS). "Therefore, we must learn to handle different cultures better—both outside and within the firm. That growth probably cannot all come organically, but we must not lose our focus or our distinctive culture. It is what makes this place special."

Hiring and Retaining Employees

The cultural issues surrounding the expansion of international personnel touched on the issue of the firm's ability to hire and retain Indian personnel as well. Infosys had seen tremendous growth in sales over the past several years and had been able to support that growth through a commensurate expansion of its headcount (see **Exhibit 14** for historical sales and employment figures). In order to rapidly grow its employee base without diluting its talent pool, Infosys had carried out a rigorous interviewing process with potential candidates. "We seek the candidates that have the highest degree of learnability," according to Murthy:

> After looking at the resumes of potential candidates, we select a relatively small number of people for testing [see **Exhibit 15** for Infosys's recruiting process and statistics]. These tests consist of a set of puzzles and math algorithms in order to gauge which candidates have the highest learnability. Those candidates that pass are then interviewed for a position with Infosys.

EXHIBIT 14   **Infosys Historical Sales and Employment Figures**

Source: Infosys.

As of March 31,	1988	1989	1990	1991	1992	1993	1994	1995	1996	1997	1998
Total Revenues											
Indian GAAP—R million	27.5	25.4	41.5	55.1	94.6	145.2	300.8	577.0	934.1	1,438.1	2,603.7
U.S. GAAP—US$ million	n/a	n/a	n/a	n/a	n/a	n/a	9.5	18.1	26.6	39.6	68.3
Total employees	73	110	136	176	300	450	573	904	1,172	1,705	2,605

EXHIBIT 15
Infosys Recruiting Process and Statistics

Source: "Infosys," Thomas Weisel Partners.

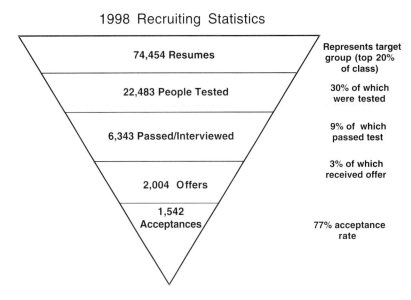

1998 Recruiting Statistics

74,454 Resumes — Represents target group (top 20% of class)

22,483 People Tested — 30% of which were tested

6,343 Passed/Interviewed — 9% of which passed test

2,004 Offers — 3% of which received offer

1,542 Acceptances — 77% acceptance rate

In the past, Infosys had been able to offer a highly meritorious career path for people due to its growth. The rapid pace of growth had allowed and even demanded that it give an increasing amount of responsibility to its employees. The challenge for the company going forward was to preserve the spirit and to offer a similar career horizon for new hires in the face of an increasing base of employees.

A U.S. Offering—to List or Not to List?

Facing these challenges in the marketplace, Infosys had a key decision to make at the start of 1999: whether to commence a stock offering in the United States. Infosys had gone public nearly six years earlier, listing on the Bombay Stock Exchange. That listing had not only fulfilled one of Murthy's original goals of completing an IPO of Infosys but had also fulfilled the goal of creating wealth for Infosys's managers and employees by creating a liquid asset out of the equity that they held. Although the exit event had already been created through the original IPO, Infosys viewed a U.S. offering as providing many benefits, according to Nilekani:

> Our main challenge is to move up the value chain by increasing our revenues per employee and by increasing our customer base. To accomplish this goal, it is essential that we enhance our brand. Because of our size and our niche market, we cannot rely on tools like advertising

and other "traditional" forms of marketing. That may work for IT consulting companies that can leverage advertising across many businesses and by doing so generate much higher revenues—but that might not work for Infosys. What we need to do is create a buzz in the market—create word-of-mouth publicity that will highlight the uniqueness of our company compared to our competitors. Currently, our competitors are perceived to be the other Indian companies in the market. We need to be viewed in relation to our "true" competitors— technology companies such as Cambridge Technology Partners in the United States. An American Depositary Receipt [ADR] offering in the United States will allow us to accomplish that goal. We may be an Indian company, but most of our customers are in the United States. The U.S. offering would allow us to create and to leverage that buzz in our customers' home market.

Secondly, an ADR offering in the United States would help accomplish other goals, such as the recruitment of international employees. Not only would the offering enhance Infosys's image with potential employees in the United States, but it would also provide us with flexibility. We would be able to offer the potential employee a completely U.S. dollar-based compensation package as the options and stock he or she would be given will be listed in the United States. Thirdly, in addition to providing currency for our employees, a listing would also provide currency for acquisitions in the United States or any another international location. Finally, it would be helpful for our current investors as well. As 26% of our investors are located in the United States and in other locations outside India, we aim to help them by gaining government approval to allow foreign investors to convert existing shares into ADRs. This increases our degrees of freedom in how we conduct business going forward.

If we decide to go ahead with the listing, the issue of which exchange to list comes up. We have to choose between the New York Stock Exchange [NYSE] and the NASDAQ. There are benefits to listing on either exchange. As the first Indian company to list in the United States, we have a responsibility to make the right decision [see **Exhibit 16** for listing considerations].

While there were clear benefits to an offering, there were also some questions surrounding the viability of a U.S. offering. First of all, it was not at all clear the company needed the extra cash that would come from an offering. More important was how the process of listing would be leveraged (see **Exhibit 1** for a stock price graph for Infosys). The company had seen its stock appreciate at 142% per annum between the IPO in 1993 and 1999, which was both a tribute to the success the company had enjoyed and a

EXHIBIT 16   Listing Considerations

Source: Infosys.

	NYSE	NASDAQ
Advantages:	• World's largest equity market • Greatest liquidity • Highly prestigious/visible • High listing standards create important perception of quality • Focus of a designated specialist • Larger institutional investor base	• Peer group: favored market for technology stocks • Low cost • Large and liquid market • Significant liquidity through market-making system (multiple market makers) • Easier to fulfill listing requirements • May avoid shadow of larger companies • Exemption from providing voting rights can be obtained
Disadvantages:	• Higher listing costs • Much smaller group of comparable firms • Mandatory to provide voting rights to ADR holders	• Not as highly visible as NYSE • Less prestigious

tremendous responsibility for management. "Remember, we have a moral obligation, to both our employees and to our shareholders, to perform to their expectations," warned Murthy.

Wall Street research analysts also offered views on Infosys and the company's valuation. (See **Exhibits 17–19** for comparable trading information, earnings forecasts, and market information.) Bob Austrian, from Banc of America Securities, highlighted some of Wall Street's views:

> I have positioned Infosys as "the Star of India," playing on the name of the gem in the Museum of Natural History in New York—an incredible object of priceless value. Blending world-class software services with an offshore model, Infosys has been the IT Star of India— the best in performance and growth, the best in transparency and managing expectations, the best in most everything in India. [See **Exhibit 20** for estimated versus actual performance.] They had a conservative discipline in everything they did. Plus, they have been riding a very favorable trend of outsourcing IT needs. The offering would be fantastic for investors as there are very few, if any, comparable ways to invest in this part of the world and there is a huge desire to invest in international markets.
>
> However, there are certainly some risks involved. First, the valuation is way out there— very rich by most measures. Second, there has been a serious shift in trends at the start of 1999, not the least of which is the Y2K boon to revenues subsiding in the near term. The ERP [enterprise resource planning] software segment had slowed down and was way out of favor at the start of the year. And the shift to e-commerce had begun, and the company needs to find a way to exploit that segment. Finally, on the company-specific side, the ongoing diligence situation is quite difficult for myself and for investors. With the company in India, there is no way to check up on them quarter to quarter, let alone week to week. These factors are not only in the minds of the investors but also the company. The last thing in the world they want to do would be to champion itself and have the market fall apart; that is very dangerous.

David Grossman, from Thomas Weisel Partners, elaborated on Infosys's prospects:

> The company was the first professional services firm to leverage in a consistent way the breadth of highly trained English-speaking technical talent in India, the cost advantages in India, and the ability to execute software development projects remotely in another country and time zone. Infosys has proven to be a master at managing offshore opportunities, especially with *new* technologies. Technology moves very fast, and Infosys is always vulnerable to the risk that it will not be capable of delivering those services in highest demand with its offshore model. Other risks are that Indian companies have historically been weak in sales and marketing, especially in the U.S. Furthermore, Infosys needs to establish a brand in the U.S. to protect its margins and drive future growth.

With all of this, Murthy asked, "The question becomes—What are our options? Does the offering really help us overcome some of our current challenges, or are there other methods that would be better—or at least less 'expensive'?"

As Murthy and Nilekani walked toward their offices, they passed by the construction site at one of the buildings of Infosys's sprawling campus. Murthy observed how construction workers were unloading large batteries to be installed as a backup for power failures. The contrast of the somewhat unreliable electricity supply in Bangalore and the campus expansion of one of the world's most advanced firms for customized software reminded Murthy of how far Infosys had come since its founding in 1981. But it also reminded Murthy of the fragility of success, especially in India. Just as the company had been on the brink of bankruptcy 10 years before, improper decisions could spell trouble for the company in 1999.

EXHIBIT 17 Comparable Trading Information (early 1999)

Source: Compiled from AT Financial, First Call, Zack's company reports, Banc Boston Robertson Stephen's estimates, and Credit Suisse First Boston estimates.

	Average Daily Volume	Shares Outst. (MM)	Market Cap. ($MM)	Calendar 1998A	Calendar 1999E	Calendar 2000E	Calendar P/E Ratios 1998A	1999E	2000E	Revenues ($MM)	LTM Revenues	Growth Rate (%)
U.S. Domestic Consulting & Systems Integration Companies												
AnswerThink Consulting Group	253	34.7	927.4	$0.20	$0.46	$0.78	133.8	58.2	34.3	103	9.0	50
Cambridge Technology Partners	3111	61.9	843.3	0.91	0.73		15.0	18.7		581	1.5	25
Dendrite International	296	25.1	530.2	0.51	0.65	0.8	41.4	32.5	26.4	113	4.7	35
International Network Services (6)	276	41.0	2,852.5	0.56	0.91	1.28	124.1	76.4	54.3	238	12.0	50
Metzler Group	742	37.0	1,166.3	0.94	1.33	1.51	33.5	23.7		249	4.7	30
Sapient	224	28.5	2,147.9	0.74	1.05		101.7	71.7	49.8	160	13.4	50
Whittman-Hart	582	55.9	1,229.8	0.37	0.52	0.72	59.5	42.3	30.6	308	4.0	35
Average:							72.7	46.2	39.1		7.0	39
U.S. Domestic & Offshore Development Companies												%
Cognizant Technology Solutions	184	9.5	245.9	$0.70	0.98	1.28	36.8	26.3	20.1	59	2.4	35
Complete Business Solutions	556	36.3	655.1	0.83	1.16	1.53	21.8	15.6	11.8	377	1.7	35
Information Management Resources	543	37.7	669.5	0.73	0.95	1.20	24.3	18.7	14.8	158	4.2	44
Mastech Corp	684	49.9	616.9	0.73	1.00	1.34	17.0	12.4	9.2	305	2.0	37
Syntel	89	39.1	320.0	0.63	0.64	0.79	13.0	12.8	10.4	168	1.9	23
Average:							22.6	17.2	13.3		2.4	35
European IT Services (These companies do not trade in the United States but do trade in European markets)												%
Cap Gemini (Paris)		68.2	11,763	3.86	4.88		44.7	35.4		4,010	2.9	30
Druid (6 London)		22.1	539	0.52	0.64		46.8	38.3		67	8.1	35
Logica (6 London)		278.9	2,911	0.16	0.20		67.3	51.3		777	3.7	25
SEMA Group (London)		459.5	5,127	0.20	0.23		57.2	48.0		1,941	2.6	25
Average:							54.0	43.3			4.3	29
Infosys Technologies Limited (3)[a]		16.0	1,213.0	$0.96	$2.31	$4.17	79.2	32.8	18.2	106	11.4	35%

[a]Infosys data as of January 11, 1999, as quoted on the Bombay Stock Exchange.

Note: Numbers in parentheses following company name indicate month of fiscal year if other than December.

EXHIBIT 18　Earnings Forecast

Source: Credit Suisse First Boston.

Income Statement—Year Ended March 31 (US$ millions)

	1996	1997	1998	1999F	2000F	2001F
Net revenues	26.61	39.59	68.33	120.82	178.16	266.59
Total revenues	26.61	39.59	68.33	120.82	178.16	266.59
Expenses						
Cost of sales	15.64	22.62	40.16	64.58	93.76	145.67
SG&A	4.35	7.38	13.23	18.66	28.41	40.43
Deferred stock compensation[a]	0.36	0.77	2.57	16.60	5.84	6.00
Total operating expenses	20.35	30.77	55.96	99.84	128.01	192.10
Operating income	6.26	8.82	12.37	20.98	50.15	74.49
Nonoperating income	1.46	1.32	0.80	1.71	4.00	5.20
Interest expenses	—	0.17	—	—	—	—
Pre-tax income	7.72	9.97	13.17	22.69	54.15	79.69
Taxes	0.89	1.32	0.77	5.13	7.58	11.16
Subsidiary preferred stock dividends	—	—	—	0.20	—	—
Net income	6.83	8.65	12.40	17.36	46.57	68.53
Net income ex-deferred stock comp.	7.18	9.41	14.98	33.97	52.41	74.54
Weighted shares (basic)	29.03	29.04	30.53	31.10	33.32	33.74
Weighted shares (diluted)	29.28	29.70	31.33	31.47	34.08	34.51
Basic EPS	0.24	0.30	0.41	0.56	1.40	2.03
Diluted EPS	0.23	0.29	0.40	0.55	1.37	1.99
CSFB EPS	0.25	0.32	0.48	1.08	1.54	2.16
Headcount						
Software professionals	957	1,396	2,182	3,132	4,432	5,932
Others	215	312	440	521	631	706
Total	1,172	1,708	2,622	3,653	5,063	6,638
Revenue/software professional	31,358	33,647	38,195	43,468	47,291	51,383
Revenue/employee	25,645	27,490	31,561	38,511	40,882	45,565

Cash Flow Statement—Year Ended March 31 (US$ millions)

	1997	1998	1999F	2000F	2001F
Cash flow from operating activities					
Profit after tax	8.64	12.41	17.36	46.57	68.54
Change in working capital	—	(2.29)	(9.77)	(7.68)	(12.37)
Net cash from operations	9.73	16.25	17.79	53.14	77.49
Cash flow from investing					
Investment in fixed assets	(7.27)	(8.44)	(23.17)	(26.47)	(37.51)
Net cash from investing	(7.35)	(8.44)	(23.17)	(26.47)	(37.51)
Cash flow from financing					
Issue of common stock	0.46	2.02	70.38	—	—
Issue of preferred stock	0.00	2.32	—	—	—
Preferred dividend	—	(0.07)	—	—	—
Long-term loan	(1.25)	—	—	—	—
Dividends paid	(1.06)	(1.47)	(3.40)	(5.24)	(7.45)
Net cash from financing	(1.85)	2.80	66.98	(5.24)	(7.45)
Currency translation effect	(1.90)	(3.51)	—	—	—
Net increase in cash & cash equivalents	0.53	10.61	61.60	21.43	32.53

[a]Under U.S. GAAP, expense recognized for the difference between exercise price and market price on date of option grant, amortized over vesting period.

EXHIBIT 19A
Market Information

Source: Compiled from Credit Suisse First Boston Research, Morgan Stanley Dean Witter, Infosys.

Infosys Beta (versus Bombay Stock Exchange)	1.2
Beta for U.S. software companies	1.46
Beta for all Indian software companies versus Bombay Stock Exchange	0.73
U.S. equity risk premium	7.50%
Indian equity risk premium[a]	10.00%
30-year U.S. Treasury bond	5.15%
Indian bonds:	
Indian government long bond (local currency)	12.15%
AAA corporate bonds (U.S.$ denominated)	8.50%

[a]Measured relative to Indian government long bonds. No data on short-term Indian government paper available.

EXHIBIT 19B
Individual Betas for Some Indian Software Companies (versus Bombay Stock Exchange)

Source: Compiled from Credit Suisse First Boston Research, Morgan Stanley Dean Witter, Infosys.

Infosys	**1.20**
Aptech	0.85
NIIT	0.96
Pentafour	1.27
Satyam Comp.	1.13
Wipro	0.95

EXHIBIT 20 **Analysts' Estimates Versus Actual Performance**

Source: Compiled from First Call data, Thomas Weisel Partners data and Infosys company financials.

	Fiscal Year 1997[a]			Fiscal Year 1998[b]			Fiscal Year 1999[c]		
	Est.	Actuals	%Δ	Est.	Actuals	%Δ	Est.	Actualsd	%Δ
Net Income (R in MM)	306	336.8	10.10%	469.6	603.6	28.50%	870	1,352.60	55.50%
EPS (R)	41.1	46.4	12.90%	31	37.7	21.60%	27.5	40.2	46.20%

[a]FY 1997 estimates reflect analysts' consensus in October 1996. EPS estimate and actual number is not adjusted for stock split.
[b]FY 1998 estimates reflect analysts' consensus in April 1997.
[c]FY 1999 estimates reflect analysts' consensus in April 1998.
[d]FY 1998 actuals reflect TWP estimates, exclude nonrecurring compensation charges, and are converted into rupees.

Case 29

Mandic BBS—an Entrepreneurial Harvesting Decision

It was April 13, 1998, and Aleksandar Mandic was on his way to lunch at one of his favorite Brazilian barbecue restaurants. As Mandic drove his BMW Series 7 through the crowded streets of São Paulo, he reflected on the phone calls he had received this morning. His Internet Service Provider (ISP) company, Mandic BBS Planejamento e Informatica S.A. (Mandic BBS), was one of the market leaders in Brazil, and the only major player that was not already tied to a Brazilian media conglomerate. Its potential sale had therefore generated considerable interest. Three different investors interested in acquiring majority stakes in Mandic BBS had called, each with many reasons why Mandic should choose them as a partner.

The first call had come from a Vice President of a U.S. investment bank that represented a number of U.S. funds wishing to increase their exposure to Latin America. Mandic, who often walked around his office barefoot and had only a modest formal education, had little common ground with the typical Wall Street banker. Nevertheless, he knew that U.S. markets had placed high valuations on Internet companies and were often willing to pay considerable prices for emerging market companies with high growth potential. Although talks were still at an early stage, he thought the U.S. investors might offer the highest price for his company. Furthermore, his experience with GP Investimentos (GP), the private equity firm that had funded his early expansion, had shown him that financial investors could often provide more than just money.

The second call was from a representative of IMPSAT, an Argentine telecommunications firm with aspirations of growth throughout Latin America. IMPSAT had been introduced to Mandic by GP, which had a business relationship with some of IMPSAT's

Professor Walter Kuemmerle and Charles M. Williams Fellow Chad Ellis prepared this case. HBS cases are developed solely as the basis for class discussion. Cases are not intended to serve as endorsements, sources of primary data, or illustrations of effective or ineffective management.

controlling shareholders, and had spoken highly of the firm to Mandic. IMPSAT offered access to technology and the opportunity for Mandic to be part of a telecommunications business that went beyond the borders of Brazil, but their primary business was providing private telecommunications networks for large companies. Mandic BBS served individuals and the bulk of its customers were in São Paulo. Was the fit as compelling as IMPSAT suggested?

The third call had come from one of Mandic's leading rivals in the on-line service business. With nimble responses, an innovative marketing strategy and a strong appeal to younger users, Mandic BBS had maintained its strong initial position in Brazil's on-line market, despite lacking a parent company with deep pockets. It was no surprise that at least one of these rivals, most of whom had spent millions of dollars and lost money trying to build market share, would be interested in buying Mandic BBS.

Mandic knew there were several other potential buyers as well, including conglomerates owned by two of Brazil's richest families. It wouldn't require too many phone calls by him or by GP to lengthen the list of potential buyers to about ten. When he first had the idea of a commercial BBS system, he never imagined he would be talking with so many potential suitors. Each had their own reasons for wanting to buy Mandic BBS, and each involved complex tradeoffs for Mandic, both the company and the entrepreneur.

Remembering that he hadn't had a vacation for years, Mandic mused that it might be easier just to let GP handle the sale. They were, after all, the professionals when it came to deals like this. Unfortunately, while Mandic's relationship with GP had been excellent, he knew he had to manage his own interests in this case. For GP the deal represented an exit; they intended to sell their 50% stake in Mandic BBS, book their profits, and reinvest the funds elsewhere. Mandic intended to retain a significant equity stake and to remain CEO. For him, the sale was not just about price but also positioning the company for future growth and ensuring his position at the helm. He also knew that for GP this was one investment among many, while for him Mandic BBS was his personal creation.

Background

Aleksandar Mandic was born to Serb parents in São Paulo in 1954. His father had emigrated from Serbia to Italy before moving to Buenos Aires, where he met and married Mandic's mother, a Russian émigrée. The couple then moved to Brazil. Mandic grew up speaking Serbian, learning Portuguese, Spanish and German later in life.

Mandic went to technical school to become an electric technician and joined Siemens Brazil in 1975. His division manufactured electric microscopes, CNC controllers and process control computers for the domestic market. Despite his modest education, Mandic was quite successful at Siemens; in 1993 he was in charge of 50 engineers.

In 1989, Mandic visited a construction site and met someone from Mannesman, a European engineering firm, who managed a computer network data system for his company. Believing such a system might benefit Siemens, Mandic approached his boss with the idea. He was told that no money was available for new computer networks and that an intra-company network-based information system would not receive support or funding from Siemens.

Convinced that providing a data exchange platform for computer users would be useful, Mandic started a bulletin board system (BBS) station at home in 1990 as a hobby. Siemens did not use it, but many of his friends there did. In order to cover his

EXHIBIT 1
Mandic BBS's
Historic Sales and
EBITDA (US$000)

Source: Mandic BBS February
1998 Business Plan.

	Sales	EBITDA
1992A	35	25
1993A	240	180
1994A	452	280
1995A	1,636	643
1996A	4,718	845
1997E	8,375	395

costs, Mandic began charging users an $8 per month fee,[1] which he hoped to justify by offering some basic services, such as data storage and simple messaging (not full e-mail) between users.

Growth over the next few years was slow but promising. Mandic incorporated the BBS in 1992, with Mandic holding 70% of the company and 30% held by a partner from a local bank. By early 1993, Mandic BBS had 400 subscribers, each paying $12 per month, either by mailing in checks or by credit card. "I remember my wife and I punched in the credit card numbers ourselves," said Mandic. (See **Exhibit 1** for Mandic's historic sales and EBITDA levels.)

What had started as a hobby was showing a profit at this point, and Mandic decided it was time to devote himself full-time to the venture. In March 1993 he left Siemens. Mandic recalled:

> It was very difficult to leave Siemens. I had spent seventeen years there, and my work enabled me to travel to Germany fairly often, which I enjoyed. I also had health benefits and a pension. But I thought if I didn't leave that I would spend the rest of my life at Siemens, because I liked the company. When I told my wife that I was going to resign, she didn't believe me. When I came home that evening and told her I had left she was shocked, but not worried.
>
> Even though I had started out small only a few years earlier I was confident. I felt that everything that had to do with communication—telephone, computers, newspapers—would do well in Brazil. There would obviously be attrition as in any industry but I knew the potential for success was there.

Mandic had hoped that his partner would also commit to the venture full-time, but he decided to remain at his banking job. The two men agreed that Mandic would buy his partner out for $30,000.

During 1994 Mandic BBS added capacity and expanded services with the result that revenues nearly doubled 1993 levels. Then, in August 1995, Embratel[2] established an Internet connection for Brazil. Mandic was the first firm to offer consumer Internet services in Brazil.

Growth during this period was rapid. From its industrial origins, Mandic was now appealing primarily to young Brazilians, particularly college students. Subscriber levels hit 10,000 in 1995 and revenues reached $2 million, and operating profits were roughly $500,000. December revenues were estimated at close to $300,000. However, competition was also beginning, with other Internet service providers (ISPs) starting operations during the year.

Up to that point, Mandic BBS had grown without any external financing. Now, with the company's recent growth and the arrival of the Internet, combined with the prospect of increased competition, Mandic decided he needed to bring in a partner to fund more aggressive expansion. He contacted a friend who worked at Bradesco, Brazil's largest commercial bank, and also spoke with some private investors. "Suddenly," Mandic recalled, "GP arrived."

[1] All Mandic fees, beginning with the original $8/month BBS fee had been charged in U.S. dollars.

[2] Embratel was the major provider of domestic and international long-distance services in Brazil.

GP Comes on the Scene

GP Investimentos was Brazil's leading private equity firm. (See **Exhibit 2** for a map of Brazil and **Exhibit 3** for a macroeconomic summary of Brazil.) Prior to its incorporation in 1993, GP's partners had invested their own capital in equity investments, taking substantial equity positions in companies such as Lojas Americanas and Brahma, two of Brazil's largest private companies in the supermarket and beer industries, respectively.

GP closed its first partnership fund, GP Capital Partners I, in April of 1994, with $100 million of the partners' own money and an additional $400 million contributed by international investors. The fund was intended to take advantage of investment opportunities in Brazil and, in some situations, elsewhere in Latin America.

Alexander Behring, HBS MBA '95, had joined GP shortly after graduation. Having seen the rapid growth and high valuations of U.S. companies such as America Online, Behring believed Brazil's on-line market offered an attractive opportunity. "Brazil offered huge growth in Internet demand," recalled Behring, "and there was virtually no technology risk, as the United States had already led the way."

EXHIBIT 2
Map of Brazil

Source: Martin Greenwald Associates. 2000. *Maps on File, Brazil.* New York: Facts on File, p. 7.03.

EXHIBIT 3   Macroeconomic Data on Brazil

Source: *CIA World Factbook.* CIA: Washington, DC, 1998, p. 65.

Economic overview

"Possessing large and well-developed agricultural, mining, manufacturing, and service sectors, Brazil's economy outweighs that of all other South American countries combined and is expanding its presence in world markets. Prior to the institution of a stabilization plan—the Plano Real (Real Plan) in mid-1994, stratospheric inflation rates had disrupted economic activity and discouraged foreign investment. Since then, tight monetary policy has brought inflation under control—consumer prices increased by less than 5% in 1997 compared to more than 1,000% in 1994. At the same time, GDP growth slowed from 5.7% in 1994 to about 3.0% in 1997 due to tighter credit.

The strong currency, another cornerstone of the Real Plan, has encouraged imports—contributing to a growing trade deficit—and restrained export growth. Brazil's more stable economy allowed it to weather the fallout in 1995 from the Mexican peso crisis relatively well. Record levels of foreign investment have flowed in, helping support the Real Plan through financial shocks in October–November 1997 that occurred in the wake of the Asian financial crisis. These shocks caused Brazil's foreign exchange reserves to drop by $8 billion to $52 billion and the stock market to decline by about 25%, although it still ended up more than 30% for the year. President Cardoso remains committed to defending the Real Plan, but he faces several key challenges domestically and abroad. His package of fiscal reforms requiring constitutional amendments has progressed slowly through the balkanized Brazilian legislature; in their absence, the government continues to run deficits and has limited room to relax its interest and exchange rate policies if it wants to keep inflation under control. Some foreign investors remain concerned about the viability of Brazil's exchange rate policy because of the country's fiscal and current account deficits. The government thus has to contend with the possibility of capital flight or a speculative attack that could draw down foreign reserves to a critical level and force a devaluation."

Source: Compiled from BNDES (Brazilian Development Bank) data.

Main Economic Indicators	1995	1996	1997
GDP (US$ billions)	705.5	775.7	800.8
Per Capita Income (US$)	4,525.0	4,912.7	5,017.2
Population (millions)	155.9	157.9	159.6
Urban Population (% of total)	78.3	78.3	78.3
Unemployment Rate (% of workforce)	4.6	5.4	5.7
Inflation (calendar year)	14.8%	9.3%	7.5%

Interest rate information: The 4/12/98 Brazilian Brady Bond yield (for a bond maturing on 4/15/2024) was 11.10%. The 4/12/98 20-year U.S. government bond yield was 6.01%. Source: Bloomberg.

Behring looked for acquisition candidates, finding five companies with reasonable size that might be for sale. He quickly identified Mandic BBS as his preferred target. "Mandic was the best guy among the companies running on-line services," Behring stated, "and he was also the largest, with about a 15% market share."

Behring called Mandic in September 1995 and, after introducing himself, asked what Mandic felt his firm was worth. Mandic answered that it was worth $10 million, a number equivalent to the sales level he anticipated reaching in 1998. Behring felt this was too high. The conversation ended, but two weeks later the men spoke again and reached a preliminary agreement. GP would pay Mandic $750,000 and inject an additional $2 million into the company to fund its expansion. GP also agreed that Mandic would receive a salary of $250,000 per year beginning in 1996. In exchange, GP received 50% of the company's equity. Behring described the valuation as largely needs based, rather than scientific. "Traditional cash flow based or multiple based valuation techniques only takes you so far. Mandic needed a $2 million injection, and we wanted shared control."

Carlos Sicupira, Managing Partner at GP, elaborated on GP's strategy of control. "We always want control. We always have the right to fire the CEO. This is despite the fact that in most cases, as with Mandic, our partner *is* the CEO." Sicupira estimated that GP had replaced the CEO in roughly half of its investments, but seldom by force. "We don't like to execute contracts," explained Sicupira. "Our business here is people. If you don't treat your people well you won't succeed. Usually we can convince our partner when a change is needed."

GP also maintained shared control in its acquisitions through a "shotgun" clause, which said that the controlling partners always vote together. If there is a disagreement that cannot be reconciled, GP can either buy out the partner or require that the partner buy them out.

Mandic wasn't concerned about GP's 50% stake because he felt he remained in charge. He was, however, worried that if the company required a further capital increase his stake could be diluted below 50%. To ensure that the company was able to expand without having any immediate cash needs which might require another contribution from GP, Mandic kept the $2 million cash in a company bank account and leased the equipment needed for expansion. GP tolerated this strategy, although the use of the money was not in line with GP's original expectations.

Once the preliminary arrangement had been made, GP moved quickly. They worked closely with Mandic's accountant and completed their due diligence within two months. The deal was completed in December 1995. Mandic recalled the early days with GP fondly. "I learned a lot from GP. They are very professional, intelligent and understand quickly. I am not good at explaining, but they understood."

Post Acquisition—Strong Performance, but Competition Threatens

With new capital on hand, Mandic BBS showed explosive growth in 1996. "After GP came in we did nothing at first but add phone lines [to our proprietary network] and sales grew accordingly," recalled Mandic. Subscriber levels grew at 10%–12% per month, faster even than Mandic had projected to GP, and for most of the year Mandic BBS was able to add customers so quickly that it could barely expand its capacity to serve them fast enough.

The rapid growth created an initial sense of euphoria, both in Mandic BBS and at GP. It soon became apparent, however, that competition was increasing. Three other ISPs of comparable size to Mandic BBS were acquired in 1996,[3] enabling them to expand and compete for Brazil's growing on-line population. Moreover, while Mandic BBS remained largely independent with limited funding, media and industrial groups with strong financial resources were acquiring the other ISPs. It was not clear to what extent these new entrants were willing to lose money buying market share. Behring recalled:

> Our deal was the trigger. There were big dogs getting into the business who had deep pockets, primarily media and telecommunications groups. They had other sources of income and could afford to lose money for five years if necessary. We knew that if someone started a price war, they could fund it.

One of Mandic's most aggressive competitors was Universo On Line (UOL), a joint venture between two of Brazil's largest communications groups, the Folha Group and the Abril Group. The Folha Group published *Folha de São Paulo (Folha)*, Brazil's largest

---

[3] ViaNetworks acquired Dialdata, Psinet acquired one ISP in Sao Paolo and one in Rio de Janeiro.

daily newspaper with a Sunday circulation of approximately one million, and intended to use it to support the growth of their on-line business. One week in June 1997, each copy of the Sunday issue contained a CD-ROM along with a full-page advertisement explaining how to use the CD-ROM to subscribe to UOL.

Mandic could not afford to match his rival by producing a million CD-ROMs. Instead, in the next Sunday's issue, he inserted his own ad in *Folha*. Mandic recalled:

> We used the same style of ad that UOL had used, and the top line told readers to "use the CD of last week." Then we gave them instructions on how they could use the UOL CD to access Mandic's Internet service. *Folha* published the ad by mistake, not realizing what we were doing.

When UOL realized what had happened, *Folha* refused to run any more Mandic BBS advertisements. Mandic felt, however, that he had prevented most of the damage that might have been done by UOL's CD promotion. Furthermore, when he could no longer run ads in *Folha,* Mandic was able to persuade rival newspapers to run opinion pieces criticizing UOL's practices and supporting Mandic as the entrepreneurial underdog. Mandic enjoyed the controversy and celebrity these battles brought him, and also felt they strengthened Mandic BBS's appeal among its core market of students and other young computer users.

Another competitor that grew rapidly in 1997 was ZAZ, a subsidiary of RBS, Brazil's third-largest media group. Launched in 1996, ZAZ was one of Brazil's first ISPs. Using its franchise system to expand its reach, ZAZ claimed to be the only ISP in Brazil with national reach, offering services in over 60 cities. Mandic BBS, by comparison, was still limited to customers within the greater São Paulo region.

The heavy spending of Mandic BBS's competitors represented a clear challenge. Growth was slower in 1997 than expected, and while Mandic could reassure himself that in Brazil's booming on-line market "slow growth" for Mandic BBS was still 5% per month, for the first time Mandic BBS was growing more slowly than its main competitors. Behring explained the concern:

> Mandic built up customers through sensible investments and profitable growth. UOL spent $34 million and bought 10% of the market. They spent $7 million last year alone on promotions and expansion. That's the kind of competition we had hoped to avoid.

Mandic and GP realized that while Mandic BBS had strong capabilities in technical areas the management team needed to include a strong marketing person if Mandic BBS was to fight successfully for market share. (See **Exhibit 4** for Mandic BBS's organization chart and **Exhibit 5** for management resumes.) Behring recalled:

> Mandic wasn't sales oriented but he was really good with bits and bytes. He'd been very successful in switching from a text interface to a graphic interface, and we felt comfortable that he could handle any technical issues. Where we could help was in providing him with marketing support.

EXHIBIT 4
Organization Chart

Source: Mandic BBS February 1998 Business Plan.

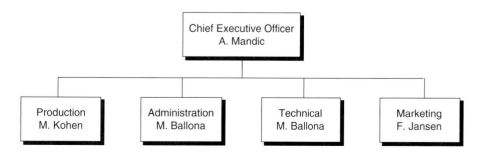

EXHIBIT 5 **Management Resumes**

Source: Mandic BBS.

Marcelo André Kohen

AEG Telefunken (1970 to 1980)

Managed computerization in a pipeline connecting an oil ship unloading port in Santa Catarina through several stations and terminals to the refinery in Paraná. Eventually left to form his own company.

Mak/Bylex S.A. (1980 to 1995)

Mak was a limited partnership that conducted projects related to electrical equipment and instrumentation for industrial use. It was purchased by British firm Cable & Wireless in 1982 and renamed Bylex S.A. at which point Kohen became CEO. In 1988 Cable & Wireless divested many of its Brazilian investments, including Bylex, after which Kohen maintained the venture independently.

Mandic BBS (1995 to present)

Joined Mandic as Production Director when the nodes were 386 diskless and the only server was a Pentium 90 MHz with 7.0 Gigabytes of disk space. Responsible for BBS operation, software development, internal systems, customer service and fraud detection.

Flavio Benicio Jansen Ferreira

Victori (1989 to 1992)

After earning his degree in Electrical Engineering, Jansen worked as an engineer for this Brazilian VSAT firm.

Modus (1992 to 1996)

Joined this small telecommunication consulting company as an engineer and became a Director and Partner in 1994. Developed extensive experience with financial products including Globus, which Modus was selling in Brazil.

Mandic BBS (1997 to present)

Marketing Director. Responsible for sales, marketing and customer service.

Marcello Ballona

Ballona began his career working for IBM, where he acquired his technical expertise. He left IBM to open his own company, a third party for call center operations. When the Brazilian economy contracted, Ballona closed his company and began working for Multicanal, a Brazilian cable TV company as a consultant.

Mandic BBS (1997 to present)

Technical and Financial Director. As Technical Director, responsible for Internet operations and new systems development. As Financial Director, responsible for all financial and administrative activities, e.g. legal and managerial reports, personnel, accounts payable and receivable and cash flow management.

GP first brought in an experienced marketing executive from IBM, but he was not successful, and was dismissed after just eight months. Sicupira described the problem:

> It was entirely our mistake. He was used to working slowly and to a mass-market approach, which wasn't right for Mandic [BBS]. So we let him go and brought in a younger guy. He had his own little marketing business and we basically bought it to make him Mandic's marketing director. He concentrated on direct marketing, using mailing lists to reach people and launching promotions where users got rewards for bringing in their friends.

Part of Mandic BBS's marketing strategy was to segment its target market through different subscription fees based on usage. Very light users, or those who wanted to test out the Internet but were unsure whether they would use it often, could pay a subscription fee of $4.95 per month. For each hour they were on-line, they would pay $2.95. Moderate users could pay $19.95 per month and receive ten free hours on-line, with additional hours costing $2.19. Heavy users could pay $39.90 per month for one hundred free hours. Finally, customers whose usage varied between months could pay $2.99 per month and would then be billed under whatever plan was cheapest each month. Mandic believed his rates represented a slight premium to the overall market; competitor rates for unlimited access (but with no proprietary content) were around $35 per month.

Mandic BBS also refined its product strategy. In its earliest days as a bulletin board provider, Mandic had had to offer his own services in order to justify the fee he was charging to users. As the customer base shifted from primarily BBS to 80% Internet, Mandic had continued to develop proprietary content. This helped convince BBS users to become Internet subscribers as well as helping Mandic BBS maintain a price premium over low-end ISPs.

In addition to Internet access, subscribers could create their own home pages and received regularly updated information on stocks and foreign exchange rates, access to wire services, message boards and chat rooms. Mandic BBS had also secured proprietary rights to third-party content, including DETRAN (official information on traffic and vehicles),[4] Revista do Tribunais (jurisprudence) and Telecheque (on-line credit information). Finally, Mandic BBS was increasing its development of corporate services, such as developing corporate home pages, group Internet access and real-time audio and video links.

There was some debate, however, over the extent to which Mandic BBS should develop content, as opposed simply to offering reliable Internet access at competitive pricing. Behring explained, "All the content we had was very low investment, or based on partnering with other organizations to get access to their content. We didn't consider high content to be a strength of the company."

Sicupira added, "We did not want Mandic to develop significant Internet content. Doing so requires a great deal of capital expenditure and involves a long development cycle. We felt that this sort of work was better-suited to the big media companies who could produce content at a lower cost and spread it over a number of different platforms."

Mandic BBS also offered its customers a twenty-four hour support service. The company hired a specialized computer service provider to handle the support functions through a dedicated team, which were trained by Mandic BBS. Mandic believed that technical support would be increasingly important as much of Brazil's growing on-line population were not computer experts and would place a high value on quick, reliable assistance.

Mandic BBS also invested in further expanding its infrastructure. In 1997 the company increased from one point of presence (POP) to nine along with more phone lines, servers and other equipment. Although this caused EBITDA to decline for the first year since the company's foundation, Mandic believed it was necessary in order to maintain Mandic BBS's competitive position. (See **Exhibit 6** for a summary of expansion from 1996 to 1997.)

The efforts paid off. In 1998, the company again showed growth at least equal to its competitors. By April, subscriber levels had reached 43,500 and sales were running at close to $10 million on an annualized basis. Market share was estimated at 7% and growing, albeit gradually. Cash flow from the business was healthy and capital needs were modest—in the absence of truly predatory competition, Mandic BBS's position as one of a handful of strong Brazilian ISPs looked secure, at least for the next twelve months.

---

[4] DETRAN was primarily used by people buying used cars in order to ensure that the car was not stolen and didn't have outstanding tickets for which, under Brazilian law, the purchaser might be held liable.

EXHIBIT 6
Perfomance—1996
and 1997

Source: Mandic BBS February
1998 Business Plan.

	1996	1997	% Change
Gross sales (US$'000)	4,755	9,685	104%
Net sales (US$'000)	4,241	8,657	104
EBITDA	845	395	−53
Branches	3	12	300
Internet subscribers	3,903	24,445	526
Mail boxes	8,000	31,380	292
Servers	7	25	257
Telephone lines (does not include BBS)	371	1,502	304
Internet channels	45	91	100
Employees Technical Department	10	12	20
Employees Administrative Department	7	8	14

The Decision to Sell

Despite the strong performance at Mandic BBS, in early 1998 GP decided it was time to exit their investment. Behring stated:

> We always sell. Our original time horizon for the investment had been about two years, and the timing seemed about right. We knew that if we would stay longer we could add to the price simply from Mandic's growth, but the market was becoming more competitive, too.

The most recent sign of how competitive the market remained was six-month-old SBT On Line, owned by Brazil's second largest television broadcasting station. SBT had announced plans to spend nearly $10 million during its ISP's first year of operations, and had already achieved a market share of roughly 6%.

Another issue for GP was the relatively small size of its investment and the opportunity cost of devoting attention to it. "Mandic [BBS] took as much of our time as Brahma," explained Sicupira, "a $180 million investment in 1989 which is worth $3 billion today." Even at its explosive rate of growth, it would be years before Mandic BBS would represent a significant position in GP's portfolio.

Mandic had his own reasons for wanting to bring in a new partner. "We did not need much capital," he explained, "but we needed a partner with technical expertise." Mandic's main concern was improving bandwidth and gaining access to satellite technology. Currently the firm had no ISDN lines or satellite links, and could only offer access up to 56K phone modems. Mandic also wanted to ensure he retained substantial control of his company, even though he knew a buyer might want to acquire more than 50%.

The Buyers

As the sole remaining independent ISP of significant size, as well as the only one currently showing profits, Mandic BBS had generated interest from a range of buyers. Mandic knew he would have to decide carefully amongst them.

LECTRON was a local competitor to Siemens in electronics with annual sales of over $800 million. Mandic had met them through an intermediary, and liked the CEO who he felt would not try to micro-manage his business. LECTRON had satellite technology and could provide some expertise in other technology improvements. They had, however, never done any business in Internet-related industries.

NewTel was the subsidiary of a large Brazilian steel company. Brazil had only just begun to dismantle the telephony monopoly of Telebras (the formerly state-owned telephone monopoly), and NewTel had been founded as a diversification effort. It had no actual business yet, but Mandic believed it had considerable financial backing and had been among the first to make a tangible offer ($14 million). Given their need for expertise as well as a new business line, Mandic knew he could probably establish a significant role for himself within the firm. A friend had introduced Mandic to NewTel.

RRK, a U.S. investment bank representing institutional investors, had contacted Mandic directly. While they had yet to make an initial offer, Mandic suspected they might ultimately offer the highest price. Before GP's investment in Mandic BBS, Mandic knew he would have been doubtful about working with purely financial investors, but GP had provided a lot of support and advice while leaving him in complete control of his operation. He didn't know what it would be like working with an unknown, and perhaps anonymous, group of U.S. institutions.

IMPSAT was an Argentine telecommunications company with operations in several countries throughout Latin America, and ambitions of being the leading Latin American telecommunications firm. IMPSAT's main business was providing private telecommunications network services to large organizations, both public and private. It did so using its own networks, which included teleports, earth stations, fibre optic and microwave links and leased satellite capacity. In February 1998, IMPSAT had become the first foreign company to win a government license to offer network services in Brazil; previously only Telebras had been able to offer such services.

Mandic had been introduced to IMPSAT by GP, who had purchased a large amount of railway assets from the company's controlling shareholders. Although GP would be unlikely to object to whatever decision Mandic reached, they had indicated they thought IMPSAT was the best choice. Indeed, IMPSAT's satellite expertise would be very useful in expanding the reach of Mandic BBS, and their corporate links could strengthen Mandic's business in that market segment. Furthermore, IMPSAT offered its subsidiaries links and services, which currently represented a third of Mandic BBS's operating costs, at roughly 10% below market prices. Nevertheless, Mandic knew from his days at Siemens that control issues could be quite different in a larger, multinational company.

Finally, one of Mandic's major competitors had argued for the logic of a merger. Growing market share rapidly had proved highly expensive, but joining the two firms would give the combined entity a market share nearly double its next rival. Combined with the financial support of its parent company, they would be in a strong position to maintain market leadership. This would, in turn, provide greater leverage in negotiations with content providers and other suppliers. Mandic respected the CEO of the rival firm, but he also knew that each of them was used to being in charge. If his firm were acquired, what were the chances he would remain in control?

Valuation

Along with deciding which partner was his ideal choice, Mandic knew he had to consider what his company was worth—as well as whether he and GP would take a second-best price in order to secure that partner. Mandic assumed his company would be valued on some multiple of annualized sales, currently running at close to $10 million. International deals had sometimes been done at quite high multiples (see **Exhibit 7**). Mandic knew that a Brazilian firm had more risk and would therefore be likely to command a lower multiple. On the other hand, the growth opportunities in Brazil were

EXHIBIT 7
Valuation
Comparisons

Source: Mandic BBS, GP
Investimentos.

Companies	Firm Value/EBITDA	Firm Value/Sales
America On-Line, Inc.	64.4	8.9
Data Transmission Network, Inc.	15.9	3.0
UUNET Technologies, Inc.	NM	23.4

AOL's equity beta between 10/96 and 4/98 was 1.13. Their market capitalization on 4/12/98 was US$15.4 billion and their Debt/(Debt+Equity) was 0.244. Source: Bloomberg.

Transaction Comparables:

At the time of the transaction, all the major acquisitions in the sector involved private companies. The only available information (which is not publicly confirmed) is shown below:

- A group of investors acquired ITNet in November 1995 for one time sales.
- Telecom paid for 20% of Microsoft network in 1995 US$625 per subscriber.
- Bertelsmann paid US$690 per subscriber for 50% of American On-Line Europe in 1995.

Other notable recent ISP transactions include the following:

Date	Target	Acquirer	Firm Value/LQA Revenue
03/26/98	Eunet	Qwest Communications	2.4
01/21/98	Erols	RCN	2.1
01/15/98	GlobalCenter	Frontier	6.1
10/13/97	Netcom	ICG	1.4
09/08/97	CompuServe	WorldCom	1.2
06/04/97	DIGEX	Intermedia	4.4
05/06/97	BBN	GTE	1.6

LaA = last quarter annualized.

considerable. Mandic had prepared financial projections (see **Exhibit 8** for projections and **Exhibit 9** for supporting assumptions) that detailed the growth he expected Mandic BBS to achieve over the next several years.

Mandic also had two initial offers on the table: $14 million from NewTel and $10 million from IMPSAT. He did not know how much maneuvering room there was with either, but at least he had a point of reference to begin with. He also had to consider how strong his negotiating position was overall. Mandic BBS was the only independent ISP of significant size and had established a distinct identity. That would make it an attractive target for a firm looking to make a rapid entry into Brazil's fledgling Internet market. A savvy buyer, however, might note that Mandic needed to sell both to secure the company's position in the face of growing competition and to meet the exit needs of GP. How he framed the negotiation might prove important.

What to Order?

As he pulled his car into the restaurant's lot and watched the valet approach, Mandic knew he would have to make some important decisions soon. If only deciding what choices to make regarding Mandic BBS were as simple as selecting a wine to go with lunch. GP had been fully supportive so far, but they wanted to sell. Choosing the right partner could be crucial for his company's success, but which characteristics made for the best partner? Some offered technology, some financial strength, some a greater degree of independence. Ultimately, one would offer the highest price. Each of these was important, but which was paramount?

EXHIBIT 8 Mandic—Business Plan: Financial Projections

Source: Mandic BBS February 1998 Business Plan.

Executive Summary	1997	1998	1999	2000	2001	2002
Market						
Users—Internet/BBS Brazil	600,000	960,619	1,440,929	2,017,300	2,622,490	3,146,988
Market growth rate %		60%	50%	40%	30%	20%
Number of Users						
Number of Mandic users (average)	21,320	58,205	118,636	200,268	291,500	390,751
Market share Mandic %	6.3%	8.2%	11.0%	12.0%	13.0%	14.0%
Capacity						
Final number of lines	1,833	3,868	7,813	11,949	16,840	21,771
Lines per user (average)	26	20	20	20	20	20
Mandic BBS Total Gross Revenue (U.S.$ 000)						
BBS subscription revenue	2,192	488	—	—	—	—
Internet subscriptions revenue	5,024	15,174	32,530	54,919	79,929	107,144
Corporate services	1,044	1,676	2,514	3,520	4,575	5,491
Advertisement	0	334	681	1,149	1,673	2,242
Other revenues	116	1,272	1,908	2,671	3,473	4,167
General total	8,376	18,943	37,633	62,259	89,650	119,044
Result (US$ 000)						
Gross operating revenue	8,376	18,943	37,633	62,259	89,650	119,044
Net operating revenue	7,552	16,850	33,474	55,380	79,744	105,889
Gross margin	5,595	11,810	23,574	39,235	56,957	76,203
EBITDA	395	2,755	12,792	24,255	38,740	54,865
EBIT	(20)	1,974	11,165	21,521	34,821	49,707
Net profit	(534)	853	6,823	13,982	24,024	36,215
Margins (% Net Operating Revenue)						
Gross margin	74.1%	70.1%	70.4%	70.8%	71.4%	72.0%
EBITDA	5.2	16.4	38.2	43.8	48.6	51.8
EBIT	−0.3	11.7	33.4	38.9	43.7	46.9
Net profit	−7.1	5.1	20.4	25.2	30.1	34.2
Investments						
Machines and equipment		1,764	3,255	3,257	3,687	3,567
Software		10	10	50	50	50
Infrastructure		0	120	120	120	120
Total		1,774	3,385	3,427	3,857	3,737
Capitalization						
Total assets	3,354	4,620	12,211	27,204	52,354	89,777
Debt	0	0	0	0	0	0
Net worth	2,408	3,261	10,084	24,066	48,090	84,304
Cash	1,382	249	3,778	15,043	36,879	72,098
Leverage (debt/(debt + net worth))	0%	0%	0%	0%	0%	0%
Net debt (cash—debt)	1,382	249	3,778	15,043	36,879	72,098

(continued)

EXHIBIT 8: (Continued) Financial Statements

	1997	1998	1999	2000	2001	2002
Result Statements (US$ 000)						
Gross Operating Revenue	8,376	18,943	37,633	62,259	89,650	119,044
Taxes and Commission Over Gross Revenue						
Direct taxes over sales	(608)	(1,449)	(2,879)	(4,763)	(6,858)	(9,107)
Banking commissions	(216)	(6440)	(1,280)	(2,117)	(3,048)	(4,047)
Total	(824)	(2,093)	(4,158)	(6,880)	(9,906)	(13,154)
Net Operating Revenue	7,552	16,850	33,474	55,380	79,744	105,889
Sales Costs						
Telephone lines rental fee	(730)	(1,608)	(2,965)	(4,514)	(5,918)	(7,144)
Telecommunications expenses	(1,050)	(2,274)	(4,635)	(7,825)	(11,388)	(15,266)
Others	(177)	(1,158)	(2,300)	(3,806)	(5,480)	(7,277)
Total	(1,957)	(5,040)	(9,900)	(16,145)	(22,787)	(29,687)
Gross Margin	5,595	11,810	23,574	39,235	56,957	76,203
Operating and Management Expenses						
Staff—top management	(586)	(667)	(741)	(889)	(889)	(889)
Staff—sales	(171)	(401)	(797)	(1,318)	(1,898)	(2,520)
Staff—systems/maintenance	(433)	(732)	(849)	(971)	(1,116)	(1,262)
Staff—management	(185)	(352)	(422)	(496)	(583)	(670)
Outsourcing	(327)	(436)	(780)	(1,161)	(1,504)	(1,798)
Customer services	(608)	(1,785)	(2,058)	(3,405)	(4,903)	(6,511)
Advertisement and marketing	(1,431)	(1,330)	(2,114)	(2,798)	(3,223)	(3,423)
Telecommunication infrastructure expenses	(670)	(831)	0	0	0	0
Other expenses	(789)	(2,521)	(3,022)	(3,943)	(4,100)	(4,264)
Total	(5,200)	(9,055)	(910,782)	(14,980)	(18,216)	(21,338)
EBITDA (operating cash flow)	395	2,755	12,792	24,255	38,740	54,865
Depreciation and amortization	(415)	(781)	(1,627)	(2,734)	(3,920)	(5,157)
EBIT (operating profit)	(20)	1,974	11,165	21,521	34,821	49,707
Financial revenues	297	163	302	1,129	3,115	6,539
Leasing payments	(223)	(864)	(1,284)	(1,782)	(2,079)	(2,194)
Financial expenses	(588)	0	0	0	0	0
EBT (earning before income tax)	(534)	1,273	10,183	20,868	35,857	54,052
Income Tax	0	(420)	(3,361)	(6,886)	(11,833)	(17,837)
Net Profit	(534)	853	6,823	13,982	24,024	36,215

EXHIBIT 8 Balance Sheet (US$ 000)

ASSETS	1997	1998	1999	2000	2001	2002
Cash and banks	1,382	249	3,778	15,043	36,879	72,098
Accounts receivable	930	2,335	4,640	7,676	11,053	14,677
Working assets	2,312	2,585	8,418	22,719	47,932	86,775
Long-term assets	88	88	88	88	88	88
Net Fixed Assets	954	1,947	3,705	4,397	4,334	2,914
Total Assets	3,354	4,620	12,211	27,204	52,354	89,777

(continued)

EXHIBIT 8 (Continued) Balance Sheet (US$ 000)

	1997	1998	1999	2000	2001	2002
LIABILITIES						
Accounts payable—suppliers	366	778	1,547	2,559	3,684	4,892
Tax payable	107	107	107	107	107	107
Labor taxes payable	29	29	29	29	29	29
Other accounts payable	64	64	64	64	64	64
Labor provisions	220	220	220	220	220	220
Clients advanced payments	—	—	—	—	—	—
Others	160	160	160	160	160	160
Short-term debt	0	0	0	0	0	0
Working liabilities	946	1,358	2,127	3,139	4,264	5,472
Long-term Liabilities	0	0	0	0	0	0
Total Liabilities	946	1,358	2,127	3,139	4,264	5,472
Capital	1,974	1,974	1,974	1,974	1,974	1,974
Accumulated profit	434	1,287	8,110	22,092	46,116	82,330
Net worth	2,408	3,261	10,084	24,066	48,090	84,304
Total Liabilities and Net Worth	**3,354**	**4,620**	**12,211**	**27,204**	**52,354**	**89,777**
CASH FLOW (US$ million)						
Operations Cash Flow						
Net profit		853	6,823	13,982	24,024	36,215
Depreciation		781	1,627	2,734	3,920	5,157
Reduction (increase) of working capital		(993)	(1,536)	(2,024)	(2,251)	(2,416)
Total		641	6,914	14,691	25,693	38,956
Investments Cash Flow						
Equipment and software investments		(1,774)	(3,265)	(3,307)	(3,737)	(3,617)
Investments—others		0	(120)	(120)	(120)	(120)
Total		(1,774)	(3,385)	(3,427)	(3,857)	(3,737)
Financing Cash Flow						
Dividends		0	0	0	0	0
Short-term debt amortization		0	0	0	0	0
Total		0	0	0	0	0
Cash—Beginning of the year		1,382	249	3,778	15,043	36,879
Total cash flow—year		(1,133)	3,529	11,265	21,836	35,219
Cash—end of the year		249	3,778	15,043	36,879	72,098
Short-term debt		0	0	0	0	0
Final cash		249	3,778	15,043	36,879	72,098

EXHIBIT 9 Assumptions for Financial Projections

Source: Mandic BBS February 1998 Business Plan.

General	• Currency: Constant US$ (no inflation considered)
Market	• Market growth: Number of Internet subscribers 39% CAGR between 1997 and 2002 (approximately half of *BusinessWeek* projection).
Revenues	• Mandic's market shares: Gradual increase from 6.3% in December 1997 to 14% in December 2002.
	• Mandic BBS service: Mandic should discontinue its BBS service during 1998 with most remaining subscribers migrating to the Internet.
	• Average revenue per BBS subscriber: Decreasing from US$16.91 in 1997 to US$14.17 (per month) during 1998.
	• Average revenue per Internet subscriber: Decreasing from US25.23 in 1997 to US$22.85 (per month) during 1998 and remaining constant thereafter.

(continued)

EXHIBIT 9 (Continued)

	• Other revenue sources:
	  o Media—US$5.74 (per year) per subscriber
	  o Corporate Services—growing at the same rate as the overall market
	  o Other revenues—growing at the same rate as the overall market

Investment	
Telephone Lines:	• 22 subscribers per line • Average cost per line/year—US$564 (decreasing 10% per year after 1998) • Communications infrastructure expense—US$378 per new line in average during 1998 (no cost thereafter)
Communication Servers:	• One new user for every additional 60 telephone lines • Unit cost US$27,000 (decreasing 10% per year after 1998)
CPU:	• One new CPU for every additional 120 telephone lines • Unit cost US$50,000 (decreasing 10% per year after 1998)
Software:	• US$10,000 year 1998/1999 • US$50,000 year 2000/2002
Infrastructure:	• US$60,000 per new branch • Two branches per year from 1999 till 2002
Cost Structure	
Direct sale tax:	• ISS (tax on revenue services) 5.00% of Gross Revenues • PIS/CONFINS 2.65% of Gross Revenues
Credit card/bank fees:	• 3.40% of Gross Revenue
Communication expenses (Embratel's Link):	• increasing in line with Gross Revenues

Personnel expenses:	• Executives
	  o One extra executive at 1998
	  o One extra executive at 2000
	  o Cost per executive equal to 1998
	• Support Staff
	  o Growing at the same rate as Gross Revenue
	  o Cost per employee equal to 1998
	• Marketing Staff
	  o Growing at the same rate as Gross Revenues
	  o Cost per employee equal to 1998
	• Systems/maintenance staff
	  o One extra per every 20,000 additional subscribers
	  o Cost per employee equal to 1998
	• Administrative staff
	  o One extra per every 50,000 additional subscribers
	  o Cost per employee equal to 1998

Marketing expenses:	• Decrease in marketing expenses during 1998 due to focus on promotions rather than mass media. After 1998, growing at 80% of Gross Revenues growth
Customer service expenses:	• Growing at the same rate as Gross Revenues
Third-party services:	• Growing at 90% of Gross Revenues growth
Depreciation:	• Equipment and machinery: 3 years • Others: 10 years
Income Tax + Social Contribution:	• 33% of EBT
Leasing finance:	• 50% of capital expenditures are financed through leasing • 100% of payments (principal + interest) are charged directly to the income statement • Leasing finance does not appear in the balance sheet • Terms are the following: 15% interest rate, 24 equal installments, no residual value

(continued)

EXHIBIT 9   (Continued)

	1997	1998	1999	2000	2001	2002
BASIC ASSUMPTIONS—REVENUE						
Total Potential Market (000) (Final)						
Internet users/BBS Brazil	600,000	960,619	1,440,929	2,017,300	2,622,490	3,146,988
Market growth rate %		60%	50%	40%	30%	20%
Market Share Mandic (Final)	6.27%	8.20%	11.00%	12.00%	13.00%	14.00%
Number of Mandic BBS users (Final)	11,755	0	0	0	0	0
Number of Mandic BBS users (average)	11,329	2,867	0	0	0	0
BBS Average Revenue (US$/user/month)	16.91	14.17	14.17	14.17	14.17	14.17
Number of Mandic Internet users (Final)	26,311	75,904	158,502	242,076	340,924	440,578
Number of Mandic Internet users (average)	9,991	55,338	118,636	200,289	291,500	390,751
Internet Average revenue (US$/user/month)	25.53	22.85	22.85	22.85	22.85	22.85
Advertisement (US$ per user)		5.74	5.74	5.74	5.74	5.74
Mandic Total Gross Revenue (US$ million)						
BBS subscription revenue	2,192	488	—	—	—	—
Internet subscription revenue	5,024	15,174	32,530	54,919	79,929	107,144
Corporate services	1,044	1,676	2,514	3,520	4,575	5,491
Advertisement	0	334	681	1,149	1,673	2,242
Other revenues	116	1,272	1,908	2,671	3,473	4,167
General Total	8,376	18,943	37,633	62,259	89,650	119,044
BUSINESS PREMISE—INVESTMENTS						
List of Effective Users per Line						
Average number for the year	26	20	20	20	20	20
Telephone Lines						
Initial number of telephone lines	877	1,833	3,868	7,813	11,949	16,840
Number of added telephone lines	956	2,035	3,945	4,135	4,891	4,931
Final number of telephone lines	1,833	3,868	7,813	11,949	16,840	21,771
Average number of telephone lines	1,355	2,851	5,841	9,881	14,394	19,305
Cost per telephone line (US$/year)	539	564	508	457	411	370
Total expense with telephone line (US$000)	730	1,608	2,965	4,514	5,918	7,144
Telecommunication Infrastructure Expenses						
Cost per telephone line (US$/year)	701	408	0	0	0	0
Total cost (US$ million)	670	831	0	0	0	0
Investment Users Connection—São Paulo (US$000)						
Communication Server—Investment		916	1,775	1,861	2,201	2,219
—Price per unit		27,000	24,300	21,870	19,683	17,715
CPU Server—Investment		848	1,479	1,396	1,486	1,348
—Price per unit		50,000	45,000	40,500	36,450	32,805
Subtotal		1,764	3,255	3,257	3,687	3,567
Software and Systems Investments		10	10	50	50	50
Infrastructure Investments		0	120	120	120	120
Total Investments		1,774	3,385	3,427	3,857	3,737

(continued)

EXHIBIT 9 (Continued)

	1997	1998	1999	2000	2001	2002
BASIC ASSUMPTIONS—COSTS						
Taxes Charged Over Gross Revenue (% Gross Revenue)						
ISS		5.00%	5.00%	5.00%	5.00%	5.00%
COFINS		2.00%	2.00%	2.00%	2.00%	2.00%
PIS		0.65%	0.65%	0.65%	0.65%	0.65%
TOTAL		7.65%	7.65%	7.65%	7.65%	7.65%
Sale Direct Costs (% Gross Revenue)						
Banking commissions		3.40%	3.40%	3.40%	3.40%	3.40%
Communications Expenses (US$000/year)						
Subtotal	1,050	2,274	4,635	7,825	11,388	15,266
Staff Expenses (including Taxes) —Summary						
Top management		667	741	889	889	889
Customer service		277	550	910	1,311	1,741
Sales		401	797	1,318	1,898	2,520
Systems/maintenance		732	849	971	1,116	1,262
Management		352	422	496	583	670
General total		2,429	3,359	4,584	5,796	7,082
Number of people		41	55	72	90	109
Advertisement		1,330	2,114	2,798	3,223	3,423
Other Expenses						
Other customer service expenses		659	1,508	2,495	3,592	4,770
Outsourcing services—US$ 000/year		436	780	1,161	1,504	1,798
ASSUMPTIONS FOR CAPITALIZATION						
Working Capital (Days of Gross Sales)						
Accounts receivable		45	45	45	45	45
Accounts payable		15	15	15	15	15
Inventory		0	0	0	0	0
Dividends (% of Net Profit)		0%	0%	0%	0%	0%
Average Interest Rates for Money Market Investments		20%	15%	12%	12%	12%
Depreciation (years)						
Machines and equipment	3	3	3	3	3	3
Others	10	10	10	10	10	10
Fixed Assets—Machines and Equipment						
Initial assets		1,360	3,134	6,399	9,705	13,442
Investments		1,774	3,265	3,307	3,737	3,617
Final assets	1,360	3,134	6,399	9,705	13,442	17,059
Initial assets depreciation		(453)	(1,045)	(2,133)	(3,235)	(4,481)
Investments depreciation		(296)	(544)	(551)	(623)	(603)
Total depreciation	(567)	(749)	(1,589)	(2,684)	(3,858)	(5,083)
Initial net assets		793	1,818	3,494	4,116	3,995
Final net assets	793	1,818	3,494	4,116	3,995	2,529
Fixed Assets—Others						
Initial assets		320	320	440	560	680
Investments		0	120	120	120	120
Final assets	320	320	440	560	680	800
Initial assets depreciation		(32)	(32)	(44)	(56)	(68)

(continued)

EXHIBIT 9   (Continued)

	1997	1998	1999	2000	2001	2002
Investments depreciation		0	(6)	(6)	(6)	(6)
Total depreciation	(159)	(32)	(38)	(50)	(62)	(74)
Initial net assets		161	129	211	281	339
Final net assets	161	129	211	281	339	385
Fixed Assets—Total						
Initial assets		1,680	3,454	6,839	10,265	14,122
Investments		1,774	3,385	3,427	3,857	3,737
Final assets	1,680	3,454	6,839	10,265	14,122	17,859
Initial assets depreciation		(453)	(1,077)	(192,177)	(3,291)	(4,549)
Investments depreciation		(296)	(550)	(557)	(629)	(609)
Total depreciation	(726)	(781)	(1,627)	(2,734)	(3,920)	(5,157)
Initial net assets		954	1,947	3,705	4,397	4,334
Final net assets	954	1,947	3,705	4,397	4,343	2,914

Appendix

Assignment Questions for Module 1

Case 1: Singulus

Case:

The case describes Singulus, the compact disc metallizer business of Leybold AG, a large German company that has been put up for sale. In April 1995, buyout firm Schroder Ventures has to decide whether to acquire the business. The investment decision is complicated by a number of factors including the fact that at this stage Singulus's assets consist primarily of intellectual property and a customer list.

Assignment Questions

1. What is the nature of the opportunity?

2. What will it take for Schroeder Ventures to make this deal happen successfully?

3. What are the major risks for Schroeder Ventures? In the short term? In the long term?

4. What price should Schroder Ventures offer for Singulus?

5. What incentives does Schroeder Ventures need to set for Singulus's management?

6. In your opinion, should Singulus offer an integrated replication line?

Case 2: Officenet (A): Making Entrepreneurship Work in Argentina

Excel Download at www.mhhe.com/kuemmerle: Officenet exhibits

Case:

The case describes the creation of Officenet, an office supply distributor in Argentina. The company serves the business-to-business market through both print and Internet-based catalogs as well as phone orders. Officenet is a pioneer in both print catalog and Internet channels. Although the company is a possible acquisition target for one of the large U.S.-based office supply distributors, the entrepreneurs have much work to do before they can realize an exit. They need to decide in which direction to grow the company and how to finance this growth. A commercial paper program seems feasible in the near future, and the entrepreneurs must decide on its size.

Assignment Questions:

1. What is your assessment of Officenet's performance to date?

2. What is the value of Officenet in October 1999?

3. The entrepreneurs are currently considering a number of strategic growth options. Which one(s) would you advise them to pursue? Why? Should they seek to grow outside of their current business at all?

4. When should the entrepreneurs plan to exit their venture? Is the sale to a large U.S.-based firm in the office supply distribution industry really such an obvious exit strategy? If not, why not?

5. How much debt should the entrepreneurs raise in the pending commercial paper program? In your opinion, how much new equity does the company need over the next two years?

Case 3: Officenet (B): After the Merger

Case:

The (B) case describes how Officenet merged with Submarino.com, a business-to-consumer Internet company in February 2000. Submarino.com sold books, CDs, and other products in Brazil, Argentina, Mexico, Spain and Portugal. In August 2000, the Officenet entrepreneurs are reconsidering the merger after a plan to take the merged entity public on Nasdaq had to be cancelled.

Assignment Question:

1. Should the entrepreneurs at Officenet push for a dissolution of the merger?

Case 4: Term Sheet Negotiations for Trendsetter, Inc.

Case:

This case describes two aspiring entrepreneurs who have just received offering documents for venture funding (known as term sheets) from two venture capital firms. Neither having experience in raising capital, the entrepreneurs are wondering how to compare the two proposals and which to choose. They need to make a decision quickly. Note that the term sheets are discussed for a U.S.-based venture rather than a venture in a different jurisdiction in order to give you a "base case." Also, venture capital firms in many different countries are gradually adopting many of the term sheet elements that are common in the United States.

Assignment Questions:

1. What are the main differences and similarities between the two term sheets?
2. If you were the entrepreneur and could not negotiate any of the terms in either term sheet, which would you prefer and why?
3. How would you seek to alter the terms in each term sheet during negotiations with each of the venture capitalists? Which terms would you seek to alter first?
4. Does it make a difference to your answers whether you expect Trendsetter to grow fast or grow slowly?
5. Does it make a difference to your wealth whether you expect to realize on Trendsetter.com through an IPO or a merger?
6. If you were an aspiring venture capitalist looking for a "blueprint" term sheet to use at your firm, which of the two term sheets would you use? Why?
7. What aspects other than term sheets would you take into consideration when choosing among potential venture capital investors?
8. If you were looking for advice on these term sheets, whom would you call? How would you know that the people you called knew what they were talking about?

Case 5: Cityspace

Excel Download at www.mhhe.com/kuemmerle: Cityspace exhibits

Case:

The case describes Cityspace, a company that presents London tourists with an interactive guidance system. System users can obtain detailed information about sights, restaurants, and events and make bookings. Cityspace seeks to raise at least 2.5 million British pounds in its second round of financing. The entrepreneurs need to decide under what terms the capital should be raised and develop a contingency plan to be invoked in the event the financing does not work as planned.

Assignment Questions:

1. What is the opportunity for Cityspace?
2. What is your assessment of the business model?
3. What is your assessment of the company's revenues and EBIT from 1998 to 2003?
4. Would you, as a venture capitalist, invest in the upcoming round of financing? Under what terms?
5. What should Meyohas and Cityspace do next?

Case 6: Internet Securities, Inc.: Financing Growth

Excel Download at www.mhhe.com/kuemmerle: Internet Securities exhibits

Case:

The case describes Internet Securities Inc. (ISI), an Internet-based information service started in 1994 that focuses on emerging markets. The founder and CEO seek to raise $12.5m to finance expansion of this rapidly growing firm. The company has yet to break even, but a number of financing alternatives seem feasible. These include sale to a financial buyer, an initial public offering, and the sale of ISI to a larger firm in the information services industry.

Assignment Questions:

1. What is Internet Securities' value in October 1998?

2. From whom should Gary Mueller raise money? Should he push for an IPO? Should he seek a financial buyer or let Internet Securities be acquired by a larger firm?

3. What advice would you give Gary on how to structure a deal with a financial buyer? With a larger firm in the same industry?

4. In your opinion, is $12.5m sufficient for Internet Securities to begin generating positive cash flows?

5. What should Gary Mueller do next?

Case 7: @Hoc: Leveraging Israeli Technology in the United States

Case:

The case describes @Hoc, an idea for an Internet software company developed by HBS MBA '99 graduates Guy Miasnik and Ly Tran. @Hoc's software, loaded into a browser, enables instant, context-sensitive information retrieval and shopping. By July 1999 the entrepreneurs have developed a high-level prototype, written a business plan, and are seeking to raise approximately US$1 to 1.5m. This case permits a discussion of expectations of venture capitalists and angel investors. For this purpose, the case contains a genuine business plan (case **Exhibit 3**).

Assignment Questions:

1. What is your assessment of @Hoc's business model? If you were a venture capitalist would you invest in @Hoc? If you were an angel would you invest? What questions would you ask the entrepreneurs about their business idea?

2. What is your assessment of the @Hoc management team? What skills are missing?

3. What is your assessment of the dual location strategy (R&D in Israel and the rest of operations in Boston)? Is this strategy sustainable? Is Boston the right location in the United States?

4. If you were to advise Guy and Ly on the following questions, what would your advice be?
   a. How much capital should they raise in July 1999?
   b. From whom?
   c. At what valuation?

5. What improvement suggestions do you have for the business plan (case **Exhibit 3**)?

Assignment Questions for Module 2

Case 8: Butler Capital Partners and Autodistribution: Putting Private Equity to Work in France

Excel Download at www.mhhe.com/kuemmerle: Butler Capital Partners and Autodistribution exhibits

Case:

The case describes a proposed buyout of Autodistribution, the leading car parts distributor in France. Autodistribution is an entrepreneurial firm. The deal became feasible because of a failed takeover battle for Autodistribution's new parent company. Private equity investor Butler Capital Partners must make an investment decision within less than three weeks. Other private equity firms are competing with Butler for the deal. Since the price for the deal is set, Butler must focus on finding an advantageous structure for all parties to secure the deal. Furthermore, Butler must assess the potential for margin improvement and expansion within France and in other European countries.

Assignment Questions:

1. Should Walter Butler submit a proposal for Autodistribution?

2. What rate of return do you expect from this investment? (Consider the assumptions for margin improvements and growth in case **Exhibit 18.**)

3. What is your assessment of Autodistribution's chances for pan-European expansion?

4. In your opinion, what are the major risks associated with this investment? What can Butler and his team do to mitigate these risks?

5. Paul-Marie Chavanne is interested in joining Autodistribution as CEO, but has not signed on yet. What kind of incentives should Butler offer Chavanne? How should these incentives be structured?

6. What should Butler's strategy be in negotiating the deal?

Case 9: Absolute Sensors

Case:

This case concerns the valuation of spin-offs. Spin-offs are becoming increasingly common as existing firms focus on, and try to cash in on some of the activities that have evolved beyond, their core businesses. Spin-offs are also interesting career alternatives for managers who are "sick and tired" of working for a parent company. Also examined is the valuation of stock options under such circumstances. Absolute Sensors (ASL) is a spin-off of a scientific consulting firm. The entrepreneur and his team must address issues such as what market(s) to target, how and from whom to raise capital, and to what extent they should engage in manufacturing their own products.

Assignment Questions:

1. Evaluate the progress of ASL's management to date. Do they possess all the capabilities needed to run and grow ASL?

2. To what extent has the role of Generics helped or hindered ASL? What are the implications for running a spin-off with close connections to its parent?

3. What will ASL need to do in order to attract outside investors? What type of investors should it seek? If you were on the board of Generics, would you want external investors to take a stake in ASL? As a venture capitalist what progress would you need to see between September 1998 and February 1999 to invest £2 million in February 1999?

4. What is the value of the options awarded to each of ASL's three directors?

Case 10: Signature Security: Providing Alarm Systems for the Countries Down Under

Excel Download at www.mhhe.com/kuemmerle: Signature Security exhibits

Case:

This case focuses on the valuation of subscription-based businesses. Empirical evidence having shown that entrepreneurs have accumulated substantial wealth through this type of business, it is useful to examine what drives valuation in a subscription-based business model.

The case describes Signature Security, a company created to roll up the electronic security industry in Australia and New Zealand. Signature was created by a team of experienced U.S. managers. Original financing was provided by Clairvest, a Canadian merchant bank. Twenty-six months after the original investment, some of the parties in the deal are reassessing their positions. In this context the investors need to value their stake in the company. Clairvest and other investors are wondering when and how they should exit their investments. Jim Covert, the CEO, is wondering whether and when he should move back to the United States. Both questions are closely related to the future strategy of the firm.

Assignment Questions:

1. What is the nature of this opportunity? Why and how did this opportunity occur?
2. How would you describe the cash flow characteristics of this business? As a potential lender, how would you assess the opportunity to finance Signature?
3. How good an investment has this been to date for the initial investors? For successive investors?
4. Should Signature continue its roll-up strategy or focus on internal growth? Why? What quantitative analysis can you carry out to determine at what point Signature should stop acquiring other companies?
5. Is this a good time for Jim Covert to return to the United States? From Covert's perspective? From the investors' perspective? From Joe Nuccio's perspective?

Case 11: Ducati & Texas Pacific Group—A "Wild Ride" Leveraged Buyout

Excel Download at www.mhhe.com/kuemmerle: Ducati exhibits

Case:

The case describes the attempt of Texas Pacific Group (TPG), a buyout firm, to purchase a controlling stake in the world's leading high-performance motorcycle company, Bologna, Italy-based Ducati Motor. At the time of the case Abel Halpern, a partner at TPG, is frustrated because a deal with the seller seems to be an ever-moving target. TPG has negotiated with the seller for almost a year. Despite costly due diligence efforts by TPG, Halpern is now ready to walk away from the deal.

Assignment Questions:

1. What is the nature of this opportunity? Could the Ducati brand be expanded beyond just motorcycles? Why? Why not?
2. How does the deal differ from a typical private equity deal in the United States? How does it differ in terms of deal flow generation, due diligence process, negotiations, and context?
3. What is the value of Ducati at the time of the deal? How much should TPG be willing to pay for 51% of the equity? Assume that TPG's target rate of return for U.S. deals is 35% (annualized).
4. The country risk premium for cross-border valuations within G7 countries is typically negligible. Even though Italy is a G7 country, should you perhaps consider applying a country risk premium in your valuation?
5. Should Abel Halpern walk away from this deal? Why? Why not?
6. If TPG pursues the deal and purchases a stake in Ducati, what critical steps must TPG take to make the deal successful? Be specific.

Case 12: Infox System GmbH

Excel Download at www.mhhe.com/kuemmerle: Infox exhibits

Case:

The case describes an opportunity for Apax, a private equity firm, to invest in a travel-related print-materials distribution business in Germany. Infox is typical of many buy-out opportunities. One of the founders seeks to exit the business and recently hired managers at Infox will have to assume an increased level of responsibility. For its investment decision Apax has to value the company and secure debt financing. In this context Apax has to assess not only the growth opportunities for Infox but also whether remaining management is up to the job.

Assignment Questions:

1. What is the nature of the opportunity? At the time of the case, what technological and other developments could threaten the Infox business model?

2. The owners are asking for DM100 million. While Martin Halusa and Michael Phillips of Apax think that this price is too high, they are at odds on what price to offer. Halusa and Phillips know that there is at least one other serious bidder. How much should Halusa and Phillips offer?

3. What is your assessment of potential future business opportunities for Infox (mentioned in the section titled "Potential Future Opportunities" of the case)? To what degree do you consider these opportunities relevant when valuing the firm?

Assignment Questions for Module 3

Case 13: Georgian Glass and Mineral Water

Case:

This case describes Georgian Glass and Mineral Water (GGMW), a company created in 1995 by a Georgian entrepreneur and Western investors in Georgia (former Soviet Union) to bottle and market the famous mineral water from the Borjomi Valley. Jacques Fleury, GGMW's newly hired CEO, faces a number of financing and operating challenges.

Assignment Questions:

1. What will it take for GGMW to succeed?

2. How much capital is needed over the next year? Over the next three years?

3. If you were ING, would you invest additional capital? At what valuation? Under what terms?

4. If you were IFC, would you invest? Under what terms?

5. What should Jacques Fleury do next?

Case 14: QI-TECH: A Chinese Technology Company for Sale

Excel Download at www.mhhe.com/kuemmerle: QI-TECH exhibits

Case:

This case focuses on the mobilization of resources in an entrepreneurial joint venture. Because joint ventures are sometimes established between large firms and entrepreneurial firms, especially in cross-border contexts, it is important to understand their strengths and weaknesses.

The case describes QI-TECH, a Chinese manufacturer of precision coordinate measurement machines. A foreign investor that holds 50% of QI-TECH must negotiate a sale with its Chinese partner and a potential buyer (a large Western measurement machine company).

For this purpose the foreign investor must value the joint venture and develop a viable deal structure and negotiation strategy.

Assignment Questions:

1. What are the objectives of the different parties on the sellers' side? Specifically, what are the objectives of Indivers? Of QI-TECH's local management? Of QQMF? Of Roger Kollbrunner?

2. What is the value of Indivers' stake in QI-TECH?

3. What negotiation strategy should Kollbrunner and Li pursue in their negotiations with Brown and Sharpe (the potential buyer)? What price should they ask?

4. What concerns might Phil James, VP of Brown and Sharpe's CMM division, have? How can the seller mitigate these concerns?

5. What should Kollbrunner do next?

6. What general lessons regarding the management of joint ventures in entrepreneurial settings can you draw from this case?

Case 15: Spotfire: Managing a Multinational Start-Up

Excel Download at www.mhhe.com/kuemmerle: Spotfire exhibits

Case:

The management of Spotfire, a recently started software company specializing in data analysis and visualization, faces a number of important challenges going forward. Though in many ways a fairly typical venture-capital-backed software company, Spotfire operates in two locations: Boston and Goteborg. Part of the class discussion is devoted to financing and coordination issues that arise from Spotfire's global expansion.

Assignment Questions:

1. What is the nature of the opportunity for Spotfire? What strategy should the company pursue over the next three to five years?

2. Spotfire expects to raise additional capital in the first half of 1999. How much capital is needed? What is the valuation of the company? Under what terms should Spotfire seek to raise capital?

3. Spotfire's development group and the rest of the firm work in geographically separate locations. Is this strategy sustainable? Why? Why not?

4. Where is Spotfire's home base location? What kind of activities (home-base-augmenting or home-base-exploiting) is Spotfire carrying out in the other location?

Case 16: Mobile Communications Tokyo, Inc.

Excel Download at www.mhhe.com/kuemmerle: Mobile Communications Tokyo exhibits

Case:

This case describes an emerging Japanese telecommunications equipment and software company. Founder and president Hatsuhiro Inoue has just seen revenues double over the last two years and expects further rapid growth. The company currently has three product lines: telecommunications hardware; telecommunications software; and Internet software. The founder needs to raise capital and is considering an initial public offering as an alternative to a private placement. Although the company could probably go public on the over-the-counter market in Tokyo, there is also the possibility of a public offering on the NASDAQ market.

Assignment Questions:

1. What strategic challenges does Mobile Communications Tokyo (MCT) face? On which lines of business would you advise Hatsuhiro Inoue to focus?

2. What are the funding needs of MCT? Would you invest at this stage? Under what terms?

3. Would you advise Inoue to go public on the Tokyo OTC market or on NASDAQ? When can MCT go public? When should it go public?

Case 17: Capital Alliance Private Equity: Creating a Private Equity Leader in Nigeria

Excel Download at www.mhhe.com/kuemmerle: Capital Alliance exhibits

Case:

The case describes the creation of the first private equity fund in Nigeria and the fund's potential first investment in GS Telecom, a Nigerian telecommunication service company. Its managers are keenly aware that a bad first investment could create a vicious circle for the fund. Thus, whether to invest and under what terms is of crucial importance.

Assignment Questions:

1. If you were in Okey Enalamah's position, would you recommend an investment in GS Telecom? If yes, under what terms and at what valuation? Should the fund acquire more than 25% of GS Telecom? Is $2m sufficient to secure GS Telecom's future?

2. What is your assessment of the returns to CAPE from an investment in GS Telecom? Should CAPE do this deal even if projected returns are low?

3. What should Enalamah do to mitigate the uncertainty regarding financial projections?

4. If you were a U.S.-pension fund manager with a mandate to invest up to $20m in Africa would you invest in CAPE? Why? Why not?

Case 18: TixToGo: Financing a Silicon Valley Start-Up

Excel Download at www.mhhe.com/kuemmerle: TixToGo exhibits

Case:

The case describes TixToGo, a Silicon Valley start-up company. TixToGo is an Internet service that enables on-line signups and payments for registrations, admissions, memberships, sponsorships, and donations. A serial entrepreneur and his partner started the company in San Francisco in early 1997. While the business model seems quite attractive, TixToGo has had difficulty gaining momentum. The founders have therefore decided to hire Lu Cordova, a manager and entrepreneur with some start-up experience, as CEO. May 18, 1999, is her first day on the job. TixToGo is also her first job as CEO of a company she did not start. The company has US$12,000 in the bank. The monthly burn rate is $30,000. Lu needs to act quickly.

Assignment Questions:

1. What is the nature of the opportunity? What are the strengths and weaknesses of the company's business model?

2. Why has TixToGo had trouble gaining momentum?

3. What should Lu Cordova do first? What next?

4. How would you value TixToGo? From whom and under what terms should the company raise funding? How much should they raise?

5. What general lessons about entrepreneurship and venture financing can you draw from this case? Be specific in your answers.

Assignment Questions for Module 4

Case 19: JAFCO America Ventures, Inc.: Building a Venture Capital Firm

Case:

The case describes the second attempt of JAFCO, a large Japanese venture capital firm, to enter the U.S. market. The U.S. subsidiary, JAV, is experiencing a challenging turnaround. Going forward, the firm's leadership needs to make a number of important decisions.

Assignment Questions:

1. What is your assessment of JAV's performance to date? What is your assessment of JAV's USIT1 fund performance to date?

2. What are JAV's challenges over the next five years?

3. Would you advise Barry Schiffman and his colleagues to move into seed-stage investing? Should they move into life sciences?

4. How can JAFCO learn from JAV?

5. How should JAFCO change its incentive system, if at all?

Case 20: Jinwoong: Financing an Entrepreneurial Firm in the Wake of the Korean Financial Crisis

Excel Download at www.mhhe.com/kuemmerle: Jinwoong Exhibits

Case:

The case describes T. P. Lee, the founder and CEO of Jinwoong, a 19-year-old Korean company that has grown into the world's largest manufacturer of camping tents. Designated by *Fortune* in 1993 one of Asia's most promising entrepreneurs, Lee faces some serious management challenges in October 1998. Largely due to the Asian (and Korean) financial crisis of 1997-1998, he must rethink his firm's financing and expansion plans. To deal with these challenges, Lee could seek outside funding from either of two groups of private equity investors or from a corporate restructuring fund set up by the Korean government. All these decisions need to be tied to Jinwoong's long-term strategy and to Lee's assessment of the different offers.

Assignment Questions:

1. Why is T. P. Lee seeking outside financing? Does he need it?

2. In your opinion, what percentage of Jinwoong should Lee sell? What should be his asking price for this stake?

3. Lee has a choice of three possible investors. Which should he pursue?

4. If you were Warburg Pincus, would you invest in Jinwoong? Why? Why not? What kind of deal would you offer Lee?

5. What general lessons about financing entrepreneurial ventures in emerging markets do you draw from this case?

Note that case **Exhibit 9** represents unconsolidated financial statements. Korean accounting rules in 1998 did not require publicly listed firms to present consolidated financial statements. The difference is that unconsolidated financial statements did not reflect the financial performance of (foreign) subsidiaries, even if they were majority-owned by the Korean parent company. Depending on the levels of accounts payable and receivable between the parent company and subsidiaries and on certain transfer pricing decisions, unconsolidated financial statements might distort a firm's true financial status. Consequently, analysis of Jinwoong should rely primarily on case **Exhibit 12,** which represents a "best effort" attempt to create consolidated figures for 1998. Briefly compare case **Exhibits 9** and **12.**

Case 21: Telewizja Wisla

Excel Download at www.mhhe.com/kuemmerle: TVW exhibits

If case is taught with focus on simulation: Crystal Ball® software download or other simulation software can be used for case analysis.

Case:

The case describes Telewizja Wisla, a television station started in Poland in 1994 by two entrepreneurs. In March 1996 the company faces a number of challenges; most important, the entrepreneurs need to raise an additional $7.4 million soon.

Assignment Questions:

1. What is the true nature of the opportunity for Telewizja Wisla? Which growth scenario (**Exhibit 10**) do you think is probable?

2. How can Claire Hurley achieve her goals despite problems with the company's current majority owners?

3. There are currently two potential investors, Bertelsmann Group and a venture capital firm. Which would you prefer?

4. Under what terms should Hurley seek to raise $7.4 million?

5. If this case is taught with focus on simulation: How could Clair Hurley effectively use scenario analysis to support her decision?

It takes only a few minutes to understand how the software (an Excel plug-in) works. Essentially, Crystal Ball allows you to make assumptions about the probability distribution of a set of inputs into an Excel formula. You need to define which inputs you want to vary and the probability distributions of these inputs. You also need to define a cell in your Excel spreadsheet that contains the output formula. You can then conveniently run a scenario analysis. Outputs are provided in a separate Excel spreadsheet generated automatically by Crystal Ball. One of the learning objectives of this case is to understand the potential (and limitations) of simulation analysis in the field of international entrepreneurship. As you prepare your valuation spreadsheet for Telewizja, think about which cells in the spreadsheet you would use as input variables for a scenario analysis and why. Run a scenario analysis using Crystal Ball and be prepared to describe the inputs and results in class. Because the case does not provide detailed information about the cost of capital, you might want to focus your analysis on determining an IRR to a prospective investor based on a certain growth and profitability scenario.

Case 22: Promise: Building a Consumer Finance Company in Japan

Excel Download at www.mhhe.com/kuemmerle: Promise exhibits

Case:

The case describes Promise, the third-largest consumer finance company in Japan. Started by an entrepreneur in 1963, Promise has kept its entrepreneurial culture alive in many ways. Its core business is providing unsecured loans of up to Yen 1 million (about US$9,000 at the time of the case) to individuals. In July 2000 Promise has approximately 2.2 million customers and faces increasing competition and a number of regulatory changes. Because of these contextual changes, management must make a number of important decisions going forward.

Assignment Questions:

1. In your opinion, what is the fair value of Promise's equity in July 2000? Why has the company done so well relative to Japanese banks?

2. The Japanese Ministry of Finance has just decided to lower the maximum interest rates for consumer finance loans to 29.2% from June 2000 onwards. In your opinion, how will this decision affect the industry's structure? What should Promise do to cope with this change?

3. Debt (with varying levels of maturity) represents 70% of Promise's balance sheet. The comparable figure for consumer finance companies in the United States is about 90%. Should Promise seek higher leverage than 70%? Why? Why not?

4. In May 1999 the Japanese Ministry of Finance permitted consumer finance companies for the first time to issue short-term commercial paper as a source of funds for loans. Should Promise make extensive use of this opportunity? Why? Why not? If not, how should Promise procure funds for expansion?

5. Takefuji, the number one competitor in the industry, has just (March 22, 2000) listed its stock on the London Stock Exchange. Should Promise do the same? Why? Why not?

6. Promise plans to expand aggressively into adjacent areas by lending to customer segments that it currently does not cover. What are the elements of this expansion plan? Is the plan feasible? Why? Why not?

Case 23: Gray Security: Building a South African Services Firm

Excel Download at www.mhhe.com/kuemmerle: Gray Security exhibits

Case:

The case describes Gray Security Services, an entrepreneurial South African firm that has recently gone through a financial restructuring with the help of Brait Capital Partners, a private equity firm. Gray provides complete security services to companies in South Africa, other African countries, and some parts of Europe. Many of Gray's clients are multinational firms. Gray is currently considering an IPO in South Africa as well as further international expansion. At this point Dick Aubin, co-founder and chairman, faces a number of important questions regarding the firm's financing and directions for future growth.

Assignment Questions:

1. What major context changes are happening in South Africa? What is your assessment of Gray's business model? In your opinion, how well will the company be able to adapt to the changing context?

2. Analyze Brait's investment in Gray. How good a deal was this for the various parties? For Gray Security? For Aubin? For Brait?

3. What is the value of Gray in January 1999?

4. Should Gray go ahead with the planned IPO in South Africa? Should Brait sell its stake in the IPO?

5. How and in which countries should Gray grow in the near future? Should Gray groom itself as an acquisition candidate or aggressively acquire other firms?

Assignment Questions for Module 5

Case 24: TCS: An Entrepreneurial Air-Express Company in Pakistan

Excel Download at www.mhhe.com/kuemmerle: TCS exhibits

Case:

The case describes Khalid Awan, co-founder of TCS, an entrepreneurial airfreight company in Pakistan. The founder has succeeded in building a sizeable company despite serious obstacles, including pressure from the public postal system, an environment prone to corruption, and a nonexistent market for venture capital. During its existence, the firm has largely followed an organic financing strategy and made extensive use of leasing contracts. However, in the aftermath of September 11, 2001, the founder faces a number of questions regarding the firm's further expansion. The tragic events of September 11 will most likely put pressure on revenues and create considerable business uncertainty. But there are also some bright spots on the horizon. The founder is also starting to think about diversifying his personal wealth, which is concentrated almost entirely in TCS. Each of the choices Awan makes will affect the firm's future financing policies and growth.

Assignment Questions:

1. Given the challenging country context of Pakistan, why has TCS done so well?

2. What is your assessment of TCS's past financing policies? Do they make sense?

3. How has the use of leasing influenced the development of TCS?

4. At the time of the case the founder of TCS is considering several possible expansion plans. Which one would you advise the entrepreneur to pursue? Should he seek external financing for this purpose? If yes, where should he raise the funds? At what valuation?

5. The case mentions that Awan has rejected past acquisition offers. In your opinion, when should he start harvesting and why? How should he do this? Should he start by selling a small or large part of TCS? Be specific in your answers.

Case 25: TelePizza

Excel Download at www.mhhe.com/kuemmerle: TelePizza exhibits

Case:

The case describes TelePizza, Spain's leading chain of pizza restaurants and delivery services. TelePizza has experienced rapid growth to about 500 stores since its creation in 1987. The company went public on the Spanish stock market in 1996. Franchising has played an important role in its expansion to date. For further growth founder and CEO Leopoldo Fernandez CEO is contemplating different strategies.

Assignment Questions:

1. Why has TelePizza done so well?

2. Leopoldo Fernandez has developed different options for growth. What is your assessment of these options? Which one(s) would you advise him to adopt? Be specific in your recommendations.

3. What implications do your recommendations regarding growth have for TelePizza's current franchising strategy?

4. What is your assessment of TelePizza's stock market valuation in October 1998?

Case 26: Sirona

Excel Download at www.mhhe.com/kuemmerle: Sirona exhibits

Case:

The case describes Sirona, the dental systems business of Siemens AG that is being sold through auction. In September 1997, buyout firm Schroder Ventures has to decide whether to make a binding offer for the business. Schroder has done extensive due diligence with support from a team of Bain & Co. consultants. There seems to be some unrealized growth potential as well as room for cost reduction at Sirona. But there is also considerable uncertainty around both the cost reduction and growth scenarios. Furthermore, there seem to be problems at Sirona subsidiaries abroad. Finally, the financing will depend on the feasibility of a high-yield offering, a first of its kind in Germany.

Assignment Questions:

1. Evaluate Schroder Ventures actions to date. What might the team have done differently? How strong is its position in the negotiations with Siemens at this point?
2. Would you advise Schroder Ventures to stick to its preliminary bid of DM800m?
3. What are your concerns regarding the financing of the deal? Namely, how do swings in the high-yield market affect this deal?
4. There are three days left before Schroder Ventures has to make a binding offer. What should the team at Schroder Ventures do next?

5. As you build your valuation model for Sirona you should obviously use any valuation method you deem appropriate. The use of Adjusted Present Value (APV) or Capital Cash Flow (CCF) methods is nevertheless suggested. In the case of CCF, you need to take the following steps.
   a. Create pro forma statements (sales and EBIT).
   b. Determine working capital needs and yearly capital expenditures.
   c. Prepare depreciation and amortization schedules. *Note:* amortization of goodwill depends on a crude assumption about purchase price. Assume that goodwill is amortized in a straight line over 20 years. To keep things simple, you might also want to assume that capital expenditures equal depreciation.
   d. Determine transaction structure (senior debt capacity, high-yield capacity, equity).
   e. Create debt, debt repayment, and interest payment schedules.
   f. Calculate capital cash flows and determine the expected asset return rate.
   g. Determine terminal value.
   h. Discount.

Also revisit steps 3, 4, 5, 6, and 7. This is an iterative process.

Case 27: VacationSpot.com & Rent-A-Holiday: Negotiating a Trans-Atlantic Merger of Start-Ups

Excel Download at www.mhhe.com/kuemmerle: VacationSpot.com exhibits

Case:

This case describes an important aspect of managing growth (and harvesting): the potential merger of two young companies. The case describes two companies in the Internet space, Seattle-based VacationSpot.com and Brussels-based Rent-A-Holiday. Both offer on-line listings and reservations for independent leisure lodging (i.e., villas, apartments, and bed and breakfasts) around the world. Both were started in 1997. At the time of the case (April 1999) the two companies are world market co-leaders and discussing a merger. Although the lodging inventory of both is quite similar, the companies' most recent post-money valuations have a ratio of approximately 9:1. Merger negotiations have come to a standstill over the valuation issue. Both sides need to decide whether to restart negotiations and what terms to propose.

Assignment Questions:

1. What is the nature of this opportunity for the two companies?

2. What is the context for Internet entrepreneurs in the United States and Europe in early 1999?

3. In your opinion, what is the value of VacationSpot.com in June 1999? What is the value of Rent-A-Holiday in June 1999?

4. Should the two companies merge? If yes, under what terms? Where should the company be headquartered? What should be the new name of the company?

5. If you were Steve Murch, would you keep Peter Ingelbrecht and Laurent Coppieters on board? For how long? If yes, what kind of incentives would you offer them? Be as specific as possible in your proposal of an incentive structure.

6. If you were an investor in Rent-A-Holiday, what would your concerns about the merger be? What would you propose to the entrepreneurs in both companies to mitigate your concerns?

Be prepared to take any of the following three positions: VacationSpot.com; Rent-A-Holiday; early investors in Rent-A-Holiday.

Case 28: Infosys: Financing an Indian Software Start-Up

Excel Download at www.mhhe.com/kuemmerle: Infosys exhibits

Case:

The case describes the financing and growth of Infosys, an Indian software start-up. Infosys defies a number of stereotypes about barriers to entrepreneurship in India. The company was founded by a small group of entrepreneurs with little equity and without backing from a large family conglomerate. Although Infosys has been quite successful recently, there was a highly uncertain period in the company's history. At the time of the case, Infosys's CEO, Narayana Murthy, and his team once again face important challenges regarding future growth and financing. Infosys's shares trade on the Bombay Stock Exchange. Murthy and his team need to decide whether to seek to list the company's shares on a U.S. stock exchange as well and, if yes, whether to list on NASDAQ or NYSE.

Assignment Questions:

1. What is your assessment of Infosys's performance to date?

2. The case describes how Infosys differs from other software companies in India. To what degree is Infosys's performance related to this fact?

3. What is your assessment of Infosys's stock price in late December 1998? What does this price imply for Infosys's growth and key operating ratios?

4. How can Infosys grow further? What competitive threats does the company face in India and abroad? What challenges does the company face if it decides to grow through acquisitions?

5. Should Infosys list on a U.S. exchange? If yes, why and on which exchange? What should Infosys's management do to mitigate the issues stated by Infosys president Nilekani in the last section of the case text?

Case 29: Mandic BBS—An Entrepreneurial Harvesting Decision

Excel Download at www.mhhe.com/kuemmerle: Mandic exhibits

Case:

The case describes Mandic BBS, one of Brazil's first Internet service providers. Mandic BBS has experienced very rapid growth, but competition is increasing and the future looks somewhat uncertain. With its venture capitalist, GP Investimentos, looking to exit their investment and with a number of suitors interested in acquiring the young company, Aleksandar Mandic must decide whether and on what terms he is willing to sell. In your analysis of the case, you might find it helpful to first assess the context and the people involved in the deal before assessing why Mandic has done so well and carrying out a valuation analysis. You might also want to think about a negotiation strategy for Aleksandar Mandic versus potential buyers and versus GP.

Assignment Questions:

1. If you were Aleksandar Mandic, would you want to sell your stake in Mandic BBS at this time? Why? Why not? If yes, what part of your stake would you want to sell?

2. Which of the potential buyers is likely to be the most attractive to Aleksandar Mandic and why?

3. There are different approaches to valuing Mandic BBS. Which approach do you prefer? Why?

4. If you had decided to sell, under what terms and at what valuation would you do so?

5. How would you approach the negotiation? With whom would you talk first? With whom would you talk next? How would you involve GP Investimentos in the negotiation?